Lecture Notes in Computer Science 1511

Edited by G. Goos, J. Hartmanis and J. van Leeuwen

Springer-Verlag Berlin Heidelberg GmbH

David R. O'Hallaron (Ed.)

Languages, Compilers, and Run-Time Systems for Scalable Computers

4th International Workshop, LCR '98
Pittsburgh, PA, USA, May 28-30, 1998
Selected Papers

 Springer

Series Editors

Gerhard Goos, Karlsruhe University, Germany
Juris Hartmanis, Cornell University, NY, USA
Jan van Leeuwen, Utrecht University, The Netherlands

Volume Editor

David R. O'Hallaron
Computer Science and Electrical and Computer Engineering
School of Computer Science, Carnegie Mellon University
5000 Forbes Avenue, Pittsburgh, PA 15213-3891, USA
E-mail: droh@cs.cmu.edu

Cataloging-in-Publication data applied for

Die Deutsche Bibliothek - CIP-Einheitsaufnahme

**Languages, compilers, and run-time systems for scalable
computers** : 4th international workshop ; selected papers / LCR '98,
Pittsburgh, PA, USA, May 28-30, 1998. David R. O'Hallaron (ed.). -
Berlin ; Heidelberg ; New York ; Barcelona ; Budapest ; Hong Kong
; London ; Milan ; Paris ; Singapore ; Tokyo : Springer, 1998
   (Lecture notes in computer science ; Vol. 1511)

CR Subject Classification (1991): F.2.2, D.1.3, D.4.4-5, C.2.2, D.3, F.1, C.2.4,
C.3

ISSN 0302-9743
ISBN 978-3-540-65172-7   ISBN 978-3-540-49530-7 (eBook)
DOI 10.1007/978-3-540-49530-7

© Springer-Verlag Berlin Heidelberg 1998

Originally published by Springer-Verlag Berlin Heidelberg New York in 1998.

Typesetting: Camera-ready by author
SPIN 10692671   06/3142 – 5 4 3 2 1 0   Printed on acid-free paper

Preface

It is a great pleasure to present this collection of papers from LCR '98, the Fourth Workshop on Languages, Compilers, and Run-time Systems for Scalable Computers. The LCR workshop is a bi-annual gathering of computer scientists who develop software systems for parallel and distributed computers. LCR is held in alternating years with the ACM Symposium on Principles and Practice of Parallel Programming (PPoPP) and draws from the same community.

This fourth meeting was held in cooperation with ACM SIGPLAN on the campus of Carnegie Mellon University, May 28–30, 1998. There were 60 registered attendees from 9 nations. A total of 47 6-page extended abstracts were submitted. There were a total of 134 reviews for an average of 2.85 reviews per submission. Submissions were rank ordered by average review score. The top 23 submissions were selected as full papers and the next 9 as short papers.

The program committee consisted of David Bakken (BBN), Ian Foster (Argonne), Thomas Gross (CMU and ETH Zurich), Charles Koelbel (Rice), Piyush Mehrotra (ICASE), David O'Hallaron, Chair (CMU), Joel Saltz (Maryland), Jaspal Subhlok (CMU), Boleslaw Szymanski (RPI), Katherine Yelick (Berkeley), and Hans Zima (Vienna).

In addition to the members of the committee, the following people chaired sessions: Lawrence Rauchwerger, Peter Brezany, Terry Pratt, Alan Sussman, Sandhya Dwarkadis and Rajiv Gupta. Also, the following people generously provided additional reviews: Sigfried Benkner, Chen Ding, Guoha Jin, Erwin Laure, Pantona Mario, Eduard Mehofer, and Bernd Wender. We very much appreciate the efforts of these dedicated volunteers.

Barbara Grandillo did a wonderful job of chairing the organizing committee and handling the local arrangements. Thomas Gross and Jaspal Subhlok made numerous suggestions. Peter Dinda, Peter Lieu, Nancy Miller, and Bwolen Yang also helped out during the workshop itself. We are very grateful for their help.

Finally I would like to thank Mary Lou Soffa at the Univ. of Pittsburgh, for her help in getting SIGPLAN support, Bolek Szymanski at RPI, who chaired the previous meeting and was always helpful and encouraging, and Alfred Hofmann at Springer, whose advice and encouragement enabled us to produce this volume.

Carnegie Mellon University   David O'Hallaron
August, 1998   LCR '98 General/Program Chair

Table of Contents

Expressing Irregular Computations
in Modern Fortran Dialects*

Jan F. Prins, Siddhartha Chatterjee, and Martin Simons

Department of Computer Science
The University of North Carolina
Chapel Hill, NC 27599-3175
{prins,sc,simons}@cs.unc.edu

Abstract. Modern dialects of Fortran enjoy wide use and good support on high-performance computers as performance-oriented programming languages. By providing the ability to express nested data parallelism in Fortran, we enable irregular computations to be incorporated into existing applications with minimal rewriting and without sacrificing performance within the regular portions of the application. Since performance of nested data-parallel computation is unpredictable and often poor using current compilers, we investigate source-to-source transformation techniques that yield Fortran 90 programs with improved performance and performance stability.

1 Introduction

Modern science and engineering disciplines make extensive use of computer simulations. As these simulations increase in size and detail, the computational costs of naive algorithms can overwhelm even the largest parallel computers available today. Fortunately, computational costs can be reduced using sophisticated modeling methods that vary model resolution as needed, coupled with sparse and adaptive solution techniques that vary computational effort in time and space as needed. Such techniques have been developed and are routinely employed in sequential computation, for example, in cosmological simulations (using adaptive n-body methods) and computational fluid dynamics (using adaptive meshing and sparse linear system solvers).

However, these so-called irregular or unstructured computations are problematic for parallel computation, where high performance requires equal distribution of work over processors and locality of reference within each processor. For many irregular computations, the distribution of work and data cannot be characterized *a priori*, as these quantities are input-dependent and/or evolve with the computation itself. Further, irregular computations are difficult to express using performance-oriented languages such as Fortran, because there is an apparent mismatch between data types such as trees, graphs, and nested sequences characteristic of irregular computations and the statically analyzable rectangular multi-dimensional arrays that are the core data types in

---

* This research was supported in part by NSF Grants #CCR-9711438 and #INT-9726317. Chatterjee is supported in part by NSF CAREER Award #CCR-9501979. Simons is supported by a research scholarship from the German Research Foundation (DFG).

D. O'Hallaron (Ed.): LCR'98, LNCS 1511, pp. 1–16, 1998.
© Springer-Verlag Berlin Heidelberg 1998

modern Fortran dialects such as Fortran 90/95 [19], and High Performance Fortran (HPF) [16]. Irregular data types can be introduced using the data abstraction facilities, with a representation exploiting pointers. Optimization of operations on such an abstract data type is currently beyond compile-time analysis, and compilers have difficulty generating high-performance parallel code for such programs. This paper primarily addresses the expression of irregular computations in Fortran 95, but does so with a particular view of the compilation and high performance execution of such computations on parallel processors.

The modern Fortran dialects enjoy increasing use and good support as mainstream performance-oriented programming languages. By providing the ability to express irregular computations as Fortran modules, and by preprocessing these modules into a form that current Fortran compilers can successfully optimize, we enable irregular computations to be incorporated into existing applications with minimal rewriting and without sacrificing performance within the regular portions of the application.

For example, consider the NAS CG (Conjugate Gradient) benchmark, which solves an unstructured sparse linear system using the method of conjugate gradients [2]. Within the distributed sample sequential Fortran solution, 79% of the lines of code are standard Fortran 77 concerned with problem construction and performance reporting. The next 16% consist of scalar and regular vector computations of the BLAS 2 variety [17], while the final 5% of the code is the irregular computation of the sparse matrix-vector product. Clearly we want to rewrite only this 5% of the code (which performs 97% of the work in the class B computation), while the remainder should be left intact for the Fortran compiler. This is not just for convenience. It is also critical for performance reasons; following Amdahl's Law, as the performance of the irregular computation improves, the performance of the regular component becomes increasingly critical for sustained high performance overall. Fortran compilers provide good compiler/annotation techniques to achieve high performance for the regular computations in the problem, and can thus provide an efficient and seamless interface between the regular and irregular portions of the computation.

We manually applied the implementation techniques described in Sect. 4 to the irregular computation in the NAS CG problem. The resultant Fortran program achieved a performance on the class B NAS CG 1.0 benchmark of 13.5 GFLOPS using a 32 processor NEC SX-4 [25]. We believe this to be the highest performance achieved for this benchmark to date. It exceeds, by a factor of 2.6, the highest performance reported in the last NPB 1.0 report [27], and is slightly faster than the 12.9 GFLOPS recently achieved using a 1024 processor Cray T3E-900 [18]. These encouraging initial results support the thesis that high-level expression and high-performance for irregular computations can be supported simultaneously in a production Fortran programming environment.

2   Expressing Irregular Computations Using Nested Data Parallelism

We adopt the data-parallel programming model of Fortran as our starting point. The data-parallel programming model has proven to be popular because of its power and simplicity. Data-parallel languages are founded on the concept of collections (such as arrays) and a means to allow programmers to express parallelism through the application of an operation independently to all elements of a collection (e.g., the elementwise addition of two arrays). Most of the common data-parallel languages, such as the array-based parallelism of Fortran 90, offer restricted data-parallel capabilities: they limit collections to multidimensional rectangular arrays, limit the type of the elements of a collection to scalar and record types, and limit the operations that can be applied in parallel to the elements of a collection to certain predefined operations rather than arbitrary user-defined functions. These limitations are aimed at enabling compile-time analysis and optimization of the work and communication for parallel execution, but make it difficult to express irregular computations in this model.

If the elements of a collection are themselves permitted to have arbitrary type, then arbitrary functions can be applied in parallel over collections. In particular, by operating on a collection of collections, it is possible to specify a parallel computation, each simultaneous operation of which in turn involves (a potentially different-sized) parallel subcomputation. This programming model, called *nested data parallelism*, combines aspects of both data parallelism and control parallelism. It retains the simple programming model and portability of the data-parallel model while being better suited for describing algorithms on irregular data structures. The utility of nested data parallelism as an expressive mechanism has been understood for a long time in the LISP, SETL [29], and APL communities, although always with a sequential execution semantics and implementation.

Nested data parallelism occurs naturally in the succinct expression of many irregular scientific problems. Consider the sparse matrix-vector product at the heart of the NAS CG benchmark. In the popular compressed sparse row (CSR) format of representing sparse matrices, the nonzero elements of an $m \times n$ sparse matrix A are represented as a sequence of m rows $[R_1, \ldots, R_m]$, where the ith row is, in turn, represented by a (possibly empty) sequence of (v, c) pairs where v is the nonzero value and $1 \leq c \leq n$ is the column in which it occurs: $R_i = [(v_1^i, c_1^i), \ldots, (v_{k_i}^i, c_{k_i}^i)]$. With a dense n-vector x represented as a simple sequence of n values, the sparse matrix-vector product $y = Ax$ may now be written as shown using the NESL notation [4]:

$$y = \{\texttt{sparse\_dot\_product}(R, x) \; : \; R \text{ in } A\}.$$

This expression specifies the application of `sparse_dot_product`, in parallel, to each row of A to yield the m element result sequence y. The sequence constructor $\{\ldots\}$ serves a dual role: it specifies parallelism (for each R in A), and it establishes the order in which the result elements are assembled into the result sequence, i.e., $y_i = $ `sparse_dot_product`(R_i, x). We obtain nested data parallelism if the body expression `sparse_dot_product`(R, x) itself specifies the parallel computation of the dot product of row R with x as the sum-reduction of a sequence of nonzero products:

$$\texttt{function sparse\_dot\_product}(R, x) = \texttt{sum}(\{v*x[c]: \; (v,c) \text{ in } R\})$$

More concisely, the complete expression could also written as follows:

$$y = \{\texttt{sum}(\{v*x[c]: \; (v,c) \text{ in } R\}): \; R \text{ in } A\}$$

where the nested parallelism is visible as nested sequence constructors in the source text.

```
MODULE Sparse_matrices

  IMPLICIT none

  TYPE Sparse_element
     REAL                                      :: val
     INTEGER                                   :: col
  END TYPE Sparse_element

  TYPE Sparse_row_p
     TYPE (Sparse_element), DIMENSION (:), POINTER :: elts
  END TYPE Sparse_row_p

  TYPE Sparse_matrix
     INTEGER                                   :: nrow, ncol
     TYPE (Sparse_row_p), DIMENSION (:), POINTER   :: rows
  END TYPE Sparse_matrix

END MODULE Sparse_matrices
```

Fig. 1. Fortran 90 definition of a nested sequence type for sparse matrices

Nested data parallelism provides a succinct and powerful notation for specifying parallel computation, including irregular parallel computations. Many more examples of efficient parallel algorithms expressed using nested data parallelism have been described in [4].

3   Nested Data Parallelism in Fortran

If we consider expressing nested data parallelism in standard imperative programming languages, we find that they either lack a data-parallel control construct (C, C++) or else lack a nested collection data type (Fortran). A data-parallel control construct can be added to C [11] or C++ [30], but the pervasive pointer semantics of these languages complicate its meaning. There is also incomplete agreement about the form of parallelism should take in these languages.

The FORALL construct, originated in HPF [16] and later added into Fortran 95, specifies data-parallel evaluation of expressions and array assignments. To ensure that there are no side effects between these parallel evaluations, functions that occur in the expressions must have the PURE attribute. Fortran 90 lacks a construct that specifies parallel evaluations. However, many compilers infer such an evaluation if specified using a conventional DO loop, possibly with an attached directive asserting the independence of iterations. FORALL constructs (or Fortran 90 loops) may be nested. To specify nested data-parallel computations with these constructs, it suffices to introduce nested aggregates, which we can do via the data abstraction mechanism of Fortran 90.

As a consequence of these language features, it is entirely possible to express nested data-parallel computations in modern Fortran dialects. For example, we might introduce the types shown in Fig. 1 to represent a sparse matrix. Sparse_element is the type of

```
SUBROUTINE smvp(a, x, y)

  USE Sparse_matrices, ONLY : Sparse_matrix

  IMPLICIT none

  TYPE (Sparse_matrix), INTENT(IN)  :: a
  REAL, DIMENSION(:), INTENT(IN)    :: x
  REAL, DIMENSION(:), INTENT(OUT)   :: y

  FORALL (i = 1:a%nrow)

    y(i) = SUM(a%rows(i)%elts%val * x(a%rows(i)%elts%col))

  END FORALL

END SUBROUTINE smvp
```

Fig. 2. Use of the derived type `Sparse_matrix` in sparse matrix-vector product.

a sparse matrix element, i.e., the (v, c) pair of the NESL example. `Sparse_row_p` is the type of vectors (1-D arrays) of sparse matrix elements, i.e., a row of the matrix. A sparse matrix is characterized by the number of rows and columns, and by the nested sequence of sparse matrix elements.

Using these definitions, the sparse matrix-vector product can be succinctly written as shown in Fig. 2. The DO loop specifies parallel evaluation of the inner products for all rows. Nested parallelism is a consequence of the use of parallel operations such as sum and elementwise multiplication, projection, and indexing.

Discussion

Earlier experiments with nested data parallelism in imperative languages include V [11], Amelia [30], and F90V [1]. For the first two of these languages the issues of side-effects in the underlying notation (C++ and C, respectively) were problematic in the potential introduction of interference between parallel iterations, and the efforts were abandoned. Fortran finesses this problem by requiring procedures used within a FORALL construct to be PURE, an attribute that can be verified statically. This renders invalid those constructions in which side effects (other than the nondeterministic orders of stores) can be observed, although such a syntactic constraint is not enforced in Fortran 90.

The specification of nested data parallelism in Fortran and NESL differ in important ways, many of them reflecting differences between the imperative and functional programming paradigms.

First, a sequence is formally a function from an index set to a value set. The NESL sequence constructor specifies parallelism over the value set of a sequence while the Fortran FORALL statement specifies parallelism over the index set of a sequence. This allows a more concise syntax and also makes explicit the shape of the common index domain shared by several collections participating in a FORALL construct.

Second, the NESL sequence constructor implicitly specifies the ordering of result elements, while this ordering is explicit in the FORALL statement. One consequence is that the restriction clause has different semantics. For instance, the NESL expression

$$v = \{i:\ i \text{ in } [1{:}n] \mid \texttt{oddp}(i)\ \}$$

yields a result sequence v of length $\lfloor n/2 \rfloor$ of odd values while the Fortran statement

$$\texttt{FORALL } (i = 1{:}n,\ \texttt{odd}(i))\ v(i) = i$$

replaces the elements in the odd-numbered positions of v.

Third, the Fortran FORALL construct provides explicit control over memory. Explicit control over memory can be quite important for performance. For example, if we were to repeatedly multiply the same sparse matrix repeatedly by different right hand sides (which is in fact exactly what happens in the CG benchmark), we could reuse a single temporary instead of freeing and allocating each time. Explicit control over memory also gives us a better interface to the regular portions of the computation.

Finally, the base types of a nested aggregate in Fortran are drawn from the Fortran data types and include multidimensional arrays and pointers. In NESL, we are restricted to simple scalar values and record types. Thus, expressing a sparse matrix as a collection of supernodes would be cumbersome in NESL. Another important difference is that we may construct nested aggregates of heterogeneous depth with Fortran, which is important, for example, in the representation of adaptive oct-tree spatial decompositions.

4   Implementation Issues

Expression of nested data-parallelism in Fortran is of limited interest and of no utility if such computations can not achieve high performance. Parallel execution and tuning for the memory hierarchy are the two basic requirements for high performance. Since the locus of activity and amount of work in a nested data-parallel computation can not be statically predicted, run-time techniques are generally required.

4.1   Implementation Strategies

There are two general strategies for the parallel execution of nested data parallelism, both consisting of a compile-time and a run-time component.

The thread-based approach. This technique conceptually spawns a different thread of computation for every parallel evaluation within a FORALL construct. The compile-time component constructs the threads from the nested loops. A run-time component dynamically schedules these threads across processors. Recent work has resulted in run-time scheduling techniques that minimize completion time and memory use of the generated threads [9, 6, 20]. Scheduling very fine-grained threads (e.g., a single multiplication in the sparse matrix-vector product example) is impractical, hence compile-time techniques are required to increase thread granularity, although this may result in lost parallelism and increased load imbalance.

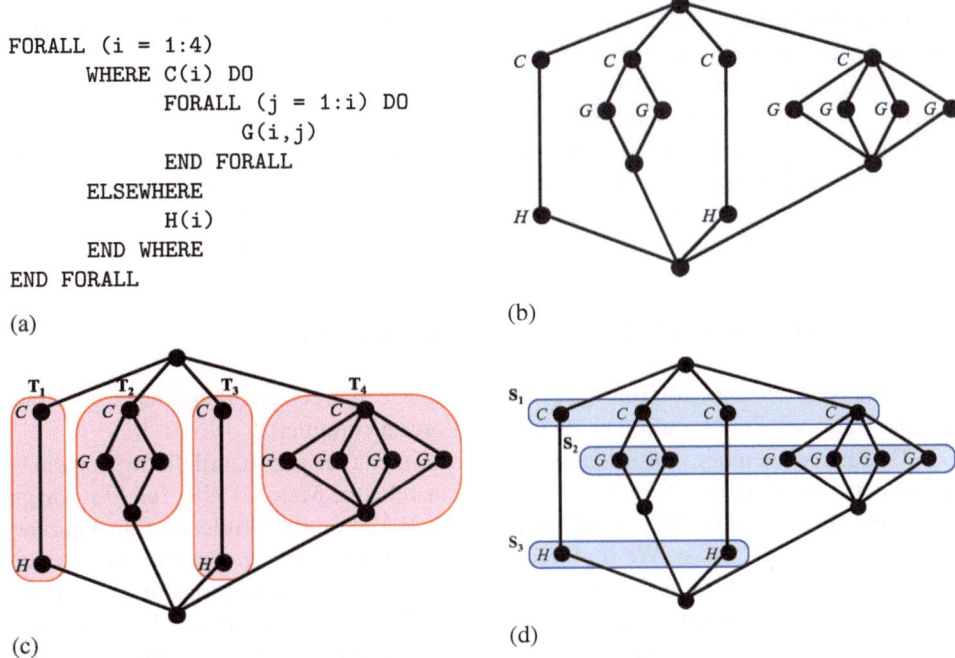

```
FORALL (i = 1:4)
     WHERE C(i) DO
          FORALL (j = 1:i) DO
               G(i,j)
          END FORALL
     ELSEWHERE
          H(i)
     END WHERE
END FORALL
```

(a)

(b)

(c)

(d)

Fig. 3. (a) Nested data-parallel program. (b) The associated dependence graph. (c) Thread decomposition of the graph. (d) Data-parallel decomposition of the graph.

The flattening approach. This technique replaces nested loops by a sequence of steps, each of which is a simple data-parallel operation. The compile-time component of this approach is a program transformation that replaces FORALL constructs with "data-parallel extensions" of their bodies and restructures the representation of nested aggregate values into a form suitable for the efficient implementation of the data-parallel operations [8,26]. The run-time component is a library of data-parallel operations closely resembling HPF-LIB, the standard library that accompanies HPF. A nested data-parallel loop that has been flattened may perform a small multiplicative factor of additional work compared with a sequential implementation. However, full parallelism and optimal load balance are easily achieved in this approach. Compile-time techniques to fuse data-parallel operations can reduce the number of barrier synchronizations, decrease space requirements, and improve reuse [12,24].

The two approaches are illustrated for a nested data-parallel computation and its associated dependence graph[1] in Fig. 3. Here G and H denote assignment statements that can not introduce additional dependences, since there can be no data dependences between iterations of FORALL loops.

In Fig. 3(c) we show a decomposition of the work into parallel threads $T_1, \dots, T_4$. In this decomposition the body of the outer FORALL loop has been serialized to increase the grain size of each thread. As a result the amount of work in each thread is quite

---

[1] We are using HPF INDEPENDENT semantics for the control dependences of a FORALL loop.

different. On the other hand, since each thread executes a larger portion of the sequential implementation, it can exhibit good locality of reference.

In Fig. 3(d) we show a decomposition of the work into sequential steps $S_1, \ldots, S_3$, each of which is a simple data-parallel operation. The advantage of this approach is that we may partition the parallelism in each operation to suit the resources. For example, we can create parallel slack at each processor to hide network or memory latencies. In this example, the dependence structure permits the parallel execution of steps S_1 and S_2, although this increases the complexity of the run time scheduler.

4.2   Nested Parallelism Using Current Fortran Compilers

What happens when we compile the Fortran 90 sparse matrix-vector product smvp shown in Fig. 2 for parallel execution using current Fortran compilers?

For shared-memory multiprocessors we examined two auto-parallelizing Fortran 90 compilers: the SGI F90 V7.2.1 compiler (beta release, March 1998) for SGI Origin class machines and the NEC FORTRAN90/SX R7.2 compiler (release 140, February 1998) for the NEC SX-4. We replaced FORALL construct in Fig. 2 with an equivalent DO loop to obtain a Fortran 90 program. Since the nested parallel loops in smvp do not define a polyhedral iteration space, many classical techniques for parallelization do not apply. However, both compilers recognize that iterations of the outer loop (over rows) are independent and, in both cases, these iterations are distributed over processors. The dot-product inner loop is compiled for serial execution or vectorized. This strategy is not always optimal, since the distribution of work over outermost iterations may be uneven or there may be insufficient parallelism in the outer iterations.

For distributed memory multiprocessors we examined one HPF compiler. This compiler failed to compile smvp because it had no support for pointers in Fortran 90 derived types. Our impression is that this situation is representative of HPF compilers in general, since the focus has been on the parallel execution of programs operating on rectangular arrays. The data distribution issues for the more complex derived types with pointers are unclear. Instead, HPF 2.0 supports the non-uniform distribution of arrays over processors. This requires the programmer to embed irregular data structures in an array and determine the appropriate mapping for the distribution.

We conclude that current Fortran compilers do not sufficiently address the problems of irregular nested data parallelism. The challenge for irregular computations is to achieve uniformly high and predictable performance in the face of dynamically varying distribution of work. We are investigating the combined use of threading and flattening techniques for this problem.

Our approach is to transform nested data parallel constructs into simple Fortran 90, providing simple integration with regular computations, and leveraging the capabilities of current Fortran compilers. This source-to-source translation restricts our options somewhat for the thread scheduling strategy. Since threads are not part of Fortran 90, the only mechanism for their (implicit) creation are loops, and the scheduling strategies we can choose from are limited by those offered by the compiler/run-time system. In this regard, standardized loop scheduling directives like the OpenMP directives [23] can improve portability.

A nested data parallel computation should be transformed into a (possibly nested) iteration space that is partitioned over threads. Dynamic scheduling can be used to tolerate variations in progress among threads. Flattening of the loop body can be used to ensure that the amount of work per thread is relatively uniform.

4.3 Example

Consider a sparse $m \times n$ matrix A with a total of r nonzeros. Implementation of the simple nested data parallelism in the procedure smvp of Fig. 2 must address many of the problems that may arise in irregular computations:

- Uneven units of work: A may contain both dense and sparse rows.
- Small units of work: A may contain rows with very few nonzeros.
- Insufficient units of work: if n is less than the number of processors and r is sufficiently large, then parallelism should be exploited within the dot products rather than between the dot products.

We constructed two implementations of smvp. The *pointer-based* implementation is obtained by direct compilation of the program in Fig. 2 using auto-parallelization. As mentioned, this results in a parallelized outer loop, in which the dot products for different rows are statically or dynamically scheduled across processors.

The *flat* implementation is obtained by flattening smvp. To flatten smvp we replace the nested sequence representation of A with a linearized representation (A', s). Here A' is an array of r pairs, indexed by val and col, partitioned into rows of A by s. Application of the flattening tranformations to the loop in Fig. 2 yields

$$y = \texttt{segmented\_sum}(A'\%\texttt{val} * x(A'\%\texttt{col}),s),$$

where segmented_sum is a data-parallel operation with efficient parallel implementations [3]. By substituting $A'\%\texttt{val} * x(A'\%\texttt{col})$ for the first argument in the body of segmented_sum, the sum and product may be fused into a *segmented dot-product*. The resulting algorithm was implemented in Fortran 90 for our two target architectures.

For the SGI Origin 200, A' is divided into $p\sigma$ sections of length $r/(p\sigma)$ where p is the number of processors and $\sigma \geq 1$ is a factor to improve the load balance in the presence of multiprogramming and operating system overhead on the processors. Sections are processed independently and dot products are computed sequentially within each section. Sums for segments spanning sections are adjusted after all sections are summed.

For the NEC SX-4, A' is divided into pq sections where q is the vector length required by the vector units [5]. Section i, $0 \leq i < pq$, occupies element $i \bmod q$ in a length q vector of thread $\lfloor i/p \rfloor$. Prefix dot-products are computed independently for all sections using a sequence of $r/(pq)$ vector additions on each processor. Segment dot-products are computed from the prefix dot-products and sums for segments spanning sections are adjusted after all sections are summed [25]. On the SX-4, σ is typically not needed since the operating system performs gang-scheduling and the threads experience very similar progress rates.

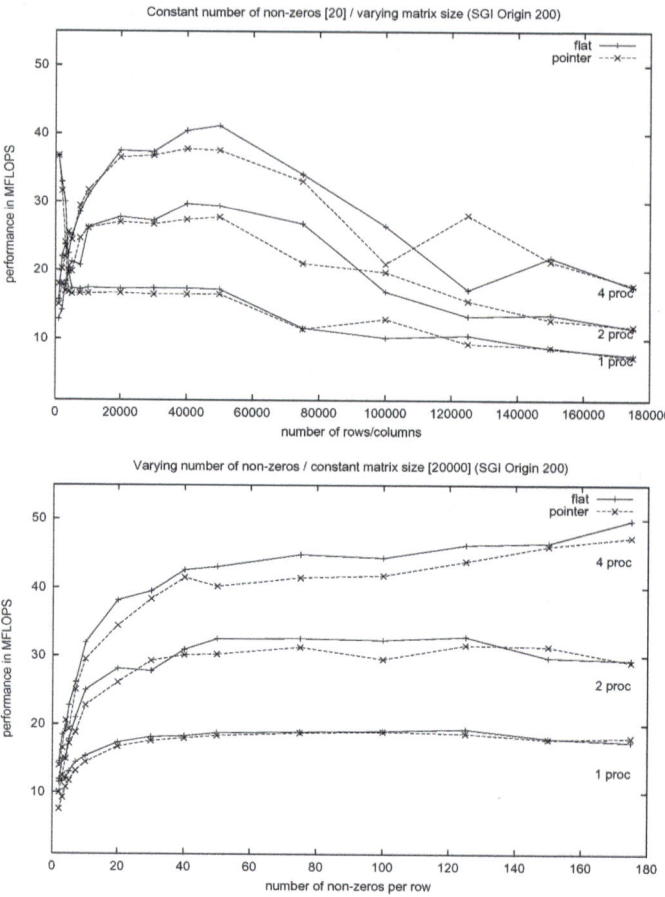

Fig. 4. Performance measurements for the pointer-based and the flattened implementations of smvp on the SGI Origin 200.

4.4   Results

The SGI Origin 200 used is a 4 processor cache-based shared memory multiprocessor. The processors are 180MHz R10000 with 1MB L2 cache per processor. The NEC SX-4 used is a 16 processor shared-memory parallel vector processor with vector length 256. Each processor has a vector unit that can perform 8 or 16 memory reads or writes per cycle. The clock rate is 125 MHz. The memory subsystem provides sufficient sustained bandwidth to simultaneously service independent references from all vector units at the maximum rate.

The performance on square sparse matrices of both implementations is shown for 1, 2, and 4 processors for the Origin 200 in Fig. 4 and for the SX-4 in Fig. 5. The top graph of each figure shows the performance as a function of problem size in megaflops

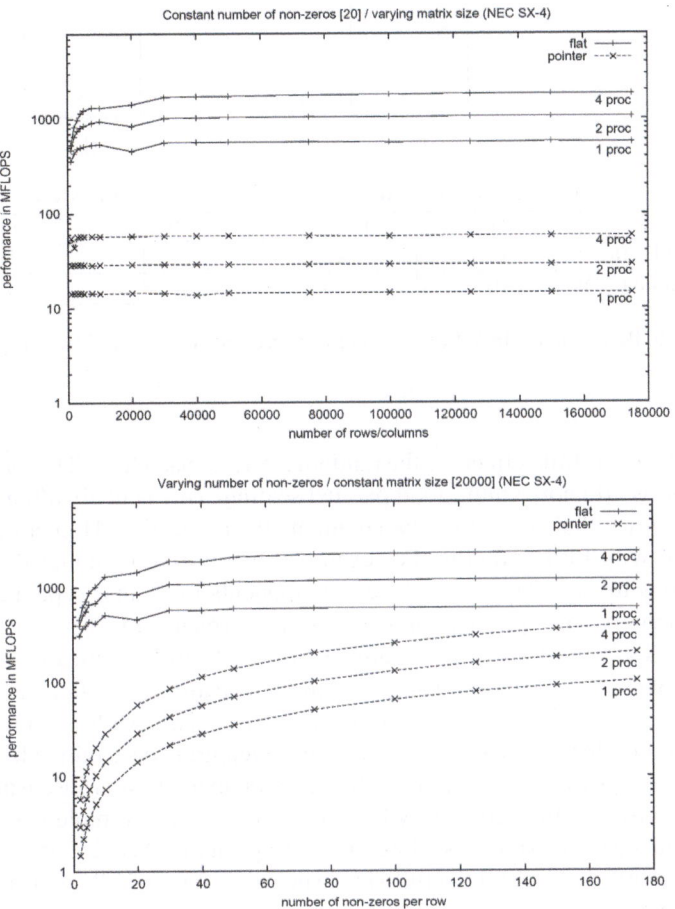

Fig. 5. Performance measurements for the pointer-based and the flattened implementations of smvp on the NEC SX-4. (Note the logarithmic scale of the y-axis.)

per second, where the number of floating point operations for the problem is $2r$. Each row contains an average of 20 nonzeros and the number of rows is varied between 1000 and 175000. The bottom graph shows the influence of the average number of nonzeros per row (r/n) on the performance of the code. To measure this, we chose a fixed matrix size ($n = 20000$) and varied the average number of nonzeros on each row between 5 and 175. In each case, the performance reported is averaged over 50 different matrices.

On the Origin 200 the flattened implementation performed at least as well as the pointer-based version over most inputs. The absolute performance of neither implementation is particularly impressive. The sparse matrix-vector problem is particularly tough for processors with limited memory bandwidth since there is no temporal locality in the use of A (within a single matrix-vector product), and the locality in reference to x diminishes with increasing n. While reordering may mitigate these effects in some

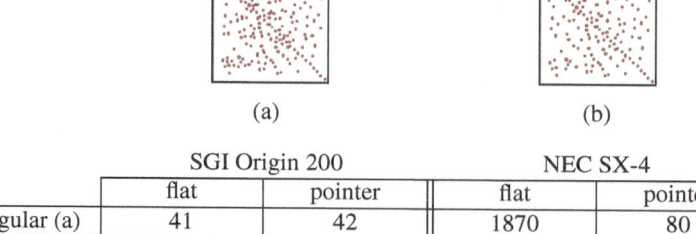

| | SGI Origin 200 | | NEC SX-4 | |
	flat	pointer	flat	pointer
regular (a)	41	42	1870	80
irregular (b)	40	26	1278	76

Fig. 6. Performance in Mflops/s using four processors on two different problems.

applications, it has little effect for the random matrices used here. The Origin 200 implementations also do not exhibit good parallel scaling. This is likely a function of limited memory bandwidth that must be shared among the processors. Higher performance can be obtained with further tuning. For example, the current compiler does not perform optimizations to map the val and col components of A into separate arrays. When applied manually, this optimization increases performance by 25% or more.

On the SX-4 the flattened implementation performs significantly better than the pointer implementation over all inputs. This is because the flattened implementation always operates on full-sized vectors (provided $r \geq pq$), while the pointer-based implementation performs vector operations whose length is determined by the number of nonzeros in a row. Hence the pointer-based implementation is insensitive to problem size but improves with average row length. For the flattened implemementation, absolute performance and parallel scaling are good primarily because the memory system has sufficient bandwidth and the full-sized vector operations fully amortize the memory access latencies.

Next, we examined the performance on two different inputs. The *regular* input is a square sparse matrix with $n = 25000$ rows. Each row has an average of 36 randomly placed nonzeros for a total of $r = 900000$ nonzeros. The *irregular* input is a square sparse matrix with $n = 25000$ rows. Each row has 20 randomly placed nonzeros, but now 20 consecutive rows near the top of A contain 20000 nonzeros each. Thus the total number of nonzeros is again 900000, but in this case nearly half of the work lies in less than 0.1% of the dot products.

The performance of the two implementations is shown in Fig. 6. The pointer-based implementation for the Origin 200 is significantly slower for the irregular problem, regardless of the thread scheduling technique used (dynamic or static). The problem is that a small "bite" of the iteration space may contain a large amount of work, leading to a load imbalance that may not be correctable using a dynamic scheduling technique. In the case of the SX-4 pointer-based implementation this effect is not as noticeable, since the dot product of a dense row operates nearly two orders of magnitude faster than the dot product of a row with few nonzeros.

The flattened implementation delivers essentially the same performance for both problems on the Origin 200. The SX-4 performance in the irregular case is reduced because dense rows span many successive sections, and incur an $O(pq)$ cost in the final sum adjustment phase that is not present for shorter rows. However, this cost is unrelated to problem size, so the disparity between the performance in the two problems vanishes with increasing problem size.

4.5 Discussion

This example provides some evidence that the flattening technique can be used in an implementation to improve the performance stability over irregular problems while maintaining or improving on the performance of the simple thread-based implementation. The flattening techniques may be particularly helpful in supporting the instruction-level and memory-level parallelism required for high performance in modern processors. The example also illustrates that dynamic thread scheduling techniques, in the simple form generated by Fortran compilers, may not be sufficient to solve load imbalance problems that may arise in irregular nested data-parallel computations.

While these irregular matrices may not be representative of typical problems, the basic characteristic of large amounts of work in small portions of the iteration space is not unusual. For example, it can arise with data structures for the adaptive spatial decomposition of a highly clustered n-body problem, or with divide-and-conquer algorithms like quicksort or quickhull [4].

5   Related Work

The facilities for data abstraction and dynamic aggregates are new in Fortran 90. Previously, Norton et al. [21], Deczyk et al. [14], and Nyland et al. [22] have experimented with these advanced features of Fortran 90 to analyze their impact on performance.

HPF 2.0 provides a MAPPED irregular distribution to support irregular computations. This is a mechanism, and makes the user responsible for developing a coherent policy for its use. Further, the ramifications of this distribution on compilation are not yet fully resolved. Our approach is fundamentally different in attempting to support well a smaller class of computations with an identifiable policy (nested data parallelism) and by preprocessing the irregular computation to avoid reliance on untested strategies in the HPF compiler. While HPF focuses on the irregular distribution of regular data structures, our approach is based on the (regular) distribution of irregular data structures.

Split-C [13] also provides a number of low-level mechanisms for expressing irregular computations. We are attempting to provide a higher level of abstraction while providing the same level of execution efficiency of low-level models.

The Chaos library [28] is a runtime library based on the inspector/executor model of executing parallel loops involving irregular array references. It is a suitable back end for the features supporting irregular parallelism in HPF 2.0. The library does not provide obvious load balancing policies, particularly for irregularly nested parallel loops. Recent work on Chaos is looking at compilation aspects of irregular parallelism.

Flattening transformations have been implemented for the languages NESL [7], Proteus [26], Amelia [30], and V [11], differing considerably in their completeness and in the associated constant factors. There has been little work on the transformation of imperative constructs such as sequential loops within a FORALL, although there do not appear to be any immediate problems. The flattening techniques are responsible for several hidden successes. Various high performance implementations are really hand-flattened nested data-parallel programs: FMA [15], radix sort [32], as well as the NAS CG implementation described in the introduction. Furthermore, the set of primitives in HPFLIB itself reflects a growing awareness and acceptance of the utility of the flattening techniques.

The mainstream performance programming languages Fortran and SISAL [10, 31] can express nested data parallelism, but currently do not address its efficient execution in a systematic way. Languages that do address this implementation currently have various disadvantages: they are not mainstream languages (NESL, Proteus); they subset or extend existing languages (Amelia, V, F90V); they do not interface well with regular computations (NESL, Proteus); they are not imperative, hence provide no control over memory (NESL, Proteus); and they are not tuned for performance at the level of Fortran (all).

6   Conclusions

Nested data parallelism in Fortran is attractive because Fortran is an established and important language for high-performance parallel scientific computation and has an active community of users. Many of these users, who are now facing the problem of implementing irregular computations on parallel computers, find that threading and flattening techniques may be quite effective and are tediously performing them manually in their codes [22, 15]. At the same time, they have substantial investments in existing code and depend on Fortran or HPF to achieve high performance on the regular portions of their computations. For them it is highly desirable to stay within the Fortran framework.

The advanced features of modern Fortran dialects, such as derived data types, modules, pointers, and the FORALL construct, together constitute a sufficient mechanism to express complex irregular computations. This makes it possible to express both irregular and regular computations within a common framework and in a familiar programming style.

How to achieve high performance from such high-level specifications is a more difficult question. The flattening technique can be effective for machines with very high and uniform shared-memory bandwidth, as that found in current parallel vector processors from NEC and SGI/Cray or the parallel multithreaded Tera machine. For cache-based shared-memory processors, the improved locality of the threading approach is a better match. The flattening techniques may help to extract threads from a nested parallel computation that, on the one hand, are sufficiently coarse grain to obtain good locality of reference and amortize scheduling overhead, and, on the other hand, are sufficiently numerous and regular in size to admit good load balance with run-time scheduling.

Thus we believe that irregular computations can be expressed in modern Fortran dialects and efficiently executed through a combination of source-to-source preprocessing, leveraging of the Fortran compilers, and runtime support. Looking ahead, we are planning to examine more complex irregular algorithms such as supernodal Cholesky factorization, and an adaptive fast n-body methods.

References

1. P. Au, M. Chakravarty, J. Darlington, Y. Guo, S. Jähnichen, G. Keller, M. Köhler, M. Simons, and W. Pfannenstiel. Enlarging the scope of vector-based computations: Extending Fortran 90 with nested data parallelism. In W. Giloi, editor, *International Conference on Advances in Parallel and Distributed Computing*, pages 66–73. IEEE, 1997.
2. D. H. Bailey, E. Barszcz, J. T. Barton, D. S. Browning, R. L. Carter, L. Dagum, R. A. Fatoohi, P. O. Frederickson, T. A. Lasinski, R. S. Schreiber, H. D. Simon, V. Venkatakrishnan, and S. K. Weeratunga. The NAS parallel benchmarks. *The International Journal of Supercomputer Applications*, 5(3):63–73, Fall 1991.
3. G. E. Blelloch. *Vector Models for Data-Parallel Computing*. The MIT Press, Cambridge, MA, 1990.
4. G. E. Blelloch. Programming parallel algorithms. *Commun. ACM*, 39(3):85–97, Mar. 1996.
5. G. E. Blelloch, S. Chatterjee, and M. Zagha. Solving linear recurrences with loop raking. *Journal of Parallel and Distributed Computing*, 25(1):91–97, Feb. 1995.
6. G. E. Blelloch, P. B. Gibbons, and Y. Matias. Provably efficient scheduling for languages with fine-grained parallelism. In *Proceedings of the 7th Annual ACM Symposium on Parallel Algorithms and Architectures*, pages 1–12, Santa Barbara, CA, June 1995.
7. G. E. Blelloch, J. C. Hardwick, J. Sipelstein, M. Zagha, and S. Chatterjee. Implementation of a portable nested data-parallel language. *Journal of Parallel and Distributed Computing*, 21(1):4–14, Apr. 1994.
8. G. E. Blelloch and G. W. Sabot. Compiling collection-oriented languages onto massively parallel computers. *Journal of Parallel and Distributed Computing*, 8(2):119–134, Feb. 1990.
9. R. D. Blumofe, C. F. Joerg, B. C. Kuszmaul, C. E. Leiserson, K. H. Randall, and Y. Zhou. Cilk: An efficient multithreaded runtime system. In *Proceedings of the Fifth ACM SIGPLAN Symposium on Principles and Practice of Parallel Programming*, pages 207–216, Santa Barbara, CA, July 1995. ACM.
10. D. Cann and J. Feo. SISAL versus FORTRAN: A comparison using the Livermore loops. In *Proceedings of Supercomputing'90*, pages 626–636, New York, NY, Nov. 1990.
11. M. M. T. Chakravarty, F.-W. Schröer, and M. Simons. V—Nested parallelism in C. In W. K. Giloi, S. Jähnichen, and B. D. Shriver, editors, *Programming Models for Massively Parallel Computers*, pages 167–174. IEEE Computer Society, 1995.
12. S. Chatterjee. Compiling nested data-parallel programs for shared-memory multiprocessors. *ACM Trans. Prog. Lang. Syst.*, 15(3):400–462, July 1993.
13. D. E. Culler, A. Dusseau, S. C. Goldstein, A. Krishnamurthy, S. Lumetta, T. von Eicken, and K. Yelick. Parallel programming in Split-C. In *Proceedings of Supercomputing '93*, pages 262–273, Nov. 1993.
14. V. K. Decyk, C. D. Norton, and B. K. Szymanski. High performance object-oriented programming in Fortran 90. *ACM Fortran Forum*, 16(1), Apr. 1997.
15. Y. C. Hu, S. L. Johnsson, and S.-H. Teng. High Performance Fortran for highly irregular problems. In *Proceedings of the Sixth ACM SIGPLAN Symposium on Principles and Practice of Parallel Programming*, pages 13–24, Las Vegas, NV, June 1997. ACM.
16. C. H. Koelbel, D. B. Loveman, R. S. Schreiber, G. L. Steele Jr., and M. E. Zosel. *The High Performance Fortran Handbook*. Scientific and Engineering Computation. The MIT Press, Cambridge, MA, 1994.

17. C. L. Lawson, R. J. Hanson, D. R. Kincaid, and F. T. Krogh. Basic linear algebra subprograms for Fortran usage. *ACM Trans. Math. Softw.*, 5(3):308–323, Sept. 1979.
18. J. McCalpin. Personal communication, Apr. 1998.
19. M. Metcalf and J. Reid. *Fortran 90/95 Explained*. Oxford University Press, 1996.
20. G. J. Narlikar and G. E. Blelloch. Space-efficient implementation of nested parallelism. In *Proceedings of the Sixth ACM SIGPLAN Symposium on Principles and Practice of Parallel Programming*, pages 25–36, Las Vegas, NV, June 1997. ACM.
21. C. D. Norton, B. K. Szymanski, and V. K. Decyk. Object-oriented parallel computation for plasma simulation. *Commun. ACM*, 38(10):88–100, Oct. 1995.
22. L. S. Nyland, S. Chatterjee, and J. F. Prins. Parallel solutions to irregular problems using HPF. First HPF UG meeting, Santa Fe, NM, Feb. 1997.
23. OpenMP Group. OpenMP: A proposed standard API for shared memory programming. White paper, OpenMP Architecture Review Board, Oct. 1997.
24. D. W. Palmer, J. F. Prins, S. Chatterjee, and R. E. Faith. Piecewise execution of nested data-parallel programs. In C.-H. Huang, P. Sadayappan, U. Banerjee, D. Gelernter, A. Nicolau, and D. Padua, editors, *Languages and Compilers for Parallel Computing*, volume 1033 of *Lecture Notes in Computer Science*, pages 346–361. Springer-Verlag, 1996.
25. J. Prins, M. Ballabio, M. Boverat, M. Hodous, and D. Maric. Fast primitives for irregular computations on the NEC SX-4. *Crosscuts*, 6(4):6–10, 1997. CSCS.
26. J. F. Prins and D. W. Palmer. Transforming high-level data-parallel programs into vector operations. In *Proceedings of the Fourth ACM SIGPLAN Symposium on Principles and Practice of Parallel Programming*, pages 119–128, San Diego, CA, May 1993.
27. S. Saini and D. Bailey. NAS Parallel Benchmark (1.0) results 1-96. Technical Report NAS-96-018, NASA Ames Research Center, Moffett Field, CA, Nov. 1996.
28. J. Saltz, R. Ponnusammy, S. Sharma, B. Moon, Y.-S. Hwang, M. Uysal, and R. Das. A manual for the CHAOS runtime library. Technical Report CS-TR-3437, Department of Computer Science, University of Maryland, College Park, MD, Mar. 1995.
29. J. T. Schwartz, R. B. K. Dewar, E. Dubinsky, and E. Schonberg. *Programming with Sets: An Introduction to SETL*. Springer-Verlag, New York, NY, 1986.
30. T. J. Sheffler and S. Chatterjee. An object-oriented approach to nested data parallelism. In *Proceedings of the Fifth Symposium on the Frontiers of Massively Parallel Computation*, pages 203–210, McLean, VA, Feb. 1995.
31. S. K. Skedzelewski. Sisal. In B. K. Szymanski, editor, *Parallel Functional Languages and Compilers*, pages 105–157. ACM Press, New York, NY, 1991.
32. M. Zagha and G. E. Blelloch. Radix sort for vector multiprocessors. In *Proceedings of Supercomputing'91*, pages 712–721, Albuquerque, NM, Nov. 1991.

Memory System Support for Irregular Applications

John Carter, Wilson Hsieh, Mark Swanson, Lixin Zhang,
Erik Brunvand, Al Davis, Chen-Chi Kuo,
Ravindra Kuramkote, Michael Parker, Lambert Schaelicke,
Leigh Stoller, and Terry Tateyama

Department of Computer Science, University of Utah

Abstract. Because irregular applications have unpredictable memory access patterns, their performance is dominated by memory behavior. The Impulse configurable memory controller will enable significant performance improvements for irregular applications, because it can be configured to optimize memory accesses on an application-by-application basis. In this paper we describe the optimizations that the Impulse controller supports for sparse matrix-vector product, an important computational kernel, and outline the transformations that the compiler and runtime system must perform to exploit these optimizations.

1 Introduction

Since 1985, microprocessor performance has improved at a rate of 60% per year; in contrast, DRAM latencies have improved by only 7% per year, and DRAM bandwidths by only 15-20% per year. One result of these trends is that it is becoming increasingly hard to make effective use of the tremendous processing power of modern microprocessors because of the difficulty of providing data in a timely fashion. For example, in a recent study of the cache behavior of the SQLserver database running on an Alphastation 8400, the system achieved only 12% of its peak memory bandwidth [11]; the resulting CPI was 2 (compared to a minimum CPI of 1/4). This factor of eight difference in performance is a compelling indication that caches are beginning to fail in their role of hiding the latency of main memory from processors. Other studies present similar results for other applications [4, 5].

Fundamentally, modern caches and memory systems are optimized for applications that sequentially access dense regions of memory. Programs with high degrees of spatial and temporal locality achieve near 100% cache hit rates, and will not be affected significantly as the latency of main memory increases. However, many important applications do not exhibit sufficient locality to achieve such high cache hit rates, such as sparse matrix, database, signal processing, multimedia, and CAD applications. Such programs consume huge amounts of memory bandwidth and cache capacity for little improvement in performance. Even applications with good spatial locality often suffer from poor cache hit rates, because of conflict misses caused by the limited size of processor caches and large working sets.

D. O'Hallaron (Ed.): LCR'98, LNCS 1511, pp. 17–26, 1998.

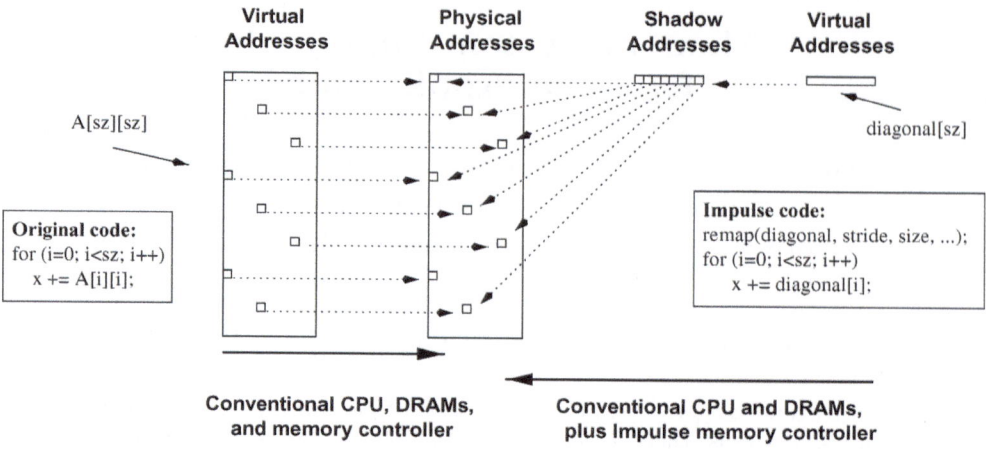

Fig. 1. Remapping shadow addresses using the Impulse memory controller. For clarity of exposition, we leave out how the Impulse controller supports non-contiguous physical pages for A.

A number of ongoing projects have proposed significant modifications to conventional CPU or DRAM designs to attack this memory problem: supporting massive multithreading [1], moving processing power on to the DRAM chips [6], or building completely programmable architectures [14]. While these projects show promise, unconventional CPU or DRAM designs will likely be slower than conventional designs, due to slow industry acceptance and the fact that processors built on current DRAM processes are 50% slower than conventional processors. In the Impulse project, we address the memory problem without modifying conventional CPUs, caches, memory busses, or DRAMs. Instead, we are building an *adaptable memory controller* that will enable programs to control how data is moved between cache and main memory at a fine grain, which will result in significantly improved memory performance for irregular applications. The Impulse memory controller implements this functionality by supporting an extra level of address translation in the memory controller.

The Impulse controller allows applications to make use of unused physical addresses, which it then translates into real physical addresses. Suppose a processor exports 32 address lines across the memory bus, but has only 1GB of memory installed. The remaining 3GB of physical address normally would be considered invalid. The Impulse controller makes use of these otherwise unused physical addresses by letting software specify *mapping functions* between these so-called *shadow addresses* and physical addresses directly backed by DRAM.

Consider a simple function that calculates the sum of the diagonal of a dense matrix, as illustrated in Figure 1. The left-hand side of the figure represents how the data would be accessed on a conventional system, where the desired diagonal elements are spread across physical memory. Each diagonal element is on a different cache line, and each such cache line contains only one useful element.

The right-hand side of the figure shows how data is accessed on an Impulse system. The application would specify that the contents of the `diagonal` vector are *gathered* using a simple strided function, using the `remap` operation. Once the `remap` operation has been performed, the memory controller knows to respond to requests for data in this shadow region by performing a gather-read operation from the physical memory storing A. The code then accesses the synthetic data structure, `diagonal`, which is mapped to a region of shadow memory. By accessing a dense structure, the application will see fewer cache misses, suffer less cache pollution, and more effectively utilize scarce bus bandwidth and cache capacity.

In Section 2, we use the sparse matrix-vector product algorithm from conjugate gradient to illustrate in detail two Impulse optimizations: (i) efficient scatter-gather access of sparse data structures and (ii) no-copy page recoloring to eliminate conflict misses between data with good locality and data with poor locality. In Section 3, we briefly discuss several other optimizations that are enabled by an Impulse memory system, describe related projects, and summarize our conclusions.

2   Sparse Matrix-Vector Multiplication

Sparse matrix-vector product is an irregular computational kernel critical to many large scientific algorithms. For example, most of the time spent performing a conjugate gradient computation [2] is spent in a sparse matrix-vector product. Similarly, the Spark98 [9] kernels are all sparse matrix-vector product codes. In this section, we describe several optimizations that Impulse enables to improve the performance of sparse matrix-vector muliplication, and sketch the transformations that the compiler and runtime system must perform to exploit these optimizations.

To avoid wasting memory, sparse matrices are generally encoded so that only non-zero elements and corresponding index arrays need to be stored. For example, the Class B input for the NAS Conjugate Gradient kernel involves a 75,000 by 75,000 sparse matrix with only 13,000,000 non-zeroes - far less than 1% of the entries. Although these encodings save tremendous amounts of memory, sparse matrix codes tend to suffer from poor memory performance because of the use of indirection vectors and the need to access sparse elements of the dense vector. In particular, when we profiled the NAS Class B conjugate gradient benchmark on a Silicon Graphics Origin 2000, we found that its L1 cache hit rate was only 58.5% and its L2 cache hit rate was only 92.7%.

Figure 2 illustrates the key inner loop and matrix encodings for conjugate gradient. Each iteration multiplies a row of the sparse matrix A with the dense vector x. On average, less than 1% of the elements of each row are non-zeroes, and these non-zeroes are "randomly" distributed. While matrix-vector product is trivially parallelizable or vectorizable, this code performs quite poorly on conventional memory systems because the accesses to x are both indirect (via the `COLUMN[]` index vector) and sparse. When $x[]$ is accessed, a conventional memory

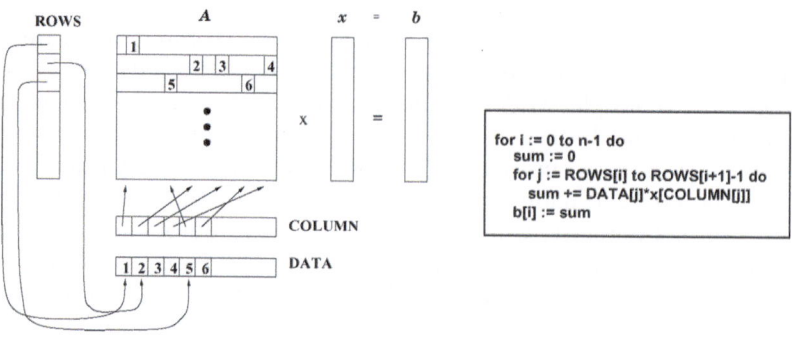

Fig. 2. Conjugate gradient's sparse matrix-vector product. The sparse matrix A is encoded using three arrays: DATA, ROWS, and COLUMN. A is encoded densely in DATA. ROWS[i] indicates where the ith row begins in DATA. COLUMN[i] indicates which column of A the element stored in DATA[i] is in, and thus which value of x must be fetched when performing the inner product.

system will fetch a cache line of data, of which only one element is used. Because of the large size of x and A and the sparse nature of accesses to x during each iteration of the loop, there will be very little reuse in the L1 cache — almost every access to x results in an L1 cache miss. If data layouts are carefully managed to avoid L2 cache conflicts between A and x, a large L2 cache can provide some reuse of x, but conventional memory systems do not provide simple mechanisms for avoiding such cache conflicts.

Because the performance of conjugate gradient is dominated by memory performance, it performs poorly on conventional architectures. Two previously studied solutions to this problem are to build main memory exclusively from fast SRAM or support massive multithreading. The Cray T916, whose main memory consists solely of fast (and expensive) SRAM, achieved 759.9 Mflops/second on the NAS CG benchmark in July 1995 [12]. The Tera MTA prototype achieves good single-node performance on the NAS conjugate gradient benchmark because its support for large numbers of cheap threads allows it to tolerate almost arbitrary memory latencies [3]. However, both of these solutions are very expensive compared to conventional hardware.

In Impulse, we take a different position — we employ off-the-shelf CPUs and memories, but build an adaptable memory controller. Our memory controller supports two major optimizations for improving the memory behavior of sparse matrix-vector product. First, it can perform scatter/gather operations, which trades temporal locality in the second-level cache for spatial locality in the first-level cache. Second, it can be used to color pages so as to better utilize physically indexed, second-level caches. We discuss these optimizations in the following two subsections.

```
setup x'[k] = x[COLUMN[k]]
for i := 0 to n-1
  sum := 0
  for j := ROWS[i] to ROWS[i+1]-1
    sum += DATA[k] * x'[j]
  b[i] := sum
```

Fig. 3. Code for sparse matrix-vector product on Impulse

2.1   Scatter/Gather

As described in Section 1, the Impulse memory controller will support scatter/gather reads and writes. We currently envision at least three forms of scatter/gather functions: (i) simple strides (ala the diagonal example), (ii) indirection vectors, and (iii) pointer chasing. The type of scatter/gather function that is relevant to conjugate gradient is the second, the use of indirection vectors.

The compiler technology necessary to exploit Impulse's support for scatter/gather is similar to that used in vectorizing compilers. Figures 3 and 4 illustrate the code generated for the inner loop of conjugate gradient by a compiler designed to exploit the Impulse memory controller. The compiler must be able to recognize the use of indirection vectors, and download to the memory controller a description of the data structure being accessed (x) and the indirection vector used to specify which elements of this structure to gather (COLUMN[]). This code can be safely hoisted outside of the inner loops, as shown in Figure 3. After performing this setup operation, the compiler will then emit accesses to the remapped version of the gathered structure (x') rather than accesses to the original structure (x).

Scatter/gather memory operations take longer than accessing a contiguous cache line, since the memory controller needs to perform multiple actual DRAM accesses to fill the x' structure. The low-level design details of the Impulse DRAM scheduler are beyond the scope of this paper – suffice it to say that it is possible to pipeline and parallelize many of the DRAM accesses required to read and write the sparse data through careful design of the controller. For optimal performance, the compiler should tell the memory controller to sequentially prefetch the elements of x' (i.e., pre-gather the next line of x'), since it can tell that x' is accessed sequentially. When all of these issues are considered, the compiler should unroll the inner loop according to the cache line size and software pipeline accesses to the multiplicand vector, as shown in Figure 4. In this example, we assume a cache line contains four doubles; for clarity we assume that each row contains a multiple of eight doubles.

These optimizations improve performance in two ways. First, fewer memory instructions need to be issued. Since the read of the indirection vector (COLUMN[]) occurs at the memory, the processor does not need to issue the read. Second, spatial locality is improved in the L1 cache. Since the memory controller packs

```
setup x'[k] = x[COLUMN[k]]
for i := 0 to n-1
  lo := ROWS[i]
  hi := ROWS[i+1]-1
  sum := DATA[lo]*x'[lo]
  for j := lo to hi step 8 do
    sum += DATA[j+4]*x'[j+4]
    sum += DATA[j+1]*x'[j+1]
    sum += DATA[j+2]*x'[j+2]
    sum += DATA[j+3]*x'[j+3]
    sum += DATA[j+8]*x'[j+8]
    sum += DATA[j+5]*x'[j+5]
    sum += DATA[j+6]*x'[j+6]
    sum += DATA[j+7]*x'[j+7]
  sum -= DATA[hi+1]*x'[hi+1]
  b[i] := sum
```

Fig. 4. Code for sparse matrix-vector product on Impulse with strip mining and software pipelining

the gathered elements into cache lines, the cache lines contain 100% useful data, rather than only one useful element each.

Since a detailed simulation of the scatter/gather capability is not yet available, we performed a simple analysis of its impact. If we examine just the inner loop of the original algorithm, it is dominated by the cost for performing three loads (to DATA[i], COLUMN[i], and x[COLUMN[i]]). If we assume a 32-byte cache line that can hold four doubles, we can see where Impulse wins in Table 1. Conv. (Best) represents the best case performance of a conventional memory system. In this case, the L2 cache is large enough to hold x and there are no L2 cache conflicts between x and any other data. Conv. (Worst) represents the worst case performance of a conventional memory system. In this case, either the L2 cache is too small to hold a significant fraction of x or frequent conflicts between x and other structures cause the useful elements of x to be conflicted out of the L2 cache before they can be reused in a subsequent iteration. Because x is not accessed directly in Impulse, its best and worst case are identical.

As we see in Table 1, Impulse eliminates four memory accesses, each of which are hits in the L2 cache, from the best case for a conventional system. In place of these four accesses, Impulse incurs the miss marked in the table with an asterisk, which is the gathered access to x'. Compared to the worst case for a conventional system, Impulse eliminates both the four L2 hits and four misses to main memory. Note that except on machines with large L2 caches and very careful data layout, the worst case is also the expected case because of the large size of x and its poor locality. If we assume that software pipelining and prefetching will hide cold misses to linearly accessed data, the misses to DATA[i], COLUMN[i], and x'[i] can be hidden. In this case, using Impulse will allow the processor to perform floating point operations as fast as the memory system can

Load	Conv. (Best)	Conv. (Worst)	Impulse
DATA[i]	miss	miss	miss
COLUMN[i]	.5 miss	.5 miss	
x[COLUMN[i]]	L2 hit	miss	
x'[i]			miss*
DATA[i+1]	L1 hit	L1 hit	L1 hit
COLUMN[i+1]	L1 hit	L1 hit	
x[COLUMN[i+1]]	L2 hit	miss	
x'[i+1]			L1 hit

Load	Conv. (Best)	Conv. (Worst)	Impulse
DATA[i+2]	L1 hit	L1 hit	L1 hit
COLUMN[i+2]	L1 hit	L1 hit	
x[COLUMN[i+2]]	L2 hit	miss	
x'[i+2]			L1 hit
DATA[i+3]	L1 hit	L1 hit	L1 hit
COLUMN[i+3]	L1 hit	L1 hit	
x[COLUMN[i+3]]	L2 hit	miss	
x'[i+3]			L1 hit

Table 1. Simple performance comparison of conventional memory systems (best and worst cases) and Impulse. The starred miss requires a gather at the memory controller.

supply two streams of dense data (x' and DATA). However, since the non-linear acccess to x[COLUMN[i]] cannot be hidden, a conventional machine will suffer frequent high latency read misses, thereby dramatically reducing performance.

It is important to note that the use of scatter/gather at the memory controller reduces temporal locality in the second-level cache. The remapped elements of x' are themselves never reused, whereas a carefully tuned implementation of CG would be able to reuse many elements of x cached in a large L2 cache. Such a situation would approach the best case column of Figure 1, modulo conflict effects in the L2 cache. In the next section, we propose a way to achieve the best case using Impulse.

2.2 Page Coloring

As an alternative to gathering elements of x, which achieves the performance indicated under the Impulse column of Table 1, Impulse allows applications to manage the layout of data in the L2 cache. In particular, on an Impulse machine, we can achieve the best-case memory performance for a conventional machine on conjugate gradient by performing *page coloring*.

Page coloring optimizes the physical memory layout of data structures so that data with good temporal locality (e.g., x) is mapped to a different part of a physically-indexed cache than data with poor temporal locality (e.g., DATA, ROW, and COLUMN). In a physically-indexed second level cache, physical pages from different data structures can wind up being mapped to the same location. As a result, data in these pages will tend to conflict with one another. For conjugate gradient, the x vector is reused within an iteration, while elements of the DATA, ROW, and COLUMN vectors are used only once each in each iteration. Thus, we would like to ensure that x does not conflict in the L2 cache with the other data structures. In the NAS CG benchmarks, x ranges from 600 kilobytes to 1.2 megabytes, and the other structures range from 100-300 megabytes. Thus, x will not fit in most processor's L1 caches, but can fit in many L2 caches.

On a conventional machine, page coloring is hard to exploit. Coloring requires that the system not map data to physical pages that have the same "color" (i.e., map to the same portion of the cache) as data with good locality. If you wish to devote a large percentage of your cache to data with good temporal locality, this effectively means that you cannot use large portions of your physical memory, which is impractical for problems with large data sets. In addition, coloring often requires data to be copied between physical pages to eliminate conflicts, which is expensive.

Impulse eliminates both of these problems, which makes page coloring simple and efficient. Since Impulse can map data structures to *shadow* physical addresses, rather than real physical addresses, and because wasting shadow address space does not waste physical memory, data with good locality can be mapped to pages that do not conflict with other data. And, because of the extra level of translation, this recoloring can be done without copying. In the case of conjugate gradient, Impulse can be used to remap x to pages that map to most of the physically-indexed L2 cache, and can remap DATA, ROWS, and COLUMNS to a small number of pages that do not conflict with either x or each other. In effect, we can use a small part of the second-level cache, e.g., two pages each for DATA, ROWS, and COLUMNS, as a stream buffer [8].

3   Conclusions

We have described two optimizations that the Impulse controller supports for irregular applications. An Impulse system can also improve the performance of dense matrix kernels. Dense matrices are tiled to improve cache behavior, but the effectiveness of tiling is limited by the fact that tiles do not necessarily occupy contiguous blocks in caches. Tile copying [7] can improve the performance of tiled algorithms by reducing cache conflicts, but the cost of copying is fairly high. The Impulse controller allows tiles to be copied *virtually*. The cost that virtual copying incurs is that read-write sharing between virtual copies requires cache flushing to maintain coherence.

An Impulse memory controller can be used to dynamically build superpages, so as to save processor TLB entries [13]. This optimization can dramatically improve the performance of applications with large working sets. Unfortunately, because the physical memory associated with a superpage must be contiguous and aligned, superpages cannot easily be used to map user data on conventional memory systems. However, by using shadow memory to map superpages, and then remapping the shadow addresses back to the non-contiguous physical addresses corresponding to the user data, Impulse can create superpages for arbitrarily shuffled user data.

An Impulse memory system also helps support efficient message passing. First, its support for scatter/gather means that the memory controller, rather than software, can handle the chore of gathering data into messages. As a result, the Impulse controller can reduce the overhead of sending a message. Second, its support for building superpages means that network interfaces need not perform complex and expensive address translation. Instead, an Impulse controller could handle the translations necessary for messages that span multiple pages.

Other research projects are looking at similar issues in designing memory systems; we briefly describe a few of them. The Morph architecture [14] is almost entirely configurable: programmable logic is embedded in virtually every datapath in the system. As a result, optimizations similar to those that we have described are possible using Morph. The Impulse project is designing hardware that will be built in an academic environment, which requires that we attack hardware outside of the processor. The RADram project at UC Davis is building a memory system that lets the memory perform computation [10]. RADram is a PIM ("processor-in-memory") project similar to IRAM [6], where the goal is to put processors close to memory. In contrast, Impulse does not seek to put a processor in memory; instead, its memory controller is programmable.

In summary, the Impulse project is developing a memory system that will help to improve the memory performance of irregular applications. We have used sparse matrix-vector product as our motivating example, but we expect that the ability to configure an Impulse memory system to various memory access patterns will be useful for a wide range of irregular problems. We are investigating both manual and automatic mechanisms for taking advantage of the flexibility that Impulse provides.

References

1. R. Alverson, D. Callahan, D. Cummings, B. Koblenz, A. Porterfield, and B. Smith. The Tera computer system. In *Proceedings of the International Conference on Supercomputing*, pages 272–277, Amsterdam, The Netherlands, June 1990.
2. D. Bailey et al. The NAS parallel benchmarks. Technical Report RNR-94-007, NASA Ames Research Center, Mar. 1994.
3. J. Boisseau, L. Carter, K. S. Gatlin, A. Majumdar, and A. Snavely. NAS benchmarks on the Tera MTA. In *Proceedings of the Multithreaded Execution Architecture and Compilation*, Las Vegas, NV, Jan. 31–Feb. 1, 1998.
4. D. Burger, J. Goodman, and A. Kagi. Memory bandwidth limitations of future microprocessors. In *Proceedings of the 23rd Annual International Symposium on Computer Architecture*, pages 78–89, May 1996.
5. A. Huang and J. Shen. The intrinsic bandwidth requirements of ordinary programs. In *Proceedings of the 7th Symposium on Architectural Support for Programming Languages and Operating Systems*, pages 105–114, Oct. 1996.

6. C. E. Kozyrakis et al. Scalable processors in the billion-transistor era: IRAM. *IEEE Computer*, pages 75–78, Sept. 1997.
7. M. S. Lam, E. E. Rothberg, and M. E. Wolf. The cache performance and optimizations of blocked algorithms. In *Proceedings of the 4th ASPLOS*, pages 63–74, Santa Clara, CA, Apr. 1991.
8. S. McKee and W. A. Wulf. Access ordering and memory-conscious cache utilization. In *Proceedings of the First IEEE Symposium on High Performance Computer Architecture*, pages 253–262, Raleigh, NC, Jan. 1995.
9. D. R. O'Hallaron. Spark98: Sparse matrix kernels for shared memory and message passing systems. Technical Report CMu-CS-97-178, Carnegie Mellon University School of Computer Science, Oct. 1997.
10. M. Oskin, F. T. Chong, and T. Sherwood. Active pages: A model of computation for intelligent memory. In *Proceedings of the 25th International Symposium on Computer Architecture*, June 1998. To appear.
11. S. E. Perl and R. Sites. Studies of Windows NT performance using dynamic execution traces. In *Proceedings of the Second Symposium on Operating System Design and Implementation*, pages 169–184, October 1996.
12. S. Saini and D. H. Bailey. NAS parallel benchmark (version 1.0) results. Technical Report NAS-96-18, NASA Ames Research Center, Moffett Field, CA, Nov. 1996.
13. M. Swanson, L. Stoller, and J. Carter. Increasing TLB reach using superpages backed by shadow memory. In *Proceedings of the 25th Annual International Symposium on Computer Architecture*, June 1998.
14. X. Zhang, A. Dasdan, M. Schulz, R. K. Gupta, and A. A. Chien. Architectural adaptation for application-specific locality optimizations. In *Proceedings of the 1997 IEEE International Conference on Computer Design*, 1997.

Menhir: An Environment for High Performance Matlab

Stéphane Chauveau, François Bodin
schauvea@irisa.fr, bodin@irisa.fr

IRISA-INRIA
Campus de Beaulieu, 35042 Rennes, FRANCE

Abstract. In this paper we present MENHIR a compiler for generating sequential or parallel code from the MATLAB language. The compiler has been designed in the context of using MATLAB as a specification language. One of the major features of MENHIR is its retargetability that allows generating parallel and sequential C or Fortran code. We present the compilation process and the target system description for MENHIR. Preliminary performances are given and compared with MCC, the MathWorks MATLAB compiler.

1 Introduction

Current approaches for the development of numerical applications are frequently decomposed in two phases. First a prototype or specification is written using a popular high level tool such as MATLAB [10,11]. Then, the application is rewritten in Fortran or C so efficiency can be achieved. When high performance is needed, the application is also parallelized. This manual process is error prone and very time consuming which makes MATLAB compilers very attractive, especially when the target is a parallel computer.

Automatically generating an efficient implementation from a MATLAB code encompasses two main aspects. First, the generated code must be efficient and able to exploit a wide range of architectures from sequential computers to parallel ones. Secondly the user must be able to change the generated code so it can be automatically inserted or exploited in an existing development environment. For instance, when the user has special data structures for implementing its matrices and the corresponding specific highly optimized libraries the compiler should be able to exploit them.

In this paper we present MENHIR (Matlab ENvironment for HIgh peRformance), a multi-target compiler for MATLAB 4.2[1]. The main feature of MENHIR is its target description system that allows addressing sequential and parallel systems. The user may add its own data structures and functions to this description, thus enabling better code generation. To exploit parallelism MENHIR relies on libraries such as ScaLapack [5].

---

[1] With a few restriction such as the operators eval, feval that take MATLAB statements as input are not supported.

D. O'Hallaron (Ed.): LCR'98, LNCS 1511, pp. 27–40, 1998.

In Section 2, we present a short summary of related tools. In Section 3, we overview the MENHIR's target system description (MTSD). In Section 4, we describe the type analysis and the code generation method used in MENHIR. Finally in Section 5, we present preliminary performance results on a set of MATLAB programs running on sequential and parallel architectures.

2   Related Works

Number of studies hava already been based on the MATLAB language. The first set of tools are interpreted MATLAB clones such as SCILAB and OCTAVE. Another class of tools proposes parallel extensions to MATLAB such as message passing in MultiMatlab [12] or a client-server mechanism in MathServer [8] or IPSC-MATLAB [4]. The main difference between those tools and MATLAB compilers is the lack of static type analysis.

Three existing compilers MCC, distributed by THE MATHWORKS INC, MATCOM [13], distributed by MATHTOOLS, and Falcon are available to generate efficient codes. The FALCON [9,7] system encompasses a compiler and an interactive environment for transforming and optimizing MATLAB programs. The Falcon project was focused on the type analysis, one of the keypoint in compiling MATLAB. MENHIR differs from these two systems by two aspects. Firstly MENHIR relies on a retargetable code generator which Falcon, MATCOM and MCC do not. Secondly, MENHIR is able to exploit parallel numerical libraries.

3   Menhir's Target System Description (MTSD)

The MTSD is a major component of MENHIR. Its goal is to describe the property and implementation details of target system. The target system, in our case, is a programming language such as Fortran, C or other and a linear algebra library. The MTSD indicates to MENHIR how to implement the matrix data structures as well as all the MATLAB operators and functions. MENHIR code generation algorithm is independent from the target system. In Table 1, we present the main constructs of the MTSD. These constructs indicate to MENHIR how to allocate and access matrices and declare the library functions which implements MATLAB operators and functions.

As shown in Table 1.b, the data structures are described in an object oriented manner. Each data structure is described in a `class` construct which members specify its properties. The fields `elem`, `shape`, `minreal`, `maxreal`, `minimag` and `maximag` respectively indicate the basic type of the elements of the data structure, the rank of the structure and a complex value interval. The `prop` field is used to declare properties about the content of the objects. These properties are declared as shown in Table 1.a. They are associated to classes, variables and expression results and propagated by the type analysis presented in Section 4.1. The identifier `bname` indicates that the data structure is inherited from class `bname`. This mechanism allows to define new classes with different properties but which share the same implementation. In example Table 1.b, the class `UTMatReal` is declared to the compiler to be an upper triangular matrix with element values in 0 to 2^{16} which is implemented with the same data structure as the real matrix (i.e. `MatReal`). The default data structures to be used by the code generator are declared as shown Table 1.c.

The declaration of the accesses to data structure elements is shown Table 2.g while code generation for memory allocation is illustrated in Table 1.j. The `assign` and `cast` constructs are provided to allow the compiler to copy and convert data structures from one type to another. Cast operations are necessary to ensure that the result of operators/functions can be converted in a format suitable to the routines exploiting the results. They are shown Table 1.f.

MATLAB operators and functions are declared as shown in Table 1.d and 1.e. The code to generate is an expression or a sequence of statements. For each parameter in the list, an attribute (*att*) and a class name (*cname*) are given. The attribute indicates how the parameter is used in the target code ; `out` for a result, `const` for a constant variable, `expr` for an expression (i.e. without an address) etc. The type indicates the data structure `class` name. Contrary to operators, MATLAB functions are declared in two parts (Table 1.e). First some target subroutines are declared. Then, they are gathered in the `function` construct. MATLAB control statements are defined similarly as shown in Table 2.h.

The conform statement iterators given in Table 2.i are used by the compiler to implement conform statement, such as the point-wise addition of two matrices, in an efficient manner that minimizes the number of temporary variables. For instance, if we consider the MATLAB expression $R = B - A * x$, an implementation based on library function calls would imply to generate the code in two parts, first $T = A * x$ and then $R = B - T$ resulting in poor performance. Instead MENHIR generates the following C code using the `loop` construct:

```
...
for (tmp136 = 1; tmp136 <= tmp128; tmp136++) {
    for (tmp135 = 1; tmp135 <= tmp127; tmp135++) {
        (*tmp133++) = ((*tmp129++)-
            ((*tmp131++)*tmp94));
    }
    tmp129 = &tmp129[tmp130];
    tmp131 = &tmp131[tmp132];
    tmp133 = &tmp133[tmp134];
}
...
```

As shown by this example, the generated code can be close to what "hand programming" would produce. In the case of parallel code generation, a similar principle, shown in Table 2.k, is used to describe the scanning of a distributed matrix local elements.

Syntax	Example
a) Properties property *name* ;	property DIAG ; property UPPERTRI ;

b) Data Structure
class *name* : *bname*
    elem = *id*
    shape = *scal,row,col,matrix*
    minreal = *constant* ;
    maxreal = *constant* ;
    minimag = *constant* ;
    maximag = *constant* ;
    prop = *list of properties*;
end
	class UTMatReal: MatReal
	    elem = Real ;
	    shape = matrix;
	    minreal = 0 ;
	    maxreal = 2^{16};
	    prop = UPPERTRI;
	end

c) Default Data Structure default *shape, elemtype* [,*prop*] = *cname*	default matrix,complex = MatComplex ; default matrix,real,DIAG = DiagMatReal ;

d) MATLAB Operators
inline *name* (*att cname var1,...*)
    => *statement 1*
    => ...
    ;
inline *res name* (*att cname var1,...*)
        "*expression*" ;
	inline real @op_add(real A,int B)
	    "(A+((double)B))" ;

e) MATLAB Functions
 	
inline *func1(parameters)*
    => code ;
    ;
function *res* = *name(parameter)*
    add *func1*;
    add *func2*;
end function
	inline C_lup_real(out MatReal MATL,
	    out MatReal MATU, ...,MatReal MATA)
	    => lup_RRI_R(&MATL,&MATU,
	        &MATP,MATA) ;
	    ;
	function [L,U,P] = lu(A)
	    add C_lup_real(L,U,P,A) ;
	end function

f) Assign and Cast Operators
inline @assign(out *cname r*,
        const *cname i*)
    => *statement 1* ;
    => ...;
    ;
inline *cname* @cast(*att cname var*)
    "*expression*"
    ;
	inline @assign(out MatReal DEST,
	        const TranspMatReal SRC)
	    => transpose_R_R(&DEST,&SRC) ;
	    ;
	inline int @cast(RowInt VAR)
	    "VAR.get(1)"
	    ;

Table 1. Target System Description Content.

Syntax	Example

g) Index Accesses
 	
`inline @get|put|...()`
  `=> statement 1 ;`
  `=> ...;`
  `;`
	`inline real @get(MatReal MAT)`
	  `"get_Rii(&MAT,I1,I2)" ;`
	`inline @put(MatReal MAT,real VAL)`
	  `=> set_Riir(&MAT,I1,I2,VAL) ;`
	  `;`

h) Matlab Control Statement
 	
`inline @do(real CPT,real START,`
    `const real STEP,real END)`
  `=> loop code(BODY);`
`;`
	`inline @do(real CPT,real START,`
	  `const real STEP,real END)`
	  `=> for(CPT=START;CPT<=END;CPT+ =STEP){`
	  `=>    BODY`
	  `=> }`
	`;`

i) Conform Statement Iterators
 	
`inline @loop(local variablelist)`
  `=> statement 1(BODY) ;`
  `=> ...;`
  `;`
	`inline @loop(local int I1,int I2)`
	  `=> for (I1=1;I1<=DIM1;I1++)`
	  `=>    for (I2=1;I2<=DIM2;I2++)`
	  `=>    {`
	  `=>       BODY`
	  `=>    }`
	  `;`

j) Memory Management, Declaration, Target Language Statements
`inline @declar(cname var)`
  `=> statement 1 ;`
  `=> ...;`
  `;`
`inline @alloc(cname var,`
    `int DIM1,int DIM2)`
  `=> statement 1 ;`
  `=> ...;`
  `;`
	`inline @declar(MatReal MAT)`
	  `=> MatReal *MAT ;`
	  `;`
	`inline @alloc(MatReal VAR,`
	    `int DIM1,int DIM2)`
	  `=> alloc_R(&VAR,DIM1,DIM2) ;`
	  `;`

k) Local scan of distributed matrix
 	
`defaccess matrix name ;`
`inline @loopinit:name(cname var)`
  `=> statement 1 ;`
  `;`
`inline @loop:name(parameter list)`
  `=> statement 1 ;`
  `;`
`inline real @get:name(cname var)`
  `"(expression)" ;`
	`defaccess matrix paralocal ;`
	`inline @loopinit:paralocal(PMatReal MAT)`
	  `=> LOCD1 = MAT.local.dim1;`
	  `=> LOCD2 = MAT.local.dim2;`
	  `;`
	`inline @loop:paralocal(..., int LOCD1,`
	    `int LOCD2)`
	  `=> STAT1`
	  `=> for (I2=1;I2<=LOCD2;I2++){`
	  `=>    for (I1=1;I1<=LOCD1;I1++) {`
	  `=>       BODY }`
	  `=>    STAT2 }`
	  `;`
	`inline real @get:paralocal(PMatReal MAT)`
	  `"(*PTR++)" ;`

Table 2. Target System Description Content.

4   Overview of Menhir's Compilation Process

MENHIR's compilation process is divided in the following steps:

1. **lexical and syntactic analysis:** this step performs the lexical and syntactic analysis of the MATLAB M-Files.
2. **identifiers analysis:** this preliminary step of the type analysis determines the nature of the identifier. The nature of an identifier can be a script file (M-file), a function or a variable. The ambiguities are resolved statically and the compiler assumes that the nature of an identifier is constant in a program unit (MATLAB allows a identifier to reference a variable and a function or a script in the same program unit).
3. **function cloning and restructuring in canonical form:** At this step, all functions are cloned and most of the special cases of MATLAB are removed by expanding them in a canonical form. Temporary variables are added to limit code expansion for large expressions. All runtime choices are expanded at that step. For instance, the statement A=B+C is expanded in:

```
if (dim1(B)==1 & dim2(B)==1) then
   if (dim1(C)==1 & dim2(C)==1) then
      A = B+C % scalar+scalar
   else
      A = B+C % scalar+matrice
   ...
```

a simple local type analysis is applied locally to each expression to avoid useless cases. Later, after the type analysis has been performed, dead code elimination is applied.
4. **type analysis and dead code elimination:** this type analysis determines the properties of each expression and variable according to the semantic of MATLAB and the target system description. If an operator or a function returns an object with special properties, they are propagated. The type analysis is completed by removing all dead codes (i.e. runtime operator/function selection that have been solved statically). The remaining conditionals added at step 3 are left as run-time checking.
5. **data structure selection:** This step selects an implementation for each variable according to the type computed in previous step and the defaults given in the MTSD (Table 1.c).
6. **operators and functions implementation selection:** At this step operator and function implementations are selected. Data structure casts are inserted to ensure that returned results can be used as input parameters of the subsequent function calls.
7. **code issue:** This step gathers the selected implementations to issue the final code.

In the following, we present in more details steps 4 and 6.

4.1   Type Analysis

The type analysis is a major component in MENHIR as its result has a great impact on the quality of the generated code. In MATLAB, all operators and functions are polymorph and the default is to implement all objects as complex matrices. Furthermore, variable types can change during the program execution and matrices can be resized by any assignment. An accurate analysis limits runtime type checking overheads and allows selecting the appropriate library methods (for instance, operators on floats instead of complex variables).

A type in MENHIR is defined as a set of possible shapes (*scalar, row vector, column vector* and *matrix*), an interval of complex value, a string, an integer status and a set of numerical properties. A class from the MTSD defines such a type. The properties are used to select optimized implementations. To illustrate this feature consider the following MATLAB statement sequence:

$$A = \texttt{triu}(\ldots);$$
$$\ldots$$
$$v = b/A;$$

MATLAB function `triu` returns a matrix that is upper triangular. To execute efficiently specialized solver (this solver does not check at runtime if matrix A is upper triangular). This is achieved in MENHIR by having the following declaration in the MTSD that use the **UPPERTRI** property that is propagated by the type analysis:

```
property UPPERTRI ;
class UTMatReal : MatReal
    prop = UPPERTRI;
end ;
inline triu_Real(out UTMatReal A, MatReal B)
        => ... ;
        ;
function [A] = triu(B)
add triu_Real;
...
end function
inline @op_matdiv(MatReal RES,
    MatReal PARAM1,
    UTMatReal PARAM2)
        => ...;
        ;
```

This powerful feature is not restricted to MATLAB functions and operators. User's libraries can be exploited in a similar fashion and new properties can be created at any time.

The type propagation algorithm is interprocedural and based on an iterative data flow solver [1,6] that is closed to the one proposed by DeRose [9]. The analysis computes a superset of the possible values for each variable and expression at each point of the program. However, in many cases, there is not enough information to propagate in a MATLAB program to compute accurately the types describing these supersets. Via directives, MENHIR allows specifying information on objects that are used by the type analysis. The most frequent directives give information about the contents (i.e. the shape, the properties or the element types) of some variables at a given point of the program. These directives cannot be regarded as global type declarations since their scope is limited and they do not specify the implementation of the objects. A variable *declared* as a scalar in a point of program can become a matrix or a vector in another point.

The second kind of directives is used to simplify the semantic of the MATLAB language. For instance the directive

$$\texttt{\%\$VAR var [,var] : [no] RESIZE/MASK}$$

allows to declare if a variable is subject to resizing or to be acceded using a mask index[2].

4.2   Code Generation

The code generation must solve three problems:

1. selecting the data structure for each variable and expression according to the type analysis
2. selecting the implementations (the methods) for MATLAB operators and functions
3. inserting data structure cast operations

These choices are interdependent. The methods whose operand data structures match more the current parameters data structures are most suitable. Conversely, it seems interesting to adapt the data structures to the methods using them. To illustrate this problem, consider the class C_1 and C_2 and the implementations of $\mathbf{F}$, $M_1 : C_1 \to C_2$ and $M_2 : C_2 \to C_1$, in the following MATLAB code:

```
for i=1:n
    B=F(A) ; C=F(B) ; A=F(C) ;
end
```

The figure 1 shows how the initial choice for the data structure of $\mathbf{A}$ can influence the remaining of the analysis.

In MENHIR, the choice of variable data structures is made first according to the result of the type analysis and to the defaults given in the MTSD. Although imperfect, this strategy is acceptable since only a few types are provided into the MTSD.

Then, the selection for operators/functions and the insertion of cast operations is made. This is performed by building *on the flight* a directed acyclic graph. Vertices correspond to variables, MATLAB operators/functions and data

---

[2] A mask variable in MATLAB is a matrix containing only 0 or 1 element values used as booleans.

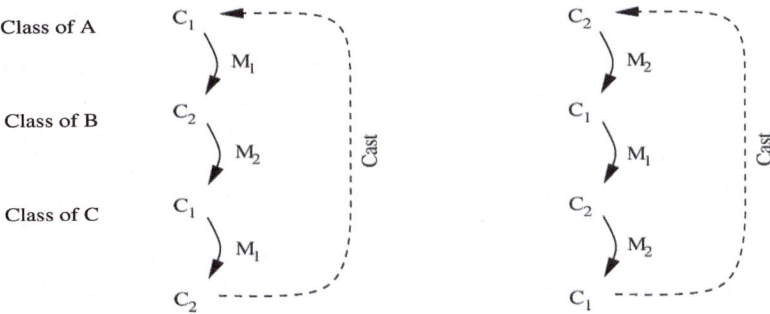

Fig. 1. Selection of the implementation according to the initial data structure of **A**

structure conversion subroutine. An example of such a graph is shown figure 2. Code generation consists in selecting a set of paths that covers all program statements and variables (indicated in gray in Figure 2).

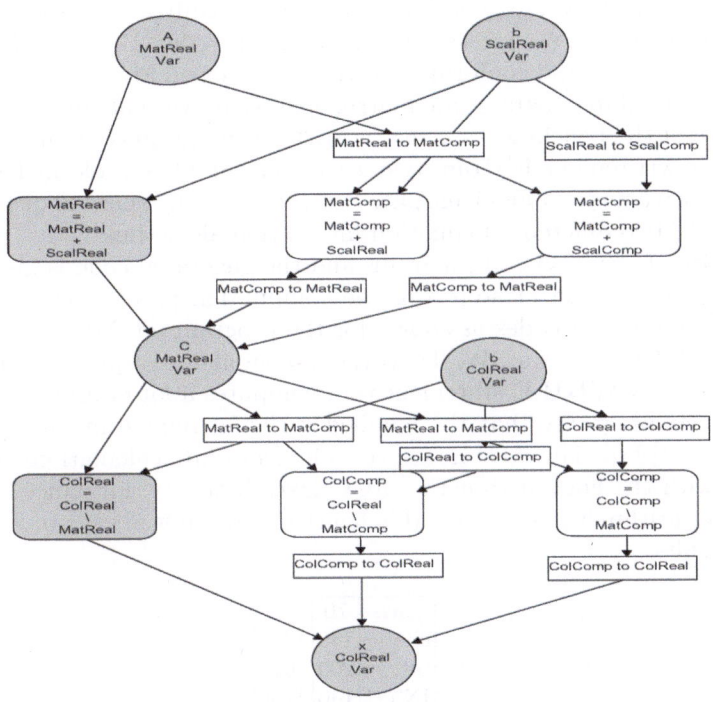

Fig. 2. Code generation graph for MATLAB code C=A+b; x=C/d;. MatComp, MatReal, ColReal, ColComp, and ScalReal, respectively denote complex matrices, float matrices, float column vectors, complex column vectors, and float scalars data structures.

A score is associated to each cast and each method according to the shapes of the data structures to which they are applied. Then, the algorithm looks for a path with a lowest score on a subset of the graph. The costly part of the algorithm is not the shortest path computation itself but the creation of the subgraphs that represents the data structures casts. Each of them depends on the type analysis result for the local value and can contain several nodes. In many cases, the construction of the graph is avoided by choosing as preset cast (i.e. applied to generic types). For more details the reader can refer to [3].

The last stage consists in assembling the codes of the selected methods for the expressions, the instructions and the casts. The syntax of the target language, except for the literals and the identifiers, is entirely described by the **MTSD**.

5   Preliminary Performances

In this section, we present preliminary performance obtained using MENHIR on a single processor Sun workstation and on a parallel computer Onyx SGI with 4 processors R10000. The sequential codes are generated using a target system description based on the Lapack library [2] while the parallel codes are obtained using ScaLapack [5]. The parallel codes are SPMD and the same data distribution (block-cyclic) is used for all matrices. Only a very few directives (20 for all benchmarks) were inserted in the MATLAB codes. Because MENHIR relies on parallel libraries and conform operations but not on MATLAB loops, program that does not exhibit coarse grain matrix operations was not run in parallel. This is the case of the benchmarks *gauss*, a MATLAB program computing a gaussian elimination written in a Fortran style, *chol*, an incomplete cholesky factorization, *pfl*, an iterative method for eigenspace decomposition by spectral dichotomy, and *INT1*, *INT4* two differential equation integration algorithms.

The size of the MATLAB programs and the generated code is given in Table 3. Cloning, performed at step 3 of the compilation process, can substantially generate large target codes as shown for the program *pfl*. MENHIR is more efficient than MCC, the MathWorks MATLAB compiler, except for *chol*. The main loop of *chol* is a **WHILE** statement that computes a lot of integer expressions. Some directives specify that the handled variables remain in the integer range $[-2^{31}, 2^{31} - 1]$ but they have no effect on intermediate calculations, which must be done with the float arithmetic. MCC gives better performance since it uses the integer arithmetic. However, this heuristic does not always produce the expected results.

gauss	70	200
chol	180	620
pfl	200	9000
INT 1	140	4700
INT 4	200	3100

Table 3. MATLAB program code sizes and corresponding generated C code sizes.

Two programs illustrate the parallel code generation: a conjugate gradient algorithm with preconditioning and a Jacobi computation.

Figure 4 gives the execution times for the conjugate gradient. On the x axis, MATLAB 4.2 and 5 correspond to the MATLAB interpreters execution time, MCC is the execution time of the code produced by the MathWorks compiler, MENHIR is the time for the sequential code generated by our compiler and ONYX$n \times m$ and PARAGON$n \times m$ are the execution times on the Onyx and the Paragon parallel computers. As it can be seen, MENHIR performs better that the interpreter and MCC except in one case, *chol*. In this case MENHIR's code contains float to integer conversions that slow down the algorithm. In general, the code produced by MENHIR is closed, for most of the benchmarks of the "hand-coded" versions of the algorithms. However, these "hand coded" versions were not aggressively optimized.

Parallel codes reach good speedups thanks to the ScaLapack library but also to the type analysis[3]. Figure 5 gives the execution times for two versions of the same version of Jacobi compiled with different MTSD. In the second version, good performance is obtained when the MTSD propagates the information that the preconditioning matrix M, shown Figures 3, is diagonal. Then, the run-time checking of this property disappears and a large amount of memory space and communication is saved.

```
. . .
m=size(A,1) ;
n=size(A,2) ;
[ M, N ] = split( A , b, 1.0, 1 ) ;
for iter = 1:max_it,
    x_1 = x;
    y = N*x + b ;
    x = M /y ;
    error = norm(x-x_1 )/norm( x );
    if ( error <= tol ), break, end
end
. . .
```

Fig. 3. Main loop of the Jacobi benchmark.

---

[3] We don't have MCC or MATLAB on the Onyx computer, so the performance numbers in sequential are not given for this architecture.

6   Conclusion

In this paper we briefly present MENHIR, a **retargetable** compiler for MAT-
LAB. The strength of MENHIR is its original target system description that allows
generating code that exploits optimized sequential and parallel libraries. Performance shows that the generated code is in most of the cases more efficient than
the one obtained by the Mathworks compiler MCC on sequential workstation.
Future work will focus on exploiting more aggressively parallelism by also considering MATLAB loops.

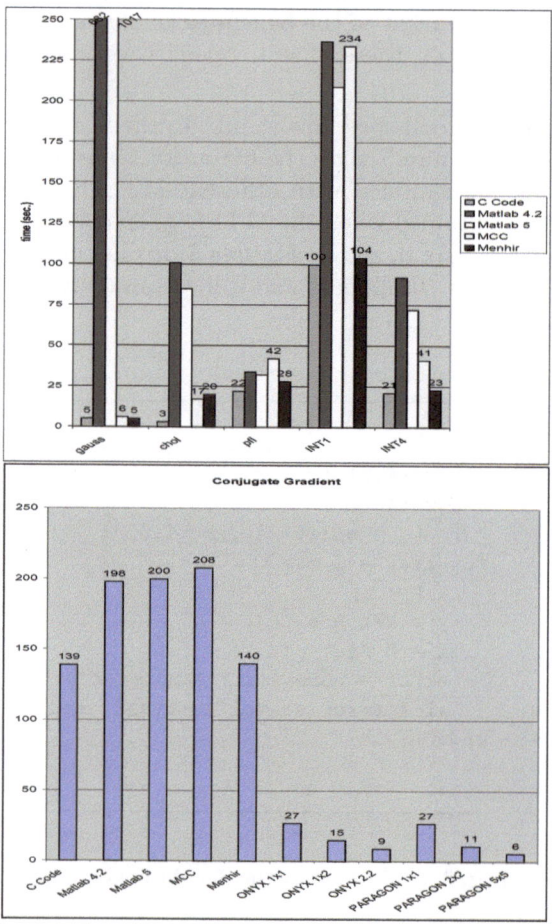

Fig. 4. Execution time in seconds of the sequential and parallel generated C codes.

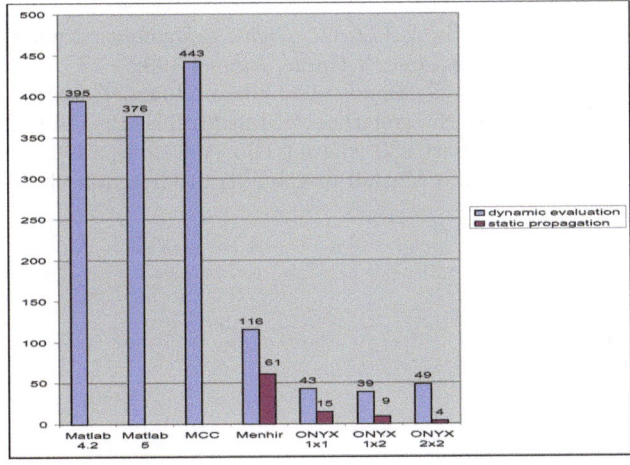

Fig. 5. Execution time in seconds for the jacobi code with and without the static propagation of the preconditioning matrix diagonal nature.

References

1. A. Aho, R. Sethi, and J. Ullman. *Compilers: Principles, Techniques and Tools.* Addisson-Wesley Publishing Compagny, 1985. 33

2. E. Anderson, Z. Bai, C. Bischof, J. Demmel, J. Dongarra, J. Du Croz, A. Greenbaum, S. Hammarling, A. McKenney, S. Ostrouchov, and D. Sorensen. *LAPACK Users' Guide.* SIAM, Philadelphia, second edition, 1995. 36

3. Stphane Chauveau. *MENHIR. un environnement pour l'excution efficace des codes Matlab (in French).* PhD thesis, Universit de Rennes 1, February 1998. 36

4. Shirish Chinchalkar. IPSC-MATLAB reference manual. Technical Report 92-106, Cornell Theory Center, September 1992. 28

5. J. Choi, J. DEmmel, I. Dhillon, J. Dongarra, S. Ostrouchov, A. Petitet, K. Stanley, D. Walker, and R.C. Whaley. ScaLAPACK: A portable linear algebra library for distributed memory computers - design issues and performance. Technical Report CS-95-283, Computer Science Dept., University of Tennesse, Knoxville, 1995. (LAPACK Working Note 95). 27, 36

6. John B. Kam and Jeffrey D. Ullman. Global data flow analysis and iterative algorithms. *Journal of the ACM*, 31(1):158–171, January 1976. 33

7. Bret Andrew Marsolf. Techniches for the interactive development of numerical linear algebra libraries for scientific computation. Master's thesis, University of Illinois at Urbana-Champaign, 1997. 28

8. M. Rezny. MATHSERVER: A client-server approach to scientific computation. Department of Mathematics, The University of Queensland, Australia. 28

9. Luis De Rose. compiler techniques for MATLAB programs. Master's thesis, University of Illinois at Urbana-Champain, 1996. 28, 33

10. INC THE MATHWORKS. *MATLAB, High-Performance Numeric Computation and Visualization Software. Reference Guide*, August 1992. 27

11. INC THE MATHWORKS. *MATLAB, High-Performance Numeric Computation and Visualization Software. User's Guide*, August 1992. 27
12. Anne E. Trefethen, Vijay S. Menon, Chi-Chao Chang, Grzegorz J. Czajkowski, Chirs Myers, and Lloyd N. Trefethen. MultiMATLAB: MATLAB on multiple processors. Technical Report 239, Cornel Theory Center, 1996. 28
13. Keren Yaron. MATCOM, a Matlab to C++ Translator, March 1996. 28

On the Automatic Parallelization of Sparse and Irregular Fortran Programs *

Yuan Lin and David Padua

Department of Computer Science, University of Illinois at Urbana-Champaign
{yuanlin,padua}©uiuc.edu

Abstract. Automatic parallelization is usually believed to be less effective at exploiting implicit parallelism in sparse/irregular programs than in their dense/regular counterparts. However, not much is really known because there have been few research reports on this topic. In this work, we have studied the possibility of using an automatic parallelizing compiler to detect the parallelism in sparse/irregular programs. The study with a collection of sparse/irregular programs led us to some common loop patterns. Based on these patterns three new techniques were derived that produced good speedups when manually applied to our benchmark codes. More importantly, these parallelization methods can be implemented in a parallelizing compiler and can be applied automatically.

1   Introduction

Sparse computations are implementations of linear algebra algorithms that store and operate on the nonzero array elements only. These algorithms are usually complex, use sophisticated data structures, and have irregular memory reference patterns. Automatic parallelization is usually believed to be less effective at exploiting implicit parallelism in sparse codes than in their dense counterparts. However, little is known because there have been few research reports on the applicability of automatic parallelism detection techniques on sparse/irregular programs.

In the work reported in this paper, we studied a collection of sparse programs written in Fortran 77. We found that, despite their irregular memory reference pattern, many loops in the sparse/irregular codes we studied are parallel. We have derived several new transformation techniques that can be applied automatically by a compiler to parallelize these loops. Manually applying these techniques to our collection of irregular programs resulted in good speedups. This strengthens our belief that automatic parallelizing techniques can work on sparse/irregular programs as well as they do on dense codes.

---

* This work is supported in part by Army contract DABT63-95-C-0097; Army contract N66001-97-C-8532; NSF contract MIP-9619351; and a Partnership Award from IBM. This work is not necessarily representative of the positions or policies of the Army or Government.

D. O'Hallaron (Ed.): LCR'98, LNCS 1511, pp. 41–56, 1998.

Table 1. Benchmark Codes

	Benchmark	Description	Origin	# of lines	Seq Exec Time (s)
1	Cholesky	Sparse cholesky factorization	HPF-2	1284	323.50
2	Euler	A multimaterial, multidiscipline 3D hydrodynamics code	HPF-2	1990	972.14
3	Gccg	Computational fluid dynamics	Univ of Vienna	407	374.27
4	Lanczos	Eigenvalues of symmetric matrices	Univ of Malaga	269	389.25
5	SpLU	Sparse LU factorization	HPF-2	363	1958
6	SparAdd	Addition of two sparse matrices	[9]	67	2.40
7	ProdMV	Product of a sparse matrix by a column vector	[9]	28	1.28
8	ProdVM	Product of a row vector by a sparse matrix	[9]	31	1.07
9	SparMul	Product of two sparse matrices	[9]	64	3.32
10	SolSys	Solution of system $U^T D U x = b$	[9]	43	4.51
11	ProdUB	Product of matrices U^{-T} and B	[9]	49	3.72

Our hope is that the techniques developed based on our limited benchmark collection also will be effective at handling most situations in an extended benchmark collection. In fact, for sparse computation, we intend to follow the approach we took for dense computation in the Polaris project[2]. The Polaris project started with a hand analysis of a program collection, the Perfect Benchmark suite. The techniques derived from the Perfect Benchmark suite proved to be quite effective with an extended collection of programs, including SPEC and Grand Challenge programs contributed by NCSA.

As in our early Polaris study, our current work focuses on loop-level parallelism in shared memory programs. We believe this is an important first step in understanding difficulties in automatic parallelization of sparse/irregular programs. For programs that can be separated into a symbolic section and a numeric section, we focus on (but do not limit ourselves to) the numeric section. Distinguishing the two sections helps us to develop transformation techniques that are key to obtaining good speedups.

This paper is organized as follows. Section 2 describes the benchmark programs we collected for this project. The important loop patterns we found are studied in Sect. 3. Section 4 discusses some newly identified transformation techniques, the effectiveness of which is evaluated in Sect. 5. Section 6 compares our work with that of others. And, Section 7 presents our conclusions.

2   The Benchmark Suite

Table 1 lists all the codes in our sparse/irregular benchmark suite[1]. We chose them for the same reason programs were chosen for the collection of HPF-2 motivating applications: "they include parallel idioms important to full-scale

Table 2. Loop Patterns

Benchmark	Indirectly Accessed Array				Others		
	Right-hand Side	Histogram Reduction	Offset and Length	Sparse and Private	Consecutively Written Array	Premature Exit Loop w. Reduction	Array Privat-ization II
1 Cholesky			√			√	√
2 Euler		√					
3 Gccg	√						
4 Lanczos	√						
5 SpLU			√	√	√		√
6 SparAdd			√	√			
7 ProdMV	√						
8 ProdVM		√					
9 SparMul			√	√			
10 SolSys	√	√					
11 ProdUB		√					

'sparse/irregular' applications"[5]. The programs in our suite are small. This enabled us to complete the hand analysis in a reasonable time. We plan to expand this collection to include larger programs. The expanded collection will be used to evaluate the parallelizing techniques once they are implemented in the Polaris parallelizing compiler.

3 Loop Patterns

3.1 Overview

Sparse/irregular programs are usually considered difficult for automatic parallelization because they use indirectly accessed arrays and the subscript values are often unknown until run-time. However, in order to better understand this problem, we studied how indirectly accessed arrays are used in our benchmark collection. Our most surprising finding is that efficient methods can be used to automatically analyze and parallelize loops with indirectly accessed arrays. We also found some important loops in our benchmarks that require the use of new techniques to parallelize. These loops do not contain indirectly accessed arrays, but do occur in sparse/irregular programs.

Table 2 summarizes the seven most important loop patterns we found in our benchmarks. A '√' means this pattern appears in the program. The patterns in columns three through six involve indirectly accessed arrays. In this paper, we call the array that appears in the subscript of another array the *subscript array* and the indirectly accessed array the *host array*.

3.2   Loop Patterns for Indirectly Accessed Arrays

Right-hand Side. In this pattern, the indirectly accessed arrays appear only on the right-hand side of assignment statements. These arrays are read-only in the enclosing loop. Thus, this loop pattern does not cause any difficulty in the automatic detection of parallelism. The pattern, illustrated in Fig. 1, appears in Gccg, Lanczos, ProdMV and SolSys.

```
do nc = nintci, nintcf
   direc2(nc) =   bp(nc)*direc1(nc)
               - bs(nc)*direc1(lcc(nc,1))
               - bw(nc)*direc1(lcc(nc,4))
               - bl(nc)*direc1(lcc(nc,5))
end do
```

Fig. 1. An Example of the *Right-hand Side* Pattern

Histogram Reduction. An example of this pattern is shown in Fig. 2, where op is a reduction operation, and expression does not contain any references to array a(). Array a() is accessed via index array x(). Because two elements of x() could have the same value, loop-carried dependence may exist. Histogram reductions are also called irregular reductions[5].

```
real  a(m)
do i = 1, n
   a(x(i)) = a(x(i)) op expression
end do
```

Fig. 2. An Example of the *Histogram Reduction* Loop

Histogram reductions are pervasive in sparse/irregular codes. There are several reasons for this. First, some typical sparse matrix computations, such as the vector/matrix multiplication in the following example, have the form of histogram reduction:

```
do i = 1, n
   do k = rowbegin(i), rowend(i)
      c(ja(k)) = c(ja(k)) + b(i) * an(i)
   end do
end do
```

Second, a large collection of irregular problems, which can be categorized as general molecular dynamics, accumulate values using histogram reduction. Four programs in the HPF-2 motivation applications(i. e. , MolDyn, NBFC, Binz and DSMC) have histogram reductions at their computation core[5]. The third reason is that the computation of structure arrays, like the index arrays used to access sparse matrix and the interaction list in molecular dynamics, often contains histogram reductions. An obvious example is the calculation of the number of nonzero elements for each row in a sparse matrix stored in column-wise form.

In Sect. 4.2, we will discuss in detail the techniques that are useful to parallelize a histogram reduction loop.

Offset and Length. In this pattern, subscript arrays are used to store offset pointers or length of segments. The host array is accessed contiguously within each segment. Figure 3 shows the basic pattern. Array offset() points to the starting position of each segment. The size of each segment is given in array length(). Figure 3(a) and (b) are two common forms of using the offset and length arrays.

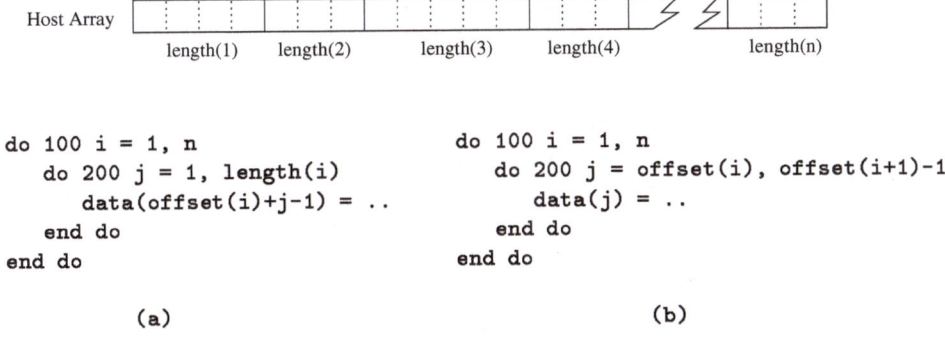

```
do 100 i = 1, n                    do 100 i = 1, n
   do 200 j = 1, length(i)            do 200 j = offset(i), offset(i+1)-1
      data(offset(i)+j-1) = ..           data(j) = ..
   end do                             end do
end do                             end do


        (a)                                (b)
```

Fig. 3. Examples of the *Offset and Length* Subscript Array

A typical example of this pattern appears in sparse matrix codes using the Compressed Column Storage(CCS) or the Compressed Row Storage(CRS) format and traversing the matrix by row or column. The CCS/CRS format was adopted by the Harwell-Boeing Matrix Collection[6] and has become very popular. We also found this pattern in the Perfect Benchmark codes DYFESM and TRFD. There are variants of CCS/CRS that reflect the structures of some specific sparse matrices. However, the basic loop patterns to access arrays represented in these variants are similar to those in Fig. 3.

This loop pattern is somewhat regular. In languages, such as Fortran 77, where the array is the basic data type and the loop is the main iterative construct, storing and accessing related data elements contiguously in an array is the natural way to program. Furthermore, this pattern has good spatial cache locality. Thus, the presence of this access pattern in sparse/irregular codes is not surprising.

Sparse and Private. In this loop pattern, array elements are accessed in a *totally irregular* manner. However, in this pattern, the array is also used as a working place which can be privatized.

A typical example of this pattern appears in the scatter and gather operation, as shown in the matrix addition code in Fig. 4, where the working place array x() is used to hold the intermediate result.

```
do i = 1, n
    /* scatter */
    do ip = ic(i), ic(i+1) - 1
        x(jc(ip)) = 0
    end do
    do ip = ia(i), ia(i+1) - 1
        x(ja(ip)) = an(ip)
    end do
    do ip = ib(i), ib(i+1) - 1
        x(jb(ip)) = x(jb(ip)) + bn(ip)
    end do
    /* gather */
    do ip = ic(i), ic(i+1) - 1
        c(ip) = x(jc(ip))
    end do
end do
```

$$\forall\, 1 \leq i \leq n, \quad \{jc(j) \mid ic(i) \leq j \leq ic(i+1) - 1\}$$
$$= \{ja(j) \mid ia(i) \leq j \leq ia(i+1) - 1\} \cup \{jb(j) \mid ib(i) \leq j \leq ib(i+1) - 1\}$$

Fig. 4. An Example of the *Sparse and Private* Pattern - Sparse Matrix Addition

Summary. Of the four loop patterns, *Right-Hand Side* is trivial to handle; *Histogram Reduction* can be recognized automatically[10], although its efficient parallelization is not as easy as it first appears; and *Offset and Length* and *Sparse and Private* can be managed by the run-time method presented in Section 4.3. Thus, we believe that a parallelizing compiler enhanced with the techniques described in this paper should be able to automatically analyze most loops containing indirectly accessed arrays in our benchmark codes.

3.3   Other Loop Patterns

The loop patterns described in this subsection do not involve indirectly accessed arrays. However, they appear in our benchmark codes and require new parallelization techniques.

Consecutively Written Array. In this pattern, array elements are written one after another in consecutive locations. However, there is no closed form expression of the array index because the value of the index is changed conditionally. This pattern is illustrated in Fig. 5.

```
        do i = 1, n
           while (...)
              if (...) then
S1:             a(j) = ...
S2:             j = j+1
              end if
           end do
        end do

( a() is write only in this pattern )
```

Fig. 5. An Example of the *Consecutively Written Array*

Current data dependence tests fail to disprove the dependence in this pattern because the index value in each iteration is determined at run-time.

Premature Exit Loop with Reduction Operations. A premature exit loop is a loop containing a **goto** or **break** statement that directs the program flow out of the loop before all iterations have been executed. Speculative execution, which is a possible parallelization method for this type of loop, may execute beyond the iteration where the loop exit occurs and cause side-effects. These overshot iterations should be recovered in order to produce the correct result. The need for rollback makes the parallelization complicated and sometimes impossible.

However, if the only operation within the premature exit loop is a reduction, as illustrated in Fig. 6, then a simple speculative parallelization transformation is possible. The basic idea is to block schedule the loop, let each processor get its own partial result and throw away the unneeded part in the cross-processor reduction phase.

Array Privatization of Type II. Array privatization is one of the most important parallelization techniques. It eliminates data dependences between different occurrences of a temporary variable or an array element across different

```
a = initvalue
do i = lower, upper
    if (cond(i)) break
    a = reduct(a,i)
end do
```

Fig. 6. An Example of the *Premature Exit Loop with Reduction Operations*

iterations[8][13]. Blume et al. [2] measured the effectiveness of privatization on the Perfect Benchmark suite.

Figure 7 shows a typical access pattern for a privatizable array.

```
                                 do i = 1, m
                                     t(i) = const
                                 end do

                    LOOP_2:      do i = 1, n
    do i = 1, n                      k = 0
        do j = 1, m                  ....
            t(j) = 0                 while (...)
        enddo           S1:             ... = t(...) op express
        .. = t(k)                   ....
    enddo                           k = k+1
                        S2:             t(k) = ...

                                    ....
                                 end while
                                 ....
                                 do j = 1, k
                        S3:          t(j) = const
    1 ≤ k ≤ m                       end do
                                 end do
```

Fig. 7. Array Privatization of Type I

Fig. 8. Array Privatization of Type II

Generally, a variable or an array can be privatized if it is defined before it is used in each loop iteration[13][8]. This traditionally has been the only kind of data item privatized by existing compliers. However, in our benchmark codes, we found another kind of privatizable array, as shown in Fig. 8, which we will refer to as type II. We call the more traditional privatizable array type I.

In this example, array t() is used as a temporary array. In each iteration of LOOP_2, the elements of t(), which are modified in S2, are always reset to const before leaving the iteration. Because the value of t() is always the same upon entering each iteration, a private copy for each iteration with the same initial value const can be used. Thus, t() is a privatizable array.

It is not surprising that people write code in this way, rather than initializing t() to 'const' at the beginning of each iteration. The reason is twofold. First, the size of t() may be very large while the number of elements modified in each iteration is relatively small, thereby creating a high cost to initialize all elements of t() in each iteration. Second, when the range of t() that will be referenced in each iteration is unknown until the array is actually being written, such as the value of k in the example, it is difficult to write initialization statements prior to the references. In this case 'resetting' rather than 'initializing' is more straightforward and unnecessary computations can be avoided. Like the pattern of *consecutively written array*, *privatizable array of type II* reflects the dynamic nature of sparse/irregular programs. We found this access pattern in CHOLESKY and SpLU.

4   New Transformation Techniques

This section describes three transformation techniques that we found important to parallelize sparse/irregular programs[1].

4.1   Parallelizing Loops Containing Consecutively Written Array

For two reasons, we want to recognize the consecutively written array.

- First, most *consecutively written* accesses can be statically detected. A parallelizing compiler should be able to parallelize the enclosing loop if there are no other dependences.
- The knowledge that all the array elements within a section are written is important for array dataflow analysis in some cases, such as the array privatization test in the following example. The array a() can be privatized if the compiler knows that a(1..k-1) is defined before entering loop j in each iteration of loop i.

```
do i = 1,  n
   k = 1
   while (..) do
      a(k) = ..
      k = k+1
   end while
   do j = 1, k-1
      .. = a(j)
   end do
end do
```

[1] We do not cover the techniques for the patterns of *Right-hand Side* and of *Premature Exit Loop with Reduction Operation*. The former is trivial to handle and the latter can be parallelized by using the associative transformation[11].

To recognize a consecutively written array, we first use the following heuristic method to find a candidate array:

1. the array is write-only in the loop,
2. the array is always written at positions specified by a same induction variable, and
3. all operations on the induction variable are increments of 1, or all are decrements of 1.

Then, we work on the control flow graph of the loop. We call all assignment statements of the candidate array (like S1 in Fig. 5) *black nodes*, and all assignments to the induction variable (like S2) *grey nodes*. The remaining nodes are called *white nodes*. The candidate array is a consecutively written array if and only if on each path between two grey nodes there is at least one black node. We can do the checking in the following way. For each grey node, we do a depth-first search from it. The boundary of this search is black nodes. If any other grey node is found before the search finishes, then the array is not a consecutively written array and the search aborts. If the search finishes for all grey nodes, then we find a consecutively written array. Because the working control flow graph is usually rather simple, the recognition phase is fast and can be integrated into the pass for induction variables processing in a parallelizing compiler.

Transformation - Array Splitting and Merging. Because positions where the elements of a consecutively written array are written in one iteration depend on the previous iteration, there is a loop-carried true dependence. We use a technique called *array splitting and merging* to parallelize this loop.

Array splitting and merging has three phases. First, a private copy of the consecutively written array is allocated on each processor. Then, all processors work on their private copies from position 1 in parallel. After the computation, each processor knows the length of its private copy of the array; hence, the starting position in the original array for each processor can be easily calculated. Finally, the private copies are copied back (merged) to the original array. Figure 9 illustrates the idea when two processors are used.

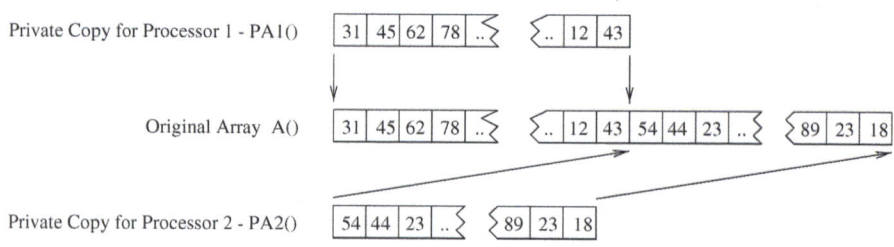

Fig. 9. An Example of Array Splitting and Merging

4.2   Histogram Reduction

In this section, we discuss four techniques that can be used to parallelize histogram reduction loops: critical section, data affiliated loops, array expansion, and reduction table.

Critical Section. We can put the accesses to shared variables in a critical section, using a lock/unlock pair. The operations on different arrays can be executed in parallel. However, this method does not exploit the parallelism within reductions. Without fast hardware support for synchronization, critical section in many cases is not a good alternative to sequential reduction.

Data Affiliated Loops. This method shares the same idea as the *owner computes* rule. It partitions data instead of loop iterations. Each processor traverses all the iterations and checks whether the data referenced in the current iteration belongs to it. If it does, the processor executes the operation; otherwise, it skips the operation. The advantage of this approach is its potential for good cache locality when block distribution is used. The disadvantage is that this method becomes too complicated when there are several indirectly accessed arrays in the loop. Also, the overhead could be high if each iteration is relatively short.

Array Expansion. In this method, each processor allocates a private copy of the whole reduction array. The parallelized loop has three phases. All the private copies are initialized to the reduction identity in the first phase. In the second phase, each processor executes the reduction operation in its own private copy in parallel. There is no inter-processor communication in this phase. The last phase does cross-processor reduction. The following example illustrates the three phases.

```
real a(1:m)
real pa(1:m,1:num_of_threads)

// phase 1
parallel do i = 1, num_of_threads
   do j = 1, m
      pa(j,i) = reduction_identity
   end do
end do

// phase 2
parallel do i = 1, n
   pa(i, thread_id) = pa(i, thread_id) op expression
end do
```

```
// phase 3
parallel do i = 1, m
   do j = 1, num_of_threads
      a(i) = a(i) op pa(i,j)
   end do
end do
```

The method works well when almost all array elements will be updated by each processor. The biggest disadvantage of this approach, however, is having to keep multiple copies of the whole array. This not only increases the memory pressure, but also introduces high overhead. When each processor touches only a small portion of the array, working on the whole array in the first and the last phase may hinder speedup.

Reduction Table. This method also uses private memory, but the required size is small. The private copy is used as a table. The number of entries is fixed. Each entry in the table has two fields: index and value. The value of an entry is accessed by using a fast hash function of the index. Thus, this can be thought of as a hash table. We call this table the *reduction table* because the value of an entry is updated by some reduction operation.

Figure 10 illustrates how reduction table is used. Processor 1 executes iterations 1 through 4, and Processor 2 executes 5 through 8.

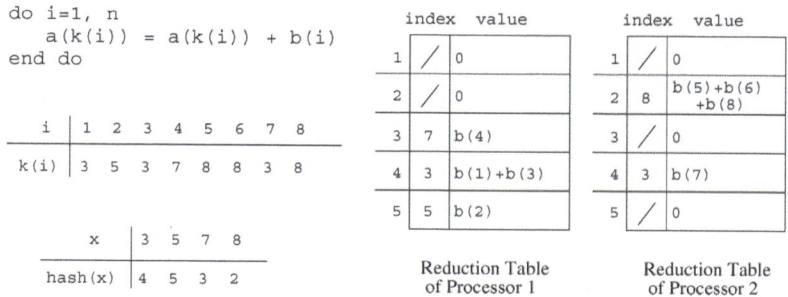

Fig. 10. An example of using reduction table

In the reduction table approach, all entries in the reduction tables are initialized to the reduction identity before entering the parallel loop. Then, each processor works on its own reduction table in parallel. Each array element is mapped to a table entry by using a hash function on the array subscript. When a reduction is to be performed, the table is looked up to find an entry that contains the same array index or, if no such entry exists, an empty entry. If the entry is available, then reduction operation is performed on the old value in the entry with the new value. If the entry is not avaialbe, which means the table is full, the operation is performed directly on the shared array within a critical section. After the parallel section, all entries whose values do not equal reduction identity are flushed out to the global array in critical sections.

This method is a hybrid of the critical section method and the array expansion method. Like the critical section method, it ensures the atomic operation on global shared variables; and, like the expansion method, it takes advantage of reduction operation. The reduction table method does not have to keep private copies of the whole reduction array. The number of table entries can be much smaller than the number of elements in the reduction array. Only those elements that are updated in the loop are kept. This method trades hash table calculations with memory operations. It may be particularly beneficial when used with a simple, fast hash function.

4.3   Loop-pattern-aware run-time dependence test

When static analysis is too complex or the subscript arrays are functions of the input data, a run-time method becomes necessary for parallelization. Some run-time tests, as proposed in [12], use shadow arrays that have the same size as the data arrays. They check and mark every read/write operation on the array elements. This kind of run-time test would introduce high overhead on modern machines where memory access is significantly slower than computation. One solution is to use hardware support[14]. However in some cases, efficient software methods are available if the information of loop patterns can be used.

Our run-time test is based on the loop patterns we discussed above and is applied to loops with indirectly accessed arrays. Of the four patterns, *right-hand side* and *histogram reduction* can always be handled statically. We, therefore, focus on the last two cases. Our run-time test can be thought of as run-time pattern matching. It relies on the compiler to detect the static syntactic pattern and uses the run-time test to verify variable constraints.

In the case of the *offset and length* pattern, a run-time test would be used to check whether two array segments overlap. Thus, only the first and last positions need to be stored, and the size of the shadow array is greatly reduced. In the case of the *sparse and private* pattern, the marking and analysis phases can be simplified because we only check the validation of privatization for these *totally irregular* arrays. For type I privatization, we mark the shadow array when a write occurs. The test immediately fails once we find a shadow that is not marked when a read occurs. For type II privatization, the shadow is marked when an array element is read or written and is cleared when the element is set to a constant. If there are still some marked elements in the shadow at the end of the inspector phase, then the test fails. In the experiment on CHOLESKY, we found that our simplified run-time test has a run-time overhead of 20% of the parallel execution time on eight processors as compared to 120% overhead of the general run-time test.

Because the new run-time test is based on the loop pattern, we call it the loop-pattern-aware run-time test. The trade-off is its conservativeness. While the general run-time test[12] can exploit almost all classes of parallelism (even partially parallelizable loop), ours may report dependence where there actually

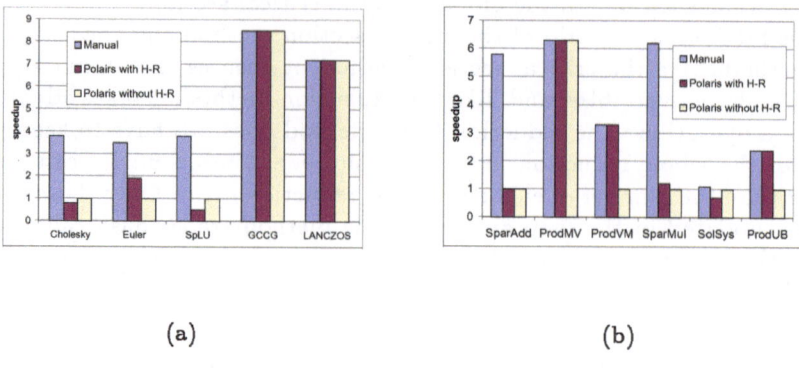

(a)   (b)

Fig. 11. Speedups of Benchmark Codes

is none. However, for the codes in our benchmark suite, the loop-pattern-aware run-time test suffices.

5   Experimental Results

Preliminary experimental results are discussed in this section. We compare the speedups obtained by manually applying the new techniques with those of the current version of Polaris, with and without histogram reduction[2]. The programs were executed in real-time mode on an SGI PowerChallenge with eight 195 MHz R10000 processors.

Figure 11(a) shows the speedups of benchmark codes for the first five programs. Parallelizing Gccg and Lanczos requires no new techniques, and our current version of Polaris does quite well on these two codes. For Cholesky, Euler and SpLU, manual transformation led to good speedups. In Cholesky and SpLU, there are several innermost loops that perform very simple histogram reductions. The overhead of array expansion transformation reduction hinders the performance. However, this transformation works well on Euler, which has large granularity in its loopbodies.

Speedups of the sparse matrix algebra kernels in our benchmark collection are shown in Fig. 11(b). ProvVM and ProdUB achieve speedup because of the parallel histogram reduction transformation. ProvMV is simple and Polaris handles it well. SparAdd and SparMul require the loop pattern aware run-time test and array privatization of type II. These new techniques produce speedups of

---

[2] SGI's parallelizing compiler, PFA, produced results very similar to Polaris without histogram reduction. We, therefore, do not include its data here. The parallelization technique for histogram reduction loops currently implemented in Polaris is the array expansion method.

Table 3. Techniques Applied to Each Code

	Code	Techniques
1	Cholesky	Associative Transformation, Loop-pattern-aware Run-time Test
2	Euler	Histogram Reduction(Array Expansion)
3	Gccg	trivial
4	Lanczos	trivial
5	SpLU	Array Splitting and Merging, Loop-pattern-aware Run-time Test
6	SparAdd	Loop-pattern-aware Run-time Test
7	ProdMV	trivial
8	ProdVM	Histogram Reduction(Array Expansion)
9	SparMul	Loop-pattern-aware Run-time Test
10	SolSys	Histogram Reduction(Reduction Table)
11	ProdUB	Histogram Reduction(Array Expansion)

around 6. SolSys has a DOALL loop, which Polaris recognized as a histogram reduction loop thereby causing the slow down.

The techniques manually applied to each code are summarized in Table 3.

6   Related Work

To our knowledge, there are very few papers in the literature that directly address the problem of automatically detecting parallelism in sequential sparse/irregular programs. The closest work we are aware of is that of Christoph Keßler[3]. Keßler is investigating the generalization of his program comprehension technique to sparse matrix codes. His approach is based on pattern matching and therefore depends on the storage scheme and algorithm used by the program. By contrast, we study the loop pattern to find the common ingredients of different algorithms and storage formats. Our approach is more general and even applicable to some 'homemade' codes that do not follow standard algorithms. Another approach is followed by Bik and Wijshoff[4]. Their solution is to generate sparse matrix programs from dense matrix programs by using their sparse compiler. Kotlyar, Pingali, and Stodghill proposed another interesting solution based on their 'data-centric-compilation' concept[7]. Although both methods can be used to produce parallel sparse programs, they can not handle existing sequential sparse codes and their applicability to programs beyond matrix computation kernels is unclear.

7   Conclusion and Future Work

In this paper, we have studied the possibility of using automatic compilers to detect the parallelism of sparse/irregular programs. The experiments with our benchmarks led us to extract some common loop patterns, which can be used to apply transformations. Three new techniques have been derived. Manual transformation using these techniques generates good speedups. More importantly, these parallelization methods can be applied automatically.

Loop-pattern-aware run-time test is used to handle the case of *offset and length* and *sparse and private* in this paper. However, we find that in some cases these patterns can be detected statically by analysis of the subscript arrays. We are currently developing techniques for this type of analysis.

References

1. Rafael Asenjo, Eladio Gutierrez, Yuan Lin, David Padua, Bill Pottenger, and Emilio Zapata. On the Automatic Parallelization of Sparse and Irregular Fortran Codes. Technical Report 1512, Univ. of Illinois at Urbana-Champaign, CSRD, Dec 1996
2. William Blume, Ramon Doallo, Rudolf Eigenmann, John Grout, Jay Hoeflinger, Thomas Lawrence, Jaejin Lee, David Padua, Yunheung Paek, Bill Pottenger, Lawrence Rauchwerger, and Peng Tu. Parallel Programming with Polaris. *IEEE Computer*, 29(12):78–82, December 1996.
3. Christoph W. Keßler, Applicability of Program Comprehension to Sparse Matrix Computations, In *PROC of 3rd EUROPAR*, Passau, German, August, 1997
4. Aart J. C. Bik and Harry A. G. Wijshoff, Automatic Data Structure Selection and Transformation for sparse Matrix Computations. *IEEE Trans. on Parallel and Distributed Systems*, Volume 7, pages 109–126, Feb. 1996
5. Ian Foster, Rob Schreiber, and Paul Havlak. HPF-2 Scope of Activities and Motivating Applications. Technical Report CRPC-TR94492, Rice University, November, 1994
6. Harwell-Boeing Sparse Matrix Collection (Release I), Matrix Market, http://http://math.nist.gov/MatrixMarket /collections/hb.html
7. Vladimir Kotlyar, Keshav Pingali, and Paul Stodghill. Compiling Parallel Code for Sparse Matrix Applications. In *Supercomputing*, November 1997
8. Zhiyuan Li, Array privatization of parallel execution of loops, In *Proc. of ICS'92*, pages 313-322, 1992
9. Sergio Pissanetzky, *Sparse Matrix Technology*, Academic Press, 1984, ISBN 0-12-557580-7
10. Bill Pottenger and Rudolf Eigenmann. Idiom Recognition in the Polaris Parallelizing Compiler. *Proceedings of the 9th ACM International Conference on Supercomputing*, Barcelona, Spain, pages 444–448, July 1995
11. Bill Pottenger, Theory, techniques, and experiments in solving recurrences in computer programs. PhD Thesis. University of Illinois at Urbana-Champaign, IL, 1997
12. Lawrence Rauchwerger, Run-time parallelization: a framework for parallel computation. PhD Thesis. University of Illinois at Urbana-Champaign, IL, 1995
13. Peng Tu and David Padua. Automatic Array Privatization. In *Proc. Sixth Workshop on Languages and Compilers for Parallel Computing, Portland, OR. Lecture Notes in Computer Science*, volume 768, pages 500–521, August 12-14, 1993.
14. Ye Zhang, Lawrence Rauchwerger, and Josep Torrellas. Hardware for Speculative Run-Time Parallelization in Distributed Shared-Memory Multiprocessors. In *Proc. of the 4th International Symposium on Hight-Performance Computer Architecture*, 1998

Loop Transformations for Hierarchical Parallelism and Locality

Vivek Sarkar

IBM Research
Thomas J. Watson Research Center
P. O. Box 704, Yorktown Heights, NY 10598, USA
vivek@watson.ibm.com

Abstract. The increasing depth of memory and parallelism hierarchies in future scalable computer systems poses many challenges to parallelizing compilers. In this paper, we address the problem of selecting and implementing iteration-reordering loop transformations for hierarchical parallelism and locality. We present a two-pass algorithm for selecting sequences of Block, Unimodular, Parallel, and Coalesce transformations for optimizing locality and parallelism for a specified *parallelism hierarchy model*. These general transformation sequences are implemented using a framework for iteration-reordering loop transformations that we developed in past work [15].

1   Introduction

The widening gap between processor speeds and memory speeds is leading to deeper memory hierarchies in current and future high-performance computer systems than ever seen before. Two levels of cache are now commonplace in many processors. The local memory serves as a third-level cache in today's parallel systems that are now being built as clusters of workstations. If we also take into account registers, TLB, and main memory, we already have computer systems today with more than five levels of memory hierarchy. With the well-established trend towards deeper memory hierarchies in the future, it should not be surprising to see computer systems with memory hierarchies that are ten levels deep within a decade from now.

In conjunction with hierarchical memories, there is a growing trend towards hierarchical parallelism. Many large-scale parallel machines are built as clusters of symmetric shared-memory multiprocessors (SMP's) as shown in figure 1, and thus have two levels of parallelism. A third level of parallelism is also exploited within each processor via instruction-level parallelism or multithreading. It is natural to expect the parallelism hierarchy to grow deeper as interconnects with smaller latencies and smaller bandwidth are used at the lower levels of the hierarchy and interconnects with larger latencies and larger bandwidth are used at the upper levels.

The increasing depths of memory and parallelism hierarchies will pose many challenges to parallelizing compilers for future scalable computer systems. In

D. O'Hallaron (Ed.): LCR'98, LNCS 1511, pp. 57–74, 1998.

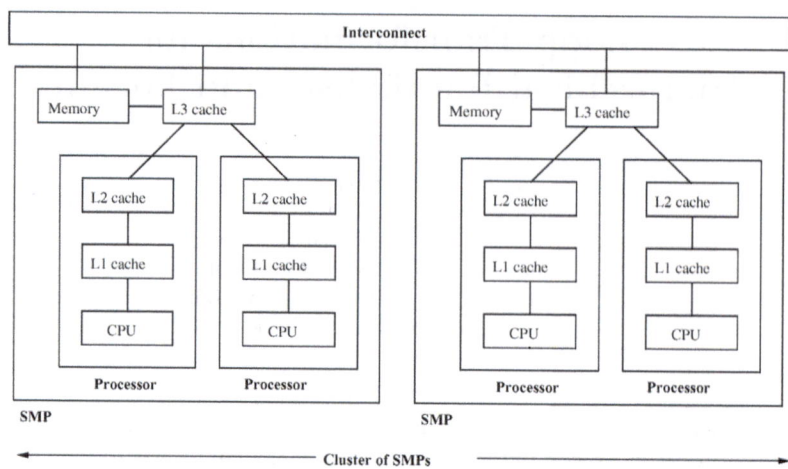

Fig. 1. A cluster of SMP's

this paper, we address the problem of selecting and implementing loop transformations for hierarchical parallelism and locality. In this paper, we restrict our attention to *iteration-reordering* loop transformations [18, 15], a special class of loop transformations that only change the execution order of loop iterations in a perfect loop nest without changing the contents of the loop body *e.g.*, unimodular loop transformations [2, 17], loop tiling/blocking [16], loop parallelization [18], loop coalescing [11], and loop interleaving [15]. Iteration-reordering loop transformations are used extensively by restructuring compilers for optimizing parallelism and data locality [16, 17, 9, 3, 13].

The past experience with iteration-reordering transformations for optimizing parallelism and locality has primarily been targeted to a single level of cache. Loop transformations for hierarchical parallelism and locality require support for transformation sequences that have not been addressed in past work, such as performing multiple levels of blocking interspersed with unimodular transformations and parallelization. In this paper, we outline a general approach for selecting transformation sequences for multiple levels of parallelism and memory hierarchy. Our approach uses the framework for iteration-reordering loop transformations reported in our past work [15]. We know of no other framework that can support these general transformation sequences that are necessary for optimizing hierarchical locality and parallelism.

We are in the process of implementing the algorithm and framework described in this paper as a prototype extension of the "high order transformer" [13, 3] component of the IBM XL Fortran product compilers for RS/6000 uniprocessors and multiprocessors. To the best of our knowledge, this is the first compiler that can support loop transformations for unbounded levels of hierarchical parallelism and locality. We believe that this capability will be essential for parallelizing compilers for future scalable computer systems.

The rest of the paper is organized as follows. Section 2 contains a brief summary of the framework for iteration-reordering loop transformations reported in our past work [15]. Section 3 outlines our algorithm for automatically selecting a loop transformation sequence for hierarchical parallelism and locality. Section 4 illustrates how our algorithm performs unimodular and parallelization transformations *after* blocking. Section 5 shows how our algorithm performs unimodular and coalescing transformations *after* parallelization. Section 6 discusses related work, and section 7 contains our conclusions.

2   Transformation Framework

This section briefly describes a general framework that can support the various loop transformation sequences discussed later in this paper. This framework builds on our past work reported in [15], and has now been completely implemented in the IBM XL Fortran product compilers [13].

We define an iteration-reordering transformation to be a sequence of template instantiations from a small but extensible kernel set of transformation templates. A *transformation template* has parameters, and providing specific values for these parameters creates a particular instantiation of this transformation template. The optimizer selects templates from this kernel set and instantiates them with specific values so as to build a desired iteration-reordering transformation as a sequence of template instantiations. The kernel set of transformation templates assumed in this paper is shown in Table 1 along with a description of their parameters.

The transformation template specifies rules for mapping dependence vectors, mapping loop bound expressions, and creating initialization statements for a transformed loop nest. The dependence vectors of a loop nest are used to test the legality of applying a transformation, with respect to the data dependence constraints of the original loop nest. When the loop nest is transformed, its dependence vectors will also change, as specified by the dependence vector mapping rules. This avoids recomputing the dependence vectors for the transformed loop nest, which is in general an expensive operation and is also intractable when the transformed loop becomes too complicated to be analyzed by a compiler (*e.g.,* after blocking and/or coalescing). The mapping rules for dependence vectors are described in [15]. Transformation of loop bounds and creation of initialization statements are actions required to generate code for the transformed loop nest. The preconditions in the loop bounds mapping rules are used to test the legality of applying a transformation, with respect to the loop bounds constraints. The mapping rules for loop bounds are also discussed in [15].

In summary, our framework treats a transformation sequence as an entity that is distinct from the loop nests on which it may be applied. Thus, transformations may be created, instantiated, composed, and destroyed, without being tied to a particular loop nest. An advantage of this framework is that it makes it easy to consider several alternative transformation sequences for a loop nest, if we choose to consider alternative algorithms in the future for selecting loop transformations for optimizing locality and parallelism.

Kernel Set of Templates	Description
Unimodular(n, M)	n is the input loop nest size (in all templates). M is the $n \times n$ *unimodular transformation matrix* specifying the desired transformation [1].
Parallelize$(n, parflag)$	$parflag[i] =$ **true** means that loop i is to be parallelized.
Block$(n, i, j, bsize)$	The range $i \ldots j$ specifies a set of contiguous loops to be blocked (tiled), and $bsize$ is a vector such that $bsize[k]$ contains an expression for the block size of loop k. Blocking can be viewed as a combination of strip mining and interchanging [18].
Coalesce(n, i, j)	The range $i \ldots j$ specifies a set of contiguous loops to be *coalesced* (or collapsed) into a single loop [12].

Table 1. Kernel Set of Transformation Templates

3   Algorithm for Selection of Hierarchical Parallelism and Locality

In this section, we outline our algorithm for automatically selecting a loop transformation sequence for hierarchical parallelism and locality. This algorithm is an outcome of our experience with selecting loop transformations for a single level of locality and parallelism [13, 3].

We assume that the target architecture is specified by a *parallelism hierarchy model* for $q \geq 1$ levels of parallelism, $\mathcal{P} = (P_1, \ldots P_q)$, numbered from outer to inner. Each P_i in turn contains a *memory hierarchy model* for $r_i \geq 1$ levels of memory hierarchy at the ith level of parallelism, $\mathcal{M}^i = (M_1^i, \ldots M_{r_i}^i)$, also numbered from outer to inner. Thus, we assume that each level of parallelism can contain multiple levels of memory hierarchy, and that each memory hierarchy level is completely contained within a single level of parallelism.

As an example, consider a parallel machine built as a cluster of SMP's, in which each SMP processor has an L1-cache and an L2-cache, and each cluster has an L3-cache. The parallelism hierarchy model for this case will then look like $\mathcal{P} = (P_1, P_2)$, with $\mathcal{M}^1 = (M_1^1)$ representing the cluster-level L3-cache, and $\mathcal{M}^2 = (M_1^2, M_1^2)$ representing the processor-level L2-cache and L1-cache. (Recall that the numbering of levels is outside-in for our parallelism hierarchy model.) The total number of memory hierarchy levels is $R = \sum_i r_i$. When each level of parallelism has the same number of memory hierarchy levels, $r_i = r$, then $R = q \times r$.

A high-level view of our algorithm for optimizing hierarchical locality and parallelism is as follows. First, we perform an *inside-out locality optimization* pass that cascades at most R pairs of Unimodular and Block transformations to obtain a sequence of $\leq 2R$ transformations of the form,

$$\sigma' = \text{Unimodular–Block–} \ldots \text{–Unimodular–Block}.$$

This transformation sequence captures the hierarchical blocking required for all R levels of memory hierarchy. Then, we perform an *outside-in parallelization* pass that appends at most q triples of Unimodular, Parallel, and Coalesce transformations *i.e.*, appends a sequence of $\leq 3q$ transformations of the form,

$$\sigma'' = \text{–Unimodular–Parallelize–Coalesce–} \ldots \text{–Unimodular–Parallelize–Coalesce}.$$

The combined sequence of transformations selected for both passes is $\sigma = \sigma'\text{–}\sigma''$ *i.e.*, σ' followed by σ''.

Our justification for performing the locality optimization pass prior to the parallelization pass is that effective cache utilization is a prerequisite for effective parallelization on parallel machines with one or more levels of cache. In general, loops that carry more locality are good candidates for serial execution (so as to exploit cache reuse), and loops that carry less locality are good candidates for parallel execution. Had we performed the parallelization pass before the locality optimization pass, we would not have locality information to distinguish among multiple candidate loops for parallelization.

However, it is possible for there to be a conflict between locality optimization and parallelization *e.g.*, there may be a single loop in the loop nest that both carries locality and is parallelizable. This conflict is addressed by using the blocking transformation, after which the inner blocked loop is executed serially to exploit cache reuse and the outer blocked loop is executed concurrently to exploit multiprocessor parallelism. The block size parameter is then selected at run-time to fine-tune the balance between locality and parallelism based on hardware parameters that might only be known at run-time such as the number of processors, cache size, etc.

Figure 2 outlines the algorithm for the first pass, *inside-out locality optimization*. As mentioned earlier, the transformation sequence built by this algorithm is a cascade of Unimodular–Block transformations, which has the net effect of *hierarchical blocking* (also referred to as *hierarchical tiling* in [10]). The algorithm works inside-out, by starting at the memory hierarchy model at the innermost level, $M_{r_i}^q$, and working outwards. Each Block transformation adds g loops to the loop nest, where g is the size of the "locality group" at that memory hierarchy level; Unimodular transformations do not change the number of loops in the nest. An important invariant for this pass is that it is always the outermost n loops that are eligible for locality transformations performed at each memory hierarchy level, where n is the number of loops in the original loop nest. In this way, the outer controlling loops of a Block transformation become eligible for

Inputs: A set of n perfectly nested loops, $\mathcal{L} = (L_1, \ldots, L_n)$, and a *parallelism hierarchy model* for q levels of parallelism $\mathcal{P} = (P_1, \ldots P_q)$. Each P_i contains a *memory hierarchy model* for r_i levels of memory hierarchy at the ith level of parallelism, $\mathcal{M}^i = (M_1^i, \ldots M_{r_i}^i)$.

Output: A sequence of loop transformations, σ', for loop nest $\mathcal{L}$ that performs hierarchical blocking for the memory hierarchy models in $\mathcal{P}$. $\mathcal{L}' = \sigma'(\mathcal{L})$ denotes the transformed loop nest obtained by applying σ' on $\mathcal{L}$.

Method:

Initialize $\mathcal{L}' := \mathcal{L}$ (with $n' = n$), and σ' to the empty sequence.
for $i := q$ **downto** 1 **do**
    for $j := r_i$ **downto** 1 **do**
      1. Let the current loop nest be $\mathcal{L}' = (L_1', \ldots, L_{n'}')$, where $n' \geq n$. Compute $F(b_1, \ldots, b_n)$, the estimated *memory cost per iteration* for memory hierarchy model M_j^i, assuming symbolic block sizes $b_1, \ldots, b_n$ for the n *outermost* loops in loop nest $\mathcal{L}'$.
      2. Identify the *locality group* G consisting of loops L_k' ($1 \leq k \leq n$) that carry locality (i.e., that have $\delta F / \delta b_k < 0$) and that can be interchanged with L_n'.
      3. Compute *estimated* block sizes $b_1, \ldots, b_n$ at compile-time as follows. If loop k has an estimated block size of $b_k = 1$, it will be removed from the locality group. Actual block sizes are computed later at run-time. The estimated block sizes $b_1, \ldots, b_n$ are computed so as to minimize $F(b_1, \ldots, b_n)$, while obeying the following constraints:
         • $1 \leq b_k \leq N_k'$, if loop L_k' is in the locality group, G. (N_k' is the number of iterations in loop L_k'.)
         • $b_k = 1$, if loop L_k' is not in the locality group, G.
         • $DL(b_1, \ldots, b_n) \leq EFFECTIVE\text{-}SIZE(M_j^i)$. The number of distinct "lines" accessed by a single block/tile of $b_1 \times \ldots \times b_n$ iterations of the n outer loops in $\mathcal{L}'$ must not exceed the effective size of the memory hierarchical model M_j^i.
      4. Update the locality goup G by removing any loops assigned $b_k = 1$ in step 3.
      5. **if** $|G| > 0$ **then** /* Let $g = |G|$ be the size of the locality group */
        (a) Append to σ' a single $n' \times n'$ Unimodular transformation containing the combination of interchange and reversal transformations required to bring the g loops in the locality group to positions $n - g + 1, \ldots, n$. Let $\mathcal{L}_U'$ represent the transformed loop nest after applying this unimodular transformation to loop nest $\mathcal{L}'$.
        (b) Append to σ' a single $n' \mapsto (n' + g)$ Block transformation for blocking loops $n - g + 1, \ldots, n$ in $\mathcal{L}_U'$. Let $\mathcal{L}_B'$ represent the transformed loop nest after applying this blocking transformation to loop nest $\mathcal{L}_U'$.
        (c) Set $\mathcal{L}' := \mathcal{L}_B'$ to represent the transformed loop nest to be used as input when optimizing locality at the next outer memory hierarchy level.
      end if
    end for
end for

Fig. 2. Inside-out algorithm for selecting a loop transformation sequence for hierarchical blocking

transformation when optimizing locality in outer levels of the memory hierarchy; the inner blocked loops in a Block transformation will not be eligible for further transformation till the parallelization pass.

Step 1 in figure 2 builds a symbolic cost function for the estimated memory cost per iteration using the approach from [4, 13]. ($b_1, \ldots, b_n$ are symbolic variables used in the cost function.) Step 2 identifies the *locality group* G for the current memory hierarchy level by extending the definition from [14, 13] so that it can apply to any memory hierarchy level. Step 3 estimates block sizes at compile-time for loops in the locality group by using the approach from [4, 13]. The "effective-size" constraint ensures that the execution of a single block of iterations will not incur any capacity or conflict misses at the current memory hierarchy level, M_j^i (assuming that the block of iterations starts with a clean cache at that level). Step 4 updates the locality group G by removing any loops that were given an estimated block size of 1. Step 5 checks if the locality group is non-empty (no transformations are created if the locality group is empty). If so, step 5.a appends a Unimodular transformation to bring the g loops in the locality group to positions $n - g + 1, \ldots, n$, the innermost positions among the outermost n loops. Step 5.b then appends a Block transformation to block the g loops in the locality group. Step 5.c updates the loop nest which now has g additional loops; the n outermost loops are thus still eligible for transformation when optimizing outer memory hierarchy levels.

Figure 3 outlines the algorithm for the second pass, *outside-in parallelization*. While algorithms for finding nested parallel loops have appeared earlier in the literature (*e.g.*, [18, 17]), the main challenge here is to perform the hierarchical parallelization in conjunction with locality transformations so as to match the structure of the given parallelism hierarchy model. In fact, when possible, our algorithm will coalesce adjacent nested parallel loops that are found at the same level of the parallelism hierarchy. Thus, the maximum nesting of parallelism generated by our algorithm will not exceed the nesting of parallelism in the machine model *i.e.*, the nesting will be at most q deep.

As mentioned earlier, the transformation sequence built by this algorithm is (in general) a cascade of Unimodular–Parallel–Coalesce transformations, which has the net effect of hierarchical nested parallelization. The Coalesce step is omitted when not required. Unimodular and Parallel transformation do not change the number of loops in the nest, but the Coalesce transformation decreases the number of loops.

The algorithm in figure 3 works outside-in by stepping through the q levels of parallelism hierarchy. Step 1 identifies the *eligible loops* for memory hierarchy level $\mathcal{M}_1^i$ *i.e.*, the outermost memory hierarchy level in parallelism level i. These are the loops that appear outside of the locality groups for memory hierarchy level $\mathcal{M}_1^i$ (or any of its inner memory hierarchy levels), but (if $i > 1$) appear inside of the locality groups for memory hierarchy level $\mathcal{M}_{r_{i-1}}^{i-1}$ (or any of its outer memory hierarchy levels). By only considering these loops as eligible for parallelization at level i, we ensure that we do not violate the hierarchical blocking transformations selected in the previous pass. Step 2 uses the parallelization

Inputs: A hierarchical blocking transformation σ', and the set of n' perfectly nested loops, $\mathcal{L}' = (L'_1, \ldots, L'_{n'})$ obtained after hierarchical blocking *i.e.*, $\mathcal{L}' = \sigma'(\mathcal{L})$. As before, the *parallelism hierarchy model* for q levels of parallelism is specified by $\mathcal{P} = (P_1, \ldots P_q)$, where each P_i contains a *memory hierarchy model* for r_i levels of memory hierarchy at the ith level of parallelism, $\mathcal{M}^i = (M^i_1, \ldots M^i_{r_i})$.

Output: An sequence of loop transformations, σ'', for loop nest $\mathcal{L}'$ that performs hierarchical parallelization for the parallelism hierarchy model $\mathcal{P}$. $\mathcal{L}'' = \sigma''(\mathcal{L}')$ denotes the transformed loop nest obtained by applying σ'' on $\mathcal{L}'$.

Method:

Initialize $\mathcal{L}'' := \mathcal{L}'$ (with $n'' = n'$), and σ'' to the empty sequence.

for $i := 1$ **to** q **do**

1. Let loops $L''_v, \ldots, L''_w$ be the *eligible loops* for memory hierarchy level $\mathcal{M}^i_1$.
2. Use the algorithm from [17] to:
   (a) First find the (unique) largest fully permutable outermost loop nest in loops $L''_v, \ldots, L''_w$.
   (b) Then find the largest set of *coalescable outermost parallel* loops that can be obtained in the fully permutable outermost loop nest identified in step 2.a.
3. Append to σ'' the (single) $n'' \times n''$ Unimodular transformation from step 2 required to obtain the largest fully permutable outermost loop nest and to reveal the largest set of coalescable outermost parallel loops.
4. Set $\mathcal{L}'' := \sigma''(\mathcal{L}')$ to represent the updated loop nest.
5. Let $L''_x, \ldots, L''_y$ be the set of coalescable outermost parallel loops in loop nest $\mathcal{L}''$ revealed by the unimodular transformation in step 2. Append to σ'' the single $n'' \mapsto n''$ Parallel transformation that parallelizes loops $L''_x, \ldots, L''_y$.
6. **if** $x < y$ **then**
   Append to σ'' the single $n'' \mapsto (n'' - (y - x))$ Coalesce transformation that coalesces the $(y - x + 1)$ parallel loops $L''_x, \ldots, L''_y$ into a single parallel loop.
   end if
7. Set $\mathcal{L}'' := \sigma''(\mathcal{L}')$ to represent the transformed loop nest after the Parallel and Coalesce transformations for use in the next iteration of the i loop.

end for

Fig. 3. Outside-in algorithm for selecting a loop transformation sequence for hierarchical parallelization

algorithm from [17] to find the (unique) largest fully permutable outermost loop nest among the eligible loops, and then to find the largest set of *coalescable outermost parallel* loops that can be obtained in this fully permutable outermost loop nest. A set of adjacent parallel loops $L''_x, \ldots, L''_y$ is said to be coalescable if it satisfies the loop bounds constraints [15] for the Coalesce transformation *i.e.*, no loop bound expression for L''_k ($x \leq k \leq y$) must use the index variable of any loop in the range $L''_x, \ldots, L''_{k-1}$. Step 3 appends to σ'' the unimodular transformation selected in step 2, and step 4 updates $\mathcal{L}''$ to reflect the output loop nest after step 2. Step 5 appends the Parallel transformation to σ'' for parallelizing loops $L''_x, \ldots, L''_y$. Step 6 appends a Coalesce transformation when multiple loops were selected in the set of coalescable outermost parallel loops identified in step 2 (*i.e.*, when $x < y$). Finally, step 7 updates $\mathcal{L}''$ to represent the output loop nest obtained after parallelization at level i.

Now that we have presented the algorithms for the inside-out locality optimization pass and the outside-in parallelization pass, the following sections use simple examples to illustrate how our framework enables implementation of the transformation sequences selected by these algorithms. Section 4 illustrates how our algorithm performs unimodular and parallelization transformations *after* blocking. Section 5 shows how our algorithm performs unimodular and coalescing transformations *after* parallelization.

4   Performing Loop Transformations after Tiling

In this section, we use a simple example program to illustrate how our compiler implements a Block–Unimodular–Parallelize transformation sequence in which unimodular and parallelization transformations are performed *after* blocking. This basic Block–Unimodular–Parallelize transformation sequence is necessary for targeting a machine with just a single level of parallelism and a single level of cache. As discussed in section 3, longer transformation sequences of this form become necessary when targeting deeper levels of memory and parallelism hierarchies.

However, even this basic Block–Unimodular–Parallelize transformation sequence cannot be supported by past work on loop transformations. A fundamental problem is that Block is not a unimodular transformation and hence the Block–Unimodular combination cannot be handled by unimodular transformation frameworks such as those described in [2, 16]. And if the Block transformation is attempted as a prepass (by rewriting the loop nest), today's compilers are unable to perform a unimodular transformation on the output loop nest generated by blocking due to its complex loop bound expressions and the fact that the block sizes may be unknown at compile-time.

The example program is a four point stencil operation shown in Figure 4(a). There are two loops in this loop nest, with index variables j and i. The set of loop-carried data dependence vectors for the original loop nest is $\{(0,1),(1,0)\}$. Since both loops carry data locality, the locality optimization pass described in section 3 will decide to block both loops. After applying the blocking transformation, we obtain the loop nest of size four shown in Figure 4(b), with loops jj and ii serving as the outer controlling loops. Variables bj and bi contain the block sizes for loops j and i, which are computed (in general) at run-time as a function of the loop iteration lengths, number of available processors, and the target processor's cache geometry.

Now consider the parallelization pass described in section 3. Since none of the outer jj or ii loops can be parallelized at this stage, a Normalize–Skew–Interchange–Parallel transformation sequence is selected after blocking to enable loop parallelization. This sequence has the effect of performing a wavefront

```
(a) INPUT LOOP NEST:
--------------------
do j = 2, n-1
   do i = 2, n-1
      A(i,j) = 0.25 * ( A(i-1,j) + A(i+1,j) + A(i,j-1) + A(i,j+1) )
   end do
end do

INPUT DEPENDENCE VECTORS = { (0,1), (1,0) }

(b) AFTER BLOCKING LOOPS j AND i WITH BLOCK SIZES bj AND bi:
-----------------------------------------------------------
do jj = 2, n-1, bj
   do ii = 2, n-1, bi
      do j = jj, min(jj+bj-1,n-1)
         do i = ii, min(ii+bi-1,n-1)
            A(i,j) = 0.25 * ( A(i-1,j) + A(i+1,j) + A(i,j-1) + A(i,j+1) )
         end do
      end do
   end do
end do

DEPENDENCE VECTORS AFTER BLOCKING =
{ (0,0,0,1), (0,0,1,0), (0,1,0,*), (1,0,*,0) }

(c) AFTER NORMALIZATION AND SKEWING LOOP iii W.R.T. LOOP jjj:
------------------------------------------------------------
do jjj = 0, (n-3)/bj
   do temp = jjj, jjj + (n-3)/bi
      iii = temp - jjj
      jj = 2 + jjj*bj
      ii = 2 + iii*bi
      do j = jj, min(jj+bj-1,n-1)
         do i = ii, min(ii+bi-1,n-1)
            A(i,j) = 0.25*(A(i-1,j)+A(i+1,j)+A(i,j-1)+A(i,j+1))
         end do
      end do
   end do
end do

DEPENDENCE VECTORS AFTER SKEWING =
{ (0,0,0,1), (0,0,1,0), (0,1,0,*), (1,1,*,0) }
```

Fig. 4. A Block-Skew Transformation Sequence

AFTER INTERCHANGING LOOPS jjj AND temp, AND PARALLELIZING LOOP jjj:

```
do temp = 0, (n-3)/bj + (n-3)/bi
   pardo jjj = max(temp-(n-3)/bi,0), min(temp,(n-3)/bj)
      iii = temp - jjj
      jj = 2 + jjj*bj
      ii = 2 + iii*bi
      do j = jj, min(jj+bj-1,n-1)
         do i = ii, min(ii+bi-1,n-1)
            A(i,j) = 0.25 * ( A(i-1,j) + A(i+1,j) + A(i,j-1) + A(i,j+1) )
         end do
      end do
   end do
end do
```

DEPENDENCE VECTORS AFTER INTERCHANGE =
{ (0,0,0,1), (0,0,1,0), (1,0,0,*), (1,1,*,0) }

DEPENDENCE VECTORS AFTER PARALLELIZATION =
{ (0,0,0,1), (0,0,1,0), (1,0,0,*), (1,*,*,0) }

Fig. 5. Result of a Block-Skew-Interchange-Parallelize Transformation Sequence

```
do temp2 = 0, (n-3)/bj2 + (n-3)/bi2
   pardo jjj2 = max(temp2-(n-3)/bi2,0), min(temp2,(n-3)/bj2)
      iii2 = temp2 - jjj2
      jj2 = 2 + jjj2*bj2
      ii2 = 2 + iii2*bi2
      do temp = 0, min(bj2-1,n-1-jj2)/bj2 + min(bi2-1,n-1-ii2)/bi2
         pardo jjj = max(temp-min(bi2-1,n-1-ii2)/bi2,0),
                     min(temp,min(bj2-1,n-1-jj2)/bj2)
            iii = temp - jjj
            jj = jj2 + jjj*bj
            ii = ii2 + iii*bi
            do j = jj, min(jj+bj-1, min(jj2+bj2-1,n-1))
               do i = ii, min(ii+bi-1, min(ii2+bi2-1,n-1))
                  A(i,j) = 0.25*(A(i-1,j)+A(i+1,j)+A(i,j-1)+A(i,j+1))
               end do
            end do
         end do
      end do
   end do
end do
```

Fig. 6. Result of a Block–Block–Unimodular–Parallelize–Unimodular–Parallelize Transformation Sequence for Hierarchical Blocking and Parallelization

transformation [8] on the outer blocked loops. The result of the Normalize and Skew transformations is shown in figure 4(c), and the final result after the Interchange and Parallelize steps is shown in figure 5. Therefore, the complete sequence of transformations performed for this example is Block–Normalize–Skew–Interchange–Parallelize, which can be viewed more generally as the Block–Unimodular–Parallelize sequence discussed at the start of this section.

One concern with the transformed code in figure 5 might be that the additional assignment statements for mapping index variables could be a source of extra overhead. However, these statements have little impact on the overall execution time because they do not appear in the innermost loop. Also, their overhead is further reduced when the transformed code is compiled by an optimizing back-end because the index mapping statements are usually translated into simple register-register operations after strength reduction and register allocation.

As mentioned earlier, longer transformation sequences may be necessary for multiple levels of parallel and memory hierarchies. As an example, figure 6 shows the output nest of six loops obtained when applying the Block–Block–Unimodular–Parallelize–Unimodular–Parallelize transformation sequence to the two-dimensional loop nest in figure 4(a). This code is too complicated for a programmer to write by hand; however, it is easy to generate this kind of code mechanically for unbounded levels of hierarchy by using our algorithm.

5   Performing Transformations on Parallel Loops

In this section, we discuss the importance of *transforming parallel loops i.e.,* transforming loop nests after some loops have been parallelized. The two-pass algorithm outlined in section 3 assumes the ability to perform unimodular transformations as well as loop coalescing [11] after parallelization. The framework described in section 2 allows these loop transformations to follow parallelization as needed.

The question of how to model transformation of parallelized loops has been largely ignored in past work because most parallelizing compilers view parallelization as the last step in a transformation sequence. The answer is not trivial. For example, note that interchanging loops $temp$ and jjj is legal for the loop nest in figure 4(c), when both $temp$ and jjj are sequential loops. However, interchanging loops $temp$ and jjj becomes illegal after loop jjj is parallelized as in figure 5. Our framework addresses this problem by treating Parallelize like another iteration-reordering loop transformation, and by using a special dependence vector mapping rule for the Parallelize transformation [15]. The transformed dependence vectors after parallelization are shown at the bottom of Figure 5. Based on these transformed vectors, we can use the standard legality test for loop interchange to recognize that interchanging loops jjj and $temp$ is illegal after loop jjj is parallelized. As we will see in the next example, there are also cases in which interchange is legal after parallelization.

```
(a) Input loop nest:
--------------------
do j = 1, n
   do k = 1, n
      do i = 1, n
         A(i,j) = A(i,j) + B(i,k) * C(k,j)
      end do
   end do
end do

INPUT DEPENDENCE VECTORS = { (0,1,0) }

(b) After blocking loops j, k, i with block sizes bj, bk, bi:
------------------------------------------------------------
do jj = 1, n, bj
   do kk = 1, n, bk
      do ii = 1, n, bi
         do j = jj, min(jj+bj-1,n)
            do k = kk, min(kk+bk-1,n)
               do i = ii, min(ii+bi-1,n)
                  A(i,j) = A(i,j) + B(i,k) * C(k,j)
               end do
            end do
         end do
      end do
   end do
end do

DEPENDENCE VECTORS AFTER BLOCKING = { (0,0,0,0,1,0), (0,1,0,0,*,0) }
```

Fig. 7. A Blocking Transformation

(a) After parallelizing loops jj and ii, and interchanging loops kk and ii:

```
pardo jj = 1, n, bj
   pardo ii = 1, n, bi
      do kk = 1, n, bk
         do j = jj, min(jj+bj-1,n)
            do k = kk, min(kk+bk-1,n)
               do i = ii, min(ii+bi-1,n)
                  A(i,j) = A(i,j) + B(i,k) * C(k,j)
               end do
            end do
         end do
      end do
   end do
end do
```

DEPENDENCE VECTORS AFTER PARALLELIZATION = {(0,0,0,0,1,0), (0,1,0,0,*,0)}

DEPENDENCE VECTORS AFTER INTERCHANGE   = {(0,0,0,0,1,0), (0,0,1,0,*,0)}

(b) After coalescing parallel loops jj and ii:

```
pardo temp = 1, (n-1+bj)/bj * (n-1+bi)/bi
   lo_j = 1 + (temp - 1) / ( (n - 1 + bi) / bi ) * bj
   hi_j = 1 + min(lo_j + bj - 1, n)
   lo_i = 1 + ((temp-((n-1+bi)/bi)*((temp-1)/((n-1+bi)/bi)))-1)*bi
   hi_i = 1 + min(hi_i + bi -1, n)
   do kk = 1, n, bk
      do j = lo_j, hi_j
         do k = kk, min(kk+bk-1,n)
            do i = lo_i, hi_i
               A(i,j) = A(i,j) + B(i,k) * C(k,j)
            end do
         end do
      end do
   end do
end do
```

DEPENDENCE VECTORS AFTER COALESCING   = {(0,0,0,1,0), (0,1,0,*,0)}

Fig. 8. Result of a Block-Parallelize-Permute-Coalesce Transformation Sequence

The example program discussed in this section is the matrix multiply loop nest shown in Figure 7(a). The ordering of loops from outer to inner in the input loop nest is j, k, i. After applying the blocking transformation selected by the locality optimization pass described in section 3, we obtain the loop nest of size six shown in Figure 7(b), with loops jj, kk, ii serving as the outer controlling loops. Variables bj, bk, and bi contain the block sizes which may be initialized at run-time, as in the previous example.

Performing the parallelization pass described in section 3 results in parallelizing loops jj and ii as shown in Figure 8(a). (For simplicity, the algorithm did not consider the possibility of parallelizing loop kk, even though its loop-carried dependence is only a sum reduction). The dependence vectors after parallelization are shown in Figure 8(a) as well. The algorithm also interchanges loops ii and kk so as to move parallel loop ii outwards as shown in Figure 8(a). Unlike the previous example in figure 5(c), this interchange of a parallel loop is legal — the legality condition can be verified by examining the dependence vectors after parallelization in Figure 8(a).

The final transformation selected for this example by the parallelization pass in section 3 is loop coalescing. The rules for transforming data dependence vectors and for generating new loop bounds and initialization statements for loop coalescing were described in [15]. The code generated by our algorithm for the transformed loop nest after the entire Block-Parallelize-Permute-Coalesce transformation sequence is shown in Figure 8(b). As before, this code is too complicated for a programmer to write by hand, but it is easy to generate mechanically by using our algorithm. Also, despite their complexity, the index mappings created for coalescing are invariant in all but the outermost loop and hence their run-time overhead is negligible.

6   Related Work

There are several papers related to loop transformations for parallelism and locality that have been published in the literature. Space limitations prevent us from discussing all these references; instead, we outline a representative subset that, to the best of our knowledge, covers the prior work related to our paper.

Lamport [8] introduced the *hyperplane method* and the *coordinate method* for loop parallelization. The framework used in [8] included dependence vectors that contain distance or direction values, and iteration-reordering transformations that can be represented by $\mathcal{Z}^n \mapsto \mathcal{Z}^n$ linear mappings. Further, the legality test for a linear mapping was based on the existence of a lexicographically negative tuple in the set of transformed dependence vectors. Therefore, the framework from [8] can be used to implement a two-step Unimod–Par transformation sequence.

Irigoin and Triolet [6] describe a framework for iteration-reordering transformations based on *supernode partitioning*, an aggregation technique achieved by hyperplane partitioning, followed by iteration space tiling across hyperplane boundaries. In this framework, data dependences are represented by *dependence cones* rather than dependence vectors. They also provide a general code generation algorithm for any linear transformation that corresponds to a unimodular change of basis [5]. Their framework incorporates loop interchange, hyperplane partitioning, and loop tiling (blocking) in a unified way, for loop nests with linear bounds expressions. Our framework takes its inspiration from this kind of unified approach to loop transformations. Their framework is more general than ours in its ability to support non-rectangular tiling through hyperplane partitioning. Our framework is more general than theirs in its ability to support non-linear transformations like loop parallelization and loop coalescing. Our framework is also more practical because it is based on dependence vectors rather than dependence cones.

Recently, *unimodular transformations* have gained popularity as a practical framework for iteration-reordering transformations. Banerjee [2] shows how transformations like loop interchange, loop reversal, and loop skewing, can be represented by a unimodular transformation matrix; however, the results in the paper are proved only for loop nests of size $= 2$, and containing constant loop bounds. Wolf and Lam [17] also show how unimodular transformations can be used to unify loop interchange, loop reversal, and loop skewing; the results in their paper are applicable to loop nests of arbitrary size and with linear bounds constraints. Therefore, the framework from [17] can be used to implement a two-step Unimod–Par transformation sequence. In other work [16], Wolf and Lam incorporate the tiling (blocking) transformation into their framework by proposing a two-step approach, where a unimodular transformation is followed by a tiling transformation. Thus, the framework from [16] can be used to implement a two-step Unimod–Block transformation sequence. More recently, McKinley, Carr, and Tseng [9] studied improvements in data locality by using the loop permutation, fusion, distribution, and reversal transformations. Their experimental results show wide applicability of these locality-improving transformations for existing Fortran 77 and Fortran 90 programs.

The key advantage of the approach reported in this paper over past work is that it allows arbitrary hierarchical composition of a large class of iteration-reordering transformations (Unimodular, Block, Parallel, Coalesce) while maintaining a uniform legality test and code generation scheme. In addition, we present an algorithm for selecting hierarchical combinations of these transformations for optimizing locality and parallelism for a specified parallelism hierarchy model.

7   Conclusions and Future Work

In this paper, we addressed the problem of selecting iteration-reordering loop transformations for hierarchical parallelism and locality. We outlined a general algorithm that can be used for selecting these transformations for a given parallelism hierarchy model. We then showed how our compiler framework can support the combinations of Block, Unimodular, Parallel, and Coalesce transformations that are required when optimizing for hierarchical parallelism and locality, and that cannot be supported by past loop transformation frameworks reported in the literature.

One of the main directions for future work is to experimentally evaluate the performance of the algorithm presented in this paper for selecting a sequence of loop transformations for a specified parallelism hierarchy model. Our prototype compiler implementation can be used to generate code for such an evaluation. However, we are still considering different possibilities for the target architecture (including simulators vs. real machines) for carrying out such a study. Other directions for future work include extending the set of transformations to include loop distribution and fusion as considered in [9, 13] and data-centric blocking transformations as considered in [7].

Acknowledgments

The author would like to thank Radhika Thekkath for her contribution to the underlying loop transformation framework [15] used in this paper, and to its initial implementation in the ASTI transformer [13] in 1992 at the IBM Santa Teresa Laboratory. The author would also like to thank Alan Adamson and other members of the Parallel Development group in the IBM Toronto Laboratory for their ongoing work on extending the ASTI optimizer component and delivering it as part of the IBM XL FORTRAN compiler products for RS/6000 uniprocessors and multiprocessors.

References

1. Utpal Banerjee. *Dependence Analysis for Supercomputing*. Kluwer Academic Publishers, Norwell, Massachusetts, 1988.
2. Utpal Banerjee. Unimodular Transformations of Double Loops. *Proceedings of the Third Workshop on Languages and Compilers for Parallel Computing*, August 1990.
3. Jyh-Herng Chow, Leonard E. Lyon, and Vivek Sarkar. Automatic Parallelization for Symmetric Shared-Memory Multiprocessors. *CASCON '96 conference*, November 1996.
4. Jeanne Ferrante, Vivek Sarkar, and Wendy Thrash. On Estimating and Enhancing Cache Effectiveness. *Lecture Notes in Computer Science*, (589):328–343, 1991. Proceedings of the Fourth International Workshop on Languages and Compilers for Parallel Computing, Santa Clara, California, USA, August 1991. Edited by U. Banerjee, D. Gelernter, A. Nicolau, D. Padua.
5. Francois Irigoin. Code generation for the hyperplane method and for loop interchange. Technical report, Ecole Nationale Superieure des Mines de Paris, October 1988. Report ENSMP-CAI-88-E102/CAI/I.
6. Francois Irigoin and Remi Triolet. Supernode Partitioning. *Conference Record of Fifteenth ACM Symposium on Principles of Programming Languages*, 1988.
7. Induprakas Kodukula, Nawaaz Ahmed, and Keshav Pingali. Data-centric Multi-level Blocking. *Proceedings of the ACM SIGPLAN '97 Conference on Programming Language Design and Implementation, Las Vegas, Nevada*, pages 346–357, June 1997.

8. L. Lamport. The Parallel Execution of DO Loops. *Communications of the ACM*, 17(2):83–93, February 1974.

9. Kathryn S. McKinley, Steve Carr, and Chau-Wen Tseng. Improving Data Locality with Loop Transformations. *ACM Transactions on Programming Languages and Systems*, 18:423–453, July 1996.

10. Nicholas Mitchell, Larry Carter, Jeanne Ferrante, and Karin Hogstedt. Quantifying the Multi-Level Nature of Tiling Interactions. In *Languages and compilers for parallel computing. Proceedings of the 10th international workshop. Held Aug., 1997 in Minneapolis, MN.*, Lecture Notes in Computer Science. Springer-Verlag, New York, 1998. (to appear).

11. Constantine Polychronopoulos. Loop Coalescing: A Compiler Transformation for Parallel Machines. Technical report, U. of Ill., January 1987. Submitted for publication to the 1987 International Conference on Parallel Processing, St. Charles, Ill.

12. Constantine D. Polychronopoulos and David J. Kuck. Guided Self-Scheduling: A Practical Scheduling Scheme for Parallel Supercomputers. *IEEE Transactions on Computers*, C-36(12), December 1987.

13. Vivek Sarkar. Automatic Selection of High Order Transformations in the IBM XL Fortran Compilers. *IBM Journal of Research and Development*, 41(3), May 1997.

14. Vivek Sarkar, Guang R. Gao, and Shaohua Han. Locality Analysis for Distributed Shared-Memory Multiprocessors. In *Languages and compilers for parallel computing. Proceedings of the 9th international workshop. Held Aug., 1996 in Santa Clara, CA.*, Lecture Notes in Computer Science. Springer-Verlag, New York, 1997.

15. Vivek Sarkar and Radhika Thekkath. A General Framework for Iteration-Reordering Loop Transformations. *Proceedings of the ACM SIGPLAN '92 Conference on Programming Language Design and Implementation*, pages 175–187, June 1992.

16. Michael E. Wolf and Monica S. Lam. A Data Locality Optimization Algorithm. *Proceedings of the ACM SIGPLAN Symposium on Programming Language Design and Implementation*, pages 30–44, June 1991.

17. Michael E. Wolf and Monica S. Lam. A Loop Transformation Theory and an Algorithm to Maximize Parallelism. *IEEE Transactions on Parallel and Distributed Systems*, 2(4):452–471, October 1991.

18. Michael J. Wolfe. *Optimizing Supercompilers for Supercomputers*. Pitman, London and The MIT Press, Cambridge, Massachusetts, 1989. In the series, Research Monographs in Parallel and Distributed Computing.

Data Flow Analysis Driven Dynamic Data Partitioning

Jodi Tims   Rajiv Gupta   Mary Lou Soffa
Department of Computer Science

University of Pittsburgh Pittsburgh, PA 15260
{jlt, gupta, soffa@cs.pitt.edu}

Abstract. The use of distributed memory architectures as an effective approach to parallel computing brings with it a more complex program development process. Finding a partitioning of program code and data that supports sufficient parallelism without incurring prohibitive communication costs is a challenging and critical step in the development of programs for distributed memory systems. Automatic data distribution techniques have the goal of placing the responsibility of determining a suitable data partitioning into the domain of the compiler. Static program analysis techniques that expose data interrelationships and derive performance estimates are central to the development of automatic data distribution heuristics. In this paper we present a data partitioning heuristic that makes use of array data flow analysis information in the modeling of data interrelationships and the estimation of costs associated with resolving interrelationships via communication. The global view provided by data flow analysis permits consideration of potential communication optimizations before data partitioning decisions are made. Our heuristic uses tiling techniques to determine data partitionings. The resulting data distributions, while still regular, are not limited to the standard BLOCK, CYCLIC and BLOCK-CYCLIC varieties. Preliminary results indicate an overall reduction in communication cost with our technique.

1   Introduction

The distributed memory approach to parallel computing offers benefits of scalability and cost effectiveness. As in shared memory systems, program development for distributed memory architectures requires the parallelization of program code in order to exploit the power of multiple processors. Distributed memory systems encounter additional complexity, however, in the need to partition data among the independent memory units of each processor. If data is distributed to the local memories in a haphazard fashion, any gains due to parallel execution of the code may well be equaled or exceeded by communication costs.

The problems of process decomposition and data distribution share a high degree of coupling. The Single-Program—Multiple-Datastream (SPMD) model of execution [5] assumed in this work, addresses this interaction by requiring that computations occur on the processor where the result operand has been

D. O'Hallaron (Ed.): LCR'98, LNCS 1511, pp. 75–90, 1998.
© Springer–Verlag Berlin Heidelberg 1998

mapped. This "owner-computes" rule simplifies program development for distributed memory architectures somewhat, in that process decomposition is implicit in the determination of a data decomposition. Even assuming the SPMD execution model, however, data distribution is a complex task. Automatic data distribution algorithms place the burden of determining a data partitioning into the domain of the compiler. This approach not only simplifies program development for distributed memory systems, but also encourages the use of nonstandard distribution patterns.

Automatic data distribution techniques fall into two primary categories. *Static data distribution* techniques [10, 12] determine a single distribution for each array variable for the duration of the program's execution. The limitation of this approach is that if data interrelationship patterns vary significantly during the course of a program, some phases of the execution will incur significant communication costs. *Dynamic data distribution* techniques [2, 3, 4, 6, 7, 13, 15, 17] address this limitation by allowing arrays to be realigned and redistributed during execution so that more of the program's interrelationships may be resolved by the data distribution. Care must be taken, however, that the communication saved by changing the data distribution is not offset or exceeded by the inherent cost of relocating data values during realignment and redistribution operations. Finding the optimal dynamic data distribution for a given program has been determined to be an NP-complete problem [14].

Existing dynamic distribution techniques share a common view that a single distribution encompasses the partitioning of multiple array variables that are used within a particular code segment, most commonly a loop nest. Using an estimate of communication cost as a basis, all interrelationships within the code segment are analyzed to determine the "best" distribution for the segment. Distribution conflicts between adjacent code segments are resolved either by sacrificing parallelism, merging distributions and inserting communication into one of the nests, or redistributing all arrays involved in both segments. After determining the data distribution, a communication optimization phase tries to reduce communication costs using techniques such as message aggregation, overlapping communication and computation, and elimination of redundant messages.

In this paper we present an automatic data partitioning heuristic that makes significant use of array data flow analysis information in the modeling of data interrelationships and the estimation of costs associated with resolving interrelationships via communication. To support the analysis required by the distribution heuristic, we develop the *Distribution Interrelationship Flowgraph (DIF)* representation of a program. The DIF supports data flow analysis and makes explicit those interrelationships that impact data distribution decisions. The global view of data interrelationships provided by data flow analysis permits consideration of potential communication optimizations before data partitioning decisions are made. This allows the partitioning heuristic to choose a data distribution that resolves data interrelationships whose communication costs would be highest if communication were required. Our heuristic uses tiling techniques [16] to determine data partitionings. The resulting data distributions, while still regular, are not limited to the standard BLOCK, CYCLIC and BLOCK_CYCLIC varieties. Experimental results indicate an overall reduction in communication cost with our technique.

The technique presented in this paper differs from existing dynamic distribution techniques in two significant ways. First, the interrelationships that affect the partitioning of an array at a program point are extracted from global data flow analysis information. Thus the interrelationships discovered are value-centric rather than location-centric and span the lifetime of the values rather than their use in a localized code segment. The precision of array analysis information realizable using interval data flow analysis techniques [9] in comparison to other methods of dependence detection (e.g., dependence vectors) enables some false interrelationships to be excluded from consideration in partitioning decisions. The nature of the interrelationship information impacts the philosophy underlying our heuristic. A data distribution refers to the partitioning of a group of values generated at a single program point and exists until those values are no longer live. This group of values may span an entire array or some regular section of the array. Distribution of array locations is an implicit side effect of the computation of new values into the locations. The computation of the new values is carried out on their owner processor(s) rather than on the owner(s) of previous values. This approach avoids the need to communicate the newly generated values if there is a change in ownership. Our technique assigns a distribution to each section of array values generated during the program's execution. Disjoint sections of the same array may have different distributions at the same program point. Decisions to redistribute array locations are implicit in assigning distributions to the sections.

The second difference in our technique concerns the integration of communication optimization information into the communication cost estimates that drive data partitioning decisions. The applicability of many communication optimizations is determined from reaching definitions data flow analysis information. This is the same data flow information used to determine data interrelationships. Thus, it is known before partitioning decisions are made whether or not certain communication optimizations can be exploited if communication of values is necessary. The savings realizable by those optimizations are incorporated into the communication cost estimates. Consequently, our technique aligns and orients the programs arrays so that those data interrelationships that will incur the highest communication costs are satisfied by the data distribution.

The remainder of this paper is organized as follows. Section 2 discusses the intermediate representation and communication cost estimates used by the partitioning heuristic. Section 3 presents our data partitioning heuristic. Section 4 summarizes experimental results. Conclusions are presented in Section 5.

2 Program Representation and Communication Costs

A program representation that supports automatic data distribution driven by array data flow analysis information must have two primary characteristics.

First, the representation must include control flow information to support the performance of data flow analysis. Secondly, the representation must make explicit those interrelationships that affect data partitioning decisions. Such interrelationships result both from the use of multiple variables within a single expression and from multiple uses of the same variable in different expressions. We have developed the *Distribution Interrelationship Flow Graph (DIF)* to meet both of these requirements.

The DIF is based upon the Control Flow Graph (CFG) representation of a program. This CFG basis enables data flow analysis to be performed and also allows the DIF to be used for phases of compilation subsequent to automatic data distribution (e.g., code generation). The CFG constructed by our heuristic is an extension of the traditional CFG in that *merge nodes* are inserted at the join points of alternate control paths. While these merge nodes in no way affect the semantics represented, they allow for the establishment of a single last distribution point for each array value in much the same manner as the *phi* nodes of Static Single Assignment form [8] provide for single last definition points. This approach serves to constrain set sizes during data flow analysis and to simplify automatic generation of communication statments at the expense of some realignment/redistribution communication at the merge nodes associated with conditional constructs. The CFG with merge nodes is referred to as the *Extended Control Flow Graph (ECFG)* representation to distinguish it from the traditional CFG representation.

Efficient generation of data flow analysis information is supported in the DIF by the addition of a set of *distribution flow edges* associated with each of a program's array variables. Distribution flow edges bypass single-entry-single-exit regions of the ECFG where an array variable is not accessed. Placement of distribution flow edges is similar to the placement of dependence flow edges in the Dependence Flow Graph (DFG) [11]. The subgraph induced by the distribution flow edges for an array variable A is termed the *Distribution Control Flow Graph of A ($DCFG_A$)*.

Explicit representation of data interrelationships in the DIF comes through the extension of the ECFG with a set of *relationship edges*. These undirected edges connect nodes in the ECFG which represent distribution points of array sections. An edge between node n and node m indicates that the distribution of the array section that originates at node n interacts with the distribution of the array section that originates at node m at some program point. Since each array definition point in the program is considered to be a distribution point, reaching definitions data flow information is used to determine the placement of relationship edges. The undirected subgraph induced by the set of relationship edges is termed the *Interrelationship Graph (IG)* of the program.

Relationship edges are labeled with ordered pairs consisting of nodes and costs. In each ordered pair, the first element is the ECFG node number at which an interrelationship represented by the edge occurs. This information is needed so that the partitioning heuristic can retrieve information about the specific reference functions involved in the interrelationship. The second element of each ordered pair is an estimate of the cost incurred if the interrelationship needs to be resolved via communication. It is assumed that the send statement of the communication is moved as far away from the actual access as possible. If the communication can be initiated outside any loops in which the access is nested, its cost is adjusted to reflect a savings realizable through message aggregation. The cost also incorporates an estimated savings attributable to the overlap of communication with computation between the send and receive statements.

Figure 1b shows the ECFG for the program example in Fig. 1a. Nodes of the ECFG have been labeled for ease of reference. The boldfaced, undirected edges are the relationship edges of the DIF and are discussed below. Figure 1c shows the subgraph induced by the distribution flow edges for array variable C. Since the middle loop nest of the program does not reference array C, $DCFG_C$ does not include any of the ECFG associated with that loop.

The relationship edges in Fig. 1b are labeled only with the ECFG node names where the relationships originate. Communication costs are discussed below. Since arrays C and D are not assigned values before they are used, it is assumed that their distributions occur at the *start* node prior to the first loop. The use of elements of array C to compute elements of array A at node **d** results in the generation of a relationship edge (a, d) labeled **d**. In an analogous manner, edges (d, i) and (a, j) with labels **i** and **j** are inserted. The final interrelationship in the example results from the use of elements from arrays A and C at node **o**. Since relationship edges are placed between the distribution points of the arrays involved in an interrelationship, the appropriate edge in this instance is (a, j). Since edge (a, j) already exists, it is given a second label, **o**, to indicate another interrelationship involving the same distribution points. When the IG is further processed by the partitioning heuristic, the single physical node, **a**, is treated as two nodes, a_C and a_D, and the single physical edge, (a, j), is treated as two logical edges, (a_C, j) and (a_D, j), since two different sets of variables are involved in the interrelationships labeling the edge.

Relationship edges are labeled with symbolic communication cost estimates derived for each relationship. As an example of these costs, consider relationship edge (d, i) labeled **i**. This interrelationship arises from the use of $a[i][j]$ to define $b[i][j]$ at node **i**. Since process decomposition is accomplished via the owner computes rule [5], the values of $a[i][j]$ will be communicated if the distribution does not resolve this interrelationship. Given that the values of $a[i][j]$ are defined prior to the loop nest in which node **i** occurs, the values involved in this communication can be aggregated and sent prior to the start of the loop nest. If there are p processors available, this results in $p(p-1)$ messages, each of length $\frac{10000}{p(p-1)}$. The expression $Transfer(\frac{10000}{p(p-1)})$ represents the time required for one of these messages. The send statement of the communication is scheduled immediately after the loop in which the values of $a[i][j]$ are computed. Thus, the communication cost is adjusted to reflect the savings due to overlapping the communication with the computation that occurs between the send statement and node **i**. This savings is represented as the expression $time(f, i)$. Thus, the symbolic communication cost derived for edge (d, i) is $p(p-1) * Transfer(\frac{10000}{p(p-1)}) - time(d, i)$.

```
for (i=1; i<1011 u++)
  for (j=1; j<101; j++)
    a[i][j] = c[i][j] + 1;
for (i=1; i<101; i++)
  for (j=1; j<101; j++)
  {
    b[i][j] = a[i][j] - 2;
    a[i][j] = d[i] * 2;
  }
for (i=1; i<101; i++)
  for (j=1; j<101; j++)
    x = a[i][j] + c[j][i]
```

(a)

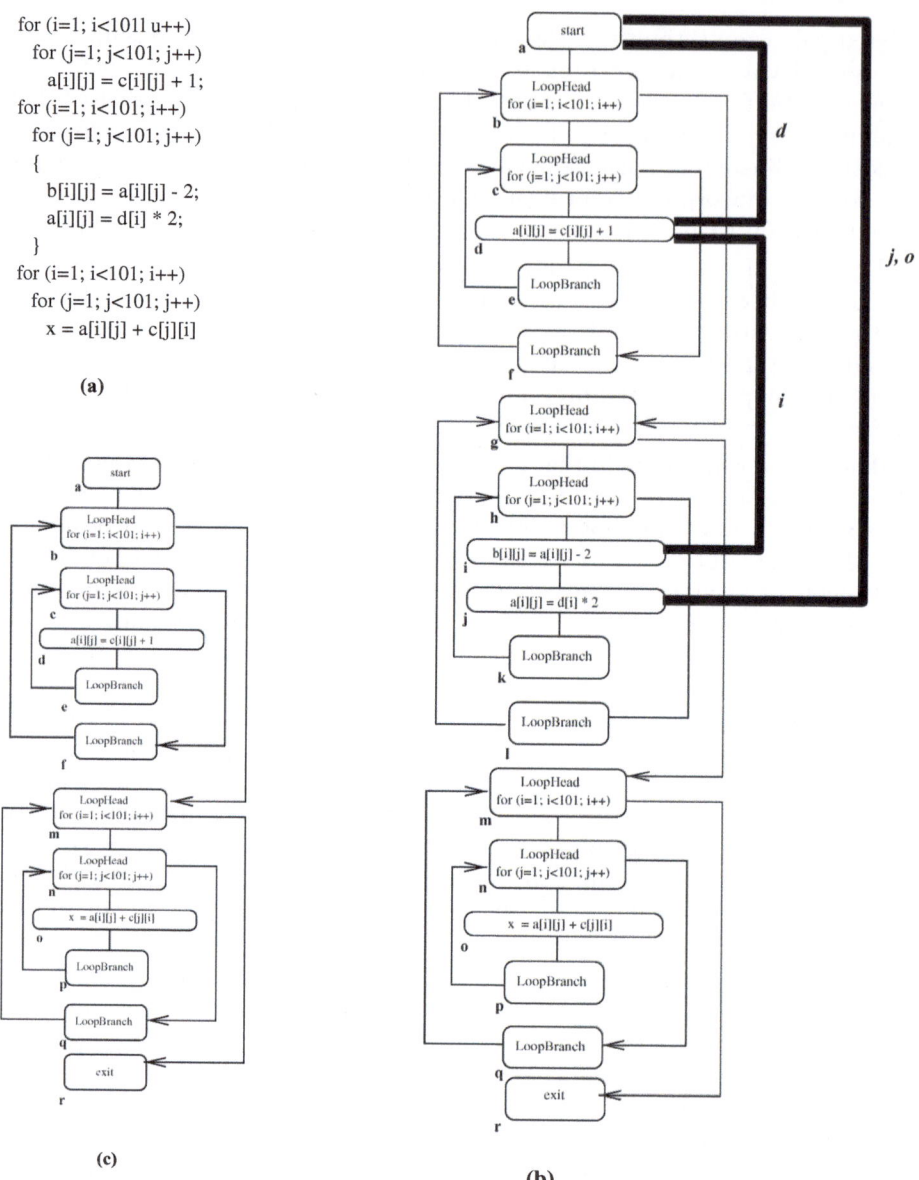

Figure 1. The Distribution Interrelationship Flowgraph

3   The Partitioning Heuristic

Determining relationship clusters. The data distribution heuristic begins by partitioning the IG into groups of related nodes termed *relationship clusters*. Each cluster is built by starting with the ECFG node closest to the ECFG end node that is not already in a cluster. An adjacent node, *d*, is added to the cluster if two conditions are met. First, d must not belong to another cluster. This condition ensures that each value is owned by a single processor at each program point. Secondly, if there is another node, e, already in the cluster that represents values also represented by d, then d will only replace e in the cluster if the highest cost interrelationship involving node d is greater than the highest cost interrelationship involving node e. This condition enables each definition point of a value to be considered as a potential redistribution point for the array locations defined there. This second condition also establishes that lower cost interrelationship edges will fall between clusters while higher cost edges will fall within clusters. Those edges between relationship clusters are not considered as data distributions are derived. Therefore it is likely that those relationships between clusters will have to be resolved via communication and thus should carry as small a cost as possible. If node d is added to the cluster, nodes adjacent to d in the IG are also considered for inclusion. The cluster is complete when there are no more nodes that satisfy the conditions.

All nodes in a cluster are mapped to a single virtual data space. Selecting a distribution for the virtual data space implicitly selects a distribution for all array sections mapped to it. Specification of a section's orientation is represented by a function π such that dimension i of the section is mapped to dimension $\pi(i)$ of the virtual data space. The alignment within a dimension is specified by a linear function, $f(x) = ax + b$, where a specifies the stride within the virtual data space between adjacent points of the section and b represents the offset of each point of the section.

Determining alignment and orientation. If the alignment and orientation of an array section represented by a node in a relationship cluster are known, the interrelationship labeling an edge to an adjacent node in the cluster can be used to determine a communication-free alignment and orientation of the array section of the adjacent node. Assume section s_1 represented by node n_1 has permutation function π_1 and alignment $f_{1,i}$ in dimension i. Let s_2 be the section represented by adjacent node n_2 in the relationship cluster. Assume that in the relationship labeling edge (n_1, n_2) that s_1 is accessed by the function R_1 in dimension i and that R_1 references index variable I. If s_2 is accessed in dimension j by function R_2 involving the same index variable I, then to avoid communication the orientation function π_2 of s_2 should specify that $\pi_2(j) = \pi_1(i)$. With respect to alignment, each coordinate in dimension i of s_1 can be mapped to a corresponding point in dimension j of s_2 via the function composition $R_2 R_1^{-1}$. In order to avoid communication, these corresponding points of s_1 and s_2 must also coincide in the virtual data space. Thus, the alignment function $f_{2,j}$ is defined by the composite function $R_2 R_1^{-1} f_{1,i}$.

If a relationship cluster is acyclic, the highest cost interrelationship on each edge can be satisfied through proper alignment and orientation of the array sections in the cluster to the virtual data space. If a relationship cluster contains a cycle, then it is possible that two conflicting alignments and orientations are required for a single array section in order to avoid communication. Such conflicts are detected by traversing the biconnected components of each relationship cluster. The starting node of each traversal is arbitrarily aligned and oriented in direct relationship to its virtual data space. As each new node is encountered during the traversal, its alignment and orientation are computed. When a cycle is detected the two partitionings computed for the node are compared. If there is a conflict, the edge in the cycle with the minimum communication cost estimate is removed from the cluster. It is assumed this relationship will be resolved via communication and it is not further considered during the partitioning process.

Figure 2 presents an example of determining alignment and orientation. The partitioned IG for the program segment of Fig. 2a is shown in Fig. 2b. The nodes of the IG are labeled to correspond to the programs statements that define each array section. Only the highest cost interrelationship that affects partitioning decisions is indicated on each edge of the IG. The cluster containing nodes 2, 5 and 10 contains no cycles and therefore no conflicts. Assume that the section at node 10 is arbitrarily given orientation $\pi_{10} = (1, 2)$ and alignment $f_{10,1}(x) = x$ and $f_{10,2}(x) = x$. Given the interrelationship $C(I, J) \Longleftrightarrow A(100 - J, I)$ on edge (10,5), the orientation of the section at node 5 is determined to be $\pi_5 = (2, 1)$. In computing the alignment of dimension two of A with dimension 1 of C, $R_{10,1}^{-1} = I$, $R_{5,2} = I$ and $f_{10,1}(x) = x$. Therefore, $f_{5,2}(x) = x$. Similarly, $R_{10,2}^{-1} = J$, $R_{5,1} = 100 - J$ and $f_{10,2}(x) = x$ yielding $f_{5,1}(x) = 100 - x$. The alignment and orientation of the section represented by node 2 are computed from the section at node 5. The section represented by node 1 is arbitrarily given an alignment and orientation that maps each point directly to the virtual data space.

Selecting tile shape and size. Once the sections of a relationship cluster have been aligned and oriented to the virtual data space, those interrelationships that have not been satisfied by the alignments and orientations chosen are examined to determine what constraints they place on the distribution of the virtual data space. Whenever two values from an array section (e.g., $B[I, J]$ and

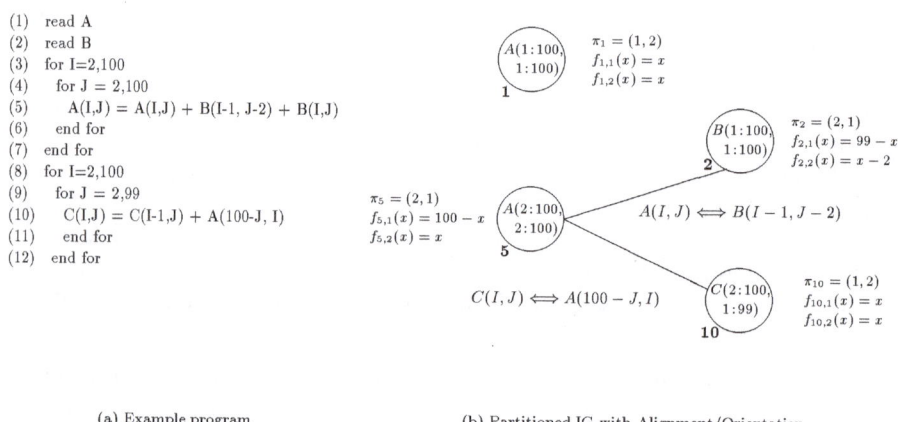

```
(1)    read A
(2)    read B
(3)    for I=2,100
(4)      for J = 2,100
(5)        A(I,J) = A(I,J) + B(I-1, J-2) + B(I,J)
(6)      end for
(7)    end for
(8)    for I=2,100
(9)      for J = 2,99
(10)       C(I,J) = C(I-1,J) + A(100-J, I)
(11)     end for
(12)   end for
```

(a) Example program   (b) Partitioned IG with Alignment/Orientation

Figure 2. Example of Determining Alignment and Orientation

$B[I-1, J-1])$ are accessed in the same statement or with a single value from another array section (e.g., $A[I, J]$), then there is a preference for the two values (i.e., $B[I, J]$ and $B[I-1, J-1]$) to reside in the same processor memory. When possible, this preference is represented in the form of a distance vector (e.g., (1,1)) and is termed a *communication dependence*. Since constraints on the distribution must be relative to the virtual data space, communication dependences derived from the reference functions of an interrelationship are transformed based upon the alignments and orientations of the array sections to that space.

Consider the relationship cluster containing nodes 2, 5 and 10 from the example in figure 2. Figure 3 shows this cluster labeled with all interrelationships. The self loop on node 10 results in the creation of a communication dependence, (1,0), specifying that $C(I, J)$ should reside with $C(I-1, J)$. Since array C is directly aligned to the virtual data space, no transformation of this dependence is required. There are 9801 non-invariant data values associated with this dependence. The interrelationships labeling edge (10,5) indicate a preference for the points defined by $A(100 - J, I)$ to reside in the same partition as those defined by $A(100 - J, I + 1)$. This gives rise to the dependence (0, -1). The orientation and alignment functions of array A indicate a transposition of dimensions and inversion in dimension 1. Thus, the transformed communication dependence is the vector (1,0). There are 10000 loop-invariant data values associated with this dependence. The two interrelationships on the edge (5,2) give rise to the dependence (1,2), indicating a preference for the points $B(I-1, J-2)$ and $B(I, J)$ to reside in the same processor memory. The reorientation indicated by π_2 and the inversion indicated by $f_{2,1}$ transform this communication dependence from (1,2) to (-2,1). There are 10000 loop-invariant values associated with this dependence. The self loop on node 2 gives rise to the communication dependence (1,2). Again, the orientation/alignment of array B results in a transformation of this vector to (-2, 1). There are 9801 loop-invariant values associated with this dependence.

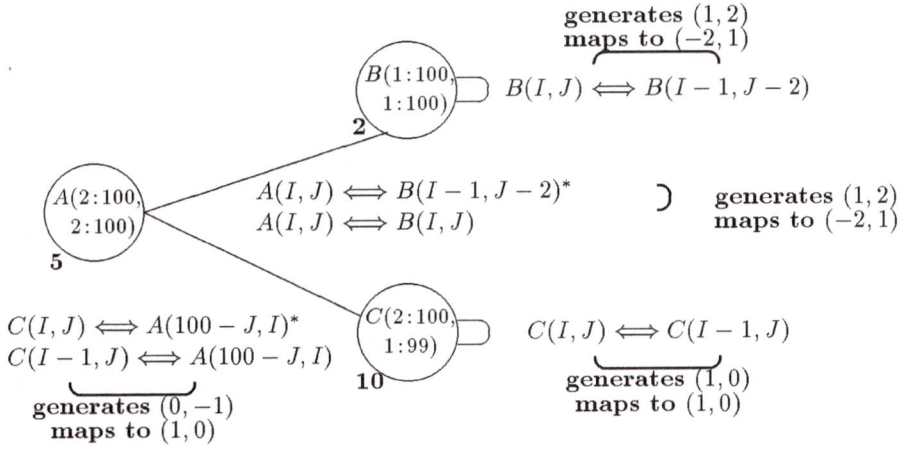

Figure 3. Example of Generating Communication Dependences

In order to minimize communication costs, tile boundaries are aligned with communication dependences. The extreme vectors [16] in the set of all dependences for a cluster are used for this purpose so that the tiles formed will encapsulate the most communication. Each tile is constrained to have length equal to some constant multiple of the length of its associated dependence vector. Determination of those constants is based upon estimates of the communication cost and parallelism derived as functions of the unknown constant multipliers. This approach enables the tradeoff between parallelism and communication inherent in some programs to be considered while determining the tile size. The communication cost function is also adjusted to reflect savings due to message aggregation when applicable.

Consider the representative tile shown in Fig. 4. The tile boundaries are formed by two dependences, $a = (a_1, a_2)$ and $b = (b_1, b_2)$, and have angles of inclination denoted by $\theta_a = \tan^{-1}(a_2/a_1)$ and $\theta_b = \tan^{-1}(b_2/b_1)$. The lengths of the sides are given as $c_1\sqrt{a_1^2 + a_2^2}$ and $c_2\sqrt{b_1^2 + b_2^2}$.

The distance vector, d, represents a communication dependence in the virtual data space. Each point in the tile is the source of an equivalent dependence. Those points that lie within the inner parallelogram will not incur any communication costs since their respective vectors lie completely within the tile. Those dependences whose source is in the boundary area between the inner and outer parallelograms will require communication to be satisfied.

The total number of communications generated within the tile is equal to the area of the boundary between the parallelograms. This boundary area is divided into three sections such that all of the communication within an area has a common destination. The areas of these sections, A_1, A_2 and A_3, are expressed as functions of the constants c_1 and c_2.

If the values being communicated for a given instance i of dependence vector d are loop invariant then those values can be aggregated into three messages of

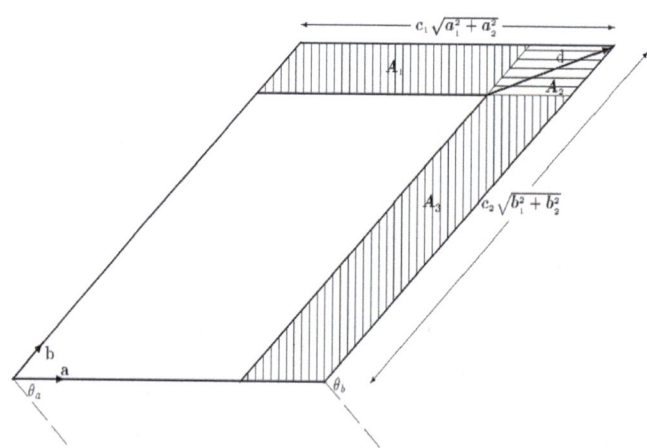

Figure 4. Representative Tile for Communication Analysis

sizes A_1, A_2 and A_3. If the values are not loop invariant then $A_1 + A_2 + A_3$ messages of size one data value (m words) are needed. The communication for instance i in a single tile follows.

$$C_t^i = \begin{cases} \sum_{i=1}^{3} Transfer(A_i * m) & \text{if invariant} \\ \sum_{i=1}^{3} A_i * Transfer(m) & \text{otherwise} \end{cases}$$

Assume the size of the data space associated with instance i is S_i. Then the number of tiles, t_i, that will be in that space is given by

$$t_i = \frac{S_i}{c_1 c_2 \sqrt{a_1^2 + a_2^2} \sqrt{b_1^2 + b_2^2} \sin(\theta_b - \theta_a)}.$$

If D is the set of all communication dependences in the cluster, then the total communication cost over all dependences is

$$C = \sum_{\text{all } d \in D} \sum_{\text{all } i} C_t^i * t_i.$$

The parallelism estimate used is an approximation based upon the size of a tile relative to the size of the virtual data space. Tile boundaries are oriented with the extreme vectors, $a = (a_1, a_2)$ and $b = (b_1, b_2)$, such that they form angles of $\theta_a = \arctan(\frac{a_2}{a_1})$ and $\theta_b = \arctan(\frac{b_2}{b_1})$ with the horizontal boundary of the virtual data space. A diagonal line segment drawn through the virtual data space and coinciding with the diagonal of the tile forms the angle θ_d with the horizontal boundary of the virtual data space such that

$$\theta_d = \arccos\left(\frac{a_1 + b_1}{\sqrt{(a_1 + b_1)^2 + (a_2 + b_2)^2}}\right)$$

The length of the line segment, L_d, passing through the virtual data space at angle θ_d is given by

$$L_d = \begin{cases} \frac{N_h}{\cos(\theta_d)} & \text{if } |\theta_d| \leq \arctan(\frac{N_v}{N_h}) \\ \frac{N_v}{\sin(\theta_d)} & \text{otherwise} \end{cases}$$

where N_h and N_v are the horizontal and vertical lengths of the virtual data space respectively.

The length of the tile diagonal, l_d, is given by the equation

$$l_d = \sqrt{(c_1 \bar{a} \cos(\theta_a) + c_2 \bar{b} \cos(\theta_b))^2 + (c_1 \bar{a} \sin(\theta_a) + c_2 \bar{b} \sin(\theta_b))^2}$$

where $\bar{a}$ and $\bar{b}$ are the lengths of vectors a and b. The parallelism estimate used is the quotient $P = \frac{L_d}{l_d}$.

Values for the constants c_1 and c_2 are determined using the method of La-Grange multipliers. Parallelism is constrained so that P is the number of available processors. The communication cost function is viewed as an objective function in multiple variables to be minimized subject to the parallelism constraint.

Representing the data distribution. The partitioning of the virtual data space is expressed as families of parallel lines that form the tiles with the chosen orientation and size. Assume that the bottom left corner of the virtual data space is the point (i_s, j_s). The two families of lines that are defined as functions of the constants $k_1, k_2 \ \epsilon Z$ follow.

1. lines with slope b_2/b_1 will pass through points

$$\left(i_s + k_1 \cos(\theta_a)c_1\sqrt{a_1^2 + a_2^2}, j_s + k_1 \sin(\theta_a)c_1\sqrt{a_1^2 + a_2^2} \right)$$

2. lines with slope a_2/a_1 will pass through points

$$\left(i_s + k_2 \cos(\theta_b)c_2\sqrt{b_1^2 + b_2^2}, j_s + k_2 \sin(\theta_b)c_2\sqrt{b_1^2 + b_2^2} \right)$$

Transformation of these families of lines into a partitioning of a related array section requires two steps. The orientation functions for the array sections must be examined to determine the relative roles of the variables i and j in the two sections. If the sections are transposed with respect to one another in the virtual data space, the roles of i and j must interchange. Secondly, any inversion (i.e., negation of i or j) or shifting for alignment purposes requires translation of the lines. This information is available as the inverse of the alignment function that mapped each array section to the virtual data space.

4   Experimental Results

To assess the effectiveness of our heuristic, we have performed an experimental evaluation using a communication emulation system [18] that gathers statistics about the actual communication resulting from a series of send statements issued by a program. The emulator is implemented as a C library routine that simulates communication in a set of physical processors. A client program of the emulator invokes the library's primary function at the point of each send statement, passing parameters of the communication in the form of a *Section Communication Descriptor (SCD)* [18]. The SCD includes the name of the array, a bounded regular section descriptor defining which elements are to be communicated and a description of the mappings of the elements to both the source and destination processors of the communication. A description of the virtual-to-real processor mapping is provided. The emulator enumerates each point that is to be communicated and determines if the source and destination processors for the point differ. The total number of points that actually result in communication and the number of messages required to send those points after aggregation opportunities are exploited is recorded. The quotient of the number of data points divided by the number of messages is also reported as a measure of the average message length.

Five test programs were chosen for evaluation of the partitioning heuristic. The program kernel ARTDIF is taken from the Hydro2D program of the SPEC95 benchmark suite. It is an astrophysical program for the computation of galactical jets using hydrodynamical Navier Stokes equations. The tomcatv grid generation program was also taken from the SPEC95 benchmark suite. The third program contains a Conjugate Gradient solver. The alternating-direction implicit (adi) program solves a tridiagonal system using cyclic reduction. Swim is a weather prediction program from the SPEC95 benchmark suite. Its procedures have been inlined to produce a single procedure for this experimentation.

The experimental evaluation compares the results of the communication emulator for each of the five test programs when compiled with the dynamic distribution technique and with a static distribution technique followed by a communication optimization phase. The compiler used to generate and optimize communications given a static data distribution is an extension to the Stanford SUIF compiler [1]. A data flow analysis based communication optimizer then performs message aggregation, redundant communication emulation and global message scheduling. For each of the five test programs, multiple static distributions were tested. The chosen distribution for each program was one that had the lowest communication cost while enabling an acceptable level of parallelism.

Figure 5 summarizes the output of the communication emulator. The results indicate a reduction in the number of messages generated and the total number of data points communicated for three of the five test programs. In the program ARTDIF, the distributions chosen by the dynamic technique are virtually identical to those chosen for the static distribution. Consequently, communication savings in this program cannot be contributed to choosing better distributions. Instead, the savings can be traced to more effective redundant communication elimination in the dynamic technique. As the dynamic heuristic creates a list of potential communications, each new entry is compared to the other entries in the list. If two different sections of the same array are both defined and used at the same program point, a union operation is performed and the intersection of the sections appears only once in the list. The data flow based communication optimizer did not uncover such redundant communications. As can be seen from the results of ARTDIF, such redundancy may not significantly impact the total number of messages required but dramatically increases the total number of data points communicated. Thus the average message length of the dynamic technique is much smaller, indicating a savings in communication cost.

The program tomcatv has two significant sources of communication savings in the dynamic distribution approach. First, some parallelism is sacrificed by the heuristic when loop-invariant communications arise in order to reduce communication costs. Secondly, the largest cluster of definition points created by the heuristic exhibits several non-vertical, non-horizontal communication dependences. The generalized tiling approach allows the set of extreme vectors to better encompass those dependences than a standard BLOCK tiling would.

The conjugate gradient program alternately accesses several one-dimensional arrays with each other and with a single two-dimensional array. When the program's one-dimensional arrays are distributed for access with the two-dimensional array, the block sizes of the one-dimensional arrays are chosen to match that of

Table 1. Results of the communication emulator for programs compiled using static and dynamic data distribution techniques

Program	total messages	total values communicated	average message size
ARTDIF (static)	18	1470576	81698.664
ARTDIF (dynamic)	16	1124	70.25
tomcatv (static)	10804	13095388	1212.087
tomcatv (dynamic)	3896	9666462	2480.611
adi (static)	23544	124692	5.296
adi (dynamic)	27700	1667354	60.123
conjugate gradient (static)	669	330735	495.372
conjugate gradient (dynamic)	243	3384	13.296
swim (static)	2469	3994204	1617.742
swim (dynamic)	4379	20072364	4583.778

the two-dimensional array. Whenever the one-dimensional arrays are reinitialized for use with each other exclusively, the block sizes are reduced so that more parallelism can be exploited. In the static case, matching one-dimensional block sizes to those of the two dimensional arrays restricts available parallelism at program points where the two-dimensional array is not accessed. Consequently, a static distribution must incur higher communication costs on the elements of the one-dimensional arrays when accessed in conjunction with the two-dimensional array.

The final two test programs in the suite performed more poorly when compiled using the dynamic distribution technique than when a static distribution was used. In the case of adi, this degradation can be traced to a common type of access pattern for array sections involving two adjacent loop nests. The first loop nest initializes an array section and the second loop nest reuses those initial values to redefine the same array elements. The use of the elements in the second loop is the only occurrence of a use for the values of the section in the first loop. However, since the heuristic demands that two definition points for the same array elements cannot be in the same partitioning cluster, the possibility exists that the two references to $x[i][j]$ in the second loop refer to values on different processors. This happened several times in this program. While any inter-cluster relationship edge has a high probability of requiring communication to resolve the interrelationship it represents, a case like the above is unnecessarily detrimental to the performance of the program.

In the case of the swim program, there are two reasons the dynamic heuristic performed poorly. First, swim has a significant number of program statements not contained in loops that assign to single array elements. The present implementation is ineffective at aligning and orienting clusters containing significant numbers of array sections with constant reference functions. A more significant source of increased communication in swim comes from a high number of messages that are generated at the merge point of a conditional control construct. If the last distribution point of an array along a control path of a conditional is given a partitioning different than the one assigned to the section at the merge node, the values must be redistributed at the merge node. Unlike redistributions upon assignment, explicit communication must be inserted to move those values. Furthermore, any values distributed by the merge node may require separate communication to resolve other interrelationships. The end result is that many points may be redistributed, only to be immediately communicated to yet another processor. Clearly this is inefficient. Extensions to the heuristic must consider the possibility of developing communication optimizations aimed at reducing communication costs at the merge points of alternate control paths.

5   Conclusion and Future Work

This paper details the development of an automatic data distribution heuristic for distributed memory parallel architectures. Through the use of global data flow analysis information and a program representation that makes explicit those data interrelationships that impact the level of communication required by a program, the heuristic selects data distributions and performs communication optimizations. Experimental results indicate a reduction in communication requirements for programs compiled using our heuristic when compared with programs compiled using a static distribution technique followed a data flow analysis based communication optimization phase.

Comparison of the effectiveness of our approach relative to other dynamic data distribution heuristics is a topic of future work. A code generator must be developed to allow execution statistics to be generated to support this work. Additional future work will center on the development of communication optimizations techniques applicable at the merge points of conditional constructs.

References

1. S.P. Amarashinge, J.M. Anderson, M.S. Lam, and C.W. Tseng. "The SUIF Compiler for Scalable Parallel Machines". In *Proceedings of the Seventh SIAM Conference on Parallel Processing for Scientific Computing*, Feb. 1995.
2. Jennifer M. Anderson and Monica S. Lam. "Global Optimizations for Parallelism and Locality on Scalable Parallel Machines". In *ACM SIGPLAN '93 Conference on Programming Language Design and Implementation*, pages 112–125, Albuquerque, NM, Jun. 1993.
3. Eduard Ayguade, Jordi Garcia, Merce Girones, M. Luz Grande, and Jesus Labarta. "Data Redistribution in an Automatic Data Distribution Tool. In *Proceedings of the 8th Workshop on Languages and Compilers for Parallel Computing*, pages 407–421, Columbus, Ohio, Aug. 1995.
4. R. Bixby, K. Kennedy, and U. Kremer. "Automatic Data Layout Using 0-1 Integer Programming". In *Proceedings of the International Conference on Parallel Architectures and Compilation Techniques (PACT94)*, pages 111–122, Montreal, Canada, Aug. 1994.
5. D. Callahan and K. Kennedy. "Compiling Programs for Distributed-Memory Multiprocessors". *The Journal of SuperComputing*, 2, 1988.

6. Barbara M. Chapman, Thomas Fahringer, and Hans P. Zima. "Automatic Support for Data Distribution on Distributed Memory Multiprocessor Systems". In *Proceedings of the 6th Workshop on Languages and Compilers for Parallel Computing*, pages 184–199, Portland, Oregon, Aug. 1993.

7. S. Chatterjee, J. R. Gilbert, R. Schreiber, and T.J. Sheffler. "Array Distribution in Data-Parallel Programs". In *Proceedings of the 7th Workshop on Languages and Compilers for Parallel Computing*, pages 76–91, 1994.

8. Ron Cytron, Jeanne Ferrante, Barry Rosen, Mark N. Wegman, and F. Kenneth Zadeck. "Efficiently Computing Static Single Assignment Form and the Control Dependence Graph". In *ACM Transactions on Programming Languages and Systems*, volume 13, pages 451–490, Oct. 1991.

9. Thomas Gross and Peter Steenkiste. "Structured Dataflow Analysis for Arrays and its Use in an Optimizing Compilers". *Software Practice and Experience*, 20(2):133–155, Feb. 1990.

10. Manish Gupta and Prithviraj Banerjee. "Demonstration of Automatic Data Partitioning Techniques for Parallelizing Compilers on Multicomputers". *IEEE Transactions on Parallel and Distributed Systems*, 3(2):179–193, Mar. 1992.

11. Richard Johnson and Keshav Pingali. "Dependence-Based Program Analysis". In *ACM SIGPLAN '93 Conference on Programming Language Design and Implementation*, pages 78–89, Jun. 1993.

12. M. Kandemir, J. Ramanujam, and A. Choudhary. "Compiler Algorithms for Optimizing Locality and Parallelism on Shared and Distributed Memory Machines". In *Proceedings of the International Conference on Parallel Architectures and Compilation Techniques (PACT97)*, San Francisco, CA, Nov. 1997.

13. Kathleen Knobe, Joan D. Lukas, and Guy L. Steele Jr. "Data Optimization: Allocation of Arrays to Reduce Communication on SIMD Machines". *Journal of Parallel and Distributed Computing*, 8:102–118, 1990.

14. Uli Kremer. "NP-completeness of Dynamic Remapping". In *Proceedings of the Fourth Workshop on Compilers for Parallel Computers*, The Netherlands, Dec. 1993.

15. Daniel J. Palermo and Prithviraj Banerjee. "Automatic Selection of Dynamic Data Partitioning Schemes for Distributed-Memory Multicomputers". In *Proceedings of the 8th Workshop on Languages and Compilers for Parallel Computing*, pages 392–406, Columbus, OH, Aug. 1996.

16. J. Ramanujam and P. Sadayappan. "Nested Loop Tiling for Distributed Memory Machines". In *5th Distributed Memory Computing Conference*, pages 1088–1096, Charleston, SC, Apr. 1990.

17. Thomas J. Sheffler, Robert Schreiber, William Pugh, John R. Gilbert, and Siddhartha Chatterjee. "Efficient Distribution Analysis via Graph Contraction". In *Frontiers '95: The 5th Symposium on the Frontiers of Massively Parallel Computation*, pages 377–391, McLean, VA, Feb. 1995.

18. X. Yuan, R. Gupta, and R. Melhem. "An Array Data Flow Analysis based Communication Optimizer". In *Proceedings of the 10th Workshop on Languages and Compilers for Parallel Computing*, Minneapolis, MN, Aug. 1997.

A Case for Combining Compile-Time and Run-Time Parallelization*

Sungdo Moon[1], Byoungro So[1], Mary W. Hall[1], and Brian Murphy[2]

[1] USC Information Sciences Institute
Marina del Rey, CA 90292, {sungdomo,bso,mhall}@isi.edu
[2] Dept. of Computer Science, Stanford University
Stanford, CA 94305, brm@cs.stanford.edu

Abstract. This paper demonstrates that significant improvements to automatic parallelization technology require that existing systems be extended in two ways: (1) they must combine high-quality compile-time analysis with low-cost run-time testing; and, (2) they must take control flow into account during analysis. We support this claim with the results of an experiment that measures the safety of parallelization at run time for loops left unparallelized by the Stanford SUIF compiler's automatic parallelization system. We present results of measurements on programs from two benchmark suites – SPECFP95 and NAS sample benchmarks – which identify inherently parallel loops in these programs that are missed by the compiler. We characterize remaining parallelization opportunities, and find that most of the loops require run-time testing, analysis of control flow, or some combination of the two. We present a new compile-time analysis technique that can be used to parallelize most of these remaining parallel loops. This technique is designed to not only improve the results of compile-time parallelization, but also to produce low-cost, directed run-time tests that allow the system to defer binding of parallelization until run-time when safety cannot be proven statically. We call this approach *predicated array data-flow analysis*. We augment array data-flow analysis, which the compiler uses to identify independent and privatizable arrays, by associating with each array data-flow value a predicate. Predicated array data-flow analysis allows the compiler to derive "optimistic" data-flow values guarded by predicates; these predicates can be used to derive a run-time test guaranteeing the safety of parallelization.

1   Introduction

Parallelizing compilers are becoming increasingly successful at exploiting coarse-grain parallelism in scientific computations, as evidenced by recent experimental results from both the Polaris system at University of Illinois and from the Stanford SUIF compiler [2, 11]. While these results are impressive overall, some of

---

* This work has been supported by DARPA Contract DABT63-95-C-0118, a fellowship from AT&T Bell Laboratories, the Air Force Materiel Command and DARPA contract F30602-95-C-0098.

D. O'Hallaron (Ed.): LCR'98, LNCS 1511, pp. 91–106, 1998.
© Springer-Verlag Berlin Heidelberg 1998

the programs presented achieve little or no speedup when executed in parallel. This observation raises again questions that have been previously addressed by experiments in the early 90s [3, 21]: is the compiler exploiting all of the inherent parallelism in a set of programs, and if not, can we identify the techniques needed to exploit remaining parallelism opportunities?

These earlier experiments motivated researchers and developers of parallelizing compilers to begin incorporating techniques for locating coarse-grain parallelism, such as array privatization and interprocedural analysis, that have significantly enhanced the effectiveness of automatic parallelization. Now that the identified techniques are performed automatically by some compilers, it is an appropriate time to revisit these questions to determine whether further improvements are possible. This paper *empirically* evaluates the remaining parallelism opportunities using an automatic run-time parallelization testing system. We augment the Lazy Privatizing Doall (LPD) test to instrument and test whether any of the candidate unparallelized loops in the program can be safely parallelized at run time [18]. The LPD test determines whether remaining loops contain data dependences (different iterations access the same memory location, where at least one of the accesses is a write), and further, whether such dependences can be safely eliminated with privatization (whereby each processor accesses a private copy of the data). The implementation is based on the automatic parallelization system that is part of the Stanford SUIF compiler. We present measurements on programs from the SPECFP95 and NAS sample benchmarks.

The results of this experiment indicate that a new analysis technique, *predicated array data-flow analysis*, can be used to parallelize most of the remaining loops missed by the compile-time analysis in the SUIF compiler. This technique extends an existing implementation of array data-flow analysis by associating with each data-flow value a predicate; analysis interprets these predicate-value pairs as describing a relationship on the data-flow value when the predicate evaluates to true. A few existing techniques incorporate predicates, most notably guarded array data-flow analysis by Gu, Li, and Lee [8]. Our approach goes beyond previous work in several ways, but the most fundamental difference is the application of these predicates to derive run-time tests used to guard safe execution of parallelized versions of loops that the compiler cannot parallelize with static analysis alone. Run-time parallelization techniques that use an inspector/executor model to test all access expressions and decide if parallelization is safe can be applied to these same loops, but such techniques can potentially introduce too much space and time overhead to make them profitable [18, 19]. The run-time tests introduced by predicated analysis are, by comparison, much simpler.

Predicated data-flow analysis unifies in a single analysis technique several different approaches that combine predicates with array data-flow values. By folding predicates into data-flow values, which we call *predicate embedding*, we can produce more precise data-flow values such as is achieved in the PIPS system by incorporating constraints derived from control-flow tests [14]. By deriving predicates from operations on the data-flow values, which we call *predicate extraction*, we can obtain breaking conditions on dependences and for privatization, such that if the conditions hold, the loop can be parallelized. The notion of breaking conditions has been suggested by Goff and by Pugh and Wonnacott [7, 17]. We discuss how such conditions can be derived in much broader ways, and present how to use these conditions both to improve compile-time analysis or as the basis for run-time tests.

The remainder of the paper is organized into three sections, related work and a conclusion. The next section presents the results of the instrumentation experiment. The subsequent section describes predicated array data-flow analysis. Section 4 presents speedup measurements from applying predicated array data-flow analysis.

2   Instrumentation

To determine remaining parallelization opportunities automatically, our system extends the LPD test to instrument multiple loops in a nest, and perform instrumentation across procedure boundaries. We are thus able to locate all the loops in the program whose iterations can be safely executed in parallel for a particular program input, possibly requiring array privatization to create private copies of an array for each processor. The run-time parallelization system [22] augments the existing automatic parallelization system that is part of the Stanford SUIF compiler. We have evaluated the system on the SPECFP95 and NAS sample benchmark suites. We used reference inputs for SPECFP95 and the small inputs for NAS. One program was omitted from our results, fpppp, due to non-standard Fortran that our compiler does not accept.

Our experiments consider two benchmark suites for which the SUIF compiler was already mostly successful at achieving good speedups. In a previous publication, SUIF achieved a speedup on seven of the SPECFP95 programs; of these seven, su2cor achieved a speedup of only 4 on 8 processors of a Digital Alphaserver 8400 [11]. The remaining six obtained a speedup of more than 6. The programs apsi, wave5 and fpppp were the only three not to obtain a speedup. In the NAS benchmark suite, only buk and fftpde failed to achieve a speedup. To obtain the results presented below, we executed the instrumented program to locate the LPD-proven parallel loops.

From the results, we see that overall the compiler was already doing a good job of parallelizing these applications. Only eight of the seventeen programs (where mgrid and applu are counted twice) contain LPD-proven parallelizable loops that the compiler missed. Once we identified the programs with remaining parallelism opportunities, we examined the LPD-proven parallelizable loops in these programs to evaluate how a parallelizing compiler might exploit this additional parallelism automatically. We characterized the requirements of these additional loops as presented in Table 1[1].

---

[1] The difference in these results as compared to a previously published version is mostly due to eliminating from the count those loops that only execute a single

Table 1. Requirements of remaining parallel loops.

Program	Total	NL	CF	BC	C+B	CI	IE	DD
apsi	19	1	12	0	6	0	0	0
mgrid	1	0	0	0	0	0	1	0
su2cor	17	0	8	5	0	4	0	0
wave5	11	0	0	7	2	0	0	2
buk	1	0	0	0	0	0	1	0
cgm	2	0	0	0	0	0	0	2
fftpde	3	0	3	0	0	0	0	0
mgrid	1	0	0	0	0	0	1	0
Total	55	1	23	12	8	4	3	4

In the table, the programs are listed in the first column, with counts appearing in the second column. The remaining seven columns provide a count of how many of the loops could potentially be parallelized with a particular technique. These techniques and requirements are defined as follows:

- **NL:** Identifies loops with nonlinear array subscript expressions, in an array reshape across procedure boundaries. These loops could be parallelized statically with some extensions to the compiler's symbolic analysis.
- **CF:** Identifies loops for which parallelization analysis fails because of control flow within the loop. The control flow paths that would result in a dependence can potentially be ruled out at compile time by associating predicates with array data-flow values during analysis and comparing predicates on reads and writes to rule out impossible control flow paths. While not in common practice, a few techniques refine their array data-flow analysis results in this way [8, 25].
- **BC:** Identifies certain loops whose safe parallelization depends on values of variables not known at compile time. For the loops in this category, it is straightforward to derive *breaking conditions* by extracting constraints on dependences directly from the dependence and privatization tests [7, 17].
- **C+B:** Identifies loops that require both of the previously described techniques. In some cases, derivation of breaking conditions is not as simple as extracting them directly from the dependence test.
- **CI:** Identifies loops that carry dependences only along certain control paths, but where the control flow test is based on array values. Such dependences can be parallelized with a simple inspector/executor that only determines control flow paths taken through the loop (a control inspector).
- **IE:** Identifies loops that can probably only be parallelized with an inspector/executor model [18]. These loops contain potential dependences on arrays with subscript expressions that include other arrays (*i.e.*, index arrays)

Parallelizing such loops is obviously not going to improve performance, and counting them skews the results.

- **DD:** Identifies loops where an inspector/executor model is probably not even suitable, because they contain dependences that occur only under certain control flow paths through the loop, and the control flow tests are based on loop-varying variables within the loop. The only approach we know that could parallelize such loops is a speculative inspector/executor model, where the loop is parallelized speculatively, and the inspector is run concurrently with executing the loop [18].

The eight programs contain a total of 55 additional parallelizable loops found by the LPD test. (Note that this number contains only loops that were executed at run time.) The two programs apsi and su2cor have the most loops, nineteen. The keys to parallelizing apsi are to take control flow tests into account during analysis and derive simple run-time tests. Several of the loops in the **CF** column have compiler-assumed dependences on scalar variables only. The bulk of the large loops in su2cor can be parallelized by taking control flow into account, with four loops in a nest requiring a control inspector. Wave5 has two large loops that require analysis that incorporates control-flow tests and introduces some run-time testing. The NAS program fftpde has large loops that can be parallelized by taking control flow into account.

Overall, we see that most of the loops require some sort of run-time testing to verify the safety of parallelization, at least 31 of the 55 loops. But rather than always reverting to a potentially expensive inspector/executor model, we see that in 24 of the 31 loops requiring run-time testing, a less expensive and more directed run-time test can potentially be derived with other techniques. We also observe from the table that taking control flow tests into account in analysis is very important, required for 31 of the 55 loops. These results indicate that there is still some room for improvement in automatic parallelization in two areas: incorporating control flow tests into analysis and extracting low-cost run-time tests wherever applicable instead of using an inspector/executor.

3   Predicated Array Data-Flow Analysis

In this section, we present an overview of predicated array data-flow analysis. A more complete treatment is found elsewhere [15]. This technique can be used to parallelize the 43 loops that fall into the CF, BC and CF+BC categories from the experiment in the previous section.

3.1   Extending Traditional Data-Flow Analysis

Traditional data-flow analysis computes what is called the *meet-over-all-paths (MOP)* solution, which produces data-flow values based on the conservative assumption that all control-flow paths through a program may be taken. Traditional analyses are also formulated on a meet-semilattice, where two data-flow values at a merge point are combined to a single data-flow value that conservatively approximates the two values. These two ways in which traditional analysis conservatively approximates the true data flow in the program may significantly limit the precision of program analysis. Predicated data-flow analysis integrates an existing data-flow analysis with an analysis on a predicate lattice to eliminate the need for many of these approximations. At the same time, analysis maintains optimistic data-flow values guarded by predicates that can be used to derive run-time tests that guarantee the safety of parallelization for loops that cannot be safely parallelized at compile time.

To make these points more concrete, we consider one straightforward way to derive useful predicates holding at a statement s (but only one of the ways considered in this paper). We can form the conjunction of control-flow tests along all paths reaching s from the beginning of the program (or from program end, if solving a problem that analyzes backward data flow). Predicates incorporating control-flow tests allow the compiler to improve data-flow information by ruling out certain control flow as impossible.

This point is illustrated by the example in Figure 1(a). The two control flow tests are identical, so any path through the loop body that includes execution of the statement $help[j] = \dots$ must also execute the statement $\dots = help[j]$. Incorporating the control-flow tests into the data-flow analysis, the compiler can prove at compile time that data-flow values corresponding to executing one but not the other statement within an iteration of the loop are infeasible. Considering only feasible data-flow values, our analysis can produce results of two kinds:

- A *meet-over-feasible-predicates solution (MOFP)* eliminates data-flow values from the traditional meet-over-all-paths solution (MOP) that the compiler can prove are infeasible. Through the MOFP solution, the compiler can improve the precision of static, compile-time analysis.
- A *value-to-predicate solution (VPS)* of a given analysis, when given a particular (optimistic) desirable data-flow value for the original problem, produces a predicate that, when true at run time, guarantees the value holds at run time. The VPS solution is derived from the MOFP solution, and can be applied by the compiler to derive run-time tests guarding safety of executing a particular optimized body of code.

Related to these solutions are operators that use values from the predicate domain to enhance the data-flow values in the original problem domain, and vice versa.

- *Predicate embedding* applies a predicate to the data-flow value it guards to produce a refined data-flow value.
- *Predicate extraction* derives a predicate from a data-flow value to produce a refined data-flow value guarded by the extracted predicate.

We illustrate how predicated array data-flow analysis uses the MOFP and VPS solutions and predicated embedding and extraction with the examples in Figures 1, and 2, loosely based on examples from our experiment. In each example, the goal is to determine whether the loop contains any array data dependences, or if so, if they can be eliminated safely with array privatization. As

for i = 1 **to** c
    for j = 1 **to** d
        if (x > 5) **then**
            help[j] = ...
    endfor
    for j = 1 **to** d
        if (x > 5) **then**
            ... = help[j]
    endfor
endfor
	for i = 1 **to** c
	    for j = 1 **to** d
	        help[j] = ...
	    endfor
	    for j = 1 **to** d
	        if (j = 1) **then**
	            ... = help[j]
	        else
	            ... = help[j-1]
	    endfor
	endfor

(a) benefits from
    MOFP solution
	(b) MOFP solution benefits
	    from predicate embedding

Fig. 1. Predicated analysis improves compile-time analysis.

part of array privatization analysis, the compiler must determine whether any read accesses are *upwards exposed* to the beginning of the iteration. If there are no upwards exposed read regions, privatization is safe. Otherwise, privatization is only possible if these upwards exposed read regions are not written by any other iteration. Predicated array data-flow analysis extends SUIF's existing array data-flow analysis implementation [12]. This analysis computes a four-tuple at each program region, $\langle$ *Read, Exposed, Write, MustWrite* $\rangle$, which are the set of array sections that may be read, may be upwards exposed, may be written and are always written, respectively. Dependence and privatization testing performs comparisons on these sets of array sections.

The notion of predicated data-flow analysis described above is not restricted to parallelization analysis. Nevertheless, our approach is particularly appropriate for array data-flow analysis for parallelization because parallelization is a high-payoff optimization (so that low-cost run-time tests are worth the run-time cost) and because predicates can introduce additional constraints into the solution of systems of linear inequalities (yielding a benefit beyond simply a more precise understanding of control flow). While most parallelizing compilers do not make explicit use of predicates in producing their optimizations, there are a few related techniques that we will describe here. The power of the predicated analysis paradigm, when applied to parallelization analysis, is that it unifies these existing techniques in a single framework, and at the same time, introduces an important new capability – deriving low-cost run-time parallelization tests to significantly increase the parallelism exposed by the compiler.

3.2 Improving Compile-Time Analysis

MOFP solution. For Figure 1(a), traditional data-flow analysis determines that there may be an upwards-exposed use of array *help* because there is a possible control flow path through the loop that references *help* without defining

```
for i = 1 to c          for i = 1 to c              for i = 1 to c
  help[i] = help[i+m]     for j = 1 to d               for j = 1 to d-1 step 2
endfor                      if (x > 5) then               help[j] = ...
                              help[j] = ...               help[j+1] = ...
                          endfor                        endfor
                          for j = 1 to d              for j = 1 to d
                            if (x > 2) then               ... = help[j]
                              ... = help[j]             endfor
                          endfor                      endfor
                        endfor
```

(a) VPS solution benefits   (b) Benefits from   (c) Benefits from extracting
    from predicate extraction   VPS solution   "optimistic" predicate

Fig. 2. Using predicated analysis in run-time parallelization.

it. That is, there is a possible path within the loop that bypasses the definition of *help* but not the references to it. An MOFP solution could discover that the predicates for the definition and reference of *help* are equivalent; thus, none of array *help* is upwards exposed. Previous work by Gu, Li and Lee, and by Tu and Padua, produce a similar such solution [8, 25].

Predicate Embedding. In examples such as in Figure 1(b), most compilers would assume that the element $help[0]$ is upwards exposed because the loop assigns to only $help[1 : d]$ but it possibly references $help[j - 1]$ and j ranges from 1 to d. But observe that the data dependence and array data-flow analyses, particularly if based on integer linear programming techniques, make use of integer constraints on scalar variables used in array accesses to determine whether two accesses in different iterations can refer to the same memory location. The compiler can utilize the constraint $j > 1$ inside the else branch of the second j loop to prove that $help[0]$ is not accessed by the loop, and, as a result, *help* can be safely privatized and the loop parallelized. The PIPS system includes such linear constraints in its data dependence and array data-flow analysis [14]. Predicated data-flow analysis that incorporates a predicate embedding operator can also derive this result and parallelize the loop at compile time.

3.3 Deriving Low-Cost Run-Time Parallelization Tests

Breaking Conditions on Data Dependences. In some cases, it is safe to parallelize a loop only for certain input data. A few researchers have considered how to derive breaking conditions on data dependences, conditions that would guarantee a data dependence does not hold at run time [7, 17]. In the example in Figure 2(a), the loop is parallelizable under the run-time condition ($m \geq c$ or $m = 0$). Pugh and Wonnacott present an integer programming solution to derive such linear constraints on the scalar variables used in array accesses directly from the constraints on the data dependence problem [17]. Predicated analysis that incorporates a predicate extraction operator can also derive this predicate and use it to guard execution of a conditionally parallelized loop at run time. Further, breaking conditions derived from predicate extraction can be propagated during analysis and used in conjunction with computing the MOFP solution described above to refine the precision of compile-time analysis.

VPS Solution. The VPS solution can go beyond previous work and be used in a more aggressive way, to enable optimizations that may only be performed conditionally. The VPS solution can provide run-time evaluable tests to guard execution of conditionally transformed code as would be useful in Figure 2(b). Here, *help* is upwards exposed for certain values of x. The VPS solution for two problems assists our analysis in parallelizing this loop. First, we consider whether a dependence exists on *help*, which occurs if there is an intersection of read and write regions and their predicates both hold. Thus, there is a dependence only if both $x > 2$ and $x > 5$ hold, which is equivalent to $x > 5$. Thus, if $NOT(x > 5)$, the loop can be parallelized as written. Second, we compare the upwards exposed read regions and the write regions to determine if privatization is safe and discover that array *help* is privatizable if $x > 5$, the only condition where an upwards exposed read intersects with a write. These two cases enable the compiler to parallelize all possible executions of the loop.

Predicate Extraction for Optimistic Assumptions. A distinguishing feature of our approach is the use of predicate extraction to introduce reasonable assumptions by the compiler to guard much more precise (i.e., optimistic) data-flow values. An example illustrating this point is the code excerpt in Figure 2(c). The first j loop accesses either $help[1 : d]$ or $help[1 : d-1]$, depending on whether d is even or odd, respectively. Thus, *help* may have an upwards exposed read of the last element if d is not even, and then this potentially upwards exposed read intersects with the subsequent write of the entire *help* array. It is only safe to privatize *help* and parallelize the loop if d is even. If the compiler separates the written region from the first loop to include two predicate-value pairs, one with predicate true containing $help[1 : d - 1]$ and one with $(d \bmod 2 = 0)$ containing $help[d]$, then it can determine at the read access that the only exposed read region is $help[d]$ with predicate $NOT(d \bmod 2 = 0)$. From this, the compiler can conditionally parallelize the loop by simply introducing the predicate $(d \bmod 2 = 0)$ to guard the parallel version. We are not aware of any other analysis-based technique that is capable of parallelizing this loop.

3.4   Description of Technique

The above presentation describes features of a prototype implementation of predicated array data-flow analysis that is part of the Stanford SUIF compiler. While space considerations preclude a formal description of predicated array data-flow analysis, we touch on what modifications to an existing array data-flow analysis are required to realize this solution. The technique is described in more detail elsewhere [15].

1. *Analysis augments array data-flow values with predicates.* Array data-flow analysis in the SUIF compiler already maintains, for a particular array, a set of regions of the array (instead of a single region that conservatively approximates all of the accesses within a loop). The SUIF compiler maintains a set of regions to avoid loss of precision when multiple very different accesses to an array occur within a loop. Our experience has shown that keeping more than one region per array, when necessary to avoid loss of precision, significantly improves precision of analysis while not introducing prohibitive cost. Since SUIF is already maintaining multiple regions per array, it is straightforward to extend each array region to have an associated predicate. Depending on the data-flow problem being solved, this predicate is interpreted as being conservative towards true (for union problems such as *Read*, *Write* and *Exposed*) or conservative towards false (for intersection problems such as *MustWrite*). That is, for union problems, analysis errs towards assuming a value holds, while for intersection problems, analysis errs towards assuming a value cannot hold.

2. *Analysis redefines key operators to correctly support predicated array data-flow values.* At a given program point, calculating upwards exposed read regions involves a subtraction of the *Exposed* regions of a body of code (such as a basic block) with the *MustWrite* regions of the preceeding body of code. The subtraction operator, as well as intersection and union operators (the meet functions for *MustWrite*, and the other data-flow problems, respectively) have been redefined for predicated array data-flow analysis. All other operators remain unchanged.

3. *The system modifies dependence and privatization tests.* These tests must derive as solutions, instead of true or false, run-time parallelization tests that can be used to guard execution of a parallelized version of the loop.

4   Experimental Results

To measure the impact of predicated array data-flow analysis at finding additional parallelism, we applied our prototype implementation to programs in the SPECFP95 benchmark suite. We have identified loops in three of the four programs for which speedup was previously limited (see discussion in 2, apsi, su2cor, and wave5, that would benefit from predicated array data-flow analysis.

We present a set of results for the three programs in Table 2 and Figure 3. The table shows a list of the major loops in these programs that were previously left sequential by the SUIF compiler but are now automatically parallelized using predicated array data-flow analysis. Figure 3 shows the speedup resulting from parallelizing these additional loops as compared to results using the base SUIF system. In performing these experiments, we encountered some limitations in the base SUIF system that interfered with our analysis, most notably the interface between the symbolic analysis and the array data-flow analysis. To focus on

Table 2. Additional loops parallelized by predicated analysis.

Loop	LOC	Coverage	Granularity	Speedup	Req.
apsi					
run-909	1281	8.40	0.037	3.56	⇐,R
run-953	1281	8.38	0.037	3.60	⇐,R
run-1015	1281	8.39	0.037	3.61	⇐,R
run-1044	1216	5.89	0.026	3.48	⇐,R
run-1083	1281	8.36	0.037	3.61	⇐,R
run-1155	1266	6.05	0.027	3.60	⇐,R
dcdtz-1331	235	4.94	0.022	3.00	⇒
dtdtz-1448	260	7.08	0.031	3.28	⇒
dudtz-1642	237	10.77	0.047	3.09	⇒
dvdtz-1784	240	7.16	0.032	3.22	⇒
dkzmh-6265	164	4.75	0.021	3.43	⇐,R
su2cor					
sweep-420	237	32.73	0.032	2.12	⇐
loops-1557	185	0.95	0.133	2.84	⇐
loops-1613	243	2.64	0.372	2.94	⇐
loops-1659	573	21.34	3.000	3.26	⇐
wave5					
fftf-5064	1154	3.84	0.053	3.46	⇐,R
fftb-5082	1147	4.05	0.055	3.21	⇐,R

issues specific to predicated data-flow analysis, we performed a few transformations by hand to parallelize some of the loops. The second group of five loops in apsi were parallelized completely automatically with no transformations to the code. The first six loops in apsi and the loops in wave5 required transformations to the original source before performing our analysis: forward substitution and cloning and loop peeling to enable forward substitution. The loops in su2cor were parallelized completely automatically.

In Table 2, the first column gives the subroutine and line number for the loop. The second column provides the number of lines of code in the loop body. All of these loops span multiple procedure boundaries, so this line count is the sum of the number of lines of code in each procedure body invoked inside the loop. Even if a procedure is invoked more than once in the loop, it is counted only once. The column labeled Coverage is a measure of the percentage of sequential execution time of the program spent in this loop body. The column labeled Granularity provides a per-invocation measure of the loop in seconds, indicating the granularity of the parallelism. (In our experience, granularities on the order of a millisecond are high enough to yield speedup.) The fifth column gives 4-processor speedups for just the loop, measured on an SGI Origin 2000 multiprocessor with 195MHz R10000 processors. The final column describes what components of the analysis are needed to parallelize each loop. The symbols ⇒ and ⇐ refer to whether predicate embedding or extraction are required, and R refers to loops that are only parallelizable under certain run-time values and require a run-time

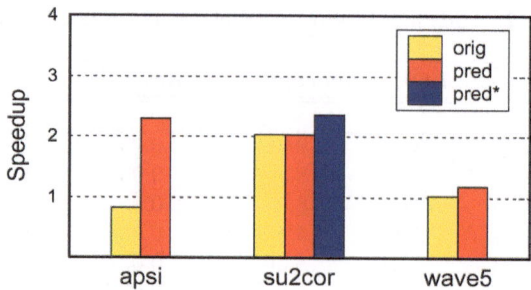

Fig. 3. Speedups due to predicated array data-flow analysis.

test. For those requiring a run-time test, we produced the parallel version using a user tool and modifications to the final output of the SUIF compiler; that is, the analysis is automated but the generation of conditionally parallel code is not.

Certainly, the most dramatic results are from apsi, which contains eleven loops benefitting from predicated array data-flow analysis, comprising 80% of the program's execution time. All of the loops cross multiple procedure boundaries, and the first six are the largest loops ever parallelized by the SUIF compiler. All of the loops obtain speedup of 3 or better on 4 processors (we believe the speedups are less than 4 because of locality issues, which we have not addressed in our experiments). We observe that every loop requires either predicate extraction or embedding, and seven of the loops require some run-time testing, either for safe parallelization, or in the case of *dkzmh-6265*, to eliminate the initialization region on a private array. Parallelizing these additional loops translates to substantial improvement in speedup for the program, 2.3 on 4 processors. Without parallelizing these loops, the 4-processor parallel program does not speed up at all.

The compiler finds four additional loops to parallelize in su2cor, comprising 58% of the program's execution time. These loops also require predicate extraction, but they can be parallelized statically. If all four loops are parallelized, such as with the second bar in Figure 3, the program speeds up only a tiny amount from the base speedup of 2 on 4 processors. However, if we sequentialize the first loop, *sweep-420*, we observe the result in the third bar labelled *pred**, a speedup of 2.4 on 4 processors. While the *sweep-420* loop is reasonably coarse-grained and makes up over 32% of the program's execution time, it executes only a few iterations and has a load imbalance problem that limits the individual loop speedup to 2.1. These problems could be mitigated if the SUIF run-time system exploited multiple levels of parallelism in a nest, but in the current system, it is more cost-effective to execute the inner loops nested inside of this one in parallel. Note that the real benefit of predicated analysis for su2cor is in parallelizing the fourth loop, which has a stunning granularity of 3 seconds per invocation.

There are also two loops in wave5, comprising roughly 8% of the program's execution time. Both require extracting a run-time test to guarantee safe parallelization. Parallelizing these loops improves the speedup from no speedup with the base compiler to a speedup of 1.2 with predicated array data-flow analysis.

5   Related Work

A number of experiments in the early 90s performed hand parallelization of benchmark programs to identify opportunities to improve the effectiveness of parallelizing compilers [3, 21]. These experiments compared hand-parallelized programs to compiler-parallelized versions, pointing to the large gap between inherent parallelism in the programs and what commercial compilers of the time were able to exploit. Blume and Eigenmann performed such a comparison for 13 programs from the Perfect benchmark suite [3]. They cited the need for compilers to incorporate array privatization and interprocedural analysis, among other things, to exploit a coarser granularity of parallelism. These early studies focused developers of commercial and research compilers to investigate incorporating these techniques, and now they are beginning to make their way into practice. As stated earlier, our experiment goes beyond these previous studies because it measures parallelism potential empirically using run-time testing. Further, now that these previously missing techniques are now performed automatically by the compiler, a new experiment can identify the next set of missing analysis techniques.

Analysis techniques exploiting predicates have been developed for specific data-flow problems including constant propagation [26], type analysis [23], symbolic analysis for parallelization [10, 4], and the array data-flow analysis described above [9, 24]. Tu and Padua present a limited sparse approach on a gated SSA graph that is demand based, only examining predicates if they might assist in loop bounds or subscript values for parallelization, a technique that appears to be no more powerful than that of Gu, Li and Lee [24]. Related to these array analysis techniques are approaches to enhance scalar symbolic analysis for parallelization. Haghighat describes an algebra on control flow predicates [10] while Blume presents a method for combining control flow predicates with ranges of scalar variables [4]. As compared to this previous work, our approach is distinguished in several ways: (1) it is capable of deriving low-cost run-time tests, consisting of arbitrary program expressions, to guard conditionally optimized code; (2) it incorporates predicates other than just control flow tests, particularly those derived from the data-flow values using predicate extraction; and, (3) it unifies a number of previous approaches in array data-flow analysis, as previously discussed.

Some previous work in run-time parallelization uses specialized techniques not based on data-flow analysis. An inspector/executor technique inspects array accesses at run time immediately prior to execution of the loop [18, 19]. The inspector decides whether to execute a parallel or sequential version of the loop. Predicated data-flow analysis instead derives run-time tests based on values of scalar variables that can be tested prior to loop execution. Thus, our approach, when applicable, leads to much more efficient tests than inspecting all of the array accesses within the loop body.

There are some similarities between our approach and much earlier work on data-flow analysis frameworks. Holley and Rosen describe a construction of qualified data-flow problems, akin to the MOFP solution, but with only a fixed, finite, disjoint set of predicates [13]. Cousot and Cousot describe a theoretical construction of a reduced cardinal power of two data-flow frameworks, in which a data-flow analysis is performed on the lattice of functions between the two original data-flow lattices, and this technique has been refined by Nielson [6, 16]. Neither of the latter two prior works were designed with predicates as one of the data-flow analysis frameworks, and none of the three techniques derives run-time tests.

Recently, additional approaches that, in some way, exploit control-flow information in data-flow analysis have been proposed [1, 5, 20]. Ammons and Larus's approach improves the precision of data-flow analysis along frequently taken control flow paths, called hot paths, by using profile information. Bodík et al. describe a demand-driven interprocedural correlation analysis that eliminates some branches by path specialization. Both approaches utilize code duplication to sharpen data-flow values but are only applicable if the information is available at compile time. Deferred data-flow analysis proposed by Sharma et al. attempts to partially perform data-flow analysis at run time, using control-flow information derived during execution.

6   Conclusion and Future Work

This paper has presented the results of an important experiment to determine whether there are remaining opportunities for improving automatic parallelization systems for a set of 16 programs from two benchmark suites. With a model where a loop's iterations can only execute in parallel if it accesses independent memory locations, possibly after privatization of array data structures, we have identified all the remaining loops not parallelized by the SUIF compiler for which parallelization is safe. Our results indicate that there is still some room for improvement in automatic parallelization in two areas: incorporating control flow tests into analysis and extracting low-cost run-time tests wherever applicable instead of using an inspector/executor. These two requirements can be met with a single new analysis technique, predicated array data-flow analysis, whereby predicates are associated with data-flow values. We have shown preliminary results that predicated array data-flow analysis can improve the speedup of three of the four programs in the SPECFP95 benchmark suite that previously did not speed up well.

In future work, we envision extending predicated data-flow analysis to derive more aggressive run-time tests to enable parallelization of additional loops. Of particular interest is parallelizing loops with run-time tests involving certain classes of loop-varying variables. Such a run-time test would execute a small portion of the loop body prior to the loop's execution. For example, this would allow the compiler to verify that a nonlinear subscript expression was monotonically increasing, even if this could not be proven at compile time. Loops requiring a control inspector could also be parallelized in this way. Neither of these techniques requires the use of shadow arrays, so this type of inspector can be significantly more efficient than the more general inspectors used by the LRPD test. Another interesting issue is how to integrate the run-time tests from predicated data-flow analysis with inspector/executor techniques. With all of thethese extensions to the predicated array data-flow analysis, the overhead of the run-time tests, because they involve executing a loop body, can become higher. For this reason, further work in this area would benefit from optimizations to hoist these inspectors out of loops and across procedure boundaries to less frequently executed portions of the code.

References

[1] AMMONS, G., AND LARUS, J. R. Improving data-flow analysis with path profiles. In *Proceedings of the ACM SIGPLAN '98 Conference on Programming Language Design and Implementation* (Montreal, Canada, June 1998), pp. 72–84.

[2] BLUME, W., DOALLO, R., EIGENMANN, R., GROUT, J., HOEFLINGER, J., LAWRENCE, T., LEE, J., PADUA, D., PAEK, Y., POTTENGER, B., RAUCHWERGER, L., AND TU, P. Parallel programming with Polaris. *IEEE Computer 29*, 12 (December 1996), 78–82.

[3] BLUME, W., AND EIGENMANN, R. Performance analysis of parallelizing compilers on the Perfect Benchmark programs. *IEEE Transaction on Parallel and Distributed Systems 3*, 6 (November 1992), 643–656.

[4] BLUME, W. J. *Symbolic Analysis Techniques for Effective Automatic Parallelization.* PhD thesis, Dept. of Computer Science, University of Illinois at Urbana-Champaign, June 1995.

[5] BODÍK, R., GUPTA, R., AND SOFFA, M. L. Interprocedural conditional branch elimination. In *Proceedings of the ACM SIGPLAN '97 Conference on Programming Language Design and Implementation* (Las Vegas, Nevada, June 1997), pp. 146–158.

[6] COUSOT, P., AND COUSOT, R. Systematic design of program anaysis frameworks. In *Conference Record of the Sixth Annual ACM Symposium on Principles of Programming Languages* (San Antonio, Texas, January 1979), pp. 269–282.

[7] GOFF, G. Practical techniques to augment dependence analysis in the presence of symbolic terms. Tech. Rep. TR92–194, Dept. of Computer Science, Rice University, October 1992.

[8] GU, J., LI, Z., AND LEE, G. Symbolic array dataflow analysis for array privatization and program parallelization. In *Proceedings of Supercomputing '95* (San Diego, California, December 1995).

[9] GU, J., LI, Z., AND LEE, G. Experience with efficient array data-flow analysis for array privatization. In *Proceedings of the Sixth ACM SIGPLAN Symposium on Principles & Practice of Parallel Programming* (Las Vegas, Nevada, June 1997), pp. 157–167.

[10] HAGHIGHAT, M. R. *Symbolic Analysis for Parallelizing Compilers.* PhD thesis, Dept. of Computer Science, University of Illinois at Urbana-Champaign, August 1994.

[11] HALL, M. W., ANDERSON, J. M., AMARASINGHE, S. P., MURPHY, B. R., LIAO, S.-W., BUGNION, E., AND LAM, M. S. Maximizing multiprocessor performance with the SUIF compiler. *IEEE Computer 29*, 12 (December 1996), 84–89.

[12] HALL, M. W., MURPHY, B. R., AMARASINGHE, S. P., LIAO, S.-W., AND LAM, M. S. Interprocedural analysis for parallelization. In *Proceedings of the 8th International Workshop on Languages and Compilers for Parallel Computing* (Columbus, Ohio, August 1995), pp. 61–80.

[13] HOLLEY, L. H., AND ROSEN, B. K. Qualified data flow problems. In *Conference Record of the Seventh Annual ACM Symposium on Principles of Programming Languages* (Las Vegas, Nevada, January 1980), pp. 68–82.

[14] IRIGOIN, F. Interprocedural analyses for programming environments. In *Proceedings of the NSF-CNRS Workshop on Environment and Tools for Parallel Scientific Programming* (September 1992).

[15] MOON, S., HALL, M. W., AND MURPHY, B. R. Predicated array data-flow analysis for run-time parallelization. In *Proceedings of the 1998 ACM International Conference on Supercomputing* (Melbourne, Australia, July 1998).

[16] NIELSON, F. Expected forms of data flow analysis. In *Programs as Data Objects*, H. Ganzinger and N. D. Jones, Eds., vol. 217 of *Lecture Notes on Computer Science*. Springer-Verlag, October 1986, pp. 172–191.

[17] PUGH, W., AND WONNACOTT, D. Eliminating false data dependences using the Omega test. In *Proceedings of the ACM SIGPLAN '92 Conference on Programming Language Design and Implementation* (San Francisco, California, June 1992), pp. 140–151.

[18] RAUCHWERGER, L., AND PADUA, D. The LRPD test: Speculative run-time parallelization of loops with privatization and reduction parallelization. In *Proceedings of the ACM SIGPLAN '95 Conference on Programming Language Design and Implementation* (La Jolla, California, June 1995), pp. 218–232.

[19] SALTZ, J. H., MIRCHANDANEY, R., AND CROWLEY, K. Run-time parallelization and scheduling of loops. *IEEE Transaction on Computers 40*, 5 (May 1991), 603–612.

[20] SHARMA, S. D., ACHARYA, A., AND SALTZ, J. Defeered data-flow analysis: Algorithms, proofs and applications. Tech. Rep. UMD–CS–TR–3845, Dept. of Computer Science, University of Maryland, November 1997.

[21] SINGH, J. P., AND HENNESSY, J. L. An empirical investigation of the effectiveness and limitations of automatic parallelization. In *Proceedings of the International Symposium on Shared Memory Multiprocessing* (April 1991).

[22] SO, B., MOON, S., AND HALL, M. W. Measuring the effectiveness of automatic parallelization in SUIF. In *Proceedings of the 1998 ACM International Conference on Supercomputing* (Melbourne, Australia, July 1998).

[23] STROM, R. E., AND YELLIN, D. M. Extending typestate checking using conditional liveness analysis. *IEEE Transaction on Software Engineering 19*, 5 (May 1993), 478–485.

[24] TU, P. *Automatic Array Privatization and Demand-driven Symbolic Analysis*. PhD thesis, Dept. of Computer Science, University of Illinois at Urbana-Champaign, May 1995.

[25] TU, P., AND PADUA, D. Automatic array privatization. In *Proceedings of the 6th International Workshop on Languages and Compilers for Parallel Computing* (Portland, Oregon, August 1993), pp. 500–521.

[26] WEGMAN, M. N., AND ZADECK, F. K. Constant propagation with conditional branches. *ACM Transaction on Programming Languages and Systems 13*, 2 (April 1991), 180–210.

Compiler and Run-Time Support for Adaptive Load Balancing in Software Distributed Shared Memory Systems *

Sotiris Ioannidis and Sandhya Dwarkadas

Department of Computer Science
University of Rochester
Rochester, NY 14627–0226
{si,sandhya}@cs.rochester.edu

Abstract. Networks of workstations offer inexpensive and highly available high performance computing environments. A critical issue for achieving good performance in any parallel system is load balancing, even more so in workstation environments where the machines might be shared among many users. In this paper, we present and evaluate a system that combines compiler and run-time support to achieve load balancing dynamically on software distributed shared memory programs. We use information provided by the compiler to help the run-time system distribute the work of the parallel loops, not only according to the relative power of the processors, but also in such a way as to minimize communication and page sharing.

1 Introduction

Clusters of workstations, whether uniprocessors or symmetric multiprocessors (SMPs), offer cost-effective and highly available parallel computing environments. Software distributed shared memory (SDSM) provides a shared memory abstraction on such distributed memory machines, with the advantage of ease-of-use. Previous work [5] has shown that an SDSM run-time can prove to be an effective target for a parallelizing compiler. The advantages of using an SDSM system include reduced complexity at compile-time, and the ability to combine compile-time and run-time information to achieve better performance ([6,18]).

One issue in achieving good performance in any parallel system is load balancing. This issue is even more critical in a workstation environment where the machines might be shared among many users. In order to maximize performance based on available resources, the parallel system must not only optimally distribute the work according to the inherent computation and communication demands of the application, but also according to available computation and communication resources.

* This work was supported in part by NSF grants CDA–9401142, CCR–9702466, and CCR–9705594; and an external research grant from Digital Equipment Corporation.

D. O'Hallaron (Ed.): LCR'98, LNCS 1511, pp. 107–122, 1998.

In this paper, we present and evaluate a system that combines compiler and run-time support to achieve load balancing dynamically on SDSM programs. The compiler provides access pattern information to the run-time at the points in the code that will be executed in parallel. The run-time uses these points to gather statistics on available computational and communication resources. Based on the access patterns across phases, as well as on available computing power, the run-time can then make intelligent decisions not only to distribute the computational load evenly, but also to maximize locality (based on current processor caching) and minimize communication overhead in the future. The result is a system that uniquely combines compile-time and run-time information to adapt both to changes in access patterns as well as to changes in computational power in order to reduce execution time.

Our target run-time system is TreadMarks [2], along with the extensions for prefetching and consistency/communication avoidance described in [6]. We implemented the necessary compiler extensions in the SUIF [1] compiler framework. Our experimental environment consists of eight DEC AlphaServer 2100 4/233 computers, each with four 21064A processors operating at 233 MHz. Preliminary results show that our system is able to adapt to changes in load, with performance within 20% of ideal.

The rest of this paper is organized as follows. Section 2 describes the run-time system, the necessary compiler support, and the algorithm used to make dynamic load balancing decisions. Section 3 presents some preliminary results. Section 4 describes related work. Finally, we present our conclusions and discuss on-going work in Section 5.

2 Design and Implementation

We first provide some background on TreadMarks [2], the run-time system we used in our implementation. We then describe the compiler support followed by the run-time support necessary for load balancing.

2.1 The Base Software DSM Library

TreadMarks [2] is an SDSM system built at Rice University. It is an efficient user-level SDSM system that runs on commonly available Unix platforms. TreadMarks provides parallel programming primitives similar to those used in hardware shared memory machines, namely, process creation, shared memory allocation, and lock and barrier synchronization. The system supports a *release consistent* (RC) memory model [10]. The programmer is required to use explicit synchronization to ensure that changes to shared data become visible. TreadMarks uses a *lazy invalidate* [14] version of RC and a *multiple-writer* protocol [3] to reduce the overhead involved in implementing the shared memory abstraction.

The underlying virtual memory hardware is used to detect accesses to shared memory. Consequently, the consistency unit is a virtual memory page. The *multiple-writer* protocol reduces the effects of false sharing with such a large consistency unit. With this protocol, two or more processors can simultaneously modify their own copy of a shared page. Their modifications are merged at the next synchronization operation in accordance with the definition of RC, thereby reducing the effects of false sharing. The merge is accomplished through the use of *diffs*. A diff is a run-length encoding of the modifications made to a page, generated by comparing the page to a copy saved prior to the modifications (called a *twin*).

With the *lazy invalidate* protocol, a process invalidates, at the time of an *acquire* synchronization operation [10], those pages for which it has received notice of modifications by other processors. On a subsequent page fault, the process fetches the *diffs* necessary to update its copy.

2.2   Compile-Time Support for Load Balancing

For the source-to-source translation from a sequential program to a parallel program using TreadMarks, we use the Stanford University Intermediate Format (SUIF) [11] compiler. The SUIF system is organized as a set of compiler passes built on top of a kernel that defines the intermediate format. The passes are implemented as separate programs that typically perform a single analysis or transformation and then write the results out to a file. The files always use the same format.

The input to the compiler is a sequential version of the code. The output that we start with is a version of the code parallelized for shared address space machines. The compiler generates a single-program, multiple-data (SPMD) program that we modified to make calls to the TreadMarks run-time library. Alternatively, the user can provide the SPMD program (instead of having the SUIF compiler generate it) by identifying the parallel loops in the program that are executed by all processors.

Our SUIF pass extracts the shared data access patterns in each of the SPMD regions, and feeds this information to the run-time system. The pass is also responsible for adding hooks in the parallelized code to allow the run-time library to change the load distribution in the parallel loops if necessary.

Access Pattern Extraction

In order to generate access pattern summaries, our SUIF pass walks through the program looking for accesses to shared memory (identified using the **sh_** prefix). A regular section [12] is then created for each such shared access. Regular section descriptors (RSDs) concisely represent the array accesses in a loop nest. The RSDs represent the accessed data as linear expressions of the upper and lower loop bounds along each dimension, and include stride information. This information is combined with the corresponding loop boundaries of that index, and the size of each dimension of the array, to determine the access pattern. Depending on the kind of data sharing among parallel tasks, we follow different strategies of load redistribution in case of imbalance. We will discuss these strategies further in Section 2.3.

Prefetching

The access pattern information can also be used to *prefetch* data [6]. The Tread-Marks library offers prefetching calls. These calls, given a range of addresses, prefetch the data contained in the pages in that range, and provide appropriate (read/write) permissions on the page. This prefetching prevents faulting and consistency actions on uncached data that is guaranteed to be accessed in the future, as well as allows communication optimization by taking advantage of bulk transfer.

Load Balancing Interface and Strategy

The run-time system needs a way of changing the amount of work assigned to each parallel task. This essentially means changing the number of loop iterations performed by each task. To accomplish this, we augment the code with calls to the run-time library before the parallel loops. This call is responsible for changing the loop bounds and consequently the amount of work done by each task.

The compiler can direct the run-time to choose between two partitioning strategies for redistributing the parallel loops. The goal is to minimize execution time by considering both the communication and the computation components.

1. Shifting of loop boundaries: This approach changes the upper and lower bounds of each parallel task, so that tasks on lightly loaded processors will end up with more work than tasks on heavily loaded processors. With this scheme, we avoid the creation of new boundaries, and therefore possible sharing, on the data accessed by our tasks. Applications with nearest neighbor sharing will benefit from this scheme. This policy, however, has the drawback of causing more communication at the time of load redistribution, since data has to be moved among all neighboring tasks rather than only from the slow processor.

2. Multiple loop bounds: This scheme is aimed at minimizing unnecessary data movement. When using this policy, each process can execute non-continuous loop indices by using multiple loop bounds. This policy possibly fragments the shared data among the processors, but reduces communication at load redistribution time. Hence, care must be taken to ensure that this fragmentation does not result in either false sharing or excess true sharing due to load redistribution.

2.3   Run-Time Load Balancing Support

The run-time library is responsible for keeping track of the progress of each process. It collects statistics about the execution time of each parallel task and adjusts the load accordingly. The execution time for each parallel task is maintained on a per-processor basis (TaskTime). The relative processing power of the processor (RelativePower) is calculated on the basis of current load distribution (RelativePower) as well as the per-processor TaskTime as described in Figure 1.

```
float    RelativePower[NumOfProcessors];
float    TaskTime[NumOfProcessors];
float    SumOfPowers;


for  all Processors i
     RelativePower[i] /= TaskTime[i];
     SumOfPowers += RelativePower[i];

for  all Processors i
     RelativePower[i] /= SumOfPowers;
```

Fig. 1. Algorithm to Determine Relative Processing Power

Each processor executes the above code prior to each parallel loop (SPMD region). It is crucial not to try to adjust too quickly to changes in execution time because sudden changes in the distribution of the data might cause the system to oscillate. To make this clear, imagine a processor that for some reason is very slow the first time we gather statistics. If we adjust the load, we will end up sending most of its work to another processor. This will cause it to be very fast the second time around, resulting in a redistribution once again. For this reason, we have added some hysteresis in our system. We redistribute the load only if the relative power remains consistently at odds with current allocation through a certain number of task creation points. Similarly, load is balanced only if the variance in relative power exceeds a threshold. If the time of the slowest process is within N% of the time of the fastest process we don't change the distribution of work. Otherwise, minor oscillations may result as communication is generated due to the adjusted load. In our experiments, we collect statistics for 10 task creation points before trying to adjust, and then if the time of the slowest process is not within 10% of the time of the fastest process, we redistribute the work. These cut-offs were heuristically determined on the basis of our experimental platform, and are a function of the amount of computation and any extra communication.

Load Balancing vs. Locality Management

Previous work [20] has shown that locality management is at least as important as load balancing. This is even more the case in software DSM where the processors are not tightly coupled, making communication expensive. Consequently, we need to avoid unnecessary movement of data and at the same time minimize page sharing. In order to deal with this problem, the run-time library uses the information supplied by the compiler about what loop distribution strategy to use. In addition, it keeps track of accesses to the shared array as declared in previous SPMD regions (in other words, the data currently cached by each processor). Changes in partitioning that might result in excess communication are avoided in favor of a small amount of load imbalance (by comparing the time to process the data locally against the time to communicate the data in order to effect a balanced computational load). We call this method *Locality-Conscious Load Balancing*.

2.4 Example

Consider the parallel loop in Figure 2. Our compiler pass transforms this loop into that in Figure 3. The new code makes a **redistribute** call to the run-time library, providing it with all the necessary information to compute the access patterns (the arrays, the types of accesses, the upper and lower bounds of the loops, as well as their stride, and the format of the expressions for the indices).

The **redistribute** computes the relative powers of the processors (using the algorithm shown in Figure 1), and then uses the access pattern information to decide how to distribute the workload.

```
int    sh_dat1[N], sh_dat2[N];

for (i = lowerbound; i < upperbound; i += stride)
    sh_dat1[a*i + b] += sh_dat2[c*i + d];
```

Fig. 2. Initial parallel loop.

3 Experimental Evaluation

3.1 Environment

Our experimental environment consists of eight DEC AlphaServer 2100 4/233 computers. Each AlphaServer is equipped with four 21064A processors operating at 233 MHz and with 256 MB of shared memory, as well as a Memory Channel network interface. Each AlphaServer runs Digital UNIX 4.0D with TruCLuster v. 1.5 extensions. The programs, the run-time library, and TreadMarks were compiled with **gcc** version 2.7.2.1 using the **-O2** optimization flag.

3.2 Load Balancing Results

We evaluate our system on two applications: a Matrix Multiply of three 256x256 shared matrices of longs (which is repeated 100 times), and Jacobi, with a matrix size of 2050x2050 floats. Jacobi is an iterative method for solving partial differential equations, with nearest-neighbor averaging as the main computation.

Our current implementation only uses the first loop redistribution policy, shifting of loop boundaries, and does not use prefetching. To test the performance of our load balancing library, we introduced an artificial load on one of the

```
int     sh_dat1[N], sh_dat2[N];

redistribute(
    list of shared arrays,  /* sh_dat1, sh_dat2 */
    list of types of accesses,  /* read/write */
    list of lower bounds,       /* lower_bound */
    list of upper bounds,       /* upper_bound */
    list of strides,            /* strides    */
    list of coefficients and
    constants for indices       /* a, c, b, d */
);

while (There are still ranges) {
    lowerbound = new lower bound for that range;
    upperbound = new upper bound for that range;
    range = range->next;

    for (i = lowerbound; i < upperbound; i += stride)
        sh_dat1[a*i + b] += sn_dat2[c*i + d];
}
```

Fig. 3. Parallel loop with added code that serves as an interface with the run-time library. The run-time system can then change the amount of work assigned to each parallel task.

processors of each SMP. This consists of a tight loop that writes on an array of 10240 longs. This load takes up 50% of the CPU time.

Our preliminary results appear in Figures 4 and 5. We present execution times on 1, 2, 4, 8, and 16 processors, using up to four SMPs. We added one artificial load for every four processors except in the case of two processors where we only added one load. The load balancing scheme we use is the shifting of loop boundaries (we do not use multiple loop bounds). The first column shows the execution times for the cases where there was no load in the system. The second column shows the execution times with the artificial load, and finally the last column is the case where the system is loaded but we are using our load balancing library.

The introduction of load slows down both Matrix Multiply and Jacobi by as much as 100% in the case of two processors (with the overhead at 4, 8, and 16 not being far off).

Our load balancing strategy provides a significant improvement in performance compared to the execution time with load. In order to determine how good the results of our load balancing algorithm are, we compare the execution times obtained using 8 processors with load and our load balance scheme, with that using 7 processors without any load. This 7-processor run serves as a bound on how well we can perform with load balancing, since that is the best we can hope to achieve (two of our eight processors are loaded, and operate at only 50%

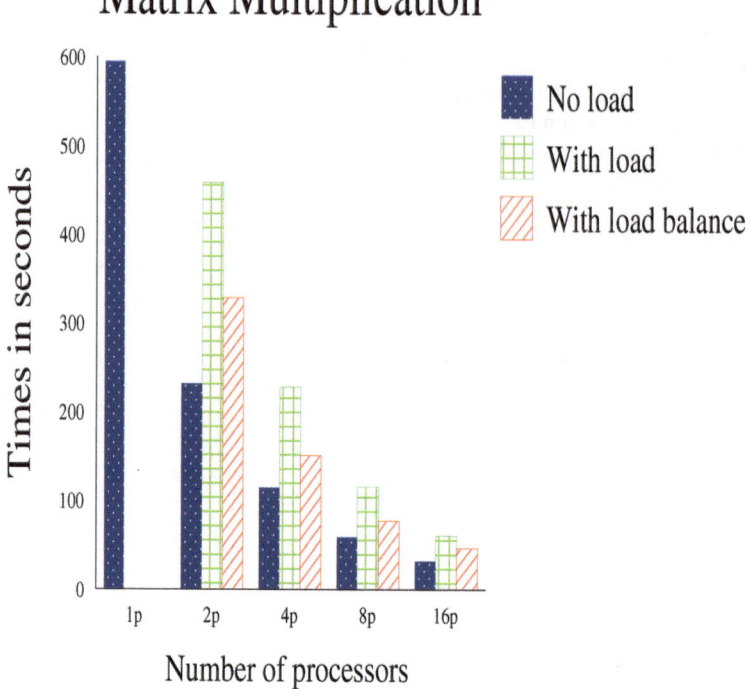

Fig. 4. Execution Times for Matrix Multiply

of their power, giving us the equivalent of seven processors). The results are presented in Figure 6. For Matrix Multiply, our load balancing algorithm is only 9% slower than the seven processor load-free case. Jacobi is 20% slower, partly due to the fact that while computation can be redistributed, communication per processor remains the same.

In Figure 7, we present a breakdown of the normalized execution time relative to that on 8 processors with no load, indicating the relative time spent in user code, in the protocol, and in communication and wait time (at synchronization points). When we use our load balancing algorithm, we reduce the time spent waiting at synchronization points relative to the execution time with load and no load balance because we have better distribution of work, and therefore improve overall performance.

Finally, we conducted experiments to determine the overhead imposed by our run-time system. We ran Matrix Multiply and Jacobi in a load-free environment with and without use of our run-time library. The results are presented in Figure 8. In the worst case, we impose less than 6% overhead.

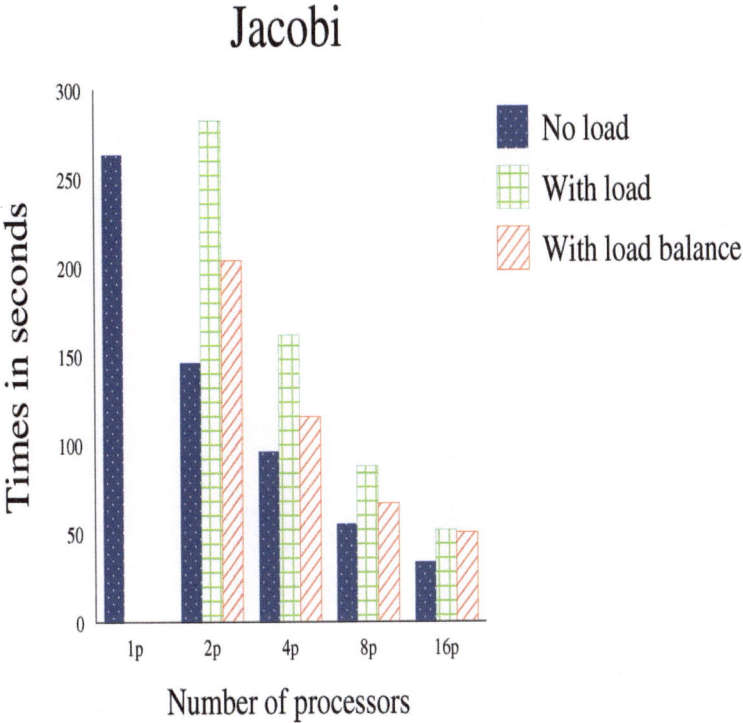

Fig. 5. Execution Times for Jacobi

3.3 Locality-Conscious Load Balancing Results

For the evaluation of our locality-conscious load balancing policy, we used Shallow, with an input size resulting in matrices of 514x514 doubles. Shallow is the shallow water benchmark from the National Center for Atmospheric Research. The code is used in weather prediction and solves difference equations on a two-dimensional grid. Shallow operates on the interior elements of the arrays and then updates the boundaries. Compiler parallelized code or a naive implementation would have each process update a part of the boundaries along each dimension in parallel. This can result in multiple processes writing the same pages, or false sharing. A smarter approach is to have the processes that normally access the boundary pages do the updates, thus eliminating false sharing. Our integrated compiler/run-time system is able to make the decision at run-time, using the access pattern information provided by the compiler. It identifies which process caches the data and can repartition the work so that it maximizes locality.

We present our results in Figure 9. In these experiments, we don't introduce any load imbalance into our system, since we want to evaluate our locality-conscious load balancing policy. We have optimized the manual parallelization to eliminate false sharing, as suggested earlier. A naive compiler parallelization that

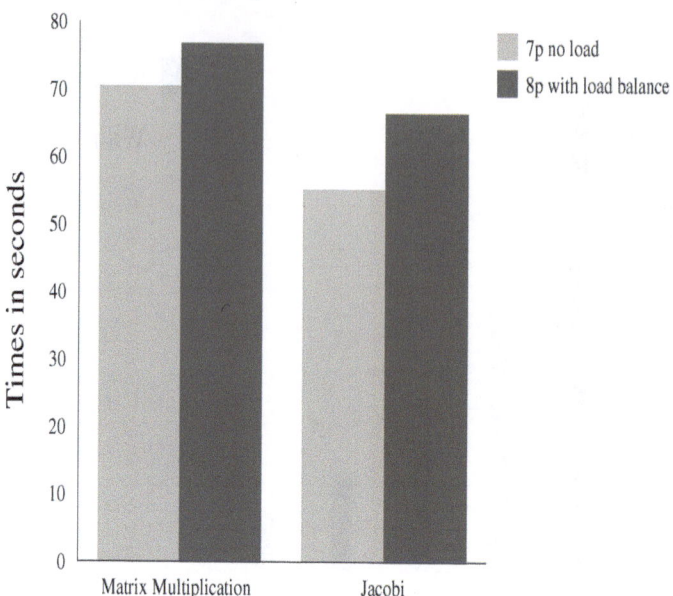

Fig. 6. Comparison of the running times of the applications using our load balancing algorithm on 8 loaded processors, compared to their performance on 7 load-free processors.

does not take data locality into account performs very poorly as the number of processors increases because of multiple writers on the boundary pages. However, when we combine the complier parallelization with our locality-conscious load balancing run-time system, the performance is equivalent to the hand-optimized code.

4   Related Work

There have been several approaches to the problems of locality management and load balancing, especially in the context of loop scheduling. Perhaps the most common approach is the **Task Queue Model**. In this scheme, there is a central queue of loop iterations. Once a processor has finished its assigned portion, more work is obtained from this queue. There are several variations, including *self-scheduling* [23], *fixed-size chunking* [15], *guided self-scheduling* [22], and *adaptive guided self-scheduling* [7].

Markatos and Le Blanc in [20], argue that locality management is more important than load balancing in thread assignment. They introduce a policy they call *Memory-Conscious Scheduling* that assigns threads to processors whose local memory holds most of the data the thread will access. Their results show

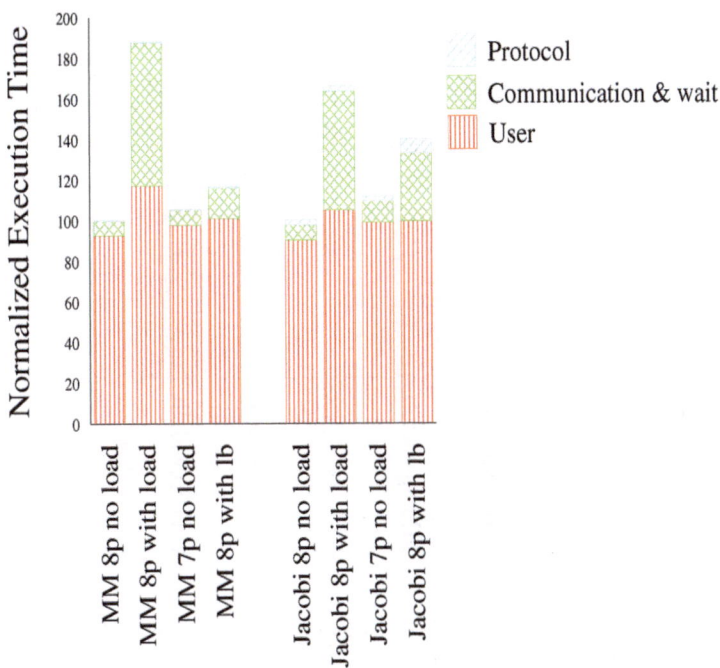

Fig. 7. Break-up of normalized time for Matrix Multiply and Jacobi into time spent in user code, communication and wait at synchronization points, and protocol time.

that the looser the interconnection network, the more important the locality management.

Based on the observation that the locality of the data that a loop accesses is very important, *affinity scheduling* was introduced in [19]. The loop iterations are divided over all the processors equally in local queues. When a processor is idle, it removes $1/k$ of the iterations in its local work queue and executes them. k is a parameter of their algorithm, which they define as P in most of their experiments, where P is the number of processors. If a processor's work queue is empty, it finds the most loaded processor and removes $1/P$ of the iterations in that processor's work queue and executes them.

Building on [19], Yan et al. in [24] suggest *adaptive affinity scheduling*. Their algorithm is similar to affinity scheduling but their run-time system can modify k during the execution of the program. When a processor is loaded, k is increased so that other processors with a lighter load can get loop iterations from the loaded processor's local work queue. They present four possible policies for changing k: an exponential adaptive mechanism, a linear adaptive mechanism, a conservative adaptive mechanism, and a greedy adaptive mechanism.

Times for MM - Jacobi without load

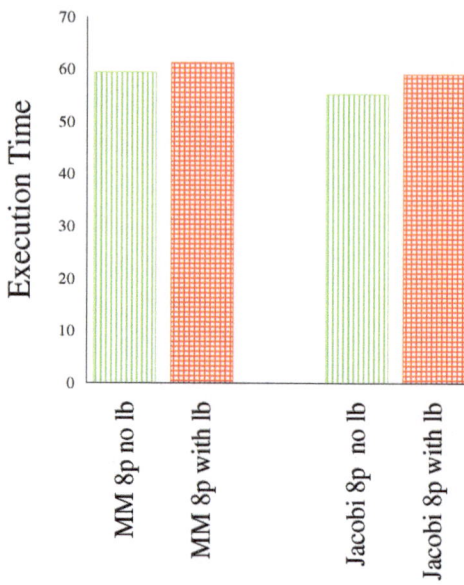

Fig. 8. Running times for Matrix Multiply and Jacobi in a load-free environment, with and without use of our run-time library.

In [4], Cierniak et al. study loop scheduling in heterogeneous environments with respect to programs, processors, and the interconnection networks. Their results indicate that taking into account the relative computation power as well as any heterogeneity in the loop format while doing the loop distribution improves the overall performance of the application. Similarly, Moon and Saltz [21] also looked at applications with irregular access patterns. To compensate for load imbalance, they examine periodic re-mapping, or re-mapping at predetermined points of the execution, and dynamic re-mapping, in which they determine if repartitioning is required at every time step.

In the context of dynamically changing environments, Edjlali et al. in [8] and Kaddoura in [13] present a run-time approach for handling such environments. Before each parallel section of the program they check if there is a need to re-map the loop. This is similar to our approach. However, their approach deals with message passing programs.

A discussion on global vs. local and distributed vs. centralized strategies for load balancing is presented in [25]. The strategies are labeled local or global based on the information they use to make load balancing decisions. Distributed and centralized refers to whether the load balancer is one master processor, or distributed among the processors. The authors argue that depending on the application and system parameters, different schemes can be the most suitable for best performance.

Shallow

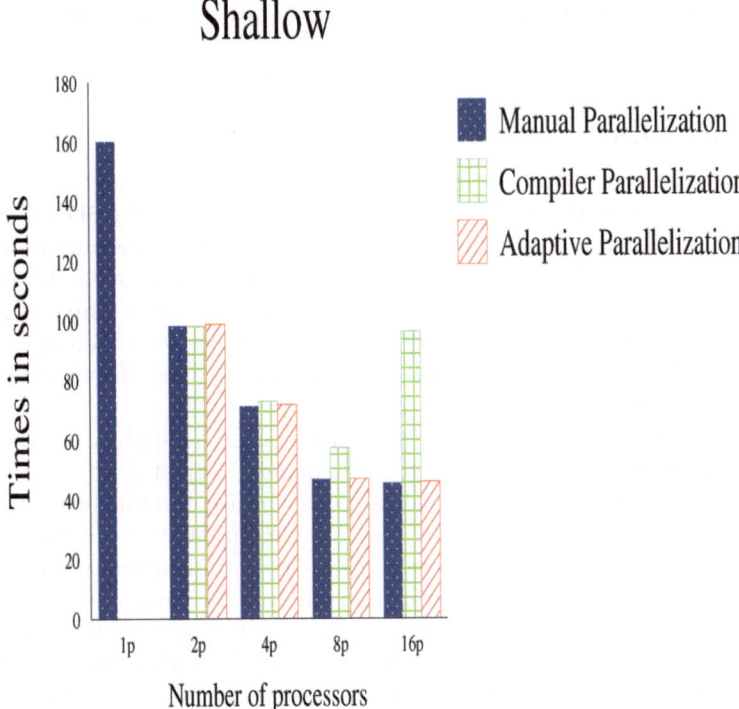

Fig. 9. Running times of the three different implementations of Shallow in seconds. The manual parallelization takes data location into account in order to avoid page sharing. The compiler parallelization does not consider data location. The adaptive parallelization uses the compiler parallelization with our run-time library, which adjusts the workload by dynamically taking the data location into account.

The system that seems most related to ours is Adapt, presented in [17]. Adapt is implemented in concert with the Distributed Filaments software kernel [9], a DSM system. It monitors communication and page faults, and dynamically modifies loop boundaries so that the processes access data that are local if possible. Adapt is able to extract access patterns by inspecting page faults. It can recognize two patterns: *nearest-neighbor* and *broadcast*. In our system, we use the compiler to extract the access patterns and provide them to the run-time system, making our approach capable of handling dynamic phase changes.

Finally, systems like Condor [16] support transparent migration of processes from one workstation to another. However, such systems don't support parallel programs efficiently.

Our system deals with software distributed shared memory programs, in contrast to closely coupled shared memory or message passing. Our load balancing method targets both irregularities of the loops as well as possible heterogeneous processors and load caused by competing programs. Furthermore, our system addresses locality management by trying to minimize communication and page sharing.

5   Conclusions

In this paper, we address the problem of load balancing in SDSM systems by coupling compile-time and run-time information. SDSM has unique characteristics that are attractive: it offers the ease of programming of a shared memory model in a widely available workstation-based message passing environment. However, multiple users and loosely connected processors challenge the performance of SDSM programs on such systems due to load imbalances and high communication latencies.

Our integrated system uses access information available at compile-time, along with run-time information, to dynamically adjust load at run-time based on the available relative processing power and communication speeds. The same access pattern information is also used to prefetch data. Preliminary results are encouraging. Performance tests on two applications and a fixed load indicate that the performance with load balance is within 9 and 20% of the ideal performance. Additionally, our system is able to partition the work so that processes attempt to limit their accesses to local data, thereby minimizing false sharing. Our system identifies regions where false sharing exists and changes the loop boundaries to avoid it. The performance on our third application, when the number of processors was high, was equivalent to the best possible workload partitioning.

Further work to collect results on a larger number of applications is necessary. In addition, for a more thorough evaluation, we need to determine the sensitivity of our strategy to dynamic changes in load, as well as to changes in the hysteresis factor used when determining when to redistribute work. The tradeoff between locality management and load must also be further investigated.

References

1. S. P. Amarasinghe, J. M. Anderson, M. S. Lam, and C. W. Tseng. The SUIF compiler for scalable parallel machines. In *Proceedings of the 7th SIAM Conference on Parallel Processing for Scientific Computing*, February 1995.
2. C. Amza, A.L. Cox, S. Dwarkadas, P. Keleher, H. Lu, R. Rajamony, and W. Zwaenepoel. TreadMarks: Shared memory computing on networks of workstations. *IEEE Computer*, 29(2):18–28, February 1996.
3. J.B. Carter, J.K. Bennett, and W. Zwaenepoel. Techniques for reducing consistency-related information in distributed shared memory systems. *ACM Transactions on Computer Systems*, 13(3):205–243, August 1995.
4. M. Cierniak, W. Li, and M. J. Zaki. Loop scheduling for heterogeneity. In *Fourth International Symposium on High Performance Distributed Computing*, August 1995.

5. A.L. Cox, S. Dwarkadas, H. Lu, and W. Zwaenepoel. Evaluating the performance of software distributed shared memory as a target for parallelizing compilers. In *Proceedings of the 11th International Parallel Processing Symposium*, pages 474–482, April 1997.

6. S. Dwarkadas, A.L. Cox, and W. Zwaenepoel. An integrated compile-time/run-time software distributed shared memory system. In *Proceedings of the 7th Symposium on Architectural Support for Programming Languages and Operating Systems*, October 1996.

7. D. L. Eage and J. Zahorjan. Adaptive guided self-scheduling. Technical Report 92-01-01, Department of Computer Science, University of Washington, January 1992.

8. G. Edjlali, G. Agrawal, A. Sussman, and J. Saltz. Data parallel programming in an adaptive environment. In *Internation Parallel Processing Symposium*, April 1995.

9. V. W. Freeh, D. K. Lowenthal, and G. R. Andrews. Distributed filaments: Efficient fine-grain parallelism on a cluster of workstations. In *Proceedings of the First USENIX Symposium on Operating System Design and Implementation*, pages 201–213, November 1994.

10. K. Gharachorloo, D. Lenoski, J. Laudon, P. Gibbons, A. Gupta, and J. Hennessy. Memory consistency and event ordering in scalable shared-memory multiprocessors. In *Proceedings of the 17th Annual International Symposium on Computer Architecture*, pages 15–26, May 1990.

11. The SUIF Group. An overview of the suif compiler system.

12. P. Havlak and K. Kennedy. An implementation of interprocedural bounded regular section analysis. *IEEE Transactions on Parallel and Distributed Systems*, 2(3):350–360, July 1991.

13. M. Kaddoura. Load balancing for regular data-parallel applications on workstation network. In *Communication and Architecture Support for Network-Based Parallel Computing*, pages 173–183, February 1997.

14. P. Keleher, A. L. Cox, and W. Zwaenepoel. Lazy release consistency for software distributed shared memory. In *Proceedings of the 19th Annual International Symposium on Computer Architecture*, pages 13–21, May 1992.

15. C. Kruskal and A. Weiss. Allocating independent subtasks on parallel processors. In *Transactions on Computer Systems*, October 1985.

16. M. Litzkow and M. Solomon. Supporting checkpointing and process migration outside the unix kernel. In *Usenix Winter Conference*, 1992.

17. D. K. Lowenthal and G. R. Andrews. An adaptive approach to data placement. In *10th International Parallel Processing Symposium*, April 1996.

18. H. Lu, A.L. Cox, S. Dwarkadas, R. Rajamony, and W. Zwaenepoel. Software distributed shared memory support for irregular applications. In *Proceedings of the 6th Symposium on the Principles and Practice of Parallel Programming*, pages 48–56, June 1996.

19. E. P. Markatos and T. J. LeBlanc. Using processor affinity in loop scheduling on shared-memory multiprocessors. *IEEETPDS*, 5(4):379–400, April 1994.

20. E. P. Markatos and T. J. LeBlanc. Load balancing versus locality management in shared-memory mult iprocessors. *PROC of the 1992 ICPP*, pages I:258–267, August 1992.

21. B. Moon and J. Saltz. Adaptive runtime support for direct simulation monte carlo methods on distributed memory architectures. In *Salable High Performance Computing Comference*, May 1994.

22. C. D. Polychronopoulos and D. J. Kuck. Guided self-scheduling: a practical scheduling scheme for parallel supercomputers. In *Transactions on Computers*, September 1992.
23. P. Tang and P. C. Yew. Processor self-scheduling: A practical scheduling scheme for parallel computers. In *International Conference On Parallel Processing*, August 1986.
24. Y. Yan, C. Jin, and X. Zhang. Adaptively scheduling parallel loops in distributed shared-memory systems. In *Transactions on parallel and sitributed systems*, volume 8, January 1997.
25. M. J. Zaki, W. Li, and S. Parthasarathy. Customized dynamic load balancing for a network of workstations. Technical Report 602, Department of Computer Science, University of Rochester, December 1995.

Efficient Interprocedural Data Placement Optimisation in a Parallel Library

Olav Beckmann and Paul H.J. Kelly

Department of Computing, Imperial College
180 Queen's Gate, London SW7 2BZ, U.K.
{ob3,phjk}@doc.ic.ac.uk

Abstract. This paper describes a combination of methods which make interprocedural data placement optimisation available to parallel libraries. We propose a delayed-evaluation, self-optimising (DESO) numerical library for a distributed-memory multicomputer. Delayed evaluation allows us to capture the control-flow of a user program from within the library at runtime, and to construct an optimised execution plan by propagating data placement constraints backwards through the DAG representing the computation to be performed.

Our strategy for optimising data placements at runtime consists of an efficient representation for data distributions, a greedy optimisation algorithm, which because of delayed evaluation can take account of the full context of operations, and of re-using the results of previous runtime optimisations on contexts we have encountered before. We show performance figures for our library on a cluster of Pentium II Linux workstations, which demonstrate that the overhead of our delayed evaluation method is very small, and which show both the parallel speedup we obtain and the benefit of the optimisations we describe.

1 Introduction

Parallelising applications by using parallel libraries is an attractive proposition because it allows users to use any top-level calling language convenient to them, such as Fortran, C, C++ or spreadsheets. Further, it has been argued [10,11] that, at least for the time being, library-oriented parallelism, i.e. the use of carefully tuned routines for core operations, is often the only way to achieve satisfactory performance. A disadvantage of accessing parallelism through libraries, however, is that we seem set to miss opportunities for optimisation across library calls.

We propose a delayed evaluation, self-optimising (DESO) parallel linear algebra library as a way of avoiding this drawback: the actual execution of function calls is delayed for as long as possible. This provides the opportunity to capture the control flow of a user program at runtime. We refer to those points in a program where execution cannot be delayed anymore as *force points*. The most common reasons for this are output or conditional tests which depend on the result of a sequence of delayed operations. On encountering a force-point,

D. O'Hallaron (Ed.): LCR'98, LNCS 1511, pp. 123–138, 1998.
© Springer-Verlag Berlin Heidelberg 1998

we can construct an optimised execution plan for the DAG representing the computation to be performed.

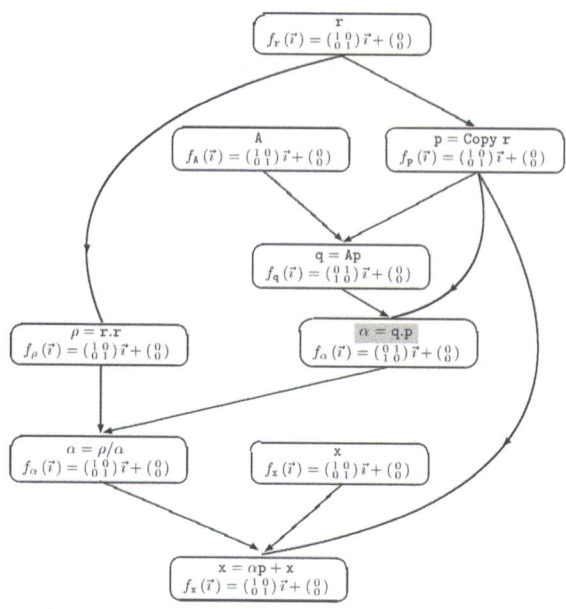

Fig. 1. DAG for the first iteration of the conjugate gradient algorithm. The "open ends" are: A, the parameter matrix, x the initial guess for a solution vector and r, the initial remainder-vector, $r = b - Ax$. The DAG has been annotated with the affine placement functions for the results of all operations. We refer to these in Section 2.1.

Example. Consider the DAG shown in Figure 1. The highlighted dot-product, $\alpha = q.p$, gives rise to a data placement conflict: If p is blocked over the rows of a mesh of processors, then the natural parallel implementation of the vector-matrix product $q = Ap$ means that q is blocked down the columns. Therefore, we need to redistribute either p or q in order to calculate the dot-product $\alpha = q.p$. If we perform the computation immediately, we have no information available about the future use of p and q to guide our choice. Delayed evaluation allows us to make a better decision by taking account of the use of p in the vector update $x = \alpha p + x$.

Key issues. The main challenge in optimising at run-time is that optimisation itself has to be very efficient. We achieve this with a combination of the following techniques:

– Working from aggregate loop nests, which have been optimised in isolation and which are not re-optimised at run-time.

- Using a purely mathematical formulation for data distributions, which allows us to calculate, rather than search for optimal distributions.
- Re-using optimised execution plans for previously encountered DAGs. A value-numbering scheme is used to recognise cases where this may be possible. The value numbers are used to index a cache of optimisation results, and we use a technique adapted from hardware dynamic branch prediction for deciding whether to further optimise DAGs we have previously encountered.

Delayed evaluation introduces runtime anti-dependence hazards which we overcome using a mechanism analogous to register renaming [18].

Related Work, Contribution of this Paper. This paper builds on related work in the field of automatic data placement [9,15], runtime parallelisation [6,17], automatic, compile-time parallelisation [3,7], interprocedural optimisation [12] and conventional compiler and architecture technology [1,8]. In our earlier paper [5] we described our method for re-using runtime-optimised execution plans in more fundamental terms. In this current paper, we add to this by describing our actual optimisation algorithm and by illustrating the benefits of our re-use strategy when combined with this particular algorithm.

Structure of this paper. We begin in Section 2 by outlining the fundamentals of our approach towards fast, runtime optimisation. Section 3 describes the optimisation algorithm we use and Section 4 presents our techniques for avoiding re-optimisation where appropriate. Finally, Section 5 shows performance results for our library. This is followed by a concluding discussion in Section 6, which includes a review of related and future work.

2 Basic Approach

2.1 Data Distributions

Our representation for data distributions is based on a combination of affine transformation functions ("alignment" in HPF [14]) and non-affine folding functions ("distribution" in HPF), together with a copying function which represents data replication.

- We *augment* the dimensionality of all arrays in an optimisation problem to the highest number of dimensions occurring in that problem: for the example shown in Figure 1, the matrix A is the array with the highest number of dimensions. We therefore augment scalars and vectors to two dimensions, treating them as 1×1 and $1 \times N$ matrices respectively. Thus we refer to the ith element of a vector as element $\binom{0}{i}$.
- Affine transformation functions act on array index vectors i and map them onto *virtual processor* indices. They take the form

$$f(i) = Ai + t \quad .\tag{1}$$

Example. The affine transformation function for mapping an N-element vector down column 0 of a virtual processor mesh is $f(\boldsymbol{i}) = \left(\begin{smallmatrix} 0 & 1 \\ 1 & 0 \end{smallmatrix}\right)\boldsymbol{i} + \left(\begin{smallmatrix} 0 \\ 0 \end{smallmatrix}\right)$, that is, vector element $\left(\begin{smallmatrix} 0 \\ i \end{smallmatrix}\right)$ is mapped to virtual processor $\left(\begin{smallmatrix} i \\ 0 \end{smallmatrix}\right)$.

- The replication of scalars and vectors, such as whether or not a vector which is mapped down the first column of a virtual processor mesh is replicated on all columns, is represented by a special copying function which we will not describe further here.
- Between any two affine placement functions f and g, we can calculate a *redistribution* function r such that $g = r \circ f$, which is itself an affine function.

We optimise with respect to affine placement functions, aiming to minimise the cost of affine redistributions.

2.2 Library Operator Placement Constraints

Each of our library operators has one or more parallel implementations. For each implementation, we formulate placement constraints as follows.

- Operators are implemented for one arbitrarily but reasonably chosen set of placements for the result and the operands. Naturally, when these placements are obeyed, the loop nest will execute correctly. As an example, for vector-matrix products, such as $\mathsf{q} = \mathsf{A}.\mathsf{p}$ in Figure 1, the chosen placements are

$$f_{\mathsf{A}}(\boldsymbol{i}) = f_{\mathsf{p}}(\boldsymbol{i}) = \left(\begin{smallmatrix} 1 & 0 \\ 0 & 1 \end{smallmatrix}\right)\boldsymbol{i} + \left(\begin{smallmatrix} 0 \\ 0 \end{smallmatrix}\right) \text{ and}$$
$$f_{\mathsf{q}}(\boldsymbol{i}) = \left(\begin{smallmatrix} 0 & 1 \\ 1 & 0 \end{smallmatrix}\right)\boldsymbol{i} + \left(\begin{smallmatrix} 0 \\ 0 \end{smallmatrix}\right) \quad .$$

  We also use the notation $A_{\mathsf{q}} = \left(\begin{smallmatrix} 0 & 1 \\ 1 & 0 \end{smallmatrix}\right)$ and $\boldsymbol{t}_{\mathsf{q}} = \left(\begin{smallmatrix} 0 \\ 0 \end{smallmatrix}\right)$.
- From that, we can calculate *constraint equations* which characterise each operator implementation by describing the relationship between the placements of the result and of the operands. In our example, we have

$$A_{\mathsf{A}} = \left(\begin{smallmatrix} 0 & 1 \\ 1 & 0 \end{smallmatrix}\right) A_{\mathsf{q}} \qquad A_{\mathsf{p}} = \left(\begin{smallmatrix} 0 & 1 \\ 1 & 0 \end{smallmatrix}\right) A_{\mathsf{q}}$$
$$t_{\mathsf{A}} = t_{\mathsf{q}} \qquad\qquad t_{\mathsf{p}} = t_{\mathsf{q}} \quad . \tag{2}$$

- For "open ends" in a DAG, i.e. for nodes representing either arrays which have already been evaluated or the result of a force, the placement is fixed and we obtain constraint equations such as (for Figure 1)

$$A_{\mathbf{r}} = \left(\begin{smallmatrix} 1 & 0 \\ 0 & 1 \end{smallmatrix}\right) \qquad t_{\mathbf{r}} = \left(\begin{smallmatrix} 0 \\ 0 \end{smallmatrix}\right) \quad . \tag{3}$$

- Our optimiser is permitted to change the placement of the result or of one of the operands of a node in the DAG at optimisation time in order to avoid data redistributions. If that happens, we re-calculate the placements for the other arrays involved in the computation at that node by means of the constraint equations described above. Further, we dynamically transform the operator's loop nest, loop bounds and communication pattern. See [3] for a basic introduction to the techniques required.

When a value is forced, the optimisation problem we need to solve consists of the union of of the equations as shown in (2) and (3) for all nodes in a DAG.

3 Optimisation

3.1 Calculating Required Redistributions

Once we have a DAG available for optimisation, our algorithm begins by calculating the affine *redistribution* functions (see Section 2.1) between the placements of arrays at the source and sink of all edges in the DAG. Let nodes in a DAG be denoted by the values they calculate. For an edge $\mathsf{a} \to \mathsf{b}$, we denote the placement of a at the source by f_a and the placement at the sink by $f_{\mathsf{a}_\mathsf{b}}$. We then define the redistribution function for this edge to be the affine function $r_{\mathsf{a} \to \mathsf{b}}$ such that

$$f_\mathsf{a} = r_{\mathsf{a} \to \mathsf{b}} \circ f_{\mathsf{a}_\mathsf{b}} \quad . \tag{4}$$

For our example in Figure 1, p is generated with distribution $f_\mathsf{p} = \left(\begin{smallmatrix} 1 & 0 \\ 0 & 1 \end{smallmatrix}\right) \boldsymbol{i} + \left(\begin{smallmatrix} 0 \\ 0 \end{smallmatrix}\right)$ and used in the dot-product $\alpha = \mathsf{q}.\mathsf{p}$ with distribution $f_{\mathsf{p}_\alpha} = \left(\begin{smallmatrix} 0 & 1 \\ 1 & 0 \end{smallmatrix}\right) \boldsymbol{i} + \left(\begin{smallmatrix} 0 \\ 0 \end{smallmatrix}\right)$, i.e. aligned with q. The redistribution function for the edge $\mathsf{p} \to \alpha$ therefore is $r_{\mathsf{p} \to \alpha}(\boldsymbol{i}) = \left(\begin{smallmatrix} 0 & 1 \\ 1 & 0 \end{smallmatrix}\right) \boldsymbol{i} + \left(\begin{smallmatrix} 0 \\ 0 \end{smallmatrix}\right)$.

3.2 A Cost Model for Redistributions

We define the *size vector* N_a of an array a to be the vector consisting of the array's data size in all dimensions, so for an $n \times m$ matrix M, we have $N_\mathsf{M} = \left(\begin{smallmatrix} n \\ m \end{smallmatrix}\right)$, and for an n-element vector v, $N_\mathsf{v} = \left(\begin{smallmatrix} 1 \\ n \end{smallmatrix}\right)$. Next, we define $\bar{r}$ to be the function obtained from a redistribution function r by substituting all diagonal elements in the matrix A with 0. For identity functions, we obtain a matrix $A = \left(\begin{smallmatrix} 0 & 0 \\ 0 & 0 \end{smallmatrix}\right)$ and for the transpose in our example, $\bar{r}_{\mathsf{p} \to \alpha} = r_{\mathsf{p} \to \alpha}$. Then, we define the weight $W_{\mathsf{a} \to \mathsf{b}}$ of an edge $\mathsf{a} \to \mathsf{b}$ as

$$W_{\mathsf{a} \to \mathsf{b}} = \|\bar{r}_{\mathsf{a} \to \mathsf{b}}(N_\mathsf{a})\|_2 \quad . \tag{5}$$

In our example, assuming that p is an n-element vector, $W_{\mathsf{p} \to \alpha} \approx n$. This model captures the amount of data movement involved in a redistribution and we have so far found it to give a sufficiently accurate reflection of which redistributions in a DAG are the most costly and should therefore be eliminated first.

3.3 The Algorithm

1. We select the edge with the highest weight. Suppose this is an edge $\mathsf{a} \to \mathsf{b}$.
2. We change the distribution at the *sink* of the edge such that the redistribution $r_{\mathsf{a} \to \mathsf{b}}$ is avoided, i.e., we substitute $f_{\mathsf{a}_\mathsf{b}} \leftarrow f_\mathsf{a}$. We then use the constraint equations at node b for calculating the resulting placement of b and any other operands and *forward-propagate* this change through the DAG.
3. We check the weight of the DAG following the change. If the weight has gone up, we abandon the change and proceed to step 4. If the weight has gone down, we jump to step 6.

4. We change the distribution at the *source* of the edge by substituting $f_b \leftarrow f_{a_b}$. We update the placements of the operands at node a and *backwards-propagate* the change through the DAG.
5. We check the weight of the DAG. If it has gone up, we abandon the change and mark the edge a → b as "attempted". Otherwise, we accept the change.
6. If the weight of the DAG has become zero, or, if the remaining weight is entirely due to edges which have already been attempted, we stop optimising. Otherwise, we have the option of optimising further. We describe in Section 4 how we decide whether or not to do this.

3.4   Related Work

Our optimisation algorithm resembles that of Feautrier [9] in that we optimise with respect to affine placement functions disregarding the non-affine mapping of virtual processors onto physical ones, and use a greedy algorithm, attempting to resolve edges with the highest weight first. However, our approach differs in that we work from aggregate data structures and use a different cost model for communication. The fact that we work at runtime and capture the control flow of a program by delayed evaluation means that we do not have to impose any restrictions on the user's source code, as is the case in [9], where programs are required to be of "static control".

4   Re-Using Execution Plans

The previous section has described our algorithm for finding an optimal execution plan for any one DAG. In real programs, essentially identical DAGs often recur. In such situations, our runtime approach is set to suffer a significant performance disadvantage over compile-time techniques unless we can reuse the results of previous optimisations we have performed. This section shows how we can ensure that our optimiser does not have to carry out any more work than an optimising compiler would have to do, unless there is the prospect of a performance benefit by doing more optimisation than would be possible with static information.

4.1   Run-Time Optimisation Strategies

We begin by discussing and comparing two different basic strategies for performing run-time optimisation. We will refer to them as "Forward Propagation Only" and "Forward And Backward Propagation". We use the following terminology: n is the number of operator calls in a sequence, a the maximum arity of operators, m is the maximum number of different methods per operator. If we work with a fixed set of data placements, s is the number of different placements, and in DAGs, d refers to the degree of the shared node (see [15]) with maximum degree.

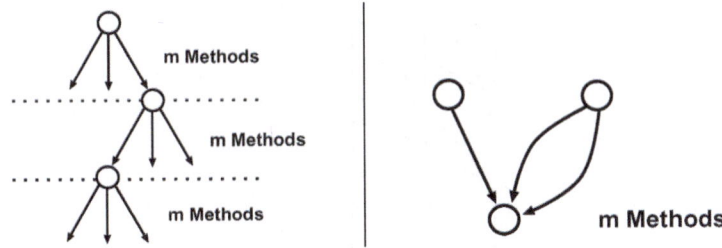

Fig. 2. Left. Optimisation of a linear stream of operators under *Forward Propagation Only*. Complexity is $\Theta(mn)$. **Right.** The only type of DAG we can recognise as such under *Forward Propagation Only*.

Forward Propagation Only. This is the only strategy open to us if we perform run-time optimisation of a sequence of library operators under *strict evaluation*: We optimise the placements for each new operator based purely on information about its ancestors.

- In Figure 2, we illustrate that the total optimisation time for a linear sequence of n operators with m different available methods per operator under this strategy has complexity $\Theta(mn)$.
- For our library (where, as stated in Section 2.2, each method captures a number of possible placements for operands), we would be able to optimise the placement of any a-ary operator in $O(a)$ time, i.e., the time for optimising any call graph would be $O(an)$.
- Linear complexity in the number of operators is probably all we can afford in a runtime system.
- However, as we already illustrated in Figure 1, the price we pay for using such an algorithm is that it may give a significantly suboptimal answer. This problem is present even for trees, but it is much worse for DAGs: Figure 2 shows the only type of DAG we can recognise as a DAG under *Forward Propagation Only*. All other DAGs can not be handled in an optimal way.

Note 1. If we choose to use *Forward Propagation Only*, there is no benefit in delaying optimisation decisions, since we already have all optimisation information available at the time when operators are called.

Forward And Backward Propagation. Delayed evaluation gives us the opportunity to propagate placement constraint information backwards through a DAG since we accumulate a full DAG before we begin to optimise.

- We illustrate in Figure 3 that this type of optimisation is much more complex than *Forward Propagation Only*.
- Mace [15] has shown it to be NP-complete for general DAGs, but presents algorithms with complexity $O((m + s^2)n)$ for trees and with complexity $O(s^{d+1}n)$ for a restricted class of DAG.

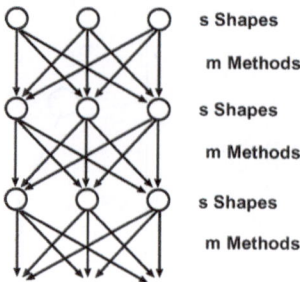

Fig. 3. Optimisation of a linear stream of operators under *Forward And Backward Propagation*. The additional complexity derives from the fact that it may be necessary to choose sub-optimal placements for one step in the calculation in order to gain optimal performance overall: we need to calculate the cost of generating each result in every possible shape, not just the cheapest for that step.

- Our own greedy optimisation algorithm does not enumerate different possible placements, but captures all distributions with one representation (see Section 2.2). This means that the complexity of our optimisation algorithm is independent of the number of possible placements we allow. Its complexity is similar to that of Gaussian elimination, i.e. $O((kn)^2)$ for some constant k. Note that this is an upper bound, the algorithm will often run in linear time.
- The point to note here is that *Forward and Backward Propagation* does give us the opportunity to find the optimal solution to a problem, provided we are prepared to spend the time required.

What we would like to do therefore is to use the full context information to derive correct, optimal placements, but to then re-use the results of such a full optimisation whenever the same optimisation problem occurs.

4.2   Recognising Opportunities for Reuse

We now deal with the problem of how to recognise a DAG, i.e. optimisation problem, which we have encountered before. The full optimisation problem, characterised by the full DAG or the resulting system of equations, is a large structure. To avoid having to traverse it to check for cache hits, we derive a hashed "value number" [1,8] for each node and use that value number to determine whether we have encountered a DAG before.

- Our value numbers have to encode data placements and placement constraints, not actual data values. For nodes which are already evaluated, we simply apply a hash function to the placement descriptor of that node. For nodes which are not yet evaluated, we have to apply a hash function to the *placement constraints* on that node.

- The key observation is that by seeking to encode all placement constraints on a node in our value numbers, we are in danger of deriving an algorithm for calculating value numbers which has the same O-complexity as *Forward and Backward Propagation* optimisation algorithms: each node in a DAG can potentially exert a placement constraint over every other node.
- Our algorithm for calculating value numbers is therefore based on *Forward Propagation Only*: we calculate value numbers for unevaluated nodes by applying a hash function to those placement constraints deriving from their immediate ancestor nodes only.
- According to Note 1, there is therefore no point in delaying the calculation of value numbers; they are generated on-the-fly, as library operators are called.
- The only way to detect hash conflicts would be to traverse the full DAGs which the value numbers represent. Apart from the fact that such a validation would have $O(n)$ complexity, it would also mean having to store full DAGs which we have previously encountered and optimised. We return to this point shortly.

4.3   When to Re-Use and When to Optimise

We now discuss when we re-use the results of previous optimisations and when we re-optimise a problem. Because our value numbers are calculated on *Forward Propagation Only* information, we have to address the problem of how to handle those cases where nodes which have identical value numbers are used in a different context later on; in other words, how to to avoid the drawbacks of *Forward Propagation Only* optimisation. This is a branch-prediction problem, and we use a technique adapted from hardware dynamic branch prediction (see [13]) for predicting heuristically whether identical value numbers will result in identical future use of the corresponding node and hence identical optimisation problems.

We store a bit, OPTIMISE, to implement a strategy of re-optimising in the following three situations:

1. A DAG has not been encountered before.
2. We have encountered a DAG before and successfully performed some optimisation when we last saw it. We "predict" that more optimisation might lead to further improvements.
3. We re-used a previously stored execution plan when we last encountered a DAG, but found this execution plan to give sub-optimal performance.

- In all other cases, we have seen the encountered DAG before, and we re-use a cached execution plan (see below).
- Point 3 deals with the problem of false cache hits, which we cannot detect directly. The run-time system automatically introduces any necessary redistributions, so the effect of using a wrong cached plan is that the number of redistributions may be larger than expected.
- The metrics which are required for deciding whether or not to invoke the optimiser therefore are (a) the success or otherwise of the optimiser in reducing

the "weight" of a DAG when we last encountered it, (b) the communication-cost of evaluating the DAG when we last encountered it, and (c) the communication cost of the 'optimal' execution plan for a DAG. We have instrumented our system such that these metrics are available.

Caching Execution Plans. Value numbers and 'dynamic branch prediction' together provide us with a fairly reliable mechanism for recognising the fact that we have encountered a node in the same context before. Assuming that we optimised the placement of that node when we first encountered it, our task is then simply to re-use the placement which the optimiser derived. We do this by using a "cache" of optimised placements, which is indexed by value numbers. Each cache entry has a valid-tag which is set by our branch prediction mechanism.

Competitive Optimisation. As we showed in Section 4.1, full optimisation based on *Forward And Backward Propagation* can be very expensive. Each time we invoke the optimiser on a DAG, we therefore only spend a limited time optimising that DAG. For a DAG which we encounter only once, this means that we only spend very little time trying to eliminate the worst redistributions. For DAGs which recur, our strategy is to gradually improve the execution plan used until our optimisation algorithm can find no further improvements.

Finally, it should be pointed out that although our value numbers are calculated on-the-fly, under *Forward Propagation Only*, we still delay the execution of DAGs we have encountered before. This is to allow new, yet unseen contexts to trigger a re-optimisation of DAGs which we have already optimised for other contexts.

Summary. We use the full optimisation information, i.e. *Forward and Backward Propagation*, to optimise. We obtain access to this information by delayed evaluation. We use a scheme based on *Forward Propagation Only*, with linear complexity in program length, to ensure that we re-use the results of previous optimisations.

5   Implementation and Performance

The implementation of our library is based on MPI. This offers portability and, MPI allows parallel libraries to be designed in such a way that they can safely be used together with other communication libraries and in user programs which themselves carry out communication [11]. In this Section, we show performance figures for our library on a cluster of desktop Pentium II Linux workstations here at Imperial College. As a benchmark we used the non-preconditioned conjugate gradient iterative algorithm. The pseudo-code for the algorithm (adapted from [4]) and the source code when implemented using our library are shown in Figure 4.

$$r^{(0)} = b - Ax^{(0)}$$

for $i = 1, \ldots, i_{max}$

$\quad \rho_{i-1} = r^{(i-1)^T} r^{(i-1)}$

$\quad$ **if** $\quad i = 1$

$\quad\quad p^{(1)} = r^{(0)}$

$\quad$ **else** $\quad \beta_{i-1} = \rho_{i-1}/\rho_{i-2}$

$\quad\quad\quad p^{(i)} = r^{(i-1)} + \beta_{(i-1)}p^{(i-1)}$

$\quad$ **endif**

$\quad q^{(i)} = Ap^{(i)}$

$\quad \alpha_i = \rho_{i-1}/p^{(i)^T} q^{(i)}$

$\quad x^{(i)} = x^{(i-1)} + \alpha_i p^{(i)}$

$\quad r^{(i)} = r^{(i-1)} - \alpha_i q^{(i)}$

$\quad$ check convergence

end

```
for(i = 1; i <= max_iter; i++) {
  if (i != 1)
    L_Dcopy(rho, &rho_o);
  L_Ddot(r, r, &rho);
  if (i == 1)
    L_Dcopy(r, &p);
  else {
    L_Ddiv(rho_o, rho, &beta);
    L_Daxpy(beta, p, r, &p);
  };
  L_Dgemv(one, A, p, zero, q, &q);
  L_Ddot(q, p, &alpha);
  L_Ddiv(alpha, rho, &alpha);
  L_Daxpy(alpha, p, x, &x);
  L_Dscal(alpha, minusone, &alpha);
  L_Daxpy(alpha, q, r, &r);
  /* Check convergence. */
};
```

Fig. 4. Pseudo-code for the conjugate gradient algorithm (left) and source code (slightly cut down) when implemented using our library.

5.1 Comparison with Sequential, Compiled Model

Figure 5 compares the performance of the single processor version of our parallel code with two different purely sequential implementations of the same algorithm. One of these uses the same BLAS kernels which our parallel code calls; these are routines which we have manually optimised for the Pentium II processor. The other version links with the Intel / ASCI Red [2] BLAS kernels.

There is virtually no distinction between the performance of our parallel code running on 1 processor and the "best effort" purely sequential version which calls our own optimised BLAS implementation. For the smallest data size in our experiment (512×512 parameter matrix), the code using our parallel library has about 10% less performance in terms of MFLOP/s, but this becomes almost indistinguishable for larger data sizes. Both the codes using our BLAS kernels do, however consistently perform somewhat better than the purely sequential code which links with the Intel / ASCI Red BLAS kernels. This demonstrates that the overhead of our delayed evaluation scheme is very small and that the baseline sequential performance of our code is very respectable.

5.2 Parallel Performance

Table 1 shows the parallel speedup we obtain with our library on a cluster of Pentium II Linux workstations. As noted in the caption of the table, these figures underestimate the actual parallel speedup we obtain. Nevertheless, a parallel speedup of 2.65 for 4 processors is encouraging, given the nature of the platform. On our current configuration, and with the problem size we used (this

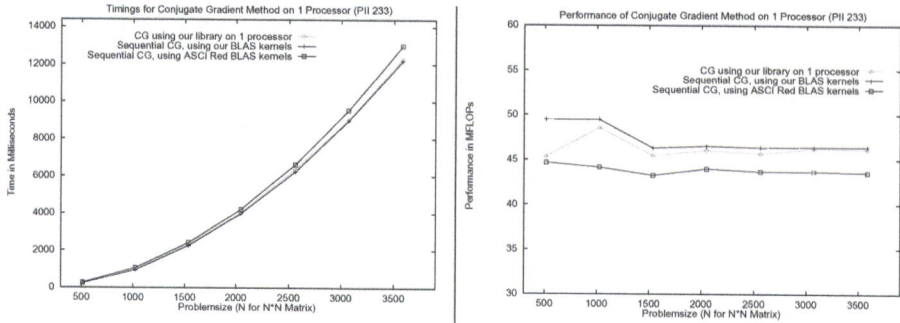

Fig. 5. Performance comparison of the single processor version of our parallel code with two different purely sequential implementations of the same algorithm on a Pentium II 233 with 128MB RAM running Linux 2.0.30. Both purely sequential codes are a direct transcription of the conjugate gradient template which is distributed with [4]; the only difference is in the underlying BLAS implementation they call.

is limited by the machine with least free RAM), our benchmark does not scale well to 9 processors.

5.3   Performance of Our Optimisations

Tables 1 and 2 show detailed measurements which break up the overall time spent by our benchmark into different categories. Note that the CG algorithm has $O(N^2)$ computation complexity, but only $O(N)$ communication complexity. This can be seen in Table 2.

- Our optimiser avoids two out of three vector transposes. This was determined by analysis and by tracing communication.
- Optimisation achieves a reduction in communication time of between 30% and 40%. We do not achieve more because a significant proportion of the communication in this algorithm is due to reduce-operations.
- Runtime overhead and optimisation time are virtually independent of the number of processors and of the problem size. We suspect that the slight differences are due to cache effects.
- With caching of optimisation results, the overall time spent by our optimiser is very small. On platforms with less powerful nodes than PII 300–233s, this aspect or our optimisation strategy is crucial. On such platforms, optimisation without re-use can easily result in overall slowdown.
- The optimisations we have described in this paper achieve speedups over the non-optimised code using our library of between 9% and 29% for reasonably large problem sizes. The overall benefit of our optimisations decreases with increasing problem size on the same number of processors. This is due to the CG algorithm's $O(N^2)$ computation complexity with only only $O(N)$ communication complexity. However, the benefit of our optimisations increases with the amount of parallelism we use to solve a problem.

	P	Comp.	Memory	Overh.	Comms.	Opt.	Total	O-Speedup	P-Speedup
N	1	21276.13	5.83	11.69	0.00	0.00	21293.65	1.00	1.00
O	1	21280.05	5.95	9.93	0.00	8.69	21304.62	1.00	1.00
C	1	21276.56	5.84	9.54	0.00	0.63	21292.57	1.00	1.00
N	4	5286.77	5.08	9.39	4047.85	0.00	9349.09	1.00	2.28
O	4	5264.42	4.39	8.15	2771.15	8.38	8056.51	1.16	2.64
C	4	5251.73	4.48	8.57	2778.93	0.62	8044.33	1.16	2.65
N	9	2625.52	5.43	10.10	3992.16	0.00	6633.23	1.00	3.21
O	9	2608.84	4.69	8.70	2516.95	9.18	5148.36	1.29	4.14
C	9	2610.86	4.63	8.49	2516.98	0.66	5141.62	1.29	4.14

Table 1. Time in milliseconds for 20 iterations of conjugate gradient, with a 4992 × 4992 parameter matrix (about 190 MB) on varying numbers of processors. N denotes timings without any optimisation, O timings with optimisation but no caching, and C timings with optimisation and caching of optimisation results. *O-Speedup* shows the speedup due to our optimisations, and *P-Speedup* the speedup due to parallelisation. All processors are Pentium IIs running Linux 2.0.32. Note however, that their specification decreases from processor 0 (dual 300 MHz, 512 MB RAM) to processor 8 (233 MHz, 64 MB). Further, processors 0–3 are connected by fast ethernet (100 Mb/s), whereas some of the remaining ones are connected by 10 Mb/s ethernet. Hence, the above numbers for parallel speedup do not actually show the full potential of our library.

6   Conclusions

We have presented an an approach to interprocedural data placement optimisation which exploits run-time control-flow information and is applicable in contexts where the calling program cannot easily be analysed statically. We present preliminary experimental evidence that the benefits can easily outweigh the run-time costs.

6.1   Run-Time vs. Compile-Time Optimisation

To see some of the relative advantages of our technique and of compile-time methods, consider the following loop, assuming that there are no force-points inside the loop and that we encounter the loop a number of times and each time force evaluation after the loop.

```
for(i = 0; i < N; ++i) {
  if <unknown conditional>
     <do A>
  else
     <do B>
}
```

This loop can have up to 2^N control-paths. A compile-time optimiser would have to find one compromise execution plan for all invocations of this loop. With our approach, we would optimise the actual DAG which has been generated on each occasion. If the number of different DAGs is high, compile-time methods

	N	Comp.	Memory	Overh.	Comms.	Opt.	Total	O-Speedup	MFLOP/s
N	1024	218.81	5.00	9.28	783.81	0.00	1016.90	1.00	45.64
O	1024	219.13	4.27	8.09	395.25	8.24	634.99	1.60	73.09
C	1024	217.79	4.35	7.99	394.27	0.61	625.01	1.63	74.26
N	2048	848.32	5.02	9.12	1522.06	0.00	2384.53	1.00	77.63
O	2048	851.87	4.26	8.24	1123.02	8.25	1995.64	1.19	92.75
C	2048	839.00	4.26	7.88	1058.75	0.61	1910.50	1.25	96.89
N	3072	2411.17	5.21	9.63	2910.47	0.00	5336.47	1.00	77.97
O	3072	2343.11	4.27	8.16	2083.26	8.11	4446.89	1.20	93.56
C	3072	2337.84	4.32	8.02	2025.89	0.62	4376.68	1.22	95.06
N	4096	4236.84	5.11	9.23	5354.08	0.00	9605.26	1.00	76.97
O	4096	4267.31	4.32	8.15	4500.90	8.34	8789.02	1.09	84.12
C	4096	4273.14	4.36	8.02	4502.32	0.62	8788.47	1.09	84.12

Table 2. Time in milliseconds for 20 iterations of conjugate gradient on four Pentium II Linux workstations, with varying problem sizes. N, O and C are as in Table 1.

would probably have the edge over ours, since we would optimise each time and could not reuse execution plans. If, however, the number of different DAGs generated is small, our execution plans for the *actual* DAGs will be superior to compile-time compromise solutions, and by reusing them, we limit the time we spend optimising.

6.2   Related Work

Most successful work on parallelising compilers for distributed-memory systems has relied on explicit control over data placement, using e.g. Fortran-D or HPF [14]. The problem for a compiler is then reduced to optimising the communications which are required.

There is a large amount of work on the problem of automatically parallelising an affine nested loop [7,9]. The first stage of that process is to map each array element and each operation onto a virtual processor, in such a way that as many non-local data accesses as possible are avoided.

We have already mentioned how our optimisation algorithm is related to that of Feautrier [9] in Section 3.4. Our approach has similarities with that of Mace [15] in that both work on aggregate arrays, rather than individual data elements. Mace gives a precise formulation of our optimisation problem in its fullest sense and shows it to be NP-complete.

Hall *et al.* [12] describe a one-pass, optimising interprocedural compilation system for Fortran D and also demonstrate the vital importance of interprocedural analysis for optimising parallelisation.

Saltz *et al.* [17] address the basic problem of how to parallelise loops where the dependence structure is not known statically. Loops are translated into an *inspector* loop which determines the dependence structure at runtime and constructs a schedule, and an *executor* loop which carries out the calculations planned by the inspector. Saltz *et al.* discuss the possibility of reusing a previously constructed schedule, but rely on user annotations for doing so. Ponnusamy *et al.* [16] propose a simple conservative model which avoids the user having to indicate to the compiler when a schedule may be reused.

Benkner *et al.* [6] describe the reuse of parallel schedules via explicit directives in HPF+: REUSE directives for indicating that the schedule computed for a certain loop can be reused and SCHEDULE variables which allow a schedule to be saved and reused in other code sections.

Value numbering schemes were pioneered by Ershov [8], who proposed the use of "convention numbers" for denoting the results of computations and avoid having to recompute them. More recent work on this subject is described by Aho *et al.* [1].

6.3   Future Work

- The most direct next step is to store cached execution plans persistently, so that they can be reused subsequently for this or similar applications.
- Although we can derive some benefit from exploiting run-time control-flow information, we also have the opportunity to make run-time optimisation decisions based on run-time properties of data; we plan to extend this work to address sparse matrices shortly.
- The run-time system has to make on-the-fly data placement decisions. An intriguing question raised by this work is to compare this with an optimal off-line schedule.

Acknowledgments. This work was partially supported by the EPSRC, under the Futurespace and CRAMP projects (references GR/J 87015 and GR/J 99117). We extend special thanks to Fujitsu and the Imperial College / Fujitsu Parallel Computing Research Centre for providing access to their AP1000 multicomputer, and to the Imperial College Parallel Computing Centre for the use of their AP3000 machine.

References

1. Alfred V. Aho, Ravi Sethi, and Jeffrey D. Ullman. *Compilers*. Addison-Wesley, Reading, Massachusetts, 1986.
2. ASCI Red Pentium Pro BLAS 1.1e. See
   http://www.cs.utk.edu/~ghenry/distrib/ and
   http://developer.intel.com/design/perftool/perflibst/.
3. Uptal Banerjee. Unimodular transformations of double loops. Technical Report TR–1036, Center for Supercomputing Research and Development (CSRD), University of Illinois at Urbana-Champaign, 1990.
4. Richard Barrett, Mike Berry, Tony Chan, Jim Demmel, June Donato, Jack Dongarra, Victor Eijkhout, Roldan Pozo, Chuck Romine, and Henk van der Vorst. *Templates for the Solution of Linear Systems: Building Blocks for Iterative Methods*. Society for Industrial and Applied Mathematics (SIAM), Philadelphia, PA, USA, 1994.

5. Olav Beckmann and Paul H J Kelly. Data distribution at run-time; re-using execution plans. To appear in Euro-Par '98, Southampton, U.K., September 1st - 4th, 1998. Proceedings will be published by Springer Verlag in the LNCS Series.

6. Siegfried Benkner, Piyush Mehrotra, John Van Rosendale, and Hans Zima. High-level management of communication schedules in HPF-like languages. Technical Report TR-97-46, Institute for Computer Applications in Science and Engineering, NASA Langley Research Center, Hampton, VA 23681, USA, September 1997.

7. Michele Dion, Cyril Randriamaro, and Yves Robert. Compiling affine nested loops: How to optimize the residual communications after the alignment phase. *Journal of Parallel and Distributed Computing*, 38(2):176–187, November 1996.

8. Andrei P. Ershov. On programming of arithmetic operations. *Communications of the ACM*, 1(8):3–6, 1958. Three figures from this article are in CACM 1(9):16.

9. Paul Feautrier. Toward automatic distribution. *Parallel Processing Letters*, 4(3):233–244, 1994.

10. William D. Gropp. Performance driven programming models. In *MPPM'97, Proceedings of the 3rd International Working Conference on Massively Parallel Programming Models*, London, U.K., November 1997. To appear.

11. William D Gropp, Ewing Lusk, and Anthony Skjellum. *Using MPI: Portable Parallel Programming with the Message-Passing Interface*. MIT Press, Cambridge, MA, USA, 1994.

12. Mary W. Hall, Seema Hiranandani, Ken Kennedy, and Chau-Wen Tseng. Interprocedural compilation of Fortran D. *Journal of Parallel and Distributed Computing*, 38:114–129, 1996.

13. John L. Hennessy and David A. Patterson. *Computer Architecture A Quantative Approach*. Morgan Kaufman, San Mateo, California, 1st edition, 1990.

14. High Performance Fortran Forum. High Performance Fortran language specification, version 1.1. TR CRPC-TR92225, Center for Research on Parallel Computation, Rice University, Houston, TX, November 1994.

15. Mary E. Mace. *Storage Patterns in Parallel Processing*. Kluwer Academic Press, 1987.

16. Ravi Ponnusamy, Joel Saltz, and Alok Choudhary. Runtime compilation techniques for data partitioning and communication schedule reuse. In *Proceedings of Supercomputing '93: Portland, Oregon, November 15–19, 1993*, pages 361–370, New York, NY 10036, USA, November 1993. ACM Press.

17. Joel H. Saltz, Ravi Mirchandaney, and Kay Crowley. Run-time parallelization and scheduling of loops. *IEEE Transactions on Computers*, 40(5):603–612, May 1991.

18. R. M. Tomasulo. An efficient algorithm for exploiting multiple arithmetic units. *IBM Journal of Research and Development*, 11(1):25–33, January 1967.

A Framework for Specializing Threads in Concurrent Run-Time Systems

Gregory D. Benson and Ronald A. Olsson

Department of Computer Science
University of California, Davis
Davis, CA 95616, USA
{benson,olsson}@cs.ucdavis.edu

Abstract. Many thread packages support only a limited number target configurations and are generally inflexible with respect to scheduling. Even configurable thread packages distance core thread operations and thread state from client code. In addition, most thread implementations duplicate some of the functionality found in concurrent language run-time systems. To address these limitations, we have developed the *Mezcla thread framework*. Unlike conventional thread packages, Mezcla enables a language implementor to generate specialized, light-weight thread systems based on the requirements of the run-time system and the functionality of the target platform. This paper presents several current techniques for implementing threads in concurrent run-time systems and evaluates their effectiveness. We then describe our experience with threads in the SR concurrent programming language. Finally, we present the design and implementation of the Mezcla thread framework with some preliminary performance results.

1   Introduction

The implementation of a programming language with concurrency semantics, such as SR [2], Java [11], and Modula-3 [19], requires an underlying thread system, that is, a set of mechanisms to create and synchronize independent execution streams. Threads are usually implemented within a language's run-time system. To date, a language implementor has had essentially two broad options for incorporating threads into a run-time system: construct a custom thread package based on low-level context switching code or use a high-level thread package. The problem is that both of these options have limitations and there is no middle ground between them.

Many thread packages support only a limited number target configurations and are generally inflexible with respect to scheduling. Even configurable thread packages distance core thread operations and thread state from client code. In addition, most thread implementations duplicate some of the functionality found in concurrent language run-time systems. In contrast, a custom thread implementation allows a run-time system to have low-level control over thread scheduling and thread state, but lacks the portability found in high-level libraries.

D. O'Hallaron (Ed.): LCR'98, LNCS 1511, pp. 139–152, 1998.
© Springer-Verlag Berlin Heidelberg 1998

To address these limitations, we have developed the *Mezcla thread framework.* Unlike conventional thread packages, Mezcla enables a language implementor to generate specialized, light-weight thread systems based on the requirements of the run-time system and the functionality of the target platform. Our work is based on the following principles:

1. Eliminate redundancies found in run-time systems and thread packages.
2. Facilitate the best match between language mechanisms and the underlying platform (architecture and operating system).
3. Allow run-time systems to be retargeted to different platforms and configurations from a single thread specification.

Mezcla allows the language implementor to choose among a variety of configuration options such as uniprocessors versus shared memory multiprocessors, or preemptive scheduling versus non-preemptive scheduling. To this end, we are developing intermediate primitives, target specifications, and a thread generation tool. The tool generates specialized code that depends on the client (run-time system) and the desired target. By generating specialized thread code, we can minimize the amount of work done on the critical path of all thread operations and expose the thread state to a run-time system. The Mezcla primitives allow the creation of custom schedulers and synchronization mechanisms that are independent of the target platform. This approach raises the status of thread implementation to that of a compiler tool rather than a library. Although our work focuses on languages used for systems applications, our techniques should work for other run-time systems that use stack-based threads.

The rest of this paper is organized as follows. Section 2 describes current alternatives for thread implementation. Section 3 discusses our experience with threads in the context of the SR run-time system. Section 4 details some fundamental problems with current thread implementation techniques. Section 5 presents the Mezcla thread framework and some results with an initial prototype. Finally, Section 6 makes some concluding remarks.

2   Thread Implementation Alternatives

As mentioned previously, many imperative languages, such as SR, Java, and Modula-3, provide constructs for concurrency. Implementations of these languages use various techniques for mapping concurrency to threads. Two common techniques are: *custom threads* and *Pthreads-style threads.*

The *custom threads* approach usually produces the most efficient implementations because user-level threads almost always outperform kernel-level threads and custom threads are tuned for a particular run-time system. Both SR and Java have implementations that use custom threads.

Packages exist to help construct custom threads systems [14,18] and a fairly portable technique for implementing user-level threads is to use the C Library routines `setjmp()` and `longjmp()`. The run-time systems based on these low-level thread building blocks generally perform well, but support only a few target configurations.

Two notable problems with user-level threads are the lack of blocking I/O support and the mismatch between the kernel scheduler and the user-level scheduler. The former problem requires sophisticated support to allow user-level threads to block on I/O operations. The latter problem can lead to poor performance on shared-memory multiprocessors if the kernel preempts a user-level thread that is holding a lock needed by other threads. Techniques such as Scheduler Activations [1], First Class User-Level Threads [16], and, more recently, Strands [23] have been used to enable better coordination between user-level scheduling and kernel scheduling. Unfortunately, all these techniques require kernel support and are currently restricted to research systems or private kernel interfaces.

The *Pthreads-style* approach is attractive from a portability standpoint. Most operating system vendors supply a Pthreads library, and usually these libraries support kernel-level threads or multiplex user-level threads onto kernel-level threads [20]. Also, many other thread systems and parallel run-time systems provide a Pthreads-style interface, such as Mach Cthreads [8], Georgia Tech Cthreads [17], Nexus [10], and Panda [7]. However, our experience has shown that Pthreads libraries generally perform much worse than custom thread implementations for basic thread operations such as thread creation, context switching, and blocking. Even Pthreads-style libraries implemented entirely in user-space tend to perform much worse than custom user-level threads [4]. Poor performance in Pthreads-style libraries is partly attributed to the generality in the Pthreads-style interface. In addition, using a Pthreads-style interface usually means giving up scheduling control. Such control may not be necessary for applications that use Pthreads directly, but a language's run-time system can often make better scheduling decisions.

Parallel run-time libraries usually provide some type of thread interface. Nexus [10] and Panda [7] have Pthreads-style interfaces; Converse [13] has a slightly lower-level interface built on top of QuickThreads [14]. Using a parallel run-time library is generally useful if one wants to take advantage of a particular communication interface. However, this approach can lead to implementations that are tightly coupled to a particular parallel run-time system. In addition, many languages do not require all the functionality found in such run-time systems. Parallel run-time systems can also introduce overhead in the core thread operations due to added functionality and indirection through procedure calls.

The approaches above have many variants. In particular, several thread packages support varying degrees of customization [6,13,12]. OpenThreads [12] is a user-level thread package that provides Pthreads-style interfaces and a meta-interface that can be used to modify the behavior of the basic thread abstractions. Among other things, the meta-interface allows a client to modify the stack allocation function, to customize the queueing mechanism for thread scheduling, and to add callback functions to various thread events for tracing and debugging.

OpenThreads is a good example of a thread package that allows a reasonable degree of customization. However, most customization is done through indirection (callback functions), the main thread interfaces are still Pthreads-style, the implementation has internal state not directly visible to the client, and there is no direct support for multiprocessors.

3 Experience with Threads in the SR Run-Time System

SR is a language for writing concurrent programs, both parallel and distributed [2]. Many of SR's abstractions correspond to modern hardware, including shared memory multiprocessors and networks of workstations. Concurrency is a fundamental notion in SR; it is used for both achieving parallelism and structuring programs. The SR run-time system uses threads not only to implement concurrency at the language-level (SR *processes*), but also to implement internal functionality. For example, threads are created to handle remote invocations and an idle thread is used to monitor I/O, to handle timer events, and to detect deadlock. Therefore, good thread performance is essential to the performance of many SR programs.

Over the last few years we have ported and re-implemented portions of the SR run-time system to support a wide range of platforms, including the Mach microkernel [5], the Panda parallel run-time library [22], and on the Flux OS Toolkit [9], which facilitates direct hardware implementation. As a result of this work we developed a portable run-time system that uses Pthreads-style interfaces and a more abstract interface to remote communication [4].

Microbenchmark	Original SR	MIT PThreads	LinuxThreads
process create/destroy	9.66	115.56	541.10
semaphore requiring context switch	1.76	14.72	32.77

Table 1. Performance of SR processes and synchronization implemented with Pthread Libraries. The test machine is a Pentium 166Mhz running Linux 2.0.24. All times are in microseconds

By using a Pthreads-style interface we gained portability, but we also introduced overhead, especially with respect to thread creation and context switching. Table 1 presents the benchmark results for some uses of key language-level mechanisms. It shows the performance of the mechanisms in the original implementation of SR, which has a custom user-level thread system and two Pthread libraries: MIT PThreads [21] (a user-level implementation), and Linux-Threads [15] (a kernel-level implementation). These microbenchmarks are based on a set of benchmarks designed to evaluate the performance of SR's concurrency mechanisms [3].

In addition, we had to give up scheduling control as well as some aspects of SR's semantics due to the inability to support thread cancellation[1]. Because Pthreads-style packages do not expose the global state of threads, we had to implement extra bookkeeping to keep track of ready threads, blocked threads, and internal run-time system threads. We also ran into problems with SR's idle thread. In the original implementation, the idle thread runs when no other threads are ready to run. As noted earlier, the idle thread is used to help detect if the running program is in local and global deadlock (distributed). We were using Solaris threads, and priorities did not work as expected. Therefore, we ran the idle thread periodically. This introduced two problems. First, the idle thread ran needlessly when there were ready threads. Second, to reduce the cost of running the idle thread too frequently we used a longer period. The longer the period, the longer it took to detect global deadlock.

4   Implementation Issues for Threads and Run-Time Systems

Based on our experience with SR and the evaluation of other language run-time systems — such as Kaffe [25], a free Java virtual machine — and several thread packages, we have identified several implementation issues that can affect both performance and functionality. Below, we outline the key issues.

4.1   Thread Control Blocks

The run-time systems for both SR and Kaffe have the notion of a *thread control block* (TCB). The TCB encapsulates language specific information about a thread as well as information for scheduling and blocking. For example, SR processes (threads) execute in the context of an SR resource (a dynamic module), therefore the SR TCB encodes the owning resource in addition to other language-specific fields (see Figure 1 for a partial listing of the SR TCB). Several fields in the TCB are also dedicated to scheduling the thread, such as a priority field, queue pointers, and a stack pointer. The Kaffe virtual machine [25] has a similar TCB layout.

Two observations can be made. First, run-time systems that employ custom user-level threads encode scheduling information inside the TCB. Adding new or different scheduling functionality generally will require modification to the TCB. For example, MultiSR, a multiprocessor version of SR [24], adds a stack lock to the TCB. Second, if a Pthreads-style thread package is used, then some thread state is hidden and a run-time system has to maintain its own thread state. Therefore, two different TCBs are required: one for the run-time system and one for thread package. For example, the SR run-time system needs to keep track of blocked threads, thus two queues are used: one for the run-time

---

[1] Most operating systems vendors now support Pthread cancellation. However, most Pthreads-style libraries still do not support general thread cancellation.

```
struct tcb_st {                 /* process control block */

    enum pr_type ptype;         /* type of process */
    enum in_type itype;         /* type of invocation if a PROC */
    char *pname;                /* proc name, or "body" or "final" */
    char *locn;                 /* current source location */
    int priority;               /* process priority */
    Sem wait;                   /* sem for initial completion */

    Ptr    stack;               /* process context and stack */
    Mutex stack_mutex;          /* is the stack free yet? */

    int status;                 /* process status */
    Procq *blocked_on;          /* list process is blocked on */
    Bool should_die;            /* is someone trying to kill this? */
    Sem waiting_killer;         /* if so, is blocked on this */

    Rinst res;                  /* resource process belongs to */
    ...
}
```

Fig. 1. Partial thread control block for SR

system and one for the thread package. Not only are queues duplicated, but both queues will require separate locks when running on a multiprocessor (see Figure 2). Similarly, in Kaffe, thread groups are used to keep track of collections of threads for combined operations. The two TCBs will also have to be related, so some form of thread-specific data is required to associate the run-time system's TCB with its corresponding thread in the thread package. This creates a level of indirection to the language-specific TCB information.

4.2   Context Switching

As described in Section 3, basic thread performance can have significant impact on the performance of programs written in concurrent languages. Many thread packages and run-time systems use the same context switch code for different types of targets (e.g., uniprocessors and multiprocessors). While this may lead to better portability, the resulting run-time systems for certain targets will exhibit less than optimal performance.

The original SR implementation uses *direct* context switch to pass control from one thread to another. The direct switch simply saves the register state and stack pointer of the current thread and then restores the register state and stack pointer of the new thread. However, in MultiSR, when a thread blocks, two context switches are required to prevent a race condition involving the blocking thread's stack. An intermediate thread with its own stack is used to unlock the

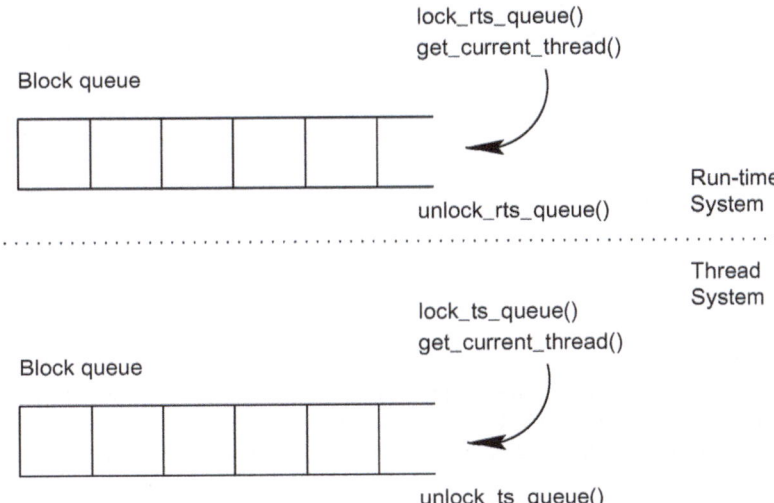

Fig. 2. Duplication in thread control block queues. Because a language run-time system does not have access to the thread state of a Pthreads-style library, the run-time system must duplicate some of the thread system's functionality. In this case, the run-time system is keeping track of where a thread is blocked. **get_current_thread()** returns a handle that is used to relate the current thread to the run-time system TCB. The TCB is then queued. On a multiprocessor, this operation must be protected by locks. The same operation is also carried out in the thread system.

blocking thread's stack and to switch to a new thread. Thus every thread switch requires two context switches (see Figure 3). A simple SR microbenchmark illustrates this cost. On a 133Mhz Pentium, a thread switch caused by blocking on a semaphore takes 2.18 microseconds with uniprocessor switching and 2.80 microseconds with multiprocessor switching, a 28% increase. The same benchmark on a 50Mhz Sparc 20 requires 13.74 microseconds and 19.28 microseconds, a 40% increase. For these benchmarks we turned off spinlocks.

By using a *preswitch* approach, in which code for the blocking thread is executed on the stack of the new thread, as used in QuickThreads [14], the second context switch for the multiprocessor thread switch can be eliminated. Keppel also describes several other techniques for efficient context switching in different settings in [14]. Additional considerations include preemptive versus non-preemptive scheduling and lock holding across context switches. The important point is that different targets require different context switch code for optimal performance, but most thread packages do not offer a choice.

4.3   Scheduling and Synchronization

Researchers have long recognized the need for application specific synchronization and scheduling [6]. Likewise, language run-time systems have special synchronization needs. For example the SR run-time system does not directly need

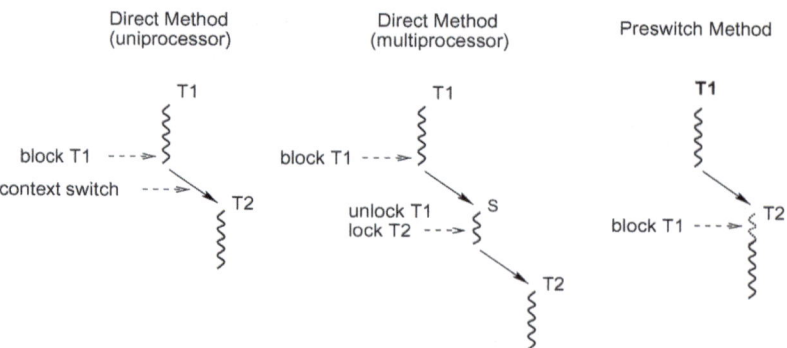

Fig. 3. Context switching methods. The direct method switches saves T1's state then restores T2's state. The preswitch method saves T1's state, switches to T2's stack, then runs a function on behalf of T1. After the function returns, T2's state is restored

support for condition variables. Instead, blocking is achieved with low-level queue operations and semaphores based on these operations. Rather than introducing a level of indirection by forcing the SR run-time system to use condition variables, it makes more sense to support SR's synchronization as directly as possible based on target primitives. For example, a `fetch-and-add` instruction can be used to implement fast semaphores.

Language run-time systems can also benefit from custom scheduling. For example, a run-time system can directly schedule threads to handle incoming network requests to reduce latency. Also, a language run-time system can schedule threads based on run-time knowledge to take advantage of processor affinity on a multiprocessor.

5   The Mezcla Thread Framework

To address the issues outlined in the previous section, we have designed a framework for generating specialized thread systems that tightly integrate language-specific thread data and operations with a particular target platform. In addition, the framework supports custom synchronization and scheduling. We are not introducing new mechanisms into Mezcla. Instead, we are using an intermediate form and target specifications to take advantage of proven techniques that work well for different thread operations on different targets. Figure 4 illustrates the general organization of the Mezcla thread framework. Below we expand on some of the details.

5.1   Thread Control Blocks

To reduce duplication in terms of time and space, Mezcla helps generate specialized TCBs. The idea is to construct TCBs that contain just the right amount of information needed for the language run-time system and for thread scheduling.

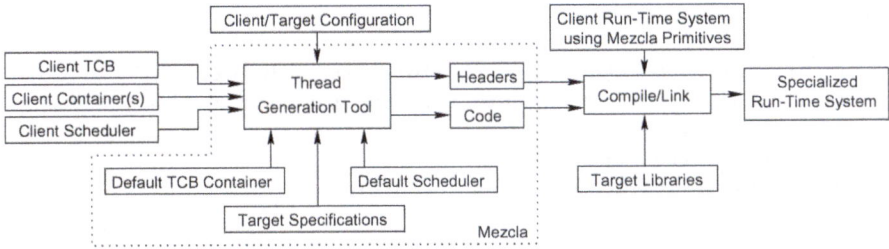

Fig. 4. The Mezcla Thread Framework

A Mezcla TCB has three components: (1) the target context fields, (2) the TCB container fields, and (3) client supplied TCB fields.

The target fields depends on configuration information provided by the client. For example, a QuickThreads context is represented by a single pointer. A stack pointer is also used for stack reuse and deallocation. For `setjmp/longjmp`, the context is a `jmp_buf`. If the target is a high-level thread system, then the context will be a handle to a thread from a target thread package.

The TCB container fields are used in storing TCBs. A common implementation is simply a `next` pointer for a simple queue. The client can specify the container fields directly, or use the Mezcla-supplied defaults. Client-supplied TCB fields are provided by the client, and thus only have meaning in the language run-time system.

5.2 Thread Primitives

Mezcla provides the client with a small set of primitives that can be mapped to different target environments. The key thread primitives appear in Figure 5. The main TCB functions provide an interface to the client for creating and scheduling threads. The locking functions are used for low-level synchronization on multiprocessors and the container functions are used to store TCBs (e.g., in block queues or a ready queue).

5.3 Thread Generation

Currently, the thread generation tool is very straightforward. It collects the appropriate TCB fields based on the configuration file (see Figure 6). Appropriate code is generated that integrates the specialized TCB into the implementation of the thread primitives for a particular target (see Figure 7). If the client supplies container functions, they are made available to the thread primitives, otherwise defaults are used. By using client-supplied containers, a run-time system can implement custom scheduling.

Currently the specified TCB container is used for both blocking threads and for the ready queue (used for scheduling). We plan to enhance the framework to allow multiple types of containers. This will allow the client to generate different

```
/* TCB Functions */

int mtf_init(mtf_tcb *main, mtf_tcb *idle, mtf_tcb *exit);
int mtf_tcb_init(mtf_tcb *tcb, mtf_tcb_func func, void *arg);
int mtf_tcb_yield(void);
void mtf_tcb_exit(void);
int mtf_tcb_block(mtf_tcb_container *container);
mtf_tcb *mtf_tcb_self(void);
int mtf_tcb_equal(mtf_tcb *tcb1, mtf_tcb *tcb2);

/* TCB Locking Functions */

void mtf_tcb_lock(mtf_tcb_lock *lock);
void mtf_tcb_unlock(mtf_tcb_lock *lock);

/* TCB Container Functions */

int mtf_tcb_container_init(mtf_tcb_container *container);
int mtf_tcb_put(mtf_tcb *tcb, mtf_tcb_container *container);
mtf_tcb *mtf_tcb_get(mtf_tcb_container *container);
```

Fig. 5. The Mezcla thread primitives

types of blocking policies for different situations. For example, a mutex-like lock may use a simple FCFS queue, while the ready queue may use multi-level queue for priority scheduling.

We are currently targeting QuickThreads [14] and context switch code from the original SR implementation [24] in non-preemptive uniprocessor and multi-processor environments. Also, we are working on a retargetable locking policy, I/O integration, and Pthreads-style emulation that will allow a run-time system to incorporate and schedule foreign threaded code (e.g., communication libraries).

5.4 Performance

To demonstrate the feasibility of the Mezcla thread framework, we have implemented a simple prototype based on the design outlined in the previous sections. To get an idea of the potential benefit of generating specialized thread systems, we wrote a benchmark that performs a thread block operation similar to the same operation found in concurrent run-time systems. Table 2 shows the cost of the block operation for MIT Pthreads, OpenThreads, and Mezcla Threads. For both MIT Pthreads and OpenThreads, we had to duplicate the queue operations as described in Section 4.1. Although part of the difference in performance is due to the added cost of duplication, both MIT Pthreads and OpenThreads also have functionality not found in Mezcla threads.

```
# TCB (thread control block) fields
tcb {
        int id;
        char name[256];
}

# TCB container fields
tcb_container {
        struct tcb *next;
}

# TCB blocking
tcb_block {
        mtf_tcb_container_put(mtf_tcb_self(), container)
}
```

Fig. 6. Client thread specification

Microbenchmark	MIT PThreads	OpenThreads	Mezcla
thread blocking	46	10.7	2.5

Table 2. Performance of thread blocking using different thread systems. Both MIT Pthreads and OpenThreads require TCB and TCB queue duplication. The test machine is a Pentium 133Mhz running Linux 2.0.24. All times are in microseconds

We incorporated Mezcla threads into the SR run-time system to demonstrate the benefits of supporting multiple types of context switching methods. Figure 8 shows the performance of two common thread operations in SR: process creation and process blocking on a semaphore. In both benchmarks, Mezcla threads use preswitch context switching method instead of the direct method to achieve better performance.

Figure 9 compares the performance of the traveling salesman problem running on the original SR implementation and on an implementation using Mezcla. We achieved about a 12% improvement in performance.

6   Conclusions

In this paper, we have evaluated several current techniques for implementing threads in concurrent run-time systems. We also described our experiences with threads in the SR concurrent programming language. Based on this work, we designed the Mezcla thread framework, which allows a language implementor to create specialized user-level thread systems. Our early performance results are

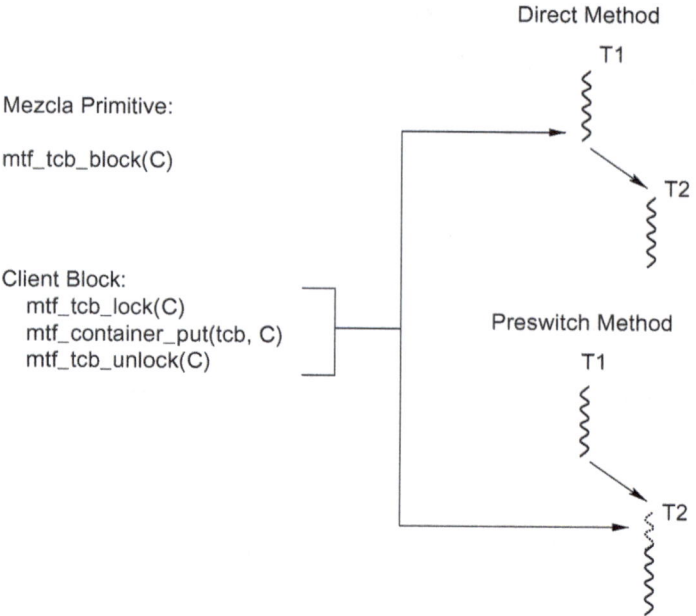

Fig. 7. Specialization using code templates

promising. We are concurrently refining the framework and integrating it into Kaffe [25], a free Java virtual machine.

References

1. T. E. Anderson, B. N. Bershad, E. D. Lazowska, and H. M. Levy. Scheduler activations: Effective kernel support for the user-level management of parallelism. *ACM Transactions on Computer Systems*, 10(1):53–70, February 1992.
2. G. R. Andrews and R. A. Olsson. *The SR Programming Language: Concurrency in Practice*. The Benjamin/Cummings Publishing Co., Redwood City, California, 1993.
3. M. S. Atkins and R. A. Olsson. Performance of multi-tasking and synchronization mechanisms in the programming language SR. *Software – Practice and Experience*, 18(9):879–895, September 1988.
4. G. D. Benson and R. A. Olsson. A portable run-time system for the SR concurrent programming language. In *Proceedings of the Workshop on Runtime Systems for Parallel Programming*, pages 21–30, Geneva, Switzerland, April 1997. Held in conjunction with the 11th International Parallel Processing Symposium (IPPS'97).
5. G.D. Benson and R.A. Olsson. *The Design of Microkernel Support for the SR Concurrent Programming Language*, chapter 17, pages 227–240. Languages, Compilers, and Run-Time Systems for Scalable Computers. Kluwer Academic Publishing, Boston, MA, 1996. B. K. Szymanski and B. Sinharoy (editors).
6. B. Bershad, E. Lazowska, and H. Levy. Presto: A system for object oriented parallel programming. *Software: Practice and Experience*, 18(8), August 1988.

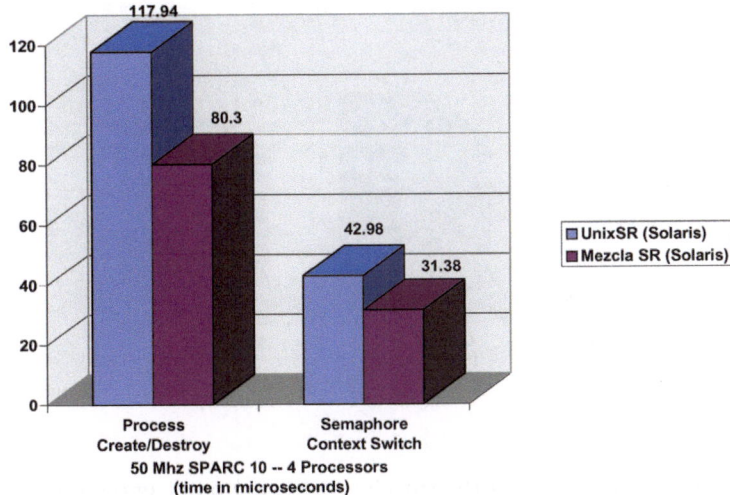

Fig. 8. The performance of Mezcla Threads on a multiprocessor

7. R. Bhoedjang, T. Rühl, R. Hofman, K. Langendoen, H. Bal, and F. Kaashoek. Panda: A portable platform to support parallel programming languages. In *Symposium on Experience with Distributed and Multiprocessor Systems IV*, pages 213–226, San Diego, California, September 1993. USENIX.
8. E. Cooper and R. Draves. C threads. Technical Report CMU-CS-88-154, Carnegie Mellon University, Department of Computer Science, 1988.
9. B. Ford, G. Back, G. Benson, J. Lepreau, O. Shivers, and A. Lin. The Flux OS Toolkit: A substrate for kernel and language research. In *Proceedings of the Sixteenth Symposium on Operating Systems Principles*, pages 38–52, St. Malo, France, October 1997.
10. I. Foster, C. Kesselman, and S. Tuecke. The Nexus approach to integrating multithreading and communication. *Journal of Parallel and Distributed Computing*, 37(1):70–82, August 1996.
11. J. Gosling, B. Joy, and G. Steele. *The Java Language Specification.* Addison-Wesley, 1996.
12. M. Haines. On designing lightweight threads for substrate software. In *The Proceeding of the Annual Technical Conference on UNIX and Advanced Computing Systems*, Anaheim, California, January 1997. USENIX.
13. L. V. Kale, Milind Bhandarkar, Narain Jagathesan, Sanjeev Krishnan, and Joshua Yelon. Converse: An interoperable framework for parallel programming. In *Proceedings of the 10th International Parallel Processing Symposium*, pages 212–217, April 1996.
14. D. Keppel. Tools and techniques for building fast portable threads package. Technical Report UW-CSE-93-05-06, University of Washington, Department of Computer Science and Engineering, May 1993.
15. X. Leroy. *LinuxThreads*, 1996. http://sunsite.unc.edu/pub/Linux/docs/faqs/Threads-FAQ/html/.

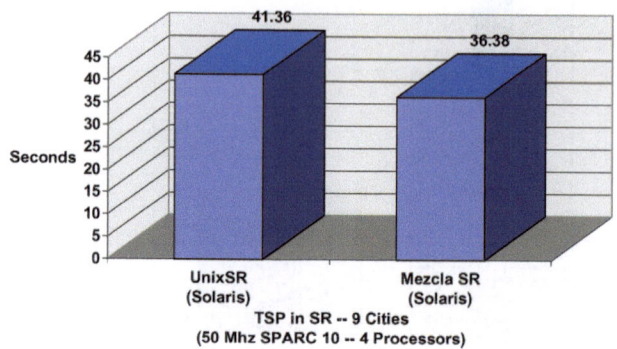

Fig. 9. The performance of the traveling salesman problem on a multiprocessor

16. B. D. Marsh, M. L. Scott, T. J. LeBlanc, and E. P. Markatos. First-class user-level threads. In *Proceedings of the Thirteenth Symposium on Operating Systems Principles*, pages 110–121, Pacific Grove, CA, October 1991.
17. B. Mukherjee. A portable and configurable threads package. Technical Report GIT-ICS-91/02, College of Computing, Georgia Institute of Technology, Atlanta, Georgia, 1991. Also appears in Proceedings of Sun User's Group Technical Conference, pages 101–112.
18. B. Mukherjee, G. Eisenhauer, and K. Ghosh. A machine independent interface for lightweight threads. Technical Report GIT-CC-93/53, College of Computing, Georgia Institute of Technology, Atlanta, Georgia, 1991.
19. G. Nelson, editor. *Systems Programming with Modula-3*. Prentice Hall, Englewood Cliffs, New Jersey, 1991.
20. M. L. Powell, S. R. Kleiman, S. Barton, D. Shah, D. Stein, and M. Weeks. SunOS multi-thread architecture. In *Proceedings of the Winter USENIX Conference*, Dallas, TX, 1991.
21. C. Provenzano. *MIT PThreads*, 1996. http://www.mit.edu:8001/people/proven/pthreads.html.
22. T. Rühl, H. Bal, G. D. Benson, R. Bhoedjang, and K. G. Langendoen. Experience with a portability layer for implementing parallel programming systems. In *Proceedings of the International Conference on Parallel and Distributed Processing Techniques and Applications*, pages 1477–1488, Sunnyvale, CA, August 1996.
23. E. G. Sirer, P. Pardyak, and B. N. Bershad. Strands: An efficient and extensible thread management architecture. Technical Report UW-CSE-97-09-01, University of Washington, Department of Computer Science and Engineering, 1997.
24. Gregg Townsend and Dave Bakken. *Porting the SR Programming Language*. Department of Computer Science, University of Arizona, 1994. From the SR distribution: http://www.cs.arizona.edu/sr/.
25. Tim Wilkinson. Kaffe - a free virtual machine to run java code. http://www.kaffe.org/.

Load Balancing with
Migrant Lightweight Threads*

David Cronk[1] and Piyush Mehrotra[2]

[1] Computer Science Department, Williamsburg, VA 23187 cronk@cs.wm.edu
[2] ICASE, NASA Langley Research Center, Hampton, VA 23681 pm@icase.edu

Abstract. The use of lightweight threads in a distributed memory environment is becoming common. As distributed lightweight threads have become popular, there has been increased interest in migrating threads across process boundaries. One possible use of thread migration is to perform dynamic load balancing. This paper introduces our implementation of a dynamic load balancing mechanism using thread migration as the means for load redistribution. We provide a brief description of the thread migration mechanism and a detailed description of the load balancing layer. We also present the performance of this load balancing mechanism on a variety of parallel applications.

1 Introduction

As distributed lightweight threads become more popular [1,8,10], the idea of mobile lightweight threads gains momentum [2,3,4,5,6,12,13]. If a multi-threaded application exhibits load imbalance, thread migration is a natural mechanism for balancing the load. When designing and implementing a load balancing mechanism based on thread migration there are several factors which must be considered.

In many distributed applications it is difficult to determine where the majority of work must be performed. This can lead to some of the processors finishing their work quickly and becoming idle, while other processors continue to have a significant amount of work to perform. This situation is known as load imbalance, and can diminish performance since idle processors are not contributing to the computation. When a load imbalance is encountered, it is often advantageous to move work from the overloaded processors to the idle processors. This moving of work is known as load balancing. Load balancing can improve overall execution time by allowing processors that would otherwise be idle to contribute to the computation. Different applications require different load balancing schemes. While some applications perform optimally when the load is distributed nearly evenly across all processors, others simply require that no processor be idle while others have sufficient work to perform.

---

* This work supported in part by the National Aeronautics and Space Administration under NASA Contract No. NAS1-97046, while the authors were in residence at ICASE, NASA Langley Research Center, Hampton VA, 23681.

D. O'Hallaron (Ed.): LCR'98, LNCS 1511, pp. 153–166, 1998.
© Springer-Verlag Berlin Heidelberg 1998

An important component of any load balancing scheme is the decision making phase. This includes the decisions of: when is a load redistribution necessary, what processors gain and lose work, and which load units are redistributed. These decisions are application dependent. That is, decision making criteria which perform well for one application may perform poorly for other applications. Therefore, any load balancing package which is to be used with a variety of applications must allow customization of the decision making phase.

In a multi-threaded application, a natural choice for units of work is the thread. This translates to thread migration being a natural choice as a means of load redistribution. That is, when a load redistribution is necessary, threads can be migrated between processors.

Thread migration allows a thread residing in one process to move to another process, possibly on a different processor. While there are different models of thread migration, our implementation allows threads to migrate at arbitrary suspension points during execution. When a thread migrates from one processor to another, its state and all associated data is moved to the destination processor. Additionally, our system supports thread migration in the presence of user-level pointers. When the migrant thread resumes on the remote processor, it continues execution as if nothing has changed, providing seamless execution as viewed by the user.

This paper discusses an implementation of dynamic load balancing using thread migration in a distributed memory environment. The system we describe here is built on top of *Chant* [10,11], which is a distributed lightweight threads package we have developed for supporting point-to-point communication between threads.

The remainder of this paper is organized as follows: Section 2 briefly describes the design of Chant while Section 3 briefly discusses our thread migration implementation. Section 4 discusses our load balancing layer including our user interface and customized load balancing. Section 5 provides performance results based on a variety of applications and in Section 6 we present some brief conclusions and future directions.

2   Chant.

Chant [10,11] is a distributed lightweight threads package we have developed for supporting point-to-point communication between threads. It was designed and implemented as a runtime system with a user interface using MPI like and Pthreads like calls.

Chant is designed as a layered system (as shown in Figure 1) where the Chant System interface makes standard communication and thread package calls for efficient communication and thread manipulation. On top of this communication and threads system interface is a layer supporting point-to-point communication. In standard communication packages such as MPI, there is no concept of any entities besides processes. This means messages can be sent only to processes, not directly to entities such as threads. Chant is designed such that a thread in

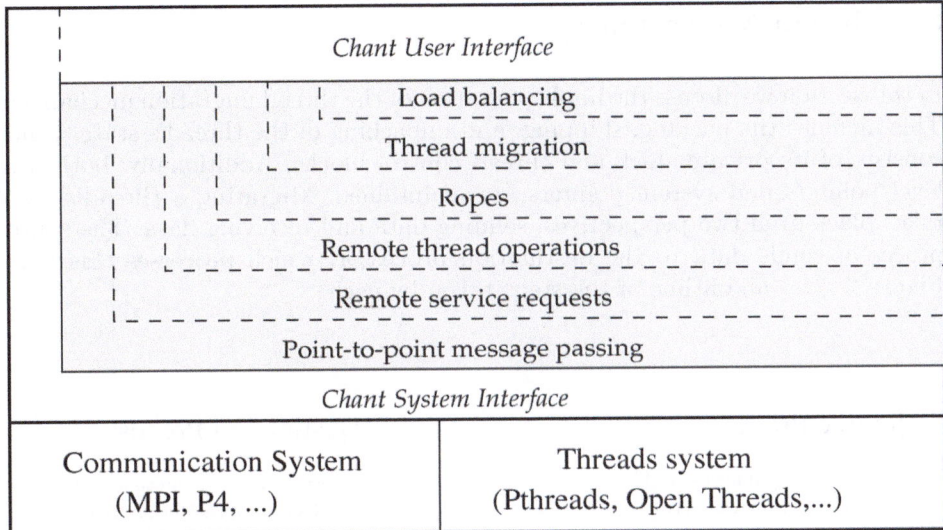

Fig. 1. Chant runtime layers and interfaces

one address space can send a message directly to a thread in another address space, with no intermediate processing of the message. On top of this layer is the Remote Service Request (RSR) layer, where one process can instruct another process to do some work. This layer is implemented by creating a system thread which simply checks for RSR messages, processes them when they arrive, and yields the processor to another thread when there are no requests to fulfill. This system thread is known as the *RSR server*.

On top of this RSR layer is built the layer for remote thread operations. This layer uses the RSR server to perform various remote thread operations such as remote thread creation. Finally there is the ropes layer which supports collective operations and indexed communication.

We use MPI and Open Threads as our communication and thread libraries. Open Threads [9] is a threads package developed by Matthew Haines at the University of Wyoming. Open Threads was chosen because it allows the user deep access into the threads system, allowing easy manipulation of the threads and the run queue. This allows us to implement thread migration and to manipulate threads for load balancing without making changes to the thread system itself.

Off the shelf threads packages use a Thread Control Block (TCB) associated with each thread. This TCB is used for keeping track of the thread's state and some other thread specific information. Since Chant also has some thread specific information which it must maintain, the use of an off the shelf threads package (as opposed to creating our own threads package) necessitates the use of two TCBs: the one associated with Open Threads and Chant's own TCB.

3   Thread Migration

In this section we discuss the implementation of the thread migration mechanism. This includes the packing, shipping, and unpacking of the thread's state, which consists of its private stack and thread control blocks. Additionally, both user level pointers and system pointers are maintained. Migrating a thread's state takes place from two perspectives, sending data and receiving data. The source processor sends data to the destination processor, which processes this data. Figure 2 gives an outline of the steps taken by each.

Source Process	Destination Process
Send size of thread's stack	Receive size of thread's stack
Send Open Threads TCB	Receive Open Threads TCB
Send Chant TCB	Receive Chant TCB
Send Thread's stack	Receive thread's stack
Receive thread's new local thread id	Send new local thread id to source
Inform other processors of new location of thread	Update pointers
Forward messages intended for thread	Repost outstanding receives

Fig. 2. Steps taken to migrate a thread

The source processor first sends a message informing the destination processor that a migrant thread is about to arrive. This message contains the size of the migrant thread's stack. The source processor then sends the Open Threads TCB followed by the Chant TCB. To complete the actual migration, the source processor sends the migrant thread's stack to the destination processor. Thus, the source processor sends four messages to the destination processor to migrate a thread. After the thread has been migrated, the source processor receives, from the destination processor, the new local thread *id* of the migrant thread. This new thread *id* is sent to all the processors allowing each processor to update the thread's location for future communication. Finally, the source processor leaves a stub of the migrant thread for the purpose of forwarding messages.

The destination processor receives a message letting it know a thread is about to arrive, including the size of said thread's stack. The destination processor then allocates memory for the arriving thread's stack, its underlying thread package's TCB, and its Chant TCB. Next the two TCBs are received and the fields updated as needed (some fields have processor specific data which must be updated to reflect the new processor on which the thread resides). Next the thread's stack is received from the source processor and stored in the newly allocated memory. Some bookkeeping is required to handle pointers and communication. Finally, the thread is added to the run queue of the destination processor. When it gets control of the processor, the thread will resume by executing the same instruction it would have executed had there been no migration, making the migration seamless.

A more detailed description of the implementation can be found in [6,7].

4   Load Balancing

In Chant, the RSR layer is implemented by creating a system thread, on each processor, which simply checks for RSR messages, processes them when they arrive, and yields the processor to another thread when there are no requests to fulfill. This system thread is known as the *RSR server*.

Our load balancing mechanism uses this *RSR server* to carry out load balancing operations. When users turn load balancing on, they specify how often the *RSR server* should attempt to perform load balancing. Since the situation where load balancing is not necessary often indicates a fairly stable system, this frequency may vary. The user can specify that the *RSR server* never attempts load balancing (on a processor by processor basis), or attempts load balancing every time it gains control of the processor. Alternatively, this frequency can vary linearly or exponentially. A linear variation means that load balancing is attempted every *nth* time the *RSR server* gets on the processor, where n starts at 1 and increases by one each time a load redistribution is not necessary. The parameter n is reset to 1 following an actual load redistribution. An exponential variation means that load balancing is attempted every *nth* time the *RSR server* gets on the processor, where n starts at 1 and doubles each time a load redistribution is not necessary. The parameter n is reset to 1 following an actual load redistribution.

When the *RSR server* gets control of the processor, it checks to see when load balancing was last performed. If it has been long enough (using the frequency discussed above) the *RSR server* makes a call to the load balancing function. If load balancing is actually performed it resets the frequency counter. If no load balancing is performed, the *RSR server* uses the user defined frequency to indicate when load balancing should be attempted again.

Different applications perform better under different load balancing schemes. That is, a load balancing scheme that performs well for one application, may perform poorly for another application. For this reason, our primary goal while designing the load balancing layer was to provide support for building customized load balancing systems tailored to specific applications. This has been accomplished by providing a default load balancing implementation which can be re-written by the user. The level of customization is left to the user, from nearly no user support, to a near 100% user implementation.

The load balancing layer is itself built with a layered approach, consisting of three sub-layers. The bottom sub-layer consists of lower level load balancing routines. These routines range from gathering state information to manipulating the run queue. The middle layer consists of load balancing commands. These commands either determine which threads to move where, or instruct the system to move specific threads to specific processors. The commands which are used for decision making can be customized by the user, while the commands which instruct the system to move threads are, by their nature, statically implemented. These commands make use of the lower level routines to make decisions and to move threads. The top-most sub-layer is the actual load balancing function. This is the function which is called by the system whenever it is to attempt load balancing. We provide a default load balancing function, but allow the user to register a customized load balancing function which may make use of the two lower layers. These layers are described in greater detail below.

4.1   Lower Level Load Balancing Routines

The lower level load balancing routines are used to set system parameters, manipulate the system, obtain and manipulate thread characteristics, obtain global state information, and manipulate the run queue.

Set System Parameters One of the most important of these routines is the one that allows load balancing to be switched on and offdynamically. This may be important for a computation which goes through phases, some of which require load balancing and some of which do not. One example would be a rendering algorithm that renders multiple images. In many such applications, the rendering stage is the only one which requires load balancing. In such a situation the user may turn load balancing on prior to rendering an image, turn it off once the image has been rendered, and turn load balancing back on when the next image is ready to be rendered.

When load balancing is turned on the user must supply three parameters. These are upper and lower thresholds and a frequency for attempting load balancing. The upper and lower thresholds are used by the default load balancing function to determine if a load redistribution is needed, but they are also available to any user supplied implementations. The frequency, as described above, is used by the system to determine when load balancing should be attempted.

Another routine which sets system parameters defines the load balancing domain, i.e., the set of processors to be involved in load balancing operations. This domain can include all the processors within the computation, or any subset of processors. This routine is called on each processor in the computation and different processors may have different load balancing domains. This domain is used for any subsequent global operations.

Manipulating the System There are two routines provided for manipulating the system. The first allows synchronization of all processors within the calling processor's load balancing domain. This routine informs all the processors within the domain to stop computation and participate in a load balancing phase. This may be useful when the load balancing domain is small and it is beneficial to have quick responses to remote queries. It may also be necessary if the load balancing scheme depends on the state of the system (within the domain) not changing during a load balancing phase.

The other routine which fits this category is the one that actually migrates threads from one processor to another. This routine takes a thread which is not on the run queue, and migrates the entire thread state to the specified processor. Upon return the thread has been added to the run queue of the destination processor. The caller must also, however, return the thread to the run queue on the source processor, so the underlying thread system can do some cleaning up following the migration.

Thread Characteristics One important characteristic of a thread is its migratability. The user may create certain special threads which should remain on the the same processor throughout its lifetime. Chant provides for this by allowing the user to specify, at thread creation time, if a thread is migratable or non-migratable. A non-migratable thread will never migrate to another processor. However, there may also be a situation where a thread should be allowed to migrate at certain times and not be allowed to migrate at other times. Thus, we provide routines for checking the migratability of thread (so one never attempts to migrate a non-migratable thread), along with routines for temporarily marking a thread as non-migratable and returning it to a migratable state.

Another important characteristic is how much a thread contributes to the overall load of of its processor. Some threads are known to have more work to perform than others. Thus, Chant provides for a thread's load to be specified at the time of its creation. Additionally, a thread may have a specified amount of work to do, such as a certain number of iterations. As the thread performs work it is known how much work it has left to do. For these reasons we provide routines for checking the amount of load threads contribute at any given time as well as a routine for altering the amount of load a thread is contributing.

Finally, communication patterns may affect the decision of which threads to migrate where. A load balancing system may wish to minimize communication overhead at the same time as it attempts to balance the load. That is, if thread A is doing a lot of communication with threads residing on the same processor as it resides, it is a poor choice for migration. If, however, thread A is doing a lot of communication with processor X, it may be a good candidate for migration to X. Therefore, we provide routines for returning the communication history of threads i.e., the number of messages which have been sent to each processor in the computation.

Global State Information There are also low level routines for returning global state information. This includes the local loads of each processor in either the domain or the entire computation. It also includes returning the communication histories of these processors.

Manipulating the Run Queue The final type of low level routines are those that manipulate the run queue. We provide routines for getting a thread from the run queue. This includes getting the thread from the front of the run queue as well as getting a specific thread from the run queue. Threads can be specified either as an offset from the front of the run queue or with a pointer to the Chant TCB. Additionally, threads can be put back on the run queue. However, threads can only be added to the end of the queue.

4.2   Load Balancing Commands

There are two types of load balancing commands: those that can be customized by the user and those which are statically implemented. Among these statically implemented commands are commands for moving threads to different processors. For these commands, threads are specified along with the processors to which these threads should be migrated.

Others of these types of commands instruct a processors to send specific amounts of work to specific processors. This can either be such that the processor is instructed to send different amounts of work to different processors, or it can be a processor requesting a certain amount of work from another processor. While these commands themselves cannot be customized by the user, their effects can. The commands simply inform a processor how to redistribute its load, but it is up to the specified processor to decide how this load redistribution should be carried out. These decisions are made by calling some other load balancing commands, which can be customized by the user.

One of these customizable commands determines which threads to migrate to a specific processor, based on a specified amount of work to be moved This command would be called by a processor that has had a certain amount of work requested by another processor, as mentioned above. The default implementation simply traverses the run queue, choosing all migratable threads until the requested load has been reached. However, a user may wish to use a more sophisticated approach. For this reason, the user may register a customized routine, which would be called in place of the default impementation.

Another, related, customizable command, decides which threads to migrate to various other processors, based on different amounts of work needing to be sent to different processors. This would be called by the processor when a specific load redistribution is requested. The default implementation simply traverses the run queue, choosing all the migratable threads until enough work has been selected to satisfy the request. Again, a more sophisticated approach may be desired, and the user can register a customized routine.

A final customizable command is called by an underloaded processor. This command decides from which processors, how much work should be requested. The default implementation simply polls all the processors in its domain, for their current load. It then chooses the most heavily loaded processor and requests work from it. The amount of work requested is the sum of all the loads divided by the total number of processors. Again, this command can be replaced by the user.

4.3   The Load Balancing Function

As mentioned above, the load balancing function is called by the system anytime it attempts to balance the system load. We provide a very simple default implementation for this function. If the local load (that is, the load of the processor calling the load balancing function) is below a user defined lower threshold, the customizable command described above is called to decide from which processors how much work is requested. If the user has not registered a customized command, this will be carried out as described above. If, however, the user has customized this command, the default load balancing function will call the user supplied command and be returned a list of processors and an amount of work to be requested from each. These results will be passed to a non-customizable command which will make the actual requests.

Thus, it is possible for the user to use the default load balancing function while customizing the load balancing commands. It is also possible for the user to customize the load balancing function while using the default load balancing commands. Finally, it is possible for the user to replace the default load balancing function and any or all of the customizable load balancing commands. The customized commands can make use the lower level load balancing routines and the other load balancing commands. By allowing such customization we hope to enable users to tailor the load balancing layer to specific applications to a degree of their choosing, from almost no customization to complete customization.

5   Performance

This section presents the performance of our system both in terms of overhead and in terms of overall execution times for a small test suite. We present the time it takes to migrate threads with varying sized stacks as well as the time it takes to forward messages following a migration. Finally, we tested our default load balancing mechanism on three applications: An artificially unbalanced traveling salesman problem, an adaptive quadrature problem using Simpson's algorithm, and a parallel volume renderer.

We ran our tests on a dedicated network of four Sun SPARCstation 20 workstations, model 612 (dual 60 MHz SuperSPARC processors). Each machine was running Solaris 2.6 with full patches. Machine *P0* was the OS server for the rest of the machines, all of which were auto clients. The experiment was set up with only a single user process running on each processor, so that the tests would not be affected by any other processes except normal system services. The machines were interconnected via a private FDDI Network and thus there was no external network traffic. We used the MPICH version 1.0.13 implementation of MPI with debug flags turned off during compilation.

5.1   Thread Migration Performance

Two sets of tests were conducted for the purpose of comparison. The first set of tests used MPI primitives with no multi-threading. In this set of tests we varied the size of a message being exchanged and measured the average message passing times. The second set of tests used threads with stack sizes corresponding to the sizes of the messages used in the first set of tests. This set of tests measured the average amount of time it took to take the thread off the run queue, migrate it to another processor, and put it back on the run queue.

Table 1 shows the results of these tests where *Size* is the size of both the message and the thread's stack. *Communication* is the average time to send a message of size m using MPI primitives (first set of tests) while *Migration* is the average time it takes to migrate a thread with a stack of size m (second set of tests). *Overhead* is simply the difference between *Communication* and *Migration*. The times are all in milliseconds.

Size (m)	Communication	Migration	Overhead
16K	4.1	7.6	3.5
32K	8.2	12.2	4.0
64K	14.3	18.4	4.1
128K	25.7	30.5	4.8
256K	49.8	54.1	4.3

Table 1. Thread migration time (in ms) with varying sized stacks

The differences in overhead for the various sizes can be attributed to experimental fluctuation. Since the migration takes place in several steps, we tried to account for this overhead. Migration is accomplished with four messages being sent to the destination processor. These messages are: an integer indicating the size of the thread's stack, the underlying thread package's thread control block (TCB), Chant's TCB, and the thread's stack. The underlying TCB has a size of 72 bytes while Chant's TCB has a size of 4400 bytes. The size of the Chant TCB is dependent upon the maximum number of processors used in the application and the maximum number of message tags that can be used for message passing. For these experiments the values were 8 and 100 respectively. These first three messages together take approximately 3.0 ms to send.

These numbers show that other than message transfer overhead, which cannot be avoided, there is very little overhead associated with the thread migration. If we could send the two TCBs as a single message we could reduce this overhead somewhat. The small additional overhead (ranging from 0.5 ms to 1.8 ms) can be attributed to table traversal for updating pointers and a list traversal for reposting pending receive operations. This overhead is only on the destination processor.

5.2 Message Forwarding Performance

The previous section only studies thread transmission overhead and overhead paid by the destination processor. This section presents the overhead associated with forwarding messages, i.e., the time it takes the source processor to forward messages to the migrant thread. These tests were run on 2, 4, and 8 processors with a varying number of messages needing to be forwarded.

	2 processors	4 processors	8 processors
No messages	5.5	8.1	13.7
1 message per proc	6.6	10.9	21.5
2 message per proc	7.8	13.6	28.6
3 message per proc	9.6	18.4	41.8
per message	+0.51	+0.64	+0.88

Table 2. Forwarding overhead and per message time (in ms.)

Table 2 shows the results of these tests where the first row is the amount of time spent when there are no messages which need to be forwarded. This is overhead associated with the forwarding algorithm itself. These numbers increase with the number of processors since each processor must be handled separately. The next three rows show the total time needed to forward all messages with 1, 2, and 3 messages per processor, respectively. The total number of messages forwarded is equal to the number of messages per processor times the number of processors. The final row indicates the average time per message for forwarding. The average amount of time it takes to forward a message increases with the number of processors. This is due to the fact that the MPI implementation we used takes longer to retrieve messages from the system buffer when there are more processors.

These times only reflect the extra time spent by the source processors. They do not take into account any effects of increased network contention or increased work on other processors. Still, these numbers show acceptable overhead associated with the forwarding algorithm and low overhead associated with the actual forwarding of the messages.

5.3   Test Applications

This section presents the overall execution times for our set of test applications. Each application has four versions:

- A sequential, non-threaded version
- A parallel non-threaded version
- A parallel multi-threaded version with no load balancing
- A parallel multi-threaded version with load balancing

TSP The first test application is an artificially unbalanced traveling salesman problem. Since we are only interested in how well our load balancing layer performs, we used a very naive algorithm, unconcerned with the relative performance of the algorithm. *Because we are concerned with the performance of the* *load balancing layer, we wanted an instance that would be significantly unbalanced.* For this reason, we created a graph which forces almost all the work to a single branch of the search tree. This causes almost all the work to be performed by a single processor in the parallel version.

Table 3 shows the results for a 13 city traveling salesman problem (TSP). The first column shows the application. The second and third columns show the time in seconds for a single processor and four processors respectively.

Implementation	1 Processor	4 Processors
Non-threaded	107.7	114.3
Multi-threaded with no load balancing	119.5	117.5
Multi-threaded with load balancing	122.4	36.9

Table 3. Execution time (in sec) for 13 city TSP

The non-threaded version runs slower on four processors due to the fact that it periodically checks to see if a message has arrived informing it of a new best solution on another processor. It does this every 10000 iterations and the comparisons alone, to see if it should check for a message, account for approximately 8.0 seconds. Timings are more consistent in the multi-threaded version because it performs a context switch every 1000 iterations, thus the single processor version incurs the comparison cost also. This table clearly shows low overhead associated with multi-threading and significant speedup achieved from load balancing.

Adaptive Quadrature The next test application is an adaptive quadrature problem using Simpson's algorithm. Again, since we are concerned with the performance of our load balancing layer, we chose a function which forces the large majority of work to be performed in the last 8th of the domain.

Implementation	1 Proc	2 Procs	4 Procs	8 Procs
Non-threaded	147.1	145.8	145.2	144.9
Multi-threaded with no load balancing	151.2	150.4	149.7	149.5
Multi-threaded with load balancing	151.9	77.0	41.1	25.0

Table 4. Execution time (in seconds) for adaptive quadrature

Table 4 shows the results for 1, 2, 4, and 8 processors. These numbers show negligible speedup for the non-threaded case with low overhead associated with the multi-threading. Once again, we see significant speedup achieved from load balancing the multi-threaded code.

Volume Rendering The final application is a volume renderer using a real life set of volume data. Though we are interested in the performance of the load balancing layer, we also want to show that the overhead does not cause performance degradation of an application which is not severely unbalanced.

Implementation	1 Proc	2 Procs	4 Procs	8 Procs
Non-threaded	364.3	185.0	115.9	62.3
Multi-threaded with no load balancing	402.2	221.8	117.5	69.0
Multi-threaded with load balancing	402.8	216.1	109.5	58.0

Table 5. Execution time (in seconds) for volume rendering

Table 5 shows the results for the volume rendering on 1, 2, 4, and 8 processors. We are still not sure why we get such poor performance for the multi-threaded implementation running on two processors. However, for four and eight processors we once again show little overhead associated with multi-threading. However, when we use load balancing, we actually show a small performance improvement for both four and eight processors. While we are pleased by this, the main result is that we did not have performance degradation associated with the load balancing layer, i.e., even for a test which is only slightly unbalanced, offering little room for improvement, the overhead associated with the load balancing layer does not exceed the benifit gained from load redistribution.

6   Conclusions and Future Work

Distributed lightweight threads have become a popular parallel programming environment. As threads have gained in popularity there has been an increased interest in mobile threads. A natural extension is using thread migration as a mechanism for dynamic load balancing.

We have implemented a simple dynamic load balancing scheme using thread migration as a means for load redistribution. We have shown that this can be done such that significant speedup can be achieved for severely unbalanced cases. Additionally, we have shown that the load balancing layer does not degrade performance for cases which are only slightly unbalanced.

In the near future we would like to run some tests with applications which are perfectly balanced, in order to further evaluate potential performance degradation associated with the load balancing. Additionally, we would like to compare the thread migration approach to some traditional load balancing methods.

References

1. Raoul Bhoedjang, Tim Rühl, Rutger Hofman, Koen Langendoen, Henri Bal, and Frans Kaashoek. Panda: A portable platform to support parallel programming languages. In *Symposium on Experiences with Distributed and Multiprocessor Systems IV*, pages 213–226, San Diego, CA, September 1993.
2. A. Black, N. Hutchinson, E. Jul, and H. Levy. Object structure in the Emerald system. In *Proceedings of the ACM Conference on Object-Oriented Programming Systems, Languages and Applications*, pages 78–86, Portland, OR, October 1986.
3. Jeremy Casas, Ravi Konuru, Steve W. Otto, Robert Prouty, and Jonathan Walpole. Adaptive load migration systems for PVM. In *Proceedings of Supercomputing*, pages 390–399, Washington D.C., November 1994. ACM/IEEE.
4. J.S. Chase, F.G. Amador, E.D. Lazowska, H.M. Levy, and R.J. Littlefield. The Amber system: Parallel programming on a network of multipocessors. In *ACM Symposium on Operating System Principles*, December 1989.
5. Nikos P. Chrisochoides. Multithreaded model for dynamic load balancing parallel adaptive PDE computations. Technical Report CTC95TR221, Cornell University, October 1995.
6. David Cronk, Matthew Haines, and Piyush Mehrotra. Thread migration in the presence of pointers. In *Proceedings of the 30th Annual Hawaii International Conference on System Sciences, vol I*, pages 292–298, Maui, HI, January 1997.
7. David Cronk and Piyush Mehrotra. Migrating communicating threads. Submitted to 1998 International Conference on Supercomputing. July 1998.
8. Ian Foster, Carl Kesselman, Robert Olson, and Steven Tuecke. Nexus: An interoperability layer for parallel and distributed computer systems. Technical Report Version 1.3, Argonne National Labs, December 1993.
9. Matthew Haines. On designing lightweight threads for substrate software. Technical Report TR-97-4, Institute for Computer Applications in Science and Engineering, January 1997.
10. Matthew Haines, David Cronk, and Piyush Mehrotra. On the design of Chant: A talking threads package. In *Proceedings of Supercomputing*, pages 350–359, Washington D.C., November 1994. ACM/IEEE.
11. Matthew Haines, Piyush Mehrotra, and David Cronk. Ropes: Support for collective operations among distributed threads. Technical Report 95-36, Institute for Computer Applications in Science and Engineering, November 1994.
12. Edward Mascarenhas and Vernon Rego. Ariadne: Architecture of a portable thread system supporting mobile processes. Technical Report CSD-TR-95-017, Purdue University, March 1995.
13. R. Namyst and J. F. Mehaut. PM^2: Parallel Multithreaded Machine. In *Proceedings of Parco '95*, Gent, Belgium, September 1995.

Integrated Task and Data Parallel Support for Dynamic Applications

James M. Rehg[1], Kathleen Knobe[1], Umakishore Ramachandran[2], Rishiyur S. Nikhil[1], and Arun Chauhan[3]

[1] Cambridge Research Laboratory[†], Compaq Computer Corporation, Cambridge, MA 02139 {rehg|knobe|nikhil}@crl.dec.com
[2] College of Computing, Georgia Institute of Technology, Atlanta GA 30332 rama@cc.gatech.edu
[3] Computer Science Department, Rice University, Houston, TX 77005 achauhan@cs.rice.edu

Abstract. There is an emerging class of real-time interactive applications that require the dynamic integration of task and data parallelism. An example is the Smart Kiosk, a free-standing computer device that provides information and entertainment to people in public spaces. The kiosk interface employs vision and speech sensing and uses an animated graphical talking face for output. Due to the interactive nature of the kiosk, the structure of its tasks and the available computational resources can vary with the number of customers and the state of the interaction. In particular, using experimental results from a color-based people tracking module, we demonstrate the existence of distinct operating regimes in the kiosk application. These regimes require dynamic trade-offs in data parallel strategy. We present a framework for the dynamic integration of task and data parallelism. Our solution has been implemented in the context of Stampede, a cluster programming system under development at the Cambridge Research Laboratory.

1 Introduction

There is an emerging class of real-time interactive applications that require dynamic integration of task and data parallelism for effective computation. The Smart Kiosk system [18,5] under development at the Cambridge Research Laboratory (CRL) is an example which motivates this work. Kiosks provide public access to information and entertainment. The CRL Smart Kiosk supports natural, human-centered interaction. It uses camera and microphone inputs to drive the behavior of a graphical talking face which speaks to its customers. It has features that we believe are typical of future scalable applications. It is both reactive and interactive, since it must respond to changes in its environment as new customers arrive and it must interact with multiple people. It is computationally demanding due to the need for real-time vision, speech, and graphics

---

[†] This work was performed at the Cambridge Research Laboratory.

D. O'Hallaron (Ed.): LCR'98, LNCS 1511, pp. 167–180, 1998.

processing. It is also highly scalable, both at the task level in supporting a variable number of users and functions, and at the data level in processing multiple video and audio streams.

Although the Smart Kiosk depends critically on integrated task and data parallel computing [1,4,9,15,3] for sufficient computational resources, existing techniques are not well-suited to this type of application. The current state-of-the-art in task and data parallelism integration [15] employs extensive off-line analysis of the memory requirements, communication patterns and scalability aspects of the tasks. This information is then used to make a static determination of the ideal distribution of work among processors.

In contrast, the computational requirements of even simple vision algorithms for the kiosk are proportional to the number of customers, which cannot be predicted in advance. This variability has a direct influence on the optimal resource assignment, as we will demonstrate. Furthermore, computational requirements that are unrelated to sensing tasks (such as database access, remote content retrieval, and conversation with the customer) will also vary as customers use the kiosk, impacting the resources available for sensing. Some previous work has been done on dynamic integration of task and data parallelism for scientific applications [3]. However, that work is focused on parallel numerical algorithms such as can be found in ScaLAPACK.

In this paper, we describe the dynamic integration of task and data parallelism for interactive real-time applications like the Smart Kiosk. This work takes place within the context of Stampede, a cluster programming system under development at CRL. Stampede is aimed at making it easy to program this emerging class of applications on clusters of SMPs, the most economically attractive scalable platforms. Stampede provides a task-parallel substrate: dynamic cluster-wide threads, together with Space-Time Memory *channels*, a high-level, flexible mechanism for threads to communicate time-sequenced data (such as video frames). Our integration of task and data parallelism is a way to dynamically organize threads and channels into task and data parallel structures based on instantaneous computational requirements and resource constraints.

We present experimental results from a color-based people tracking algorithm that demonstrate the existence of distinct operating regimes requiring dynamic trade-offs in data parallel strategy. Strictly static strategy may not be optimal since transitions among these regimes only become apparent during execution. We describe an approach to this problem using a combination of on-line adaptation and off-line analysis. The best strategy for each regime is determined off-line. Changes in state that indicate a transition between regimes trigger a change to the new regime-specific optimal strategy.

2   The Smart Kiosk: A Dynamic Vision Application

This work is motivated by the computational requirements of a class of dynamic, interactive computer vision applications. We introduce this class through a specific example: a vision-based user-interface for a Smart Kiosk [18,13]. A

Smart Kiosk is a free-standing computerized device that is capable of interacting with multiple people in a public environment, providing information and entertainment.

We are exploring a social interface paradigm for kiosks. In this paradigm, vision and speech sensing provide user input while a graphical speaking agent provides the kiosk's output. A description of the project, including results from a recent public installation, can be found in [5]. A related kiosk application is described in [7].

Figure 1 shows a picture of our most recent Smart Kiosk prototype. The camera at the top of the device acquires images of people standing in front of the kiosk display. The kiosk employs vision techniques to track and identify people based on their motion and clothing color [13]. The estimated position of multiple users drives the behavior of an animated graphical face, called DECface [17], which occupies the upper left corner of the display.

Vision techniques support two kiosk behaviors which are characteristic of public interactions between humans. First, the kiosk greets people as they approach the display. Second, during an interaction with multiple users DECface exhibits natural gaze behavior, glancing in each person's direction on a regular basis. Future versions of

Fig. 1. The Smart Kiosk

the kiosk will include speech processing and face detection and recognition.

There is currently a great deal of interest in vision- and speech-based user-interfaces (see the recent collections [6,8]). We believe the Smart Kiosk to be representative of a broad class of emerging applications in surveillance, autonomous agents, and intelligent vehicles and rooms.

A key attribute of the Smart Kiosk application is the real-time processing and generation of multimedia data. Video and speech processing combined with computer graphics rendering and speech synthesis are critical components of a human-centered style of interaction. The number and bandwidth of these data streams results in dramatic computational requirements for the kiosk application. However, there is significant task-level parallelism as a result of the loose coupling between data streams. This can be exploited to improve performance. Unfortunately the complex data sharing patterns between tasks in the application make the development of a parallel implementation challenging.

One source of complexity arises when tasks share streams of input data which they sample at different rates. For example, a figure tracking task may need to sample every frame in an image sequence in order to accurately estimate the motion of a particular user. A face recognition task, in contrast, could be run much less frequently. Differences in these sampling rates complicate the recycling and management of the frame buffers that hold the video input data.

The dynamics of the set of tasks that make up the kiosk application is a second source of complexity. These dynamics are a direct result of the interactive nature of the application. A task such as face recognition, for example, is only performed if a user has been detected in the scene. Thus, whether a task in the application is active or not can depend upon the state of the external world and the inputs the system has received. This variability also complicates frame buffer management. In particular, it raises the question of which image frames in an input video sequence a newly-activated task should be allowed to see.

2.1   Color-Based Tracking Example

The Smart Kiosk application can be viewed as a dynamic collection of tasks that process streams of input data at different sampling rates. To explore this point further, we focus on a subpart of the Smart Kiosk application that tracks multiple people in an image sequence based on the color of their shirts.

Figure 2 shows the task graph for a color-based person tracking algorithm taken from [13]. It was used in our first Smart Kiosk prototype, which is described in [18]. It tracks multiple people in the vicinity of the kiosk by comparing each video frame against a set of previously defined histogram models of shirt colors. There are four distinct tasks: *digitizer, change detection, histogram,* and *target detection,* which are shown as elliptical nodes in the diagram. The inputs and outputs for these tasks are shown as rectangles. For example, the *histogram* task reads video frames and writes color histograms. The *target detection* task is based on a modified version of the standard histogram intersection algorithm described in [16].

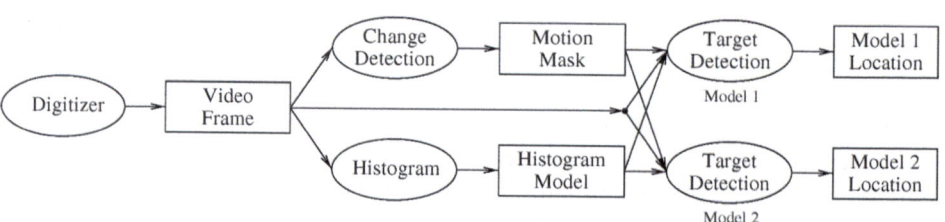

Fig. 2. Task graph for the color-based tracker. Ellipses denote *tasks*, implemented as threads. Rectangles denote *channels* which hold streams of data flowing between tasks.

Figure 3 illustrates the flow of data in the color tracker by following a single image through the task graph. Processing begins at the *digitizer* task, which generates the video frame shown in Figure 3(a). The *change detection* task subtracts a previously acquired background image from this frame to produce a motion mask (b) showing the foreground objects and their shadows. Similarly, the *histogram* task produces a histogram model (c) of the video frame (a). Figure (c) shows an 8 by 8 bin histogram of the normalized red and green pixel values from the input frame, rendered as an intensity image. The brightness of each square bin reflects the number of pixels it contains.

Each instantiation of the *target detection* task compares the image histogram in Figure 3(c) to a previously defined model histogram, resulting in a backprojection image. There is a separate backprojection image for each model. Figure (d) shows the sum of the two backprojection images for the two targets. Each pixel in a backprojection image encodes the likelihood that its corresponding image pixel belongs to a particular color model. Connected component analysis and peak detection on the smoothed backprojection images results in the detected positions of the two models, shown with crosses in (e).

Parallelism at both the task and the data level are visible in the diagram of Figure 2. Task parallelism arises when distinct tasks can be executed simultaneously. It is most obvious in the *change detection* and *histogram* tasks, which have no data dependencies and can therefore be performed in parallel. It is also present in the form of pipelining, where for example the *histogram* and *target detection* tasks can be performed simultaneously on different frames of an image sequence.

Data parallelism occurs when a single task can be replicated over distributed data. The *target detection* task is data parallel, since it performs the same operation for each color model in the application. The search for a set of models can be performed in parallel by multiple instances of the *target detection* task. For example, Figure 2 illustrates a parallel search for two models. Similarly, data parallelism at the pixel level can be exploited in many image processing tasks, such as *change detection* or *histogram*, by subdividing a single frame into regions and processing them in parallel.

In designing a parallel implementation of the color tracker we could focus on task parallelism, data parallelism, or some combination of the two. Our experimental results in Section 5 confirm our hypothesis that in this application's dynamic environment, we need to combine task and data parallelism and, moreover, that the combined structure must vary dynamically.

3   Stampede

In this section we briefly describe Stampede, the programming system within which we explore integrated task and data parallelism (a more detailed description may be found in [11]). Stampede is currently based entirely on C library calls, *i.e.*, it is implemented as a run-time system, with calls from standard C.

Stampede extends the well-known POSIX dynamic threads model [10] from SMPs to clusters of SMPs, which constitute the most economically attractive scalable platforms today. It provides various "shared-memory" facilities for threads to share data uniformly and consistently across clusters.

More pertinent to the current discussion, Stampede provides a high-level, concurrent, distributed data structure called *Space-Time Memory* (STM), which

(a) Video Frame

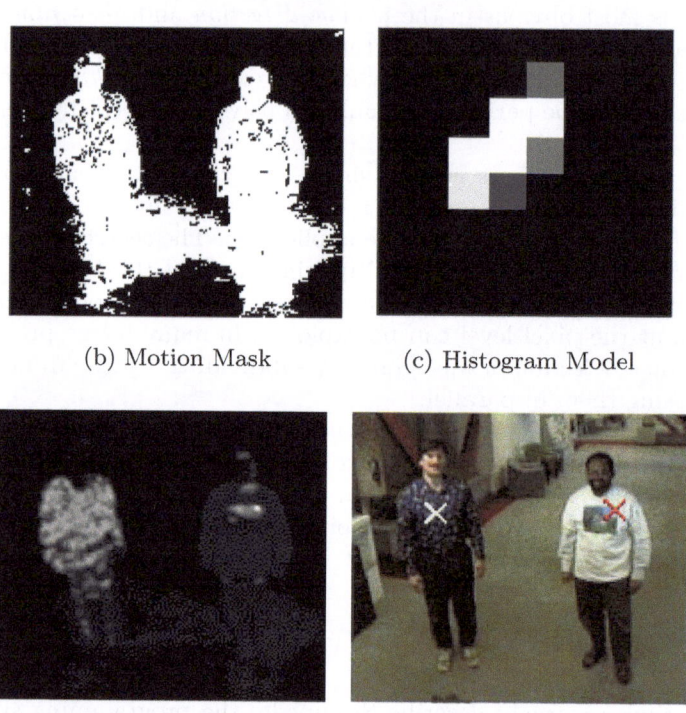

(b) Motion Mask   (c) Histogram Model

(d) Backprojection Image   (e) Model Locations

Fig. 3. Data flow in the color tracker of Figure 2 during a search for two models, corresponding to the two figures in the input frame (a). The final output is the positions of the detected targets in (e). Intermediate results are shown in (b)–(d).

allows threads to produce and consume time-sequenced data in flexible ways, addressing the complex "buffer management" problem that arises in managing temporally indexed data streams as in the Smart Kiosk application. There are four sources of this complexity:

- streams become temporally sparser as we move up the analysis hierarchy, from low-level vision processing tasks to high-level recognition tasks;
- threads may not access items in strict stream order;
- threads may combine streams using temporal correlation (*e.g.*, stereo vision, or combining vision and sound), and
- the hierarchy itself is dynamic, involving newly created threads that may re-examine earlier data.

Traditional data structures such as streams, queues and lists are not sufficiently expressive to handle these features.

Stampede's Space-Time Memory (STM) is our solution to this problem. The key construct in STM is the *channel*, which is a location-transparent collection of objects indexed by time. The API has operations to create a channel dynamically, and for a thread to *attach* and *detach* a channel. Each attachment is known as a *connection*, and a thread may have multiple connections to the same channel. Figure 4 shows an overview of how channels are used. A thread can *put* a data

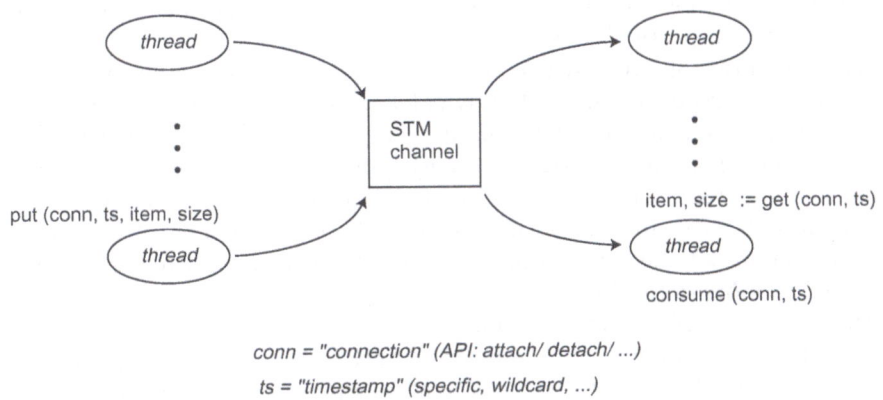

conn = "connection" (API: attach/ detach/ ...)

ts = "timestamp" (specific, wildcard, ...)

Fig. 4. Overview of Stampede channels.

item into a channel *via* a given output connection using the call:

```
spd_channel_put_item (o_connection, timestamp, buf_p, buf_size, ...)
```

The item is described by the pointer buf_p and its buf_size in bytes. A channel cannot have more than one item with the same timestamp, but there is no constraint that items be put into the channel in increasing or contiguous timestamp order. Indeed, to increase throughput, a module may contain replicated threads that pull items from a common input channel, process them, and put items into a common output channel. Depending on the relative speed of the threads and the particular events they recognize, it may happen that items are placed into the output channel "out of order". Channels can be created to hold a bounded or unbounded number of items. The `put` call takes an additional flag that allows it to block or to return immediately with an error code, if a bounded output channel is full.

A thread can *get* an item from a channel *via* a given connection using the call:

```
spd_channel_get_item (i_connection, timestamp,
                      & buf_p, & buf_size,
                      & timestamp_range, ...);
```

The `timestamp` can specify a particular value, or it can be a wildcard requesting the newest/oldest value currently in the channel, or the newest value not previously gotten over any connection, *etc.* As in the `put` call, a flag parameter specifies whether to block if a suitable item is currently unavailable, or to return immediately with an error code. The parameters `buf_p` and `buf_size` can be used to pass in a buffer to receive the item or, by passing NULL in `buf_p`, the application can ask Stampede to allocate a buffer. The `timestamp_range` parameter returns the timestamp of the item returned, if available; if unavailable, it returns the timestamps of the "neighboring" available items, if any.

The `put` and `get` operations are atomic. Even though a channel is a distributed data structure and multiple threads across the cluster may simultaneously be performing operations on the channel, these operations appear to all threads as if they occur in a particular serial order.

The semantics of `put` and `get` are copy-in and copy-out, respectively. Thus, after a `put`, a thread may immediately safely re-use its buffer. Similarly, after a successful `get`, a client can safely modify the copy of the object that it received without interfering with the channel or with other threads. Of course, an application can still pass a datum by reference– it merely passes a reference to the object through STM, instead of the datum itself. The notion of a "reference" can be based on any of the "shared-memory" mechanisms supported by Stampede, described in more detail in [11].

Puts and gets, with copying semantics, are of course reminiscent of message-passing. However, unlike message-passing, these are location-independent operations on a distributed data structure. These operations are one-sided: there is no "destination" thread/ process in a `put`, nor any "source" thread/ process in a `get`. The abstraction is one of concurrently putting items into and getting items from a temporally ordered collection, not of communicating between processes. Additional information about STM can be found in [14].

4   Integration of Task and Data Parallelism

In this section, we examine the integration of task and data parallelism in the context of the color tracker application from Figure 2. We will discuss both static and dynamic integration strategies within the Stampede framework.

For tasks like the color tracker there is a basic performance tradeoff between latency and throughput. Since the digitizer can generate images significantly faster than the downstream tasks can process them, pipeline parallelism can be used to increase throughput. Alternatively, a data parallel implementation of the target detection task can be used to remove the bottleneck and reduce latency. An earlier set of experiments described in [14] addressed throughput issues for the color tracker. The integration of task and data parallelism makes it possible to address latency and throughput in a single framework.

We introduce a framework for performing tasks with collections of data parallel threads. The key idea is that any node in the task graph can be replaced with a subgraph consisting of multiple worker threads that exactly duplicates the task's behavior on its input and output channels.

We will describe the general form of the data parallel subgraph which may be applied to any node in the task graph. The details of its operation will depend upon the application. For example, the color tracker operates on two data types, image frames and target color models, and three distinct approaches to data parallelism are possible as a result. The tracker data space can be characterized as the cross product of frames, pixels in each frame, and models. Correspondingly, there are three possible strategies for exploiting data parallelism: distribute distinct whole frames, distribute parts of the same frame, and distribute models.

Distributing distinct frames is equivalent to pipelining and would increase throughput. Since the focus of this work is on latency we address the other two strategies. In distributing parts of the same frame each data parallel thread searches in distinct image regions for all of the models. Alternatively, in distributing models, each thread searches the entire frame for a distinct subset of target models. Combinations of these two approaches are also possible.

4.1   Static Data Parallel Strategy

We begin by describing a static data parallel strategy to introduce three basic components: *splitter*, *worker*, and *joiner* threads. The structure is illustrated in Figure 5. For some task T we execute N instances of the task concurrently, each on approximately one Nth of the data. A data parallel worker thread performs each instance. The splitter thread reads from the input channels for task T and converts a single chunk of work into N data parallel chunks, one for each of the workers. The joiner combines the N partial results from the workers into a single result, which it places on T's output channels.

The splitter and joiner threads provide the interface between the worker threads and the rest of the task graph. They ensure that the data parallelism within T is not visible to the rest of the application.

The extent of the data parallelism employed is determined by the number of workers. Each worker implements a parameterized version of the original application code, designed to work on arbitrary chunks. Distribution across pixels and models can be accomplished by passing image regions or subsets of models to the workers, respectively. Note that distribution across whole frames can also be handled easily: the splitter reads multiple frames and passes them to the workers, and the joiner places the processed frames on its output channel.

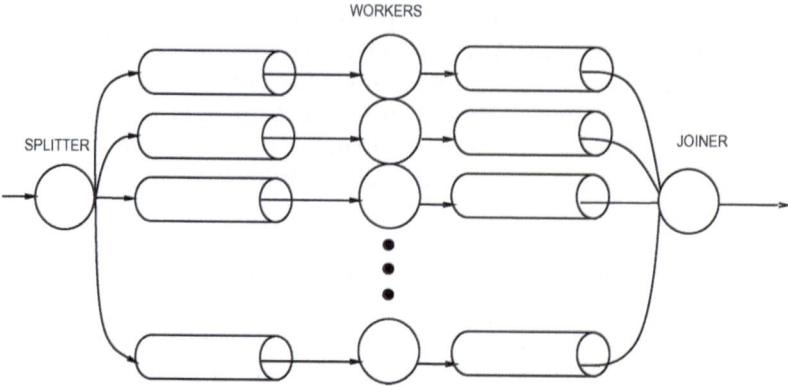

Fig. 5. Static task and data parallelism

The data parallel approach of Figure 5 is *static* in that there is a fixed assignment of chunks to workers and a fixed number of worker threads. Note however that the splitter does not have to wait until one set of chunks has been completed before sending the next set of chunks to the workers.

4.2   Dynamic Data Parallel Strategy

The static assignment of chunks to workers is unnecessarily restrictive. It limits the flexibility of the splitter to respond to changes in the task and makes it difficult to vary the number of workers. In the color tracking application, for example, the splitter's strategy should vary with the number of targets, as we demonstrate experimentally in Section 5.

Figure 6 illustrates a dynamic data parallel architecture that avoids the limitations of the static approach. Here a single *work queue* acts as the source of chunks for all of the worker threads, supporting the dynamic assignment of chunks based on worker availability. This strategy minimizes latency and makes it easier to vary the number of worker threads, N, during execution.

The splitter divides an item of work into M chunks, where we no longer require $M = N$ and, in fact, M may vary with each item provided that $M \leq M_{\mathrm{max}}$. In the static scenario the joiner knew the number of chunks for each item and where to find them. Here, the splitter communicates its data parallel strategy for each item, including the number of chunks, to the joiner through the *controller queue*. The workers communicate with the joiner through M_{max} *done channels*. The splitter tags each chunk with its target done channel. (Chunk i goes to done channel i). This mechanism allows any worker to process any chunk since the done channels act as a sorting network for the results. The joiner reads the partial results from the appropriate done channels, combines them, and outputs the complete result.

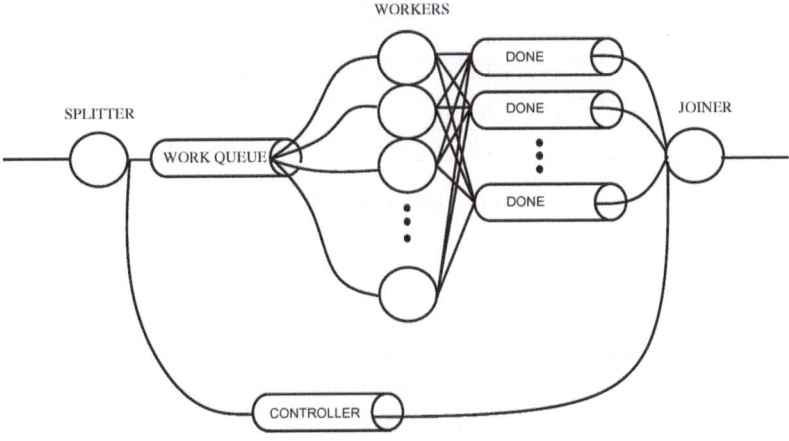

Fig. 6. Dynamic task and data parallelism

Although the individual components are application specific, the data parallel architecture described here is general and may be applied to any task in the task graph. In our current implementation, the splitter, joiner, and worker threads are explicitly created at the application level. Our next goal is to automate the generation of data parallel subgraphs. For each data parallel task, the user will define a chunk data type and supply parameterized splitter, worker, and joiner methods. The abstraction would automatically create the necessary channels and threads by invoking these application-provided methods to generate the structure depicted in Figure 6. The specific configuration would depend upon resource availability.

5   Experimental Results

We implemented the color tracker application from Section 2.1 within the Stampede framework and conducted a series of data parallel experiments. We applied the dynamic parallel architecture of Figure 6 to the target detection task in the color tracker application. STM channels were used to implement the communication between splitter, worker, and joiner threads. More information about this implementation can be found in [12].

We experimentally evaluated three data parallel strategies for the target detection task which is the performance bottleneck in the color tracker (see Figure 2). The cost of target detection is dominated by the histogram backprojection (HB) algorithm [16] which generates the back projection images depicted in Figure 3(e). In HB, each pixel in the input image is compared to each of the target models, which are color histograms. This comparison step results in a set of images, one for each target, in which each pixel location has been labeled with the likelihood that it came from that target model. After smoothing these

	Total Models		
	1	8	
Partitions	MP = 1	MP = 8	MP = 1
FP = 1	0.876 (1)	1.857 (8)	6.850 (1)
FP = 4	0.275 (4)	2.155 (32)	2.033 (4)

Table 1. Timing results in seconds/frame for the backprojection task with one and eight target models.

images to reduce the effects of image noise, connected components analysis is used to identify blobs corresponding to the location of each target in the image.

In parallelizing the HB algorithm for a single frame we can divide the data by target models and by image regions. For a small number of target models, distribution over regions is the only option, but as the number of models increases there is a choice. We would expect distributing over regions to result in increased overhead over processing whole frames. For example, there are certain set-up costs involved in processing a region of pixels regardless of its size. In addition, there are book-keeping costs involved in partitioning a frame of pixel data into regions for processing. This expectation is borne out by the experimental timing results given in Table 1. These results demonstrate the superiority of distributing over models in the eight target case.

Table 1 shows the total time to detect all targets in a single frame. In this experiment there were two regimes, in which the total number of models was one and eight. The model and frame data are both partitioned. MP gives the number of partitions of the models and FP the number of partitions of the frames. The total number of chunks in each experiment (shown in parentheses) is the product of MP and FP. For example, in the case MP = 8 and FP = 1 each of eight chunks searched for a single model across the entire frame. The experiments were performed using four worker threads on a four processor SMP, the DIGITAL AlphaServer 4100.

In the case where total models is one (first column), we tested the sequential approach of searching the entire frame in one chunk (FP = 1) against the data parallel strategy of dividing the frame across four chunks (FP = 4). The parallel approach was faster, as expected, by more than a factor of three.

In the case of eight total models (second column) we tested four combinations of two strategies, corresponding to partitioning the data across models (MP = 8) and across frames (FP = 4). The three parallel approaches corresponding to 8, 32, and 4 chunks were all more than three times faster than the sequential approach in the upper right of the table, which corresponds to a single chunk. As expected, the division across models was 17 percent faster than the division across pixels due to the increased overhead in the region case.

These results demonstrate that dynamic data parallel strategies are required even for a relatively simple vision algorithm. In this example the optimal strategy depends upon the number of targets. Below some threshold we should divide over regions, above it we should divide over models.

The color tracker itself makes up only a small part of the complete kiosk application. As additional vision, speech, and graphics functionalities are implemented, an even more complex set of dynamic choices will have to be made.

6   Conclusions and Future Work

There is a class of emerging applications that requires the integration of task and data parallelism. However, these applications are not well suited to static techniques because they exhibit wide variability over time. In some cases this variability is over a small number of distinct regimes each of which is amenable to static techniques. For example, in the case of the color tracker, each regime corresponds to a specific number of people in front of the kiosk.

We have experimentally demonstrated the need for a dynamic approach in even fairly simple algorithms such as the vision-based color tracker. We have described and implemented a mechanism for integrating task and data parallelism which supports dynamic changes in strategy.

The next step is to provide a higher level of support for generating these data parallel structures. This involves the addition of data parallel data types and methods to our API, through which the application can specify a variety of data parallel strategies. We plan to allow the application to provide a table which identifies the correct strategy for each of its operating regimes. The runtime system can then switch strategies by querying the table as the application progresses. A key issue is to identify the types of state variables that may be useful in indexing the different operating regimes.

We are interested in exploring the use of machine learning techniques to identify optimal strategies and operating regimes (see [2] for an application of learning techniques to dynamic packet routing.) A key issue is the identification of metrics for measuring the quality of competing data parallel solutions. One possibility is to look at flow control issues such as a build-up of unread items on channels suggesting a bottleneck.

Acknowledgments

We would like to thank the members of the Scalable Group at CRL, especially Robert H. Halstead, Jr., Leonidas Kontothanassis, Christopher Joerg, and James Hicks for their comments and support.

References

1. R. Bagrodia, M. Chandy, and M. Dhagat. UC: A set-based language for data parallel programs. *J. of Parallel and Distributed Computing*, Aug. 1995.

2. J. A. Boyan and M. L. Littman. Packet routing in dynamically changing networks: A reinforcement learning approach. In *Advances in Neural Information Processing Systems 6*, 1994.

3. S. Chakrabarti, J. Demmel, and K. Yelick. Models and scheduling algorithms for mixed data and task parallel programs. *J. of Parallel and Distributed Computing*, 47:168–184, 1997.

4. K. M. Chandy, I. Foster, K. Kennedy, C. Koelbel, and C.-W. Tseng. Integrated support for task and data parallelism. *Intl. J. of Supercomputer Applications*, 1994.

5. A. D. Christian and B. L. Avery. Digital smart kiosk project. In *ACM SIGCHI '98*, pages 155–162, Los Angeles, CA, April 18–23 1998.

6. R. Cipolla and A. Pentland, editors. *Computer Vision for Human-Machine Interaction*. Cambridge University Press, 1998. In press.

7. T. Darrell, G. Gordon, J. Woodfill, and M. Harville. A virtual mirror interface using real-time robust face tracking. In *Proc of 3rd Intl. Conf. on Automatic Face and Gesture Recognition*, pages 616–621, Nara, Japan, April 1998.

8. *Proc. of Third Intl. Conf. on Automatic Face and Gesture Recognition*, Nara, Japan, April 14–16 1998. IEEE Computer Society.

9. I. Foster, D. Kohr, R. Krishnaiyer, and A. Choudhary. A library-based approach to task parallelism in a data-parallel language. *J. of Parallel and Distributed Computing*, 1996.

10. IEEE. Threads standard POSIX 1003.1c-1995 (also ISO/IEC 9945-1:1996), 1996.

11. R. S. Nikhil, U. Ramachandran, J. M. Rehg, R. H. Halstead, Jr., C. F. Joerg, and L. Kontothanassis. Stampede: A Programming System for Emerging Scalable Interactive Multimedia Applications. In *Proc. Eleventh Intl. Wkshp. on Languages and Compilers for Parallel Computing*, Chapel Hill NC, Aug. 7-9 1998. See also Technical Report 98/1, Cambridge Research Lab., Compaq Computer Corp.

12. J. M. Rehg, K. Knobe, U. Ramachandran, R. S. Nikhil, and A. Chauhan. Integrated task and data parallel support for dynamic applications. Technical Report CRL 98/3, Compaq Computer Corporation Cambridge Research Lab, Cambridge MA, May 1998.

13. J. M. Rehg, M. Loughlin, and K. Waters. Vision for a smart kiosk. In *Computer Vision and Pattern Recognition*, pages 690–696, San Juan, Puerto Rico, 1997.

14. J. M. Rehg, U. Ramachandran, R. H. Halstead, Jr., C. Joerg, L. Kontothanassis, and R. S. Nikhil. Space-time memory: A parallel programming abstraction for dynamic vision applications. Technical Report CRL 97/2, Digital Equipment Corp. Cambridge Research Lab, April 1997.

15. J. Subhlok and G. Vondran. Optimal latency - throughput tradeoffs for data parallel pipelines. *Proc. 8th Symposium on Parallel Algorithms and Architecture (SPAA)*, June 1996.

16. M. Swain and D. Ballard. Color indexing. *Intl J. of Computer Vision*, 7(1):11–32, 1991.

17. K. Waters and T. Levergood. An automatic lip-synchronization algorithm for synthetic faces. *Multimedia Tools and Applications*, 1(4):349–366, Nov 1995.

18. K. Waters, J. M. Rehg, M. Loughlin, S. B. Kang, and D. Terzopoulos. Visual sensing of humans for active public interfaces. Technical Report CRL 96/5, Digital Equipment Corp. Cambridge Research Lab, 1996. To appear in *Computer Vision for Human-Machine Interaction*, Cambridge University Press. In press.

Supporting Self-Adaptivity for SPMD Message-Passing Applications

M. Cermele, M. Colajanni, and S. Tucci

Dipartimento di Informatica, Sistemi e Produzione
Università di Roma "Tor Vergata", Italy 00133
{cermele, colajanni, tucci}@uniroma2.it

Abstract. Real parallel applications find little benefits from code portability that does not guarantee acceptable efficiency. In this paper, we describe the new features of a framework that allows the development of Single Program Multiple Data (SPMD) applications adaptable to different distributed-memory machines, varying from traditional parallel computers to networks of workstations. Special programming primitives providing indirect accesses to the platform and data domain guarantee code portability and open the way to runtime optimizations carried out by a scheduler and a runtime support.

1 Introduction

The SPMD paradigm is the most widely adopted model for a large class of problems. However, this programming paradigm does not facilitate portability because it requires the choice of a specific domain decomposition, and the insertion of communications and parallel primitives in a decomposition dependent way. If we want a parallel application to be portable with efficiency (*performance portability*), the best domain decomposition and communication pattern cannot be chosen during implementation. Although standard message-passing libraries, such as PVM and MPI, guarantee *code portability*, performance portability requires more sophisticated frameworks. They have to provide an abstract machine for the parallel implementation and a runtime environment for adapting the application to the status of the actual platform. The solution can be at different levels of abstraction going from explicit tools to transparent supports. The former approach leads to parallel programs that we call *reconfigurable* because the adaptivity is achieved at the price of some programming overhead. The latter solution makes a program *self-adaptable* to various platforms without any programming effort greater than the parallelization itself.

This paper proposes a method to add self-adaptivity to SPMD message-passing applications running on multicomputers, clusters or distributed systems, where each (possibly, heterogeneous and nondedicated) node has its own local memory. The focus is on the new features of the Dame framework that was initially proposed for cluster computing to dynamically switch from one type of data-distribution to another type [9]. With respect to that version, now Dame includes a new *abstract machine interface* and a new *scheduler* that improve

D. O'Hallaron (Ed.): LCR'98, LNCS 1511, pp. 181–194, 1998.
© Springer-Verlag Berlin Heidelberg 1998

transparency and enlarge the class of applications and target machines. This paper describes the role of those components in achieving self-adaptivity, while does not present other features under implementation, such as the capability of dynamically changing the number of processes that actually carry out computation, the new algorithms for mapping the application's communication pattern onto the active nodes, the automatic method to choose the frequency of activation of the reconfiguration support.

Section 2 describes the basic approach, the programming paradigm and the abstract machine interface. Section 3 outlines how the scheduler adapts the application to the platform status at startup. Section 4 details the operations of the runtime scheduling. Section 5 discusses related works. The paper is concluded by some final remarks.

2   Abstract Machine Interface

The simplicity of the SPMD model is preserved if the programmer can assume a regular and homogeneous environment. The question whether a support can provide easy-to-use parallelism, facilitate the portability and not sacrifice performance requires a decision about the most appropriate level of abstraction. The proposed levels go from an abstract machine that hides only system and network heterogeneity such as in PVM and MPI, to an explicit use of facilities for load balancing such as in ADM [4] and DRMS [17], until the more abstract Linda machine that hides distributed memory [3]. The solution suggested in this paper is an intermediate degree of abstraction that guarantees code portability without sacrificing performance portability. The Dame abstract machine emulates the main features of a distributed memory parallel computer. It hides system heterogeneity, node nonuniformity, actual (typically, irregular) domain decomposition and the underlying architecture, however it still requires the explicit insertion of communication primitives. The programmer or the supercompiler can refer to a *virtual platform* and a *virtual data-distribution*. The virtual platform consists of homogeneous nodes with the same static computational power. Each node executes one SPMD thread that has its own address space. The need for any data placed in the memory of other nodes requires explicit message-passing. The virtual data-distribution is regular because each node is supposed to have the same amount of data items. The programmer can choose the virtual data-distribution which is most appropriate to the application without caring of the platform. Presently, Dame manages one- and two-dimensional decompositions with block, cyclic, or intermediate decomposition formats [5].

The complexity of portable parallel computing is effectively hidden in the *Dame Library* (DML). The DML primitives are simpler than standard message-passing constructs because they refer to the virtual platform and virtual data-distribution. These primitives, providing *indirect accesses* to the platform and data domain, replace any SPMD operation (e.g., system inquiry, domain inquiry, communication) that typically depends on the platform and/or data-distribution. This choice guarantees code portability and allows the dynamic reconfigurations that are at the basis of performance portability. Indirect accesses to data items were previously proposed in CHAOS [19] and Multiblock Parti libraries [1] to manage irregular parallel applications. Here we outline the primitives that are relevant to dealing with data parallelism without taking care of the distributed platform and related issues.

System inquiries. System inquiries give information about the number of nodes involved in computation. Moreover, these primitives are crucial for establishing the role of each node when it executes an SPMD program. The library provides the programmer with primitives for node identification which are based on the subset of data domain they own. A process is not referred in the code through explicit Cartesian coordinates or static identifier such as pid, but always through a formula like 'node(s) holding certain data items', where this information is given by the *data inquiry* primitives.

Data inquiries. These are the key primitives that support the decomposition independence of Dame applications since the programmer is never required to specify exactly data locations and bounds of local domain. The *data inquiry* primitives have typically three arguments: $<domain>$, $<row\ index>$, $<column\ index>$, where the indexes can refer to the local or global domain or can be the wildcard -1. For example, dml_f(A,i,j) applies the primitive f to the local or global entry (i, j) of the matrix A, while dml_f(A,k,-1) refers to all the row k. Let us distinguish the data inquiry primitives into five classes.

  – *Owner identifiers* return the node or set of nodes that hold a specified data set. The former primitive dml_which_node(A,i,j) returns the node identifier to which the global entry (i, j) is assigned. The wildcard parameter is not allowed for this function.

  The latter primitive dml_which_set(A,i1,i2,j1,j2) returns the set of node identifiers that contain the subdomain delimited by the rows $i1 - i2$ and by the columns $j1 - j2$. The wildcard parameter -1 can be used in any of the last four input positions. Depending on the position, the meaning is either from the beginning or until the end. For example, dml_which_set(A,i1,-1,j1,-1) denotes all nodes containing the submatrix starting from row $i1$ and column $j1$. Moreover, dml_which_set(A,i,i,-1,-1) denotes all nodes containing row i.

  – *Local data extractors* get from the global data domain the part contained in the address space of the calling node or set of nodes.

  – *Index conversion* functions consist of three primitives: *local-to-global, global-to-local, local loop ranges*.
  Local-to-global primitives take as input a local row (column) index and return the equivalent global row (column) index.
  Dual results are given by the *global-to-local* conversion functions. For example, dml_gtol(A,i,-1) translates the global row index i into the equivalent global row index within the address space of the calling node. Local-to-global and global-to-local primitives return a negative value (that is, error) if the input index is out of the local domain range.

The index conversion class contains also *proximity* primitives that are mainly used to iterate over the local data domain. They compute lower and upper bounds of index loops by taking as input an array and a row (column) global index and returning the closest local index. For example, `dml_close(A,i,-1)` translates the global row index i into the local row index h which is closest to i. Let us consider that the global identifiers of the first and last rows held by the calling node are $i1$ and $i2$, respectively. Three cases are in order. If $i < i1$, the primitive returns $h = 0$; if $i > i2$, it returns the local index of the last row located in the calling node; otherwise, it behaves analogously to `dml_gtol(A,i,-1)`.

- *Owned domain bounds* take the global domain name as input parameter and return the local or global index of the first and last row (column) of the subdomain contained in the address space of the calling node. The primitives returning the global indexes are `dml_gminX(A)`, `dml_gmaxX(A)`, `dml_gminY(A)`, `dml_gmaxY(A)`, while the local indexes are obtained by analogous primitives such as `dml_lminX(A)`.
- *Locality predicates* take as input a global index and execute locality tests. For example, `dml_in_mynode(A,i,-1)` returns true if a part of row i is located in the address space of the calling node.

Communications. Dame communications conform to the PVM/MPI standard by supporting three classes of communications: point-to-point, multicast, gather. All these primitives are based on the send-receive mechanism provided by PVM or MPI.

The use is slightly different and in some sense simplified. Evaluation of the destination nodes and message transmission has to be seen as an atomic action in the sense that no reconfiguration primitive can occur between these two operations. The destination nodes must be always evaluated before the communication through the owner identifier primitives.

A point-to-point communication of a data d to the node owning the (i, j) entry is done through the couple `dest=dml_which_node(A,i,j)` and `dml_send(tag,d,dest)`. A multicast to the nodes having a portion of column h is done through `mdest=dml_which_set(A,-1,-1,h,h)` and `dml_mcast(tag,d,mdest)`, where `mdest` is an integer array containing the process identifiers to be sent to (the number of these processes are specified in the first position of the array). Keeping message transmission and destination evaluation as an atomic action allows to compute at runtime the actual scope of each communication.

Interface primitives. They represent the only non-transparent interface between the abstract machine and the support that guarantees adaptivity. The `dml_init` and `dml_end` primitives initialize and close the Dame environment, while `dml_check_load` activates the runtime scheduler. This last function will be discussed in Section 4.

There is no complexity of converting legacy MPI/PVM applications to the Dame library because self-adaptivity simplifies SPMD programming. Let us consider the example in Figure 1. It contains a naive SPMD code where the nodes

```
% if row k is in my_node, sum the local entries %
if ((k/dimblock)==(mynode/p1))
   {for(j=0; j<dimblock; j++)
       sum = sum + Loc_A[k%dimblock][j] };
       ......
% if A[k][h] is in my_node, send it to the nodes %
% owning column h %
if (h/dimblock)==(mynode%p1)
   {if (k/dimblock)==(mynode/p1)
      {for(i=0;i<(p1-1);i++)
          mdest[i]=(mynode+(i+1)*p2)%numnodes;

      x=Loc_A[k%dimblock][h/dimblock];
      mcast(tag,x,mdest) };

   else receive(tag,x) };
```

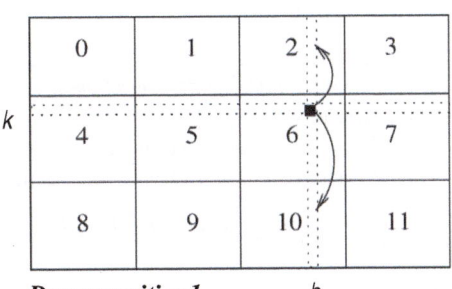

Decomposition1   *h*

SPMD program

Fig. 1. An example of SPMD program.

owning a portion of row k evaluate the sum of their local entries, and the node having the $A(k, h)$ entry sends it to each node containing elements of column h. Note that tedious and error-prone operations, such as the evaluation of the iterative loop bounds, conditional checks and communications, are replaced by simple calls to DML primitives. Moreover, if we want to execute the program of Figure 1 on an irregular platform where the nodes have different speeds, the SPMD program does not work well because it strictly refers to a block decomposed matrix which is uniformly mapped onto a $p_1 \times p_2$ mesh.

On the other hand, the Dame version of the same algorithm (Figure 2) is independent of the actual platform and data-distribution. The same program can be executed without requiring changes and recompilations. If necessary, Dame scheduler achieves the nonuniform data-distribution shown in *Decomposition2*, and the same Dame code is able to self-adapt to this balanced decomposition. Node behavior is different depending on data-distributions. As example, for *Decomposition1* the $A(k, h)$ entry is sent by node 6 to nodes 2 and 10, for *Decomposition2*, the same entry is sent by node 4 to nodes 1 and 11.

Dame achieves self-adaptivity by intervening in all phases of program's life. We have already seen the peculiarities of the Dame implementation style. The compilation does not alter the program's independence, because it generates a code that leaves unset all indirect accesses to the platform and data domain. The runtime support translates the Dame primitives referring to the abstract parallel machine into explicit accesses to actual data locations and active nodes. Modifications of the active platform and data-distribution do not require any adjustment of the high level code because the semantic flexibility of the indirect

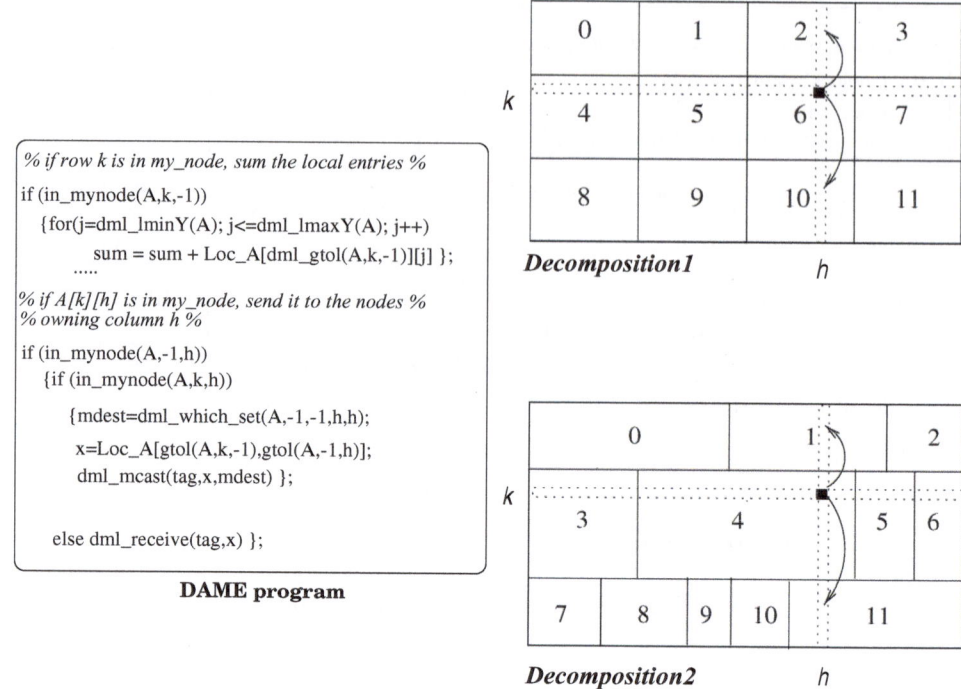

```
% if row k is in my_node, sum the local entries %
if (in_mynode(A,k,-1))
   {for(j=dml_lminY(A); j<=dml_lmaxY(A); j++)
        sum = sum + Loc_A[dml_gtol(A,k,-1)][j] };
   .....
% if A[k][h] is in my_node, send it to the nodes %
% owning column h %
if (in_mynode(A,-1,h))
   {if (in_mynode(A,k,h))

      {mdest=dml_which_set(A,-1,-1,h,h);

      x=Loc_A[gtol(A,k,-1),gtol(A,-1,h)];

      dml_mcast(tag,x,mdest) };


   else dml_receive(tag,x) };
```

DAME program

Decomposition1   *h*

Decomposition2   *h*

Fig. 2. The same program of Figure 1 written in Dame.

accesses allows the library runtime support to take different actions at different time for the same primitive call. When the scheduler modifies the actual platform and/or data-distribution, the application is indirectly informed through the updated results of the Dame primitives.

An interesting property is that the semantic flexibility does not introduce big overhead to the underlying layers. Table 1 shows that the cost of the decomposition-independent Dame primitives is equivalent to the cost of analogous constructs that are explicitly implemented in PVM and MPI on the basis of a single data-distribution.

The slightly higher time of some Dame primitives is entirely rewarded by the simplicity of implementation and self-adaptivity of the code. Moreover, that overhead becomes quite negligible when the primitives are used in a real contest. To this purpose, we compare the execution time of a *template* implementing a portion of the LU factorization algorithm (identification of the nodes owning the pivot column and evaluation of the multipliers). The transmission times are quite comparable because the Dame communications are based on PVM or MPI layers. The cost due to the dynamic evaluation of the destinations is much lower than any message transmission and does not affect the overall performance.

Table 1. Execution time (μsec., as average of 100 runs) of some programming primitives.

Class	Primitive	PVM	Dame-PVM	MPI	Dame-MPI
System inquiry	`dml_my_node`	< 0.001	< 0.001	< 0.001	< 0.001
	`dml_which_set`$(A,k,\text{-}1)$	0.23	0.48	0.37	0.59
Data inquiry	`dml_lmaxX(A)`/`dml_gmaxY(A)`	0.01	0.01	0.01	0.01
	`dml_gtol`$(A,\text{-}1,k)$	0.18	0.23	0.22	0.28
	`if(dml_in_mynode`$(A,k,\text{-}1))$	0.8	0.9	0.8	0.9
	template	33	34	33	34
Communication	`dml_send` (single data)	$1.3E+3$	$1.3E+3$	$1.1E+3$	$1.1E+3$

3   Initial Adaptivity

The *initial adaptivity* is guaranteed at startup time by the scheduler through three main activities:

- choice of the *active platform* that is, the set of nodes that actually carry out computation at a certain time;
- mapping of the communication pattern of the application onto the topology of the active platform;
- mapping of the virtual data-distribution onto the nodes of the active platform.

3.1   Active Platform

The user chooses the maximum set of machines that participate in computation at startup time. This set, called *maximum platform*, may differ from the active platform. For example, a node of the platform could be excluded because it does not provide adequate efficiency or because an external application with higher priority requires exclusive use of this node. If the platform is static that is, we are guaranteed that all the initial nodes provide the same computational power, the active platform does not change at runtime. Otherwise, if the real platform is dynamic, we could have various active platforms during computation.

The algorithm that chooses the initial active platform works on the basis of three kinds of startup information. Some of them are provided by the user at startup (U), others are typically set once and for all (O), others are automatically get by the scheduler (A).

Maximum platform (U).

This is the maximum set of machines that can participate in the computation. Typically, there is a list of default machines from which the user can select the maximum set for that computation. The set chosen at startup does not vary at runtime. The Dame scheduler, differently from the Piranha scheduler [3], does not try to dynamically acquire machines external to the maximum set. Hence, the active platform is always a subset of the maximum platform.

Startup platform conditions (A).

The scheduler evaluates the status of each node of the maximum platform such as availability, computational power and, if the nodes belong to a platform distributed among multiple subnetworks, mean inter-communication times.

Exclusion thresholds (O).

There are three set of thresholds that are useful when the actual platform is not a traditional parallel machine: *power threshold* Π, *latency threshold* Λ, *sharing thresholds* ϑ_i^D and ϑ_i^N.

In a heterogeneous platform, the nodes may have different computational powers. The scheduler excludes from the initial active platform the nodes that offer a relative power so small that the ratio between that value and the average platform speed is below Π.

In a platform where the nodes have different inter-communication times, the threshold Λ is used to exclude from the initial active platform the nodes that are connected so slowly to cause a bottleneck for the application.

When the platform is used as a parallel compute server and by individual users, the scheduler requires for each node i a couple of *sharing threshold* ϑ_i^D and ϑ_i^N that is, the maximum percentage of power that the parallel application is allowed to employ on node i during day-time and night-time, respectively. When an external application requires more power than that specified by the sharing threshold value, the scheduler withdrawals the parallel application from that node. Typically, each node has its default ϑ_i^D and ϑ_i^N values that can be changed only upon explicit request at startup. These values are negotiated when the parallel user asks for accounts on non-property machines. The use of shared thresholds provides a twofold contribution. They reduce suspicious look at a shared use of resources, and allow a flexible degree of obtrusiveness of the Dame applications. For example, if the shared threshold for each node is close to zero, Dame behaves similarly to frameworks such as Condor [16] and Piranha [3] that leave a node as soon as an interactive user logs in.

3.2 Mapping Algorithms

Once defined the active platform, central to the scheduler role are the notions of *embedding* and *data mapping*. The scheduler binds the application's communication pattern to the active platform topology, and the virtual data-distribution to the data-distribution that best adapt itself to the status of each node.

The problem of embedding the communication pattern onto the active platform is highly simplified thanks to the assumption that the number of nodes of the active platform coincides with the number of active application threads.

Analogously, the data mapping is simplified because the computational domain has a fine granularity. Hence, data entries can be almost optimally assigned with no computational effort. Embedding and data mapping require the following user's information.

1. *Virtual data-distribution.*
   The programmer has implemented the SPMD application on the basis of this distribution. Two parameters characterize the division that has to be made on the computational domain: the *decomposition dimension* and the *decomposition format*. Presently, Dame manages one-dimensional (by row or column) and two-dimensional decompositions, and pure block, cyclic, or intermediate combinations of decomposition formats. Other frameworks that provide nonuniform data-distributions for cluster-based computing consider only static decompositions [8], block decompositions [12] or are not transparent to the user [4].
   One-dimensional decompositions typically lead to applications with lower number of communications. The advantage of two-dimensional decompositions is a smaller granularity of the items that can be reconfigured and, hence, a potential better load balancing. This choice is especially recommended for irregular applications. It should be noted that a parallel program implemented on the basis of a two-dimensional decomposition can run even for one-dimensional decompositions, whereas the opposite does not hold.

2. *Actual topology.*
   Various topologies are proposed in literature. However, the topologies of existing platforms are rather restricted. Presently, the scheduler manages most common topologies such as *hypercube* (e.g., Ncube2), *two-dimensional mesh* (e.g., Paragon), *single-line cluster* (e.g., nodes in the same physical network connected through one line such as Ethernet), *multiple-lines cluster* (e.g., IBM SP-2, or a Myrinet cluster where multiple lines connect the nodes), *multi-cluster* (e.g., a distributed system where the nodes belong to different physical subnetworks).

3. *Communication pattern.*
   Each SPMD message-passing application follows a prevalent pattern to exchange information among nodes. For the embedding task, the scheduler takes into account common patterns: *master/slave, near-neighbor, multicast, irregular*.

4   Dynamic Adaptivity

The dynamic adaptivity of the SPMD application is guaranteed by a *runtime environment* that consists of a dynamic activation of the scheduler to manage load and platform reconfigurations, and a runtime support that adapts the effects of Dame primitives in a transparent way, thereby masking any modification to the high-level code. The runtime scheduler aims to solve dynamic load imbalance due to the platform and/or to the application.

In particular, at runtime the scheduler copes with external factors such as active set modifications and relative node power variations when the platform is shared among multiple users. The internal factors are due to irregular applications. (As example, we have investigated the WaTor algorithm [5] and large scale molecular dynamics.) The overall process of platform and workload reconfiguration is hidden to the programmer. Moreover, the new version of the runtime scheduler uses a decision support system that automatically chooses the frequency of activation on the basis of information monitored at runtime [6].

The runtime scheduler maintains the workload proportional to the computational power of each node through migrations of data items from overloaded to underloaded nodes. Although the decision is centralized, a possible remapping is not performed by the master node that only indicates to each process which data are to be sent or received. The SPMD paradigm allows a very light-weight reconfiguration: only the local data of a process need to be moved during the migration phase. At the end of this phase, the data domain is partitioned in proportion to the power of each node.

We designed the support in a modular way so that different load balancing strategies can be easily plugged in. The dynamic load balancing model is similar to that given in [21]. It consists of four phases that can be implemented in different ways:

1. *Activation mechanism.*
   Various protocols such as synchronous/asynchronous and implicit/explicit have different degrees of interference between the support and internal processes. We propose a partial transparent framework that does not leave any responsibility for data reconfiguration to the programmer, however it requires the programmer to specify the place of the application where the support has to be activated through the `dml_check_load()` primitive. The activation interval can be chosen by the programmer or automatically set by the support [6].

2. *Load monitoring.*
   Once the support has been activated, each process evaluates the status of the external workload on its node. This phase is usually executed in a distributed way. We use two active methods for load monitoring. The alternatives regard the ways in which the load parameter can be evaluated. The first method exploits Unix system information. One can obtain different kinds of information about current computational power such as average number of tasks in the run queue, one-minute load average, rate of CPU context switches. Following Kunz's results [15], we use the number of tasks in the run queue as basis for measuring the external workload.

   An available alternative estimates the current load through a synthetic micro-benchmark that is, a purposely implemented function which gives an immediate estimate about the available capacity. The code of the micro-benchmark is specifically designed for scientific-based programs. Other classes of parallel applications would require different micro-benchmarks. The Unix call is faster in the evaluation of the load but requires some additional computations to evaluate the available capacity. Moreover, this estimate causes some approximation in the load information.

3. *Decision.*
   This phase takes two important decisions: *whether* to redistribute and *how* to redistribute. We implemented policies which are based on a centralized approach. The reconfiguration master is responsible for collecting the load parameters, executing one decision policy, and broadcasting the results to the internal processes. This message consists of three parts: *operation* (to reconfigure or not), *node information* (map of sender and receiver nodes), *data information* (map of data to transmit). Even if a centralized approach tends to be more time consuming and less feasible than distributed strategies as the number of processors in the system becomes large, we preferred a central scheme such as in [18,2,20] because it guarantees the consistency of a generic SPMD application, and allows the master to keep track of the global load situation to evaluate the relative capacities. Various decision policies can be used in Dame. They use different state information, such as instantaneous workload variation, present and past load, maximum system imbalance.

4. *Data reconfiguration.*
   When the runtime scheduler decides a data reconfiguration, each application process has to be blocked. Data migrations occur in a distributed way among the nodes that own parts of neighbor data domain. In this way, the scheduler ensures the locality of data-distribution after the reconfiguration. The scheduler is in charge of the flow control of messages for data migrations. If a one-dimensional data distribution is used, each node communicates with the two neighbor nodes. For two-dimensional data distributions, data exchanges occur first horizontally and then, if necessary, vertically.

In our current implementation, the framework follows a master/slave policy. It is activated explicitly by a call to the `dml_check_load()` function that we provide together with the run-time support. When this function is activated, each process independently evaluates the load status of its node, and transmits the new parameters to the reconfiguration master process.

Although an explicit activation of the runtime scheduler partially violates the transparency requirement that frameworks such as Dame should satisfy, the programmer's task is very limited. The check-load points are specified by the programmer if the application is parallelized by hand, or may be automatically chosen by the compiler if the application is automatically parallelized by frameworks such as HPF. However, even in this latter case, an explicit intervention of the user through some directive seems the most efficient choice because the admissible check-load points risk to be too many and the insertion of a `dml_check_load` call in each of them is impractical because of excessive overhead. Additional considerations for the automatic insertion of check-load points are discussed in [12].

5   Related Work

Dame provides a new *abstract machine interface* consisting of a programming model, a language to use it and a runtime support. From the portability point of view, it is not important if the parallelization is done by hand or automatically because the main goal is that the programmer or the supercompiler refers the implementation to the abstract machine. The code is adapted to the real platform by the *scheduler* that monitors the platform status and workload conditions. As the runtime environment does not force any adjustment on the high level code and does not require programmer's intervention, the Dame program can be considered *self-adaptable*. This property differentiates this version of Dame from other projects oriented to SPMD message-passing applications [17,9,12].

The focus on the SPMD model is the main difference among Dame solutions and the approaches of other projects that aim at a self-adaptable parallel code, but in the context of task migration [4,11] and thread migration [10] solutions, object-oriented parallelism [2,13], special languages such as Linda [3] and Dataparallel C [18], or multidisciplinary applications [7].

The DRMS support [17] achieves reconfigurable SPMD codes but not a true self-adaptivity because most responsibility for node and data repartitioning is still left to the programmer. More related to Dame's goals is the Adaptive Multiblock Parti (AMP) project [12]. An AMP programmer explicitly activates the reconfiguration support through the `remap` function. Unlike the `dml_check_load` primitive that specifies only the reconfiguration points and the domains to be reconfigured, the `remap` function requires also an explicit update of all variables and data structures that reconfiguration may affect. For this reason, a complete self-adaptivity could be achieved by the ongoing project of integrating AMP with a supercompiler, such as HPF [14], that can autonomously indicate the variables in the `remap` function.

The integration of Dame with a supercompiler would mainly address programming issues than reconfiguration aspects. The main reason is that the `dml_check_load` function is designed in such a way that it does not require the explicit specification of the data structures subject to modifications. Indeed, the semantic flexibility of Dame primitives already allows the code to self-adapt to runtime variations thus masking them to the programmer and high-level program. Another important difference of Dame from related projects is the possibility of automatically choosing the load balancing interval. Such a solution is useful to increase the degree of transparency and to optimize the performance of the load balancing support.

6   Conclusions

The importance of frameworks that guarantee self-adaptivity of SPMD applications has a twofold motivation. This paradigm is the most widely adopted for parallel programs (some estimations say about 80%) and represents the typical output of supercompilers. Moreover, the typical platform on which executing a parallel application is changing with respect to that of some years ago. Interconnected or shared platforms are becoming popular. Therefore, it is likely that a modern programmer or a supercompiler does not (want to) know the exact platform on which its application will run, but wants that code and performance portability is guaranteed at least for some large class of platforms.

This paper presents the Dame solution that enriches SPMD message-passing applications with self-adaptivity for the broad class of platforms consisting of nodes with local memory. This attribute is achieved with no additional efforts on the programmer. To preserve the simplicity of the SPMD model, we provide the programmer with an *abstract machine interface*, a *scheduler*, and a *runtime environment*. The abstract machine interface provides the programmer with a regular platform and data decomposition model. The scheduler adapts the computation written for the abstract machine to the real platform. The runtime environment performs platform reconfiguration and translates the primitives referring to the virtual platform and virtual decomposition into accesses to the actual platform.

Dame simplifies SPMD programming and provides code portability without sacrificing performance. The experimental results demonstrate that using the Dame primitives does not add significant overheads to a PVM/MPI code that is not even reconfigurable. Moreover, we verified that the benefits of Dame adaptivity are more appreciable when the platform is subject to intense power variations.

We are examining how to enrich Dame with a dynamic fault recovery mechanism. Another interesting development is the integration of Dame adaptivity mechanisms into a supercompiler such as HPF to generate portable SPMD code that does not require explicitly message passing and local memory management.

Acknowledgements

This research is supported by the Italian Ministry of University and Scientific Research in the framework of the project *High Performance Systems for Distributed Applications*.

References

1. G. Agrawal, A. Sussman, J. Saltz, "An integrated runtime and compile-time approach for parallelizing structured and block structured applications", *IEEE Trans. on Parallel and Distributed Systems*, v. 6, n. 7, pp. 747–754, July 1995.
2. J.N.C. Árabe, A. Beguelin, B. Lowekamp, E. Seligman, M. Starkey, P. Stephan, "Dome: Parallel programming in a distributed computing environment", Proc. *10th Int. Parallel Processing Symposium* (IPPS'96), Honolulu, April 1996.
3. N. Carriero, D. Kaminsky, "Adaptive parallelism and Piranha", *IEEE Computer*, v. 28, n. 1, Jan. 1995.
4. J. Casas, R. Konuru, S.W. Otto, R. Prouty, J. Walpole, "Adaptive load migration systems for PVM", *Proceedings of Supercomputing '94*, Washington, DC, pp. 390–399, Nov. 1994.

5. M. Cermele, M. Colajanni, "Nonuniform and dynamic domain decomposition for hypercomputing", *Parallel Computing*, v. 23, n. 6, pp. 697–718, June 1997.
6. M. Cermele, M. Colajanni, and S. Tucci, "Check-load interval analysis for balancing distributed SPMD applications", Proc. of *Int. Conf. on Parallel and Distributed Techniques and Applications*, Las Vegas, v. 1, pp 432–442, June 1997
7. B. Chapman, M. Haines, P. Mehrotra, H. Zima, J. Van Rosendale, "Opus: A coordination language for multidisciplinary applications", Tech. Rep. TR-97-30, ICASE, June 1997.
8. A.L. Cheung, A.P. Reeves, "High performance computing on a cluster of workstations", Proc. *1st Int. Symp. on High-Performance Distributed Computing*, Syracuse, NY, pp. 152–160, Sept. 1992.
9. M. Colajanni, M. Cermele, "Dame: An environment for preserving efficiency of data parallel computations on distributed systems", *IEEE Concurrency*, v. 5, n. 1, pp. 41–55, Jan.-Mar. 1997.
10. D. Cronk, M. Haines, P. Mehrotra, "Thread migration in the presence of pointers", Tech. Rep. TR-96-73, ICASE, Dec. 1996.
11. P. Dinda, D. O'Hallaron, J. Subhlok, J. Webb, B. Yang, "Language and run-time support for network parallel computing", Proc *8th Int. Work. on Languages and Compilers for Parallel Computing* (LCPC'95), Columbus, OH, Aug. 1995.
12. G. Edjlali, G. Agrawal, A. Sussman, J. Humphries, J. Saltz, "Runtime and compiler support for programming in adaptive parallel environments", *Scientific Programming*, v. 6, Jan. 1997.
13. A.S. Grimshaw, J.B. Weissman, W.T. Strayer, "Portable run-time support for dynamic object-oriented parallel processing", *ACM Trans. on Comp. Systems*, v. 14, n. 2, pp. 139–170, May 1996.
14. C. Koelbel, D. Loveman, R. Schreiber, G. Steele, M. Zosel, *The High Performance Fortran Handbook*, MIT Press, Cambridge, MA, 1993.
15. T. Kunz, "The influence of different workload descriptions on a heuristic load balancing scheme", *IEEE Trans. on Software Engineering*, vol. 17, no. 7, pp. 725–730, July 1991.
16. M. Litzkow, M. Livny , M.W. Mutka, "Condor - A Hunter of Idle Workstations", *Proc. of the 8th International Conference of Distributed Computing Systems*, pp. 104-111, June 1988.
17. J.E. Moreira, K. Eswar, R.B. Konuru, V.K. Naik, "Supporting dynamic data and processor repartitioning for irregular applications", Proc. *IRREGULAR'96*, Santa Barbara, pp. 237–248, Aug. 1996.
18. N. Nedeljkovic, M.J. Quinn, "Data-parallel programming on a network of heterogeneous workstations", *Concurrency: Practice and Experience*, v. 5, n. 4 , pp. 257–268, June 1993.
19. R. Ponnusamy, J. Saltz, A. Choudhary, Y.-S. Hwang, G. Fox, "Runtime support and compilation methods for user-specified irregular data distributions", *IEEE Trans. on Parallel and Distributed Systems*, v. 6, n. 8, pp. 815–829, Aug. 1995.
20. B.S. Siegell, "Automatic generation of parallel programs with dynamic load balancing for a network of workstations", Tech. Report CMU-CS-95-168, Carnegie Mellon University, May 1995.
21. M.H. Willebeek-LeMair, and A.P. Reeves, "Strategies for dynamic load balancing on highly parallel computers", *IEEE Trans. on Parallel and Distributed Systems*, vol. 4, no. 9, pp. 979–993, Sept. 1993.

Evaluating the Effectiveness of a Parallelizing Compiler

Dixie Hisley[1], Gagan Agrawal[2], and Lori Pollock[2]

[1] High Performance Computing Division
U.S. Army Research Laboratory
Aberdeen Proving Ground, MD 21005
[2] Computer and Information Sciences
University of Delaware
Newark, DE 19716

Abstract. An important question of concern for both compiler writers and computational scientists is: How does the existing compiler technology, when implemented in a production level tool, help in achieving improved performance for real scientific and engineering applications on state-of-the-art parallel systems? In this paper, we evaluate the effectiveness of the SGI compiler in parallelizing OVERFLOW, a 40,000 line production CFD code, on a 32 processor Origin 2000. Based upon our experimental results and user experiences, we describe some desirable properties of the compilation technology and software tools that would be helpful to the applications community.

1 Introduction

Compiling for parallelism has been an important research area within computer science for the past twenty years. A large number of researchers has made significant contributions to the development of fundamental dependence analyses [9] and compilation and code-improvement techniques for vector machines [1], shared memory parallel machines [3], distributed memory message passing machines [11] and distributed shared memory machines [2]. An important, yet still inadequately answered, question of concern to the compiler researchers as well as the computational scientists is:

To what extent can this compiler technology, when implemented in a production-level compiler, help the applications programmers effectively exploit the state-of-the-art parallel systems?

Academic parallelizing compiler research initially focused on developing theoretical foundations [9], followed by development of prototypes which were tested on small (typically single loop-nest) templates [11], and more recently, more integrated systems have been evaluated using some of the SPEC and SPLASH benchmarks [6], typically the codes with a few thousand lines.

In this paper, we report on our experiences in parallelizing a computational fluid dynamics (CFD) code called OVERFLOW [5], running on the distributed shared memory parallel machine, Origin 2000, using SGI's compilation system.

D. O'Hallaron (Ed.): LCR'98, LNCS 1511, pp. 195–204, 1998.

OVERFLOW is a production code consisting of 861 procedures in 45 subdirectories and a total of 40,000 lines of code. Thus, it represents an order of magnitude higher level of complexity than most of the codes previously used for evaluating parallelizing compilers. Moreover, an important limitation of the evaluation performed using the academic prototypes rather than production codes is that compilers are not responsible for generating correct codes for any possible input, and this can sometimes allow them to optimize some of the cases more aggressively.

Based upon our results and experience, we make recommendations along the following lines: (1) What additional research or results from the compiler researchers could potentially help compiler vendors and the applications community? (2) Besides compilers, what additional tools or environments would be useful to the applications community involved in a parallelization effort of this kind? and (3) How should the application scientists go about using compilers and tools to achieve good performance with a reasonable effort?

The rest of this paper is organized as follows. Section 2 presents background information on the Origin 2000 architecture and programming environment, the OVERFLOW code, and the CFD demonstration problem. Section 3 details the experimental study performed with the automatic parallelizing compiler and the user-inserted compiler directives. Performance results are given for the beta and released version of the F77 V7.2 compiler. Additional profiling data, such as cache misses, false sharing counts and synchronization costs, using SGI's hardware support for event counts are also presented. Section 4 discusses the results and provides recommendations for compiler researchers, tool development, and application scientists. Finally, conclusions are presented in Section 5.

2   Background

In this section, we give further details of the Origin 2000 system, the SGI parallelizing compiler used for our study and the OVERFLOW code.

2.1   Origin 2000

The Origin 2000 is a distributed shared memory (DSM) architecture. The Origin 2000 utilized for this study is part of the Army Research Laboratory's (ARL) Major Shared Resource Center (MSRC) supercomputing assets. It is configured with 16 nodes, each of which has 2 195 Mhz IP27 processors and 800 Mbytes of main memory. The Origin nodes are connected together by a scalable fast ethernet interconnection network. The memory associated with each node is physically distinct, however, the directory-based cache coherence protocol is at the heart of a layer of abstraction that allows the user to see the memory across nodes as one logical memory space. The access time to all memory is not uniform, but instead depends on the data distribution and the network topology.

We believe that a DSM system like the Origin 2000 is an important and interesting architecture to target for our study on the effectiveness of parallelizing compilers. We expect that distributed shared memory machines will be machines of choice for applications programmers who rely on parallelizing compilers and need to use a large system. Unlike centralized shared memory machines, these systems are scalable to large configurations. For example, the Origin 2000 is expandable to 1024 processors (512 nodes) and 1 TB of main memory. Message passing parallel machines are also scalable like the DSM systems, however, the compilers for DSM systems have had considerable more success with a variety of applications [4], as compared to the academic and production level compilers for message passing systems [8,12,10]. Since such systems provide a shared address space to the programmer, most of the techniques for compiling centralized shared memory machines are applicable to these systems. Compiling for shared memory machines is almost two decades old as a research topic, so we can expect sufficient technology transfer to the compiler vendors.

2.2 Parallel Programming Environment

The Origin 2000 can be programmed as a distributed shared memory machine, by parallelizing individual loops (which we will refer to as the *loop-level parallelism*), or as a message passing machine by creating a SPMD version of the code. We are interested in focusing on using the Origin 2000 as a distributed shared memory machine, its main intended use.

Loop-level parallelism can be achieved by: 1) using hand-inserted data parallel compiler directives, 2) using hand-inserted task parallel compiler directives, or 3) by using automatic compiler parallelization. These techniques may be used singly or in combination with each other. One advantage of loop-level parallelization is that it can be done incrementally, while checking for correctness and performance increases.

For our experimental study, we first used a beta version, and then the official released version, of SGI's FTN77 V7.2 compiler with the Power Fortran Analyzer (-pfa). The SGI compiler allows the automatic parallelizing option (-pfa) to be applied to selected subroutines. All OVERFLOW program modules were compiled with the application binary interface (ABI) set to -64 and the instruction set architecture set to MIPS IV (-mips4). Also, all modules were compiled with the highest level of optimization (-O3), which invokes aggressive optimizations including software pipelining, intrafile inlining, interprocedural analysis (inlining, common block array padding, constant propagation, dead function elimination, alias analysis, etc.) and loop nest optimizations (for example, loop fission and loop fusion). Overall, this parallelizing compiler incorporates a number of the advanced optimization techniques developed within the past few years, and therefore, it serves as a good candidate for this experimental study.

2.3 OVERFLOW

OVERFLOW originated at the NASA Ames Research Center in the sequential F3D/Chimera CFD code developed by Joseph Steger. Over the years, a number of people have made significant contributions that have taken the Chimera overlapped grid capability from a research vehicle to a production code status. The OVERFLOW documentation, written by Pieter Buning [5], identifies these individuals and their contributions.

OVERFLOW is a thin-layer Reynolds-averaged Navier Stokes solver that utilizes a finite volume, implicit, factored diagonal scheme. In this study, code options were selected that produce second order spatial accuracy, first order temporal accuracy, local time-stepping, central differencing in all directions, and Baldwin-Lomax turbulence modeling [3] plus Degani-Schiff cutoff criteria. OVERFLOW has been tuned for optimizing memory accesses on a single processor RISC-based system.

For computational testing purposes, we selected a demonstration geometry that has been previously studied and is well-documented in terms of experimental results. The geometry is an ogive-cylinder body configuration. The configuration was tested at Mach = 1.2 and at an angle of attack of 14 degrees. For timing comparison purposes, a 50-iteration sequential run was benchmarked at a wall clock time of 15:07 minutes.

We believe that OVERFLOW is an interesting code for the study of parallelizing compilers for at least two reasons. First, it is a regular code; optimizing and parallelizing compiler technology is the most well developed and has seen the most success in prototypes on regular codes. Secondly, the developers of the code, Buning, et al., carefully hand-parallelized sections of this code, which allows a comparison of the compiler-parallelized and hand-parallelized versions.

3   Experimental Study

In this section, we first report on the execution and compilation times obtained using SGI's FTN77 automatic parallelizing compiler. The results obtained from the beta release of SGI's FTN77 parallelizing We then report on various other performance measures that the Origin 2000 enables through its profiling tools perfex and speedshop.

3.1   Execution Times of the Parallel Versions

The results obtained from the beta release of SGI's FTN77 parallelizing compiler are summarized in Figure 1. All reported numbers are in minutes. #PROCS refers to the number of processors used. Though we had a 32 processor machine, we have reported results from a maximum of 31 processors. This is because the version of operating system we used (Irix 6.4) employs one processor to run all the system daemons. In ths figure shown, pfa refers to automatic compiler parallelization and mp means that only the loops with user-inserted compiler directives are parallelized, i.e., automatic parallelization is not performed. +c.d. refers to the use of hand-inserted compiler directives and -c.d. implies that compiler directives are commented out, i.e., they are not seen by the compiler. ALL_ON indicates that all 861 subroutines in OVERFLOW were compiled with the features given in parentheses. OBJ_MP_ON indicates that only 220 of the

#PROCS	ALL_ON (+pfa, +c.d.)	OBJ_MP_ON (+pfa, -c.d.)	OBJ_MP_ON (+mp, +c.d.)	OBJ_MP_ON (+pfa, +c.d.)
1		15:07	15:08	15:20
4		13:48	6:41	4:42
8		13:43	4:48	2:47
16	126:20+	13:43	4:12	2:01
31		13:45	3:58	1:35

Fig. 1. OVERFLOW (50 iterations) FTN77 V7.2 Beta Compiler

original 861 subroutines were compiled with the features given in parentheses; the other routines had no compiler directives and no effort was made to parallelize them through the compiler. This subset of 220 subroutines was chosen with two considerations. First, only a very small fraction of the overall time in the sequential run was spent in the remaining subroutines, and second, the other subroutines did not appear to have parallel loops.

The second column shows what happens when pfa is used on all of the subroutines in OVERFLOW including those with hand-inserted compiler directives (+c.d.). The generated executable appears to get into an infinite loop. This job was repeated and left to run overnight and still did not complete after 24 hours. The run had to be manually aborted.

The third column shows the timings generated when pfa is used on a carefully selected subset of the subroutines (220 out of 861), but with the user-inserted compiler directives commented out (-c.d.). Parallel speedup is practically nil and there is no noticeable scalability. This can have one of two implications: either the compiler is unable to find any parallelism by itself, or the parallelism obtained on a certain set of loops is offset by the slow-down that the compiler causes on other loops.

The fourth column uses an option to the Fortran compiler (-mp) that only produces parallel code for the loops preceded by user-inserted compiler directives. No automatic parallelism is attempted by the compiler. The timings show reasonable speedup.

The final column presents the timings that are obtained when the -pfa option is used on the selected subset of subroutines and the user-inserted compiler directives are also turned on. This column produces the best level of speedup and scalability. Note that on 31 processors, the speedup with the combination of user directives and compiler analysis is nearly 2.5 times better speedup than what could be obtained from just the user directives.

These results are very interesting in view of the results in the third column. In the third column, we had shown that the compiler, without any involvement

#PROCS	ALL_ON (+pfa, +c.d.)	OBJ_MP_ON (+pfa, -c.d.)	OBJ_MP_ON (+mp, +c.d.)	OBJ_MP_ON (+pfa, +c.d.)
1	16:50	15:12	16:21	15:59
4	6:35	13:51	6:09	5:18
8	4:07	14:00	4:48	3:04
16	1:51	13:53	4:13	2:09
31	1:41	15:38	4:06	1:36

Fig. 2. OVERFLOW (50 iterations) FTN77 V7.2 Released Compiler

from the user, produced almost negligible parallel speedup. The results from the third and fifth versions together imply that while the compiler is able to find sufficient speedup on a number of loops, it also generates code for other loops that results in a substantial slow-down. If additional user-directives are provided, this slow-down does not occur.

After these results were obtained with the beta version of the compiler, the official released version of the compiler was made available. The runs performed above were repeated; the same notation and definitions apply. The results are reported in Figure 2.

The most notable result is that the compiler no longer produces code that appears to get into an infinite loop for the second column. The rest of the trends are the same as for the beta compiler. The speedups obtained by turning on -pfa for all the subroutines (second column) as compared to a select subset of subroutines (last column) are similar. Applying the parallelizing compilation option to the remaining 641 routines does not produce any better overall speedup, which implies that the assumption made about focusing on the 220 subroutines was reasonable.

3.2   Compilation Times

We also measured the compilation times for the four different versions, using the official released version of the FTN77 V7.2 compiler. The compilation times are reported in the Figure 3. The version in the fourth column, which does not attempt any automatic parallelization, has the minimum compilation time. The versions in the third and the fifth column have almost identical compilation time. Both these versions performed automatic compiler analysis on 220 of the 861 procedures. The version in the second column has the highest compilation time, since it attempts to parallelize code in all of the 861 procedures.

Several interesting observations can be made from the compilation times reported here. If automatic parallelization is attempted on select subroutines

Version	ALL_ON (+pfa, +c.d.)	OBJ_MP_ON (+pfa, -c.d.)	OBJ_MP_ON (+mp, +c.d.)	OBJ_MP_ON (+pfa, +c.d.)
Compilation Time	29:59	12:40	8:22	12:52

Fig. 3. Compilation Times for the different versions

where most of the computation time is spent, the compilation overhead is relatively low. The compilation time went up by only 51% in going from the version in fourth column to the version in the third column. However, if automatic parallelization is attempted on all the subroutines, the net compilation cost increases significantly. The compilation time went up by 135% in going from the version in the third column to the version in the second column, whereas the speed-up achieved did not increase at all.

3.3 Additional Experimental Data and Analysis

The R10000 design in the Origin2000 provides hardware support for counting various types of events, such as cache misses, memory coherence operations, and graduated (completed) floating point operations. These counters are useful for gaining insight into where and how time is spent in an application and for discovering performance bottlenecks.

Common sources of poor scaling in any shared memory parallel machines are: load imbalance, excessive synchronization costs, and false sharing. Load imbalance can be checked by determining whether all threads issue a similar number of graduated floating point operations. Excessive synchronization costs are determined by examining whether the counts of store conditionals are high. Finally, if false sharing is a problem, then the counts of store exclusive to shared blocks should be high.

In our experimental study, we obtained event counts for floating point operations, synchronization, and false sharing. The counts showed that approximately 30% of the overall run time cost was being spent on floating point operations, while false sharing accounted for an order of magnitude less run time, and synchronization costs accounted for yet another order of magnitude less run time. These results show that synchronization costs or the false sharing are not the factors behind the limited speedup achieved on this code. The count for floating point operations showed that the last processor was always performing much more work than the others, signifying load imbalance. Assuming that all sequential portions of the code are executed on the last processor, this results shows that either the code does not have enough parallelism, or additional effort is required in extracting parallelism from other loops.

We also did an approximation study of the speedup achievable on this code using the speedup on 2 processors and the Amdahl's law. Details of this analysis will be included in the final version of the paper.

4   Discussion

Our experience with the parallelizing compiler in this study has been both positive and negative. Without any user-directives for parallelization, the compiler failed to provide any speedup on 31 processors. However, combined with additional user-directives, the compiler parallelized code performed significantly better than the code with only user-inserted parallelism. Based upon our results and our experiences in producing and analyzing our results, we can make the following recommendations.

Recommendations for Compiler Researchers: A user not sufficiently familiar with parallel machines and/or the details of the sequential code, and not having a version of the code with hand-inserted parallel directives, will only achieve the performance shown in the third columns in Figures 1 and 2, and will therefore be extremely disappointed with the use of the parallelizing compiler. When compiler tries to parallelize certain additional loops (which were parallelized by user-directives in other runs), the performance degrades below the performance when these loops were not parallelized. This implies that while attempting to parallelize certain loops, the compiler generates code that performs much worse than the sequential code, and results in substantial overall slow-down for the entire code.

Our experiments suggest that an important aspect for a parallelizing compiler is to disallow parallelization of certain loops, which are difficult to analyze, to avoid degrading the performance of the overall code. We are not aware of any research publications that focus on this aspect of the compilers. The compiler community has historically focused on developing new techniques for parallelizing loops, and has always presented positive results from certain set of loops or codes. There is a lack of reports that explain negative results, i.e., the loops for which the compiler generated worse than sequential code, and how such behavior can be avoided.

Recommendations for Developing Additional Tools: We believe that our results also strongly motivate the need for production-level tools of two types. The first is the interactive parallelizing environments, such as the Parascope Editor [7], which can allow the the compiler and the knowledgeable application programmers to work together on achieving the best possible parallelism. The ability to see what sections of the code have already been parallelized by the compiler is the key to the application programmer being able to effectively use his/her effort in parallelizing the code. The second kind of tools are the tools for profiling the execution of the code, which can allow the programmers to gather information about where time is spent in the code. Such tools are available on SGI, however, they can be improved in two directions: 1) Ability to better visualize the distribution of time graphically and 2) Integration with the compilers, especially graphically presenting the comparison of the time spent on the various parts of the code, in sequential and compiler parallelized versions.

Recommendations for Application Scientists: Our study suggests that while the application programmers cannot fully rely on the compilers to parallelize the code, they can use the compiler's abilities in conjunction with their own parallelization of the parts of the code, and other tools which may be available. More over, if the compilation time is of concern, it is important to profile the code, understand where most of the execution time is spent, and then attempt automatic parallelization on loop nests or subroutines where most of the execution time is spent.

5 Conclusions

We believe that the usefulness of advanced compiler technology for the application programmers community needs to be evaluated through experiences with large, production-level application codes. In this paper, we have presented one such experiemental study, by parallelizing a production CFD code OVERFLOW on the SGI Origin 2000. Our results have been both positive and negative for parallelizing compilers. When the automatic parallelization capabilities of the compiler were combined with some additional user-inserted compiler directives, impressive speedups were obtained. However, without any additional user-inserted directives, the compiler parallelized code resulted in only small speedups on 31 processors. Based upon our results, we have made recommendations for the compiler researchers, tools developers and application programmers.

Acknowledgements:

Gagan Agrawal was supported in part by NSF CAREER award.

References

1. Randy Allen and Ken Kennedy. Automatic translation of Fortran programs to vector form. *ACM Transactions on Programming Languages and Systems*, 9(4):491–542, October 1987.
2. J.M. Anderson, S.P. Amarasinghe, and M.S. Lam. Data and computation transformations for multiprocessors. In *Proceedings of the Fifth ACM SIGPLAN Symposium on Principles & Practice of Parallel Programming (PPOPP)*, pages 166–178. ACM Press, July 1995. ACM SIGPLAN Notices, Vol. 30, No. 8.
3. Utpal Banerjee, Rudolf Eigenmann, Alexandru Nicolau, and David A. Padua. Automatic program parallelization. *Proceedings of the IEEE*, 81(2):211–243, February 1993. In Special Section on Languages and Compilers for Parallel Machines.
4. S. Chandra and J. R. Larus. Optimizing Communication in HPF Programs for Fine-Grain Distributed Shared Memory. In *Proc. of the Sixth ACM SIGPLAN Symp. on Principles and Practice of Parallel Programming (PPOPP'97)*, pages 100–111, June 1997.
5. P. Buning *et al.* Overflow user's manual. Technical report, NASA-Ames Research Center, 1995.

6. M. W. Hall, S. Amarsinghe, B. R. Murphy, S. Liao, and Monica Lam. Detecting Course-Grain Parallelism using an Interprocedural Parallelizing Compiler. In *Proceedings Supercomputing '95*, December 1995.

7. Mary W. Hall, Timothy J. Harvey, Ken Kennedy, Nathaniel McIntosh, Kathryn S. McKinley, Jeffrey D. Oldham, Michael H. Paleczny, and Gerald Roth. Experiences using the ParaScope editor: an interactive parallel programming tool. In *Proceedings of the Fourth ACM SIGPLAN Symposium on Principles & Practice of Parallel Programming (PPOPP)*, pages 33–43, May 1993. ACM SIGPLAN Notices, Vol. 28, No. 7.

8. Seema Hiranandani, Ken Kennedy, and Chau-Wen Tseng. Compiling Fortran D for MIMD distributed-memory machines. *Communications of the ACM*, 35(8):66–80, August 1992.

9. D.J. Kuck, R.H. Kuhn, D.A. Padua, B. Leasure, and M. Wolfe. Dependence graphs and compiler optimizations. In *Proceedings of the Eighth ACM Symposium on Principles of Programming Languages*, pages 207–218. ACM Press, 1981.

10. Larry Meadows and Douglas Miles. Migrating CM Fortran applications to HPF. In *Proceedings of the Fifth Symposium on Frontiers of Massively Parallel Computation*, pages 37–40, February 1995.

11. C.-W. Tseng, S. Hiranandani, and K. Kennedy. Preliminary experiences with the Fortran D compiler. In *Proceedings Supercomputing '93*, pages 338–350. IEEE Computer Society Press, November 1993.

12. Gene Wagenbreth. APR's approach to high performance fortran for distributed memory multiprocessor systems. In *Proceedings of the Fifth Symposium on Frontiers of Massively Parallel Computation*, pages 41–45, February 1995.

Comparing Reference Counting and Global Mark-and-Sweep on Parallel Computers

Hirotaka Yamamoto, Kenjiro Taura, and Akinori Yonezawa

Department of Information Science, University of Tokyo,
Hongo 7-3-1, Bunkyo-ku, Tokyo, Japan
{ymmt,tau,yonezawa}@is.s.u-tokyo.ac.jp

Abstract. We compare two dynamic memory management schemes for distributed-memory parallel computers, one based on reference counting and the other based on global mark-and-sweep. We present a simple model in which one can analyze performance of the two types of GC schemes, and show experimental results. The two important observations drawn from the analysis are: 1) the performance of reference counting largely depends on shapes of data structures; specifically, it is bad when applications use deeply nested data structures such as distributed trees. 2) the cost of reference counting has a portion that is independent of the heap size while that of global mark-and-sweep does not. We confirmed these observations through experiments using three parallel applications.

1 Introduction

Most of the proposed algorithms and implementations of garbage collection (GC) on distributed-memory parallel computers can be classified into two groups: *Reference Counting* and *Global Mark-and-Sweep*[13]. Reference counting has often been considered superior to global mark-and-sweep because it does not require any synchronization, but previous arguments are often superficial, not confirmed by experiments, and lack a macroscopic viewpoint on the *overall efficiency* of these two collection schemes.

This paper reports a performance comparison of these two schemes, with simple analyses on the overall efficiency of both reference counting and global mark-and-sweep, and experimental results. Experiments have been done on a parallel computer in which processes communicate solely via message passing, using three parallel applications.

Observations drawn from the analyses and experimental results include:

- Performance of reference counting is sensitive to the "shape" of distributed data structure to be collected. More specifically, it is bad when the application uses deeply nested distributed data structures, such as distributed trees.
- For applications that do not heavily use such deeply nested structures, performance of a simple global mark-and-sweep and a reference counting are comparable.

D. O'Hallaron (Ed.): LCR'98, LNCS 1511, pp. 205–218, 1998.

The rest of this paper is organized as follows. Section 2 specifies the algorithms and implementations we used, then Sect. 3 analyze the performance of both reference counting and global mark-and-sweep on a simple model. Section 4 shows the results of the experiments we did to confirm our analyses. After briefly discussing other performance studies of distributed garbage collections in Sect. 5, we finally summarize our claim and state future work in Sect. 6.

2   Collection Algorithms and Implementations

2.1   Local Collector and Entry Table

Like other collectors, our reference counting and global mark-and-sweep consist of two levels — *local* and *global*. Reference counting-based collectors are often combined with a local tracing collector and keep track of reference counts only for remote references , since managing reference counts on every pointer duplication and deletion will incur very large overhead. Global mark-and-sweep also often has a local collector besides the global collector to collect local garbage quickly.

To prevent local collections from reclaiming objects that may still be referenced by other processors, an *entry table* is used. An entry table keeps pointers of an object until a global collector (either a reference counter or a global marker) finds that the object is no longer remotely referenced. The local collector simply considers the entry table as a root of a local collection.

Local collections in our collectors are co-scheduled, that is, when one processor performs a local collection, it requests all processors to perform a local collection. This does not require any synchronization, but it merely try to do local collections at the same time on all processors. This appears to entail excessive local collections at a glance and may be a waste of time; we confirmed, however, that this does not degrade performance of the applications we tested, and in fact often *improves* it, because scheduling local collections independently disturbs the synchronization performed by the applications. Further accounts on this issue whether local collections should be synchronized or not have been published in separate papers[16,18].

Garbage collections generally equip a strategy that adjusts the heap size according to the amount of live data, and dynamically expands heap (i.e., request memory from OS) when needed. When heap is exhausted, garbage collection is triggered if the application has made enough allocations since the last collection. Otherwise, heap is expanded. In [16], we have presented an adaptation of this strategy to distributed-memory parallel computers, but for the purpose of experiments in this paper, we simply give a fixed heap size when the application starts. As will be described in Sect. 4, we compare reference counting and global mark-and-sweep giving the same amount of memory.

We implemented our collectors by extending Boehm's conservative garbage collection library[5,6], which runs mainly on uniprocessor systems.

2.2   Reference Counting

In reference counting collectors, each processor increments a reference count of an object when it sends a reference to another processor and decrements a reference count of an object when it no longer uses a remote reference to the object. Objects whose reference count reached zero are unregistered from the entry table and thus can be reclaimed by a local collector. Actual implementations are more complicated to deal with communication delays and our algorithm is a variant of Weighted Reference Counting[3,17], which do not send any message when it duplicates a remote reference in contrast to naive reference countings. Details are unimportant for the purpose of this paper, though.

The question is how does a processor detect remote references that it will no longer use. Typical reference counting-based collectors on distributed environments, including ours, *detect them by local collections*; a local collection traverses objects from its local root (including its entry table) and, as a by-product of this traversal, finds remote references that are no longer reachable from its local root. It then sends "delete messages" to the owner of such references. Upon reception of a delete message, the receiver processor decrements the reference count of the corresponding object. Reference counting scheme we focus in this paper should thus be called a *hybrid* of a local tracing collector and a remote reference counting.

The overhead involved in the above hybrid scheme seems very small; it merely adds a small amount of communication overhead to each local collection. At the first glance, it seems as efficient as local mark-and-sweep on uniprocessors, and therefore more involved schemes, such as global mark-and-sweep, are unnecessary (or necessary only for collecting cycles). A careful analysis and experiments reveal that this is not quite right, however.

Leaving detailed discussion to Sect. 3, here we just illustrate a situation in which a reference counting can become very inefficient. Consider a distributed binary tree, in which all references between a parent and a child are remote, and the reference count of the root node has just become zero. The first local collection after this point only reclaims its root node, because reference counts of other nodes are still non-zero. This local collection not only retains these objects, but also spends time to traverse these (garbage) objects. Thus, the *efficiency* of this local collection – space reclaimed per work – can be as bad as reclaiming a single node by traversing the rest of the entire tree. The second collection only reclaims two nodes at the second level from the root, whose reference counts now become zero, again spending time to traverse the rest of the tree, and the third one reclaims four objects at the third level, and so forth. This is, of course, an overly pessimistic scenario, but the point we would like to clarify is that hybrid schemes of this form retain objects that could be reclaimed by one stroke of global mark-and-sweep, spending a considerable amount of time to mark them repeatedly.

2.3 Global Mark-and-Sweep

Our global collector is a natural extension to a mark-and-sweep collector on uniprocessors, which has been described in [16]. Upon a global collection, each processor starts marking from its local root (excluding its entry table) and traces remote references by sending "mark messages" to traverse the entire object graph. Objects that are not marked when marking finishes are reclaimed.

A global collector requires global coordination of all processors to detect the termination of this global marking, which has been deprecated by many studies that naive global mark-and-sweep is worse and less scalable than reference counting. We claim, however, that arguments like this lack a macroscopic viewpoint on the cost of garbage collection. A garbage collection scheme, or any memory management scheme in general, is more efficient than another as long as it reclaims a larger amount of memory with the same amount of work. In the next section, we analyze how much work is required to collect the same amount of garbage for both reference counting and global mark-and-sweep.

There remains a question as to which of local/global collections should be performed when heap overflows. We adaptively choose one by comparing the efficiency (space reclaimed per work) of the last local collection and the last global collection. A global collection is also performed when otherwise heap was expanded in the original algorithm, because we suppress heap expansion as mentioned above.

3   Performance Analysis on a Simple Model

3.1   Cost of Garbage Collection

A major goal of garbage collection is to reclaim larger amount of memory with less amount of work; in other words, to minimize the cost of garbage collection, which is defined as:

$$\text{Cost} = \frac{\text{Time spent on GC}}{\text{Amount of Allocated Memory}} . \tag{1}$$

The amount of allocated memory becomes equal to the amount of reclaimed memory if the application runs for sufficiently long term and reuses reclaimed memory many times. Therefore the cost of garbage collection can also be expressed as:

$$\text{Cost} = \frac{\text{Time spent on GC}}{\text{Amount of Reclaimed Memory}} . \tag{2}$$

For example, the cost of a tracing collector on uniprocessor systems is:

$$C_{\text{local}} = \frac{\alpha_{\text{local}} L}{H - L} \tag{3}$$

where H is the heap size, L is the amount of live objects, and α_{local} is a constant, which represents a cost to traverse one word of memory.[1] Obviously, given a larger heap, the cost of GC on uniprocessors becomes smaller.

In the rest of this section, we extend this argument to the cost of reference counting and global mark-and-sweep, assuming following simple behavior of applications.

- Applications repeat the same computation many ($= n$) times.
- Applications allocate A bytes of objects during one period of computation, and then discards all of them when it reaches the end of the period.

3.2   Analysis of Reference Counting

Depth of Garbage. As mentioned in Sect. 2, the intuitive explanation of the possible bad performance is that nodes near leaves of a distributed tree are marked many times until their reference counts become zero. Below, we formalize this intuition. First we define the *depth of a garbage object* as the minimum number that satisfies the following constraints:

- If the reference count of a garbage object o is zero, the depth of o is zero.
- If a garbage object o is referenced by a *local* reference from an object of depth d, the depth of o is at least d.
- If a garbage object o is referenced by a *remote* reference by an object of depth d, the depth of o is at least $d + 1$.

The definition captures our intuition that objects that are put at the end of a long chain of remote references are "deep". Figure 1 shows a graph of garbage objects and their depths. Under this definition, an object whose depth is d when it becomes garbage survives d local collections after it becomes garbage, and is collected by the $(d + 1)$th local collection.

Impact of Deep Garbage. Letting G_i be the total size of objects that are allocated in a period and whose depths are i when becoming garbage. Thus we have $A = \sum_{i \geq 0} G_i$. The application repeat the computation n times, thus the total amount of allocated memory is:

$$nA = n \sum_{i \geq 0} G_i \ . \tag{4}$$

Since garbage at depth d is marked d times until reclaimed, the total work required to reclaim all objects is:

$$W_{\mathrm{rc}} = \alpha_{\mathrm{local}} mL + \alpha_{\mathrm{local}} n \sum_{i \geq 0} i G_i \ , \tag{5}$$

---

[1] The cost for sweeping is ignored. In fact, it merely adds a small constant to (3) because the time spent on sweeping is proportional to the amount of allocated memory.

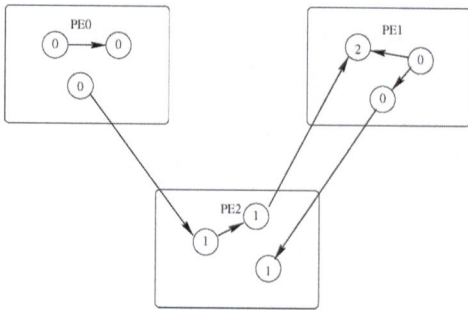

Fig. 1. Depth of Garbage. Squares, circles, and arrows represent processors, objects, and references (either remote or local) respectively. Numbers in circles are the depths of objects.

where m is the number of GCs performed during n periods of computation, which is determined by the heap size and live objects. The first term $(\alpha_{\text{local}} mL)$ represents the amount of work for live objects, and the second term $(\alpha_{\text{local}} n \sum_{i \geq 0} iG_i)$ for garbage.[2]

The total number of GCs (m) is determined as follows. Since objects at depth i when they become garbage will survive i local GCs, and the amount of such garbage allocated during two successive GCs is $\frac{n}{m} G_i$, the total amount of such garbage (originally at depth i) just before a local GC (T_{G_i}) is:

$$T_{G_i} = (i + 1) \frac{n}{m} G_i \ . \tag{6}$$

Therefore the total amount of garbage (T_G) just before a local GC is:

$$T_G = \frac{n}{m} \sum_{i \geq 0} (i + 1) G_i \ . \tag{7}$$

From the fact that T_G is equal to $H - L$,

$$m = \frac{(\sum_{i \geq 0} iG_i + \sum_{i \geq 0} G_i) n}{H - L} \ . \tag{8}$$

Thus, the cost of reference counting is:

$$C_{\text{rc}} = \frac{W_{\text{rc}}}{nA} = C_{\text{local}}(\bar{d} + 1) + \alpha_{\text{local}} \bar{d} \qquad \text{where } \bar{d} = \frac{\sum_{i \geq 0} iG_i}{\sum_{i \geq 0} G_i} \ . \tag{9}$$

$\bar{d}$ indicates the average depth of garbage. $(\bar{d} + 1) C_{\text{local}}$ is the cost to mark live objects and $\alpha_{\text{local}} \bar{d}$ is the cost to mark garbage.

---

[2] For simplicity, we do not include the amount of work required to send/receive delete messages. It would add a constant (depending on applications) to the cost of reference counting (C_{rc}).

Again, the first term represents the cost for marking live objects and the second term for dead objects. It is intuitive that the first term decreases as the heap becomes large and that the second term is proportional to the average depth of garbage ($\bar{d}$), because an object at depth d will get marked d times after it becomes garbage. Less intuitively, the first term also increases as $\bar{d}$. This is because deep garbage survives local GCs many times, hence occupies a part of heap. Therefore, deep garbage shrinks effective heap size that are available for allocation, making GCs more frequent.

Two important interpretations of this result are:

- When the average depth of garbage ($\bar{d}$) is very close to zero, $C_{rc} \approx C_{local}$, which means reference counting is as efficient as uniprocessor garbage collection. When $\bar{d}$ is large, however, this no longer holds; C_{rc} is much larger than the cost of uniprocessor garbage collection (C_{local}), especially when $\bar{d}$ is large or the heap is large (hence C_{local} is very small).
- The cost cannot be less than $\alpha_{local}\bar{d}$ no mater how large is the heap, because $\alpha_{local}\bar{d}$ is independent of the heap size. More specifically, the cost approaches a constant ($\alpha_{local}\bar{d}$) as the heap size (H) becomes sufficiently large.

3.3   Analysis of Global Mark-and-Sweep

Cost of Global Collection. Global mark-and-sweep works only on live objects, therefore we can express the cost of global mark-and-sweep as:

$$C_{gms} = \frac{\alpha_{gms}L}{H - L} = \frac{\alpha_{gms}}{\alpha_{local}}C_{local} \; , \qquad (10)$$

where α_{gms} is a constant, which represents an average cost to traverse a remote/local reference. Apparently, this does not capture dependencies on the number of processors which affects the cost for synchronization, communication latency of the network, the proportion of remote references to local references, or load in-balancing among processors which results in increase of idle time during GC. These are simply represented as an increase in α_{gms}. α_{gms} remains being a constant and independent of the heap size, however, as long as we use the same application and the same number of processors on the same machine to compare global mark-and-sweep and reference counting. Experiments in the next section are limited to meet these conditions.[3]

The cost of global mark-and-sweep thus may be several times as large as that of a local collector, but it retains a preferable feature of local GC, namely, larger heaps will reduce the cost of global mark-and-sweep.

Cost of Local Collections. As mentioned in Sect. 2, we use a local collector together with a global collector expecting that the local collector is often more efficient than the global collector.

---

[3] We agree that some of these conditions are to be removed to get more detailed characteristics of global mark-and-sweep. Our analysis is, however, still usable for the purpose of comparing two GC schemes.

A local collector used with a global collector can reclaim only garbage at depth zero (G_0). Assuming that a global collection is performed every m local collections, we can calculate the total amount of work of m local collections at:

$$W_{\text{lgc}} = \alpha_{\text{local}} \sum_{j=1}^{m} j \sum_{i>1} G_i = \alpha_{\text{local}} \frac{m(m+1)}{2} \sum_{i>1} G_i \ , \tag{11}$$

since the amount of garbage to be marked by local collector increases by $\sum_{i>1} G_i$ for every local collection. The average cost of m local collections is thus:

$$C_{\text{lgc}} = \frac{\alpha_{\text{local}}(m+1) \sum_{i>1} G_i}{2G_0} \tag{12}$$

Equation (12) indicates that:

- The cost of local collection gets worse as m becomes large.
- The cost of local collection depends on proportion of local garbage (G_0) to the other ($\sum_{i>1} G_i$); specifically, it is often bad when applications heavily use remote references.

In our implementation, however, one of local/global collection that seems to be better than another will be selected and performed dynamically. Thus the cost of local collection will never excess that of global collection. In addition, since the cost of global collection becomes smaller as heap becomes larger, the whole performance of global mark-and-sweep gets better with larger heaps.

4   Experiments

We performed experiments to compare the performance of the two distributed garbage collectors and to confirm our analyses. We used three parallel applications (Bin-tree, Puzzle, and N-body) written in a concurrent object oriented language ABCL/f in the experiments on Sun's Ultra Enterprise 10000.

4.1   Environments

ABCL/f is a concurrent object-oriented language proposed by Taura et al.[15]. It supports concurrent objects and dynamic thread creation via future call of procedures and methods. A concurrent object can be dynamically created on any processor and shared among multiple processors via remote references. Besides concurrent objects, a special object called *communication channel* is created by a remote procedure/method call to communicate the result value of the invocation. Objects that can be shared among processors thus consist of this concurrent objects and communication channels.

Sun Ultra Enterprise 10000 consists of 64 Ultra SPARC I processors operating at 250MHz, and 6 G-bytes shared-memory. We emulated distributed-memory parallel computers by running ABCL/f on a communication layer using shared-memory of a group of processes. The shared-memory has never been used except for message-passing purposes. We used only 48 processors out of 64 in experiments not to be disturbed by other system processes.

4.2   Applications

Bin-tree makes a binary tree spanning all processors whose height is 13, and traverses every node of the tree once. The construction and traverse of a tree is executed successively 60 times. Upon creating a new tree, the old tree becomes garbage. The majority of garbage therefore consists of the binary trees and communication channels.

Puzzle solves an 8-puzzle (small version of 15-puzzle) whose shortest solution is 17 steps using distributed list successively 30 times. Communication in 8-puzzle is very frequent so that it makes a number of garbage communication channels.

N-body solves N-body problem that contains 8000 objects using a hierarchical oct-tree structure[2]. It successively simulates the problem for 60 steps and replaces the old tree with a new tree for each step. Similar to Bin-tree, N-body generates distributed tree structures; it also generates, however, much more local garbage than Bin-tree while computing.

4.3   Results

To confirm the observations drawn from our analyses, we measured for each application 1) the distribution of garbage, and 2) time spent on GC for both reference counting and global mark-and-sweep.

The distribution of garbage is measured by running each application for only a single period of computation, and then repeatedly performing local collections of reference counting, without making any allocation thereafter. The amount of memory reclaimed by $(i + 1)$th local collection gives the amount of garbage at depth i (G_i). The result is shown in Fig. 2.

From Fig. 2(a), it is clear that Bin-tree generates a considerable amount of *deep* garbage, which required many local collections to be collected. Figure 2(c), on the other hand, indicates that most garbage generated by N-body is shallow and thus can be efficiently reclaimed by the reference counting. Note that garbage of depth 0 is special in that they can be collected without reference counting; a simple local collection that is used in the global garbage collection suffices.

Figure 3 shows the time spent on GC in each application. GC time is totaled over all (48) processors. LGC, RRC, and GGC are elapsed time in local collections, sending and receiving delete messages, and global collections, respectively. The x-axis represents the heap size of one processor, where L refers to the minimum heap size required to run that application. L is measured by invoking global mark-and-sweep very eagerly and frequently. Each application was then run with various heap sizes ranging from $2L$ to $8L$. L was 6M bytes for Bin-tree, 2.5M bytes for Puzzle, and 5.5M bytes for N-body.

Global mark-and-sweep was better in two applications, and most notably, was significantly better in Bin-tree. In addition, when the heap size increases, global mark-and-sweep consistently becomes better, whereas reference counting does not.

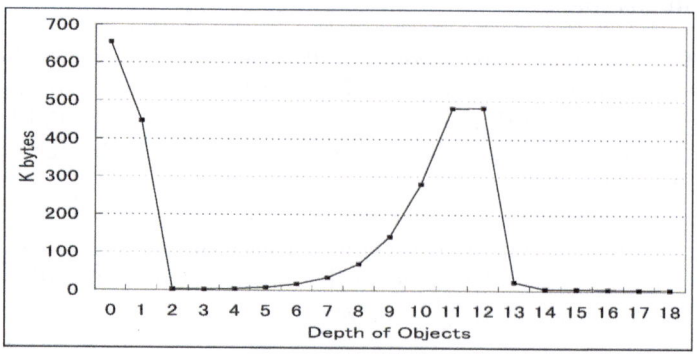

(a) Bin-tree

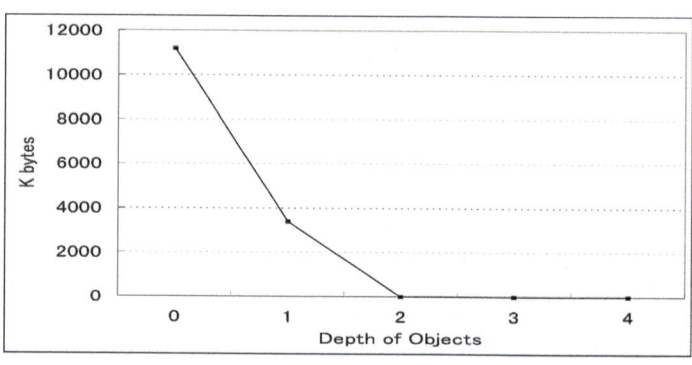

(b) Puzzle

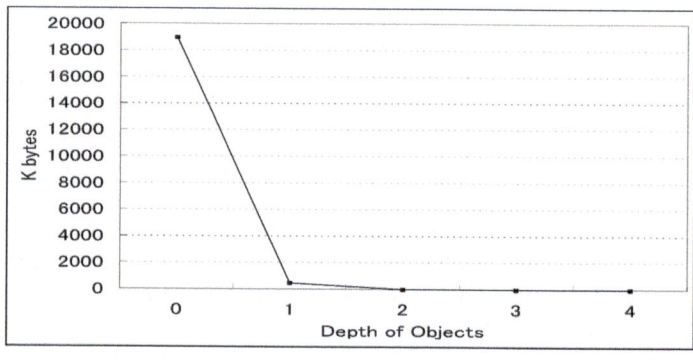

(c) N-body

Fig. 2. Distribution of Garbage. The x-axis indicates the depth of garbage whose amount is shown by the y-axis.

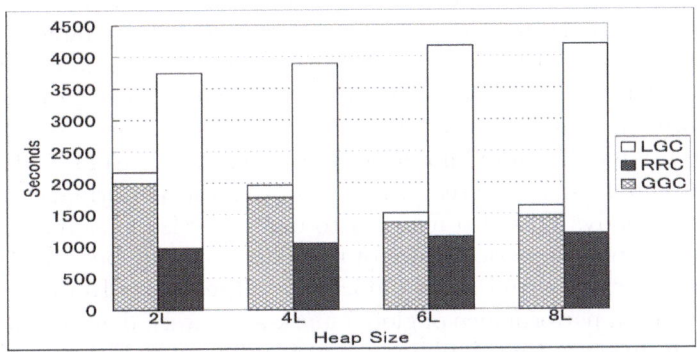

(a) Bin-tree

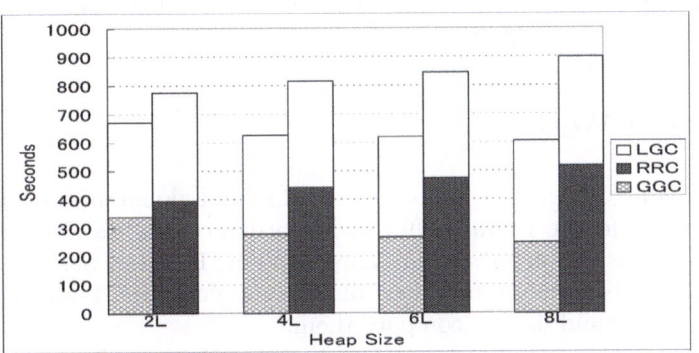

(b) Puzzle

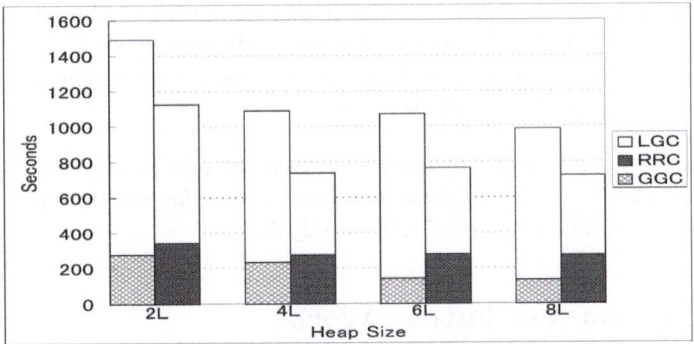

(c) N-body

Fig. 3. Elapsed Time in GC. Vertical bars represent the time spent on GC; left bars represent the time of global mark-and-sweep, and right bars represent the time of reference counting.

These results match fairly well to our experimental results; as to Bin-tree and Puzzle where the weighted average of depth of garbage are larger than that of N-body, reference counting performed worse than global mark-and-sweep as our analyses predicted. As to N-body, on the other hand, most garbage is shallow and reference counting performed better.

Moreover, larger heaps did not improve the performance of reference counting in Bin-tree and Puzzle, whereas they improved the performance of reference counting in N-body. This also matches to our analysis of reference counting in which we predicted the performance of reference counting becomes independent of the heap size when $\bar{d}$ and H are sufficiently large, like in Bin-tree and Puzzle.

The presented performance of global mark-and-sweep does not fit our prediction so much, in sense that doubling heap size did not half the total time spent on global mark-and-sweep. We guess that there are some inherent overheads in Boehm's library when handling so large heaps, and this is probably also why the performance of reference counting was gradually getting worse as heap became larger in Bin-tree and Puzzle.

5   Related Work

A number of algorithms for reference counting and global mark-and-sweep have been proposed in the literature[9,13]. Performance studies are rare, presumably because most of them are not implemented. Existing performance studies [10,14,16,19] only show performance of either a global mark-and-sweep or a reference counting and do not compare them.

Most of previous works about distributed garbage collection schemes have been saying that:

– Reference counting can do local collections independently and can incrementally reclaim global garbage without any difficulties, whereas global mark-and-sweep requires global coordination of all processors.
– Naive reference counting-based collectors cannot reclaim cyclic garbage while mark-and-sweep based collectors can.

These statements are correct; however, they do not clearly explain *the difference between performance of these two collection schemes*, or explain it without experiments or sufficiently convincing analysis.

6   Conclusion and Future Work

Analysis shown in Sect. 3 clarified that the efficiency of (hybrid) reference counting schemes can potentially be very bad. Experimental results in Sect. 4.3 confirmed that a reference counting could perform much worse than a (fairly unsophisticated) global mark-and-sweep.

A better understanding on the benefit of reference counting is:

- It is as efficient as uniprocessor mark-and-sweep, *as long as most distributed garbage is shallow*, (i.e., not put at the end of a long chain of remote references).
- Reference counting does not require *any extra implementation effort* to make it latency-tolerant, because communication latency is naturally masked by the application. Notice that while the global mark-and-sweep presented in this paper may be sensitive to latency, it is certainly possible to make a global mark-and-sweep latency-tolerant, in ways described in [7] or [10], for example. Hence, the real benefit is that the latency tolerance comes free for reference counting.

To summarize, it will be a choice in environments where communication latency is very long, or we know that most distributed garbage is shallow. They will be the case, for example, in distributed server-client computing in which most references direct from a client to the server, hence long chains of remote references are rarely created. This was not the case, on the other hand, in parallel applications in which deeply nested data structures are often created and the latency of communication is typically much smaller than that of LAN. Interestingly enough, the situation may be changing in distributed computing environments too, with the emerging low-latency interconnect technologies [4,8] and global computing paradigms[1].

We are now planning to:

- adapt our analysis to other GC algorithms such as Hughes' time-stamp based global collector[7], indirect reference counting[12], or generational local collector[11],
- perform more experiments using realistic applications and true distributed-memory computers,
- and extend our analysis of global mark-and-sweep.

Acknowledgment

A discussion with Takashi Chikayama was a start to extend our previous incomplete work. Naoki Kobayashi gave us lots of invaluable comments on drafts of this paper. We are also thankful to the anonymous referees for their insightful comments. We extend our thanks to many people who read and commented on earlier versions of this paper: Tomio Kamada, Toshio Endo, and Norifumi Gotoh.

References

1. A. D. Alexandrov, M. Ibel, K. E. Schauser, and C. J. Scheiman. SuperWeb: Research Issues in Java-Based Global Computing. *Concurrency: Practice and Experience*, June 1997.
2. Josh Barnes and Piet Hut. A hierarchical $O(N \log N)$ force-calculation algorithm. *Nature*, (324):446–449, 1986.

3. David I. Bevan. Distributed garbage collection using reference counting. In *Parallel Architectures and Languages Europe*, number 258 in Lecture Notes in Computer Science, pages 176–187. Springer-Verlag, 1987.

4. Nanette J. Boden, Danny Cohen, Robert E. Felderman, Alan E. Kulawik, Charles L. Seitz, Jakov N. Seizovic, and Wen-King Su. Myrinet: A gigabit-per-second local area network. *IEEE Micro*, 15(1):29–36, February 1995.

5. Hans-Juergen Boehm. Space efficient conservative garbage collection. In *Conference on Programming Language Design and Implementation*, SIGPLAN NOTICES, pages 197–206. ACM, June 1993.

6. Hans-Juergen Boehm and David Chase. A proposal for garbage-collector-safe c compilation. *The Journal of C Language Translation*, 4(2):126–141, December 1992.

7. John Hughes. A distributed garbage collection algorithm. In *Proceedings of Functional Programming Languages and Computer Architecture*, number 201 in Lecture Notes in Computer Science, pages 256–272. Springer-Verlag, 1985.

8. IEEE Computer Society, New York, USA. *IEEE Standard for Scalable Coherent Interface (SCI)*, August 1993.

9. Richard Jones and Rafael Lins. *Garbage Collection, Algorithms for Automatic Dynamic Memory Management*. Joen Wiley & Sons, 1996.

10. Tomio Kamada, Satoshi Matsuoka, and Akinori Yonezawa. Efficient parallel global garbage collection on massively parallel computers. In *Proceedings of SuperComputing*, pages 79–88, 1994.

11. Henry Lieberman and Carl Hewitt. A real-time garbage collector based on the lifetimes of objects. *Communications of the ACM*, June 1983.

12. Jose M. Piquer. Indirect reference-counting, a distributed garbage collection algorithm. In *Parallel Architectures and Languages Europe, Lecture Notes in Computer Science*, number 365,366, pages 150–165. Springer-Verlag, June 1991.

13. David Plainfossé and Marc Shapiro. A survey of distributed garbage collection techniques. In *Proceedings of International Workshop on Memory Management*, number 986 in Lecture Notes in Computer Science. Springer-Verlag, 1995.

14. Kazuaki Rokusawa and Nobuyuki Ichiyoshi. Evaluation of remote reference management in a distributed KL1 implementation. *IPSJ SIG Notes 96-PRO-8 (SWoPP'96 PRO)*, 96:13–18, August 1996. (in Japanese).

15. Kenjiro Taura, Satoshi Matsuoka, and Akinori Yonezawa. ABCL/f :a future-based polymorphic typed concurrent object-oriented language — its design and implementation. In *Specification of Parallel Algorithms*, DIMACS, pages 275–291, 1994.

16. Kenjiro Taura and Akinori Yonezawa. An effective garbage collection strategy for parallel programming languages on large scale distributed-memory machines. In *Proceedings of Principles and Practice of Parallel Programming*, SIGPLAN, pages 264–275. ACM, June 1997.

17. Paul Watson and Ian Watson. An efficient garbage collection scheme for parallel computer architectures. In *Parallel Architectures and Languages Europe*, number 258 in Lecture Notes in Computer Science, pages 432–443. Springer-Verlag, 1987.

18. Hirotaka Yamamoto, Kenjiro Taura, and Akinori Yonezawa. A performance comparison between reference count and distributed marking for global garbage collection scheme on distributed-memory machines. *IPSJ SIG Notes 97-PRO-14 (SWoPP'97 PRO)*, 97(78):109–114, August 1997. (in Japanese).

19. Masahiro Yasugi. Evaluation of distributed concurrent garbage collection on a data-driven parallel computer. In *Proceedings of Joint Symposium on Parallel Processing*, volume 97, pages 345–352, May 1997.

Design of the GODIVA Performance Measurement System *

Terrence W. Pratt

CESDIS
NASA Goddard Space Flight Center
Greenbelt, Maryland
pratt@cesdis.gsfc.nasa.gov

Abstract. GODIVA (GODdard Instrumentation Visualizer and Analyzer) is a software system for instrumentation and performance analysis of large Fortran and C science codes executing on scalable parallel systems, including traditional MPPs and Beowulf-class clusters. The system consists of an annotation "language" used to add annotations to Fortran or C codes, a preprocessor for translating annotated codes into standard Fortran or C with embedded calls to the Godiva run-time library, the run-time library itself, and a set of postprocessors for generating analyses of instrumentation data collected during program execution. This paper provides an overview of the system and discusses several of the most important and unique design decisions that differentiate Godiva from other performance measurement systems.

1 Introduction

Godiva is a new software system for performance measurement and analysis. Work on Godiva began in 1995 and the first version became available in April 1996. Godiva Version 3.4 is currently in regular use by the author on the Goddard 1088- processor SGI/Cray T3E, two Beowulf-class machines at Goddard (networked PC's running parallel Linux), and uniprocessor Sun workstations. This paper represents the first public presentation of the system. It provides a brief overview of the system structure and then focuses on discussion of several of the key design decisions that differentiate Godiva from other performance measurement systems, such as Pablo, AIMS, Paradyn, and the SGI/Cray Apprentice and PAT tools. A companion paper[3] describes in greater detail the novel aspects of Godiva that target the analysis of data and data flow. The complete Godiva User's Manual may be viewed on the Web[2].

The development of Godiva is part of a larger project within the NASA HPCC Program in Earth and Space Science (HPCC/ESS). This program is

* This work was supported by the NASA HPCC Project in Earth and Space Science, through Task 31 at the Center of Excellence in Space Data and Information Sciences (CESDIS) at the NASA Goddard Space Flight Center. CESDIS is operated by the Universities Space Research Association (USRA), a university consortium, under contract to NASA.

D. O'Hallaron (Ed.): LCR'98, LNCS 1511, pp. 219–228, 1998.

currently funding nine "Grand Challenge" science teams at U.S. universities together with a cooperative agreement with SGI/Cray that has placed a T3E at Goddard, primarily for use by the Grand Challenge teams to run large science simulation programs in various areas of Earth and space science. Performance milestones, stated in terms of 10, 50, and 100 Gflop/s sustained computation rates, are an important aspect of this program. As part of the HPCC/ESS program, the author heads a small research activity to study new methods for understanding the performance of these large science simulation codes on scalable parallel systems. The goal of this "Performance Evaluation Project" is to understand in depth how these ESS codes perform on the current scalable parallel systems, such as the T3E, with an eye to later NASA procurements of large scalable systems to support ESS research activity. For more detail about this project see sdcd.gsfc.nasa.gov/ESS.

Within this programmatic context, the Performance Evaluation Project is attempting to do a comprehensive analysis of about a dozen large science codes, produced by the Grand Challenge teams and submitted to the NASA HPCC/ESS project for distribution through the HPCC Software Exchange. The Godiva software is being used to support this activity. Godiva is not yet available for general distribution.

The requirement that Godiva be useful for the comprehensive analysis of large production science codes, and that it be useful on a traditional MPP with 500+ processors, has played an important role in some of the design decisions discussed below. Because the concept of a "Beowulf" system (a networked cluster of PC's running parallel Linux) was invented by Thomas Sterling at CESDIS as part of the NASA HPCC/ESS project and implemented in two major systems currently at Goddard, there also has been continuing interest in using Godiva to compare performance of traditional MPPs and Beowulf-class machines on ESS codes. This requirement has also been important in the Godiva design.

2 Overview of Godiva Structure and Use

The Godiva software system has a structure typical of many performance measurement tools: preprocessor, run-time library, and postprocessor, but with several unique elements. We begin with a brief overview of how Godiva is used.

The Godiva user begins with a source code in Fortran or C. Special Godiva annotations are inserted into the source code by the user to identify elements to be counted and timed in various ways. The number and complexity of these annotations may range from a simple counting and timing of the executions of one or more code segments to a complete data flow analysis of the entire code executing in parallel on hundreds of processors.

The annotated source code is fed to the preprocessor, which reads the annotations and processes them. Some annotations are data descriptions, which are tabled for later use. Most other annotations generate calls to routines in the Godiva run-time library. The preprocessor produces as its output a Fortran or C source program. A key design element is that the preprocessor does not process any of the underlying program's source code; the preprocessor only looks at Godiva annotations and skips over the source code itself.

The source program produced by the preprocessor can be compiled by the user with whatever optimization or other compilation options are desired. Because Godiva annotations only introduce subroutine/function calls and are usually placed outside of inner loops, most compiler optimizations of inner loops are not affected by the instrumentation. Godiva annotations appear as comments to the Fortran compiler (in C, they are simply removed by the Godiva preprocessor).

The compiled object code is next linked with the Godiva run-time library (more accurately described as a run-time "package" consisting of both data structures and routines). The object code is then run and the Godiva library routines generate the desired statistics and other measurements. To avoid the need for frequent recompilation, various elements of Godiva tracing are controlled by a run-time Godiva input file, which can be modified and the code rerun without source code changes.

Execution of the program on a parallel system produces one trace output file for each processor. The Godiva post-processors are used to produce various tables and histograms from each trace file, again controlled by a list of user choices. Graphical output is produced as data and command files for the widely available *gnuplot* graphical plotting and display tool.

Annotating a Source Code

The Godiva preprocessor recognizes about thirty different types of annotations, including the following:

1. *Data declarations:* annotations **global/local/defblks/undef** for defining "interesting" global and local arrays.
2. *Subprogram interfaces:* annotations **main/rstart/arg/formal-arg** for defining main program and subprogram names and data passed in a subprogram call.
3. *Code segments:* annotations **kstart/kend** delimiting "interesting" code segments that should be timed and counted.
4. *Activity within a code segment:* annotations **in/out/inout** describing data flow in and out of code segments, **read/write/open/close/seek** describing input/output activity, **send/recv/bcast/recvany** describing parallel communication, **flops** for flop counts, and the like.
5. *Cache alignments:* annotations **cache/endcache/in/out/inout** allowing display of where array slices fall in cache.
6. *Asynchronous counters and timers:* annotations **count/timeron/timeroff** for counters and timers that may be used anywhere.
7. *Trace control:* Annotations **traceon/traceoff** to toggle tracing on/off.

Example. Annotation of a Fortran 77 routine for matrix multiplication might look like this. The user-provided Godiva annotations are comments that begin with the tag "!...". Explanatory comments follow "–" and are not part of the annotation.

```
!...rstart matmul              -- define a routine matmul
      subroutine matmul (A,B,C,n)
!...formal-arg 1 = A,B,C         -- first arg of interest is #1
      real A(n,n), B(n,n), C(n,n)
!...local [8](n,n) :: A,B,C      -- each array elem has 8 bytes
!...defblks               -- data def lib calls go here
c
!...kstart                -- begin interesting code seg
!...in (*,*) :: A,B           -- use the declared array dims
!...out (*,*) :: C
!...flops [n*n*n*2]                -- count 2 flops per loop iter
      do i = 1,n
        do j = 1,n
          C(i,j) = 0.0
          do k = 1,n
            C(i,j) =  C(i,j) + A(i,k) * B(k,j)
          enddo
        enddo
      enddo
!...kend                  -- end of timed segment
      return
      end
```

This annotated code would be combined with other annotated routines and the main program (which must always be included) and run through the Godiva preprocessor to produce the source code to be compiled. After compilation and linking with the Godiva run-time library, the object file is ready for execution.

Executing the Annotated Code

A run-time options file is read by the Godiva library routines at the start of execution. The options available in this file allow the program to be executed in a variety of configurations without recompilation. Options include setting the trace file name and path, setting points at which to toggle tracing on and off during the run, getting a "progress display" of the number of traced segments executed, choosing a time step size for time-histograms (to control the level of detail in histograms), and setting a point at which to end tracing completely, possibly coupled with termination of the run. For *live-dead* data flow analysis, a particularly costly tracing option, the option may be used or disabled. Most of the basic trace data gathering is always done during execution; only live-dead analysis may be disabled in the current version of Godiva.

For example, in the *matmul* code above, execution would cause the loop nest to be timed on each execution and the number of executions counted. At each execution, the 'flops' expression would be evaluated and the value added to the flops total for the segment. Also the formal argument arrays A, B, and C would be associated with the actual argument arrays back in the calling program, and the volume of *in* and *out* data for the code segment would be computed and tallied, both for the segment and for the individual actual parameter arrays. At the user's option, the *in-out* data flow information could also be used in tracking the *live-dead* data throughout execution in each of the actual arrays corresponding to the formal arrays A, B, and C.

Generating Results from Trace Files

When execution is complete, each parallel process will have generated its own trace file (named with the user chosen file name appended with a node number). Trace file size is determined by the run-time trace options chosen and the execution path followed. The Godiva postprocessor reads a second options file created by the user (which specifies the output tables and histograms the user wants to see) and then applies these options in postprocessing a trace file to produce usable results. The same options may be applied to all trace files, or separate options may be chosen for different trace files. Options include the following (chosen by including the tag word in the options file for the postprocessor):

ksegs: Summarize the timing and data flow activity for each annotated code segment (kseg).

flops: Summarize the flop counts, timings, and flop/sec rates for each kseg.

blocks: Summarize data block activity – sizes of blocks and data flow volumes.

ios: Summarize input/output activity and send/receive activity.

mpi: Summarize parallel communication and synchronization activity.

histos: Generate a set of histograms (displayed using gnuplot) which show variations in kseg execution rates, flop rates, and communication volumes during execution.

cache: Generate a set of snapshot plots showing layout in cache of data segments.

mem: Generate a set of histograms showing variations in live-dead-allocated data volumes during execution for each data block.

Of course, each option only generates displays of data that the user gathered through annotations. For example in the *matmul* code, the choice of the postprocessing options **ksegs**, **flops**, and **blocks** would cause tables to be produced which summarized the total number of times the kseg in *matmul* was executed, the total time taken, the average time/execution, the total and average volume of *in-out* data for these executions, the total flops counted and the average flop/sec rate for the loop nest. Choice of the **histos** option would generate histogram files showing the pattern of execution of the kseg, the variations in flop rate over time, and the variations in *in-out* data volume. If the *live-dead* data analysis option were chosen during execution, so that *live-dead* data was actually collected, then choice of the **mem** option would also allow a look at variations in the amount of *live-dead* data in each data block during execution, including the effect of the references, during execution of *matmul*, to arrays A and B (keeping the values alive) and the setting of new values in array C (making the old values dead and creating new live values).

3   Design Choices: Pro's and Con's

Because of its total reliance on user provided annotations of applications codes, the Godiva design represents one extreme in the design space of performance measurement systems for scalable computers. The major contribution of this paper lies in the identification of some of the key design choices in Godiva and discussion of the advantages and disadvantages of these choices as they have played out in practice over the past two years. We believe other designers might benefit from our experience. In this section, we address some of these choices, starting with the most obviously controversial.

Choice 1: Manual user annotation of source codes. The user is responsible for identifying what to instrument and measure and for providing the details of exactly how to count many elements such as flops and data volumes. The alternative design would provide automatic measurement of these elements.

Advantages: Annotations have proven to be a remarkably flexible instrumentation technique. In our experience, each new large code has unique measurement issues. Annotations have allowed many unforeseen measurement problems to be successfully addressed. Annotations also allow careful user control of the tradeoff between the cost of measurement and the detail of measurement: a fast run to gather basic information about a code, or a slower run to gather more detail about a particular part of a code.

In addition, note that Godiva is a rapidly evolving prototype. We want to keep the software design simple so that its rapid evolution may continue as we gain experience. As the design matures and stabilizes it will be relatively easy to scan the source code and automatically generate many of the annotations now generated manually.

Disadvantages: Manual annotation of some code elements such as flops counts and the shape of in/out/inout data slices can be tedious, error-prone, and time consuming.

Choice 2: All instrumentation is at the source code level. Godiva counts and measures things that are visible in the source code, such as code segments and user data objects. Flop counting is a good example. With the **flops** annotation, the user specifies the flop count to associate with a particular code segment. No attempt to access hardware flop counters is made in the current system (although later versions will provide this access as an option).

Advantages: All instrumentation results are immediately in terms of source code constructs such as routines, arrays, code segments, I/O statements, MPI calls, and the like.

Disadvantages: If a compiler radically reorganizes a code segment, the instrumentation could be wrong. If accurate hardware or OS measurements are available they are ignored (with the exception of the use of OS timers).

Choice 3: Preprocessor scans only annotations, not source code.

Advantages: Annotations may be used to creatively "lie" about the source code, for example, in specifying counts and data volumes. This option can sometimes be useful to answer "what if" questions about a code without actually changing the code, or to ignore some pathological code component whose accurate measurement might skew the measurements desired.

Disadvantages: Annotations can inadvertently "lie" about the source code, through user error. No cross checking is provided.

Choice 4: Tracing results are aggregated on-the-fly during execution.
Originally we thought it would be best to generate time-stamped event traces during execution, to be postprocessed later into aggregate statistics of various kinds. Version 1 of Godiva did this; it was a mistake. The event trace files were far too large to save for any length of time and they took a lot of time to generate.

Advantages: Because the trace data is aggregated during execution, trace files are relatively small. On-the-fly trace data aggregation scales well to larger, longer running codes.

Disadvantages: To see different aggregations of the data, the code may need to be rerun.

Choice 5: Single node performance gets as much attention as parallel activity.
Annotations are provided in Godiva that allow detailed analysis of loops, library function calls, cache layouts, and other on-node code activities that often dominate performance issues in real codes.

Advantages: This has turned out to be a major strength of Godiva. In several codes we have used Godiva to look deeply into performance issues of key loops. It is possible to instrument relatively easily most on-node code segments and count and time the key elements.

Disadvantages: Accurate timing of small, frequently executed segments can introduce a prohibitive measurement cost and severe timing measurement errors. Annotation of complex loops may be quite tedious.

Choice 6: Data and data flow get as much attention as computation and control flow.
Perhaps the most unique Godiva annotations are those that allow a complete instrumentation of the data flow (of slices of major arrays) in a code (see [3]). Annotations can be used to track the flow of data through the major levels of the storage/ memory hierarchy (secondary storage to remote memories to local memory and through the processor cache).

Advantages: In parallel machines, data flow is a major element in many performance issues. The ability to accurately describe and track this data flow can provide deep insight into how a code behaves.

Disadvantages: Annotating data flow accurately is the most difficult and tedious of the Godiva instrumentation options, and a full data flow analysis can add significant overhead to a run.

Choice 7: Measuring application code "stress patterns" gets as much attention as measuring system performance. Much of the Godiva design is concerned with providing ways to understand and characterize how large science application codes "stress" scalable parallel machines. These stress patterns are independent of the machine "response" (in terms of good or bad performance). By attempting to quantify these stress patterns we hope to gain a deeper understanding of how different applications codes differ in their stress patterns.

Advantages: The ability to easily "quantify" performance related stress patterns in a code provides a deeper understanding of the code's behavior, and allows the "response" of different machines to be understood in terms of these patterns rather than simply in terms of overall timings. Issues of scaling and load balance may also be understood more fully in terms of these patterns.

Disadvantages: Gathering a comprehensive and accurate picture of the stress patterns produced by an applications code using only annotations can be tedious and error prone.

4   Comparison with Other Systems

Browne, Dongarra, and London[1] have recently completed a useful comparison of several major performance measurement systems for scalable parallel machines that have broadly similar goals to the Godiva effort. AIMS, Nupshot, Pablo, Paradyn, VAMPIR, and VT (see the references in [1]) are the systems reviewed. In addition we have used the SGI/Cray Apprentice and PAT tools for the T3E. In general, these other systems provide much more sophisticated graphical user interfaces, reflecting their maturity and the level of effort involved in their construction. For the most part, these systems allow the user to choose various types of code constructs to be measured (MPI calls, loops, I/O) and then the system automatically inserts the instrumentation required. For many types of analysis, such as a detailed understanding of patterns of MPI parallel communication and synchronization, one of these other tools will be superior to Godiva in both ease of use and detail of analysis. In our work on the T3E, we often use both the SGI/Cray tools and Godiva in studying a code's performance.

Godiva differs from these tools primarily in its emphasis on user annotations and in its features for analysis of data and data flow. For some types of analysis, Godiva provides more flexibility and user control. However, Godiva clearly suffers in the simplicity of its user interface and its lack of automatic instrumentation.

5   Conclusions

Full technical details of the Godiva design and use may be found in the Godiva User's Manual[2]. After two years of rapid evolution of the Godiva design based on practical experience with earlier versions, our evaluation of the current design is this, using the same evaluation framework used by Browne, Dongarra, and London [1].

Portability: Godiva has a relatively simple interface to the operating system and compilers. It is written entirely in standard C and uses only a few system services (timers, processor numbers, I/O). The preprocessor does not scan source code and generates only Fortran 77 or standard C subroutine/function calls as output. This combination has allowed relatively easy porting to several machines (in a few hours typically).

Versatility: The current annotation set in Godiva 3.4 provides a fairly comprehensive set of instrumentation capabilities to measure both on-node and off-node performance, and to probe a code either broadly across all of its components or deeply within a single component. The Godiva annotation scheme allows precise user control over exactly what is instrumented and measured in a code. This provides excellent flexibility in adapting to unforeseen measurement requirements and in balancing the cost of tracing against the detail desired. In addition (although this is not an option for the user but a benefit in a prototype) the relatively simple Godiva software structure has allowed repeated extension to meet new requirements through the addition of new annotation forms, new library control options, and new postprocessing options.

Usability: The lack of a graphical user interface and of automatic insertion of instrumentation is a detriment to usability. The straightforward annotation syntax and the flexible set of run-time and postprocessing options, however, have proven to make the system reasonably easy to use for most analyses of interest.

Speed in analysis is important to usability. The Godiva run-time library is fast for most analyses, usually adding only a few percent to overall execution time. At the opposite extreme, data flow analysis is the most time-consuming form of analysis during execution (because of the need to track all elements of all arrays being traced) and a full data flow analysis with live-dead data tracking can more than double execution time. In most cases, the user can adjust the amount of data-flow tracing to get an acceptable level of tracing overhead. The Godiva preprocessor and postprocessors are extremely fast (although speed here is usually not an issue).

Scalability: Godiva has been used on codes as large as 40K lines, involving dozens of routines and hundreds of arrays and code segments, during runs that take 15–30 minutes on machines of up to 512 processors. It has proven to be easy to make simple analyses on larger codes. Comprehensive annotation of larger codes has proven to be tedious and error-prone.

Robustness: Considerable attention is placed on robustness in the internal software design, in that much checking is done for user and system errors that might cause a software failure. However, because the prototype has been rapidly evolving through use and is not intended for general distribution, systematic testing has not been performed for all options.

The Godiva software has benefited from the chance to rapidly evolve the design during use analyzing the actual target codes and machines of interest. A number of features that appeared initially to be of value have been either extensively modified or deleted based on experience, and new features have been added. We expect the system to continue to evolve, although somewhat more slowly, in the future.

References

1. S. Browne, J. Dongarra, and K. London. Review of performance analysis tools for mpi parallel programs. Technical Report CEWES MSRC/PET TR/98-02, CEWES Major Shared Resource Center, Vicksburg, MS, January 1998.
2. T. Pratt. *Godiva Users Manual, Version 3.4*. CESDIS, 1997. see the System Performance Evaluation icon at sdcd.gsfc.nasa.gov/ESS.
3. T. Pratt. Using godiva for data flow analysis. In *2nd SIGMETRICS Symposium on Parallel and Distributed Tools*, Welches, Oregon, August 1998. ACM.

Instrumentation Database for Performance Analysis of Parallel Scientific Applications [*]

Jeffrey Nesheiwat and Boleslaw K. Szymanski
E-mail: {neshj, szymansk}@cs.rpi.edu

Rensselaer Polytechnic Institute
Department of Computer Science
Troy, NY 12180-3590, USA

Abstract. Parallel codes, especially scientific applications, have increased the need for performance analysis tools. In this paper we present an approach that addresses some of the difficulties inherent to the analysis of parallel codes. To this end we examine the three components that comprise performance analysis: instrumentation, visualization, and analysis. The essence of our approach is to use a database to capture instrumentation data. We discuss how this approach influences the design of performance analysis components. We further motivate our approach with an example using a sparse matrix vector product code. We conclude by discussing some of the key implementation issues and outlining future plans.

1 Introduction

Performance analysis has become a vital part of the software development process, given the complex nature of scientific applications and the changing landscape of computer architectures. The difficulties inherent to analyzing the performance of sequential programs are exacerbated when we move to parallel codes [2].

A problem inherent to most profiling systems is *the probe effect*, [5] where adding instrumentation alters the performance of the application. Not only are the timings of events tainted, but control flows governed by asynchronous events are altered. Probing the state of the machine is not sufficient enough for localizing bottlenecks with respect to the executing program. Moreover, parallel codes, like sequential codes, behave differently depending on the inputs they act on. Input vectors and machine state have a dramatic effect on where bottlenecks are found.

Traditional performance tools simply probe the state of the machine and provide little or no way to map instrumentation data to actual source code. It is far more useful to map a potential bottleneck to a given loop, module, or other program construct. Moreover, some algorithms lend themselves well to specific architectures. There is a need for a standard instrumentation and

---

[*] This work was partially supported by NSF Grant CCR-9527151. The content does not necessarily reflect the position or policy of the U.S. Government.

D. O'Hallaron (Ed.): LCR'98, LNCS 1511, pp. 229–242, 1998.

analysis tool that can collect generic data that supports comparative analysis. Mapping performance data to source code and architecture helps ensure that a given architecture is appropriate.

In this paper we outline an approach to performance analysis that addresses these issues. This will be preceded by an overview of the central components of performance analysis tools, namely: instrumentation, visualization, and analysis. We also discuss some existing tools and their approach to these key areas.

The essence of our approach is to exploit database technology to collect and organize instrumentation data. The collected data can be queried by the user to derive meaningful performance information. At the same time, a database interface shields the user from being overwhelmed by the sheer volume of the collected data. Our approach is illustrated by instrumenting a portion of the Spark98 [8] code. This is a sparse matrix vector product kernel that operates on meshes, modeling ground movement in the San Fernando Valley during an earthquake.

2   Tool Components

A performance tool must closely approximate the process of analyzing a program's performance. This involves instrumenting the program, visualizing the data, and lastly analyzing the data.

2.1   Instrumentation

Instrumentation can be defined as the steps taken to gather performance data. These can be counters showing how frequently a module is invoked, timers showing how much time was spent executing, or timers measuring communication and synchronization delays. The granularity of these data range from individual program statements up to the state of the machine. Instrumentation can be introduced at various levels:

Hardware: Hardware can be used to count the number of mathematical operations, monitor network utilization, time critical events, etc.

Kernel: Special facilities can be provided by the kernel and operating system to monitor system call usage and probe the state of the machine using timed interrupts.

Compiler: Instrumentation can be added to a program without modifying the original program text by having the compiler collect information about the program structure and linking in profiling libraries that extend the functionality of standard libraries.

Binary: Some tools, e.g., *Paradyn* [7], actually modify the binary image of an executing program to collect timing and frequency information for critical areas of the program. This technique involves overwriting a portion of the binary with a jump to a module that will start/stop a timer or increment a counter.

Source: When other means are not available or appropriate, adding code to the program is the easiest way to collect performance data. This can be as simple as adding timers and counters to measure specific regions of the code where bottlenecks are likely to exist.

There are advantages and drawbacks to instrumenting at each of these levels. Hardware provides the most accurate and fine grain data, however it is costly to implement, not portable, and cannot be easily modified. Many supercomputers provide hardware instrumentation facilities. All of the other methods provide varying degrees of granularity and invasiveness. In short, they all suffer from the *Probe Effect* to varying degrees. This goes beyond the issue of tainting timing data, it also alters the control flow of the program. Asynchronous events governed by the program's execution are now governed by the program and its accompanying instrumentation. Periodically probing the state of the machine will generate a lot of data which are difficult to reconcile with the source program. Most sampling facilities included as part of the operating system provide no mapping to the executing program. Instrumenting at the binary level is dynamic, in that it can be added and removed during execution. This technique is only applicable to long running programs. In recent years, the use of object oriented languages for parallel programming has increased, exacerbating the need for new instrumentation techniques.

There is also an issue of *data scalability*. The amount of instrumentation data collected is usually proportional to the execution time of the program and to the number of processors used. In some cases, tools such as *AIMS* [5] collect and write instrumentation data to disk at a rate of megabytes per second. Overwhelming system resources by such a flood of data will invariably affect measured performance.

Performance analysis usually begins with running the program and determining if the performance is acceptable. If not, the modules of the program are profiled to determine where the majority of time is being spent. Time critical modules are further examined to find which loops and communication events are consuming the most time. To facilitate this top down approach we generate the program's control flow hierarchy [6] at compile time (Figure-1).

A control flow hierarchy is tightly coupled with the structure of the program and it ensures data scalability since the structure of the program does not change with the execution time or the size of input data. Moreover, instrumentation data associated with this hierarchy maps to the source code nicely. This technique can be extended to support object oriented programs. A control flow hierarchy, once captured by a database schema, allows queries to the instrumentation database to be cast in terms of source code features. The mapping of control flow hierarchy onto a database schema is a fundamental feature of our approach.

2.2 Visualization

A great deal of effort has gone into performance visualization. There are a large number of tools on many platforms that provide visual displays of performance

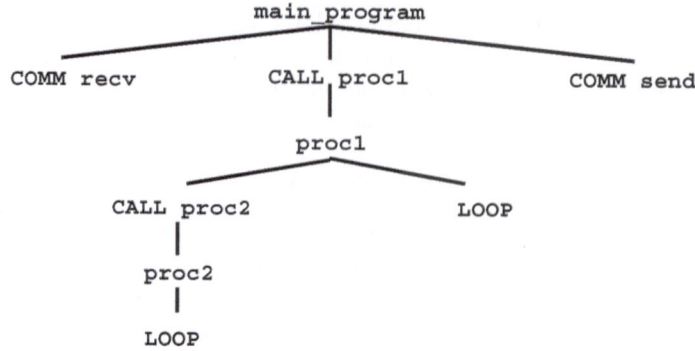

Fig. 1. Sample control flow hierarchy generated at compile time.

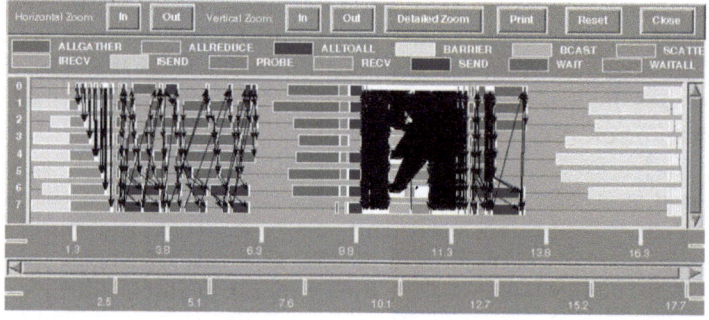

Fig. 2. Upshot visualization of mesh partitioning algorithm using 8 processors. High degrees of interprocessor communication render this an ineffective way to visualize performance.

data [3]. Similar to data scalability, there is the notion of *visual scalability*. Most visualizations work well for programs that run for a short time on a small number of processors. As these quantities increase, the visual display becomes less useful and more overwhelming to the user. A good example of this effect is *Upshot* [9], the performance visualization tool that is distributed with the *MPI* library. It uses Gantt charts to display the status for each processor. Such a display becomes overwhelming for programs with large running times, high interprocessor communication, or that use many processors (Figure-2).

Apprentice [5], the performance tool that runs on Cray supercomputers, does an excellent job at ensuring visual scalability. It shows module performance relative to other modules. The values it displays are maintained as running sums, thus ensuring scalable displays.

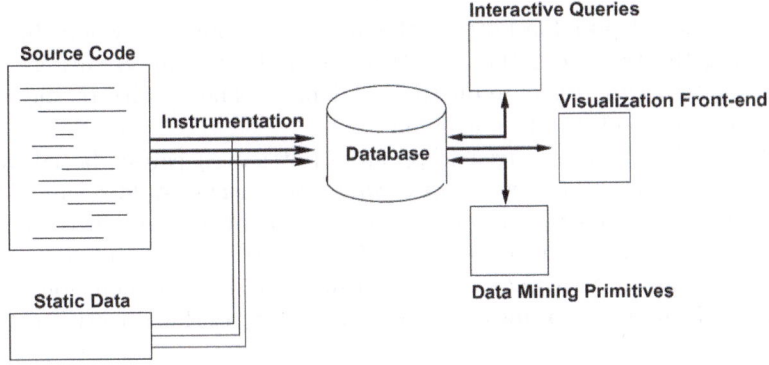

Fig. 3. Instrumentation database architecture.

Another technique is to provide the user with multiple performance views. This is desirable because it allows the user to visualize properties relevant to the program being analyzed. For example, if a program is communication intensive, network visualizations are going to be most useful; whereas if a program is compute bound, processor utilization views would be useful. Apprentice provides the user with multiple performance views such as: call graphs, histograms, tables, and even source code views. Ideally, the user should be able to define what information is visualized. This is achieved in our approach because an instrumentation database provides a standard representation for instrumentation data that can be queried by the user.

2.3   Analysis

Analysis involves more than drawing conclusions. It involves breaking down and organizing available information, thus enabling the user to draw multiple conclusions. It is here that our instrumentation database approach is most useful. A framework for understanding a program's performance can be formed based on instrumentation data collected in a scalable way. This information in conjunction with static data about the architecture, program, and inputs can be used to derive an integrated view of the program's performance across multiple runs and architectures.

In our approach, the instrumentation database (Figure-3) archives collected performance data for a given program. As the program is run repeatedly with different parameters, the database can be used to derive multiple conclusions about overall performance. The hierarchical instrumentation and static data captured by the database schema make it possible to map performance to actual source code and run-time environment.

Some tools automate the actual analysis of a program by using expert systems, artificial intelligence, or, as is the the case of *Paradyn*, a W^3 search tree

[4]. This is a tree of possible bottleneck causes and condition when they occur. By traversing the tree from the root through nodes where conditions are satisfied, the system will converge on the bottleneck. The quality of the result is dependant on how well the tree is defined.

A W^3 search traverses a tree of possible bottleneck causes based on proving hypotheses as to *what, where and when* bottlenecks could occur. The tree and answers are defined by the programmer. In contrast, our instrumentation database approach does not automate analysis. Instead, it ensures that the user has access to information necessary to draw meaningful conclusions about a program's performance. To this end, there are three interfaces to the instrumentation database:

1. An *interactive query language* allows the user to retrieve specific information from the database. The information required to analyze a program is embedded in the source code in a complex way. It is for this reason that the user should have direct access to the database. Queries provide an expressive means through which the user can sift through large amounts of information without being overwhelmed. It is up to the user to determine what information is relevant.
2. *Data mining primitives* built on top of the interactive query language provide a set of powerful queries that derive performance characteristics based on trends in the raw instrumentation data. These primitives can be extended to meet more specialized needs.
3. A *front-end visualization tool* to display general performance information graphically. This can be useful for *zooming* into the instrumentation hierarchy to determine where the majority of execution time is spent within the program. The limitation of this tool is that it can only visualize general information. Since the front-end visualizes query results, it can be easily extended to provide specialized views.

These interfaces shield the user from the sheer volume of collected data while providing the means for deriving meaningful performance information.

3   Sparse Matrix Vector Product Example

Spark98 is a set of kernels for Sparse Matrix Vector Product (SMVP) computations [8]. The kernels run a number of shared and distributed memory implementations of a SMVP problem. The matrices are derived from finite element simulation of ground movement in the San Fernando Valley during an earthquake. The Spark98 kernels are well suited to illustrate the basics of the instrumentation database approach. The small size makes working with the codes easy. Multiple parallel and sequential implementations are useful for comparative analysis. Lastly, the kernels are a realistic representation of a large class of scientific applications. The example presented in this section is a subset of the sequential implementation of the SMVP problem.

3.1   Instrumentation

A control flow hierarchy is generated automatically at run-time. In this example, we generate hierarchies for a subset of the sequential Spark98 code. Figure-4 shows the `main` module and its accompanying control flow hierarchy. The subsequent figures show hierarchies for other modules.

Each node in the *control flow hierarchy*, CFH for short, maps to a performance critical event in the program. These events are of the following four types:

PROC which maps procedure definitions. These are high-level probes that collect module level instrumentation data.

LOOP that collects data for all iteratation constructs.

CALL which measures performance for function calls. This is useful for analyzing library routines, system calls, or other opaque structures.

COMM that instruments blocking send and receive instructions.

In a fully instrumented program, data is collected for each of these events. To ensure data scalability individual data points are not collected. Instead running statistics are continually refined every time a probe is encountered. Once the statistics are updated, the data point is discarded. In this way, each probe's information is of fixed size. The CFH's size is solely a function of the program structure, hence data scalability is ensured. This data is collected by calls to an instrumentation application programmer's interface (API), as shown in table-1.

OPERATION	PARAMETERS	DESCRIPTION
INIT	IDB-FILE, CFG-FILE	Initializes data structures, reads configuration file (CFG-FILE). Prepares database (IDB-FILE) for writing.
CLOSE	NONE	Flushes data structures to database and deallocates storage
START	PROBE-ID, PROBE-TYPE	Allocates data structures for probe if needed. Starts probe timers, increments counter and begins collecting noise reduction data.
STOP	PROBE-ID	Stops timer, updates noise reduction data

Table 1. Instrumentation API

Specialized performance data can be derived, or inferred, from a minimal set of statistical data collected at run time (see table-2).

A database schema can capture these control flow hierarchies and their accompanying statistical data which vary with each run of the program. The

DATA	DESCRIPTION
AVG	Average time spent executing event
MIN	Shortest time spent executing event
MAX	Longest time spent executing event
TIME	Time spent on current execution of event
SDEV	Standard deviation of measured times
COUNT/ITER	Number of times event was executed

Table 2. Statistics collected by each probe for a given PROC, CALL, LOOP, or COMM event.

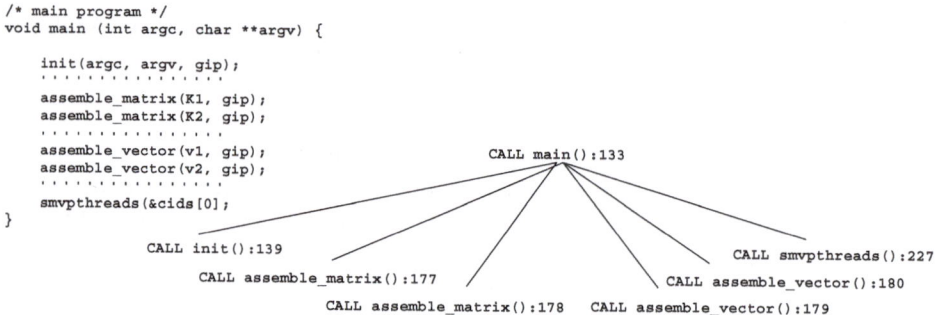

Fig. 4. A fragment of the Spark98 `main` program and its accompanying control flow hierarchy.

schema is also augmented with static information such as target architecture, compile options, and inputs. In this case the input refers to the mesh read in by the Spark98 kernel. The kernels are distributed with three differently sized meshes that model ground movement at different sampling rates.

3.2 Analysis

The database is populated when the program is run. To form a general view of the program's performance, we permute parameters, such as mesh that is used or optimization levels. Once populated, queries can be issued to the database to determine the performance characteristics of the program. Queries originate from one of three sources. A front-end visualization tool can query the database to generate its graphical views. A set of *canned queries* can be used to extract information across multiple runs of the same program. This is particularly useful in determining which inputs are particularly well suited to the program. Lastly, the database can be queried directly using an interactive query language. Since

```
void *smvpthread(void *a)
{
    ....................................................
    for (i=0;i<gip->iters; i++) {
        /* w1 = K1*v1 */
        zero_vector(w1, 0, gip->nodes);
        local_smvp(gip->nodes, K1, gip->matrixcol,
            v1, w1, 0, gip->nodes, id, gip);

        /* w2 = K1*v2 */
        zero_vector(v2, 0, gip->nodes);
        local_smvp(gip->nodes, K2, gip->matrixcol,
            v2, w2, 0, gip->nodes, id, gip);
    }
    ...........................................................
    return NULL;
}
```

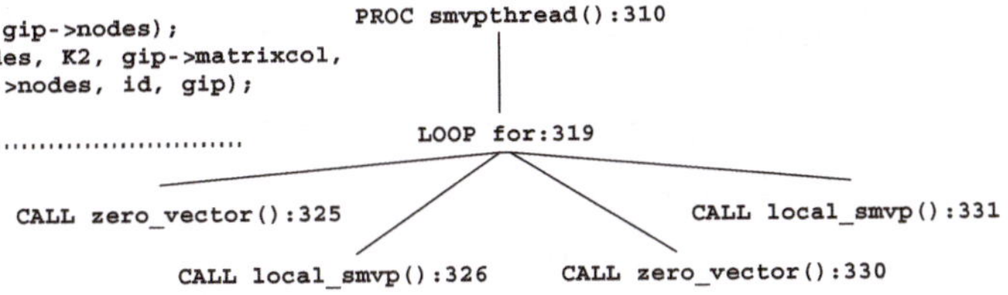

PROC smvpthread():310

LOOP for:319

CALL zero_vector():325   CALL local_smvp():331

CALL local_smvp():326   CALL zero_vector():330

Fig. 5. A fragment of the `smvpthread` module and its accompanying control flow hierarchy.

the program is instrumented evenly, all parts of the program incur similar delays thus preserving the relative timings of events, even on different architectures.

Noise Reduction Performance tools strive to collect accurate data with as little intrusion to the executing program as possible. Various noise reduction techniques are used to ensure that the collected data is accurate. Instrumented programs suffer from a *dialation effect* which causes the program to take longer to execute because of the instrumentation overhead. Dialation and noise are reduced by factoring out instrumentation costs, efficient implementation, and selective instrumentation of only portions of the program.

Each probe in the CFH has noise associated with it. This noise is a function of two parameters; the nesting level of probes from the root node, and the number of times that these probes are executed. Each time a probe is encountered, data is collected and stored in the CFH, incurring an overhead on every PROC, CALL, LOOP, and COMM event. We employ two techniques to minimize and factor out this noise.

Each probe measures how long it takes to complete its own instrumentation activities. This information is stored locally for each probe in the CFH as its cumulative overhead contribution. The total noise of the program can be factored out by summing these values for all nested probes. For example, to factor out the total noise for the program, simply sum these values for every node in the CFH and subtract the resulting value from the time stored at the root node. The best way to eliminate instrumentation overhead is to avoid instrumenting at all. There are many regions of a program that do not need to be instrumented because the code is provably optimal or is simply not in the critical execution path and will not impact performance significantly. Instrumentation at the source code level can be inserted selectively to probe only those areas of the program that are of

```
void assemble_matrix(double (*K)[DOF][DOF], struct gi *gip)
{
    .....................................................
    for (i=0;i<gip->matrixlen; i++) {
        for (j=0;j<DOF;j++) {
            for (k=0;k<DOF;k++) {
                K[i][j][k] = 0.0;
            }
        }
    }
    for (elem = 0;elem<gip->elems;elem++) {
        for (j=0;j<gip->corners;j++) {
            for (k=0;i<gip->corners;k++) {
                ...........................................
                while (gip->matrixcol[templ] != gip->vertex[elem][k]) {
                    ...........................................
                }
                for (l=0;l<3;l++) {
                    for (m=0;m<3;m++) {
                        K[templ][l][m++];
                    }
                }
            }
        }
    }
}
```

PROC assemble_matrix():347

LOOP for:351   LOOP for:358

LOOP for:352   LOOP for:359

LOOP for:353   LOOP for:360

LOOP while:367   LOOP for:375

LOOP for:376

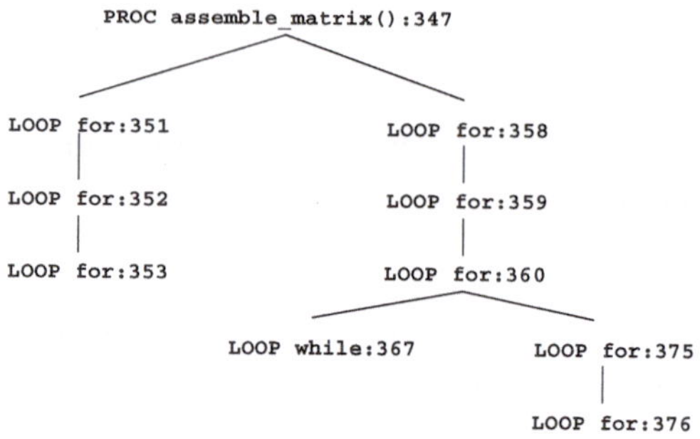

Fig. 6. A fragment of the `assemble_matrix` module and its accompanying control flow hierarchy.

interest. Figure-7 illustrates the notion of blackening out loops. Trivial loops are the most common source of noise, by blackening them out, we avoid unnecessary probing thus reducing noise and dialation.

Derived Attributes Given the information in table 3, simple queries can be issued to the instrumentation database to ascertain which function has the longest running time.

Function	Running Time
local_smvp()	50.37s
assemble_matrix()	23.21s
zero_vector()	00.69s

Table 3. Running times of selected Spark98 functions measured using `gprof`.

(a).   **(b).**

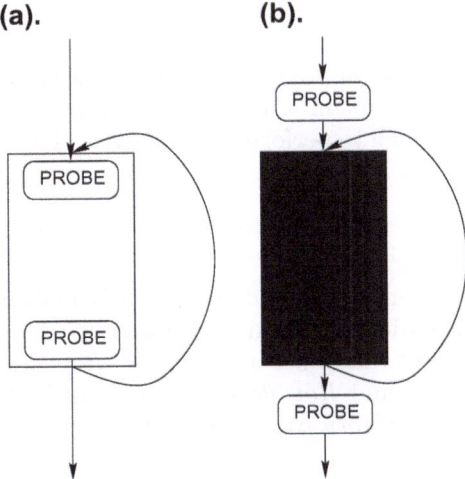

Fig. 7. (a). Whitebox loop instrumentation collects instrumentation data for each iteration of the loop. (b). Blackbox loop instrumentation collects instrumentation data once, treating the loop as a single event.

Q1 = SELECT procedure
        FROM   runs(Spark98, Nodes=1,
                    Arch='Solaris_25', mesh='sf5.1.pack')
        WHERE run_time = MAX(procedure.run_time)

This query would return the database tuples containing probe data corresponding to the control flow hierarchy rooted at `local_smvp`, the function with the longest running time. This is the first step in a top down analysis. The next step would be to find the bottleneck within this function.

Q2 = SELECT Event
        FROM   Q1
        WHERE run_time = MAX(event.run_time)

This simple example does not show the full analytic capabilities of our approach. It shows how a relational *view* is formed using the `run()` portion of the FROM part in Q1. It also shows how metrics that we do not explicitly collect can be derived, or inferred, from the collected data. In this example, the search for the function with the longest run time is restricted to sequential runs of the Spark98 kernel for a specific architecture and mesh. The SQL syntax can be extended to provide easier interface to database contents.

4   Conclusion

In this paper we lay out an approach for instrumenting and analyzing the performance of parallel programs in a data scalable way. Our initial work suggests that this is a valid approach to performance analysis. The next step is to address some fundamental design issues.

4.1   Design Issues

The instrumentation techniques outlined previously make it possible to collect a small amount of information from which performance data can be derived. This gives rise to two questions that must be answered: *How do we represent this data internally in a database?* and *How do we extend our instrumentation approach to deal with distributed memory parallel programs?*

Schema Design. The data to be stored in the instrumentation database falls into one of three categories:

1. *Static Data* which associates program executions with static information such as: architecture, input vector, compiler, etc.
2. *Probe Data* contains actual statistical information about each probe, namely MIN, MAX, AVG, SDEV, TIME, COUNT, NOISE, etc.
3. *CFH Data* defines how all probes for a given run are related to each other. This hierarchy resembles the control flow graph of the program. It differs in that the only nodes represented correspond to CALL, PROC, LOOP, and COMM events.

A relational database is ideal for storing tabular information[1] such as the *Static Data* or the *Probe Table* as shown in figure-8. Relational databases are not adequate for storing graph based information, such as the CFH, in such a way that it can be efficiently queried. Object-oriented databases are particularly well suited to storing and querying graph data. An object oriented database will be used to capture the control flow hierarchy and traditional relations will be used to store statistical and static information. In this way, queries can be cast in terms of how probes are interconnected across multiple control flow hierarchies representing different runs.

Parallel Support. For parallel programs, collecting the instrumentation data globally would necessitate syncronizing the data gathering and could lead to resource contention. To avoid these difficulties, each processor in our approach maintains its own CFH and probe data. After execution, the local data for each processor are coalesced during the post-processing phase (see figure-9).

Two other possible approaches involve communicating all data to a singe node for on-the-fly processing or having each processor write output sequentially using synchronization barriers [10]. The disadvantage to these methods is that network load and processor synchronization is adversely affected during run time.

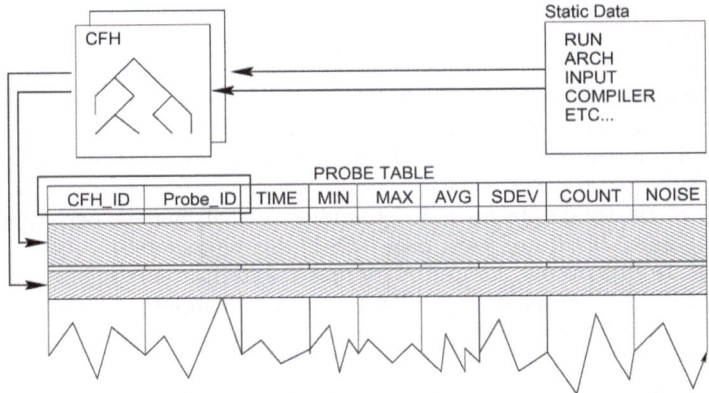

Fig. 8. Static Data is associated with numerous Control Flow Heirarchies, one for each run of the program. A CFH is associated with the Probe Table. The CFH provides parent and child pointer information for each probe. The dotted box around the first two entries in the Probe Table signifies that the CFH_ID and the PROBE_ID together act as the primary key for indexing probes. This means that no two entries in the database will have the same values for these two attributes.

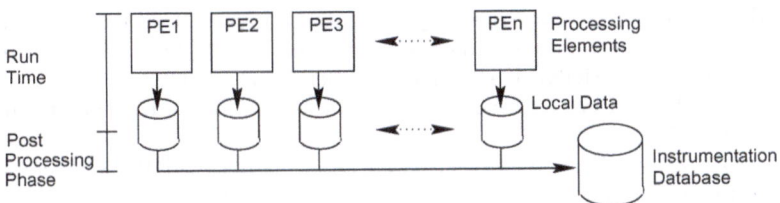

Fig. 9. Each processing element collects instrumentation data locally at run-time. This data is merged into the instrumentation database after the program has completed executing.

4.2   Future Work

The described approach is in its early stages of development and much of the work remains to be done. Short term goals include automating the instrumentation process. This will allow larger codes to be analyzed. Schema design and implementation must be completed to facilitate basic query development and ultimately data mining primitives. Long term goals include building support for object oriented parallel languages, extending SQL syntax to support basic analysis semantics, and developing front-end visualization tools.

References

1. Elmasri and Navathe. *Fundamentals of Database Systems Second Edition*. The Benjamin/Cummings Publishing Company, Inc., 1994. 240
2. Michael T. Heath. *Visualization of Parallel and Distributed Systems*, chapter 31. McGraw-Hill, 1996. 229
3. Michael T. Heath and Jennifer A. Etheridge. Visualizing the performance of parallel programs. *IEEE Software*, pages 29–39, September 1991. 232
4. Jeffrey K. Hollingsworth, James E. Lumpp Jr., and Barton P. Miller. Techniques for performance measurement of parallel programs. Computer Sciences Department, University of Wisconin and Department of Electrical Engineering, University of Kentucky. 234
5. Anna Hondroudakis. Performance analaysis tools for parallel programs. Technical report, Edinburgh Parallel Computing Centre, The University of Edinburgh, July 1995. 229, 231, 232
6. Kei-Chun Li and Kang Zhang. Stamp: A stopwatch approach for monitoring performance of parallel programs. Department of Computing, Macquarie University, 1996. 231
7. Barton P. Miller, Mark D. Callaghan Jeffrey K. Hollingsworth, Jonathan M. Cargille, R. Bruce Irvin, Karen L. Karavanik, Krishna Kunchithapadam, and Tia Newhall. The paradyn parallel performance measurement tools. *IEEE Computer*, 28(11), November 1995. Special Issue on Performance Analysis Tools for Parallel and Distributed Computer Systems. 230
8. David R. O'Hallaron. Spark98: Sparse matrix kernels for shared memory and message passing systems. Technical Report CMU-CS-97-178, School of Computer Sciences, Carnegie Mellon University, October 1997. 230, 234
9. Peter S. Pacheco. *Parallel Programming with MPI*. Morgan Kaufmann Publishers, Inc., 1997. 232
10. Marc Snir, Steve W. Otto, Steven Huss-Lederman, David W. Walker, and Jack Dongarra. *MPI: The Complete Reference*. The MIT Press, 1996. 240

A Performance Prediction Framework for Data Intensive Applications on Large Scale Parallel Machines*

Mustafa Uysal, Tahsin M. Kurc, Alan Sussman, and Joel Saltz

UMIACS and Department of Computer Science
University of Maryland
College Park, MD 20742
{uysal,kurc,als,saltz}@cs.umd.edu

Abstract. This paper presents a simulation-based performance prediction framework for large scale data-intensive applications on large scale machines. Our framework consists of two components: application emulators and a suite of simulators. Application emulators provide a parameterized model of data access and computation patterns of the applications and enable changing of critical application components (input data partitioning, data declustering, processing structure, etc.) easily and flexibly. Our suite of simulators model the I/O and communication subsystems with good accuracy and execute quickly on a high-performance workstation to allow performance prediction of large scale parallel machine configurations. The key to efficient simulation of very large scale configurations is a technique called *loosely-coupled simulation* where the processing structure of the application is embedded in the simulator, while preserving data dependencies and data distributions. We evaluate our performance prediction tool using a set of three data-intensive applications.

1 Introduction

In recent years, data-intensive parallel applications [1,2,5,6,8] have emerged as one of the leading consumers of cycles on parallel machines. The main distinction of these applications from more traditional compute-intensive applications is that they access and perform operations on huge amounts of disk-resident data. It is critical that future parallel machines be designed to accommodate the characteristics of data-intensive applications. Conversely, application developers need tools to predict the performance of their applications on existing and future parallel machines.

In this paper we present a simulation-based framework for performance prediction of large scale data-intensive applications on large scale parallel machines.

---

* This research was supported by the Department of Defense, Advanced Research Projects Agency and Office of Naval Research, under contract No. N66001-97-C-8534, by NSF under contracts #BIR9318183, #ACI-9619020 (UC Subcontract #10152408) and #CDA9401151, by ARPA under contract No. #DABT63-94-C-0049 (Caltech subcontract #9503), and by grants from IBM and Digital Equipment Corporation.

D. O'Hallaron (Ed.): LCR'98, LNCS 1511, pp. 243–258, 1998.

Our framework consists of two components: *application emulators* and *a suite of simulators*. We have developed application emulators that accurately capture the behavior of three data-intensive applications that represent three typical classes of data-intensive applications, in a sufficient level of detail for performing performance prediction for large scale parallel machines. Emulators provide parameterized models of these applications, which make it possible to scale applications in a controlled way. We have also developed a set of simulation models that are both sufficiently accurate and execute quickly, so are capable of simulating parallel machine configurations of up to thousands of processors on a high-performance workstation. These simulators model the I/O and communication subsystems of the parallel machine at a sufficiently detailed level for accuracy in predicting application performance, while providing relatively coarse grain models of the execution of instructions within each processor. We describe a new technique, *loosely coupled simulation*, that embeds the processing structure of the application in the form of *work flow graphs* into the simulator while preserving the application workload. This technique allows accurate, yet relatively inexpensive performance prediction for very large scale parallel machines.

The rest of the paper is organized as follows. Section 2 presents the class of applications for which we have developed application emulators. Section 3 describes in detail what an application emulator is, and presents an application emulator for one of the applications as an example. In Section 4, we present the suite of simulation models we have developed and discuss the various tradeoffs that can be made between accuracy of prediction and speed of simulation. In particular, we discuss the issues involved in coupling application emulators to simulators, and describe loosely-coupled simulation as an efficient technique for interaction between an application emulator and a simulator. Section 5 presents an experimental evaluation of the simulation models. Related work is briefly summarized in Section 6, and we conclude in Section 7.

2   Data Intensive Applications Suite

In this section we briefly describe the data intensive applications that have motivated this work.

2.1   Remote Sensing - Titan and Pathfinder

Titan [6] is a parallel shared-nothing database server designed to handle satellite data. The input data for Titan are sensor readings from the entire surface of the earth taken from the AVHRR sensor on the NOAA-7 series of satellites. The satellite orbits the earth in a polar orbit, and the sensor sweeps the surface of the earth gathering readings in different bands of the electro-magnetic spectrum. Each sensor reading is associated with a position (longitude and latitude) and the time the reading was recorded for indexing purposes. In a typical operation for Titan, user issues a query to specify the data of interest in space and time. Data intersecting the query are retrieved from disks and processed to generate the output. The output is a two-dimensional multi-band image generated by various types of aggregation operations on the sensor readings, with the resolution of its pixels selected by the query.

Titan operates on data-blocks, which are formed by groups of spatially close sensor readings. When a query is received, a list of data-block requests for each processor is generated. Each list contains read requests for the data-blocks that are stored on the local disks of the processor and that intersect the query window. The operation of Titan on a parallel machine employs a peer-to-peer architecture. Input data-blocks are distributed across the local disks of all processors and each processor is involved in retrieval and processing of data-blocks. The 2D output image is also partitioned among all processors, and each processor is responsible for processing data-blocks that fall into its local subregion of the image. Processors perform retrieval, processing and exchange of data-blocks in a completely asynchronous manner [6]. In this processing loop, a processor issues disk reads, sends and receives data-blocks to and from other processors, and performs the computation required to process the retrieved data-blocks. Non-blocking I/O and communication operations are used to hide latency and overlap these operations with computation. The data-blocks are the atomic units of I/O and communication. That is, even if a data-block partially intersects with the query window and/or the subregion of the output image assigned to a processor, the entire data-block is retrieved from disk and is exchanged between processors.

Pathfinder [1] is very similar to Titan except that it always processes *all* the input data that is available for a particular time period, over the entire surface of the earth. In addition, the operation of Pathfinder on a parallel machine employs a client/server architecture with separate I/O nodes and compute nodes.

2.2 Virtual Microscope

The Virtual Microscope [8] is designed to emulate the behavior of a high-power light microscope. The input data for the Virtual Microscope are digitized images of full microscope slides under high power. Each slide consists of several focal planes. The output of a query into the Virtual Microscope is a multi-band 2D image of a region of a slide in a particular focal plane at the desired magnification level (less than or equal to the magnification of the input images). The server part of the software running on the parallel machine employs a peer-to-peer architecture. As in Titan and Pathfinder, input data is partitioned into data-blocks and distributed across the disks on the parallel machine. In a typical operation, multiple clients can simultaneously send queries to the server. When a query is received, each processor in the server retrieves the blocks that intersect with the query from its disks, processes these blocks, and sends them to the client. There is no communication or coordination between server processors. Different processors can even operate on different queries at the same time.

3   Application Emulators

An application emulator is a program that, when run, exhibits computational and data access patterns that closely resemble the patterns observed when executing a particular class of applications. In practice, an emulator is a simplified version of the real application, but contains all the necessary communication, computation and I/O characteristics of the application required for the performance prediction study. Using an emulator results in less accurate performance estimations than using full application, but it is more robust and enables fast performance predictions for rapid prototyping of new machines. An application emulator models the computation and data access patterns of the full application in a parameterized way. Adjusting the values of the parameters makes it possible to generate various application scenarios within a single class of applications.

In a simulation-based performance prediction framework, application emulator provides a specification of the behavior of the application to the simulator. Using an application emulator has several advantages over using traces from actual program runs or running the full application on the simulator. First, a trace is static and represents the behavior of the application for a single run on a particular configuration of the machine. Since an application emulator is a program that can be run on the simulator, it can model the dynamic nature of an application and can be used for different machine configurations. Second, running a real application may complicate the task of the simulator unnecessarily. By abstracting away parts of the application that are not critical to predicting performance, an application emulator can allow an efficient simulation without getting bogged down in the unimportant details of the application. Third, execution of a complete application requires the availability of real input data. Since the application behavior is only emulated, an application emulator does not necessarily require real input data, but can also emulate the characteristics of the actual data. This can enable performance studies of applications on large machine configurations with large datasets. Fourth, the level of abstraction in the emulator can be controlled by the user. An application emulator without a great amount of detail can be used for rapid prototyping of the performance of the application on a new machine configuration; while a highly detailed emulator can be used, for instance, to study different parallelization strategies for the application.

In this work we target a framework that enables the studying of large scale applications and large scale machines (consisting of several thousands of processors). For this reason, application emulators developed in this work do not provide very detailed models of applications in order to conduct performance prediction studies in reasonable amount of time. However, they model the salient characteristics of each application class in a parameterized and flexible way, thus making it possible to generate various application scenarios within the same class of applications and to emulate the behavior of application with larger datasets for large scale machines. We now describe the emulator for Titan in more detail.

3.1 Case Study: An Application Emulator for Titan

Titan has three major components that characterize the I/O, communication and processing patterns in this class of applications: *input data set(s)*, *output data set(s)*, and *the processing loop*.

Input data: As we discussed in Section 2.1, Titan operates on data-blocks. Although each data-block contains the same number of input elements (sensor readings), the spatial extent of each data-block varies. This is because of the characteristics of the satellite orbit and the AVHRR sensor, which causes the extent of data-blocks containing sensor readings near the earth's poles to be larger than that of data-blocks near the equator. In addition, there are more spatially overlapping data-blocks near the poles than near equator. Thus, each Titan data-block and the distribution of the data-blocks through the input attribute space are somewhat irregular. The irregular nature of the input data also determines the irregular communication and computation patterns of Titan. In the emulator, a data-block is represented by four parameters. A *bounding rectangle* represents the spatial extent of a data-block. The *disk id, offset into the disk*, and *block size* are used to emulate I/O patterns. Synthetic data-blocks are generated using simple parameterized functions. In this way, the number of data-blocks can be scaled for large scale machines quickly, while preserving the important characteristics of such satellite input data, as described above. Using simple functions also allows us to change the input characteristics in a controlled way. A user can control the partitioning of input data into blocks, the number of data-blocks, and the distribution of the data-blocks through the input attribute space to generate different application scenarios.

Titan uses Moon's *minimax* algorithm [12] to distribute data-blocks across the disks in the machine. This algorithm achieves good load balance in disk accesses for a wide class of queries. However, it takes a long time to decluster even a moderate number of blocks across a small number of disks [6]. In the emulator, a simple round-robin assignment strategy has been employed to decluster the blocks across the available disks quickly. We are therefore trading off accuracy in modeling the application for efficiency in performing the emulation. Nevertheless, not much accuracy is lost, since we have observed that a round-robin assignment achieves good load balance (but not always as good as the minimax algorithm, especially for queries with small spatial extent).

Output data: Titan implements a workload partitioning strategy. The output, which is a 2D image bounded by the spatial extent of the query in longitude and latitude, is partitioned among processors. Processors are (logically) organized into a 2D grid. This grid is superimposed on the output grid to create rectangular subregions of the output with equal areas. In the emulator, the output is represented by a 2D rectangle bounded by the spatial extent of the input query. The number of processors in each dimension of the 2D processor grid is controlled by the user.

Processing loop: The most important characteristic of the processing loop of Titan is that all disk reads, message sends and receives are non-blocking operations. Despite this seemingly very dynamic structure, there do exist dependencies between operations. First, all message send operations on a data-block depend on the completion of the disk read for that data-block. A completed disk read operation can initiate message send operations to other nodes if the retrieved data-block intersects with their output regions. Moreover, if a data-block intersects with the local output image, then it is enqueued for processing locally. Initiation of receive operations in a processor does not depend directly on the reads or sends in that processor. However, completion of a receive operation depends on the corresponding send operation on the processor that has the data-block on its local disks. When a data-block is received, it is enqueued for processing. The emulator retains the dependencies between operations when generating events for the simulator.

The processing time of a data-block depends on the data values in the data-block. Our simulators model the I/O and communication subsystems of the parallel machine at a sufficiently detailed level, while providing relatively coarse grain models of the execution of instructions within each processor. Therefore, the emulators only have to capture the I/O and communication patterns of the applications accurately, as well as completely capturing the dependency patterns between operations, but do not have to model all the details of the computations performed. Each data-block in our applications is assumed to take the same amount of time to be processed, without regard to the data values it contains. This value is provided to the emulator by the user.

Figures 1(a)-(d) compare the behavior of the Titan emulator with that of the full Titan application. Titan currently runs on 15 nodes of the IBM SP2 at the University of Maryland [6]. Its input data consists of 60 days (24 GBytes) of AVHRR data distributed across the 60 disks attached to the nodes (4 local disks per node). Experiments were carried out using queries covering four regions of the earth: *World, North America, South America, Africa* [6], accessing either 10 or 60 days of data. We should note here that since we target performance prediction for large scale machines, we do not require that the application emulator precisely capture the data access and computation patterns exhibited by the application, but want to capture the behavior of the application when input parameters are changed and when the input dataset size is scaled. Figures 1 (a) and (b) show the total number of I/O, communication and computation operations performed by the Titan emulator and by Titan for the different queries. Figures 1 (c) and (d) show the execution times for the emulator and Titan on the SP2. When the application emulator is executed on the real machine, it performs actual non-blocking read, send and receive operations. However, the processing for a data-block is emulated by a constant delay, which was modeled as the average processing time for data-blocks accessed in several queries by Titan. For this reason, the execution times of the application emulator and the real application may not be close to each other for some queries, such as for the *World* query. However, as is seen from the figures, the application emulator exhibits similar behavior to that of the real application, and consistently matches the application across different queries as well as when the input dataset is scaled.

4   Simulation Models

Our main objective is to develop a simulation framework that is capable of simulating a parallel machine consisting of thousands of processors. We specifically target a data intensive application workload that can process multiple terabytes of data. We require efficient simulators that can run on moderately equipped, readily available hardware, such as a high-performance workstation. The relatively complicated processing structure of the target applications, which seek to

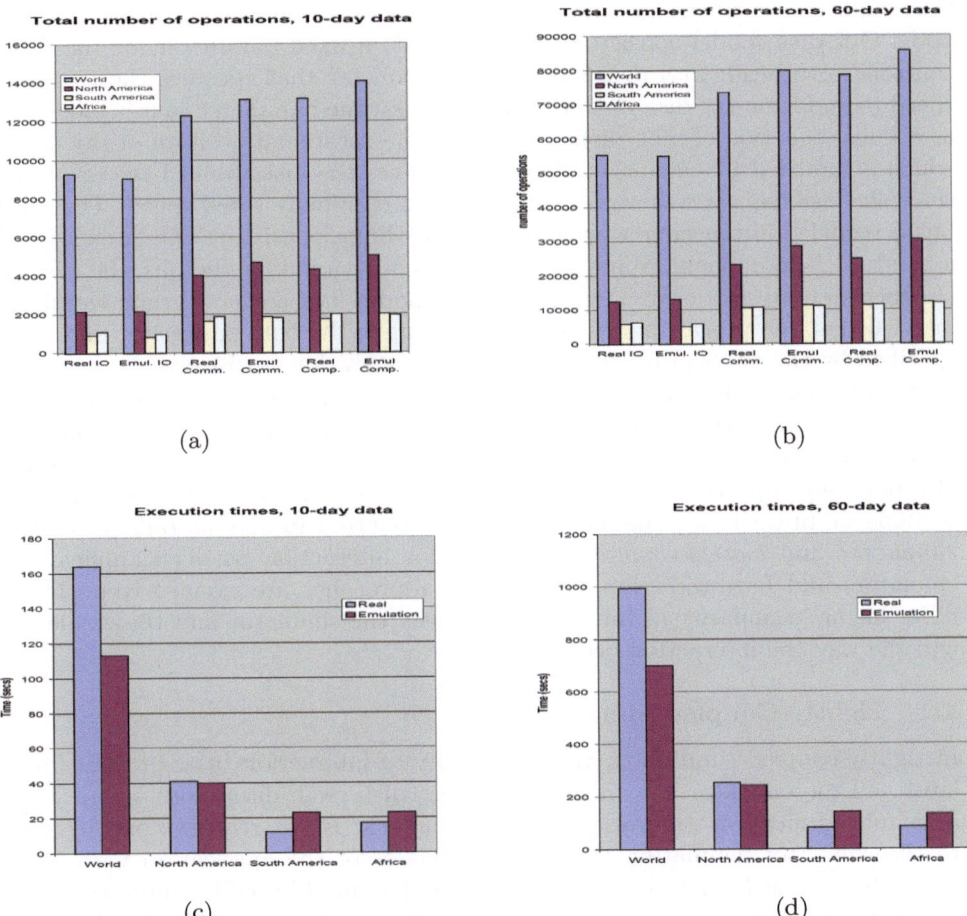

Fig. 1. Comparison of Titan emulator with real Titan in terms of total number of operations for (a) 10-day and (b) 60-day data, and execution time for (c) 10-day and (d) 60-day data.

overlap computation, communication, and I/O to attain high levels of performance, exacerbates the efficiency problem. A typical simulation of a large scale parallel machine needs to deal with hundreds of thousands of pending I/O operations as well as millions of outstanding messages between the processors. This section addresses these simulation efficiency issues.

4.1   Hardware Models

In order to achieve high levels of efficiency, we employ coarse grain hardware models for the network, disk, I/O bus, and processor. We assume that each node is connected to its peers by dedicated point-to-point links. The time to transfer a message of size L over a network link is modeled as $T = \alpha + L/\beta$ where α and β represent the wire latency and bandwidth, respectively. We neither model the network topology nor link congestion, but we do model end-point congestion that might occur when multiple nodes attempt to transfer messages to a single node. Our disk model consists of four parts: 1) a fixed parameter for the disk controller overhead, 2) a disk bandwidth parameter that specifies the transfer speed to and from the disk media, 3) a disk seek-time parameter that is modeled as a linear function of seek distance, and 4) the rotational position of the disk, which is modeled by calculating how many times the disk would have revolved since the last request was served, at the disk's nominally rated speed. The I/O bus is modeled in the same way as the network links, consisting of a latency and a bandwidth component. When multiple devices contend for the bus, the effects of congestion are modeled. The processor is modeled at a coarse grain; the time interval that the processor was busy computing is the only parameter and it is specified by the application emulator for each operation performed.

Unfortunately, having only coarse grain hardware models is not sufficient to model the performance of data intensive applications for very large configurations. Interaction between application emulators and the hardware simulator also plays an important role in the efficiency of the simulation. In the next two sections we present two different approaches, referred to here as *tightly-coupled simulation* and *loosely-coupled simulation*, for interaction between application emulators and hardware simulators. Both approaches are event-driven. They differ in the granularity of interaction between the simulator and the emulator and the way the interaction occurs.

4.2   Tightly-Coupled Simulation

In tightly-coupled simulation, the granularity of interaction between the simulator and the emulator is a single event (e.g., disk read, data-block send). Just as a full application program does, the emulator issues requests one by one to the simulator, emulating the actual behavior of the application with calls to the filesystem for I/O and to the message passing library for interprocessor communication. Our simulator library provides an API for both blocking and non-blocking I/O and communication operations, as well as calls to check the completion of these operations. If the calls are asynchronous calls, such as a non-blocking send, the simulator returns a request id, and the emulator uses that id to check the status of the request later. Each application (emulator) process running on a node of the simulated target machine is implemented by a thread, which is referred to as *emulator thread*. Emulator threads are responsible for simulating the behavior of the applications with respect to the input data. In addition to emulator threads, the combined system has a simulator thread that runs the main simulation engine. It is responsible for processing requests received from emulator threads, keeping track of simulated time, and scheduling emulator threads to make sure that events happen in logical clock order.

4.3   Loosely-Coupled Simulation

Interaction between the emulator and the simulator in tightly-coupled simulation closely resembles the interaction between an application and a real machine.

However, this approach has several drawbacks which make it unsuitable for simulation of large scale machines. First, the number of emulator threads increases with the number of processors. Handling a large number of threads becomes very costly for the simulator, as it has to schedule emulator threads to ensure correct logical ordering of events. Second, as hardware configurations get larger, message and I/O tables for outstanding non-blocking operations grow very large, becoming very costly to manage and slowing down the network model, which must check for end-point congestion. Moreover, each emulator thread has to maintain local data structures to keep track of outstanding non-blocking operations, replicating the simulator's work and increasing memory requirements. As in a real machine, the status of non-blocking operations is determined by explicitly checking with the simulator; for multiple terabyte datasets, the overheads for these checks become enormous and contribute both to processing time and to the number of context switches between emulator and simulator threads.

To address these efficiency issues, we introduce a technique called *loosely-coupled simulation*. Loosely coupled simulation is currently applicable to applications with a processing loop similar to the one described in Section 2.1, although we are working on applying it to other types of applications. The key idea in loosely-coupled simulation is to embed the processing loop of the application and its dependency structure, modeled by *work flow graphs*, into the simulator. Therefore only two threads are required; a simulator thread and an emulator thread. As in tightly-coupled simulation, the emulator thread is responsible for generating events and the simulator thread is responsible for processing these events. However, unlike tightly-coupled simulation, the emulator and the simulator interact in distinct phases, called *epochs*, rather than interacting at every event.

Modeling the Application Processing Structure: Work Flow Graphs

A *work flow graph* describes the dependencies between operations performed on a single data-block. A node in the graph represents an operation performed on the data-block. In our current set of applications, there are four types of operations: *read*, *send*, *receive*, and *compute*. The directed graph edges represent the dependencies between these operations. For example, an edge from a read operation to a send operation indicates that a send operation on a data-block should start after the read operation is completed. In the applications considered in this work, there are no dependencies between operations performed on different data-blocks neither within the same processor nor across different processors. As a result, work flow graphs impose a partial order on events, and in a sense describe the *life cycle* of a single data-block. Work flow graphs for Titan, Pathfinder, and the Virtual Microscope are illustrated in Figure 2.

The basic skeleton of a work flow graph is independent of specific instances of input data, output data and machine configuration. This skeleton depends on the characteristics of the application. The skeleton is embedded in the simulator. However, we need to parameterize work flow graphs to reflect the behavior of the application for a specific instance of input data, output data and machine configuration. For example, the number of send operations performed on a data-block

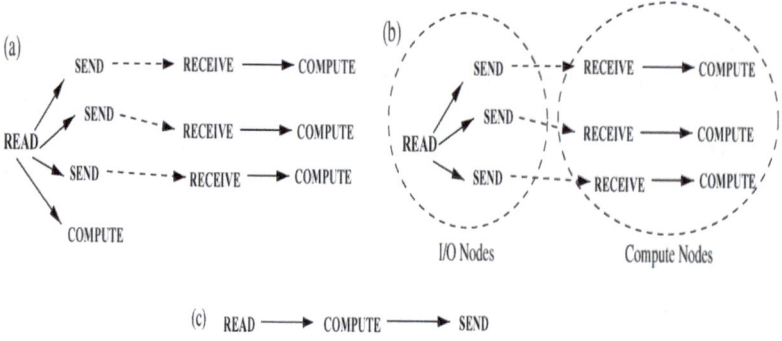

Fig. 2. Work flow graphs for (a) Titan, (b) Pathfinder, (c) Virtual Microscope. The dashed circles for Pathfinder denote the operations performed on client and server nodes. Solid arrows denote dependencies within a processor, while dashed arrows denote inter-processor dependencies

in Titan depends on the spatial extent of the data-block and the partitioning of the output data structure across the processors. Parameterization of work flow graphs is done by the application emulators.

Epoch-Based Interaction between Emulator and Simulator

In epoch-based interaction, the emulator and the simulator interact in distinct phases, called *epochs*, instead of interacting for each event. In an epoch, the emulator passes the simulator a set of events for each simulated processor at the same time, along with the dependency information shown in Figure 2. The simulator then processes all the events, without invoking the emulator for each event. The simulator is responsible for determining the order in which these events are executed, while enforcing the dependencies. As a result, the emulator does not need to keep track of completed and outstanding events. When the simulator finishes processing all the events for a particular processor, it requests another set of events for that processor from the emulator. There are two main reasons for having the emulator pass the events in epochs rather than passing all the events at once. The first reason is to decrease the memory requirements of the simulator by limiting the number of events passed at the same time. The second is to give some control also to the emulator over the order in which events are executed. The operations represented by events in distinct epochs cannot be executed concurrently. This gives the emulator the ability to impose dependencies that cannot be represented as work flow graphs. For example, in the Virtual Microscope, processing of separate queries is currently not overlapped. The emulator generates events for these queries in distinct epochs, thus imposing this dependency.

In an epoch, the emulator passes the simulator the events for a set of data-blocks for each simulated processor. For the current suite of applications, the emulator encodes the following information for each data-block: *disk number, block size, list of consumer processors,* and *data-block computation time.* The *disk number* denotes the local disk where the block is stored, and implicitly indicates a read operation for that disk. The *block size* is used to estimate I/O and communication time. The *list of consumer processors* denotes the processors that will process this data-block (including the processor doing the I/O for the data-block if the block is processed locally). Thus, the list encodes the send operations to be issued for the data-block. It also implicitly encodes the corresponding receive and compute operations, since a send operation always has a matching receive and a received block is always processed (see Fig. 2).

Note that the total number of events generated and processed are the same for both the loosely-coupled and tightly-coupled simulation models. However, the order in which these events are processed may be different because of the different interactions between the simulator and application emulator in each model. To evaluate the efficiency and accuracy of these two approaches, we have developed two simulators, LC-SIM and TC-SIM, for loosely-coupled and tightly-coupled simulation, respectively. Both simulators employ the same hardware models, differing only in the way that they interact with the emulator.

5   Experimental Evaluation of Simulation Models

In this section, we present an experimental evaluation of our simulation models. We focus on simulation speed and the accuracy of the models as the machine configuration and datasets for the application scale. Our target platforms are distributed memory machines in which each node has local disks.

To evaluate the accuracy of the simulation models, we used two IBM SP machines with different configurations. The first machine is a 16-node IBM SP2 at the University of Maryland (UMD). Each node of this machine has a peak performance of 266 MFlops, 128 MB of main memory and six local disks, which are connected to the memory bus with two fast-wide SCSI buses (20 MB/s) – 3 disks on each bus. Nodes are interconnected through the High Performance Switch (HPS) with 40 MB/s peak bandwidth per node. In these experiments, the data sets were distributed across 15 nodes of the machine, on four disks per node. The second machine is a 128-node SP at the San Diego Supercomputing Center (SDSC). Each node of this machine has a peak performance of 640 MFlops, 256 Mbytes of main memory and one disk. All nodes are interconnected by a newer version of the HPS with 110 MB/s peak bandwidth per node. In the validation experiments described below, we have compared the execution times of the application emulators estimated by the simulators with the actual execution times of the application emulators running on these machines. Over all our experiments, the number of data-blocks for the Titan and Pathfinder applications was varied from 3.5K (4 days of satellite data) to 14115K, (2.6 Terabytes for 42 years of data). For the Virtual Microscope, the number of blocks was scaled from 5K (2 slides, 1 focal plane each) to 128000K blocks (5120 slides, 10 focal planes each) of size 384 terabytes. For Titan, we have used the "world query" that accesses all the blocks [6]. For the Virtual Microscope emulation, we generated a set of random queries. The number of simultaneous queries processed was scaled with the number of nodes in the machine.

Table 1 shows the validation results for TC-SIM and LC-SIM on the UMD SP. For Pathfinder, we fixed the number of compute nodes per I/O node to

Emulator	Data set	IBM SP2	TC-SIM	LC-SIM
Titan	9K blocks	113	105 (7%)	100 (12%)
	27K blocks	347	322 (7%)	306 (12%)
Pathfinder	9K blocks	166	153 (8%)	149 (10%)
	27K blocks	497	467 (6%)	452 (9%)
Virtual	5K blocks (200 queries)	127	122 (4%)	119 (6%)
Microscope	7.5K blocks (400 queries)	243	236 (3%)	234 (4%)

Table 1. Accuracy of the simulation models. All timings are in seconds. IBM SP2 figures represent the actual execution time of the emulators on 15 nodes of the UMD SP. The numbers in parentheses denote the percent error in estimating the actual runtime.

three in all measurements. The values in parentheses indicate the percent error in estimated execution times and are calculated as ratio of the difference between real execution time and estimated execution time to real execution time. As is seen from the table, the error of the predictions versus the actual execution times remains under 9% for TC-SIM and under 13% for LC-SIM for all the applications. As expected TC-SIM is more accurate than LC-SIM, because the interaction between the emulator and simulator more closely resembles the interaction between emulator and the real machine.

Figures 3 (a)-(d) show the validation results for LC-SIM on the SDSC SP. For the Titan application, we ran two different scenarios with the application emulators. For the first scenario, the input data size is scaled with the machine size (Fig. 3(a)). In this case, the input data size was varied from 14K datablocks (16 days of satellite data) to 91K data-blocks (100 days). For the second scenario, the input data size is fixed at 14K data-blocks and the machine size is scaled (Fig. 3(b)). For the Pathfinder application, we varied the ratio of I/O nodes to compute nodes on 64 processors (Fig. 3(c)). The number of data-blocks was fixed at 3.5K, which was the largest number of data blocks that could be stored on the machine configuration with the smallest number of I/O nodes. For the Virtual Microscope application, we scaled the number of data-blocks from 10K to 64K, and scaled the number of queries from 160 to 1000 along with the machine size (Fig. 3(d)). As is seen from the figures, the estimated execution times are very close to the actual execution times for all application scenarios and for all machine sizes. The percent error remains below 4% for all cases. Our validation results show that we do not lose much from accuracy from using the loosely-coupled simulation model.

The execution times for the simulators for up to 128 processors are presented in Table 2. We ran our simulations on Digital Alpha 2100 4/275 workstations with 256 MB of memory. For LC-SIM, the application emulator was run on one workstation, while the simulator was run on a different workstation. The data exchange between the two programs was carried out using the Unix socket interface. As is seen in the table, TC-SIM executes for almost one hour to simulate even the smallest machine configuration. It runs for more than 32 hours for performance estimation of Titan on 128 processors. This shows that TC-SIM is only feasible for simulating a fairly small numbers of processors. LC-SIM, on

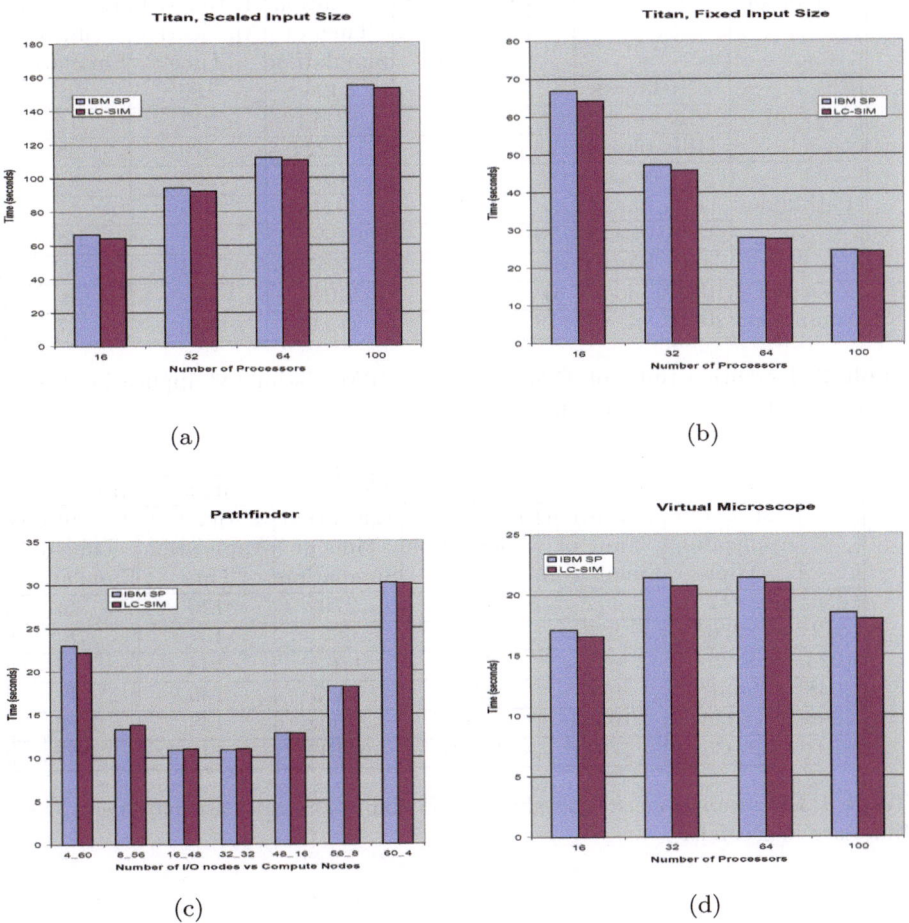

Fig. 3. Accuracy of LC-SIM when simulating the application emulators running on the SDSC IBM SP machine. All results are in seconds. (a) Titan application, scaled input size. (b) Titan application, fixed input size. (c) Pathfinder, fixed input size, varying the ratio of IO nodes to compute nodes. The x-axis labels show the number of I/O nodes versus number of compute nodes. (d) Virtual microscope, scaled input data size and number of queries.

the other hand, can simulate all machine configurations, even with very large datasets, in very little time (less than two minutes).

The execution times for LC-SIM when simulating very large scale machines are displayed in Table 3. We were able to do performance predictions for very large machines (8K processors, 32K disks) running applications with very large datasets (up to 384 terabytes) in less than 22 hours. These results show that performance prediction for large scale machines can be done in a reasonable amount of time on workstations using LC-SIM.

Emulator	Data set	P	TC-SIM		LC-SIM	
			Estimated Application Time	Execution Time of Simulation	Estimated Application Time	Execution Time of Simulation
Titan	27K blocks	32	211	3426	182	6
	55K blocks	64	285	13154	217	14
	110K blocks	128	604	116224	420	28
Pathfinder	55K blocks	32	551	11595	496	22
	110K blocks	64	718	30446	579	57
	220K blocks	128	1020	97992	881	126
Virtual Microscope	500K blocks	32	135	7155	118	4
	1000K blocks	64	145	14097	126	8
	2000K blocks	128	158	37534	138	17

Table 2. Execution times of TC-SIM and LC-SIM. Estimated application times and simulator execution times are in seconds.

P	Titan		Pathfinder		Virtual Microscope	
	Estimated Application Time	Execution Time of Simulation	Estimated Application Time	Execution Time of Simulation	Estimated Application Time	Execution Time of Simulation
256	1147	172	1579	270	136	36
512	2276	520	2342	685	137	78
1024	4525	1454	4621	1762	144	189
2048	9031	4897	9177	5032	136	498
4096	18028	16388	18274	24562	142	1481
8192	36035	77641	36437	65137	148	4873

Table 3. Execution times for loosely coupled simulation. Both estimated and execution times are in seconds.

6   Related Work

Performance prediction of applications on parallel machines is a widely studied area. Previous work in this area mainly focused on performance prediction of compute intensive scientific applications, but has taken several approaches. In [4,7,15], applications are modeled by a set of equations as a function of size of the input and number of processors. In [16,17], applications are modeled as directed graphs (i.e. task graphs). The graph representation models the data and control flow in the application. The performance estimation is done by traversing the graph. Although these approaches are fast, so are feasible for large machine configurations and datasets, it is very difficult to model the dynamic and data dependent nature of applications (such as the ones we want to model) by equations or graphs. In addition, the graph modeling the application may grow very large for large scale machines. Traces obtained from application runs are used in [9,11]. The main drawback of using traces is that a trace only represents the behavior of the application on a particular configuration of the machine, and cannot be used when the machine configuration is changed. An alternative approach to using traces or analytical models is to use simulators that run application programs. A variety of such simulators are available [3,10,13,14]. In general, application source or binary codes must be augmented or the application is required to use the simulator API so that events can be passed to the simulator so that simulated time can progress. In order to increase the efficiency of simulation, most simulators use the *direct-execution technique*, in which the application code is executed on the host machine on which the simulator runs, and only the operations that cannot be run on the host machine, plus other events of interest, are captured by the simulator and simulated. Moreover, the simulators can employ less detailed architectural models for less accurate but fast simulation, or use parallel machines to run the simulators [3,13].

Our work differs from previous work in several ways. In our work we specifically target large scale data-intensive applications on large scale machines. The application emulators presented in this paper lie in between pure analytical models and full applications. They provide a simpler, but parameterized, model of the application by abstracting away the details not related to a performance prediction study. Since an application emulator is a program, it preserves the dynamic nature of the application, and can be simulated using any simulator that can run the full application. The loosely-coupled simulation model reduces the number of interactions between the simulator and the application emulator by embedding the application processing structure into the simulator. As our experimental results show, our optimizations enable simulation of large scale machines on workstations.

7 Conclusions

In this paper, we have presented a performance prediction framework for data-intensive applications running on large scale machines. We have have implemented a performance prediction tool, which contains two components; *application emulators* and *architecture simulators*. We have developed application emulators that capture data access and computation patterns for three data-intensive applications. Emulators allow the critical components of applications to be changed and scaled easily, enabling performance prediction studies for large scale configurations. We have developed simulation models that are both sufficiently accurate and execute quickly. We presented a new technique, called *loosely coupled simulation*, that makes it possible to simulate large scale machines (up to several thousands of processors) inexpensively and accurately. Our preliminary results are very encouraging. We were able to model application datasets of up to 384 terabytes in size and run simulations that involve 8K processors on typical high performance workstations.

Acknowledgements

We would like to thank Jeff Hollingsworth and Hyeonsang Eom for their invaluable discussions about performance prediction on large scale machines.

References

1. A. Acharya, M. Uysal, R. Bennett, A. Mendelson, M. Beynon, J. K. Hollings-worth, J. Saltz, and A. Sussman. Tuning the performance of I/O intensive parallel applications. In *Proc. of IOPADS'96*. ACM Press, May 1996.
2. R. Agrawal and J. Shafer. Parallel mining of association rules. *IEEE Transactions on Knowledge and Data Engineering*, 8(6):962–9, Dec. 1996.
3. R. Bagrodia, S. Docy, and A. Kahn. Parallel simulation of parallel file systems and I/O programs. In *Proceedings of the 1997 ACM/IEEE SC97 Conference*. ACM Press, Nov. 1997.
4. J. Brehm, M. Madhukar, E. Smirni, and L. Dowdy. PerPreT - a performance prediction tool for massively parallel systems. In *Proceedings of the Joint Conference on Performance Tools / MMB 1995*, pages 284–298. Springer-Verlag, Sept. 1995.
5. C. F. Cerco and T. Cole. User's guide to the CE-QUAL-ICM three-dimensional eutrophication model, release version 1.0. Technical Report EL-95-15, US Army Corps of Engineers Water Experiment Station, Vicksburg, MS, 1995.
6. C. Chang, B. Moon, A. Acharya, C. Shock, A. Sussman, and J. Saltz. Titan: a high-performance remote-sensing database. In *Proceedings of the 13th International Conference on Data Engineering*, Apr. 1997.
7. M. J. Clement and M. J. Quinn. Using analytical performance prediction for architectural scaling. Technical Report TR BYU-NCL-95-102, Networked Computing Lab, Brigham Young University, 1995.
8. R. Ferreira, B. Moon, J. Humphries, A. Sussman, J. Saltz, R. Miller, and A. Demarzo. The Virtual Microscope. In *Proc. of the 1997 AMIA Annual Fall Symposium*, pages 449–453. American Medical Informatics Association, Oct. 1997.
9. A. Gürsoy and L. V. Kalé. Simulating message-driven programs. In *Proceedings of Int. Conference on Parallel Processing*, volume III, pages 223–230, Aug. 1996.
10. S. Herrod. Tango lite: A multiprocessor simulation environment. Technical report, Computer Systems Laboratory, Stanford University, 1993.
11. C. L. Mendes. Performance prediction by trace transformation. In *Fifth Brazilian Symposium on Computer Architecture*, Sept. 1993.
12. B. Moon and J. H. Saltz. Scalability analysis of declustering methods for multidimensional range queries. *IEEE Transactions on Knowledge and Data Engineering*, 10(2):310–327, March/April 1998.
13. S. Reinhardt, M. Hill, J. Larus, A. Lebeck, J. Lewis, and D. Wood. The Wisconsin Wind Tunnel: Virtual prototyping of parallel computers. In *Proc. of the 1993 ACM SIGMETRICS Conf. on Measuring and Modeling of Computer Systems*, 1993.
14. M. Rosenblum, S. Herrod, E. Witchel, and A. Gupta. Complete computer system simulation: The SimOS approach. *IEEE Parallel and Distributed Technology*, 3(4):34–43, Winter 1995.
15. J. M. Schopf. Structural prediction models for high-performance distributed applications. In *Cluster Computing Conference*, 1997.
16. J. Simon and J.-M. Wierum. Accurate performance prediction for massively parallel systems and its applications. In *Proceedings of Euro-Par'96*, volume 1124 of *LNCS*, pages 675–688. Springer-Verlag, Aug. 1996.
17. Y. Yan, X. Zhang, and Y. Song. An effective and practical performance prediction model for parallel computing on non-dedicated heterogeneous NOW. *Journal of Parallel and Distributed Computing*, 38:63–80, Oct. 1996.

MARS: A Distributed Memory Approach to Shared Memory Compilation

M.F.P. O'Boyle

Department of Computer Science
University of Edinburgh
King's Buildings
Mayfield Rd.
Edinburgh EH9 3JZ UK
mob@dcs.ed.ac.uk
WWW home page: http://www.dcs.ed.ac.uk/home/mob

Abstract. This paper describes an automatic parallelising compiler, MARS, targeted for shared memory machines. It uses a data partitioning approach, traditionally used for distributed memory machines, in order to globally reduce overheads such as communication and synchronisation. Its high-level linear algebraic representation allows direct application of, for instance, unimodular transformations and global application of data transformation. Although a data based approach allows global analysis and in many instances outperforms local, loop-oriented parallelisation approaches, we have identified two particular problems when applying data parallelism to sequential Fortran 77 as opposed to data parallel dialects tailored to distributed memory targets. This paper describes two techniques to overcome these problems and evaluates their applicability. Preliminary results, on two SPECf92 benchmarks, show that with these optimisations, MARS outperforms existing state-of-the art loop based auto-parallelisation approaches.

1 Introduction

Traditionally, shared memory compilation and distributed memory compilation have shared little commonality due to the differing underlying communication models. Shared memory parallelisation focussed on discovering independent loop iterations, while distributed memory compilation was primarily focussed at partitioning data so that appropriate message passing code could be inserted. With the advent of distributed shared memory architectures such as the SGi Origin, Convex Exemplar which have a single shared address space, but memory which is physically distributed, there is merging of the these two approaches.

This paper describes an auto-parallelising compiler, MARS, which uses the core idea of distributed memory autoparallelisation, i.e. data partition, as its basis for parallelising code for shared address space machines. By explicitly considering the automatic partitioning of data, issues such as locality and synchronisation are naturally incorporated. This paper does not describe MARS's

D. O'Hallaron (Ed.): LCR'98, LNCS 1511, pp. 259–274, 1998.

Loop Nest (1)	System of Inequalities (2)
| ```
Do i = 1,n
  Do j = 1,n
    Do k = 1,i
      a(i,j) = a(i,j) + b(i,k) *c(j,k)
    Enddo
  Enddo
Enddo
``` | $$\begin{bmatrix} -1 & 0 & 0 \\ 0 & -1 & 0 \\ 0 & 0 & -1 \\ \hline 1 & 0 & 0 \\ 0 & 1 & 0 \\ -1 & 0 & 1 \end{bmatrix} \begin{bmatrix} i \\ j \\ k \end{bmatrix} \leq \begin{bmatrix} -1 \\ -1 \\ -1 \\ n \\ n \\ 0 \end{bmatrix}$$ |
| Access Matrix (3) | Polyhedron (4) |
| $$\begin{bmatrix} 1 & 0 & 0 \\ 0 & 1 & 0 \end{bmatrix}_a \begin{bmatrix} i \\ j \\ k \end{bmatrix}$$ | |

Fig. 1. Linear Representation

automatic data partitioning algorithm [15] nor its strategy [3]; instead it describes the benefits and drawbacks to a data partitioning approach and develops new optimisations to improve its performance. MARS is not alone in trying to globally parallelise programs. The Jasmine compiler [1] uses an affinity graph to determine how to parallelise loop nests. The SUIF compiler [11] also considers data layout, but only after program parallelisation has taken place. Other compilers such as VFC [2] consider data layout explicitly, but are targeted towards distributed memory systems and consider data parallel language input rather than sequential FORTRAN.

MARS uses a linear algebraic representation as its core internal representation. Recent work in program transformation including [12,7], has focussed on linear algebraic loop and data transformations and therefore such an internal representation allows direct application of new techniques within MARS.

The following section describes the overall compiler infra-structure. This is followed by a section describing the particular approach used by MARS in auto-parallelisation. Sections 4 and 5 identify particular problems with this approach and develop techniques to overcome this. Section 6 applies the newly developed techniques to two example benchmarks and compares them with the existing approach and a state of the art commercial auto-parallelising compiler. Section 7 provides some concluding remarks.

2   Compiler Infra-Structure

At the heart of the MARS compiler is an extended linear algebraic framework. This is a high level abstraction of the key components of data parallelism, namely
```

iteration spaces, arrays and access functions. Iteration spaces and the index domain of the arrays are represented as integer lattice points within convex polyhedra, stored as an ordered set of linear constraints. Access functions are stored as linear transformations on the iteration vector.

In figure 1 the loop nest in box 1 can be considered graphically as shown in box 4. The loop indices, or *iterators*, can be represented as an $M \times 1$ column vector J where M is the number of enclosing loops. The loop ranges, or affine bounds of the iterators, can be described by a system of inequalities defining the *polyhedron* $AJ \leq b$, where A is a $(\ell \times M)$ integer matrix and b an $(\ell \times 1)$ vector. The integer values taken on by J define the *iteration space* of the loop. For example, box 2 shows the internal representation of the loop nest iteration space shown in box 1.

The range of array elements declared in a program can be similarly described. The *formal indices* $\mathcal{I}$ describe the array index domain which can be represented by a $N \times 1$ column vector $\mathcal{I}$, where N is the dimension of array A. The formal indices have a certain range which describe the size of the array, or *index space*, as follows: $A\mathcal{I} \leq b$ where A is a $(2N \times N)$ integer matrix and b an $(2N \times 1)$ vector. The integer values taken on by $\mathcal{I}$ define the index space of the indices. Finally, the third component, array access, can be straightforwardly described. by $\mathcal{U}J + u$ where $\mathcal{U}$ is a $N \times M$ matrix and u is a $N \times 1$ vector. As an example, box 3 shows the internal representation of the reference to array a.

This representation allows high-level rapid analysis of program structure and the simple application of high level transformations. For instance, unimodular and non-singular loop transformations are implemented as a simple matrix multiplication with the appropriate loop constraint matrix and enclosed access matrices. As MARS is a data based approach to parallelisation, data transformations such as data partitioning, alignment, array padding etc. can also be similarly achieved, this time by multiplication of the appropriate index domain and all corresponding accesses.

The overall structure of the MARS compiler can be seen in figure 2. Fortran is read in by the Sage++[4] front-end to produce a decorated abstract syntax tree which is then translated in the augmented linear algebraic framework. This framework allows non-affine objects to be represented but this is beyond the scope of this paper. The parallelisation strategy is based on global data partitioning and is described in [3]. The current version of MARS uses separate analysis and transformation engines to make the optimisation process more modular and orthogonal. Once the appropriate transformations have taken place, the Sage++ parse tree is regenerated and unparsed to give a transformed parallel program. Different "parallel wrappers" are placed around the code depending on the target. At present MARS targets shared memory machines including the SGi family of parallel machines, KSR and the SVM software platforms KOAN [13] and VOTE.

Due to its algebraic nature, existing packages such as the Omega Test (Omega Calculator) and PIP can readily be used to perform high level analysis for array section analysis and loop generation respectively. In order that MARS may also

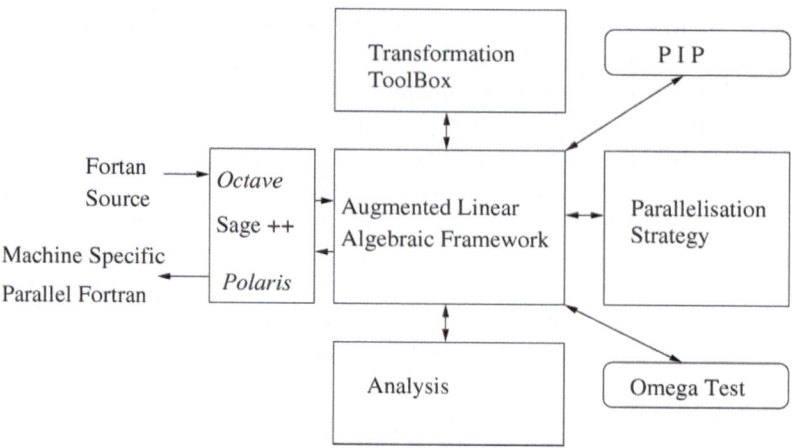

Fig. 2. MARS Structure

be used as a straightforward transformation engine, links to two further front ends, Octave and Polaris, are currently under development.

3   Data Parallel Approach

MARS has a data rather than loop orientated parallelisation strategy. Once an automatic global data partitioning decision has been made, the work is partitioned and scheduled to processors, such that each processor is responsible for calculation of a sub-portion of each of the global arrays. The underlying model of computation is SPMD, i.e. there is but one fork at the beginning of the program and one join at the end. Thus, all loops are partitioned, whether they execute in parallel or sequentially depends on whether there is any synchronisation within. Typically, it is not possible to actually allocate portions of an array to a physical processor in distributed shared memory. However, if an array portion is first written on one particular processor, this will become its home, assuming an allocation on first write policy. The main benefits of this approach are briefly summarised thus:

Communication and Synchronisation Communication and synchronisation are due to the references or the source and a sink of a dependence being scheduled to separate processors. MARS explicitly considers the layout of data and hence the amount of communication and synchronisation when parallelising the application program. This helps reduce the amount of communication and allows the insertion of the minimal number of synchronisation points [18].

Memory Coherence The owner-computes scheduling of data guarantees that only one processor will write to a particular cache line or page. This prevents invalidation traffic due to write misses on other processors. As the scheduling of data and work is compile-time known, it is possible for the insertion of local invalidation calls if supported by the hardware. In [16], a technique developed within MARS, can, in certain instances, completely eliminate invalidation based coherence traffic.

Global Analysis Arrays frequently persist throughout large sections of a program and their layout in memory will determine the costs described below. MARS applies a global data partitioning phase which trades off the differing data layout requirements of the entire program. This is in stark contrast to loop based parallelisation, where each loop nest is treated in isolation. It has the overall effect of providing affinity based parallelisation, where costs between loop nests are explicitly considered.

Applying owner-computes scheduling to sequential F77, implies that each statement has its own local iteration space, guaranteeing that the write access is to local data. Difficulties arise when there is more than one statement in a loop nest each having a different local iteration space. Such problems are not encountered in data parallel languages such as HPF, HPF+ [2] or other data-parallel forms [6] as, implicitly, there is but one statement per loop in when using, say, the FORALL loop. This is one of the draw-backs to a data-based approach which can be overcome with loop generation techniques [5]. In the following sections, we concentrate on two particular phenomena which, however, in our experience cause difficulties in a number of codes.

4   Scalars

The naive treatment of scalars within multiple-statement loop nests can introduce unnecessary work and cross-processor dependences, completely destroying available parallelism. Arrays are distributed across the processors but scalars are frequently replicated, each processor having its own copy. This has the advantage that frequently read scalars are guaranteed to be local, eliminating cross-processor dependences and hence reduces communication and synchronisation overhead. However, when writing to a scalar within a simple loop, replication means that all iterations of that loop must be executed by all processors. This in itself is not a problem, as the alternative of just one processor executing the loop and sending the results to others, can frequently be more expensive as the other processors remain idle until the result is available incurring additional synchronisation and communication.

The problem occurs in loops where there are potential parallel writes to an array in one statement and a scalar assignment in other. If there is a data dependence between them, preventing loop distribution, then the decision to replicate scalar variables introduces unnecessary cross-processor dependences. Consider the code fragment from vpenta in figure 3 row 1 column 1. MARS decides to partition the code on the second dimension generating the code in row 1 column 2. The assignment to X(J,K) refers to local data and thus cannot introduce a cross-processor dependence. As RLD is replicated, it must perform all iterations

```
DO K = KL,KU

  RLD = C(J,K) - RLD1*X(J-1,K)
  RLDI = 1./RLD

  X(J,K) = (D(J,K) -
     RLD1*Y(J-1,K))*RLDI

ENDDO
```

```
DO K = KL,KU

  RLD = C(J,K) - RLD1*X(J-1,K)
  RLDI = 1./RLD
  call mp_barrier()
  if ((-1) * k + lo1 .le. 0) then
   if (k + (-1) * hi1 .le. 0) then
    X(J,K) = (D(J,K) -
       RLD1*Y(J-1,K))*RLDI

ENDDO
```

```
DO K = KL,KU
 if ((-1) * k + lo1 .le. 0) then
  if (k + (-1) * hi1 .le. 0) then
   RLD = C(J,K) - RLD1*X(J-1,K)
 if ((-1) * k + lo1 .le. 0) then
  if (k + (-1) * hi1 .le. 0) then
   RLDI = 1./RLD
 if ((-1) * k + lo1 .le. 0) then
  if (k + (-1) * hi1 .le. 0) then
    X(J,K) = (D(J,K) -
       RLD1*Y(J-1,K))*RLDI

ENDDO
```

```
DO K = max(KL,lo1), min(KU,hi1)
  RLD = C(J,K) - RLD1*X(J-1,K)
  RLDI = 1./RLD
  X(J,K) = (D(J,K) -
       RLD1*Y(J-1,K))*RLDI

ENDDO
```

Fig. 3. Scalar Treatment

of the K loop, and therefore will refer to non-local elements of X, introducing a cross-processor dependence [18]. The following subsections describe a technique whereby the scalars are evaluated in a smaller number of iterations. This eliminates unnecessary work and cross-processor dependences, giving eventually the code in row 2 column 2.

4.1   Possible Solutions

In this section we will briefly consider three alternative solutions to the problem of scalar treatment and provide motivation for the preferred choice.

The three solutions considered are:

- Scalar Privatisation
- Forward Substitution
- Propagation of Constraints

The most obvious solution is to try standard *scalar privatisation*. In loop based parallelisation approaches, scalars can introduce cross-iteration dependences preventing parallelisation. If it can be shown that values are not used on subsequent iterations, then they can be privatised eliminating cross-iteration dependence. For further details on this well known optimisation see [9].

```
Do i = 1,n
  a = f(i)
  b(i) = b(i) +a
  b(n-i+1) = b(n-i+1)+a
Enddo
```

Fig. 4. Invalid Scalar Privatisation

The problem in applying this technique to data parallel computation is that a scalar is privatised with respect to a loop. More specifically, there will be a private copy corresponding to a group of loop iterations which are to be executed by a particular processor. This implicitly assumes that each statement within a loop body has the same local iteration space, which is not the case with owner computes scheduling.

As a simple counter example, consider the program in figure 4. This loop can be executed in parallel using data parallelism but it is not loop parallel. Scalar privatisation where a separate copy is associated with each group of loop iterations will be incorrect when executed in parallel.

Forward substitution of a scalar definition to all uses, even when legal to do so, can introduce redundant computation. It means that the amount of work associated with the evaluation of a scalar is replicated for each use. Consider the simple example in figure 5, typical of N-body type problems. Substituting for **a** in this case doubles the amount of work. As scalars within loops are frequently inserted to store computed values needed in more than one array assignment, such substitution is unnecessarily expensive and will not be considered further.

The final solution considered here, is to restrict the number of iterations within which a scalar is evaluated based on statements referring to it. This is readily obtained by merging the local iteration spaces of each statement referring to the scalar and propagating it to the definition. Although the resulting code is correct and may eliminate synchronisation, it is very inefficient. MARS, however, has an optimisation loop generation phase which propagates statement constraints up to the appropriate enclosing loops. This frequently gives code similar to the loop/array privatisation employed in loop-based parallelisation approaches. However, in those cases where each statement has a different local iteration space, then the union of these constraints must be propagated to the definition of the scalar and the loop bounds appropriately updated. The following sub-sections describe this process in more detail.

4.2   Proposed Solution

The basic idea is to determine those iterations where a scalar is used and to only evaluate the scalar in those instances; a related approach is described in [10]. It can be considered to be dead iteration removal, similar to dead code elimination. We restrict this procedure to cases where the usages are at the same or lesser deep loop nest level to the definition. In those cases where the definition is at a greater

Original	Forward Sub.

`Do i = 1,n`
`  a = expensiveFunction(i)`
`  x(y(i))= x(y(i)) + a`
`  x(z(i))= x(z(i)) + a`
`Enddo`
	`Do i = 1,n`
	`  x(y(i))= x(y(i)) + expensiveFunction(i)`
	`  x(z(i))= x(z(i)) + expensiveFunction(i)`
	`Enddo`

Fig. 5. Scalar Forward Substitution

depth, then we implicitly require the last value which is considered in section 4.3. We further restrict attention to those cases where there is no cross-iteration flow-dependence on the scalar value. This eliminates the possibility of upwardly exposed reads to a scalar [14]. Multiple reaching definitions are, however, allowed where they arise from separate branches within an `if` statement.

Once the global data partition has been determined, the local iteration spaces for each statement can be derived. Thus, each statement $\mathcal{S}$ has an associated local iteration space which will be denoted by $A\underline{J} \leq b$ or the constraint set $C_{\mathcal{S}}$. We are interested in those statements consisting of array assignments referring to one or more scalars. We shall denote these by $\mathcal{S}^u$ and will be indexed by $k \in 1, \ldots, n$ i.e. $\mathcal{S}_k^u$ is a particular statement with a usage or read reference to a particular scalar. If we denote $\mathcal{S}^d$ to be the statement defining such a scalar then we determine the new local iteration space of the scalar definition to be

$$C'_{\mathcal{S}^d} = \bigcup_k (C_{\mathcal{S}^d} \cap C_{\mathcal{S}_k^u}) \tag{1}$$

As we restrict attention to same or higher loop nest depth we have the condition:

$$dim(J^d) \leq dim(J^u), \forall u \tag{2}$$

and as we restrict attention to the case where there is no cross-iteration flow dependence:

$$\delta^f = \mathbf{0} \tag{3}$$

Once the new constraint set of the definition is calculated, frequently there will be constraints on iterators not in scope at this level e.g. when the definition is at a higher loop nest depth than the usage. Such iterators will be eliminated by fourier-motzkin elimination and the remaining constraints form the new local iteration space.

In the case of scalar definitions referring to other scalars, the propagation of constraints will have to be repeated. If we just consider array definitions, they will propagate constraints to the definitions of any scalar referred to, forming the first modified iteration space of the relevant scalar assignment. If that scalar definition refers to another scalar, then it too must propagate its newly modified iteration space to the definition of the scalar it is referring to and so on. For example, consider the program in figure 1. The constraint on `RLDI` from its usage is propagated to the definition of RLD. The number of times this process needs to be applied is equal to the number of scalar definitions within the loop of interest plus one. It does not need to iterate as we consider only those scalars where there is no cross-iteration flow dependence.

4.3   Copy Out

If there are possibly exposed reads to a scalar then we must introduce copy out code. For example, consider the program in figure 1. If there were a subsequent reference to RLD before another definition, each local copy of RLD would have to have the final value ($k = KU$) of RLD. The final value calculated by a particular processor must now be communicated to those processors requiring its value. This will require a non-local access, introducing a cross-processor dependence and hence a synchronisation point. Rather than determining the location of all exposed usages, we simplify the problem and copy the value to all processors, if there exists an exposed usage. Copy-out code in a data parallel approach differs from that used in scalar privatisation, as the processor evaluating the last iteration depends on the local iteration space.

Given the last iteration J_L, the processor z with local iteration space $A\underline{J_z} \leq b$ executing this iteration is the one satisfying the condition:

$$(A\underline{J_z} \leq b \wedge \underline{J_z} = J_L) \neq \emptyset \tag{4}$$

One problem arising from copy-out code is that we need to refer to a remote processors private variable, which by definition is not possible. Declaring private scalars as a p sized shared array where each processor z normally refers only to the zth element allows remote access to a copy-out value where necessary. In order to avoid false-sharing, such an array should be padded to the size of coherence unit - and indeed MARS already employs such a technique when parallelising scalar reductions. To illustrate this point consider the code in figure 6. The first column shows part of the wrapper MARS produces for generating parallel SPMD code around the code fragment shown in figure 1. If copy-out code is required, we have the result in column 2. Note that the scalars are now declared as shared padded arrays and that each local value of RLD(1,myid) has the same last value calculated by processor myid = NUM_PROCS.

4.4   Synchronisation

One of the largest potential benefits is that barriers within loops can in certain cases be eliminated. If scheduling, which takes place before synchronisation placement [3], incorporates constraint propagation, it should mark each array reference as being local or non-local, releaving the synchronisation phase from this requirement. Determination of local/non-local is straightforward and is based on the local iteration space of each . Those array elements that are local, LE, are given directly by the data partition i.e.

Original	Shared Variable.

<pre>REAL RLD,RLDI
.
C$DOACROSS Local (RLD,RLDI,myid,k)
 	
Do myid = 1, NUM_PROC
.
 	
.
DO K = max(KL,lo1), min(KU,hi1)
 RLD = C(J,K) - RLD1*X(J-1,K)
 RLDI = 1./RLD
 X(J,K) = (D(J,K) -
       RLD1*Y(J-1,K))*RLDI
 	
ENDDO
.
 	
.
Enddo</pre>
	<pre>REAL RLD(pad,MAX_NUM_PROCS)
	REAL RLDI
	.
	
	C$DOACROSS Local (RLDI,myid,k)
	C$DOACROSS Shared a
	
	Do myid = 1, NUM_PROC
	.
	
	.
	DO K = max(KL,lo1), min(KU,hi1)
	 RLD(1,myid) = C(J,K)
	- RLD1*X(J-1,K)
	 RLDI = 1./RLD(1,myid)
	 X(J,K) = (D(J,K) -
	          RLD1(1,myid)*Y(J-1,K))*RLDI
	
	ENDDO
	
	call mp_barrier()
	Do k = 1, NUM_PROCS
	 RLD(1,myid) = RLD(1,NUM_PROCS)
	Enddo
	
	Enddo</pre>

Fig. 6. Copy Out

$$A\underline{\mathcal{I}} \le b \tag{5}$$

Given the new constrained iteration space $A\underline{J} \le b$ and access function $\mathcal{U}J$ we can determine those array elements accessed in each of the array references to give the array section of each reference AS. If AS is a subset of LE then the reference is local otherwise it is non-local.

4.5   Algorithm

Although the above technique will eliminate unnecessary work and possibly eliminate excessive synchronisation, the new constraints will be manifest as if statements surrounding a statement within a loop body. Excessive evaluation of if statements can be avoided by propagating the constraints to the lexically enclosing loop body. In [5], we describe a technique to perform such a task when considering array assignments, and the approach can readily be adapted for our current task. The algorithm in figure 7 firstly examines the deepest loop nests and determines the local constraints on array statements referring to scalars. If, at this point exposed reads exist, requiring copy-out code, then the scalars

Forall Loops L, deepest loop first
1. Determine Schedule ∀ statements S, given data partition P, determine local iteration space/constraint set $C_S = A\underline{J} \leq b$.
2. Check Exposed Reads If there exists exposed reads redeclare scalar as shared padded array and update all scalar references.
3. Propagation phase: ∀ statements S with read references to *scalar*, propagate C_S to definition of *scalar*.
4. Determine Union of Constraints: Calculate new C_S for definition of *scalar*. For each array ref, determine if local.
5. Consider Scalar Definitions: Repeat stages 1 to 3 for each scalar assignment in reverse order.
6. Annotation pass: ∀ statements S propagate C_S and a pointer to S to the outermost parent loop L in which C_S remains invariant.
7. Loop generation: ∀ loop L, generate irredundant bounds for the affine part of L. Reconstruct directly bounds corresponding to non-affine constraints.
8. Copy-Out If copy-out insert copy-out code at highest legal loop level

Fig. 7. Scalar Algorithm

involved must be redeclared as shared arrays. The constraints are propagated and a new constraint set determined for the scalar assignments. This is repeated for each scalar definition in the loop nest. Once this is complete, the next two steps generate efficient loop bounds. Copy-out code is inserted where necessary.

Applying the algorithm to figure 1 after the propagation of constraints we have the program in row 2 column 1. Applying the loop generation phase, which propagates statement constraints up to the enclosing loops, we have the program in row 2 column 2.

5   Data Reshaping

At the heart of a data parallel approach, is the need to consistently apply a data layout to all affected portions of the code. However, difficulties arise when an array is linearised or reshaped as it has not previously been generally possible to statically determine the local programs. This frequently occurs across procedure boundaries [8]. At present, MARS has to calculate the new upper and lower bounds of the local iteration space at the beginning of each subroutine if there is a possibility of reshaped array access. Synchronisation points also need to be inserted due to possible data redistribution and hence cross-processor dependences. Not only does reshaping incur communication and synchronisation, but potentially write misses and invalidation traffic. In [17], an extension to the MARS transformation toolbox is proposed, namely rank-modifying transformations. This allows the propagation of data transformations in the presence of reshaped array access. If this is combined with loop restructuring, where the inverse data transformation is applied to the enclosing loop structure, then in the particular case of the partitioning data transformation, it allows efficient code

Original	Data Transformation	Loop Transformation

Real A(0:1,0:3)
Real B(0:7)
Equivalence(A,B)
.
.
.
Do j = 0,3
  Do i = 0,1
    A(i,j) = B(i +2*j)
          + C(i,j)
  Enddo
Enddo
Do j = 0,7
  B(j) = j*3
Enddo
	Real A(0:1,0:4)
	Real B(0:9)
	Equivalence(A,B)
	.
	.
	.
	Do j = 0,3
	  Do i = 0,1
	    A(i,i+j) = B(3*i+2*j)
	          + C(i,j)
	  Enddo
	Enddo
	Do j = 0,7
	  B(3*mod(j,2)+2*(j/2))
	    = j*3
	Enddo
		Real A(0:1,0:4)
		Real B(0:9)
		Equivalence(A,B)
		.
		.
		.
		Do j = 0,3
		  Do i = 0,1
		    A(i,i+j)=B(3*i +2*j)
		          + C(i,j)
		  Enddo
		Enddo
		Do j = 0,3
		  Do i = 0,1
		    B(3*i+2*j)=3*i+6*j
		  Enddo
		Enddo

Fig. 8. Linearised Aliasing

to be produced. This eliminates the need for any data redistribution and consequent synchronisation, communication and invalidation overhead. The next section briefly describes a technique to apply data layout transformations to arrays and shows how loops may be restructured to improve performance.

5.1   Data Transformations on Linearised Arrays

Data transformations such as alignment and partitioning must be applied to every reference to the particular array throughout the program. Difficulties occur when linearised references exist. Let $\mathcal{I}_1$ be the index space of the array to be transformed and $\mathcal{I}_2$ be the linearised space where:

$$\mathcal{I}_2 = L\mathcal{I}_1 \tag{6}$$

and L is the linearising transformation. We therefore have [1]:

$$\mathcal{I}_1 = L^\dagger \mathcal{I}_2 \tag{7}$$

If we wish to apply a non-singular data transformation $\mathcal{A}$ globally, this gives the new index domain $\mathcal{I}_1'$

$$\mathcal{I}_1' = \mathcal{A}\mathcal{I}_1 \tag{8}$$

and from equation 6 we have

$$\mathcal{I}_2' = L'\mathcal{I}_1' \tag{9}$$

---

[1] where †denotes pseudo-inverse

and therefore

$$\mathcal{I}'_2 = L'\mathcal{I}'_1 = L'\mathcal{AI}_1 = L'\mathcal{AL}^\dagger\mathcal{I}_2 \tag{10}$$

Thus, when applying $\mathcal{A}$ to the index domain $\mathcal{I}_1$, we must apply $L'\mathcal{AL}^\dagger$ to the linearised domain $\mathcal{I}_2$. Now, given two references $\mathcal{U}_1$ and $\mathcal{U}_2$, where $\mathcal{U}_2$ is a linearised reference, then on applying $\mathcal{A}$ we have as usual $\mathcal{U}'_1 = \mathcal{AU}_1$. However for the linearised access we have:

$$\mathcal{U}'_2 = L'\mathcal{AL}^\dagger\mathcal{U}_2 \tag{11}$$

L and L' and their inverses are readily derived from the array bounds before and after applying $\mathcal{A}$. E.g., for a two dimensional array we have

$$L = \begin{bmatrix} 1 & n \end{bmatrix} \quad \text{and} \quad L' = \begin{bmatrix} 1 & n' \end{bmatrix} \tag{12}$$

To illustrate this, consider the example in figure 8 column 1. Let A have the value:

$$\mathcal{A} = \begin{bmatrix} 1 & 0 \\ 1 & 1 \end{bmatrix} \tag{13}$$

that is, a simple data skew which is applied to the array A. This is in fact a data alignment transformation; the same applies to data partitioning. The access to array A in the first loop is readily found:

$$\begin{bmatrix} 1 & 0 \\ 1 & 1 \end{bmatrix} \times \begin{bmatrix} 1 & 0 \\ 0 & 1 \end{bmatrix} \begin{bmatrix} j \\ i \end{bmatrix} = \begin{bmatrix} 1 & 0 \\ 1 & 1 \end{bmatrix} \begin{bmatrix} j \\ i \end{bmatrix} \tag{14}$$

i.e., A(i, i + j) which is shown in figure 8, column 2. To update the equivalenced access to array b, we need to determine L' and $L^\dagger$.

Examining the original array bounds we have:

$$L = \begin{bmatrix} 1 & 2 \end{bmatrix} \quad \text{and} \quad L^\dagger = \begin{bmatrix} (\cdot)\%2 & (\cdot)/2 \end{bmatrix}^T \tag{15}$$

Applying $\mathcal{A}$ gives the new array bounds A(0:1,0:4). Hence

$$L' = \begin{bmatrix} 1 & 2 \end{bmatrix} \tag{16}$$

If we apply $L'\mathcal{AL}^\dagger$ to the linearised access to B in the first loop we get:

$$\begin{bmatrix} 1 & 2 \end{bmatrix} \times \begin{bmatrix} 1 & 0 \\ 1 & 1 \end{bmatrix} \times \begin{bmatrix} (\cdot)\%2 \\ (\cdot)/2 \end{bmatrix} \times [2,1] \begin{bmatrix} j \\ i \end{bmatrix}$$

$$= [2*j, 3*i] \tag{17}$$

i.e., A(3*i +2*j) which is shown in figure 8 column 2. Repeating the procedure for the second loop we have:

$$\begin{bmatrix} 1 & 2 \end{bmatrix} \times \begin{bmatrix} 1 & 0 \\ 1 & 1 \end{bmatrix} \times \begin{bmatrix} (\cdot)\%2 \\ (\cdot)/2 \end{bmatrix} \times [1][j]$$

$$= [3*(j\%2) + 2*(j/2)] \tag{18}$$

i.e., A(3*mod(j,2) +2 *(j/2)). Thus, our formulation allows systematic application of data transformations such as data alignment even in the presence of linearised array accesses.

5.2   Reducing Access Overhead for Linearised Arrays

Although correct, the program in figure 4, column 2 is far from ideal due to the % and / operators. We wish to remove these by introducing two new iterator variables corresponding to $j\%2$ and $j/2$. The % and / operators are introduced by rank-increasing transformation such as S or, in this case, the $L^\dagger$ matrix in equation 10. If we can apply a transformation such that S or $L^\dagger$ are eliminated, then the corresponding $j\%2$ and $j/2$ will be also be eliminated.

Let T be defined as follows:

$$T = \mathcal{U}^{-1} L^\dagger \mathcal{U}, \qquad (19)$$

and

$$T^{-1} = \mathcal{U}^{-1} L \mathcal{U} \qquad (20)$$

Applying this transformation to array accesses $\mathcal{U}_2'$ (defined in equation 11) gives the new access matrix:

$$\mathcal{U}_2' T^{-1} = L' A L^\dagger \mathcal{U} T^{-1} = L' A L^\dagger \mathcal{U} \mathcal{U}^{-1} L \mathcal{U} = L' A \mathcal{U} \qquad (21)$$

which is free from any rank-increasing matrices. Applying such a transformation to the second loop, gives the code in column 3 of figure 8. Thus, by combining loop and data transformations within one framework, we can can readily restructure programs so as to partially undo the effect of previous transformations.

6   Experiments

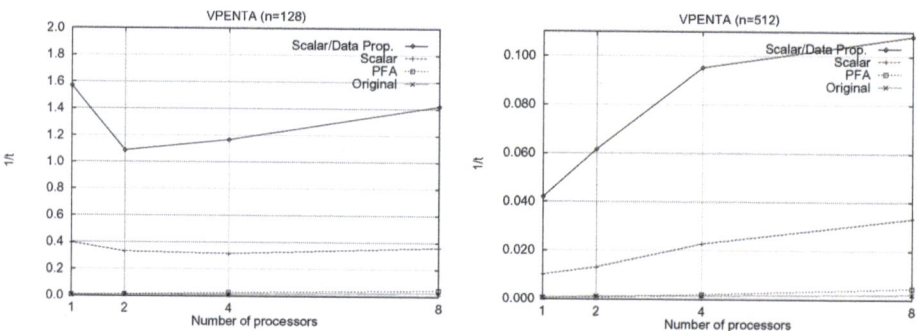

Fig. 9. Vpenta

In order to demonstrate the usefulness of a data parallel approach MARS was compared to the automatic paralleliser PFA which uses a traditional loop based fork+join approach to parallelisation. Both compilers were applied to the Specf92 benchmark programs **vpenta** and **btrix** and executed on an SGI Origin 200 on

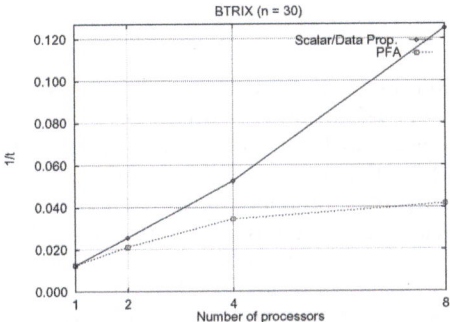

Fig. 10. Btrix

varying processor sizes. Although the data sizes for vpenta is fixed at 128 in the benchmark, a different data size was also considered to see how the two approaches scaled with data size. Three versions of MARS were tested on the vpenta benchmark: the basic version (Original), with restricted scalar evaluation (Scalar) and with data transformation propagation (Scalar/Data Prop.) and the results compared to PFA (PFA). Both PFA and the original basic version of MARS have almost identically poor performance. The addition of restricted scalar evaluation improved MARS's performance by up to a factor of 10, while the new version, with both restricted scalar evaluation and static propagation of data partitioning across reshaped arrays, gave the best performance; over twenty times as fast as PFA on eight processors. The graphs in figure 9 shows PFA versus the three versions of MARS for two differing data sizes(n =128,512) and varying processor size. The y-axis represents 1/time giving a measure of speedup. In the case of btrix only the benchmark data size of ($n = 30$) was considered due to the size of the arrays and just the modified version of MARS (Scalar/Data Prop.) compared against PFA. Once again, MARS outperforms PFA, this time by up to a factor of 3.

7   Conclusion

This paper has described certain aspects of MARS, a shared memory compiler that uses data layout as a starting point for global parallelisation of applications. It has a high-level linear algebraic representation which allows direct application of non-singular loop and data transformations. It provides, automatically, affinity style scheduling and enables aggressive synchronisation and locality optimisations to be applied. This paper described two frequently occurring problems with such an approach, namely scheduling of scalars and data reshaping. It described two techniques to overcome these problems and initial experimental results are highly encouraging. Future work will consider whether the constraint propagation techniques employed can be extended to further eliminate synchronisation.

References

1. Abdelrahman T., Manjikian N., Liu G. and Tandri S., **Locality Enhancement for Large-Scale Shared-Memory Multiprocessors**, LCR 98,Fourth Workshop on Languages, Compilers and Runtime Systems, Springer-Verlag, 1998.
2. Beckner S., Neuhold C., Egger M., Sajari K., Sipkova V. and Velkov B., **VFC The Vienna HPF+ Compiler** Compilers for Parallel Computers Sweden, July 1998 .
3. Bodin F. and O'Boyle M.F.P., **A Compiler Strategy for SVM** Third Workshop on Languages, Compilers and Runtime Systems, New York, Kluwer Press, May 1995.
4. Bodin F., Beckman P., Gannon D. and Srinivas J.G.S., **Sage++: A Class Library for Building Fortran and C++ Restructuring Tools**, Second Object-Oriented Numerics Conference, Oregon (USA), April 1994.
5. Chamski Z. and O'Boyle M.F.P., **Practical Loop Generation** HICSS-29, Hawaii International Conference on System Sciences, *IEEE Press*, Hawaii, January 1996.
6. Choudhary A., Fox G., Hiranandani S., Kennedy K., Koelbel C., Ranka S. and Tseng C.-W., **Unified Compilation of Fortran 77D and 90D**, ACM Letters on Programming Languages and Systems Vol2 Nos 1-4, March - December 1993.
7. Cierniak M. and Li W., **Unifying Data and Control Transformations for Distributed Shared-Memory Machines**, Programming Language Design and Implementation, June 1995.
8. M. Cierniak and W. Li. **Validity of Interprocedural Data Remapping**, Technical Report 642, Department of Computer Science, University of Rochester, November 1996.
9. Cytron R. and Ferrante J., **What's in a name or the value of renaming for parallelism detection and storage allocation**, Proc ICPP, 1987.
10. Gupta M., **On privatization for Data-Parallel Execution** IPPS '98, *IEEE Press*, Geneva, April 1998
11. Hall M., Anderson J., Amarsinghe S., Murphy B., Liao S., Bugnion E. and Lam M., **Maximizing multiprocessor performance with the SUIF compiler**, IEEE Computer 29(12):84-89,1996.
12. Kandemir M., Ramanujam J. and Choudhary A., **A Compiler Algorithm for Optimizing Locality in Loop Nests**, Proc. of International Conference on Supercomputing g, ACM Press, Vienna, July 1997
13. Lahjomri Z. and Priol T., **Koan : A Shared Virtual Memory for the iPSC/2 Hypercube**, Proceedings of CONPAR/VAPP92, Lyon, September 1992.
14. Li Z., **Array Privatization for Parallel Execution of Loops**, ICS, 6th ACM International Conference on Supercomputing, *ACM Press*, Washington, July 1992.
15. O'Boyle M.F.P., **A Data Partitioning Algorithm for Distributed Memory Compilation**, PARLE '94: Parallel Architectures and Languages Europe, LNCS 817 *Springer-Verlag*, Athens July 1994.
16. O'Boyle M.F.P., Ford R.W and Nisbet A.P., **A Compiler Algorithm to Reduce Invalidation Latency in Virtual Shared Memory Systems**, PACT '96, Parallel Architectures and Compiler Technology, *IEEE Press*, Boston, October 1996.
17. O'Boyle M.F.P. and P.M.W. Knijnenburg,**Integrating Loop and Data Transformations for Global Optimisation** , *to appear* PACT '98, Parallel Architectures and Compiler Technology, *IEEE Press*, Paris, October 1998.
18. O'Boyle M.F.P., Kervella L. and Bodin F., **Synchronisation Minimisation in a SPMD Execution Model**, Journal of Parallel and Distributed Computing Vol 29. 196-210, *Academic Press Inc.*, September 1995.

More on Scheduling Block-Cyclic Array Redistribution[*]

Frédéric Desprez[1], Stéphane Domas[1], Jack Dongarra[2,3],
Antoine Petitet[2], Cyril Randriamaro[1], and Yves Robert[1]

[1] LIP, Ecole Normale Supérieure de Lyon, 69364 Lyon Cedex 07, France
[desprez, sdomas, crandria, yrobert]@ens-lyon.fr,
[2] Department of Computer Science, University of Tennessee, Knoxville, TN
37996-1301, USA
[dongarra,petitet]@cs.utk.edu
[3] Mathematical Sciences Section, Oak Ridge National Laboratory, Oak Ridge, TN
37831, USA

Abstract. This article is devoted to the run-time redistribution of one-dimensional arrays that are distributed in a block-cyclic fashion over a processor grid. In a previous paper, we have reported how to derive optimal schedules made up of successive communication-steps. In this paper we assume that successive steps may overlap. We show how to obtain an optimal scheduling for the most general case, namely, moving from a CYCLIC(r) distribution on a P-processor grid to a CYCLIC(s) distribution on a Q-processor grid, for *arbitrary* values of the redistribution parameters P, Q, r, and s. We use graph-theoretic algorithms, and modular algebra techniques to derive these optimal schedulings.

Key-words: distributed arrays, block-cyclic distribution, redistribution, asynchronous communications, scheduling, HPF.

1 Introduction

Run-time redistribution of arrays that are distributed in a block-cyclic fashion over a multidimensional processor grid is a difficult problem that has recently received considerable attention. Solving this redistribution problem requires first to generate the messages to be exchanged and second to schedule these messages so that communication overhead is minimized. Rather than providing a detailed motivation and a survey of the existing literature, we refer the reader to [4,5,2].

The redistribution problem is to redistribute an array X with a CYCLIC(r) distribution on a P-processor grid to a same-size array Y with a CYCLIC(s) distribution on a Q-processor grid. This amounts to perform the HPF assignment $Y = X$.

Without loss of generality, we focus on one-dimensional redistribution problems in this article. Although we usually deal with multidimensional arrays in

---

[*] This work was supported in part by the CNRS–ENS Lyon–INRIA project *ReMaP*; and by the Eureka Project *EuroTOPS*.

D. O'Hallaron (Ed.): LCR'98, LNCS 1511, pp. 275–287, 1998.
© Springer-Verlag Berlin Heidelberg 1998

high-performance computing, the problem reduces to the "tensor product" of the individual dimensions. This is because HPF does not allow more than one loop variable in an ALIGN directive. Therefore, multidimensional assignments and redistributions are treated as several independent one-dimensional problem instances.

In a previous paper [2], we have reported how to derive optimal schedules made up of successive communication-steps, assuming a synchronization at the end of each step. The goal was to minimize either the number of steps, or the total cost of the redistribution computed as follows: for each step, the cost is (proportional to) the length of the longest message; the total cost is the sum of the cost of all steps.

In this paper we assume that successive steps may overlap. We show how to obtain an optimal scheduling using this new hypothesis that models more adequately state-of-the-art distributed-memory machines. Now the meaning of a "communication step" is simply that at any time-step, each processor sends/receives at most one message, thereby optimizing the amount of buffering and minimizing contention on communication ports. The construction of our optimal schedules relies on graph-theoretic algorithms, and on modular algebra techniques.

Notations

The main variables used in the next sections are listed in Table 1. The abbreviations "N.M." and "S/R" are used in a few communication tables. They respectively mean "Number of Messages" and "Sender/Receiver".

Table 1. Main notations in the paper.

variable	definition
P	The number of processors in the source grid
Q	The number of processors in the target grid
r	The block factor of the source distribution
s	The block factor of the target distribution
X	The array to be redistributed
M	The (global) size of X
L	The least common multiple of Pr and Qs
m	The number of slices of L data elements in array X

Consider an array $X[0...M-1]$ of size M that is distributed according to the block cyclic distribution CYCLIC(r) onto a linear grid of P processors (numbered from $p = 0$ to $p = P - 1$). Our goal is to redistribute X into an array Y distributed according to the block-cyclic distribution CYCLIC(s) onto Q processors (numbered from $q = 0$ to $q = Q - 1$). For simplicity, we assume that the size M of X is a multiple of $L = lcm(Pr, Qs)$, the least common multiple of Pr and Qs:

this is because the redistribution pattern repeats after each slice of L elements. Therefore, assuming an even number of slices in X will enable us (without loss of generality) to avoid discussing side effects. Let $m = M \div L$ be the number of slices.

Definition 1. *We let* $(P, r) \rightarrow (Q, s)$ *denote the redistribution problem from an original grid of P processors with distribution* CYCLIC(r) *to a target grid of Q processors with distribution* CYCLIC(s), *and assuming a single-slice vector of length $L = lcm(Pr, Qs)$ to be redistributed. Any indicated message length must be understood as a unit length (to be multiplied by the number of slices for actual vectors). Finally, we assume that r and s are relatively prime, that is, $\gcd(r, s) = 1$ (this handy simplification causes no loss of generality [2]).*

2   Motivating Example

Example 1. Consider an example with $P = Q = 6$ processors, $r = 2$, and $s = 3$. Note that the new grid of Q processors can be identical to, or disjoint of, the original grid of P processors. All communications are summarized in Table 2, which we refer to as a *communication grid*. Note that we view the source and target processor grids as disjoint in Table 2 (even if it may not actually be the case).

We see that each source processor $p \in \{0, 2, 3, 5\} \subset \mathcal{P} = \{0, 1, \ldots, P - 1\}$ sends 3 messages and that each processor $q \in \mathcal{Q} = \{0, 1, \ldots, Q - 1\}$ receives 4 messages. But each source processor $p \in \{1, 4\} \subset \mathcal{P}$ sends 6 messages. Hence there is no need to use a full all-to-all communication scheme that would require 6 steps, with a total of 6 messages to be sent per processor (or more precisely, 5 messages and a local copy). Rather, we should try to schedule the communication more efficiently.

Table 2. Communication grid for $P = Q = 6$, $r = 2$, and $s = 3$. Message lengths are indicated for a vector X of size $L = 36$.

S/R	0	1	2	3	4	5	N.M.
0	2	-	2	-	2	-	3
1	1	1	1	1	1	1	6
2	-	2	-	2	-	2	3
3	2	-	2	-	2	-	3
4	1	1	1	1	1	1	6
5	-	2	-	2	-	2	3
N.M.	4	4	4	4	4	4	

Figure 1 gives the optimal communication schedule for Example 1 when communication steps do not overlap. The horizontal axis represents time, and any pair "p, q" means that processor p in $\mathcal{P}$ sends a message to processor q in

$\mathcal{Q}$. For example, during the third time-step, processor 1 in $\mathcal{P}$ sends a message to processor 1 in $\mathcal{Q}$ and processor 4 in $\mathcal{P}$ sends a message to processor 2 in $\mathcal{Q}$. We obtain there a total of 9 time-steps, which is optimal with the non-overlapping assumption, but which can be further reduced if we suppress this assumption. Table 2 shows that each processor completes its own communications in 6 time steps. If we allow the communication steps to overlap, we can pack the smaller communications to fill the "holes" in the schedule. This is what we do in Figure 2: we obtain an optimal schedule with 6 time steps. The communication links of the processors are always used and we do not have to split any message. It can be checked in Figure 2 that each processor sends/receives at most one message at any time-step.

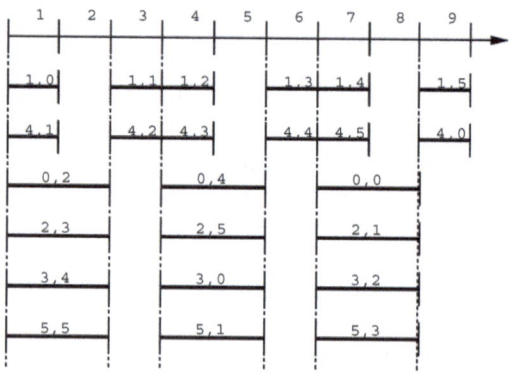

Fig. 1. Communication Scheduling for Example 1 (without overlap of time steps).

3   The Overlapped Redistribution Problem

3.1   Communication Model

According to the previous discussion, we concentrate on "overlapped schedules". The rules are the following:

- At any time-step, each sending processor is sending at most one message.
- At any time-step, each receiving processor is receiving at most one message.

This model is oriented to one-port communication machines, but is well-suited to any architectural platform because it minimizes the amount of buffering that has to be managed by the hardware or operating system.

To compute the cost of a redistribution, we simply take the delay between the initiation of the first message and the termination of the last one. The cost

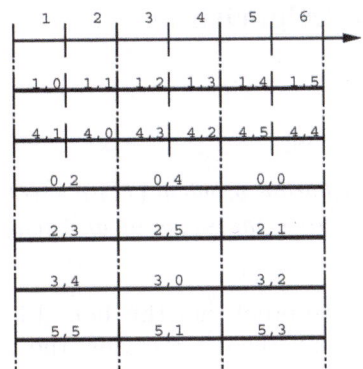

Fig. 2. Communication Scheduling for Example 1 (with overlap of time steps).

of each message is simply modeled by its length. For Example 1, the total cost is 6 as shown in Figure 2.

As for startups, we do not take them into account in the cost (because of the asynchronism, there is no way of determining the cost of a schedule including start-ups). This is not a limitation for long messages or for new-generation machines which exhibit a reduced communication start-up, but it may induce a problem for redistributing short messages on machines with a high communication start-up. Hence, another objective in the redistribution problem is to minimize the number of start-ups, which amounts to minimizing the number of messages that are sent/received. Therefore, a secondary goal when designing a good schedule is to "decompose" or "split" as few messages as possible. Of course this is an algorithmic issue, not an implementation issue (the system may well split all messages into packets).

The obvious bound is that we need as many time-steps as the sum of the entries in any row or column of the communication grid. We state this formally as follows:

Lemma 1. *For a redistribution problem* $(P, r) \rightarrow (Q, s)$, *the length of any schedule is at least*

$$T_{opt} = \max\{\frac{L}{P}, \frac{L}{Q}\}.$$

Surprisingly, this bound cannot be met in all instances of the problem, unless we split some messages into smaller ones (note that the bound was met in Example 1). We use two main approaches to solve the redistribution problem: one uses graph-theoretic algorithms, and the other relies on modular algebra techniques.

4   Graph-Theoretic Algorithms

4.1   Complexity

Our first result is the following:

Theorem 1. *For a redistribution problem* $(P, r) \rightarrow (Q, s)$, *assume that we split each message of length* x *into* x *messages of unit length. Then the bound* T_{opt} *can be achieved.*

Proof. We give a constructive proof that this bound is tight. To do so, we borrow some material from graph theory. We view the communication grid as a multigraph $G = (V, E)$, where

- $V = \mathcal{P} \cup \mathcal{Q}$, where $\mathcal{P} = \{0, 1, \ldots, p-1\}$ is the set of sending processors, and $\mathcal{Q} = \{0, 1, \ldots, q-1\}$ is the set of receiving processors; and
- if the entry (p, q) in the communication grid is a nonzero integer x, we add x identical edges from p to q.

G is a bipartite multigraph (all edges link a vertex in $\mathcal{P}$ to a vertex in $\mathcal{Q}$). The degree of G, defined as the maximum degree of its vertices, is $d_G = T_{opt}$. According to König's edge coloring theorem, the edge coloring number of a bipartite graph is equal to its degree (see [3, vol. 2, p.1666] or Berge [1, p. 238]). This means that the edges of a bipartite graph can be partitioned in d_G disjoint edge matchings. A constructive proof is as follows: repeatedly extract from E a maximum matching that saturates all maximum degree nodes. At each iteration, the existence of such a maximum matching is guaranteed (see Berge [1, p. 130]). To define the schedule, we simply let the matchings at each iteration represent the communication steps.

Remark 1. The proof of Theorem 1 gives a bound for the complexity of determining the optimal schedule. The best known algorithm for weighted, bipartite matching has cost $O(|V|^3)$ (Hungarian method, [3, vol. 1, p.206]). Since there are at most $T_{opt} \leq rs \max\{P, Q\}$ iterations to construct the schedule, we have a procedure in $O(rs(|P| + |Q|)^4)$ to construct an optimal schedule.

The main drawback of the previous approach is that all messages are split into unit-length messages, therefore leading to a high number of start-ups. A natural question is the following: is it possible to design a schedule whose execution time is T_{opt} and for which no message is split into pieces? The answer is negative, as shown in the next section.

4.2   A Counter-Example

As a proof to the impossibility to always reach the optimal schedule without cutting messages, we take the following example: $P = Q = 15$, $r = 3$, $s = 5$ and $L = 225$. Generating the communication grid, we see that 15 unit-length

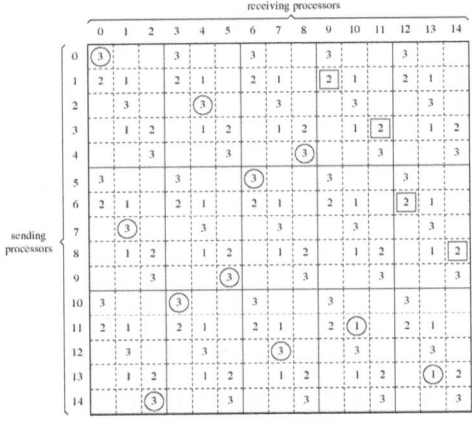

Fig. 3. Communication grid for $P = Q = 15$, $r = 3$ and $s = 5$.

data are sent by all the processors in $\mathcal{P}$, and received by all the processors in $\mathcal{Q}$. This implies that $T_{opt} = 15$ and that $15 = L/T_{opt}$ communications must be simultaneously in progress at any time-step $t \in [0, 15[$. Thus each processor must be sending a message at any time-step. We proceed by contradiction: assume for a while that there exists an optimal schedule in T_{opt} without cutting any message.

First, we reduce the problem to $t \in [0, 3[$. Indeed, nine processors out of fifteen must send five messages of size three. Thus, we want to determine a combination of communications that strictly fit into 3 time-steps. Hence, we must choose 9 communications of size 3. These are circled in Figure 3. The 6 remaining sending processors must be kept busy. We have the choice to send 6 messages of size 2 and 6 messages of size 1, or 18 messages of size 1.

- In the first case, it implies that 6 processors must be sending a message of size 2 at the same time. If we look at the communication grid in Figure 3, we can only select 4 processors.
- In the second case, it implies that 6 processors must be sending a message of size 1 at the same time. If we look at the communication grid in Figure 3, we can only select 4 processors.

Thus, it is impossible to find a solution for $t \in [0, 3[$. But, for $t \in [0, 6[$, we can find a combination of communications that strictly fits in 6 time-steps. The solution is shown in Figure 4. Unfortunately, $15 \bmod 6 = 3$ and we have proved that we cannot find a solution in 3 time-steps. Finally, there are no solutions for $t \in [0, 9[$ since $6 = lcm(3, 2, 1)$. Thus, it is impossible to find a schedule in 15 time-steps.

4.3   An Efficient Heuristic

We have implemented a heuristic to design a schedule that runs in T_{opt} time-steps and split as few messages as possible (if any). We use a greedy strategy to fill up

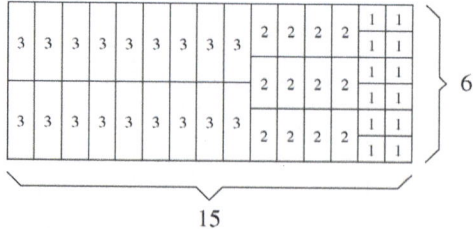

Fig. 4. A solution for the first 6 time-steps.

the schedule table. The algorithm has the ability to exchange some communications within the schedule in order to place possibly remaining communications. As the number of these exchanges is combinatorial, we have set a parameter that fix the maximum number of exchanges. The heuristic is guaranteed if we allow for a high number of exchanges. However, very fast convergence has been observed in practice. In Table 3, we give some cases in which our algorithm does not produce an optimal schedule. The T_{opt} column gives the optimal schedule time. The T_{algo} gives the schedule time given by our algorithm without any exchange of remaining packets. At last, the T_{algo}^{ech} gives the schedule time with at least $min(P, Q)$ remaining packets that are exchanged. It is important to point out that most cases are dealt without any exchange, as in the last example in Table 3.

Table 3. Schedule time for different parameters P, Q, r and s.

Parameters					T_{opt}	T_{algo}	T_{algo}^{ech}
P	r	Q	s	L			
15	4	12	3	180	15	18	15
15	4	16	3	240	16	23	17
15	2	14	3	210	15	19	16
15	2	16	3	240	16	22	17
16	9	18	5	720	45	49	46
15	9	18	5	270	18	20	18
15	16	18	32	2800	192	208	192
15	16	9	32	1440	160	174	160
14	17	19	33	149226	10659	10659	-

5   Modular Algebra Techniques

Using modular algebra techniques as in [2], we have the following result:

Proposition 1. *We have the following case analysis:*

- *if* $\gcd(r, Q) = \gcd(s, P) = 1$, *we are always able to derive a schedule whose execution time is* T_{opt} *and which splits no message at all*
- *otherwise, let* $\gcd(s, P) = s'$ *and* $\gcd(r, Q) = r'$. *We are able to derive a schedule whose execution time is* T_{opt} *and which splits no message at all under the condition*

$$\left(s' < r' \text{ and } \frac{P}{s'} \leq \frac{Q}{r'}\right) \quad \text{or} \quad \left(s' > r' \text{ and } \frac{P}{s'} \geq \frac{Q}{r'}\right)$$

Proof. — Since $\gcd(r, s) = 1$, we introduce integers u and v such that

$$ru - sv = 1.$$

In our previous paper [2], we defined classes by

$$class(k) = \{\begin{pmatrix} p \\ q \end{pmatrix} = \lambda \begin{pmatrix} s \\ r \end{pmatrix} + k \begin{pmatrix} u \\ v \end{pmatrix} \bmod \begin{pmatrix} P \\ Q \end{pmatrix}; \ 0 \leq \lambda < \frac{PQ}{g}\},$$

for $0 \leq k < g$.

In [2] we showed that a schedule based upon classes is optimal when $\gcd(r, Q) = \gcd(s, P) = 1$.

- Otherwise, assume that $g > r + s - 1$. Consider $r < s$, $s' = \gcd(s, P)$, $r' = \gcd(r, Q)$, $P = s'P'$, $Q = r'Q'$, and $g_0 = \gcd(P', Q')$. Then $g = \gcd(Pr, Qs) = r's'g_0$. The communication table is divided into subtables of size $s' \times r'$.

Now, we propose to find an optimal scheduling inside such subtables.

Lemma 2. *We can assume that* $g_0 = 1$.

We define a new class by $class(k)$ with the elements of a subtable:

$$class'(k) = \{(p, q) \in class(k); 0 \leq p < s'; 0 \leq q < r'\}$$

Lemma 3. *With such conditions, for* $1 - r \leq k < s - 1$, *each communication class* $class'(k)$ *contains one element only:* $class'(k) = (p_k,\ q_k)$.

Proof. By definition, if $(p, q) \in class'(k)$ then $(p, q) \in class(k)$, so

$$\begin{pmatrix} p \\ q \end{pmatrix} = \lambda \begin{pmatrix} s \\ r \end{pmatrix} + k \begin{pmatrix} u \\ v \end{pmatrix} \bmod \begin{pmatrix} P \\ Q \end{pmatrix}; \ 0 \leq \lambda < \frac{PQ}{g};$$

While $s' = \gcd(s, P)$ and $r' = \gcd(r, Q)$, then

$$\begin{pmatrix} p \\ q \end{pmatrix} = \lambda \begin{pmatrix} s' \\ r' \end{pmatrix} + k \begin{pmatrix} u \\ v \end{pmatrix} \bmod \begin{pmatrix} P \\ Q \end{pmatrix}; 0 \leq \lambda$$

As $0 \le p < s'$ and $0 \le q < r'$, then $\lambda = 0$. In addition, by definition of s' and r', $\gcd(s', P) = s'$ and $\gcd(r', Q) = r'$, hence

$$\binom{p}{q} = k \binom{u}{v} \quad \begin{matrix} \bmod s' \\ \bmod r' \end{matrix}$$

Now consider $(p', q') \in class'(k)$, so

$$\binom{p'}{q'} = k' \binom{u}{v} \quad \begin{matrix} \bmod s' \\ \bmod r' \end{matrix}$$

it implies

$$\begin{matrix} ku = k'u \bmod s' \\ kv = k'v \bmod r' \end{matrix} \Rightarrow \begin{matrix} (k - k')u = \alpha s' \\ (k - k')v = \beta r' \end{matrix} \Rightarrow \begin{matrix} s' | (k - k') \text{ because } \gcd(s', u) = 1 \\ r' | (k - k') \text{ because } \gcd(r', v) = 1 \end{matrix}$$

then $r's' | (k - k')$. $1 - r \le k, k' < s - 1$, then $0 < |k - k'| < g$. $g = r's'$ so $k = k'$.

Lemma 4. *For any $k \in [1 - r, s - 1]$, there is no contention (i.e. same sender or same receiver) between class'(k) and class'(k + x), where $x \in [1, r' - 1]$*

Proof. Consider a contention between senders of $class'(k)$ and $class'(k+x)$, then, if $(p, q) = class'(k)$ then $class'(k + x) = (p', q') = (p, q')$. Hence $p = ku \bmod s' = (k+x)u \bmod s'$ so $xu \bmod s' = 0$. In the same way, there is a contention between receivers of $class'(k)$ and $class'(k + x)$ iff $xv \bmod r' = 0$. Assuming that $r' < s'$, if $x > 0$ a contention implies $x \ge r'$.

Lemma 5. *Sending messages by classes from class'(1 − r) to class'(s − 1) generates no contention.*

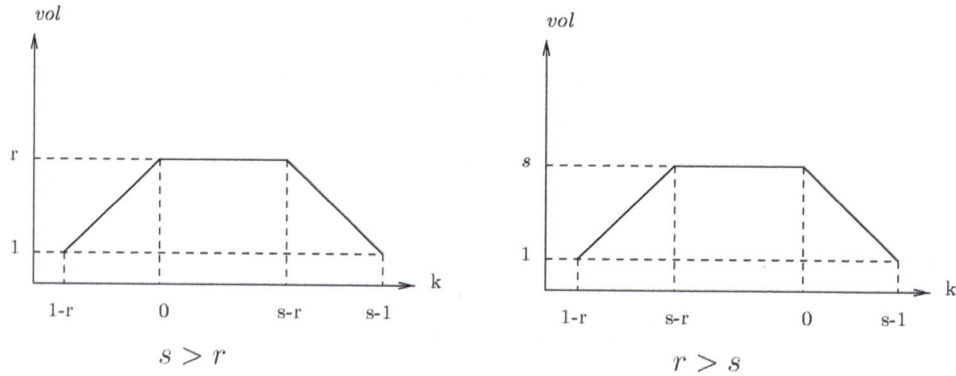

Fig. 5. The piecewise linear function *vol*.

Proof. In paper [2], it is proved that function $vol(k)$ given by Figure 5 for $k \in [1 - r, s - 1]$ represents the size of each communication in $class(k)$, for a vector of length $L = lcm(Pr, Qs)$. While $class'(k) \subset class(k)$ this result is still correct for $class'(k)$.

During the first step of that schedule, the r' communications in $class'(k)$ with $k \in [1 - r, -r + r']$ can be performed in the same time (lemma 4) shows that there is no contention).

$$vol(1 - r) = 1$$
$$vol(-r + 2) = 2$$
$$vol(-r + 3) = 3$$
$$\vdots$$
$$vol(-r + r' - 1) = r' - 1$$
$$vol(-r + r') = r'$$

The next step is composed by the next r' communications in $class'(k)$ (i.e. $k \in [1-r+r', -r+2r'])$ during that step due to the same lemma, for any $k \in [1-r+r', -r+2r']$, $class'(k)$ generates no contention with any $class'(k')$ where $k' \in [k+1, -r+2r']$ or $k' \in [k-r'+1, k-1]$. Because sizes are sorted, communications in $class'(k' \le k - r')$ are already performed when the communication of $class'(k)$ begins. Hence, there is no contention at all during the execution of the first two steps. In the same way, we can prove that there in no contention during the next steps up to messages of size r, and then when the message size decreases:

$$vol(1 - r + r') = r' + 1 \ (r) \quad vol(s - 2r') = r \qquad vol(s - r') = r'$$
$$\vdots \qquad\qquad (r) \ \vdots \qquad\qquad\qquad vol(s - r' - 1) = r' - 1$$
$$vol(-1) = r - 1 \qquad (r) \ vol(r - s) = r \qquad \vdots$$
$$vol(0) = r \qquad\qquad (r) \ vol(r - s + 1) = r - 1 \ vol(s - 3) = 3$$
$$\vdots \qquad\qquad (r) \ \vdots \qquad\qquad\qquad vol(s - 2) = 2$$
$$vol(-r + 2r') = r \qquad (r) \ vol(s - r' - 1) = r' \quad vol(s - 1) = 1$$

Lemma 6. *If an optimal schedule is found in a $s' \times r'$ grid, an optimal schedule can be found for the $P \times Q$ grid if $s' > r'$ and $\frac{P}{s'} \ge \frac{Q}{r'}$.*

Proof. The idea is to perform schedule in boxes by diagonals.

Example 2. Consider the following example where $P = 15$, $Q = 6$, $r = 3$, and $s = 5$, $r' = \gcd(3, 6) = 3$, and $s' = \gcd(5, 15) = 5$. As shown in Table 4, the communication table is divided into boxes of size 5×3. In that example, the communication in two diagonal boxes can be performed in the same time with no contention: there is no intersection between the set of senders (or receivers) of the boxes. While the number of sender is greater than the number of receiver, it is the maximum number of boxes that can be taken: when communications are performed in a box, all receivers are always receiving. Then, performing communication by boxes in the same diagonal is optimal. Hence, it is easy to

Table 4. Communication grid for $P = 15$, $Q = 6$, $r = 3$, and $s = 5$. Message lengths are indicated for a vector X of size $L = 225$.

Send/Recv.	0	1	2	3	4	5	Nbr of msg.
0	3	-	-	3	-	-	5
1	2	1	-	2	1	-	10
2	-	3	-	-	3	-	5
3	-	1	2	-	1	2	10
4	-	-	3	-	-	3	5
5	3	-	-	3	-	-	10
6	2	1	-	2	1	-	5
7	-	3	-	-	3	-	10
8	-	1	2	-	1	2	5
9	-	-	3	-	-	3	10
10	3	-	-	3	-	-	5
11	2	1	-	2	1	-	10
12	-	3	-	-	3	-	5
13	-	1	2	-	1	2	10
14	-	-	3	-	-	3	5
Nbr of msg.	6	9	6	6	9	6	

prove that the algorithm by boxes in diagonals is optimal under the condition

$$\left(s' < r' \text{ and } \frac{P}{s'} \le \frac{Q}{r'} \right) \quad \text{or} \quad \left(s' > r' \text{ and } \frac{P}{s'} \ge \frac{Q}{r'} \right)$$

Note that Proposition 1 covers a wide range of cases. And because the proof is constructive, we can easily implement a schedule based upon modular techniques. Also note that it is a sufficient but not necessary condition to derive an optimal schedule. For example, with $P = 12$, $Q = 8$, $r = 4$, and $s = 3$ (see [2]), $r' = \gcd(4, 8) = 4$, and $s' = \gcd(3, 12) = 3$. The condition is not true but there exists an optimal schedule in time $T_{opt} = 6$.

6   Conclusion

In this article, we have extended our previous work devoted to general redistribution problem, that is, moving from a CYCLIC(r) distribution on a P-processor grid to a CYCLIC(s) distribution on a Q-processor grid.

In our previous paper [2], we have constructed a schedule that is optimal both in terms of the number of steps and of the total cost, but with a synchronization between each communication step. In this article, we have presented several results to schedule the messages with the only rule that each processor can send/receive at most one message per time-step. An implementation of our algorithm is currently under development for a future release of ScaLAPACK.

References

1. Claude Berge. *Graphes et hypergraphes*. Dunod, 1970. English translation by Elsevier, Amsterdam (1985).
2. Frédéric Desprez, Jack Dongarra, Antoine Petitet, Cyril Randriamaro, and Yves Robert. Scheduling block-cyclic array redistribution. *IEEE Trans. Parallel Distributed Systems*, 9(2):192–205, 1998.
3. R.L. Graham, M. Grötschel, and L. Lovász. *Handbook of combinatorics*. Elsevier, 1995.
4. David W. Walker and Steve W. Otto. Redistribution of block-cyclic data distributions using MPI. *Concurrency: Practice and Experience*, 8(9):707–728, 1996.
5. Lei Wang, James M. Stichnoth, and Siddhartha Chatterjee. Runtime performance of parallel array assignment: an empirical study. In *1996 ACM/IEEE Supercomputing Conference*. http://www.supercomp.org/sc96/proceedings, 1996.

Flexible and Optimized IDL Compilation for Distributed Applications

Eric Eide, Jay Lepreau, and James L. Simister

University of Utah Department of Computer Science
3190 MEB, Salt Lake City, Utah 84112

flick@cs.utah.edu, http://www.cs.utah.edu/projects/flux/flick/

Abstract. The author of a distributed system is often faced with a dilemma when writing the system's communication code. If the code is written by hand (e.g., using Active Messages) or partly by hand (e.g., using MPI) then the speed of the application may be maximized, but the human effort required to implement and maintain the system is greatly increased. On the other hand, if the code is generated using a high-level tool (e.g., a CORBA IDL compiler) then programmer effort will be reduced, but the performance of the application may be intolerably poor. The tradeoff between system performance and development effort arises because existing communication middleware is inefficient, imposes excessive presentation layer overhead, and therefore fails to expose much of the underlying network performance to application code. Moreover, there is often a mismatch between the desired communication style of the application (e.g., asynchronous message passing) and the communication style of the code produced by an IDL compiler (synchronous remote procedure call). We believe that this need not be the case, but that established optimizing compiler technology can be applied and extended to attack these domain-specific problems.

We have implemented *Flick*, a flexible and optimizing IDL compiler, and are using it to explore techniques for producing high-performance code for distributed and parallel applications. Flick produces optimized code for marshaling and unmarshaling data; experiments show that Flick-generated stubs can marshal data between 2 and 17 times as fast as stubs produced by other IDL compilers. Further, because Flick is implemented as a "kit" of components, it is possible to extend the compiler to produce stylized code for many different application interfaces and underlying transport layers. In this paper we outline a novel approach for producing "decomposed" stubs for a distributed global memory service.

This research was supported in part by the Defense Advanced Research Projects Agency, monitored by the Department of the Army under contract number DABT63–94–C–0058, and Air Force Research Laboratory, Rome Research Site, USAF, under agreement number F30602–96–2–0269. The U.S. Government is authorized to reproduce and distribute reprints for Governmental purposes notwithstanding any copyright annotation hereon.

D. O'Hallaron (Ed.): LCR'98, LNCS 1511, pp. 288–302, 1998.

1   Introduction

Modern computer networks are becoming increasingly fast, and modern operating systems are now supporting efficient, lightweight communication mechanisms such as shared memory-based intra-node communication channels [1], highly optimized kernel IPC paths [22, 11], and new inter-node communication models such as active messages [31] and sender-based protocols [5, 30]. As Clark and Tennenhouse predicted in 1990 [8], these improvements in low-level communication systems have moved the performance bottlenecks for distributed applications out of the network and operating system layers and into the applications themselves [19, 20].

It is now possible to write high-performance, distributed applications that efficiently utilize network bandwidth. However, in order to *realize* the benefits of modern communication networks, the authors of parallel and distributed applications are generally forced to write their applications' communication code by hand. In order to squeeze the necessary performance out of the communication code, programmers must often write their own routines to marshal and unmarshal data, to dispatch and receive messages, and to handle communication failures. Writing this code requires a great amount of effort, is error-prone, and places a significant maintenance burden on the application programmer. Unfortunately, all this effort is necessary because today's high-level tools for producing communication code are inadequate for the demands of high-performance distributed applications.

An *interface definition language* (IDL) compiler is one tool for producing communication code with minimal programmer effort. An IDL compiler reads a high-level specification of an interface to a software component, and from that produces "stubs": functions that encapsulate the communication between the *client* that invokes an operation and the *server* that implements the operation. The stubs output by the IDL compiler hide the details of communication and allow the client and server to interact through a procedural interface. For example, consider the following CORBA [24] IDL specification of a simple file server:

```
interface FS {
  typedef sequence<octet> content;

  content read(in string filename);
  void    write(in string filename, in content data);
};
```

Given this interface, a CORBA IDL compiler for C will generate the following stub prototypes for the **read** and **write** operations:[1]

---

[1] For clarity, we have omitted the declaration of the **FS** object type and the declaration of the **FS_content** type.

```
FS_content *FS_read(FS obj,
                    CORBA_char *filename,
                    CORBA_Environment *env);

void FS_write(FS obj,
              CORBA_char *filename, FS_content *data,
              CORBA_Environment *env);
```

The compiler will also output implementations of the **FS_read** and **FS_write** stubs that implement *remote procedure call* (RPC) [4] or *remote method invocation* (RMI) semantics: the client that invokes **FS_read** or **FS_write** will block until the server replies to the client's request. From the client's point of view, the **FS_read** and **FS_write** functions behave like normal, local procedure calls.

IDLs and IDL compilers can increase programmer productivity and eliminate the errors that are common in hand-written communication code. Traditionally, however, this benefit has come at a cost: poor optimization of the IDL-derived code. The code generated by existing IDL compilers like **rpcgen** [29] contains a great deal of overhead; Schmidt et al. [19] and others have quantified this overhead for a number of existing CORBA implementations. This overhead is often not a problem for applications that make infrequent RPC calls; similarly, it is often not a problem if the underlying network layers are slow (thus causing the network or operating system layers to be the performance bottleneck). However, the inefficiency of IDL-derived code can make it completely unsuitable for use in an application that demands maximum RPC performance. For this reason, the designers of highly distributed and parallel applications have been unable to take advantage of tools that ease the creation of communication code.

Beyond the substantial concerns about performance, there is a further and perhaps more significant barrier to the use of IDL compilers for many distributed applications: namely, that traditional IDL compilers can produce only RPC or RMI stubs. Many distributed applications require greater control over their communication; other applications simply have communication patterns that do not easily mesh with traditional RPC semantics. In order to support these kinds of applications, an IDL compiler must be flexible: it must give the application writer a great deal of control over the stubs that are generated by the IDL compiler. This level of control is also required in order to provide a migration path for existing applications already written to other communication models such as MPI [23].

We believe that parallel and distributed applications would be improved if they were designed to use either IDLs or other languages incorporating optimized presentation layer code, and that the barriers described above can be eliminated by bringing well-established compiler techniques to bear on the domain of IDL compilation. To explore these ideas we have implemented *Flick* [10], the Flexible IDL Compiler Kit. Flick is a "toolkit" of compiler components that may be specialized for particular IDLs, stub styles, and transport systems. Flick has three separate front ends that parse interface specifications written in the CORBA [24], ONC RPC (a.k.a. Sun RPC) [28], and MIG [26] IDLs. A specification in any of these languages is sent through a series of separate compiler passes to produce optimized CORBA-, rpcgen-, or MIG-style C stubs communicating via TCP, Mach [1] messages, Trapeze [2] messages, or Fluke [15] kernel IPC. Section 2 summarizes the structure of Flick, and Sec. 3 describes how we are extending Flick to create specialized, "decomposed" stubs for a class of distributed applications heretofore unsupported by traditional IDL compilers. Our new IDL compilation techniques provide fine-grained control over communication and will soon be applied to generating stubs for Khazana [6], a distributed global memory service.

2   Flick

Figure 1 shows the design of the Flick IDL compiler. Flick is organized like a traditional language compiler with separate front ends, intermediate code generators, and back ends.

The first phase of the compiler is the *front end*, which reads an IDL specification and produces an intermediate file called an Abstract Object Interface (AOI). The second phase, the *presentation generator*, reads the AOI file produced by the front end and outputs a file that describes the programmer's interface to the stubs that will be generated by the compiler. This is called the *presentation* of the interface. A presentation is a "programmer's contract" that describes everything an application programmer must know in order to use the functions and data type declarations created by an IDL compiler. This contract includes such things as the names of the generated functions, the types of their arguments, the memory allocation conventions, and so on.

Consider the stub prototypes shown previously for the **read** and **write** operations of our simple filesystem interface. Those prototypes conform to the CORBA specification for mapping IDL constructs onto the C programming language. However, that mapping is not the only possible mapping, nor it is necessarily the most useful one. Previous experiments [13, 14] have shown that by modifying the mapping from IDL to stub, a programmer can adapt the stubs to better meet the needs of a particular system. Section 3 will explore this idea further.

Flick provides support for different presentation styles through its multiple presentation generators. Each presentation generator implements a specific presentation style for a particular programming language (e.g., the CORBA C language mapping). The output of the presentation generator is another intermediate file, called a Presentation in C (PRES_C) file.

The third and final phase of the compiler, the *back end*, transforms the presentation description into the source code that will implement client/server communication. Each of Flick's back ends is specialized for a particular communications infrastructure (e.g., CORBA IIOP or Mach typed messages). The back end decides the internals of the stubs — message format, message data encoding, and underlying transport facility — and finally produces the optimized stub code.

Flick's back ends apply numerous domain-specific optimizations to reduce the overheads that typically hinder IDL-based communication. For instance, Flick analyzes the overall storage requirements of every message and for each produces

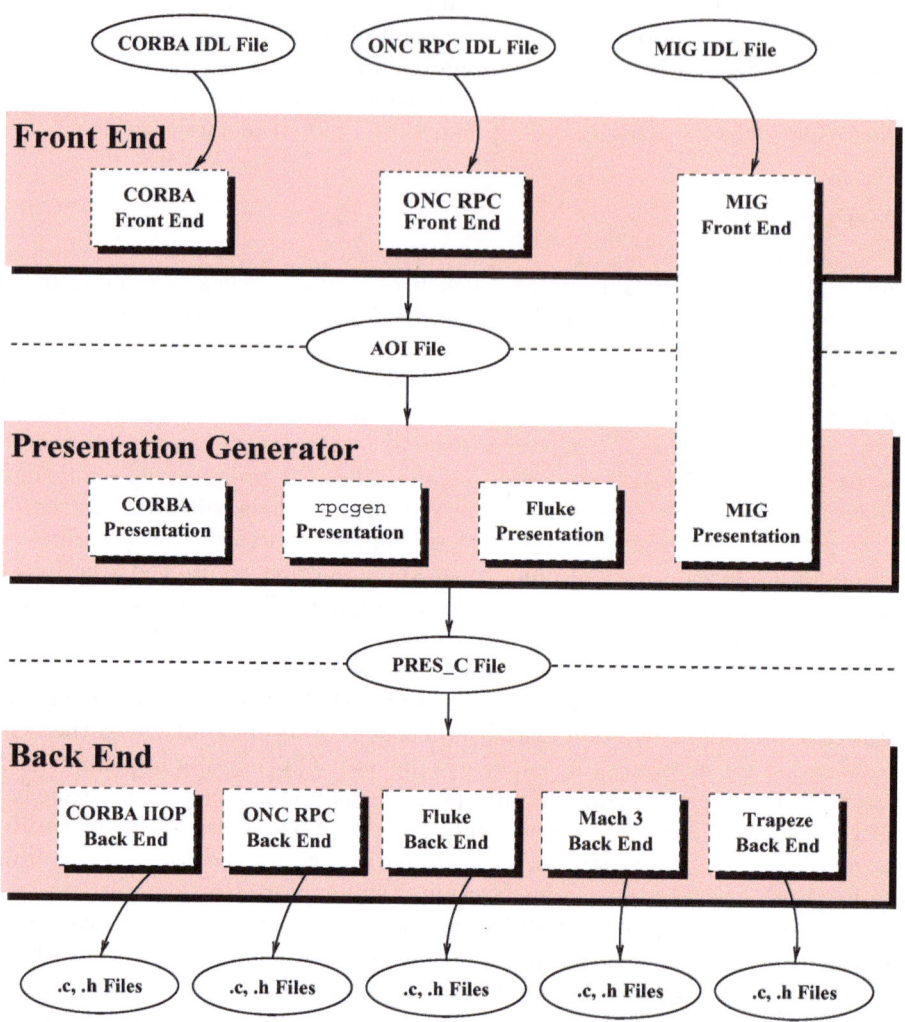

Fig. 1. The components of the Flick IDL compiler. Flick is implemented as three separate compiler passes which communicate through intermediate files. Each pass is primarily implemented by a large library of code which is specialized in order to create particular compiler components.

efficient memory allocation code. Flick also exploits opportunities to copy objects with efficient copy routines; for example, arrays of integers may be copied with memcpy when Flick is able to determine that no byte-swapping or other presentation layer conversion is required. Previous experiments with Flick [10] show that Flick-generated stubs can marshal data between 2 and 17 times as fast as stubs generated by other IDL compilers. This reduction in presentation layer overhead results in significant end-to-end throughput improvements for applications running on stock operating systems, communicating over TCP.

3   IDL Compilation for a Global Memory Service

As described in Sec. 2, the *presentation* of an interface is a description of everything that client or server code must know in order to use the stubs and other code output by an IDL compiler. There may be many different presentations of a single interface; that is, there are many different ways of translating an IDL specification into bits of code to implement the interface. Traditional IDL compilers produce RPC stubs, but this is not the only possible way to implement an interface, and may in fact be a bad match with the needs of particular distributed or parallel applications. This section presents one such application and describes a novel presentation style for CORBA IDL that we are implementing within Flick, thus allowing Flick to accommodate the application in a way that traditional IDL compilers cannot.

3.1   Khazana

The application is Khazana [6], a "global memory service" being developed by Carter et al. at the University of Utah. Khazana is a middleware layer for distributed applications that provides the abstraction of a distributed, persistent, globally shared store in which applications may save state. Khazana is implemented as a collection of peer processes; there is no single "server" process. Instead, all of the Khazana processes cooperate in order to provide the illusion of a single shared resource.

Khazana processes communicate by exchanging asynchronous messages. Although there are conceptual requests and replies, Khazana nodes must be able to process events after a request is sent but before the corresponding reply is received. When responding to a request, a Khazana node may discover that it needs to forward the message to another node (e.g., the home node of some requested Khazana memory page). A node may also discover that it can only service part of a request, and that the request needs to be "pushed back" onto the queue of incoming requests along with the partial results that have been so far computed.

The current implementation of Khazana uses hand-coded functions to handle the exchange of messages between nodes, perform asynchronous sends and receives, and save partially handled requests. The Khazana implementors, however, anticipate that as development continues, the number of message types will

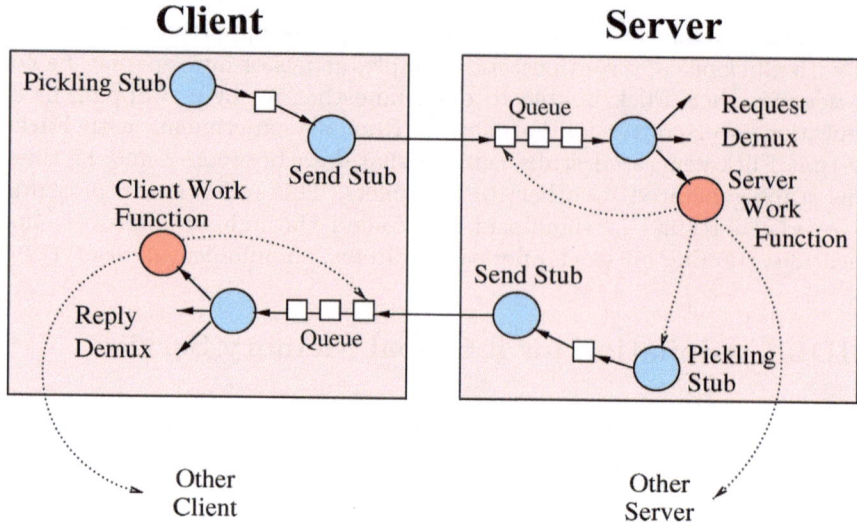

Fig. 2. A new presentation style for CORBA interfaces. Unlike the standard presentation of CORBA interfaces, this new presentation allows for asynchronous requests and replies, efficient message forwarding, and saving intermediate results.

increase and that the burden of writing all the messaging code will be overwhelming. For this reason they are interested in using Flick to generate the Khazana communication stubs — but the generated code must meet the requirements outlined above. The design of Khazana is incompatible with the traditional presentation of IDL interfaces as simple, synchronous RPC stubs.

3.2 Decomposed Stubs: A New Presentation Style for CORBA

We have therefore designed a new presentation style for CORBA IDL specifications that breaks apart traditional RPC stubs and better meets the needs of Khazana. This new presentation style is illustrated in Fig. 2 and consists of:

- *pickling stubs*, to marshal (encode) request and reply messages;
- *unpickling stubs*, to unmarshal (decode) request and reply messages;
- *send stubs*, to transmit pickled messages to other nodes;
- *server work functions*, to handle received requests;
- *client work functions*, to handle received replies; and
- *continuation stubs*, to postpone the processing of messages.

The stub and function prototypes generated by Flick for this new "decomposed" presentation style are summarized in Table 1.

Table 1. Summary of the stubs and functions that are part of Flick's "decomposed" CORBA presentation style. The italicized elements (e.g., *Interface*) are replaced with the appropriate names and elements from the input IDL file.

| Pickling Stubs | ```
Interface_Request Interface_operation_encode_request(
      in and inout parameters,
      CORBA_Environment *env);
Interface_Reply Interface_operation_encode_reply(
      return and inout and out parameters,
      CORBA_Environment *env);
Interface_Reply Interface_operation_encode_exception(
      CORBA_Environment *reply_env,
      CORBA_Environment *env);
``` |
| Unpickling Stubs | ```
void Interface_operation_decode_request(
      Interface_Request msg,
      in and inout parameters,
      CORBA_Environment *env);
void Interface_operation_decode_reply(
      Interface_Reply msg,
      return and inout and out parameters,
      CORBA_Environment *env);
``` |
| Send Stubs | ```
void Interface_send_request(
      Interface target, Interface_Request msg,
      Invocation_id inv_id, Client client,
      CORBA_Environment *env);
void Interface_send_reply(
      Client client, Interface_Reply msg,
      Invocation_id inv_id, Interface target,
      CORBA_Environment *env);
``` |
| Work Functions | ```
void Interface_operation_do_request(
      Interface target, Interface_Request msg,
      Invocation_id inv_id, Client client);
void Interface_operation_do_reply(
      Client client, Interface_Reply msg,
      Invocation_id inv_id, Interface target);
``` |
| Continuation Stubs | ```
typedef void Interface_Request_Continuer(...);
typedef void Interface_Reply_Continuer(...);
void Interface_operation_continue_request(
      Interface target, Interface_Request msg,
      Invocation_id inv_id, Client client,
      Interface_Request_Continuer func, void *data);
void Interface_operation_continue_reply(
      Client client, Interface_Reply msg,
      Invocation_id inv_id, Interface target,
      Interface_Reply_Continuer func, void *data);
``` |
```

Pickling and Unpickling Stubs. Each operation in the IDL specification results in three "pickling" stubs: one to marshal operation requests, a second to marshal ordinary operation replies, and a third to marshal exceptional (error-signaling) replies. A pickling stub takes as parameters the data to be encoded, followed by a standard CORBA environment parameter used to communicate exceptions back to the caller (i.e., errors that occur as the message is being encoded). The pickled message is returned by the stub so that the application can send the message at a later time; that is, the encoding and transmission events are decoupled. Note that the type of the pickled message is specific to a single interface (object type); this helps prevent programming errors in which a request or reply is sent to an object of an inappropriate type. Also note that the returned message is opaque. This allows each of Flick's back ends to choose a message format, data encoding, and implementation that is best suited to the application's requirements and the underlying transport facility (e.g., CORBA IIOP messages, or some more specialized system).

Each operation also results in two "unpickling" stubs: one to unmarshal requests and one to unmarshal replies (ordinary or exceptional). An unpickling stub takes a pickled message, parameters into which the message data will be decoded (the CORBA inout, out, and return values), and a CORBA environment parameter that allows the unpickling stub to report decoding errors to the application.

Pickling and unpickling stubs provide applications with greater control over the handling of messages and enable certain application-specific optimizations that are not possible within a traditional RPC model. For example, a message can be pickled once and then sent to multiple targets; also, common replies can be premarshaled and cached, thus reducing response times. An especially useful optimization for Khazana is that a message can be redirected to another node without the overhead of decoding and re-encoding the message (assuming that the message data is not needed in order to make the forwarding decision).

Send Stubs. Once a request or reply message has been marshaled, an application transmits the message by invoking the appropriate send stub. Two send stubs are defined for each CORBA interface (object type): one for requests and another for replies. Unlike a traditional RPC stub, a send stub returns immediately after the message has been sent; it does not wait for a reply.

Also unlike a traditional RPC stub, the send stubs produced by Flick take two special parameters as shown in Table 1: an *invocation identifier* and a *client reference*. These parameters are unique to Flick's "decomposed" stub presentation style and are not standard CORBA stub parameters. An invocation identifier (Invocation_id) corresponds to a single message transmission event and is used to connect a reply with its associated request. The application is responsible for providing invocation identifiers to the send stubs; this allows for application-specific optimizations in the generation and management of the identifiers. A client reference (Client) is a CORBA pseudo-object [24], managed by the communications runtime layer, that provides additional contextual information for handling requests and replies. A client reference serves two primary functions. First, it locates the entity that will receive the reply for a given request. Keeping explicit client references makes it possible, for instance, for one node to forward a request message to another node and direct the eventual reply back to the original requester. Second, the client reference allows the application to save state from the time a request is sent until the corresponding reply is received. A process can allocate as many client references as it needs and associate them with request transmission events as it sees fit. Then, whenever a reply message is received, the runtime locates the client reference that was provided with the original request, and gives that reference to the function that will process the newly received reply.

Server and Client Work Functions. The server and client work functions are the functions that ultimately receive and service request and reply messages, respectively. Traditional RPC presentations contain server work functions only; traditional clients process requests and replies synchronously. In contrast, Flick's decomposed stub presentation allows replies to be handled asynchronously, and therefore, clients must contain explicit functions to receive and handle incoming replies. A server work function receives the pickled representation of the request that it is to service. This makes it straightforward and efficient for a Khazana node to forward the request to another node, or to delay local processing. If the request is to be handled immediately, the server work function will invoke the unpickling stub to extract the request data. Similarly, a client work function receives a pickled reply message so that it may choose to handle the reply immediately, forward the reply (to another client), or delay processing by invoking a continuation stub.

Continuation Stubs. While handling a request or reply, a client or server work function may need to postpone processing — for instance, a server handling a request may find that it needs data from another server before it can continue. To allow applications to handle these situations gracefully, Flick produces two "continuation" stubs for each operation: one for the request and another for the reply. These are essentially normal send stubs, except that they direct the message back into the node's own message queue. Each continuation stub accepts a pickled message, a pointer to the function that will be invoked to service the continued message (i.e., a special work function), and an opaque pointer that allows the application to pass arbitrary state information along to the function that will resume processing.[2]

Dispatch Functions. Given an interface specification, Flick also produces the server dispatch function that is invoked to demultiplex incoming requests, and a client dispatch function that is invoked to demultiplex incoming replies. These

---

[2] We have not yet specified the interface that allows the application to tell the runtime layer when the new work function should be invoked.

functions, however, are not properly part of the presentation because they are visible only to the runtime layers, not to application code.

3.3 Decomposed Stubs for Distributed Applications

We expect that this new presentation style for CORBA interfaces will be useful not only to Khazana but also to other, similar parallel and distributed applications. Since this new style is more like traditional message-passing, we believe that it will be useful as a migration path for applications that wish to move away from hand-written communication code and toward the use of higher-level tools. This will reduce the application writers' burden and eliminate what is currently an error-prone process, without compromising application performance.

4 Related Work

Recent work by Schmidt et al. [19, 27] has quantified the impact of presentation layer overhead for rpcgen and two commercial CORBA implementations. On average, due to inefficiencies at the presentation and transport layers, compiler-generated stubs achieved only 16–80% of the throughput of hand-coded stubs.

To address these and similar performance issues, several attempts have been made to improve the code generated by IDL compilers. These are discussed in our earlier paper on Flick [10]. In summary, these other IDL compilers are either not very flexible (e.g., Mach's MIG compiler [26]) or they generate very slow code (e.g., ILU [21]).

Like Flick, the Concert/C distributed programming system [3] quite fully develops the concept of flexible presentation. The primary purpose of flexible presentation in Concert is to handle the vagaries of RPC mappings to different target languages, striving for a "minimal contract" in order to achieve maximal interoperability between target languages. However, this technique is not leveraged for optimizations. In earlier work [14, 13] we concentrated on leveraging Flick's explicit separation of presentation from interface in order to produce application-specialized stubs. We showed that programmer-supplied interface annotations that coerce the "programmer's contract" to applications' needs could provide up to an order of magnitude speedup in RPC performance.

The CORBA Event Service [25] is an Object Management Group standard for decoupling requests and replies between CORBA objects. The specification defines an *event channel* as an object that mediates communication between sets of suppliers and consumers. Because an event channel is a heavyweight object, it can provide many services — but these extra services may come at a price. To make use of any channel services, including asynchronous messaging, clients and servers must be specially written to communicate through event channels. This is in contrast to Flick's decomposed stubs which allow a client or server (or both) to use asynchronous messaging without cooperation or knowledge from the other side. Also, because event channels interpose on communication, they may introduce overheads that are not present in Flick's optimized stubs.

Asynchronous communication and message forwarding are not new ideas. Anderson et al. [2] describe these same mechanisms for a Global Memory Service [12] built on top of Trapeze. However, their work focuses on the transport layer rather than the presentation and application layers. Further, they provide no support for automatically generating stubs to exploit asynchronous communication and message forwarding. Our work focuses on presenting these mechanisms to the application and automatically generating the appropriate stubs. We believe that our work is complementary to that of Anderson et al.; Flick can leverage the benefits of an efficient transport system to produce optimized communication stubs.

For parallel applications, there are a large number of specialized programming languages such as CC++ [7], Fortran M [16], and Split-C [9]. In most of these cases the language handles marshaling and unmarshaling of parameters. However, it is our belief that the techniques used by Flick, and possibly even its code, could be incorporated into the compilers for these languages to substantially reduce presentation layer costs, e.g., by minimizing data copying. There are also a large number of parallel runtime systems providing various levels of abstraction and functionality, such as MPI [23], PVM [18], and Nexus [17]. Typically, these systems require the programmer to write the marshaling code by hand, although they do abstract away byte-swapping in order to accommodate heterogeneous machines. We believe these provide an attractive target for optimizations provided by Flick.

5 Conclusion

High-level tools such as IDL compilers can greatly reduce the effort and time required to implement distributed and parallel systems. Unfortunately, the limits of traditional IDL compilation often prevent the use of such tools in applications that require maximum performance. Traditional IDL compilers may produce stubs that have excessive presentation layer overheads; furthermore, traditional RPC stubs are not a good match for the needs of many modern systems.

We have described Flick, a novel, modular, and flexible IDL compiler that generates optimized code for a variety of stub styles and transport mechanisms. We have described how Flick is being adapted to meet the needs of a particular distributed application, Khazana, and provide a new style of CORBA-based stubs that are appropriate for other similar systems. The work presented here is currently in progress.

Availability

Complete Flick source code and documentation are available at http://www. cs.utah.edu/projects/flux/flick/.

References

[1] M. Accetta, R. Baron, W. Bolosky, D. Golub, R. Rashid, A. Tevanian, and M. Young. Mach: A new kernel foundation for UNIX development. In *Proc. of the Summer 1986 USENIX Conf.*, pages 93–112, June 1986.

[2] D. C. Anderson, J. S. Chase, S. Gadde, A. J. Gallatin, K. G. Yocum, and M. J. Feeley. Cheating the I/O bottleneck: Network storage with Trapeze/Myrinet. In *Proc. of the USENIX 1998 Annual Technical Conf.*, pages 143–154, New Orleans, LA, July 1998.

[3] J. S. Auerbach and J. R. Russell. The Concert signature representation: IDL as an intermediate language. In *Proc. of the Workshop on Interface Definition Languages*, pages 1–12, Jan. 1994.

[4] A. D. Birrell and B. J. Nelson. Implementing remote procedure calls. *ACM Transactions on Computer Systems*, 2(1), Feb. 1984.

[5] G. Buzzard, D. Jacobson, M. Mackey, S. Marovich, and J. Wilkes. An implementation of the Hamlyn sender-managed interface architecture. In *Proc. of the Second Symp. on Operating Systems Design and Implementation*, pages 245–259, Seattle, WA, Oct. 1996. USENIX Assoc.

[6] J. Carter, A. Ranganathan, and S. Susarla. Khazana: An infrastructure for building distributed services. In *Proc. of the Eighteenth International Conf. on Distributed Computing Systems*, May 1998.

[7] K. M. Chandy and C. Kesselman. CC++: A declarative concurrent object oriented programming notation. Technical Report CS-TR-92-01, California Institute of Technology, Mar. 1993.

[8] D. D. Clark and D. L. Tennenhouse. Architectural considerations for a new generation of protocols. In *Proc. of the SIGCOMM '90 Symp.*, pages 200–208, 1990.

[9] D. E. Culler, A. Dusseau, S. C. Goldstein, A. Krishnamurthy, S. Lumetta, T. von Eicken, and K. Yelick. Parallel programming in Split-C. In *Proceedings of Supercomputing '93*, pages 262–273, Portland, OR, Nov. 1993.

[10] E. Eide, K. Frei, B. Ford, J. Lepreau, and G. Lindstrom. Flick: A flexible, optimizing IDL compiler. In *Proc. ACM SIGPLAN Conf. on Programming Language Design and Implementation*, pages 44–56, Las Vegas, NV, June 1997.

[11] D. R. Engler, M. F. Kaashoek, and J. O'Toole Jr. Exokernel: An operating system architecture for application-level resource management. In *Proc. of the 15th ACM Symp. on Operating Systems Principles*, pages 251–266, Copper Mountain, CO, Dec. 1995.

[12] M. J. Feeley, W. E. Morgan, F. H. Pighin, A. R. Karlin, and H. M. Levy. Implementing global memory management in a workstation cluster. In *Proc. of the 15th ACM Symp. on Operating Systems Principles*, pages 201–212, Copper Mountain, CO, Dec. 1995.

[13] B. Ford, M. Hibler, and J. Lepreau. Using annotated interface definitions to optimize RPC. Technical Report UUCS-95-014, University of Utah Department of Computer Science, Mar. 1995.

[14] B. Ford, M. Hibler, and J. Lepreau. Using annotated interface definitions to optimize RPC. In *Proc. of the 15th ACM Symp. on Operating Systems Principles*, page 232, 1995. Poster.

[15] B. Ford, M. Hibler, J. Lepreau, P. Tullmann, G. Back, and S. Clawson. Microkernels meet recursive virtual machines. In *Proc. of the Second Symp. on Operating Systems Design and Implementation*, pages 137–151, Seattle, WA, Oct. 1996. USENIX Assoc.

[16] I. T. Foster and K. M. Chandy. Fortran M: A language for modular parallel programming. *Journal of Parallel and Distributed Computing*, 25(1), Feb. 1995.

[17] I. T. Foster, C. Kesselman, and S. Tuecke. The Nexus task-parallel runtime system. In *Proceedings of First International Workshop on Parallel Processing*, pages 457–462, 1994.

[18] G. Geist and V. Sunderam. The PVM system: Supercomputer level concurrent computation on a heterogenous network of workstations. In *Sixth Annual Distributed-Memory Computer Conference*, pages 258–261, 1991.

[19] A. Gokhale and D. C. Schmidt. Measuring the performance of communication middleware on high-speed networks. *Computer Communication Review*, 26(4), Oct. 1996.

[20] A. Gokhale and D. C. Schmidt. Optimizing the performance of the CORBA Internet Inter-ORB Protocol over ATM. Technical Report WUCS–97–09, Washington University Department of Computer Science, St. Louis, MO, 1997.

[21] B. Janssen and M. Spreitzer. *ILU 2.0alpha8 Reference Manual*. Xerox Corporation, May 1996. `ftp://ftp.parc.xerox.com/pub/ilu/ilu.html`.

[22] J. Liedtke. Improving IPC by kernel design. In *Proc. of the 14th ACM Symp. on Operating Systems Principles*, Asheville, NC, Dec. 1993.

[23] Message Passing Interface Forum. *MPI-2: Extensions to the Message-Passing Interface*, July 1997. `http://www.mpi-forum.org/`.

[24] Object Management Group. *The Common Object Request Broker: Architecture and Specification*, 2.0 edition, July 1995.

[25] Object Management Group. Event service specification. In *CORBAservices Specification*, chapter 4. Object Management Group, Dec. 1997.

[26] Open Software Foundation and Carnegie Mellon University, Cambridge, MA. *Mach 3 Server Writer's Guide*, Jan. 1992.

[27] D. C. Schmidt, T. Harrison, and E. Al-Shaer. Object-oriented components for high-speed network programming. In *Proceedings of the First Conference on Object-Oriented Technologies and Systems*, Monterey, CA, June 1995. USENIX Assoc.

[28] R. Srinivasan. RPC: Remote procedure call protocol specification version 2. Technical Report RFC 1831, Sun Microsystems, Inc., Aug. 1995.

[29] Sun Microsystems, Inc. *ONC+ Developer's Guide*, Nov. 1995.

[30] M. R. Swanson and L. B. Stoller. Direct deposit: A basic user-level protocol for carpet clusters. Technical Report UUCS-95-003, University of Utah Department of Computer Science, Mar. 1995.

[31] T. von Eicken, D. E. Culler, S. C. Goldstein, and K. E. Schauser. Active messages: A mechanism for integrated communication and computation. In *Proc. of the 19th International Symp. on Computer Architecture*, pages 256–266, May 1992.

QoS Aspect Languages and Their Runtime Integration

Joseph P. Loyall, David E. Bakken, Richard E. Schantz, John A. Zinky,
David A. Karr, Rodrigo Vanegas, and Kenneth R. Anderson

BBN Technologies/GTE Internetworking, Cambridge, MA 02138, USA
{jloyall, dbakken, schantz, jzinky, vanegas, dkarr, kanderson}@bbn.com
http://www.dist-systems/bbn/com

Abstract. Distributed object middleware, such as CORBA, hides sys-
tem- and network-specific characteristics of objects behind functional
interface specifications. This simplifies development and maintenance of
distributed objects, contributing to their growing acceptance. Critical
applications have Quality of Service (QoS) requirements, however, such
as real-time performance, dependability, or security, that are hidden by
middleware. Because of this, application developers often bypass distributed object systems, thus gaining little or no advantage from the middleware. We have developed Quality Objects (QuO), a framework for developing distributed applications with QoS requirements. QuO provides a
set of aspect languages, called Quality Description Languages (QDL), for
specifying possible QoS states, the system resources and mechanisms for
measuring and controlling QoS, and behavior for adapting to changing
levels of available QoS at runtime. This paper describes QuO's aspect
languages, their usage, and how they interact with the QuO runtime
system to form the QuO framework.

1 Introduction

Distributed object middleware, such as CORBA [5], hides system- and network-
specific characteristics of objects behind Interface Description Language (IDL)
specifications, which describe how clients and objects interact functionally, i.e.,
the methods that can be invoked on an object and the types of data that can be
exchanged. This simplifies development and maintenance by promoting abstract
design, code reuse, and interoperability, and has contributed to the growth and
acceptance of distributed object computing. However, many distributed applications have quality of service (QoS) requirements in addition to their functional
requirements. Applications such as multimedia, video-on-demand, national security, military, health care, medical, and financial systems often have critical
requirements such as real-time performance, synchronization of data, security,
and dependability. Current commercial distributed object middleware products
fall short of supporting QoS requirements because they hide the details necessary to specify, measure, and control QoS and to adapt to changing levels of
QoS. Because of this, developers of critical applications often find themselves

D. O'Hallaron (Ed.): LCR'98, LNCS 1511, pp. 303–318, 1998.
© Springer-Verlag Berlin Heidelberg 1998

programming around the distributed object abstraction and gaining little or no advantage from middleware. The problem gets worse as the number and diversity of distributed applications increase and as applications are distributed over wide-area networks (WANs), which are inherently more dynamic, unpredictable, and unreliable than LANs.

We have developed Quality Objects (QuO) [7,4], a framework for developing distributed applications with QoS requirements. QuO provides the ability to specify, monitor, and control aspects of the QoS in an application, and to adapt to changing levels of QoS at runtime. A major component of the QuO framework is a set of Quality Description Languages (QDL) for specifying possible QoS states, the system resources and mechanisms for measuring and providing QoS, and behavior for adapting to changes in QoS. This QoS specification, monitoring, and adaptation are *aspects* of the program that would normally have to be distributed throughout the program, *cross-cutting* the components and objects comprising the functional decomposition of the program. Because of this, the QuO framework and QDL represent an instance of *aspect-oriented programming* (AOP) [1]. AOP allows programmers to divide an application into both functional components and aspects, more global concerns that cross-cut the functional decomposition. QDL consists of aspect languages for describing aspects of a program related to QoS: providing it, monitoring it, and adapting to changing levels of it.

In this paper, we describe QuO's aspect languages; how they are used to specify, measure, control, and adapt to QoS; and how they interact with the QuO runtime system to form the QuO framework.

2   Overview of Aspect-Oriented Programming

In Aspect-Oriented Programming (AOP) [1], a program is divided into aspects of concern, each of which is programmed separately in a language suitable for expressing the particular aspect. The application is constructed by weaving the aspects together into a single, executable application using code generators. Aspectual decomposition is different from, but complementary to, functional decomposition. In functional decomposition, problems are divided into procedures, objects, modules, etc., each of which is programmed to hide its implementation and expose its functional interface. Each functional module is usually compiled into a specific section of code in the application's executable code.

In contrast, aspectual decomposition divides a problem into aspects, i.e., global concerns that cut across functional module boundaries, such as distribution, synchronization, or security. The executable code that deals with each of these aspects does not exist in a specific section, but occurs throughout the application's executable code. Traditionally, programmers would pepper code throughout each module to satisfy each aspect, until the modules become tangled with concerns. AOP avoids the "tangling of concerns" phenomenon [1] by providing abstractions that correspond to the different aspects. AOP allows programmers to divide an application into both function components and aspects.

Code generators, called weavers, distribute the aspect code into the proper places throughout the application.

QuO provides an example of aspect-oriented programming. QuO allows an application developer to specify the aspects of QoS contracts, system state monitoring and control, alternate implementations, and adaptation strategies which would traditionally be interleaved throughout a critical application. QuO's code generators weave these together into a single application.

3 Overview of QuO

QuO is a framework supporting the development of distributed applications with QoS requirements. QuO provides the ability to specify, monitor, and control aspects of the QoS in an application, similar to the way in which application code and IDL, ORBs, and operating systems specify, monitor, and control the functional behavior. We give a brief overview of QuO in this section. More detailed discussion can be found in [7].

3.1 Execution Model of a QuO Application

In a traditional CORBA application, a client makes a method call on a remote object through its functional interface. The call is processed by an ORB proxy on the client's host, which marshals the clients data, and passes it to an ORB on the client's host. The ORB delivers the call to an ORB on the object's host, where an ORB proxy unmarshals the data and delivers it to the remote object. The client sees it strictly as a functional method call.

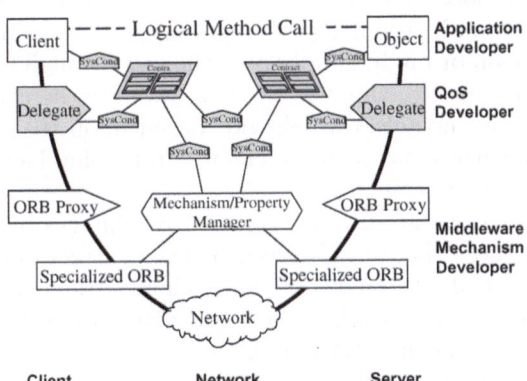

Fig. 1. A remote method invocation in a QuO application

As indicated in Figure 1, a QuO application adds additional steps to this process. In addition to the client program, ORB, and remote object (all components of a CORBA application), a QuO application adds the following components:

- Contracts, which specify the level of service desired by a client, the level of service an object expects to provide, operating regions indicating possible measured QoS, and actions to take when the level of QoS changes.
- Delegates, which act as local wrappers for remote objects. Each delegate provides an interface identical to that of its remote object, but provides locally adaptive behavior based upon the current state of QoS in the system.
- System condition objects, which link QuO contracts to resources, mechanisms, objects, and ORBs in the system. These allow QuO to measure and control QoS.

QuO applications also include property managers, mechanisms, specialized ORBs, and ORB wrappers that provide non-functional (i.e., QoS-related) capabilities. QuO replaces the bind function provided by many CORBA ORBs with *connect*. When a client calls connect to bind to a remote object, QuO instantiates the appropriate delegate and contract, and hooks up the client, delegate, contract, system condition objects, and ORB proxy.

Figure 2 illustrates the steps that can occur during a remote method call in a QuO application. When a client calls a remote method, the call is passed to the object's local delegate instead (1). This is transparent to the client, since the remote object and the delegate have the same interface. The delegate can trigger contract evaluation (2), which grabs the current value of all system conditions (3) measuring aspects of the system's state. The contract consists of a set of nested regions which describe the relevant possible states of QoS in the system. Each of these regions is defined by a predicate on the values of system condition objects. The contract evaluates the predicates to determine which regions are active (i.e., their predicates are true) and passes the list to the delegate (4).

The delegate chooses how to process the method call based upon the current regions (5). For example, the delegate might choose between alternate methods, might buffer the call, or might simply pass the call through to the remote object. Upon a method return (6), the delegate can evaluate the contract to obtain the current QoS regions and select a behavior based upon the current regions. The delegate finally returns control to the client (8), passing back any return values, **out**, and **inout** parameters.

Contract evaluation can also be triggered by changes in some system condition objects, i.e., those that are observed by the contract (7). Other system condition objects, especially those whose values change frequently, are non-observed and do not trigger contract evaluation. Regardless of how contract evaluation is triggered (by a method call/return or change in a system condition), a transition from one active region to another can trigger transition behavior, which consists of client callbacks or method calls on system condition objects.

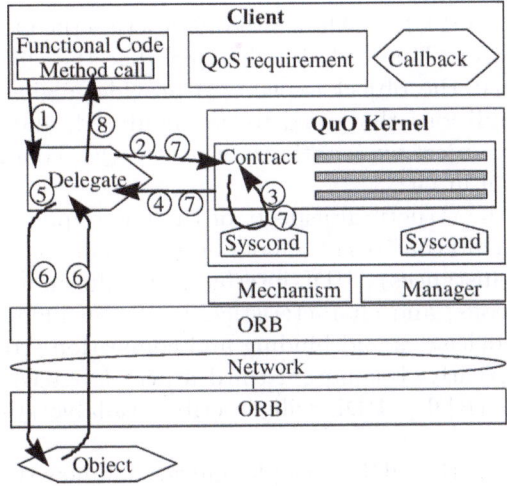

Fig. 2. Example remote method call in a QuO application

3.2 The QuO Toolkit for Building QuO Applications

As indicated in Figure 1, the development of QuO applications requires an additional role over those necessary to build a distributed application:

- Application developers who develop functional code for the clients and distributed objects;
- QoS developers who develop QuO contracts, system condition objects, callback mechanisms, and object delegate behavior; and
- Mechanism developers who develop system components, ORB wrappers, mechanisms, and libraries providing access to or control of system- or ORB-level capabilities.

To support the added role of QoS developer, we are developing a QuO toolkit, which consists of the following components:

- A suite of Quality Description Languages (QDL) for describing contracts, system condition objects, and the adaptive behavior of objects and delegates
- The QuO kernel, which coordinates evaluation of contracts and monitoring of system condition objects
- Code generators which weave together QDL descriptions, the QuO kernel code, and client code to produce a single application program.

The QuO kernel and runtime system are described in detail in [15].

4 The QuO Aspect Languages and Code Generators

QuO currently provides two aspect languages, collectively called Quality Description Languages (QDL): a Contract Description Language (CDL) and a Structure

Description Language (SDL). CDL is used to describe the QoS contract between a client and an object. This includes the QoS that the client desires from the object; the QoS that the object expects to provide; regions of possible levels of QoS; system conditions that need to be monitored; and behavior to invoke when client desires, object expectations, or actual QoS conditions change. CDL is described in detail in [4].

SDL describes the structural aspects of the QuO application. This includes the implementation alternatives of remote object, including alternate implementations (i.e., object instances) of IDL interfaces and alternate methods on specific objects, their tradeoffs, and characteristics. It also includes the local adaptive behavior of object delegates and binding and connection strategies.

We are also currently designing a third aspect language, the Resource Description Language (RDL). RDL will describe available system resources and their status.

Figure 3 illustrates the QDL aspect languages and how the QuO code generators weave them together to create QuO applications. We currently have parsers and code generators for IDL, CDL, and SDL. The code generators generate Java code for the following:

- contract classes
- connection code that creates or locates the appropriate contract instances, delegates, and system condition objects, and hooks them up
- code that is woven into the QuO runtime code for triggering and performing contract evaluation, grabbing the values of system condition objects, etc.

In addition, the code generators generate code for both client-side and server-side object delegate code. They generate delegates written in both Java and C++ code, to interface to client code written in either of these languages.

4.1   Contract Description Language (CDL)

CDL is a language for specifying a QoS contract between a client and object in an application. The contract describes the QoS that the client desires and that the object expects to provide in terms of a set of operating regions; behavior to invoke to adapt to or notify of changes in QoS; and interfaces to elements of the system that can be used to measure and control QoS. In this section we briefly describe CDL, by example. A more complete discussion of CDL, including its syntax and semantics, is provided in [4].

Elements of a CDL contract. A QuO contract consists of the following:

- a set of nested operating regions, each representing a possible state of QoS. Each region has a predicate indicating whether it is active (the predicate is true) or not (the predicate is false).
- transitions for each level of regions, specifying behavior to trigger when the active region changes.

- references to system condition objects for measuring and controlling QoS. These are either passed in as parameters to the contract or declared local to the contract. System condition objects are used in the predicates of regions to get values of system resources, object or client state, etc. and used in transitions to access QoS controls and mechanisms.
- callbacks for notifying the client or object. Callbacks are passed in as parameters to the contract and are used in transitions.

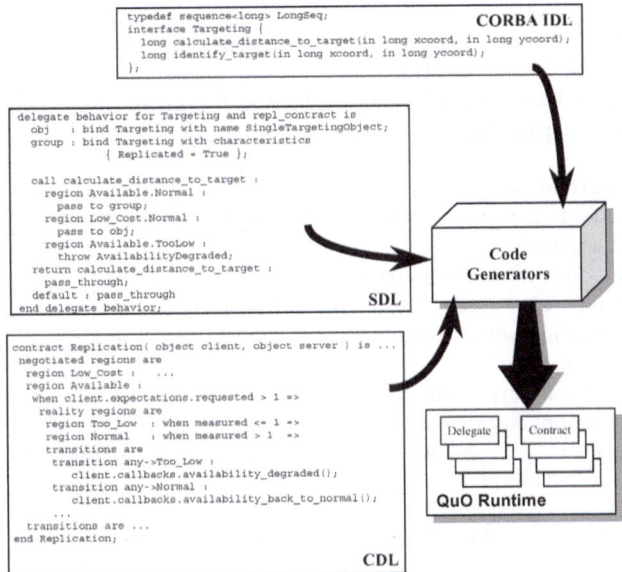

Fig. 3. The QuO code generators

The contract organizes the possible states of QoS, the information needed to monitor and control it, the actions to take when QoS changes, and the times at which information is available. The nesting of regions can be used to arrange regions according to logical groupings of information or time. For example, the contract in Figure 3 contains two sets of nested regions, an outer nesting called negotiated regions and an inner nesting called reality regions. The negotiated regions represent the QoS desired by the client and the QoS that the remote object expects to provide and their predicates consist of system condition objects that interface to the client and object. The reality regions represent the QoS measured in the system and have predicates consisting of system condition objects that interface to system resources. This grouping distinguishes the QoS associated with operating modes of the client and object, which will likely change infrequently, from the measured QoS of the system, which will probably change more frequently.

A programmer programs a contract class in CDL. At runtime, a connection between a client and an object is established, creating an object delegate instance, and creating a contract instance and passing in pointers to the client's expectations, client's callbacks, and any other necessary system condition objects or callbacks. Any system condition objects local to the contract instance are created and connected to the contract instance.

```
contract Replication(
  syscond ValueSC ValueSCImpl ClientExpectedReplicas,
  callback AvailCB ClientCallback,
  syscond ValueSC ValueSCImpl MeasuredNumberReplicas,
  syscond ReplSC ReplSCImpl ReplMgr ) is

  negotiated regions are
    region Low_Cost : when ClientExpectedReplicas == 1 =>
      reality regions are
        region Low : when MeasuredNumberReplicas < 1 =>
        region Normal : when MeasuredNumberReplicas == 1 =>
        region High : when MeasuredNumberReplicas > 1 =>
        transitions are
          transition any->Low : ClientCallback.availability_degraded();
          transition any->Normal : ClientCallback.availability_back_to_normal()
          transition any->High : ClientCallback.resources_being_wasted();
        end transitions;
      end reality regions;
    region Available : when ClientExpectedReplicas >= 2 =>
      reality regions are
        region Low : when MeasuredNumberReplicas < ClientExpectedReplicas =>
        region Normal : when MeasuredNumberReplicas >= ClientExpectedReplicas =
        transitions are
          transition any->Low : ClientCallback.availability_degraded();
          transition any->Normal : ClientCallback.availability_back_to_normal();
        end transitions;
      end reality regions;
    transitions are
      transition Low_Cost->Available :
        ReplMgr.adjust_degree_of_replication(ClientExpectedReplicas);
      transition Available->Low_Cost :
        ReplMgr.adjust_degree_of_replication(ClientExpectedReplicas);
    end transitions;
  end negotiated regions;
end repl_contract;
```

Fig. 4. A Sample CDL Contract - Replication

A simple CDL example contract. Figure 4 illustrates a sample CDL contract with CDL keywords in boldface. This contract specifies and controls replication for a QuO application. The client has two operating modes, one in which it desires a high level of availability from the remote object and another in which it does not require the high level of availability and desires to use fewer resources. This contract is simple, the client either requests one replica (encoded as the Low_Cost region) or more than one replica (encoded as the Available region). Each negotiated region has a set of reality regions, representing when the measured replication is lower than, higher than, or exactly as desired.

The negotiated region predicates use the client's expectation system condition object, ClientExpectedReplicas. It is passed as an argument to the contract because it is probably shared by all the contracts in which the client is involved, and therefore must be created outside the contract. The reality region predicates use a system condition object called MeasuredNumberReplicas, which observes the actual number of replicas.

The reality region transitions notify the client about changes in the number of replicas. The negotiated region transitions access mechanism routines to control the level of replication. A transition to either of the Low regions notifies the client via the callback method `availability_degraded`. A transition to either of the Normal regions notifies the client via the callback method `availability_back_to_normal`. The keyword `any` is used to indicate that the contract and client don't care in which region the transition originated. Callback behavior is specified in the callback code (probably in the client or a separate object).

The negotiated region transitions use a replication policy manager system condition object, `ReplMgr`, that is passed into the contract. When the client changes its desired replication, causing a transition between negotiated regions, the method `adjust_degree_of_replication` is called to suggest a new level of replication.

4.2   The Structure Description Language (SDL)

SDL allows a QuO programmer to specify adaptation alternatives and strategies based upon the QoS measured in the system. Currently, SDL allows a program to specify behaviors to invoke for method calls and/or returns based upon the current regions of contracts when the calls or returns occur. Later versions of SDL will also allow QuO programmers to specify QuO connections, i.e., the contracts, delegates, system condition objects, remote objects, and clients that need to be created or located and how they are hooked together to create a QuO application.

Elements of an SDL description. An SDL description is essentially a large table, in textual form, associating method calls or returns with contract regions, and specifying behavior for each relevant association. It consists of the following:

- a list of interfaces and contracts for which the SDL description is specifying adaptive behavior
- a list of method calls and/or returns, each of which must be a method on one of the interfaces. These are the method calls and returns for which the QuO programmer wants to specify adaptive behavior
- inside each method call and return, a list of contract regions, each of which is a region on one of the contracts listed above. These represent the states of QoS that can trigger the adaptive behavior for method calls and returns.
- inside each method and contract region association, a behavior specification. The specified behavior can choose between alternate object bindings, choose between alternate methods on an object, create new bindings, throw an exception, or execute a section of code.
- default behavior specifications. These can be specified within a method call or return specification, to be used for that method call or return and any other contract regions not enumerated. A default behavior can also be specified to be used for any method calls that aren't explicitly listed.

The code generator creates a delegate for each interface in the SDL description. Each delegate acts as a local wrapper around a remote object and presents an interface to the client with the same methods and argument types as are compiled from the remote object's IDL interface. However, it also generates two dispatch statements, i.e., `switch` statements in Java and C++, within each method, one for the call and one for the return. The dispatch statement checks the current regions of the relevant contracts and dispatches the proper behavior. The code inside each case of the dispatch statement is generated from the behavior specifications in the SDL description.

```
interface Targeting {
  long calculate_distance_to_target(long x, long y);
};
```

Fig. 5. Simple IDL for a targeting interface

A simple SDL example. As an example, consider the SDL description in Figure 6. This is a simple SDL description with only one interface, `Targeting`, specified in Figure 5, and one contract, `Replication`, specified in Figure 4.

This SDL description creates two bindings for the delegate, one to a specific object (known by a CORBA name server as `SingleTargetObject`) and a second to a replicated object group, i.e., an object tagged with the characteristic that it is replicated. Since these bindings are specified at the beginning of the SDL description, i.e., before the behavior table, they are established upon delegate creation. That is, the delegate code generated by the code generator will establish

```
delegate behavior for Targeting and Replication is
  obj : bind Targeting with name SingleTargetingObject;
  group : bind Targeting with characteristics { Replicated = True };

  call calculate_distance_to_target :
    region Available.Normal :
      pass to group;
    region Low_Cost.Normal :
      pass to obj;
    region Available.Low :
      throw AvailabilityDegraded;
    default :
      pass to obj;
  return calculate_distance_to_target :
    pass through;
  default :
    pass to obj;
end delegate behavior;
```

Fig. 6. SDL that chooses between replicated and non-replicated server objects

these bindings upon creation and initialization of the delegate. As described below, the SDL language also permits dynamic binding to objects.

Following the binding section is the behavior table, arranged as a list of method calls and returns, with region names nested inside them, finally with behavior descriptions nested inside them. The SDL description in Figure 6 essentially chooses between sending a remote method call to a single object or to an object group based upon whether the client desires and is getting availability through object replication.

When the `calculate_distance_to_target` method is called, the delegate checks the Replication contract and chooses one of the following behaviors:

- When the client desires availability and is receiving it, i.e., the contract is in the `Available` negotiated region and the `Normal` reality region, the method call is passed to the object group
- When the client does not desire availability and everything is okay, i.e., the contract is in the `Low_Cost` negotiated region and the `Normal` reality region, the method call is passed to the object
- When the client desires higher availability than what is measured, i.e., the contract is in the `Available` negotiated region and the `Low` reality region, the delegate chooses to throw an exception. This can save the cost of a remote method call when the measured QoS indicates the call is likely to fail or the client needs to be notified immediately of an exception.
- When the method returns, any value returned is passed through to the client.
- For all other method calls, i.e., the `default` behavior, the delegate will pass the method call through to the corresponding method on `obj`.

Overview of SDL features and semantics. Structure descriptions written in SDL have the following form:

```
delegate behavior for interfaces interface_list
                and contracts contract_list is
    local_variable_declarations
    adaptive_behavior_descriptions
    default_behavior_description
end delegate behavior;
```

The header specifies the interfaces for which delegates need to be generated and the contracts that determine their behaviors. The code generated from SDL code builds a delegate object for each interface in *interface_list*, containing a dispatch statement for the regions in each contract in *contract_list*.

The next section, i.e., *local_variable_declarations*, contains a list of statements binding local variables to remote objects. The current version of SDL allows a delegate to bind to remote objects by interface type, by name, or by QoS characteristics. Bindings in the declaration section of an SDL description, as illustrated in Figure 6, are established when a delegate is created and initialized. In the behavior description parts of the SDL description, the variables can be used to refer to the local objects. The variables can be rebound in the behavior descriptions.

The *adaptive_behavior_descriptions* section describes the dispatch statements for the generated delegates. It takes one of the following forms:

```
call method_name : region_behavior_list default_behavior
return method_name : region_behavior_list default_behavior
```

The first form specifies the behavior to perform when a client calls a remote method. The second specifies the behavior to perform upon the return from a remote method call. The *method_name* can be simply the name of a unique method in one of the interfaces or can be an interface name followed by a method on that interface.

The *region_behavior_list* is a list of contract regions, inside of each is nested a behavior specification. Each element of *region_behavior_list* is of the following form:

```
            region region_name : behavior_statement_list
```

The *region_name* is the name of a unique region in one of the contracts or the name of a contract followed by the name of a region in that contract.

The *default_behavior* statement above is simply the keyword **default:** followed by a *behavior_statement_list*.

A *behavior_statement_list* is a list of alternative behaviors. SDL currently supports the following specifications of behavior in a *behavior_statement_list*:

Choosing between methods and/or remote objects. The delegate uses SDL's `pass` primitive to pass the method call through to any method on any remote object to which the delegate is bound. This statement is one of the following forms:

```
pass to var;
pass to var.method;
pass to method;
pass through;
```

If *var* is specified, the delegate passes the method call through to the remote object to which *var* is bound (*var* must be bound in the declaration section). If *var.method* is specified, the method call is still passed to the remote object bound to *var*, but to the alternate method *method*, which must currently take the same number and type of arguments as the original method.

The third and fourth forms of the `pass` statement are only meaningful if the delegate has a binding to only one remote object. The `pass through` statement passes the method call to the corresponding method on the remote object. The `pass to` *method* passes the call to the alternate method on the remote object. If the delegate has bindings to more than one remote object (i.e., either the delegate header specifies more than one interface type or there are binding statements in the *local_variable_declarations* section), the semantics of the third and fourth forms are undefined.

Throwing an exception. A statement of the form

`throw` *exception*;

can be used to throw an exception without making a remote call.

Breaking and/or establishing a binding to a remote object. The delegate can choose to rebind any of its bindings or establish a new binding in order to try and improve QoS, access a service previously not available, etc. The following statement specifies this:

`rebind` [*var*] [`exclusive`] [`to` *iface*] [`with name` *name* | `with characteristics` *ch_list*] ;

This rebind statement breaks and/or establishes bindings to objects at runtime by interface type, by name, or by QoS characteristics. Using this feature, a remote connection that is not satisfying its expected QoS can be broken and reestablished with different mechanisms, a different object, or a different implementation of an interface.

The optional keyword `exclusive` tells the QuO runtime to rebind to an object different from the current binding. Without the `exclusive` keyword, the QuO runtime is free to bind again to the same object, providing it has the specified interface (*iface*), name (*name*), or characteristics (*ch_list*).

The characteristics are currently specified by a list of keyword/value pairs, as illustrated in Figure 6. The list can use any relative operator, e.g., $<$ or $<=$, to specify the values that the keyword can take.

Java or C++ functionality. The behavior description can specify Java and/or C++ code that is placed verbatim into the proper delegate, i.e., the Java delegate or the C++ delegate. Using this, the delegate can perform arbitrary local processing in place of, or in addition to, the remote call. This is specified by the following statements:

Java_code   *code*

C++_code   *code*

The programmer uses SDL to specify behavior for relevant method calls, method returns, and QoS regions. In addition, the programmer can use SDL's default statement to specify behavior for all other QoS regions for a method, or for all other methods. For example, the SDL code in Figure 3 specifies default behavior (i.e., pass through) for all other methods in the **Targeting** interface other than **calculate_distance_to_target**.

5   Related Work

QuO contracts are an example of open implementation [2,3], which provides programmers control over previously hidden or internal aspects of an application, such as alternate implementations of an algorithm, insight or control over choice of data structures, or control of scheduling. QuO contracts provide programmers control of implementation details affecting QoS.

As discussed in Section 2, QuO also represents an example of Aspect-Oriented Programming [1], in which a program is divided into aspects of concern, each of which is programmed separately in a language suitable for expressing the particular aspect. The application is constructed by weaving (using code generators) the aspects together into a single, executable application. QuO allows an application developer to separate the aspects of functional behavior, QoS contracts, system state monitoring and control, and alternate implementation and adaptation which would traditionally be interleaved throughout a critical application. QuO's code generators weave these together into a single application.

There are several other groups that have developed or are developing languages for describing aspects of QoS. The QUASAR project is working on techniques for specifying application-level QoS using the Z specification language and translating it into resource reservation requests [9]. Leue describes the use of other formal specification languages, specifically Specification and Description Language (SDL), Message Sequence Charts (MSCs), and temporal logic, to specify QoS[10].

Frølund and Koistinen describe a specification language, QoS Modeling Language (QML), for specifying QoS [11]. QML is an extension of the Unified Modeling Language (UML) [12]. QML includes concepts of QoS contract types and contracts, similar to QuO's QDL, although QML's contract type and contract concerns a particular dimension of QoS, such as performance or availability. In contrast, a contract in QDL represents more of an application client's view of QoS, combining the QoS desires of the client, the service that an object expects to provide, the resources throughout the system that must be monitored and controlled, and adaptations to adjust to changes in QoS. A contract in QDL does not have to be limited to only one QoS dimension, e.g., a contract might describe aspects of both availability and security, and it does not have to fully describe a QoS dimension, e.g., performance might be captured fully in several contracts describing managed communication, algorithm processing time, and response time.

BeeHive provides a set of service-specific application programming interfaces (APIs), through which objects can request QoS from an underlying resource manager [13]. They are currently developing APIs for real-time, fault-tolerance, and security requirements. Each API allows an object to request a requirement in application terms, e.g., Mean Time to Failure for fault-tolerance. The resource manager translates each request into low-level resource requests.

Monteiro et al. describe a technique for specifying QoS for congestion in networks [14]. The technique involves selecting a set of quantifiable parameters that comprise the QoS. Then the upper and lower bounds for a correct operating interval are selected, followed by the upper and lower values of an interval in which service is degraded, but the degradation is acceptable. These values are combined into a matrix which defines the service contract between a client and a service provider. The contracts they describe map naturally into CDL; we simply use a programming language syntax in contrast to their matrix notation. The concept of operating regions is implicit in their notion of intervals, but they only support three intervals, normal operating range, degraded but acceptable, and unacceptable (implicit), whereas QuO does not limit the number or types of regions. In addition, there doesn't seem to be any provision for adaptation to changing levels of service.

6   Conclusions

Distributed object applications, especially those with critical requirements, need to be able to specify and control the QoS provided them, monitor it, and adapt as QoS changes. QuO provides a framework for describing, controlling, monitoring, and adapting to changes in QoS. Central to the QuO framework is QDL, a suite of aspect languages for describing aspects of QoS and adaptation. QDL supports the specification of QoS contracts between clients and objects, adaptive behavior on the client and object side, and the system resources that must be observed to monitor QoS. In this paper, we described the QDL aspect languages, concentrating on the Contract Description Language, CDL, and the Structure Description Language, SDL. Each of these enables a QuO programmer to specify aspects of a QuO application, i.e., QoS contracts in CDL and adaptive behavior based upon states of Qos in SDL. A set of code generators generates Java and C++ code from these description languages and weaves the generated code into the QuO runtime and application code.

References

1. Gregor Kiczales, John Irwin, John Lamping, Jean-Marc Loingtier, Cristina Videria Lopes, Chris Maeda, Anurag Mendhekar: Aspect-Oriented Programming. ACM Computing Surveys **28(4es)** (1996)
2. Gregor Kiczales: Beyond the Black Box: Open Implementation. IEEE Software (1996)
3. Chris Maeda, Arthur Lee, Gail Murphy, Gregor Kiczales: Open Implementation Analysis and Design
4. Joseph P. Loyall, Richard E. Schantz, John A. Zinky, David E. Bakken: Specifying and Measuring Quality of Service in Distributed Object Systems. Proceedings of the First International Symposium on Object-oriented Real-time distributed Computing (ISORC '98) (1998) 43-52
5. Object Management Group: CORBA 2.0, July 96 revision, OMG Document 96-08-04 (1996).
6. Lixia Zhang, Steve Deering, Deborah Estrin, Scott Shenker, Daniel Zappala: RSVP: A New Resource ReSerVation Protocol. IEEE Network (1993)
7. John A. Zinky, David E. Bakken, Richard E. Schantz: Architectural Support for Quality of Service for CORBA Objects. Theory and Practice of Object Systems, **3(1)** (1997)
8. Sean Landis, Silvano Maffeis: Constructing Reliable Distributed Communications Systems with CORBA. Theory and Practice of Object Systems, **3(1)** (1997)
9. Richard Staelhli, Jonathan Walpole, David Maier: Quality of Service Specification for Multimedia Presentations. Multimedia Systems, **3(5/6)** (November, 1995)
10. Stefan Leue: QoS Specification based on SDL/MSC and Temporal Logic. G. v. Bochmann, J. de Meer, and A. Vogel (eds.), Proceedings of the Montreal Workshop on Multimedia Applications and Quality of Service Verification, Montreal, May 31 - June 2, 1994
11. Svend Frølund, Jari Koistinen: Quality of Service Specification in Distributed Object Systems Design. submitted to COOTS 98.
12. Grady Booch, Ivar Jacobson, Jim Rumbaugh: Unified Modeling Language, Rational Software Corporation, version 1.0, (1997)
13. John A. Stankovic, Sang H. Son, Joerg Lieberherr: BeeHive: Global Multimedia Database Support for Dependable, Real-Time Applications. Computer Science Report No. CS-97-08, University of Virginia (April 21, 1997)
14. Edmundo Monteiro, Fernando Boavida, Gonzalo Quadros, Vasco Freitas: Specification, Quantification and Provision of Quality of Service and Congestion Control for New Communication Services. Proceedings of the 16th AFCEA Europe Symposium, AFCEA(Association for Communications, Electronics, Intelligence & Information Systems Professionals)/IEEE COMSOC/IEE, Brussels, Belgium, (October 18-20, 1995) 58-68
15. Rodrigo Vanegas, John A. Zinky, Joseph P. Loyall, David Karr, Richard E. Schantz, David E. Bakken: QuO's Runtime Support for Quality of Service in Distributed Objects. Middleware'98: IFIP International Conference on Distributed Systems Platforms and Open Distributed Processing, The Lake District, England (September 15-18, 1998)

The Statistical Properties of Host Load

Peter A. Dinda

Carnegie Mellon University
5000 Forbes Avenue, Pittsburgh, PA 15213, USA
pdinda@cs.cmu.edu

Abstract. Understanding how host load changes over time is instrumental in predicting the execution time of tasks or jobs, such as in dynamic load balancing and distributed soft real-time systems. To improve this understanding, we collected week-long, 1 Hz resolution Unix load average traces on 38 different machines including production and research cluster machines, compute servers, and desktop workstations Separate sets of traces were collected at two different times of the year. The traces capture all of the dynamic load information available to user-level programs on these machines. We present a detailed statistical analysis of these traces here, including summary statistics, distributions, and time series analysis results. Two significant new results are that load is self-similar and that it displays epochal behavior. All of the traces exhibit a high degree of self similarity with Hurst parameters ranging from .63 to .97, strongly biased toward the top of that range. The traces also display epochal behavior in that the local frequency content of the load signal remains quite stable for long periods of time (150-450 seconds mean) and changes abruptly at epoch boundaries.

1 Introduction

The distributed computing environments to which most users have access consist of a collection of loosely interconnected hosts running vendor operating systems. Tasks are initiated independently by users and are scheduled locally by a vendor supplied operating system; there is no global scheduler that controls access to the hosts. As users run their jobs the computational load on the individual hosts changes over time.

Deciding how to map computations to hosts in systems with such dynamically changing loads (what we will call the *mapping problem*) is a basic problem that arises in a number of important contexts, such as dynamically load-balancing the tasks in a parallel program [20,1,22], and scheduling tasks to meet deadlines in a distributed soft real-time system [12,18,19].

Host load has a significant effect on running time. Indeed, the running time of a compute bound task is directly related to the average load it encounters during execution. Determining a good mapping of a task requires a prediction, either implicit or explicit, of the load on the prospective remote hosts to which the task could be mapped. Making such predictions demands an understanding of the qualitative and quantitative properties

Effort sponsored in part by the Advanced Research Projects Agency and Rome Laboratory, Air Force Materiel Command, USAF, under agreement number F30602-96-1-0287, in part by the National Science Foundation under Grant CMS-9318163, and in part by a grant from the Intel Corporation. The U.S. Government is authorized to reproduce and distribute reprints for Governmental purposes notwithstanding any copyright annotation thereon. The views and conclusions contained herein are those of the authors and should not be interpreted as necessarily representing the official policies or endorsements, either expressed or implied, of the Advanced Research Projects Agency, Rome Laboratory, or the U.S. Government.

of load on real systems. If the tasks to be mapped are short, this understanding of load should extend to correspondingly fine resolutions. Unfortunately, to date there has been little work on characterizing the properties of load at fine resolutions. The available studies concentrate on understanding functions of load, such as availability [17] or job durations [6,14,8]. Furthermore, they deal with the coarse grain behavior of load — how it changes over minutes, hours and days.

This paper is a first step to a better understanding the properties of load on real systems at fine resolutions. We collected week-long, 1 Hz resolution traces of the Unix load average on 38 different machines that we classify as production and research cluster machines, compute servers, or desktop workstations. We collected two sets of such traces at different times of the year. The 1 Hz sample rate is sufficient to capture all of the dynamic load information that is available to user-level programs running on these machines. In this paper, we present a detailed statistical analysis of the first set of traces, taken in August, 1997. The results are similar for the second set, so we have omitted them to save space. We also contemplate the implications of those properties for the mapping problem.

The basic question is whether load traces that might seem at first glance to be random and unpredictable might have structure that could be exploited by a mapping algorithm. Our results suggest that load traces do indeed have some structure in the form of clearly identifiable properties. In essence, our results characterize how load varies, which should be of interest not only to developers of mapping and prediction algorithms, but also to those who need to generate realistic synthetic loads in simulators or to those doing analytic work. Here is a summary of our results and their implications:

(1) The traces exhibit low means but very high standard deviations and maximums. Only four traces had mean loads near 1.0. The standard deviation is typically at least as large as the mean, while the maximums can be as much as two orders of magnitude larger. The implication is that these machines have plenty of cycles to spare to execute jobs, but the execution time of these jobs will vary drastically.

(2) Standard deviation and maximum, which are absolute measures of variation, are positively correlated with the mean, so a machine with a high mean load will also tend to have a large standard deviation and maximum. However, these measures do not grow as quickly as the mean, so their corresponding relative measures actually *shrink* as the mean increases. The implication is that if the mapping problem assumes a relative metric, it may not be unreasonable to use the host with higher mean load.

(3) The traces have complex, rough, and often multimodal distributions that are not well fitted by analytic distributions such as the normal or exponential distributions. Even for the traces which exhibit unimodally distributed load, the normal distribution's tail is too short while the exponential distribution's tail is too long. The implication is that modeling and simulation that assumes convenient analytical load distributions may be flawed.

(4) Time series analysis of the traces shows that load is strongly correlated over time. The autocorrelation function typically decays very slowly while the periodogram shows a broad, almost noise-like combination of all frequency components. An important implication is that history-based load prediction schemes seem very feasible. However, the complex frequency domain behavior suggests that linear modeling schemes may have difficulty. From a modeling point of view, it is clearly important that these dependencies between successive load measurements are captured.

(5) The traces are self-similar. Their Hurst parameters range from .63 to .97, with a strong bias toward the top of that range. This tells us that load varies in complex ways on all time scales and is long term dependent. This has several important implications.

First, smoothing load by averaging over an interval results in much smaller decreases in variance than if load were not long range dependent. Variance decays with increasing interval length m and Hurst parameter H as m^{2H-2}. This is $m^{-1.0}$ for signals without long range dependence and $m^{-0.74}$ to $m^{-0.06}$ for the range of H we measured. This suggests that task migration in the face of adverse load conditions may be preferable to waiting for the adversity to be ameliorated over the long term. The self-similarity result also suggests certain modeling approaches, such as fractional ARIMA models [9,7,3] which can capture this property.

(6) The traces display epochal behavior. The local frequency content of the load signal remains quite stable for long periods of time (150-450 seconds mean) and changes abruptly at the boundaries of such epochs. This suggests that the problem of predicting load may be able to be decomposed into a sequence of smaller subproblems.

2   Measurement Methodology

The load on a Unix system at any given instant is the number of processes that are running or are ready to run, which is the length of the ready queue maintained by the scheduler. The kernel samples the length of the the ready queue at some rate and exponentially averages some number of previous samples to produce a load average which can be accessed from a user program.

We developed a small tool to sample the Digital Unix (DUX) one minute load average at one second intervals and log the resulting time series to a data file. The 1 Hz sample rate was arrived at by subjecting DUX systems to varying loads and sampling at progressively higher rates to determine the rate at which DUX actually updated the value. DUX updates the value at a rate of $1/2$ Hz, thus we chose a 1 Hz sample rate by the Nyquist criterion. This choice of sample rate means we capture all of the dynamic load information the operating system makes available to user programs. We ran this trace collection tool on 38 hosts belonging to the Computing, Media, and Communication Laboratory (CMCL) at CMU and the Pittsburgh Supercomputing Center (PSC) for slightly more than one week in late August, 1997. A second set of week-long traces was acquired on almost exactly the same set of machines in late February and early March, 1998. The results of the statistical analysis were similar for the two sets of traces. In this paper, we concentrate on the August 1997 set.

All of the hosts in the August 1997 set were DEC Alpha DUX machines, and they form four classes:

- *Production Cluster*: 13 hosts of the PSC's "Supercluster", including two front-end machines (axpfea, axpfeb), four interactive machines (axp0 through axp3), and seven batch machines scheduled by a DQS [13] variant (axp4 through axp10.)
- *Research Cluster*: eight machines in an experimental cluster in the CMCL (manchester-1 through manchester-8.)
- *Compute servers*: two high performance large memory machines used by the CMCL group as compute servers for simulations and the like (mojave and sahara.)
- *Desktops*: 15 desktop workstations owned by members of the CMCL (aphrodite through zeno.)

3   Statistical Analysis

We analyzed the individual load traces using summary statistics, histograms, fitting of analytic distributions, and time series analysis. The picture that emerges is that load varies over a wide range in very complex ways. Load distributions are rough and frequently

	Mean Load	Sdev Load	COV Load	Max Load	Max/Mean Load	Mean Epoch	Sdev Epoch	COV Epoch	Hurst Param
Mean Load	1.00								
Sdev Load	0.53	1.00							
COV Load	-0.49	-0.22	1.00						
Max Load	0.60	0.18	-0.32	1.00					
Max/Mean Load	-0.36	-0.39	0.51	0.03	1.00				
Mean Epoch	-0.04	-0.10	-0.19	0.08	-0.05	1.00			
Sdev Epoch	-0.02	-0.10	-0.20	0.09	-0.06	0.99	1.00		
COV Epoch	0.07	-0.11	-0.23	0.15	-0.02	0.95	0.96	1.00	
Hurst Param	0.45	0.58	-0.21	0.03	-0.49	0.08	0.10	0.18	1.00

Fig. 1. Correlation coefficients (CCs) between all of the discussed statistical properties.

multimodal. Even traces with unimodal histograms are not well fitted by common analytic distributions, which have tails that are either too short or too long. Time series analysis shows that load is strongly correlated over time, but also has complex, almost noise-like frequency domain behavior.

We summarized each of our load traces in terms of our statistical measures and computed their correlations to determine how the measures are related. Figure 1 contains the results. Each cell of the table is the correlation coefficient (CC) between the row measure and the column measure, computed over the 38 load traces. We will refer back to the highlighted cells throughout the paper. It is important to note that these cross correlations can serve as a basis for clustering load traces into rough equivalence classes.

Summary Statistics: Summarizing each load trace in terms of its mean, standard deviation, and maximum and minimum illustrates the extent to which load varies. Figure 2 shows the mean load and the +/- one standard deviation points for each of the traces. As we might expect, the mean load on desktop machines is significantly lower than on other machines. However, we can also see a lack of uniformity within each class, despite the long duration of the traces. This is most clear among the Production Cluster machines, where four machines seem to be doing most of the work. This lack of uniformity even over long time scales shows clear opportunity for load balancing or resource management systems.

From Figure 2 we can also see that desktop machines have smaller standard deviations than the other machines. Indeed, the standard deviation, which shows how much load varies in *absolute* terms, grows with increasing mean load (CC=0.53 from Figure 1.) However, in *relative* terms, variance shrinks with increasing mean load. This can be seen in Figure 3, which plots the coefficient of variation (the standard deviation divided by the mean, abbreviated as the COV) and the mean load for each of the load traces. Here we can see that desktop machines, with their smaller mean loads, have large COVs compared to the other classes of machines. The CC between mean load and the COV of load is -0.49. It is clear that as load increases, it varies *less* in relative terms and *more* in absolute terms.

This difference between absolute and relative behavior also holds true for the maximum load. Figure 4 shows the minimum, maximum, and mean load for each of the traces. The minimum load is, not surprisingly, zero in every case. The maximum load is positively correlated with the mean load (CC=0.60 in Figure 1.) Figure 5 plots the ratio max/mean and the mean load for each of the traces. It is clear that this relative measure is inversely related to mean load, and Figure 1 shows that the CC is -0.36. It is also important to notice that while the differences in maximum load between the hosts

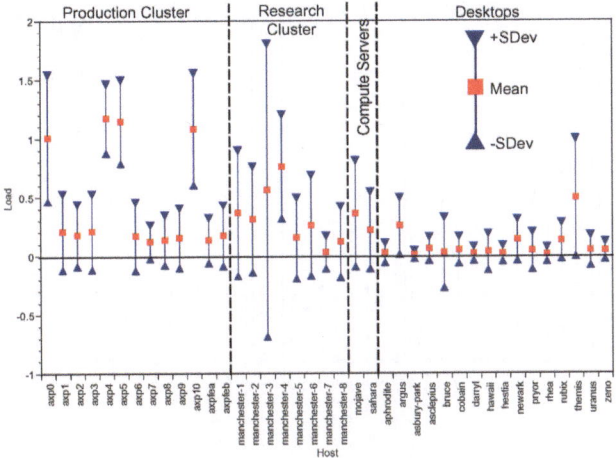

Fig. 2. Mean load +/- one standard deviation.

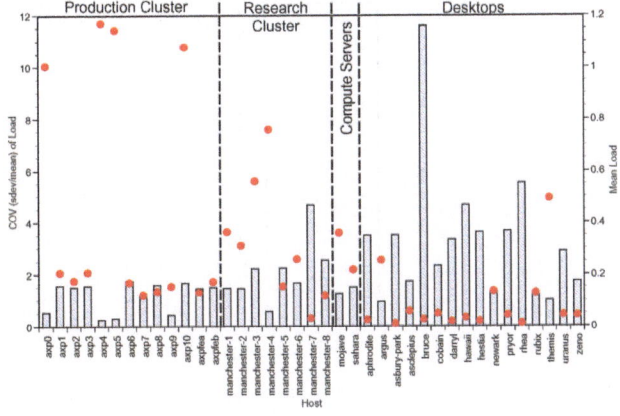

Fig. 3. COV of load and mean load.

are rather small (Figure 4), the differences in the max/mean ratio can be quite large (Figure 5.) Desktops are clearly more surprising machines in relative terms.

With respect to the mapping problem, the implication of the differences between relative and absolute measures of variability is that lightly loaded (low mean load) hosts are not always preferable over heavily loaded hosts. For example, if the performance metric is itself a relative one (that the execution time not vary much relative to the mean execution time, say), then a more heavily loaded host may be preferable.

Distributions: We next treated each trace as a realization of an independent, identically distributed (IID) stochastic process. Such a process is completely described by its proba-

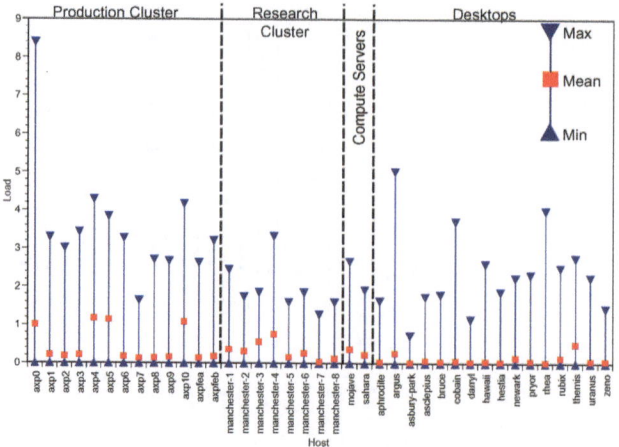

Fig. 4. Minimum, maximum, and mean load.

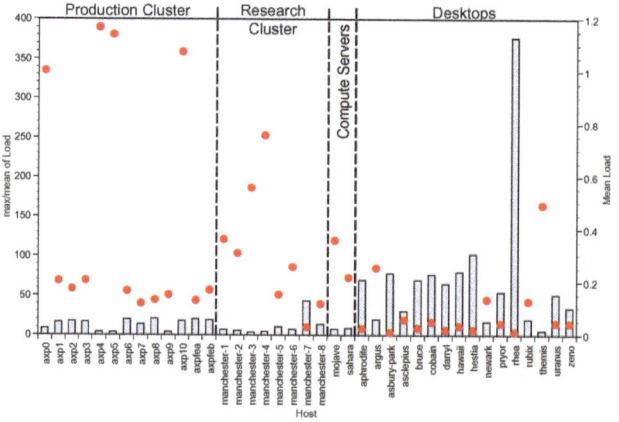

Fig. 5. Maximum to mean load ratios and mean load.

bility distribution function (pdf), which does not change over time. Since we have a vast number of data points for each trace, histograms closely approximate this underlying pdf. We examined the histograms of each of our load traces and fitted normal and exponential distributions to them. To illustrate the following discussion, Figure 6 shows the histograms of load measurements on (a) axp0 and (b) axp7 on August 19, 1997 (86400 samples each.) Axp0 has a high mean load, while axp7 is much more lightly loaded.

Some of the traces, especially those with high mean loads, have multimodal histograms. Figure 6(a) is an example of such a multimodal distribution while Figure 6(b) shows a unimodal distribution. Typically, the modes are integer multiples of 1.0 (and occasionally 0.5.) One explanation for this behavior is that jobs on these machines are for the most part compute bound and thus the ready queue length corresponds to the number of jobs. This seems plausible for the cluster machines, which run scientific workloads

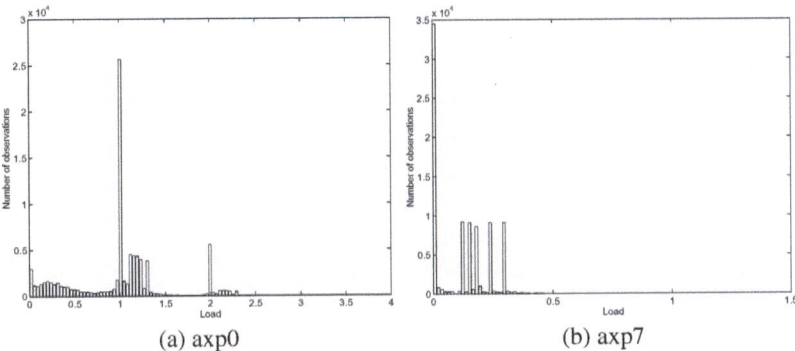

Fig. 6. Histograms for load on axp0 and axp7 on August 19, 1997.

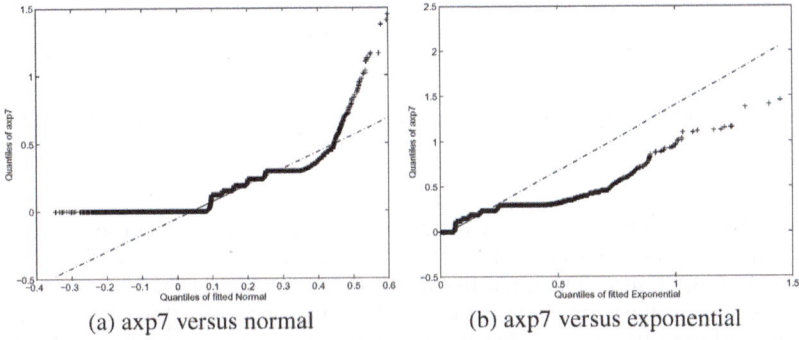

Fig. 7. Quantile-quantile plots for axp7 trace of August 19, 1997.

for the most part. However, such multimodal distributions were also noticed on the some of the other machines.

The rough appearance of the histograms (consider Figure 6(b)) is due to the fact that the underlying quantity being measured (ready queue length) is discrete. Load typically takes on 600-3000 unique values in these traces. Shannon's entropy measure [21] indicates that the load traces can be encoded in 1.4 to 8.48 bits per value, depending on the trace. These observations and the histograms suggest that load spends most of its time in one of a small number of levels.

The histograms share very few common characteristics and did not conform well to the analytic distributions we fit to them. Quantile-quantile plots are a powerful way to assess how a distribution fits data (cf. [11], pp. 196–200.) The quantiles (the α quantile of a pdf (or histogram) is the value x at which 100α % of the probability (or data) falls to the left of x) of the data set are plotted against the quantiles of the hypothetical analytic distribution. Regardless of the choice of parameters, the plot will be linear if the data fits the distribution.

We fitted normal and exponential distributions to each of the load traces. The fits are atrocious for the multimodal traces, and we do not discuss them here. For the unimodal traces, the fits are slightly better. Figure 7 shows quantile-quantile plots for (a) normal and

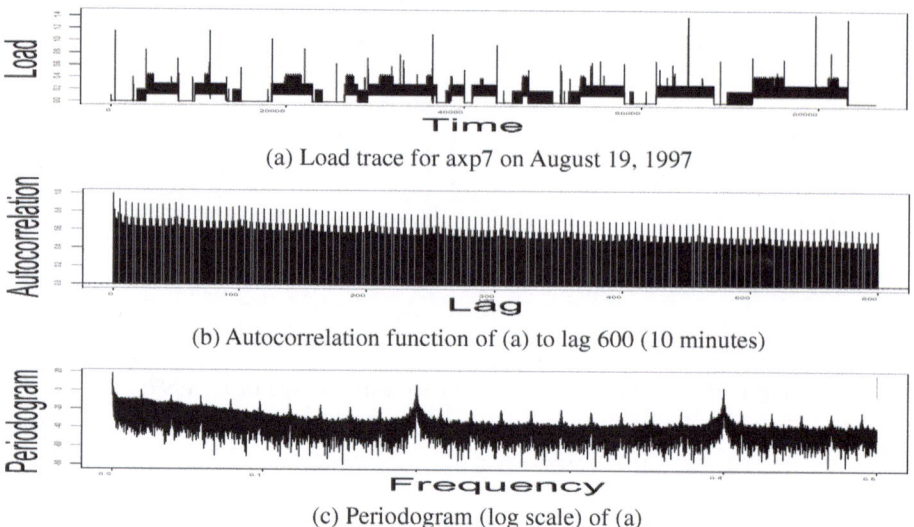

(a) Load trace for axp7 on August 19, 1997

(b) Autocorrelation function of (a) to lag 600 (10 minutes)

(c) Periodogram (log scale) of (a)

Fig. 8. Time series analysis of axp7 load trace collected on August 19, 1997.

(b) exponential distributions fitted to the unimodal axp7 load trace of Figure 6(b). Neither the normal or exponential distribution correctly captures the tails of the load traces. This can be seen in the figure. The quantiles of the data grow faster than those of the normal distribution toward the right sides of Figures 7(a). This indicates that the data has a longer or heavier tail than the normal distribution. Conversely, the quantiles of the data grow more slowly than those of the exponential distribution, as can be seen in Figures 7(b). This indicates that the data has a shorter tail than the exponential distribution. Notice that the exponential distribution goes as e^{-x} while the normal distribution goes as e^{-x^2}.

There are two implications of these complex distributions. First, simulation studies and analytic results predicated on simple, analytic distributions may produce erroneous results. Clearly, trace-driven simulation studies are to be preferred. The second implication is that prediction algorithms should not only reduce the overall variance of the load signal, but also produce errors that are better fit an analytic distribution. One reason for this is to make confidence intervals easier to compute.

Time Series Analysis: We examined the autocorrelation function, partial autocorrelation function, and periodogram of each of the load traces. These time series analysis tools show that past load values have a strong influence on future load values. For illustration, Figure 8 shows (a) the axp7 load trace collected on August 19, 1997, (b) its autocorrelation function to a lag of 600, and (c) its periodogram. The autocorrelation function, which ranges from -1 to 1, shows how well a load value at time t is linearly correlated with its corresponding load value at time $t + \Delta$ — in effect, how well the value at time t predicts the value at time $t + \Delta$. Autocorrelation is a function of Δ, and in the figure we show the results for $0 \leq \Delta \leq 600$. Notice that even at $\Delta = 600$ seconds, values are still strongly correlated. This very strong, long range correlation is common to each of the load traces. For space reasons, we do not discuss the partial autocorrelation results here. However, it is important to note that the behavior of the autocorrelation and partial autocorrelation functions is instrumental to the Box-Jenkins linear time series model identification process [4].

The periodogram of a load trace is the magnitude of the Fourier transform of the load data, which we plot on a log scale (Figure 8(c).) The periodogram shows the contribution of different frequencies (horizontal axis) to the signal. What is clear in the figure, and is true of all of the load traces, is that there are significant contributions from all frequencies — the signal looks much like noise. We believe the two noticeable peaks to be artifacts of the kernel sample rate — the kernel is not sampling the length of the ready queue frequently enough to avoid aliasing. Only a few of the other traces exhibit the smaller peaks, but they all share the broad noise-like appearance of this trace.

There are several implications of this time series analysis. First, the existence of such strong autocorrelation implies that load prediction based on past load values is feasible. It also suggests that simulation models and analytical work that eschews this very clear dependence may be in error. Finally, the almost noise-like periodograms suggest that quite complex, possibly nonlinear models will be necessary to produce or predict load.

4   Self-Similarity

The key observation of this section is that each of the load traces exhibits a high degree of self-similarity. This is significant for two reasons. First, it means that load varies significantly across all time-scales — it is not the case that increasing smoothing of the load quickly tames its variance. A job will have a great deal of variance in its running time regardless of how long it is. Second, it suggests that load is difficult to model and predict well. In particular, self-similarity is indicative of long memory, possibly non-stationary stochastic processes such as fractional ARIMA models [9,7,3], and fitting such models to data and evaluating them can be quite expensive.

Figure 9 visually demonstrates the self similarity of the axp7 load trace. The top graph in the figure plots the load on this machine versus time for 10 days. Each subsequent graph "zooms in" on the highlighted central 25% of the previous graph, until we reach the bottom graph, which shows the central 60 seconds of the trace. The plots are scaled to make the behavior on each time scale obvious. In particular, over longer time scales, wider scales are necessary. Intuitively, a self-similar signal is one that looks similar on different time scales given this rescaling. Although the behavior on the different graphs is not identical, we can clearly see that there is significant variation on all time scales.

An important point is that as we smooth the signal (as we do visually as we "zoom out" toward the top of the page in Figure 9), the load signal strongly resists becoming uniform. This suggests that low frequency components are significant in the overall mix of the signal, or, equivalently, that there is significant long range dependence. It is this property of self-similar signals that most strongly differentiates them and causes significant modeling difficulty.

Self-similarity is more than intuition — it is a well defined mathematical statement about the relationship of the autocorrelation functions of increasingly smoothed versions of certain kinds of long-memory stochastic processes. These stochastic processes model the sort of the mechanisms that give rise to self-similar signals. We shall avoid a mathematical treatment here, but interested readers may want to consult [15] or [16] for a treatment in the context of networking or [2] for its connection to fractal geometry, or [3] for a treatment from a linear time series point of view.

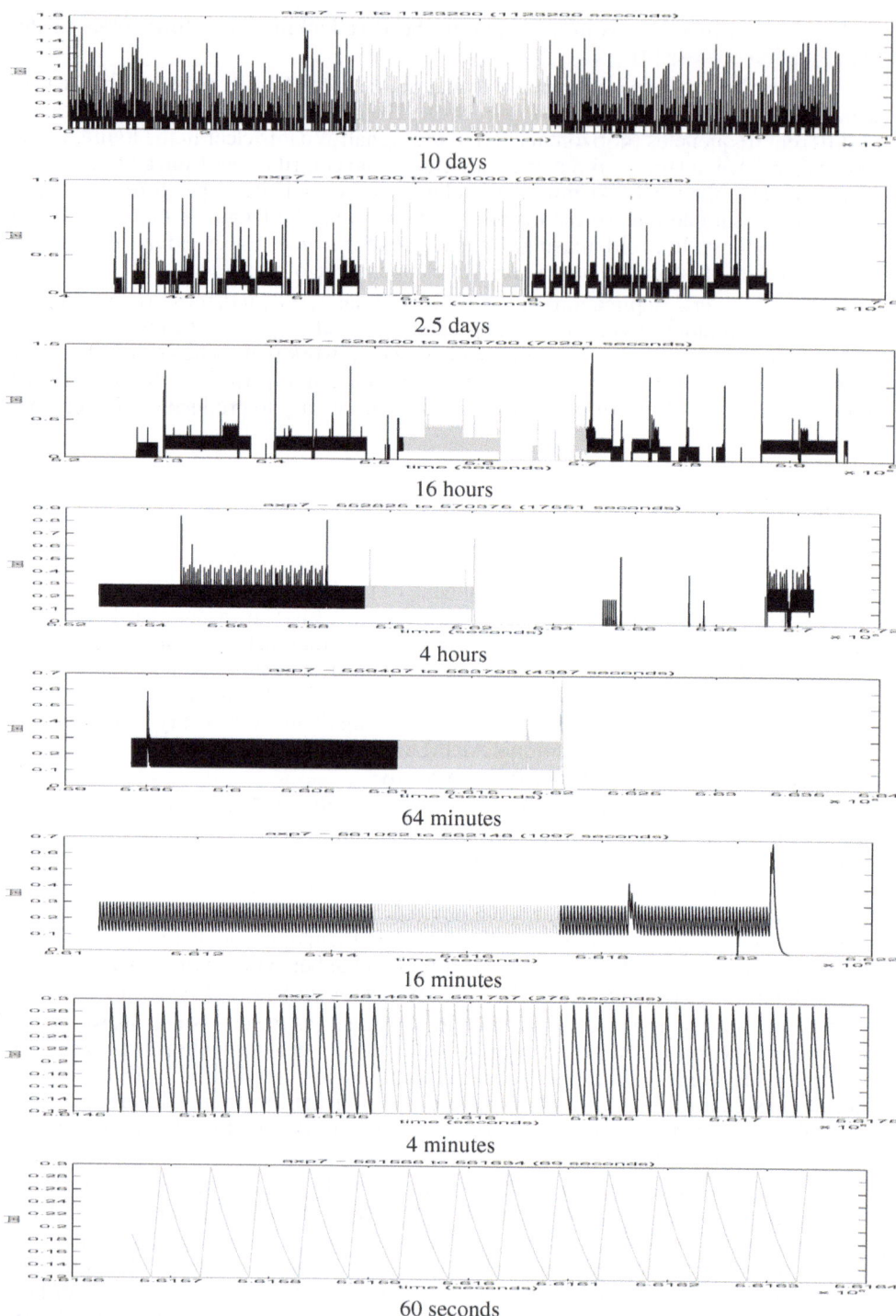

Fig. 9. Visual representation of self-similarity. Each graph plots load versus time and "zooms in" on the middle quarter

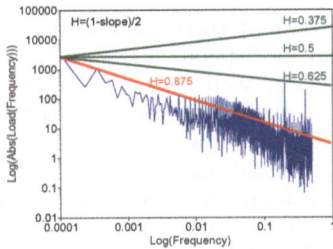

Fig. 10. Meaning of the Hurst parameter in frequency domain.

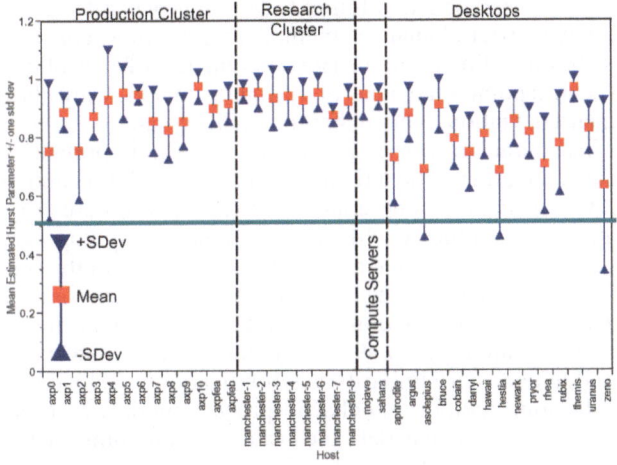

Fig. 11. Mean Hurst parameter estimates for traces +/- one standard deviation.

The degree and nature of the self-similarity of a sequence is summarized by the Hurst parameter, H [10]. Intuitively, H describes the relative contribution of low and high frequency components to the signal. Consider Figure 10, which plots the periodogram (the magnitude of the Fourier transform) of the axp7 load trace of August 19, 1997 on a log-log scale. In this transformed form, we can describe the trend with a line of slope $-\beta$ (meaning that the periodogram decays hyperbolically with frequency ω as $\omega^{-\beta}$. The Hurst parameter H is then defined as $H = (1 + \beta)/2$. As we can see in Figure 10, $H = 0.5$ corresponds to a line of zero slope. This is the uncorrelated noise case, where all frequencies make a roughly equal contribution. As H increases beyond 0.5, we see that low frequencies make more of a contribution. Similarly, as H decreases below 0.5, low frequencies make less of a contribution. $H > 0.5$ indicates self-similarity with positive near neighbor correlation, while $H < 0.5$ indicates self-similarity with negative near neighbor correlation.

We examined each of the 38 load traces for self-similarity and estimated each one's Hurst parameter. There are many different estimators for the Hurst parameter [23], but there is no consensus on how to best estimate the Hurst parameter of a measured series. The most common technique is to use several Hurst parameter estimators and try to find agreement among them. The four Hurst parameter estimators we used were R/S analysis, the variance-time method, dispersional analysis, and power spectral analysis. A description of these estimators as well as several others may be found in [2]. The advantage of these estimators is that they make no assumptions about the stochastic process that generated the sequence. However, they also cannot provide confidence intervals for their estimates. Estimators such as the Whittle estimator [3] can provide confidence intervals, but a stochastic process model must be assumed over which an H can be found that maximizes its likelihood.

We implemented R/S analysis and the variance-time method using Matlab and performed dispersional analysis and power spectral analysis by hand on graphs prepared via Matlab. We validated each method by examining degenerate series with known H and series with specific H generated using the random midpoint displacement method. The dispersional analysis method was found to be rather weak for H values less than about 0.8 and the power spectral analysis method gave the most consistent results.

Figure 11 presents our estimates of the Hurst parameters of each of the 38 load traces. In the graph, each central point is the mean of the four estimates, while the outlying points are at +/- one standard deviation. Notice that for small H values, the standard deviation is high due to the inaccuracy of dispersional analysis. The important point is that the mean Hurst estimates are all significantly above the $H = 0.5$ line and except for three traces with low H values, their +/- one standard deviation points are also above the line.

The traces exhibit self-similarity with Hurst parameters ranging from 0.63 to 0.97, with a strong bias toward the top of that range. On examination of the correlation coefficients (CCs) of Figure 1, we can see that the Hurst parameter has some correlation with mean load (CC=0.45), standard deviation of load (CC=0.58), and is inversely correlated with the max/mean load ratio (CC=-0.49). The latter seems somewhat surprising.

As we discussed above, self-similarity has implications for load modeling and for load smoothing. The long memory stochastic process models that can capture self-similarity tend to be expensive to fit to data and evaluate. Smoothing the load (by mapping large units of computations instead of small units, for example) may be misguided since variance may not decline with increasing smoothing intervals as quickly as quickly as expected. Consider smoothing load by averaging over an interval of length m. Without long range dependence ($H = 0.5$), variance would decay with m as $m^{-1.0}$, while with long range dependence, as m^{2H-2} or $m^{-0.74}$ and $m^{-0.06}$ for the range of Hurst parameters we measured.

5   Epochal Behavior

The key observation in this section is that while load changes in complex ways, the manner in which it changes remains relatively constant for relatively long periods of time. We refer to a period of time in which this stability holds true as an epoch. For example, the load signal could be a 0.25 Hz Sin wave for a minute and a 0.125 Hz sawtooth wave the next minute — each minute is an epoch. That these epochs exist and are long is significant because it suggests that modeling load can be simplified by modeling epochs separately from modeling the behavior within an epoch. Similarly, it suggests a two stage prediction process.

The spectrogram representation of a load trace immediately highlights the epochal behavior we discuss in this section. A spectrogram combines the frequency domain and time domain representations of a time series. It shows how the frequency domain changes locally (for a small segment of the signal) over time. For our purposes, this local frequency domain information is the "manner in which [the load] changes" to which we

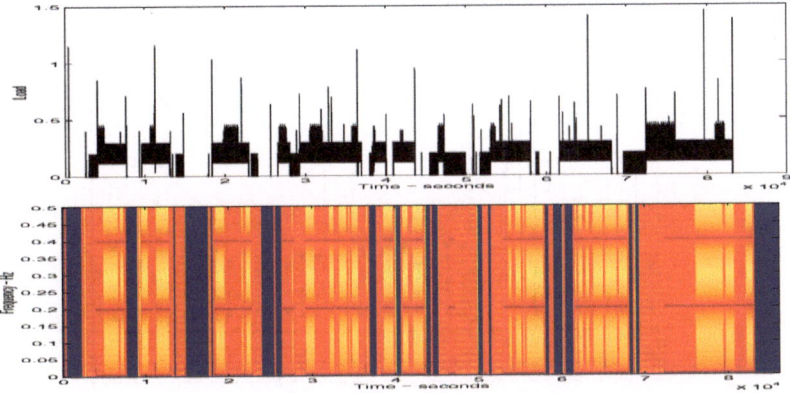

Fig. 12. Time domain and spectrogram representations of load for host axp7 on August 19, 1997.

referred earlier. To form a spectrogram, we slide a window of length w over the series, and at each offset k, we Fourier-transform the w elements in the window to give us w complex Fourier coefficients. Since our load series is real-valued, only the first $w/2$ of these coefficients are needed. We form a plot where the x coordinate is the offset k, the y coordinate is the coefficient number, $1, 2, \ldots, w/2$ and the z coordinate is the magnitude of the coefficient. To simplify presentation, we collapse to two dimensions by mapping the logarithm of the z coordinate (the magnitude of the coefficient) to color. The spectrogram is basically a midpoint in the tradeoff between purely time-domain or frequency-domain representations. Along the x axis we see the effects of time and along the y axis we see the effects of frequency.

Figure 12 shows a representative case, a 24 hour trace from the PSC host axp7, taken on August 19, 1997. The top graph shows the time domain representation, while the bottom graph shows the corresponding spectrogram representation. What is important to note (and which occurs in all the spectrograms of all the traces) are the relatively wide vertical bands. These indicate that the frequency domain of the underlying signal stays relatively stable for long periods of time. We refer to the width of a band as the duration of that frequency epoch.

That these epochs exist can be explained by programs executing different phases, programs being started and shut down, and the like. The frequency content within an epoch contains energy at higher frequencies because of events that happen on smaller time-frames, such as user input, device driver execution, and daemon execution.

We can algorithmically find the edges of these epochs by computing the difference in adjacent spectra in the spectrogram and then looking for those offsets where the differences exceed a threshold. Specifically, we compute the sum of mean squared errors for each pair of adjacent spectra. The elements of this error vector are compared to an epsilon (5% here) times the mean of the vector. Where this threshold is exceeded, a new epoch is considered to begin. Having found the epochs, we can examine their statistics. Figure 13 shows the mean epoch length and the +/- one standard deviation levels for each of the load traces. The mean epoch length ranges from about 150 seconds to over 450 seconds, depending on which trace. The standard deviations are also relatively high (80 seconds to over 600 seconds.) It is the Production Cluster class which is clearly different when it comes to epoch length. The machines in this class tend to have much higher

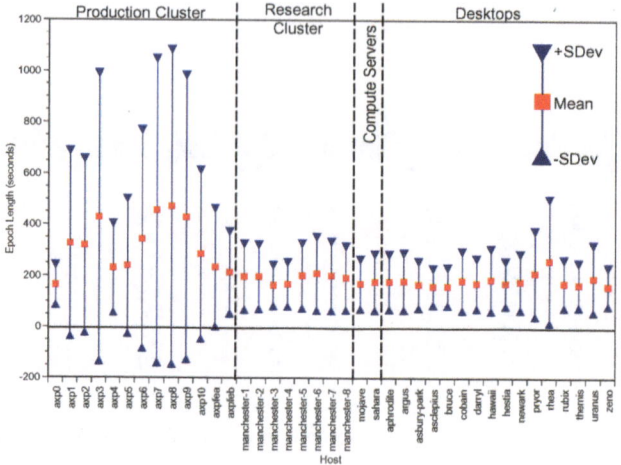

Fig. 13. Mean epoch length +/- one standard deviation.

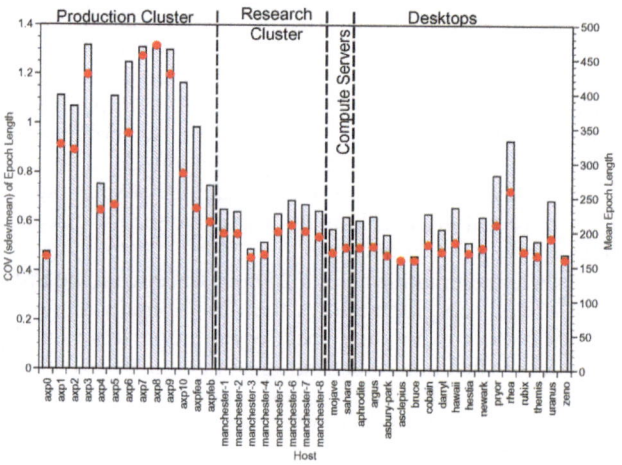

Fig. 14. COV of epoch length and mean epoch length.

means and standard deviations than the other machines. One explanation might be that most of the machines run batch-scheduled scientific jobs which may well have longer computation phases and running times. However, two of the interactive machines also exhibit high means and standard deviations. Interestingly, there is no correlation of the mean epoch length and standard deviation to the mean load or to the Hurst parameter, as can be seen in Figure 1.

The standard deviations of epoch length in Figure 13 give us an absolute measure of the variance of epoch length. Figure 14 shows the coefficient of variance (COV) of epoch length and mean epoch length for each trace. The COV is our relative measure of epoch length variance. Unlike with load (Section 3), these absolute and relative measures of epoch length variance are *both* positively correlated with the mean epoch length. In addition, the correlation is especially strong (CC=0.99 for standard deviation and CC=0.95 for COV). As epoch length increases, it varies more in both absolute and relative terms. The statistical properties of epoch lengths are independent of the statistical properties of load.

The implication of long epoch lengths is that the problem of predicting load may be able to be decomposed into a segmentation problem (finding the epochs) and a sequence of smaller prediction subproblems (predicting load within each epoch.)

Lack of seasonality: It is important to note that the epochal behavior of the load traces is not the same thing as seasonality in the time series analysis sense [5,4]. Seasonality means that there are dominant (or at least visible) underlying periodic signals on top of which are layered other signals. It is not unreasonable to expect seasonality given that other studies [17] have found that availability of compute resources to change regularly over the hours of the working day and the days of the working week. However, examination of the power spectrums and autocorrelations of the load traces suggests that load does *not* exhibit seasonality. We feel this does not contradict the earlier results — the fluctuation of resources simply is not sufficiently periodic to qualify as seasonality in the strict time series sense.

6   Conclusions and Future Work

We collected long, fine grain load measurements on a wide variety of machines at two different times of the year. The results of an extensive statistical analysis of these traces and their implications are the following:

1. The traces exhibit low means but very high standard deviations and maximums. This implies that these machines have plenty of cycles to spare to execute jobs, but the execution time of these jobs will vary drastically.
2. Absolute measures of variation are positively correlated with the mean while relative measures are negatively correlated. This suggests that it may not be unreasonable to map tasks to heavily loaded machines under some performance metrics.
3. The traces have complex, rough, and often multimodal distributions that are not well fitted by analytic distributions such as the normal or exponential distributions, which are particularly inept at capturing the tail of the distribution. This implies that modeling and simulation that assumes convenient analytical load distributions may be flawed. Trace-driven simulation may be preferable.
4. Load is strongly correlated over time, but has a broad, almost noise-like frequency spectrum. This implies that history-based load prediction schemes are feasible, but that linear methods may have difficulty. Realistic load models should capture this dependence, or trace-driven simulation should be used.
5. The traces are self-similar with relatively high Hurst parameters. This means that load smoothing will decrease variance much more slowly than expected. It may be preferable to migrate tasks in the face of adverse load conditions instead of waiting for the adversity to be ameliorated over the long term. Self-similarity also suggests certain modeling approaches such as fractional ARIMA models [9,7,3] and non-linear models which can capture the self similarity property.
6. The traces display epochal behavior in that the local frequency content of the load signal remains quite stable for long periods of time and changes abruptly at the boundaries of such epochs. This suggests that the problem of predicting load may be able to be decomposed into a sequence of smaller subproblems.

We are currently exploring how well the hierarchy of linear time series models [4] perform for short term prediction of load. Part of this work involves quantifying the benefit of capturing the self-similarity of load using fractional ARIMA models [7,9,3]. Initial results show that fractional models provide as much as a 40% improvement in prediction error and rarely perform worse than their non-fractional counterparts.

References

1. ARABE, J., BEGUELIN, A., LOWEKAMP, B., E. SELIGMAN, M. S., AND STEPHAN, P. Dome: Parallel programming in a heterogeneous multi-user environment. Tech. Rep. CMU-CS-95-137, Carnegie Mellon University, School of Computer Science, April 1995.
2. BASSINGTHWAIGHTE, J. B., BEARD, D. A., PERCIVAL, D. B., AND RAYMOND, G. M. Fractal structures and processes. In *Chaos and the Changing Nature of Science and Medicine: An Introduction* (April 1995), D. E. Herbert, Ed., no. 376 in AIP Conference Proceedings, American Institute of Physics, pp. 54–79.
3. BERAN, J. Statistical methods for data with long-range dependence. *Statistical Science 7*, 4 (1992), 404–427.
4. BOX, G. E. P., JENKINS, G. M., AND REINSEL, G. *Time Series Analysis: Forecasting and Control*, 3rd ed. Prentice Hall, 1994.
5. BROCKWELL, P. J., AND DAVIS, R. A. *Introduction to Time Series and Forecasting*. Springer-Verlag, 1996.
6. EAGER, D. L., LAZOWSKA, E. D., AND ZAHORJAN, J. The limited performance benefits of migrating active processes for load sharing. In *SIGMETRICS '88* (May 1988), pp. 63–72.
7. GRANGER, C. W. J., AND JOYEUX, R. An introduction to long-memory time series models and fractional differencing. *Journal of Time Series Analysis 1*, 1 (1980), 15–29.
8. HARCHOL-BALTER, M., AND DOWNEY, A. B. Exploiting process lifetime distributions for dynamic load balancing. In *Proceedings of ACM SIGMETRICS '96* (May 1996), pp. 13–24.
9. HOSKING, J. R. M. Fractional differencing. *Biometrika 68*, 1 (1981), 165–76.
10. HURST, H. E. Long-term storage capacity of reservoirs. *Transactions of the American Society of Civil Engineers 116* (1951), 770–808.
11. JAIN, R. *The Art of Computer Systems Performance Analysis*. John Wiley and Sons, Inc., 1991.
12. JENSEN, E. D. A real-time manifesto. http://www.realtime-os.com, 1996.
13. KAPLAN, J. A., AND NELSON, M. L. A comparison of queueing, cluster, and distributed computing systems. Tech. Rep. NASA TM 109025 (Revision 1), NASA Langley Research Center, June 1994.
14. LELAND, W. E., AND OTT, T. J. Load-balancing heuristics and process behavior. In *Proceedings of Performance and ACM SIGMETRICS* (1986), vol. 14, pp. 54–69.
15. LELAND, W. E., TAQQU, M. S., WILLINGER, W., AND WILSON, D. V. On the self-similar nature of ethernet traffic. In *Proceedings of ACM SIGCOMM '93* (September 1993).
16. MORIN, P. R. The impact of self-similarity on network performance analysis. Tech. Rep. Computer Science 95.495, Carleton University, December 1995.
17. MUTKA, M. W., AND LIVNY, M. The available capacity of a privately owned workstation environment. *Performance Evaluation 12*, 4 (July 1991), 269–284.
18. OBJECT MANAGEMENT GROUP. Realtime corba: A white paper. http://www.omg.org, December 1996. In Progess.
19. POLZE, A., FOHLER, G., AND WERNER, M. Predictable network computing. In *Proceedings of the 17th International Conference on Distributed Computing Systems (ICDCS '97)* (May 1997), pp. 423–431.
20. RINARD, M., SCALES, D., AND LAM, M. Jade: A high-level machine-independent language for parallel programming. *IEEE Computer 26*, 6 (June 1993), 28–38.
21. SHANNON, C. E. A mathematical theory of communication. *Bell System Tech. J. 27* (1948), 379–423, 623–656.
22. SIEGELL, B., AND STEENKISTE, P. Automatic generation of parallel programs with dynamic load balancing. In *Proceedings of the Third International Symposium on High-Performance Distributed Computing* (August 1994).
23. TAQQU, M. S., TEVEROVSKY, V., AND WILLINGER, W. Estimators for long-range dependence: An empirical study. *Fractals 3*, 4 (1995), 785–798.

Locality Enhancement for Large-Scale Shared-Memory Multiprocessors

Tarek Abdelrahman[1], Naraig Manjikian[2], Gary Liu[3], and S. Tandri[3]

[1] Department of Electrical and Computer Engineering
University of Toronto
Toronto, Ontario, Canada M5S 3G4
[2] Department of Electrical and Computer Engineering
Queens University
Kingston, Ontario, Canada K7L 3N6
[3] IBM Canada, Ltd
Toronto, Ontario, Canada M3C 1V7

Abstract. This paper gives an overview of locality enhancement techniques used by the *Jasmine* compiler, currently under development at the University of Toronto. These techniques enhance memory locality, cache locality across loop nests (inter-loop-nest cache locality) and cache locality within a loop nest (intra-loop-nest cache locality) in dense-matrix scientific applications. The compiler also exploits machine-specific features to further enhance locality. Experimental evaluation of these techniques on different multiprocessor platforms indicates that they are effective in improving overall performance of benchmarks; some of the techniques improve parallel execution time by up to 6 times.

1 Introduction

Large-scale Shared-memory Multiprocessors (LSMs) are being increasingly used as platforms for high-performance scientific computing. A typical LSM consists of processors, caches, physically-distributed memory and an interconnection network, as shown in Figure 1. The memory is physically distributed to achieve scalability to reasonably large numbers of processors. Nonetheless, the hardware supports a shared address space that allows a processor to transparently access memory through the network. Caches are used to mitigate the latency of accessing both local and remote memory. The hardware also enforces cache coherence. Examples of LSMs include the Stanford Flash [8], the University of Toronto NUMAchine [17], the HP/Convex Exemplar [4], and the SGI Origin 2000 [6].

Today's parallelizing compilers are capable of detecting loop-level parallelism in scientific applications, but often favor greater parallelism over locality, resulting in parallel code with poor performance [3,5]. Hence, a key challenge facing the parallelizing compilers research community today is how to restructure code and data to effectively exploit locality of reference while maintaining parallelism. This is particularly the case for LSMs, where the physically-distributed shared memory and the use of high-speed caches dictate careful attention to memory and cache locality, yet the large number of processors requires a high degree of parallelism. To address this issue, we have investigated new code and data

D. O'Hallaron (Ed.): LCR'98, LNCS 1511, pp. 335–342, 1998.
© Springer-Verlag Berlin Heidelberg 1998

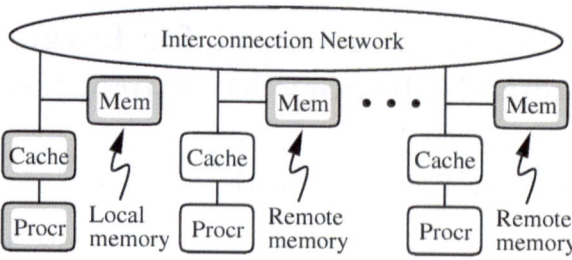

Fig. 1. A large-scale shared-memory multiprocessor.

transformations that enhance cache and memory locality in scientific programs while preserving compiler-detected parallelism. We have prototyped these transformations in the *Jasmine* compiler at the University of Toronto. The goal of this paper is to give an overview of these transformations and to present recent experimental evaluation of their effectiveness in improving the parallel performance of applications on state-of-the-art LSMs.

There are 4 types of locality enhancement techniques employed by Jasmine. They are: memory locality enhancement (described in Section 2); inter-loop-nest locality enhancement (Section 3); intra-loop-nest locality enhancement (Section 4); and machine-specific locality enhancement (Section 5).

2   Memory Locality Enhancement

The placement of data in the physically-distributed shared memory of a LSM system has been traditionally delegated to the operating system. Page placement policies, such as "first-hit" and "round-robin" place pages in memory as these pages are initially accessed [9]. Unfortunately, operating system policies are oblivious to applications' data access patterns and manage data at too coarse of a granularity. It is too often the case that these policies fail to enhance memory locality, cause contention and hot-spots, and lead to poor performance [1,9].

Data partitioning is an approach used by compilers for distributed memory multiprocessors, such as High-Performance Fortran (HPF), to map array data onto separate address spaces. Although such partitioning of an array is not necessary on a LSM because of the presence of a single coherent address space, data partitioning can be used to enhance memory locality—the compiler can place an array partition in the physical memory of the processor that uses this partition the most. Furthermore, data partitioning can eliminate false sharing, reduce memory contention and enhance cache locality across loop nests [15]. However, the task of selecting good data partitions requires the programmer to understand both the target machine architecture and data access patterns in the program [7]. Consequently, porting programs to different machines and tuning them for performance becomes a tedious and laborious process.

Hence, we designed and implemented an algorithm for automatically deriving computation and data partitions in dense-matrix scientific applications on LSMs [16]. The algorithm derives partitions taking into account not only the non-uniformity of memory accesses, but also shared memory effects, such as synchronization, memory contention and false sharing. It is used by Jasmine to place array data in the memory modules of a multiprocessor so as to enhance memory locality, reduce false-sharing, avoid contention and minimize the cost of synchronization. The algorithm consists of two main phases. In the first phase,

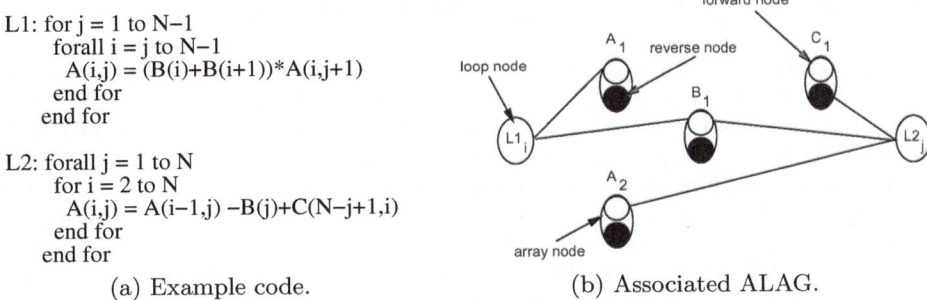

```
L1: for j = 1 to N−1
      forall i = j to N−1
        A(i,j) = (B(i)+B(i+1))*A(i,j+1)
      end for
    end for

L2: forall j = 1 to N
      for i = 2 to N
        A(i,j) = A(i−1,j) −B(j)+C(N−j+1,i)
      end for
    end for
```

(a) Example code.   (b) Associated ALAG.

Fig. 2. An example code and its ALAG.

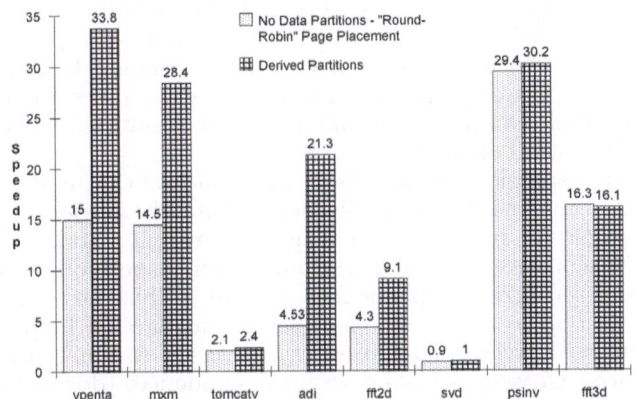

Fig. 3. Performance of benchmarks with and without CDP.

affinity relationships are established between parallel loops and array data using array references in the program. These relationships are captured by the Array-Loop Affinity Graph, or the ALAG. Each node in this graph represents either a parallel loop or an array dimension. Edges are introduced when the subscript expression in an array dimension contains the iterator of a parallel loop. Figure 2 shows a short program segment and its associated ALAG. The nodes in the ALAG are assigned initial distribution attributes and an iterative algorithm is used to derive *static* partitions. These partitions may not be optimal for some arrays that stand to be distributed differently in different loop nests. Hence, in the second phase of the algorithm, the static partitions for such arrays are re-evaluated to determine if *dynamic* partitions are more profitable. It is in this phase the machine-specific parameters and shared-memory effects are taken into account. The details of the algorithm are presented in [16].

The speedup (with respect to sequential execution) of 8 benchmarks applications on a 32-processor Convex SPP-1000 multiprocessor is shown in Figure 3. The parallel speedup of the applications using our derived computation and data partitions is superior to their speedup using operating system policies (about 2 times better on average for the applications). A more complete set of results on overall performance, on the importance of taking shared memory effects into account and on the computational efficiency of our approach is presented in [16].

3   Inter-Loop-Nest Locality Enhancement

Programs often contain sequences of parallel loop nests which reuse a common set of data. Hence, in addition to exploiting loop-level parallelism, a parallelizing compiler must restructure loops to effectively translate this reuse into cache locality. Existing techniques employ loop transformations which exploit data reuse within individual loop nests (e.g., tiling and loop permutations). Unfortunately, the benefit of these transformations is limited because there is often little reuse within a loop nest, or because today's large caches are capable of capturing what reuse exists [13]. In contrast, there exists considerable unexploited reuse *between* loop nests; the volume of data accessed in one loop nest is normally larger than the cache, causing data to be ejected from the cache before it can be reused in a subsequent loop nest.

Loop fusion is used to combine a sequence of parallel loop nests into a single loop nest and enhance *inter-loop-nest locality*. In addition, fusion increases the granularity of parallelism when the resulting loop nest is parallel, and it also eliminates barrier synchronization between the original loop nests. However, data dependences between iterations from different loop nests may become loop-carried in the fused loop nest, and may make the resulting fusion illegal, or may prevent parallelization of the fused loop.

We present a transformation called *shift-and-peel* that enables the compiler to apply fusion and maintain parallelism despite the presence of dependences that would otherwise render fusion illegal or prevent parallelization [12]. The transformation consists of two operation, which respectively overcome fusion-preventing and serializing dependences. Figure 4 illustrates the application of *shifting* and *peeling* to a pair of one-dimensional parallel loops. Backward dependences (upward arrows) that prevent fusion are eliminated by alignment of iterations spaces. Cross-processor forward dependences (downward arrows) that prevent parallelization are eliminated by peeling their sink statements, as shown in the figure. Peeling enables the main blocks of fused iterations to be executed in parallel. The individual peeled statements are collected into smaller independent blocks that are executed after all main blocks have been executed. The details of the technique are in [12].

The speedup of 3 applications on the Convex SPP-1000 is shown in Figure 5 and it indicates that shift-and-peel improves parallel performance by 10%-30%. In one application, spem, there are 11 loop nest sequences which require our shift-and-peel transformation to enable legal fusion and subsequent parallelization. The longest sequence consisted of 10 loop nests, and most of the sequences contain 4 or more loop nests. The total data size for the application is 70 MBytes, which exceeds the total cache capacity of all processors and necessitates the use of inter-loop-nest locality enhancement.

4   Intra-Loop-Nest Locality Enhancement

Complex loop nest structures often consist of an outermost loop surrounding an inner sequence of loop nests. The shift-and-peel transformation enhances inter-loop-nest locality for the inner sequence of nest by fusing it into a single loop nest. This allows the reuse that may be carried by the outermost loop to further be exploited using *tiling*. Tiling re-orders and blocks iterations of the original loop into units of tiles to reduce the number of inner-loop iterations between uses

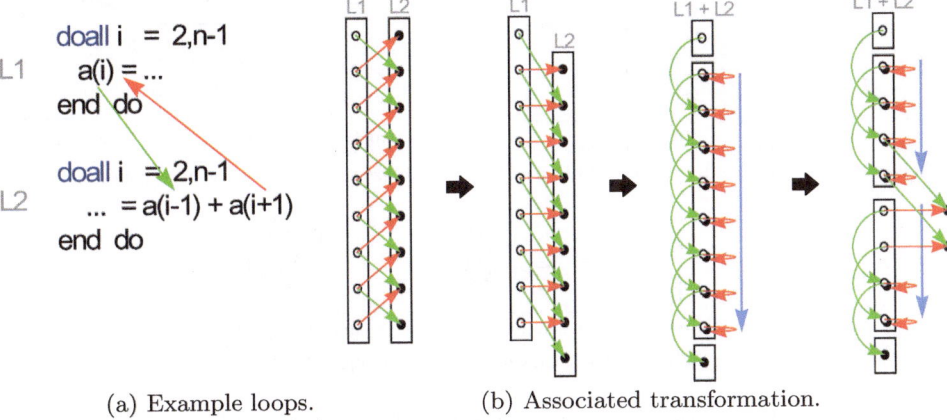

(a) Example loops.   (b) Associated transformation.

Fig. 4. The shift-and-peel transformation.

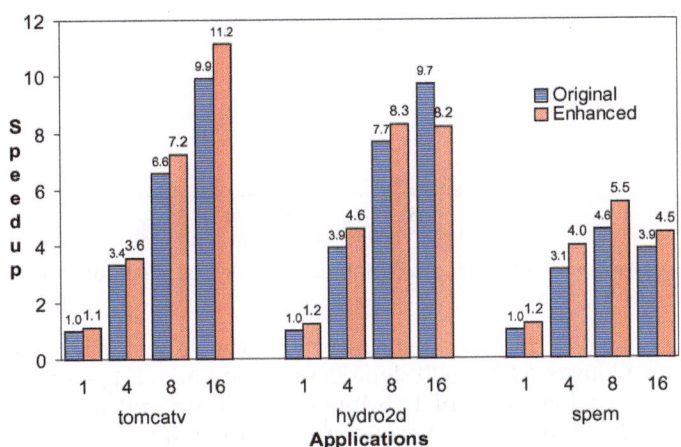

Fig. 5. The performance of applications with and without shift-and-peel.

of the same data. However, data dependences in a loop nest are often such that tiling violates the semantics of the original loop. It becomes necessary to use *loop skewing* to enable tiling, which introduces dependences that limit parallelism to *wavefronts* in the tiled iteration space. Skewing also modifies the data access patterns such that there is data reuse between adjacent tiles, as well as the data reuse that is captured within individual tiles, as shown in Figure 6 for the well-known SOR kernel.

Traditionally, dynamic scheduling has been used to execute wavefront parallelism [18]. However, dynamic scheduling does not exploit the reuse between adjacent tiles. We adapt block and cyclic static scheduling strategies in order to exploit this reuse in tiled loop nests on LSMs [11]. Our strategies also enable the use of small tiles to increase the degree of parallelism on each wavefront. The strategies are described in [11].

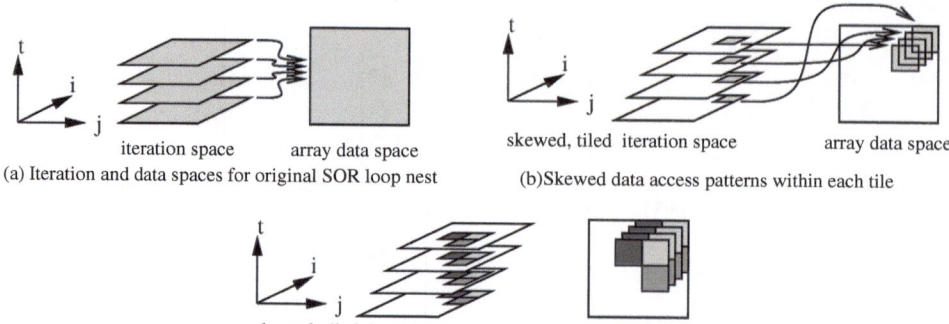

(a) Iteration and data spaces for original SOR loop nest

(b)Skewed data access patterns within each tile

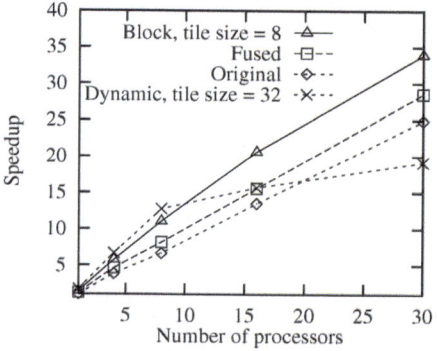

(c) Overlapping array regions swept by adjacent tiles

Fig. 6. Data access patterns that result after skewing and tiling of SOR.

Fig. 7. The performance of 2048 × 2048 Jacobi with and without our wavefront scheduling.

The use of our block scheduling strategy for the Jacobi PDE solver kernel on a 30-processor Convex SPP-1000 demonstrates its advantage over the dynamic strategy. The kernel consists of two inner loop nests and an outer loop which carries reuse. The shift-and-peel transformation is required in order to fuse the two inner loop nests. Loop skewing is required prior to tiling, which gives rise to wavefront parallelism. Figure 7 shows the speedup of the original Jacobi, the speedup after fusion but without tiling, the speedup after tiling with dynamic scheduling and the speedup after tiling with our adapted block scheduling. The best performance for a large number of processors is obtained by fusing and by using our adapted block scheduling strategy. Although not shown in the graph (for the sake of readability), dynamic scheduling with a small tile size performs far worse.

5   Machine-Specific Locality Enhancement

Several research and commercial LSMs incorporate architectural features that offer additional opportunities for locality enhancement. For example, the NU-MAchine multiprocessor [17] supports block transfers from memory to a third level cache which operates at main memory speed, called the Network Cache

(NC). Similarly, the POW network-of-workstation multiprocessor [14] supports coherent memory-to-memory prefetching in a single address space. The Jasmine compiler exploits these features to reduce the latency of remote memory accesses in parallel loops. This is done by transferring to the local memory of a processor (i.e., the NC associated with a processor in NUMAchine, or the local workstation memory in POW) the remote data which is accessed by iterations assigned to the processor [10]. The data partitions automatically derived by our algorithm (or otherwise specified by the programmer) are utilized to determine local and remote data for each processor. In addition, computation partitions and array references are used to determine iterations of a parallel loop that access only lo-cal data (referred to as *local-computation*) and iterations that also access remote data. The iterations that access remote data are removed from the parallel loop and are inserted after the local-computation. An asynchronous transfer of the remote data is initiated before the local-computation to overlap remote access latency with the local-computations and make remote data local.

The speedup of `Jacobi` on POW (8 RS6000 workstations connected by Fast Ethernet and using the TreadMarks [2] software) is shown in Figure 8 with and without computation-communication overlap. The performance of the first par-allel loop in `Jacobi` is shown in Figure 8(a) and overall performance is shown in Figure 8(b). The overlap transformation benefits both parallel loop performance and overall performance by about 30%.

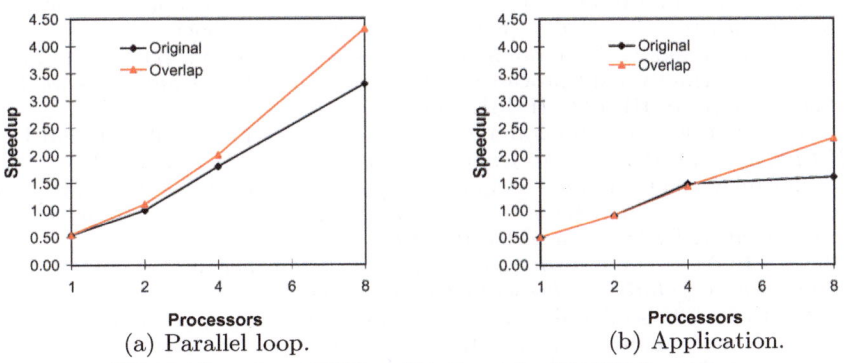

(a) Parallel loop.   (b) Application.

Fig. 8. Speedup of 512×512 `Jacobi` with 640 iterations.

6   Concluding Remarks

Compiler techniques that enhance locality are critical for obtaining high perfor-mance levels on LSMs. This paper gave an overview of code and data transfor-mations used by the Jasmine compiler to enhance memory and cache locality. These techniques address not only the relevant architectural issues of LSMs (physically-distributed memory, cache, contention, etc.) but also characteristics of real applications (sequences of loop nest and complex dependences). Expe-rimental evaluation of these transformations on state-of-the-art multiprocessors demonstrates their effectiveness in improving overall performance of applicati-ons.

References

1. T. Abdelrahman and T. Wong. Compiler support for array distribution on NUMA shared memory multiprocessors. *The Journal of Supercomputing*, to appear, 1998.
2. C. Amza, A. Cox, et al. Treadmarks: shared memory computing on networks of workstations. *IEEE Computer*, 29(12):78–82, 1996.
3. W. Blume, R. Doallo, R. Eigenmann, J. Grout, J. Hoeflinger, T. Lawrence, J. Lee, D. Padua, Y. Paek, B. Pottenger, L. Rauchwerger, and P. Tu. Parallel programming with Polaris. *IEEE Computer*, 29(12):78–82, 1996.
4. Convex Computer Corporation. *Convex Exemplar System Overview*. Richardson, TX, USA, 1994.
5. M. Hall, J. Anderson, S. Amarasinghe, B. Murphy, S. Liao, E. Bugnion, and M. Lam. Maximizing multiprocessor performance with the SUIF compiler. *IEEE Computer*, 29(12):84–89, 1996.
6. Silicon Graphics Inc. *The SGI Origin 20000*. Mountain View, CA, 1996.
7. K. Kennedy and U. Kremer. Automatic data layout for High Performance Fortran. In *Proc. of Supercomputing*, pages 2090–2114, 1995.
8. J. Kuskin, D. Ofelt, M. Heinrich, et al. The Stanford FLASH multiprocessor. In *Proc. of the 21st Annual Int'l Symposium on Computer Architecture*, pages 302–313, 1994.
9. R. LaRowe Jr., J. Wilkes, and C. Ellis. Exploiting operating system support for dynamic page placement on a NUMA shared memory multiprocessor. In *Proc. of the 3rd ACM Symposium on Principles and Practice of Parallel Programming*, pages 122–132, 1991.
10. G. Liu and T. Abdelrahman. Computation-communication overlap on network-of-workstation multiprocessors. In *Proc. of the Int'l Conference on Parallel and Distributed Processing Techniques and Applications*, to appear, 1998.
11. N. Manjikian and T. Abdelrahman. Scheduling of wavefront parallelism on scalable shared memory multiprocessors. In *Proc. of the Int'l Conference on Parallel Processing*, pages III–122–III–131, 1996.
12. N. Manjikian and T. Abdelrahman. Fusion of loops for parallelism and locality. *IEEE Trans. on Parallel and Distributed Systems*, 8(2):193–209, 1997.
13. K. McKinley and O. Temam. A quantitative analysis of loop nest locality. In *Proc. of the 7th Int'l Conference on Architectural Support for Programming Languages and Operating Systems*, pages 94–104, 1996.
14. The POW multiprocessor project. University of Toronto. *http://www.eecg.toronto.edu/parallel/sigpow*, 1995.
15. S. Tandri and T. Abdelrahman. Computation and data partitioning on scalable shared memory multiprocessors. In *Proc. of the Int'l Conference on Parallel and Distributed Processing Techniques and Applications*, pages 41–50, 1995.
16. S. Tandri and T. Abdelrahman. Automatic partitioning of data and computation on scalable shared memory multiprocessors. In *Proc. of the Int'l Conference on Parallel Processing*, pages 64–73, 1997.
17. Z. Vranesic, S. Brown, et al. The NUMAchine multiprocessor. Technical Report CSRI-324, Computer Systems Research Institute, University of Toronto, 1995.
18. M. Wolf. *Improving locality and parallelism in nested loops*. PhD thesis, Department of Computer Science, Stanford University, 1992.

Language and Compiler Support for Out-of-Core Irregular Applications on Distributed-Memory Multiprocessors*

Peter Brezany[1], Alok Choudhary[2], and Minh Dang[1]

[1] Institute for Software Technology and Parallel Systems, University of Vienna
Liechtensteinstrasse 22, A-1090 Vienna, EM: {brezany,dang}@par.univie.ac.at
[2] ECE Department, Northwestern University, Evanston, EM: choudhar@ece.nwu.edu

Abstract. Current virtual memory systems provided for scalable computer systems typically offer poor performance for scientific applications when an application's working data set does not fit in main memory. As a result, programmers who wish to solve "out-of-core" problems efficiently typically write a separate version of the parallel program with explicit I/O operations. This task is onerous and extremely difficult if the application includes indirect data references. A promising approach is to develop a language support and a compiler system on top of an advanced runtime system which can automatically transform an appropriate in-core program to efficiently operate on out-of-core data. This approach is presented in this paper. Our proposals are discussed in the context of HPF and its compilation environment.

1 Introduction

A wide class of scientific and engineering applications, called *irregular applications*, greatly benefit from the advent of powerful parallel computers. However, the efficient parallelization of irregular applications for distributed-memory multiprocessors (*DMMPs*) is still a challenging problem. In such applications, access patterns to major data arrays are only known at runtime, which requires runtime preprocessing and analysis in order to determine the data access patterns and consequently, to find what data must be communicated and where it is located.

The standard strategy for processing parallel loops with irregular accesses, developed by Saltz, Mehrotra, and Koelbel [9], generates three code phases, called the *work distributor, the inspector,* and *the executor.* Optionally, a dynamic *partitioner* can be applied to the loop [2,12].

---

* The work described in this paper is being carried out as part of the research project "Aurora" supported by the Austrian Research Foundation.

D. O'Hallaron (Ed.): LCR'98, LNCS 1511, pp. 343–350, 1998.

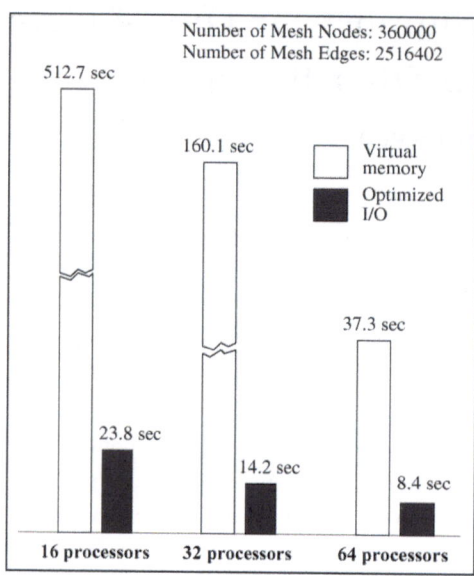

Fig. 1. Optimized file I/O vs. VM

Large scale irregular applications involve large data structures. Runtime preprocessing provided for these applications results in construction of additional large data structures which increase the memory usage of the program substantially. Consequently, a parallel program may quickly run out of memory. Therefore, some data structures must be stored on disks and fetched during the execution of the program. Such applications and data structures are called *out-of-core (OOC) applications* and *OOC data structures*, respectively. The performance of an OOC program strongly depends on how fast the processors, the program runs on, can access data from disks. Traditionally, in scientific computations, OOC problems are handled in two different ways: (1) virtual memory (VM) which allows the in-core program version to be run on larger data sets, and (2) specific OOC techniques which explicitly interface file I/O and focus on its optimization. Although VM is an elegant solution (it provides the programming comfort and ensures the program correctness), it has been observed that the performance of scientific applications that rely on virtual memory is generally poor due to frequent paging in and out of data.

In our recent papers [3,4], we describe the *runtime support* CHAOS+ we have developed for parallelization of irregular OOC applications on DMMPs. Fig. 1 shows the performance improvement obtained by the OOC version[1] of the Euler 3-D solver which was built on top of CHAOS+ against VM on the Intel Paragon. Although the interface to CHAOS+ is a level higher than the interface to a parallel file system and the interface to a communication library, it is still difficult for the application programmer to develop efficient OOC irregular programs. A promising approach is to develop a language support and a compiler system on top of an advanced runtime system which can automatically transform an appropriate in-core program to efficiently operate on OOC data. This approach is discussed in this paper.

---

[1] Only indirection arrays were out-of-core in this program version.

In Section 2, we describe the language directives available to the programmer which provide useful information to the compiler. These directives are proposed as a part of the language HPF$^+$ [5]. Section 3 presents basic and advanced compiler methods to transform the OOC program and insert communication and I/O. Experimental results are discussed in Section 4. We review related work and conclude in Sections 5 and 6.

2   Language Support

The DISTRIBUTE directive in HPF partitions an array among processors by specifying which elements of the array are mapped to each processor. This results in each processor storing a local array which is called the *distribution segment.*

In order to allocate memory and handle accesses to OOC arrays, the HPF compiler needs information about which arrays are out-of-core and also the maximum amount of in-core memory that is allowed to be allocated for each array. The user may provide this information by a directive of the following form:

!HPF+$ [*dist_spec,*] OUT_OF_CORE [, IN_MEM (*ic_portion_spec*)] :: $ar_1, .., ar_k$

where ar_i specify array identifiers, and the optional part *dist_spec* represents an HPF *distribution-specification* annotation. The keyword OUT_OF_CORE indicates that all ar_i are out-of-core arrays.

In the second optional part, the keyword IN_MEM indicates that only the array portions of the global shape that corresponds to *ic_portion_spec* are allowed to be kept in main memory. During computation, each processor brings a section of ar_i into its memory part, called *in-core local array (ICLA)*, and operates on it and stores it back, if necessary. The shape of ICLA is computed from *ic_portion_spec*.

If the data for an OOC array comes from an input file or is to be written to an output file then the file name must be specified. For this the ASSOCIATE directive ([7]) is used.

The OUT_OF_CORE directives can be introduced in the specification part of the program unit or can immediately precede the parallel loop specification. For example, in Fig. 2, arrays X, Y, EDGE1 and EDGE2 will be handled as OOC arrays in the loop L which represents a sweep over the edges of an unstructured mesh. The data for X comes from the file 'X_file.dat'. ICLAs of shape ($\lceil K/M \rceil$) are allocated for EDGE1 and EDGE2 on each processor. The shape of ICLAs allocated for X and Y is determined by the programming environment.

```
!HPF$ PROCESSORS P(M)
REAL X(NNODE), Y(NNODE); INTEGER EDGE1(NEDGE), EDGE2(NEDGE)
!HPF$ DISTRIBUTE (BLOCK) ONTO P :: X, Y, EDGE1, EDGE2
...
... X and Y are data arrays, EDGE1 and EDGE2 are indirection arrays ...
!HPF+$ ASSOCIATE ('X_file.dat', X)
... ASSOCIATE directives for Y, EDGE1, and EDGE2 ...
!HPF+$ OUT_OF_CORE :: X, Y
!HPF+$ OUT_OF_CORE, IN_MEM (K) :: EDGE1, EDGE2
!HPF+$ INDEPENDENT, REDUCTION (Y), USE (SPECTRAL_PART(X,Y))
L:  DO I = 1, NEDGE
       ...

           Y(EDGE1(I)) = Y(EDGE1(I)) + F(X(EDGE1(I)),X(EDGE2(I)))
           Y(EDGE2(I)) = Y(EDGE2(I)) − F(X(EDGE1(I)),X(EDGE2(I)))
    END DO
```

Fig. 2. Code for Out-of-Core Unstructured Mesh in HPF Extension

HPF+ enables the user to specify a partitioning strategy either for all or a selected set of arrays. We illustrate this approach by the example in Fig. 2. The USE clause of the INDEPENDENT loop enables the programmer to select a partitioner from those provided in the environment (in the example, this is SPECTRAL_PART) and the arrays (in the example, X and Y) to which it is applied.

3   Compilation Strategies

The compilation process consists of four steps: (1) processing the input HPF+ program by the front end, program normalization, and initial program analysis, (2) basic restructuring, (3) optimizations, and (4) target code generation. In the first part of this section, we describe the basic restructuring strategy and then discuss several optimizing techniques.

3.1   Basic Parallelization Strategy

The out-of-core parallelization strategy is a natural extension of the inspector-executor approach. The set of iterations assigned to each processor by the work distributor is split into a number of *iteration tiles*. Sections of arrays referenced in each tile, called *data tiles*, are small enough to fit into local memory of that processor. The inspector-executor strategy is then applied to each iteration tile.

Generally, the code generated for an OOC data-parallel loop consists of four phases which are connected by control flow depicted in Fig. 3. In the following we describe briefly each phase[2].

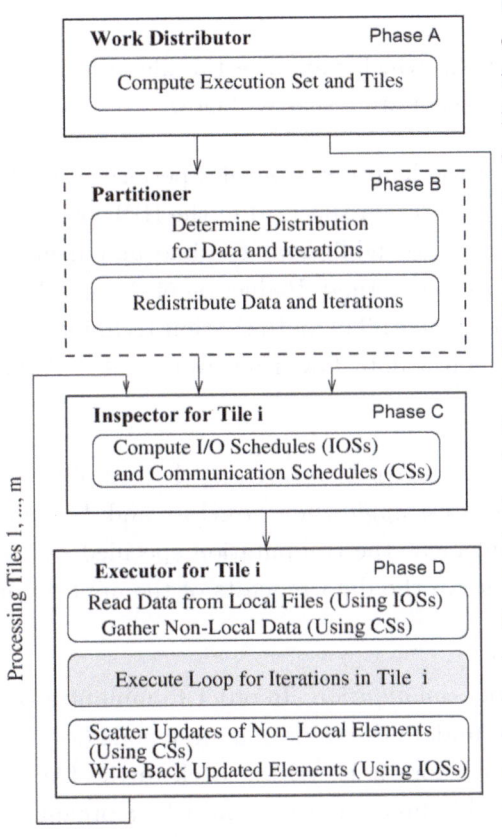

Fig. 3. Computing Phases

A. Default initial data and work distribution   Initially, the iterations and data and indirection arrays are distributed among processors in block fashion. The distribution segment of each OOC array belonging to a processor is stored in a separate *local file* of this processor[3]. Next, an ICLA is allocated for each OOC indirection array. Moreover, the iteration set assigned to a processor, called the *execution set* of this processor, is blockwise split into a number of iteration tiles. The result of this operation depends on the shape of ICLAs allocated for the indirection arrays.

B. OOC Partitioning   This optional phase involves the use of a disk-oriented partitioner which uses OOC data (for example, the node coordinates of the mesh) to determine a new data and work distribution. The data and indirection arrays are then redistributed. The redistribution results into the modification of the local files storing the corresponding distribution segments.

C. OOC Inspector   This preprocessing phase results in computation of *I/O schedules* which describe the required I/O operations and *communication schedules* which describe the required communication. The inspector phase also computes the shape of ICLAs for the data arrays.

---

[2] This compilation strategy is based on the CHAOS+ runtime support.
[3] We consider the Local Placement Execution Model [6].

D. OOC Executor   Once preprocessing is completed, we are in a position to carry out the necessary memory allocation, I/O, communication, and computation, following the plan established by the inspector.

A simplified compilation scheme can be applied to the OOC applications in which data arrays can fit in main memory, while indirection arrays are OOC.

3.2   Optimizations

We have proposed a set of optimizations which minimize the file access costs and other runtime overheads. Some of them are discussed below.

Redundancy elimination. Execution of the loop iteration tiles performed in the execution phase corresponds to the computation specified in the HPF program. On the other hand, other phases introduce additional runtime and memory overhead associated with the parallelization method. Reduction of this overhead is a crucial issue in the compiler development. The optimization techniques we apply to OOC problems are based upon a data flow framework called Partial Redundancy Elimination.

Hiding I/O latency. To overlap time expensive I/O accesses, the compiler can generate a code for two types of processes: *application processes* and *I/O processes*. The application processes implement the computation specified by the original program. The I/O processes serve the data requests of the application processes.

Eliminating extra file I/O by reordering computation. In order to minimize I/O and communication, it is important to update the value of a mesh node (see Fig. 2) for the maximum number of times before it is written back to the file. To achieve this goal the loop iterations and indirection arrays must be reorganized. Our approach [4] is based on a loop transformation called the *loop renumbering*.

4   Performance Results

This section presents the performance of the unstructured mesh linear equation solver GCCG which is a part of the program package FIRE [1]. The application was hand-coded using the methods described in Section 3. All the experiments were carried out on the Intel Paragon. To be able to compare the performance of OOC program versions with the in-core versions using the Paragon's virtual memory system, the programs operated on big unstructured meshes. So, the paging mechanism of Paragon was activated in some experiments. The performance of this solver for different number of processors and tiles is given in Table 1. We compare the performance of the implementation which includes overlapping I/O with communication and computation with the solution in which the application process is blocked while waiting on I/O. Each I/O process was running on the same node as the corresponding application process. The experimental results show a big performance improvement obtained by the OOC versions against virtual memory. The performance was significantly improved by overlapping I/O with computation and communication.

360000 mesh elements						
number of processors	4	4	8	8	16	16
number of tiles	8	16	4	8	2	4
non-overlapping	207.5	257.8	136.9	196.5	109.7	184.3
overlapping	122.9	167.8	90.1	171.3	82.3	149.0
in-core with paging	627.3		328.5		290.3	

Table 1. Performance of the OOC GCCG Solver (time in seconds).

5   Related Work

Compiling OOC data-parallel programs is a relatively new topic and there has been little research in this area. Bordawekar, Choudhary, and Thakur [11] have worked on compiler methods for out-of-core HPF regular programs. Cormen and Colvin have worked on a compiler for out-of-core C*, called ViC* [8]. Paleczny, Kennedy, and Koelbel [10] propose a compiler support and programmer I/O directives which provide information to the compiler about data tiles for OOC regular programs.

6   Conclusions

The difficulty of efficiently handling out-of-core irregular problems limits the performance of distributed-memory multiprocessors. Since coding out-of-core version of an irregular problem might be a very difficult task and virtual memory does not perform well in irregular programs, there is a need for compiler-directed explicit I/O approach.

In this paper, we have presented a preliminary design for addressing these problems which is based on an HPF compilation system and the advanced run-time support CHAOS+. We have evaluated the effectiveness and feasibility of this approach on an out-of-core irregular kernel and compared its performance with the corresponding in-core versions supported by virtual memory. The results achieved are encouraging.

References

1. G. Bachler and R. Greimel. Parallel CFD in the Industrial Environment. *UNICOM Seminars*, London, 1994.
2. P. Brezany and V. Sipkova. Coupling Parallel Data and Work Partitioners to the Vienna Fortran Compilation System. In *Proceedings of the Conference EUROSIM – HPCN Challenges 1996*. North Holland, Elsevier, June 1996.
3. P. Brezany, A. Choudhary, and M. Dang. Parallelization of Irregular Out-of-Core Applications for Distributed-Memory Systems. *Proc. of HCPN 97, Vienna*, April 1997, Springer-Verlag, LNCS 1225.
4. P. Brezany, A. Choudhary, and M. Dang. Parallelization of Irregular Codes Including Out-of-Core Data and Index Arrays. In *Proceedings of the conference "Parallel Computing 1997 - PARCO'97"*, North Holland, Elsevier, April 1998.
5. B. M. Chapman, P. Mehrotra, and H. P. Zima. Extending HPF for advanced data parallel applications. *TR 94-7*, Univ. of Vienna, 1994.
6. A. Choudhary, et al. PASSION: Parallel and Scalable Software for Input-Output. *CRPC-TR94483*, Rice University, Houston, 1994.
7. A. Choudhary, C. Koelbel, and K. Kennedy. Preliminary Proposal to Provide Support for OOC Arrays in HPF. *Document of the HPFF*, Sep. 7, 1995.
8. T. H. Cormen and A. Colvin. ViC*: A Preprocessor for Virtual-Memory C*. TR: PCS-TR94-243, Dept. of Computer Science, Dartmouth College, Nov. 1994.
9. C. Koelbel, P. Mehrotra, J. Saltz, and S. Berryman. Parallel Loops on Distributed Machines. In *Proceedings of the 5th Distributed Memory Computing Conference*, Charleston, pages 1097–1119, IEEE Comp. Soc. Press, April 1990.
10. M. Paleczny, K. Kennedy, and C. Koelbel. Compiler Support for Out-of-Core Arrays on Parallel Machines. In *Proceedings of the 7th Symposium on the Frontiers of Massively Parallel Computation, McLean, VA*, pages 110-118, February 1995.
11. R. Thakur, R. Bordawekar, and A. Choudhary. Compiler and Runtime Support for Out-of-Core HPF Programs. In *Proceedings of the 1994 ACM International Conference on Supercomputing*, pages 382–391, Manchester, July 1994.
12. R. Ponnusamy, et al. A Manual for the CHAOS Runtime Library. *Technical Report*, University of Maryland, May 1994.

Detection of Races and Control-Flow Nondeterminism

Mingdong Feng and Chung Kwong Yuen

School of Computing
National University of Singapore
Kent Ridge, Singapore 119260
{fengmd,yuenck}@iscs.nus.edu.sg

Abstract. When either of two concurrent accesses of the same data is not in its critical section, a "race condition" occurs. Previous race-detection techniques are only applicable to parallel programs without using critical sections, or to parallel programs with critical sections implemented by mutex locks. This paper presents a race-detection algorithm, called the PROTECT algorithm, for parallel programs where critical sections are defined in a higher-level programming construct – "critical region". Both the time and space complexity of the PROTECT algorithm is improved over ones of the previous race-detection algorithms. If the control-flow of a parallel execution on a given input is deterministic, then a single-run of any race-detection algorithm guarantees to find out all races. In the presence of nondeterministic control-flow, a single-run of any race-detection algorithm cannot find out all races. We present another algorithm, called the ALTER algorithm, which either guarantees to detect any nondeterministic control-flow in a program using critical regions, or certifies that the program is control-flow deterministic, thereafter all races can be detected by the PROTECT algorithm.

1 Introduction

In multithreaded systems, several threads can access and manipulate the same data concurrently. If the outcome of the execution depends on the particular order in which access take place, a *race condition* occurs. Since different runs of the same program may produce different results depending on the scheduling of the threads, debugging is extremely difficult in the presence of races. Therefore it is desirable to detect races automatically.

Race detection has been studied extensively in the past [11]. Techniques can be classified into two categories: ones for a parallel program which doesn't have any critical sections; and ones for a parallel program with critical sections.

Examples of the race-detection algorithms in the first category are [12, 3, 15, 8, 5]. Running one of these algorithms *once* is able to detect all races in a parallel program on a given input. We call this property as *single-run property*. The single-run property is desirable because even if the thread scheduling varies from runs to runs, the race detection is independent of the scheduling. Among

D. O'Halloron (Ed.): LCR'98, LNCS 1511, pp. 351–358, 1998.

these algorithms, the SP-BAGS algorithm [5] is the best in terms of time and space usage, taking almost linear time and space compared with the original program's serial execution without race detection.

Example of the race-detection algorithms in the second category are [4, 9, 13, 14, 1]. None of these algorithms holds the single-run property. This is because critical sections allow a shared location to be updated in some nondeterministic fashion depending on the scheduling. The order of two critical sections being executed can be different in two executions of the same program on the same given input. Therefore the value stored in the shared location may be nondeterministic. If the value is used in the boolean expression of a control statement, for example, if, while or for statement, to determine which branch to be taken, then *control-flow* of the program execution is produced nondeterministically. Different runs of the same program with the same input may execute different parts of the program, thus the program execution also becomes nondeterministic. In general, the problem of finding all races in a program using critical sections is proved to be NP-hard [10], partly because enumerating all possible control-flows of a parallel program cannot be achieved in polynomial time.

Moreover, the performance of all race-detection algorithms in the second category is worse than the algorithms in the first category. These algorithms assume a parallel program using mutex locks for critical sections, therefore, the time and space complexity of these algorithms is related to the total number of different lock acquisition patterns, which is non-linear compared with the original program's serial execution without race detection.

The contributions of this paper are two-fold. First, we show that if the critical section is enforced by a high-level programming construct, *critical region* [7, 6], rather than locks, then the time and space complexity of the corresponding race-detection algorithm, which we call the PROTECT algorithm, can be reduced to almost linear complexity, same as the SP-BAGS algorithm in the first category. For a program that runs in T time serially and uses v shared-memory locations, the PROTECT algorithm runs in $O(T\,\alpha(v, v))$ time where α is Tarjan's functional inverse of Ackermann's function [16], a very slowly growing function which, for all practical purposes, is bounded above by 4.

Second, we propose another algorithm, called the ALTER algorithm, to detect the control-flow nondeterminism in a parallel program. The control-flow nondeterminism is the main cause of the failure of the single-run property. The ALTER algorithm runs a parallel program with the same given input twice, and either guarantees to detect any nondeterministic control-flow in the program, or certifies that the program is control-flow deterministic. If a program's control-flow is deterministic, then the single-run property holds. If the program doesn't exhibit any races when further checked by the PROTECT algorithm, then we can certify that the program using the critical regions is race-free for any runs on the given input. If the ALTER algorithm finds nondeterministic control-flow, then the PROTECT algorithm can only check races in the particular run of the parallel program. The ALTER algorithm runs in $O(T\,\alpha(v, v))$ time, almost linearly with the original program's serial execution.

We have initial implementations of both PROTECT and ALTER algorithms for shared-memory programs written in Cilk multithreaded programming language [2]. In the following, Section 2 gives an overview of the SP-BAGS algorithm, and introduces the programming construct **guard** for critical regions. Sections 3 and 4 present the the PROTECT and ALTER algorithms respectively and state their correctness. Section 5 concludes the paper.

2   Preliminaries

In this section we give an overview of the algorithm and data structures used in the SP-BAGS algorithms. We then explain the **guard** construct used in our discussion of race-detection algorithms.

The SP-BAGS algorithm works by executing a Cilk program on a given input in serial, depth-first order. This execution order mirrors that of normal C programs: every subcomputation that is spawned executes completely before the thread that spawned it continues. While executing the program, SP-BAGS maintains a disjoint-set data structure, which allows it to determine the series/parallel relation between the currently executing thread and any previously executed thread in $O(\alpha(v, v))$ amortized time, where v is the number of shared-memory locations. In addition, SP-BAGS maintains two shadow spaces of shared memory, called *reader* and *writer*, in which the ID of the "most parallel" thread which either read from or wrote to each memory location is kept. As the program executes, each access to location l is checked for a race against previous accesses by using the data structure described above to determine the series/parallel relation of the current thread to $reader[l]$ and $writer[l]$. For a Cilk program that runs in T time serially and references v shared memory locations, the SP-BAGS algorithm runs in $O(T \alpha(v, v))$ time and $O(v)$ space.

Protected memory operations are normally achieved by encapsulating them into critical sections. Mutex locks are normally used to protect the execution of critical sections mutually exclusive. However, the possibilities that a location is protected by one or more locks, and that several locations are protected by a same lock, make the race-detection algorithms complex both in time and space. Here, we use the *critical region* concept [7, 6], and introduce a **guard** construct. The **guard** construct takes a list of arguments as memory locations being protected, and a statement that is executed atomically on the guarded locations. The **guard** allows atomic execution of any number of memory operations on any number of memory locations. Accesses of shared variables not in the guarded argument list are performed non-atomically in the statement. The runtime system guarantees that operations on a guarded memory location in a guarded statement are performed atomically, therefore no race exists between concurrent threads executing their guarded statements on the same memory location. On the other hand, concurrent accesses to a guarded memory location without using the **guard** construct constitute races. Races cause non-atomic execution of critical regions, and they are failures in programs that access and update shared data in critical regions.

3   The Protect Algorithm

In this section, we present the PROTECT algorithm, which extends the SP-BAGS algorithm to detect races in Cilk programs using `guard`.

`write` a non-guarded shared location l by thread e:
    if $reader(l) \parallel e$ **or** $writer(l) \parallel e$ **or** $guarded\text{-}reader(l) \parallel e$ **or** $guarded\text{-}writer(l) \parallel e$
        then a race exists
    $writer(l) \leftarrow F$

`read` a non-guarded shared location l by thread e:
    if $writer(l) \parallel e$ **or** $guarded\text{-}writer(l) \parallel e$
        then a race exists
    if $reader(l) \prec e$
        then $reader(l) \leftarrow F$

`write` a guarded shared location l by thread e:
    if $reader(l) \parallel e$ **or** $writer(l) \parallel e$
        then a race exists
    if $guarded\text{-}writer(l) \prec e$
        then $guarded\text{-}writer(l) \leftarrow F$

`read` a guarded shared location l by thread e:
    if $writer(l) \parallel e$
        then a race exists
    if $guarded\text{-}reader(l) \prec e$
        then $guarded\text{-}reader(l) \leftarrow F$

Figure 1. The PROTECT algorithm for race detection in Cilk programs containing guarded reads and writes.

The PROTECT algorithm in Figure 1 uses two more shadow space *guarded-reader* and *guarded-writer*, which stores the IDs of the recent reader and writer in guarded statements. We call these two shadow space as *guarded shadow space*, in contrast to the two *non-guarded shadow space*, i.e., *reader* and *writer*. For normal non-guarded reads and writes, both the guarded and non-guarded shadow space need be examined for race detection respectively. For guarded reads and writes, only the non-guarded shadow space is examined for race detection. Since the PROTECT algorithm is extended from the SP-BAGS algorithm, the race involved two non-guarded accesses are detected as usual.

Theorem 1. *The PROTECT algorithm detects a race in the serial depth-first execution of a Cilk program containing guarded reads and writes if and only if a race exists.*   □

Theorem 2. *Consider a Cilk program that executes in time T on one processor, references v shared memory locations. The* PROTECT *algorithm can check this program for races in $O(T \alpha(v, v))$ time and $O(v)$ space.*   □

The PROTECT algorithm either finds race bugs in the Cilk code, or certify that the Cilk code is race-free in its serial depth-first execution. Since the control-flow of a program containing `guard` construct can be different from runs to runs, the PROTECT algorithm can not guarantee that the Cilk code is race-free for all executions of the same program with the same input. In light of this problem, we have designed another algorithm to identify whether a Cilk program containing `guard` is deterministic. If so, we are able to extend our guarantee that any possible executions of those deterministic programs are race-free.

4   The Alter Algorithm

In this section, we present the ALTER algorithm to detect whether the program control-flow may vary from runs to runs on a given input. This algorithm locates pieces of code in the program which are not checked by one run of any race-direction algorithms, and makes the programmer aware of hidden races which may exist in those pieces of code.

A location l is called a *directly nondeterministic location* at an execution point p if the value of l read at p is set by different threads in two executions of the same program with the same input. In other words, at p in one execution, l has the value written by thread e_1, while in another execution of the same program, l has value written by thread e_2 where $e_2 \neq e_1$. Without loss of generality, we assume e_1 is executed before e_2 in the serial depth-first execution. Then, we should have $e_1 \parallel e_2$ because otherwise the value written by e_1 is overwritten by e_2 in all executions. Since $e_1 \parallel e_2$, their writes to l should be protected by `guard`, otherwise race on l occurs. A location l is called an *indirectly nondeterministic location* if it is assigned to a value calculated with reference to a directly or another indirectly nondeterministic location.

The ALTER algorithm needs to execute the same Cilk program twice (i.e., two runs) in the serial depth-first order on the same given input, and it either points out where the nondeterminism stems from in the program, or it certifies that the program is deterministic on the given input, therefore race-free for all possible executions on the same input. The *first-run* executes the Cilk program in the *serial child-first execution* and the *second-run* executes the Cilk program in the *serial parent-first execution*. In the serial child-first execution, once a `spawn` statement occurs, the child thread is executed before the next parent thread. In the serial parent-first execution, once `spawn` occurs, the next parent thread is executed till the `sync` statement before the child thread.

Figure 2 shows the ALTER algorithm for both runs. The algorithm needs a shadow space *nondeterministic* for all memory locations used in the program, both the shared and local memory locations. For any location l, *nondeterministic(l)* is initially FALSE because we assume all variables are deterministic from the beginning. As the algorithm executes, *nondeterministic(l)* is set

---

write u into a guarded shared location l by e:
    if *guarded-writer*$(l) \prec e$
      then *nondeterministic*$(l) \leftarrow$ FALSE
    if u is evaluated with reference to any location l'
        where *nondeterministic*$(l') =$ TRUE
      then *nondeterministic*$(l) \leftarrow$ TRUE

read a guarded shared location l by e:
    if *guarded-writer*$(l) \parallel e$
      then *nondeterministic*$(l) \leftarrow$ TRUE

---

write u into a non-guarded or non-shared location l:
    if u is evaluated with reference to any location l'
        where *nondeterministic*$(l') =$ TRUE
      then *nondeterministic*$(l) \leftarrow$ TRUE

---

branch on u:
    if u is evaluated with reference to any location l
        where *nondeterministic*$(l) =$ TRUE
    then nondeterministic control-flow exists

Figure 2. The ALTER algorithm detects the deviation of the program control-flow. In the first-run, a spawned child thread always executes before the next parent thread, while in the second-run, the next parent thread always executes before the spawned child thread till the **sync** statement. The *nondeterministic* shadow space is set when the location becomes directly or indirectly deterministic.

to TRUE when l becomes a directly or indirectly nondeterministic location. The situation when l becomes a directly nondeterministic location takes place when the currently-executing guarded reader or a guarded writer of l finds *guarded-writer*(l) is logically in parallel, which means there are concurrent writers, therefore the value of l becomes nondeterministic. If the current writer finds *guarded-writer*(l) in series with the current thread, which means there is no concurrent writer before the current writer in any surrounding sync block, therefore *nondeterministic*(l) is set to FALSE because location l becomes deterministic. The situation when l becomes an indirectly nondeterministic location takes place when an assignment of l assigns a value evaluated with reference to other known directly or indirectly nondeterministic memory locations. During its execution, the ALTER algorithm also examines every branching instruction in the parallel program to see whether the branching expression is evaluated with the reference to any known nondeterministic memory locations. If so, a warning is issued because this is the case where a nondeterministic control-flow may occur.

We can give an informal explanations why two runs are needed. The first-run detects the occurrences of readers *after* any concurrent writer, while the second-run detects the occurrences of readers *before* any concurrent writer. For two threads e_1 and e_2, suppose $e_1 \parallel e_2$, and e_1 writes location l, and e_2 reads l.

Then, the value of l read by e_2 is nondeterministic. If e_1 executes before e_2 in a serial depth-first child-first execution order (i.e., the first-run), e_2 can simply check the nondeterminism of l by checking whether e_1 is logically in series or parallel. If e_1 executes after e_2 in order in a serial depth-first child-first execution, then the first-run can not identify the value read by e_2 being nondeterministic because the write of e_1 has not yet happened when e_2 executes. But in a serial depth-first parent-first execution order (i.e., the second-run), e_2 executes after e_1, therefore, the second-run can identify l being a directly nondeterministic location.

Theorem 3. *The* ALTER *algorithm issues a nondeterminism warning if and only if nondeterministic control-flow exists.*   □

Theorem 4. *Consider a Cilk program that executes in time T on one processor, references v shared memory locations. The* ALTER *algorithm can check this program for control-flow nondeterminism in $O(T\,\alpha(v,v))$ time and $O(v)$ space.*   □

5   Conclusion

We have presented two algorithms. The PROTECT algorithm detects races in a program using critical regions in one execution order. The ALTER algorithm detects whether the control-flow of a program using critical regions is deterministic. If deterministic, the PROTECT algorithm guarantees that all races have been detected. In our implementation of both algorithms, we combine the PROTECT algorithm with the ALTER program such that both control-flow determinism and races are detected at the same time. We will present timing of our implementations in the full version of this paper.

Many extensions to this work are possible. If two branches of the branch instruction write the same value to shared locations, then the nondeterministic control-flow detected by the ALTER algorithm however won't affect the single-run property. We are currently experimenting user annotations to assist the ALTER algorithm avoiding false alarms. It is conceivable to combine the ALTER algorithm with other race-detection algorithms. We are more interested in using our techniques to detect race in real programs, for example, many server programs which are written in multithreaded fashion. We are also integrating our implementations into a debugging tool for parallel programming.

Acknowledgments

Thanks are due to Charles Leiserson for introducing this topic and many help discussions, when the first author was a postdoctoral fellow in MIT Laboratory of Computer Science.

References

1. Guang-Ien Cheng, Mingdong Feng, Charles E. Leiserson, Keith H. Randall, and Andrew F. Stark. Detecting data races in Cilk programs that use locks. In *Proceedings of the Tenth Annual ACM Symposium on Parallel Algorithms and Architectures (SPAA)*, June 1998.
2. *Cilk-5.1 Reference Manual.* Available on the Internet from "http://theory.lcs.mit.edu/~cilk".
3. Anne Dinning and Edith Schonberg. An empirical comparison of monitoring algorithms for access anomaly detection. In *Proceedings of the Second ACM SIGPLAN Symposium on Principles & Practice of Parallel Programming (PPoPP)*, pages 1–10. ACM Press, 1990.
4. Anne Dinning and Edith Schonberg. Detecting access anomalies in programs with critical sections. In *Proceedings of the ACM/ONR Workshop on Parallel and Distributed Debugging*, pages 85–96. ACM Press, May 1991.
5. Mingdong Feng and Charles E. Leiserson. Efficient detection of determinacy races in Cilk programs. In *Proceedings of the Ninth Annual ACM Symposium on Parallel Algorithms and Architectures (SPAA)*, pages 1–11, Newport, Rhode Island, June 1997.
6. P. Brinch Hansen. Structured multiprogramming. *Communication of the ACM*, 15(7):574–578, July 1972.
7. C. A. R. Hoare. Towards a theory of parallel programming. In C. A. Hoare and R. H. Perrott, editors, *Operating Systems Techniques*, pages 61–71. Academic Press, London, 1972.
8. John Mellor-Crummey. On-the-fly detection of data races for programs with nested fork-join parallelism. In *Proceedings of Supercomputing'91*, pages 24–33. IEEE Computer Society Press, 1991.
9. Robert H. B. Netzer and Sanhoy Ghosh. Efficient race condition detection for shared-memory programs with post/wait synchronization. In *Proceedings of the 1992 International Conference on Parallel Processing*, St. Charles, Illinois, August 1992.
10. Robert H. B. Netzer and Barton P. Miller. On the complexity of event ordering for shared-memory parallel program executions. In *Proceedings of the 1990 International Conference on Parallel Processing*, pages II: 93–97, August 1990.
11. Robert H. B. Netzer and Barton P. Miller. What are race conditions? *ACM Letters on Programming Languages and Systems*, 1(1):74–88, March 1992.
12. Itzhak Nudler and Larry Rudolph. Tools for the efficient development of efficient parallel programs. In *Proceedings of the First Israeli Conference on Computer Systems Engineering*, May 1986.
13. Dejan Perković and Peter Keleher. Online data-race detection via coherency guarantees. In *Proceedings of the Second USENIX Symposium on Operating Systems Design and Implementation (OSDI)*, Seattle, Washington, October 1996.
14. Stefan Savage, Michael Burrows, Greg Nelson, Patric Sobalvarro, and Thomas Anderson. Eraser: A dynamic race detector for multi-threaded programs. In *Proceedings of the Sixteenth ACM Symposium on Operating Systems Principles (SOSP)*, October 1997.
15. Guy L. Steele Jr. Making asynchronous parallelism safe for the world. In *Proceedings of the Seventeenth Annual ACM Symposium on Principles of Programming Languages (POPL)*, pages 218–231. ACM Press, 1990.
16. Robert Endre Tarjan. Applications of path compression on balanced trees. *Journal of the Association for Computing Machinery*, 26(4):690–715, October 1979.

Improving Locality in Out-of-Core Computations Using Data Layout Transformations

M. Kandemir[1], A. Choudhary[2], and J. Ramanujam[3]

[1] EECS Dept., Syracuse University, Syracuse, NY 13244 (mtk@ece.nwu.edu)
[2] ECE Dept., Northwestern University, Evanston, IL 60208 (choudhar@ece.nwu.edu)
[3] ECE Dept., Louisiana State University, Baton Rouge, LA 70803 (jxr@ee.lsu.edu)

Abstract. Programs accessing disk-resident arrays, called out-of-core programs, perform poorly in general due to an excessive number of I/O calls and insufficient help from compilers. In order to alleviate this problem, we propose a data layout optimization in this paper. Experimental results provide evidence that our method is effective for out-of-core nests whose data sizes far exceed the size of memory.

1   Introduction

An important characteristic of out-of-core computations is that the large data structures they access do not fit in main memory. Consequently, the data has to be stored on disk, and brought into memory only when they are to be processed. The time spent on these disk accesses is the primary determinant of the performance of out-of-core programs. Two main issues related with these large data structures are (1) when and how to transfer them between different levels of memory hierarchy, and (2) how to operate on them. It is certainly true that over the years, the I/O subsystems of parallel machines have evolved from simple-minded architectures that reserve a single processor for I/O to sophisticated systems where a number of I/O nodes can collectively perform I/O on behalf of all compute nodes. However, in general, it has been difficult to exploit these capabilities.

Several aspects of of the software support system for out-of-core computations have been addressed so far. Most of the previous research has focused on operating systems, parallel file systems, run-time libraries and applications themselves. In particular, run-time libraries and parallel file systems have received a lot of attention recently, resulting in a number of powerful and fast run-time libraries as well as a few commercial parallel file systems. In spite of these advances, it is very important for the user to exploit this capacity; inserting calls to library functions is tedious, error-prone and results in programs whose performance varies widely from machine to machine. Even in cases where a user is allowed to convey semantic information to the library, the programmer faces the burden of ensuring that what is provided is indeed correct.

In this paper we offer a less widely studied alternative to deal with the I/O problem at the software level. Instead of relying on programmer-supplied information to the run-time libraries and parallel file systems, we use techniques based on compiler analysis to obtain high-level information about the data access behavior of the scientific codes. After the information is collected, the compiler can plug it into a run-time system and/or parallel file system. Thus our approach is based on the idea of dividing responsibility between compiler and run-time system. This, in principle, should work as current optimizing compilers for shared and distributed memory machines are successful in detecting the data access behavior of scientific programs. Using the relevant information, a compiler can restructure the code such that I/O will be less of a bottleneck. In low-level terms, this restructuring of code should result in two improvements: first, the number of accesses to

D. O'Hallaron (Ed.): LCR'98, LNCS 1511, pp. 359–366, 1998.

the disk subsystem should be reduced; secondly, the volume of data transferred between memory and disk system should be reduced. Overall, these reductions will lead to reduced I/O overhead, which in turn, hopefully, will reduce the execution time of the codes.

The rest of this paper is organized as follows. In Section 2, we elaborate on why cache memory oriented techniques may not work well for I/O intensive applications, and motivate the need for data-oriented techniques to improve the performance. In Section 3 we present an overview of our data restructuring framework. In Section 4, we give preliminary experimental results on three example kernels. In Section 5 we discuss related work and conclude the paper in Section 6.

2 Existing Techniques

Our main goal is to improve the file locality exhibited by out-of-core programs. Of course, a simple way of looking at this problem is to think of the disk subsystem as yet another level in the memory hierarchy, and apply the code restructuring techniques [7] available for optimizing the performance of cache–main memory hierarchy. While in some cases this approach can work reasonably well, the observation of the following fact is important: The techniques developed for optimizing cache–main memory performance are access pattern oriented; that is the main goal there is to change the access pattern of the program (specifically the order of the loops in programs) to obtain an optimized program such that the majority of data accesses is satisfied from cache instead of memory. Improving data locality *indirectly* by changing the access pattern is problematic for main memory–disk hierarchy because of two points:

(1) The applications that use memory–disk hierarchy frequently are I/O intensive. They do I/O either because the data that they handle are too big to fit in the memory as in out-of-core computations or the data should be written into (read from) disk in regular intervals as in check-pointing, or visualization or a combination of both. The main issue here is the data itself; that is, the restructuring techniques should focus more on the data (instead of the access pattern) and seek ways to improve the transfer of data between disk and memory.

(2) Restructuring techniques for cache memories are in general limited by data dependences. That is, data dependences may prevent some locality optimizations from taking place. In the case of cache memories, this is fine for many programs. But for I/O intensive programs, traditional loop restructuring techniques are not sufficient since the penalty for going to the disk instead of memory can be very severe.

Thus, it is important for restructuring techniques for I/O intensive programs to be "data-oriented" rather than "control-oriented" (e.g., program dependences). With these issues in mind, we offer a program restructuring technique based on data layout transformations for out-of-core dense matrix computations. Specifically, our technique detects the optimal layouts in files and memory for out-of-core arrays referenced in a program. The overall effect is a much better I/O performance in terms of the number of I/O calls, the I/O volume and hence the execution time.

In order to explain the problem with loop transformation based techniques in detail, we consider *loop permutation* [7], a well-known transformation to improve locality in loop nests. Assuming column-major layouts, the locality of the code in Figure 1(a) will be poor, because successive iterations of the innermost loop touch different columns of the array. Loop permutation can improve the performance by *interchanging* the order of the loops; the resulting code shown in Figure 1(b) has good locality. Unfortunately, loop interchange may not be possible in every case. Consider the code in Figure 1(a) again, this time assuming that there is another right hand side reference A(i-1,j+1). In this case, the data dependence [7] due to this and the left hand side reference prevents loop interchange.

Our objective is to derive an optimized out-of-core version of a program from its in-core version. Specifically, we would like to determine optimal file layouts for the arrays referenced in the program. The input to our framework is a program annotated (by user or compiler) using compiler directives that indicate which arrays are out-of-core. The output is a layout–optimized program which includes I/O calls to a run-time system as well as communication calls (for message-passing machines).

Since the size of an out-of-core array is larger than the memory available, the array should be divided into chunks such that each chunk can fit into memory. At a time, for a given array, only a single data chunk can be brought from file into memory, can be operated on and (if it is modified) stored back in file. In handling a data chunk, there are two main issues: (1) how to read/write it from (into) file efficiently; and (2) how to process it efficiently. The first issue is very important as file I/O is much more expensive as compared to memory or processor operations in terms of latency. An efficient compilation framework should minimize the file access time. This can be achieved by reducing the number of I/O calls as well as the volume of the transferred data. Reducing the number of I/O calls is more important, because it is the dominant factor. The second issue is related to the efficient use of memory which is a valuable resource in out-of-core computations. In essence, the elements of a data chunk that are brought into memory should be reused as much as possible before they are stored back on file. There is no point in bringing a data chunk when the ongoing computation will use only a part of it.

To see how the compilation of out-of-core arrays is handled, we again consider the program in Figure 1(a), assuming that the reference $A(i-1,j+1)$ is also there. Suppose that A is an $n \times n$ out-of-core array and resides in a file with a column-major layout and brought into memory in chunks whose sizes and orientations are dictated by the innermost loop. Assuming that M is the size of memory allocated for this array and at most n consecutive items can be read/written in a single I/O call, to read a chunk of size $(M/n) \times n$ from file into memory (as shown in Figure 2(a)) will entail n I/O calls, each of which is for a sub-column of data of size M/n. For the entire execution of the code, n^3/M I/O calls should be issued. Of course, one might think of bringing a chunk of size $n \times (M/n)$ (instead of size of $(M/n) \times n$) by issuing only M/n I/O calls (instead of n) for it (see Figure 2(b)). Unfortunately, this is not very useful, as due to the access pattern, most of the data in this chunk will not be assigned new values as they are themselves dependent on the data which will be residing in file. The source of the problem here is that the data should not be stored as column-major in file. Rather, if it is stored as row-major as illustrated in Figure 2(c), then an $(M/n) \times n$ size data chunk can be brought into memory and operated on by issuing only M/n I/O calls. Therefore, it is possible to minimize the number of I/O calls by changing the file layout of the data.

To see the difference in performance between column-major and row-major file layouts quantitatively, consider Figure 3. The figure on the left shows (on a log scale) the number of I/O calls issued by the two versions (column-major and row-major file layouts) for different input sizes (n) between 2K and 10K elements. The memory size (M) is fixed at 4M elements for illustrative purposes. We note that when the input size is increased, the gap between the number of I/O calls in the two versions widens. The figure on the right illustrates the number of I/O calls when the memory size is varied and the input size is fixed at 4K elements. As one would expect, 16M elements is the minimum memory size to accommodate all the data. These figures indicate that with *a careful choice of file layouts,* huge savings can be obtained in the number of I/O calls issued in an application.

More importantly, file layout transformations, in most cases, do not get affected by data dependences; because they do not change the access order, they just rename the data points (array elements). This gives the file layout transformations a capability to optimize some loop nests where iteration space based optimization techniques fail due to existing data dependences.

We note that what we have done for this nest is *tiling*, a well-known transformation technique [7]. However, instead of tiling the iteration space first and then focusing on the data requirements of individual tiles, we first tile the data space and then execute all the iterations that assign new values

```
DO i = 2, n                        DO j = 2, n
  DO j = 2, n                        DO i = 2, n
    A(i,j) = A(i-1,j) + A(i,j-1)       A(i,j) = A(i-1,j) + A(i,j-1)
  END DO                             END DO
END DO                             END DO
```

              (a)   (b)

Fig. 1. (a) Original program. (b) Transformed program. [The transformed program exhibits good spatial locality for column-major memory layout].

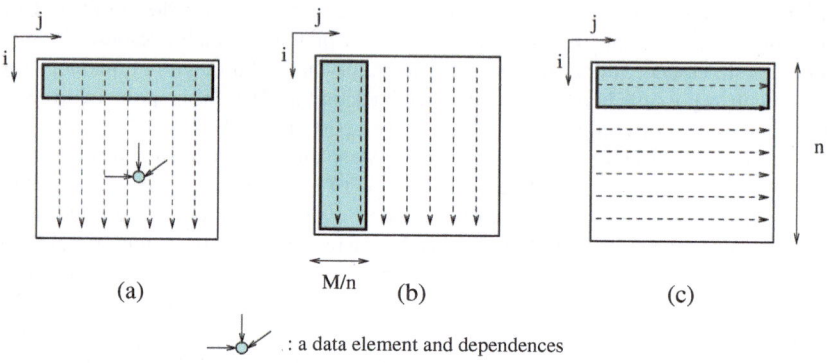

              (a)   M/n   (b)   (c)

: a data element and dependences

Fig. 2. Different memory layouts of the array accessed in Figure 1. [The shaded block in each figure denotes a data tile (chunk). The dashed arrows indicate the storage order of the array. Except near the boundaries, each data element is dependent on three others. An example data element and its dependences are also shown].

to the elements of the tile currently stored in memory. Our file layout transformation allows us to read an $(M/n) \times n$ data tile by issuing just M/n I/O calls. In this example, a simple column-major to row-major layout conversion (i.e., a dimension permutation) is sufficient to optimize the layout. In general, a compiler may have to deal with more complex data layouts. In the next section, we focus on detecting optimal file layouts automatically by using a simple linear algebra techniques using hyperplanes.

3   Layout Restructuring Framework

In this section, we outline a method using which an optimizing compiler can restructure array layouts. The method was originally developed for in-core computations to determine memory layouts for optimal cache performance; but with appropriate modifications it can be adapted for out-of-core programs. In the out-of-core computation domain, this approach reduces the number of I/O calls as well as the volume of data transferred between disk and memory. The details of the approach can be found in [4]. In order to keep the presentation simple, we focus only on two-dimensional out-of-core arrays. However, our method works with arrays of any dimensionality.

3.1   Preliminaries

We focus on programs where array subscript expressions and loop bounds are affine functions of enclosing loop indices or constants. Under this assumption, each array reference to an m-dimensional array that occurs in a k-deep loop nest can be represented by $L\bar{I} + \bar{o}$, where the access (or reference) matrix L is of size $m \times k$ and the offset vector $\bar{o}$ is of size m. For example, the reference A(i-1,j) in Figure 1(a) can be represented by $L\bar{I} + \bar{o}$, where

$$L = \begin{pmatrix} 1 & 0 \\ 0 & 1 \end{pmatrix}, \bar{I} = \begin{pmatrix} i \\ j \end{pmatrix}, \bar{o} = \begin{pmatrix} -1 \\ 0 \end{pmatrix}$$

Notice that access pattern in the innermost loop is captured by the last column of L.

3.2   Hyperplanes and File Layouts

In an m-dimensional data space, a *hyperplane* can be defined as a set of tuples

$$\{(a_1, a_2, ..., a_m) \mid g_1 a_1 + g_2 a_2 + ... + g_m a_m = c\}$$

where $g_1, g_2, ..., g_m$ are rational numbers called hyperplane coefficients and c is a rational number called hyperplane constant [6]. For convenience, we use a row vector $g^T = (g_1, g_2, ..., g_n)$ to denote an hyperplane family (for different values of c) whereas $\bar{g}$ corresponds to the column vector representation of the same hyperplane family. At least one of the hyperplane coefficients should be non-zero.

In a two-dimensional data space, the hyperplanes are defined by (g_1, g_2). We can think of a hyperplane family as parallel lines for a fixed coefficient set and different values of c. An important property of the hyperplanes is that two data points (array elements) (a, b) and (c, d) belong to the same hyperplane if

$$(g_1, g_2) \begin{pmatrix} a \\ b \end{pmatrix} = (g_1, g_2) \begin{pmatrix} c \\ d \end{pmatrix} \tag{1}$$

For example, $(g_1, g_2) = (0, 1)$ indicates that two elements belong to the same hyperplane as long as they have the same value for the column index (i.e., the second dimension); the value for the row index does not matter.

It is important to note that a hyperplane family can be used to partially define the file layout of an out-of-core array. In a two-dimensional case $(0, 1)$ is sufficient to indicate that the elements in a column of the array (i.e., the elements in a hyperplane with a specific c value) will be stored *consecutively* in file and will have *spatial locality*. The relative order of these columns are not important provided the array is large enough compared to the memory size which is the case in out-of-core computations. Similarly, the hyperplane vectors $(1, 0)$ and $(1, -1)$ correspond to row-major and diagonal file layouts, respectively.

3.3   Determining Optimal File Layouts

The following claim gives us a simple method to determine optimal file layout for a given reference to have spatial locality in the innermost loop (see [4] for the proof).

Claim. Consider a reference $L\bar{I} + \bar{o}$ to a two-dimensional array inside a loop nest of depth k where

$$L = \begin{pmatrix} a_{11} & a_{12} & \cdots & a_{1k} \\ a_{21} & a_{22} & \cdots & a_{2k} \end{pmatrix}$$

In order to have spatial locality in the innermost loop, this array should have a layout represented by a hyperplane (g_1, g_2) such that $(g_1, g_2) \in Ker\{(a_{1k}, a_{2k})^T\}$.

Returning to our example in Figure 1(a), using this result, we have $(g_1, g_2) \in Ker\{(0, 1)^T\}$ which means $(g_1, g_2) = (1, 0)$ is the spanning vector for that Ker set (null set). This vector corresponds to the row-major layout; therefore, in order to have spatial locality in the innermost loop, the array should have a row-major file layout

4   Preliminary Results

In this section, we present performance results for three example programs: an out-of-core matrix transpose nest, an out-of-core matrix multiplication nest, and the Fast Fourier Transform (FFT). For each case, we report the I/O times on an Intel Paragon message-passing machine. The machine that we used had 56 compute nodes, 3 service nodes, and one HIPPI node. Each compute node is an Intel i860 XP microprocessor with 32 MBytes of memory.

Matrix transpose: Figure 4(a) shows the I/O times for an out-of-core matrix transpose nest which transposes an out-of-core array into another. Each array is of size 2048×2048 double elements and only 256 KBytes of the memory of each compute node is used. Note that this small amount of memory makes the problem out-of-core. We conducted experiments with 4, 8, and 16 processors. The results show that optimizing file layouts can lead to huge savings in I/O times. The super-linear speedups in this case are due to memory effects.

Matrix multiplication: Figure 4(b) shows the I/O times for an out-of-core matrix multiplication routine that computes C = A $\times$ B, where A, B, and C are 2048×2048 out-of-core matrices. The results here are not as impressive as those of the matrix-transpose example. The reason is that due to the access pattern of the loop nest, only two of the three arrays could be layout-optimized. The improvements are between 6% and 26%.

FFT: The fast Fourier Transform (FFT) is widely used in several scientific and engineering problems. The 2-D out-of-core FFT consists of three steps: (1) 1-D out-of-core FFT, (2) 2-D out-of-core transpose, and (3) 1-D out-of-core FFT. The 1-D FFT steps consist of reading data from a two-dimensional out-of-core array and applying 1-D FFT on each of the columns. Of course, in order to perform 1-D out-of-core FFTs the data on disk should be strip-mined into processors memory. After this, the processed columns are written to the file. In the transpose step, the out-of-core array is staged into memory, transposed and written to file. The innermost loop of the transpose routine uses two files that are accessed by all processors. In the original program, file layout for these two arrays is column-major. The transpose is performed by reading a rectangular data tile from one of the files, transposing it in the local memory, and writing it in the other file. Since both the files are column-major, optimizing the block dimension for one array has a negative impact on I/O performance of the other array, resulting in the poor I/O performance observed in Figure 5(a) and the poor overall performance shown in Figure 5(b) (for 2048×2048 double arrays). If we store one of the arrays in row-major order the I/O performance of both the arrays improve. This is evident from Figures 5(a) and (b).

5   Related Work

Due to lack of space, we discuss related work on compilation of dense matrix codes which access out-of-core arrays. Brezany et al. [1] perform I/O optimizations in out-of-core compilation in a compilation framework with a runtime system called VIPIOS. The user provides hints for the I/O

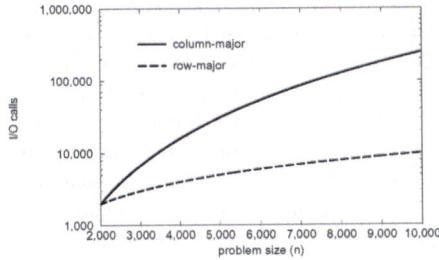
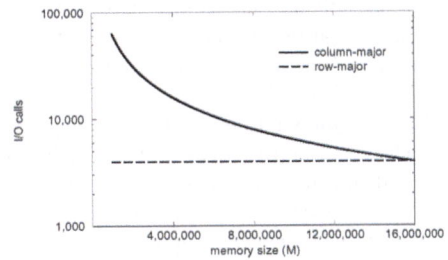

Fig. 3. The number of I/O calls in example shown in Figure 1 as a function of the input size (left) and the memory size (right).

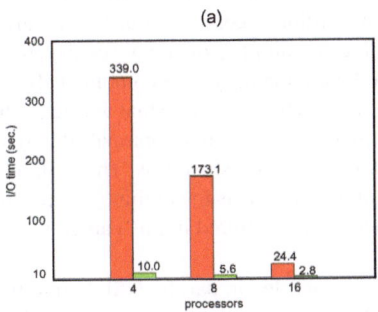
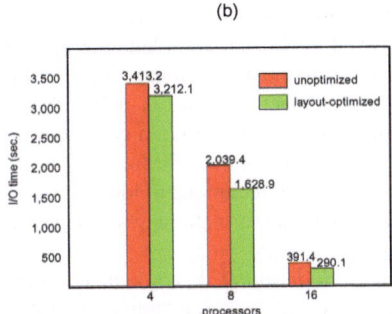

Fig. 4. I/O times (in seconds) on Intel Paragon for (a) matrix transpose and (b) matrix multiplication.

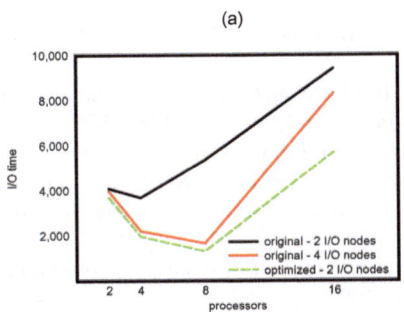
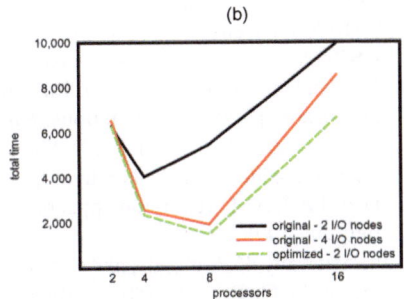

Fig. 5. Performance of the FFT on Intel Paragon (all times are in seconds).

modes, I/O distribution etc., using the language constructs. Paleczny et al.[5] incorporate out-of-core compilation techniques with Fortran D. The main philosophy behind their approach is to choreograph I/O from disks along with the corresponding computation. Their idea, however, is based on computation re-ordering, and therefore is different from ours. Cormen and Colvin [2] introduce ViC* (Virtual C*), a preprocessor which transforms a C* program that uses out-of-core data structures into a program with appropriate library calls from the ViC* library in order to read/write data from/to disks. Finally, the previous work of the authors [3] considered unified loop and file layout transformations. However, the search space for possible file layout transformations was restricted to the dimension-wise transformations (e.g., from column-major to row-major). As against to that work, the approach presented in this paper uses a more powerful technique based on hyperplanes.

6   Summary and Ongoing Work

In this paper, we have presented an approach that can optimize file layouts of multi-dimensional out-of-core arrays. The approach can work with a large set of layouts which can be expressed using hyperplanes. In practice, the technique can optimize affine accesses to out-of-core arrays in two different yet complementary ways: (1) by reducing the number of file accesses, and (2) by reducing the data volume transferred between disk and main memory. The combined effect of these is a reduction in I/O as well as the overall execution time. The main issue that we are dealing with currently is to design a conflict resolution scheme that can decide near-optimal file layouts in cases where an out-of-core array is accessed with conflicting access patterns. This will allow us to apply our technique to longer programs. Another important issue is to combine computation reordering transformations with the layout optimization technique offered in this paper.

Acknowledgments A. Choudhary and M. Kandemir are supported in part by NSF Young Investigator Award CCR-9357840 and NSF CCR-9509143. J. Ramanujam is supported in part by an NSF Young Investigator Award CCR-9457768 and by an NSF grant CCR-9210422.

References

1. P. Brezany, T. Muck, and E. Schikuta. Language, compiler and parallel database support for I/O intensive applications, In *Proc. HPCN 95,* May 1995.
2. T.H. Cormen, and A. Colvin. ViC*: A preprocessor for virtual memory C*. Dartmouth College CS Tech. Rep. PCS-TR94-243, Nov. 1994.
3. M. Kandemir, A. Choudhary, J. Ramanujam, and R. Bordawekar. Compilation techniques for out-of-core parallel computations. *Parallel Computing,* 24(3-4):597–628, June 1998.
4. M. Kandemir, A. Choudhary, N. Shenoy, P. Banerjee, and J. Ramanujam. A data layout optimization technique based on hyperplanes. Tech. Rep. CPDC-TR-97-04, Northwestern Univ., Dec. 1997. A short version appears in *Proc. ACM International Conference on Supercomputing,* Jul. 1998.
5. M. Paleczny, K. Kennedy, and C. Koelbel. Compiler support for out-of-core arrays on parallel machines. CRPC TR 94509-S, Rice University, Dec. 1994.
6. J. Ramanujam, and P. Sadayappan. Compile-time techniques for data distribution in distributed memory machines. In *IEEE Trans. Par. & Dist. Sys.,* 2(4):472–482, Oct. 1991.
7. M. Wolfe. *High Performance Compilers for Parallel Computing,* Addison-Wesley, 1996.

Optimizing Computational and Spatial Overheads in Complex Transformed Loops

Dattatraya Kulkarni[1] and Michael Stumm[2]

[1] IBM Toronto Laboratory, Toronto, CANADA M3C 1V7
dkulki@vnet.ibm.com
[2] Department of Electrical and Computer Engineering, University of Toronto, Toronto,
CANADA M5S 3G4
stumm@eecg.toronto.edu

Abstract. In this paper, we stress the need for aggressive loop transformation techniques, such as CDA (Computation Decomposition and Alignment), that have improved ability to optimize nested loops. Unfortunately, these types of aggressive techniques may also generate complex nested loops with relatively higher overheads. In this paper, we demonstrate that the computational and spatial overhead in complex transformed loops can be effectively reduced, often by simple techniques.

1 Introduction

Techniques for linearly transforming nested loops have matured immensely during the past several years [1,5,8,9,11] to the point where today's production compilers can transform arbitrary perfect loop nests with affine references to arrays and pointer structures that have a single level of indirection [4]. However, we believe that more aggressive techniques are necessary in order to exploit the performance of uniprocessor and multiprocessor systems to the fullest degree possible. The need for more aggressive transformation techniques is even more critical when considering the forthcoming processors with over 1GHz clock frequency. On these processors, the miss penalties for memory references will be large enough to warrant program transformations that improve locality of reference at the cost of a higher computational and spatial overhead in the transformed code. In fact, these processors may well require a new family of optimizations, capable of hiding the multiple cycle latency to access cache memory.

Several groups have been involved in research exploring extensions to the linear loop transformation framework [2,3,6,10]. The extended frameworks are considerably more aggressive and more powerful than the linear loop transformation framework, because the transformations in the new frameworks can alter not only the *execution order* of the iterations, but also the *composition* of the new iterations [7]. In particular, they *i*) examine computation structures in loops at much finer granularity, *ii*) explore transformation spaces left unexplored by linear loop transformations, and *iii*) consider loops that are not perfectly nested.

One undesirable side effect of improved transformation capability is increased code complexity of the transformed loops. The transformed loops may have complex loop

D. O'Hallaron (Ed.): LCR'98, LNCS 1511, pp. 367–377, 1998.
© Springer-Verlag Berlin Heidelberg 1998

control structures and higher computational and spatial overhead when compared to linearly transformed loops. The overhead in linearly transformed loop nests tends to be small relative to the execution time of the original loop. Therefore, it has sufficed for the compilers to use only traditional optimization techniques to minimize the overhead of linearly transformed loops. In the extended frameworks, however, the overhead created is much more significant, requiring techniques to reduce the overhead as much as possible. In this paper we demonstrate that simple techniques exist that can substantially reduce the overhead in complex transformed loops.

2   CDA: A Representative Extended Transformation Framework

Computation Decomposition and Alignment (CDA) is a representative example of a framework that extends the linear loop transformation framework [3,7]. We use it here to illustrate our techniques and thus briefly describe it first in this section.

A CDA transformation consists of two stages. In the first stage, *Computation Decomposition* decomposes the loop body initially into its individual statements, and then optionally the individual statements into statements of finer granularity. A statement is decomposed by rewriting it as a sequence of smaller statements that produce the same result as the original statement. In doing so, it is necessary to introduce temporary variables to pass intermediate results between the new statements. For example, the statement $a = b + c + d + e$ can be partitioned into $t = d + e$ and $a = b + c + t$, where t is a temporary variable used to pass the result of the first statement to the second. A statement can be decomposed multiple times into possibly many statements. The choice of which sub-expressions to elevate to the status of statements is a key decision in CDA optimization and is determined largely by the specific optimization objective being pursued.

A sequence of decompositions produces a new loop body that can have more statements than the original, but the loop references and loop bounds remain unchanged. For each new statement S, there is a *computation space*, $CS(S)$, which is an integer space that represents all execution instances of statement S in the loop.

In the second stage of CDA, *Computation Alignment* applies a separate linear transformation to each of the computation spaces. The set of all transformed computation spaces together defines the new iteration space. Unlike the original iteration space, the new iteration space may be non-convex, so the corresponding new loop may have complex bounds.

Figure 1 illustrates the application of a simple CDA transformation. Computation decomposition first splits the loop body into two statements S_1 and S_2. Statement S_1 is further decomposed into two smaller statements $S_{1.1}$ and $S_{1.2}$, using a temporary array t to pass the result of $S_{1.1}$ to $S_{1.2}$. The result is a loop with 3 statements in the body:

$$S_{1.1} : t(i,j) = A(i-1,j) + A(i-1,j-1) + B(i-1,j)$$
$$S_{1.2} : A(i,j) = t(i,j) + B(i,j+1) + A(i,j-1)$$
$$S_2 : B(i,j-1) = A(i,j-1) + B(i,j)$$

This computation decomposition effectively partitions the iteration space into three computation spaces, namely $CS(S_{1.1}), CS(S_{1.2})$ and $CS(S_2)$. The particular decomposition for S_1 was chosen so that it separates all $(i-1,*)$ references into a new statement, $S_{1.1}$.

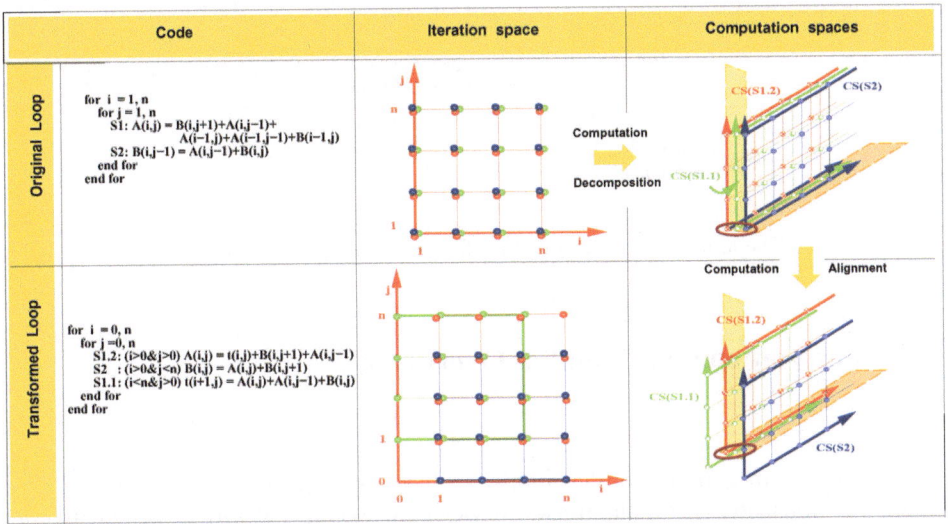

Fig. 1. Application of a simple CDA transformation.

This will allow a subsequent transformation to modify the $(i-1, *)$ references into $(i, *)$ references, without affecting the other references in S_1 that are now in $S_{1.2}$.

The three computation spaces are computationally aligned by applying transformations

$$T_{1.1} = \begin{bmatrix} 1 & 0 & -1 \\ 0 & 1 & 0 \\ 0 & 0 & 1 \end{bmatrix} \quad T_{1.2} = \begin{bmatrix} 1 & 0 & 0 \\ 0 & 1 & 0 \\ 0 & 0 & 1 \end{bmatrix} \text{ and } T_2 = \begin{bmatrix} 1 & 0 & 0 \\ 0 & 1 & -1 \\ 0 & 0 & 1 \end{bmatrix}$$

to $CS(S_{1.1})$, $CS(S_{1.2})$ and $CS(S_2)$, respectively. As a result, computation spaces $CS(S_{1.1})$ and $CS(S_2)$ move relative to $CS(S_{1.2})$, since $T_{1.2}$ is the identity matrix. $CS(S_{1.1})$ moves one stride in direction i so that the $(i-1, *)$ references in $S_{1.1}$ change to $(i, *)$ references. $CS(S_2)$ moves one stride in direction j so that the $B(i, j-1)$ reference changes to $B(i, j)$. The transformations thus align the computation spaces so that most references are aligned to $A(i, j)$. Figure 1 shows the transformed computation spaces and highlights three computations that are now executed in one iteration. The new iteration space is defined by the projection of the transformed computation spaces onto a plane. Iteration (i, j) in the new iteration space now has new, different instances of $S_{1.2}$, S_2 and $S_{1.1}$ computations, namely those that were originally in iterations (i, j), $(i, j+1)$ and $(i+1, j)$, respectively. The new iteration space is non-convex, and the limits of the new, transformed loop correspond to the convex hull of this new iteration space. An iteration now no longer necessarily entails the execution of all three statements. The transformed loop thus requires guards that allow a statement to be executed only if appropriate.

$$for \ \ i = 0, n$$
$$\quad for \ \ j = 0, n$$
$$\qquad U(i,j) = c(0) * U(i,j)$$
$$\qquad R(i,j) = c(0) * R(i,j)$$
$$\quad end \ for$$
$$end \ for$$

Fig. 2. The loop used to illustrate the effect of techniques to reduce overheads.

3   Computational and Spatial Overheads

The overheads in complex nested loops, such as those generated by applying CDA transformations, are: i) computational overhead due to empty iterations and guard computations, and ii) spatial overhead for storing temporary variables. In this paper, we briefly outline techniques to reduce both types of overheads. We illustrate the generated overheads and the effectiveness of the techniques to reduce them on the nested loops that result from applying two different CDA transformations on the loop of Figure 2. The loop is deliberately chosen to be simple so that the transformed loops demonstrate only the overheads and none of the benefits.

The transformed iteration space for the first transformation is shown on the left hand side of Figure 3, where one of the computation spaces is applied an offset alignment of (k, k), where k is a positive integer. The left hand side of Figure 4 shows the transformed iteration space for the second transformation, where one of the computation spaces is skewed with respect to the other. We will refer to the CDA transformed loops as *Loop 1* and *Loop 2*, respectively.

The overhead for these two loops was measured on a Sun workstation with hyper-SPARC CPU, and is shown in Figure 3. For the purpose of the experiments, the loop size n was set to 1000 and k was set to 5, unless otherwise specified. The overhead of *Loop 1* with the loop bounds generated by a simplistic algorithm that generates the subsumption of the union of computation spaces is shown as the first five bars on the right hand side of Figure 3. The overhead increases slightly with large k's, due to increasing number of empty iterations and guard computations. For $k = 5$, the overhead is about 22% of the execution time of the original loop. The last five bars on the right hand side of Figure 3 correspond to *Loop 1* optimized using the techniques outlined in the following sections; the overhead is then less than 0.1% of the original loop.

The overheads can also be reduced significantly when the alignments are more general than offsets. The overhead of *Loop 2* with the bounds generated by the simplistic algorithm mentioned above is shown as the first bar on the right hand side of Figure 4. The overhead can be much higher than when using offset alignments (nearly 78% of the original loop in this case), since nearly one quarter of the iterations are empty. However, the overhead is reduced to about 5% of the original loop when *Loop 2* is optimized by removing empty iterations and guards, using the techniques outlined next.

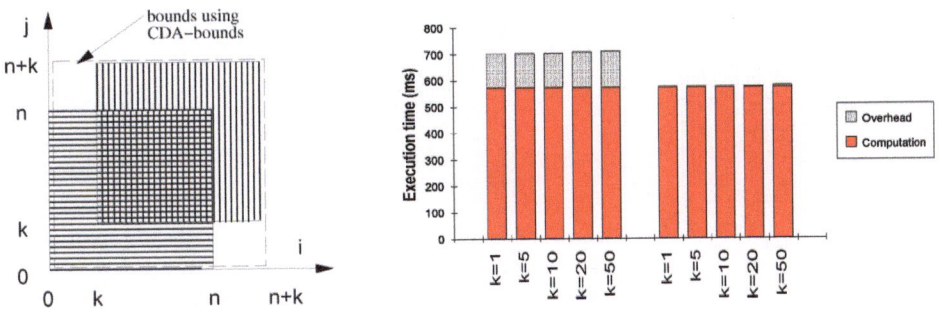

Fig. 3. Overheads in a CDA transformed loop with offset alignments (k, k). The bars on the left correspond to the execution times of *Loop 1* with overheads, whereas the bars on the right correspond to the execution times of *Loop 1* after reducing overheads with the techniques described in this paper.

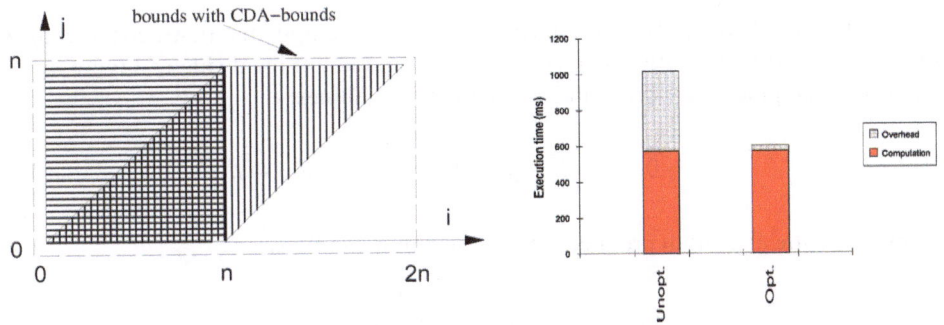

Fig. 4. Overheads in *Loop 2*, CDA-transformed with a linear alignment.

4   Removing Empty Iterations

The iteration space of a CDA transformed loop is the union of the transformed computation spaces projected onto an integer space (which we refer to as the union of computation spaces for conciseness). It is desirable to derive tight loop bounds so that a CDA transformed loop scans integer points in the smallest convex polytope containing the union of computation spaces. With tighter loop bounds, the overhead of empty iterations and the guard computations they contain is reduced.

While deriving tight loop bounds, it is desirable to keep the CDA transformed loop perfectly nested, because it may be necessary to apply other loop transformations in later stages, and most transformations require that the loop be perfectly nested. In order to obtain a perfectly nested CDA transformed loop, the polytope that the loop scans must be convex.[3] Our algorithm removes empty iterations by finding the convex-hull of the union of computation spaces. When the union is a convex polytope itself, then

---

[3] Only in some cases do non-convex polytopes correspond to perfect nestings.

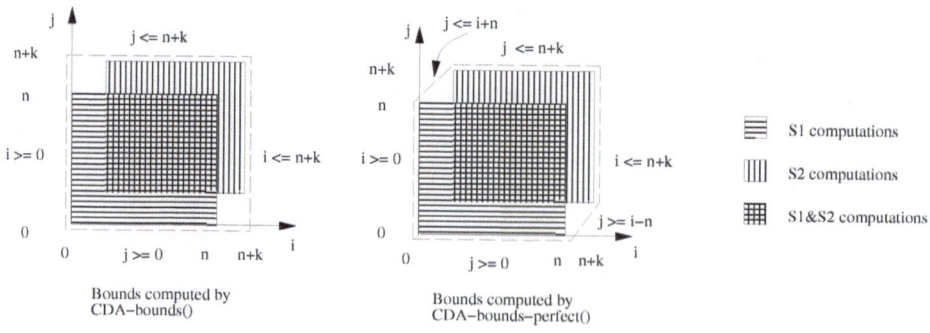

Fig. 5. Empty iterations in an iteration space with tight bounds.

the derived loop bounds are exact in that the transformed loop does not have any empty iterations.

As an example of applying our technique to reduce empty iterations, consider again the transformed computation spaces for *Loop 2* on the left hand side of Figure 4. The algorithm computes the convex-hull as defined by the lines:

$$i = 0, \quad i = 2n, \quad j = 0, \quad j = n, \quad j = i - n$$

from which the algorithm produces the following inequalities:

$$i \geq 0, \quad i \leq 2n, \quad j \geq 0, \quad j \leq n, \quad j \geq i - n$$

After variable elimination, these inequalities provide the loop bounds,

$$0 \leq i \leq 2n, \quad max(0, i - n) \leq j \leq n$$

These inequalities bound the shaded area in the figure. The loop bounds are exact in this case, since the union is a convex polygon, so it no longer includes empty iterations.

In some cases, the bounds derived using our algorithm may not remove all empty iterations. Consider the union of the computation spaces of *Loop 1* depicted on the left hand side of Figure 3, where the union is a non-convex polygon. The dotted lines on the left hand side of Figure 5 show the loop bounds that are derived by the simplistic algorithm. The dotted lines at the center of the figure show the bounds obtained by our algorithm.

Figure 6 compares the overhead of the unoptimized *Loops 1* and *2* with the overhead of the optimized loops, where the bounds are derived using our algorithm. The reduction in the overhead of *Loop 1* (of Figure 3) is not significant, since it contains only a small number of empty iterations. The application of our algorithm to *Loop 2* (of Figure 4) reduces the overhead by about 45%, since nearly one quarter of its iterations were empty.

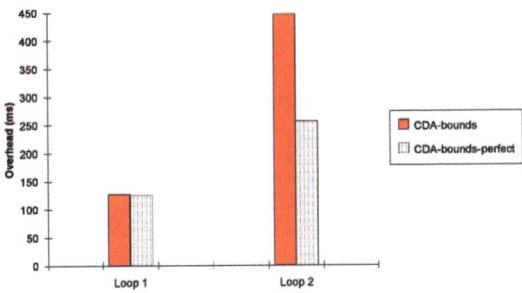

Fig. 6. Performance benefits of eliminating empty iterations.

5   Reducing the Overhead of Guard Computations

Guards are often necessary in CDA transformed loops, both to step off empty iterations and to prevent inappropriate computations from executing in the new iterations. Guards may incur considerable run-time overhead, but in many cases it is possible to remove them. Here, we outline a relatively simple technique that incrementally removes guards from selected regions of the union of computation spaces; however it results in non-perfectly nested loop nests. It is targeted primarily towards CDA transformations, where the intersection of the computation spaces makes up a large portion of the union of the computation spaces. We illustrate the technique with an example, namely the transformed iteration space on the left of Figure 7. The CDA transformations in the figure are such that the computation space of statement S_2 is moved up by k in the I_2 direction with respect to the computation space of statement S_1, and the computation space of statement S_3 is moved right by k in the I_1 direction with respect to the computation space of statement S_1. We refer to the CDA transformed loop corresponding to this iteration space as *Loop 3*. Our algorithm removes guards using the following steps:

1. The bounds of the intersection of the computation spaces are derived. For instance, the shaded area in Figure 7 is the intersection of the three computation spaces. The iterations in the intersection require the execution of all three statements S_1, S_2 and S_3. Therefore, if we partition the new iteration space to separate out the intersection, the code generated for the iterations in the intersection does not require any guards.
2. The iteration space is partitioned along the first dimension I_1 so as to delineate the intersection in that dimension. In our example, the CDA transformed iteration space of Figure 7 is divided into three partitions, namely, L_1, L_2 and L_3, based on the fact that the I_1 bounds for the intersection are k and n. Partition L_1 has iterations with I_1 values between 0 and $k-1$; partition L_2 has iterations with I_1 values between k and n, (the two I_1 bounds for the intersection); and partition L_3 has iterations with the I_1 values between $n+1$ and $n+k$.
3. Code is generated for partition L_2. This code consists of a sequence of subnests. The first subnest includes those iterations with I_2 values that do not belong to the intersection, thus requiring guards. The second subnest includes the iterations that

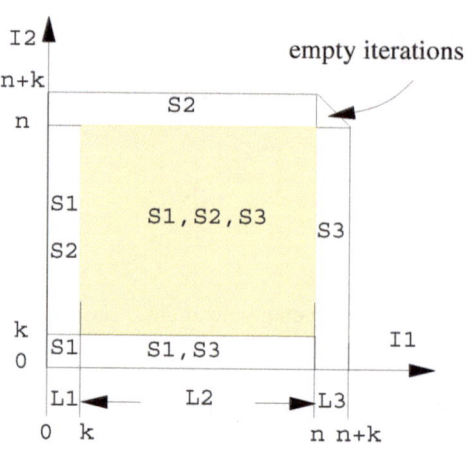

```
// Code for L1
  ...

// code for L2

for I1 = k, n
  for I2 = 0, k-1
    g(S1)   S1:
    g(S2)   S2:
    g(S3)   S3:
  end for
  for I2 = k, n
            S1:
            S2:
            S3:
  end for
  for I2 = n+1, n+k
    g(S1)   S1:
    g(S2)   S2:
    g(S3)   S3:
  end for
end for

// code for L3
  ...
```

Fig. 7. Transformed computations spaces to illustrate steps in algorithm to remove guards. The transformed loop corresponding to the transformed computation spaces is called *Loop 3*.

belong to the intersection. This code constitutes most of the iterations of the loop that need to be executed and require no guards. The final subnest includes those iterations with I_2 values higher than those of the intersection, thus requiring guards again. The three subnests for our example are shown on the right hand side of Figure 7. Note that the subnest corresponding to the intersection does not have any guard computations.

4. The algorithm is applied recursively to remove guards from partitions L_1 and L_3. The iterations in these partitions contain only a subset of the statements of the original loop body. Thus, only a subset of the computation spaces participate in the intersections of these partitions. Recursive application of the algorithm to partition L_1, does not partition it further along I_1, since the intersection of computation spaces for S_1 and S_2 spans the entire I_1 bounds of L_1. The intersection in L_1 has I_2 bounds of k and n, and guards can be similarly removed from L_1.

The result of applying the guard removal algorithm is thus a sequence of loop nests, which typically are imperfectly nested. The right hand side of Figure 7 shows a template of the code generated for the transformed computation spaces on the left hand side.

Figure 8 shows the effectiveness of the guard removal algorithm. The dark bars correspond to the overhead of CDA transformed code with guards, where the algorithm to remove empty iterations was applied to remove as many empty iterations as possible. The grey bars correspond to code for which the guard removal algorithm was applied. The figure shows that additional removal of guards can reduce the overhead substantially, when the loops are transformed by offset alignments. The reduction in overhead for *Loop 2* was not as large as for *Loops 1* and *3*, since the code for *Loop 2* continues to have

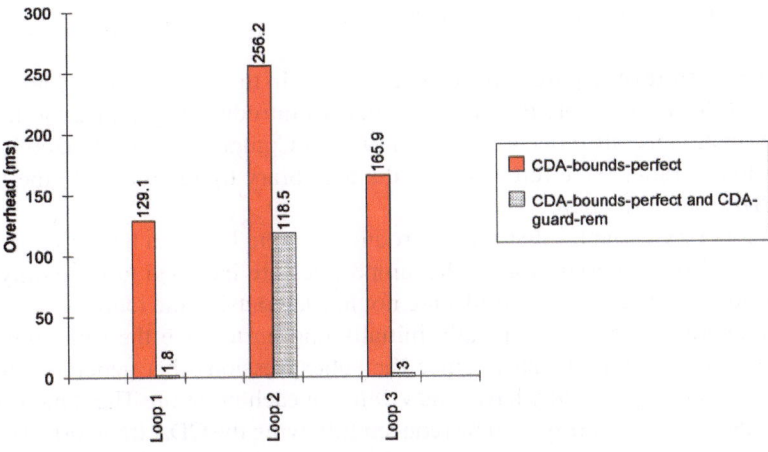

Fig. 8. Performance benefits of removing guards.

guards in nearly one quarter of the iterations, but the benefits of applying the guard removal algorithm is still significant.[4]

6 Optimization of Spatial Overhead for Temporaries

The temporary variables introduced during Computation Decomposition may increase the number of references to memory and may add to space requirements and the cache footprint. A number of optimizations can reduce some of these overheads.

– Temporaries needed in a loop may be replaced by dead variables, which are not used in the later flow of the program.
– While decomposing a statement, it is possible to eliminate the need for temporary variables altogether by using the lhs array elements to store the intermediate results. Such a replacement is legal if the dependence relations remain legal. Even though a Computation Decomposition does not modify dependences, eliminating the temporary variable this way can modify dependences. For example, it is legal to replace $t(i,j)$ by $a(i,j)$ in the following decomposition,

$$a(i,j) = a(i,j) + a(i-1,j) + a(i,j-1) \quad \Rightarrow \quad \begin{array}{l} a(i,j) \\ \cancel{t(i,j)} = a(i,j) + a(i-1,j) \\ a(i,j) \\ a(i,j) = \cancel{t(i,j)} + a(i,j-1) \end{array}$$

However, such a replacement would be illegal in the following decomposition, because $a(i,j)$ would be modified before it is used in the second statement so the temporary variable needs to be retained.

[4] These iterations correspond to the region bounded by $0 \leq i \leq n$ and $i+1 \leq j \leq n$ on the left of Figure 4.

$$a(i,j) = a(i,j) + a(i-1,j) + a(i,j-1) \quad \begin{aligned} t(i,j) &= a(i-1,j) + a(i,j-1) \\ \Rightarrow a(i,j) &= t(i,j) + a(i,j) \end{aligned}$$

Hence, storage requirements can be reduced in this way for only some decompositions. Moreover, note that the dependences introduced by replacing the temporary variable can constrain later opportunities for Computation Alignment. It is therefore better to replace the references to the temporary by references to the lhs after the CDA transformation.

- Temporary variables that were introduced in one loop can be reused in subsequent loops. This is possible since the temporaries are intended to store only the results inside a loop, and these results are not needed outside the loop.
- Temporary arrays are typically initially chosen to have the same dimension and size as the iteration space, since the subexpressions that generate values for the temporaries potentially have a new value in each iteration. The dimension and size of the temporary arrays can be reduced following the CDA transformation. It is only necessary to have as many storage locations as there are iterations between when the temporary is defined and when it is used. For simple offset alignments, the size of the temporary arrays can be just a fraction of the size of the iteration space. For example, consider the decomposition of a statement S in a two dimensional loop into statements S_1 and S_2. The results of S_1 are stored in a temporary array t. When statement S_1 is aligned to statement S_2 along the outer loop level by an offset c, then t need only be of size $c \times n$, assuming n iterations in the inner loop.

7   Concluding Remarks

In this paper, we observed the need for aggressive transformation techniques that have improved ability to optimize nested loops, but that may also generate complex nested loops with attendant overhead. We demonstrated that the computational and spatial overhead in these complex transformed loops can be effectively reduced, often by simple techniques. We believe that with the reduction in overhead achieved using the techniques we have described, complex loop transformations become suitable for integration into production compilers.

References

1. Banerjee, U. (1990) Unimodular transformations of double loops. In *Proceedings of Third Workshop on Programming Languages and Compilers for Parallel Computing*, Irvine, CA, August 1990.
2. Kelly, W. and Pugh, W. (1992) A framework for unifying reordering transformations. Technical Report UMIACS-TR-92-126, University of Maryland, 1992.
3. Kulkarni, D. (1997) CDA: Computation Decomposition and Alignment. PhD thesis, Department of Computer Science, University of Toronto, 1997.
4. Kulkarni, D. et al. (1997) XL Fortran Compiler for IBM SMP Systems. *AIXpert Magazine*, December 1997.
5. Kulkarni, D., Kumar, K.G., Basu, A., and Paulraj, A. (1991) Loop partitioning for distributed memory multiprocessors as unimodular transformations. In *Proceedings of the 1991 ACM International Conference on Supercomputing*, Cologne, Germany, June 1991.

6. Kulkarni, D. and Stumm, M. (1995) CDA loop transformations. In *Chapter 3, Languages, compilers and run-time systems for scalable computers, B.K. Szymanski and B. Sinharoy (eds)*, pages 29–42, Boston, May 1995. Kluwer Academic Publishers.

7. Kulkarni, D. and Stumm, M. (1997) Linear and Extended Linear Transformations for Shared Memory Multiprocessors. *The Computer Journal*, 40(6), pp. 373-387, December 1997.

8. Kumar, K.G., Kulkarni, D., and Basu, A. (1992) Deriving good transformations for mapping nested loops on hierarchical parallel machines in polynomial time. In *Proceedings of the 1992 ACM International Conference on Supercomputing*, Washington, July 1992.

9. Li, W. and Pingali, K. (1994) A singular loop transformation framework based on non-singular matrice. *International Journal of Parallel Programming*, 22(2), 1994.

10. Torres, J. and Ayguade, E. (1993) Partitioning the statement per iteration space using non-singular matrices. In *Proceedings of 1993 International Conference on Supercomputing, Tokyo, Japan, July 1993.*, 1993.

11. Wolf, M and Lam, M. (1991) A loop transformation theory and an algorithm to maximize parallelism. *IEEE Trans. Parallel Distributed Systems*, 2(4):452–471, 1991.

Building a Conservative Parallel Simulation with Existing Component Libraries

Chu-Cheow Lim and Yoke-Hean Low

Gintic Institute of Manufacturing Technology
71 Nanyang Drive, Singapore 638075, Singapore
Email: {cclim,yhlow}@gintic.gov.sg

Abstract. Our application is a parallel discrete event simulation of a wafer fabrication plant. When implementing such an application using a conservative protocol [2] on a shared-memory multiprocessor, an effective approach is for the programmer to use a general parallel runtime library, and implement optimizations specific to the simulation application. We initially evaluated four runtime libraries [9] and found Active Threads [3] to be most suitable and efficient for thread-creation and synchronization. But Active Threads' memory management does not scale well. We therefore added a different memory management library called Vmalloc [7] to provide a more efficient way to dynamically allocate and deallocate objects. For parallel application development, it is good news that there are public-domain research libraries which are both efficient and stable enough to build applications on shared-memory multiprocessor. The ability to use independent component libraries cannot be over-emphasized, and is very relevant to making parallel programming easier and more accessible to application programmers.

1. Introduction

The background of this work is from an ongoing collaborative project[*] between the Gintic Institute of Manufacturing Technology and the School of Applied Science in Nanyang Technological University, Singapore. The objective of our project is to study how parallel and distributed simulation techniques can be applied in a virtual factory simulation [8]. The simulations will be plant-wide, and include the modeling of manufacturing and business processes, and communications network. Such a simulation environment will allow one to model and analyze the effects of different system configurations and control policies on actual system performance. The initial focus is the electronics industry, because it is a major contributor to the manufacturing

---

[*] This research is supported by National Science and Technology Board, Singapore, under project: *Parallel And Distributed Simulation of Virtual Factory Implementation*. The project is currently located in the Centre for Advanced Information Systems, School of Applied Science, Nanyang Technological University, Singapore.

D. O'Hallaron (Ed.): LCR'98, LNCS 1511, pp. 378-385, 1998.

sector in Singapore. We therefore begin our study with a parallel discrete event simulation of a wafer fabrication plant (without considering the business process and communications aspect). We chose Active Threads [3] as the parallel runtime library from a comparison study of four runtime libraries [9] with a simplified model. We then proceeded to elaborate the model based on the Sematech datasets [11]. Each machine set in the model shares a common queue, and executes a realistic set of rules to decide which wafer-lot should be scheduled next. The program then requires efficient dynamic allocation and deallocation of objects. Because Active Threads' memory library calls do not scale well, we use a different memory management library called Vmalloc [7]. From the point of view of parallel application development, it is encouraging that there are efficient research libraries which can be used as independent and complementary components to build parallel applications on shared-memory multiprocessor.

The rest of the paper is organized as follows. Section 2 covers our application in more details, in particular the simulation protocol and simulation benchmark used. Section 3 summarizes our evaluation of four parallel runtime packages, and the selection of Active Threads. We also present the initial performance timings, and examine the memory allocation overheads. In Section 4, we describe how the Vmalloc library fits nicely as a component in our application and then new performance results are presented. We conclude our study and outline the future directions of our project in Section 5.

2. Parallel Discrete Event Simulation: Protocol and Model

In this paper, we adopted a parallel simulation protocol that executes in super-steps. The algorithm was modified from the one first proposed in [2]. It is a conservative algorithm because at each super-step, a logical process (LP) can only process the events that are safe to be simulated. We selected this algorithm in our initial experiments because it is simple to implement, compared to the optimistic protocols.

The algorithm is given in Figure 1. At each super-step, the events whose simulation time is smaller than the SafeTime are processed. In the original algorithm, the calculation of SafeTime, which is set to be the maximum of InClock and the global simulation time (GST), uses both local and global information. In the modified algorithm, if we let T_i be the minimum of the local time of those LP's which has a link to LP_i, the calculation of SafeTime for LP_i is set to be the maximum of GST and T_i. This is calculated at the beginning of a super-step. The assumption is that all the earlier messages already sent out by an LP is earlier or equal to its local time, and that all future messages will be later or equal to its local time. We are therefore guaranteed that in the current super-step, no further message earlier than SafeTime will be sent to LP_i.

In order to decide when to terminate the simulation, at each super-step's barrier synchronization, we calculate a GST value which is defined as the minimum of all queued events' time and the timestamp of all messages that have been sent but not yet received. Therefore, it is the smallest timestamp of any event in the whole system and so no event can be generated with a smaller timestamp than GST. The global reduction operation to calculate GST is done at the super-step barrier.

```
Initialize the links between LP's and each LP's state.

for all InternalEvent ie caused by InitialState do
   OrderInsert(ie@OccurrenceTime(ie), lp[i].event_q);  endfor
for all ExternalEvent ee by InitialState do
   OrderInsert(ee@lp[i].local_time, NewBuff[k,j])
       where ee is for LP k and LP i connected to jth input link of LP k;
endfor

while (GST <= endtime) do
  /* calculate SafeTime */
  SafeTime = infinity
  for each LP k, s.t. LP k has a directed link to LP i
       SafeTime = min (SafeTime, LP k's local time)       endfor
  SafeTime = max(GST, SafeTime)
  lp[i].out = infinity     /* To keep track of timestamp of generated events */

  /* simulate all safe events */
  while (FirstElementTime(lp[i].event_q) <= SafeTime) do

      /* dequeue an event and process it */
      e = RemoveFirstElem(lp[i].event_q);
      Set LP i's local time to TimeStamp(e);
      lp[i].state = Simulate(e);
      /* enqueue new internal events */
      for all InternalEvent ie caused by Simulate(e) do
           OrderInsert(ie@OccurenceTime(ie), lp[i].event_q);  endfor
      /* output external events */
      for all ExternalEvent ee caused by Simulate(e) do
           OrderInsert(ee@lp[i].local_time, NewBuff[k,j])
               where ee is for LP k and LP i connected to jth input link of LP k;
           lp[i].out = min(lp[i].out, TimeStamp(ee));
      endfor
  endwhile

  /* calculate smallest timestamp of any event in this LP */
  if (lp[i].event_q !=empty) then MinTime = FirstElementTime(lp[i].event_q);
  else MinTime = infinity;  endif
  MinTime = min(lp[i].out, MinTime);

  /* global reduction to calculate new GST, after all LP's synchronize at a barrier */
  GST = min_reduce(MinTime);
endwhile
```

Figure 1: Super-step parallel simulation algorithm

From the above discussion, it can be seen that our algorithm guarantees that there is no violation of causality. The major difference between our algorithm and other super-step based parallel simulation algorithms (e.g. YAWNS [10]), is the calculation of the SafeTime. In [10], only the global information (i.e., GST) is used to determine up to what simulation time the current super-step can simulate.

To show that deadlock cannot occur, we note that for each LP, we have SafeTime $\geq$ GST. Since GST is the smallest timestamp of any event in the whole system, at least those events with a timestamp equal to GST will be executed in the current super-step. In each super-step, there must be at least one event with a timestamp equal to GST, so the simulation will progress and deadlock will not occur.

2.1 Manufacturing Simulation Benchmark

Our simulation model of a manufacturing plant is built from the Sematech datasets. We have however made two major simplifications. The first is to remove the bottlenecks due to choice of protocol and inherent parallelism in the model because our main aim is to study the implementation overheads.

In the original dataset, each production route is specified by a sequence of processing steps. Different steps may share a machine set. When each machine set is treated as an LP, and consecutive steps from machine set k to machine set i corresponds to a directed link from LP k to LP i, the resulting graph of LP's has a complex structure. We therefore assume that the processing steps do not share any machine set, and each production route is now a simple pipeline.

The second simplification is that we only implement one type of machines – lot-processing machines. In wafer fabrication, the wafers move from one machine to the next in terms of lot's. Sematech specifies that there are machines which (a) process wafers within a lot individually, (b) process a wafer-lot as a whole, and (c) group multiple lot's into a batch for processing.

Even though we implement only lot-processing machines, we do incorporate the rules which simulationists normally associate with each machine set. The rules include: (a) a dispatching rule to decide how the waiting lot's (in the common queue for a machine set) are prioritized for scheduling, (b) a setup rule to decide if the setup of an available machine (within a set) is suitable for a waiting lot, or if the setup is to be changed, and (c) a time-out to prevent wafer-lot's from waiting indefinitely.

The simulation model has a generator which releases lot's into the production routes, as specified by the dataset, and a collector to gather all the completed lot's. We have an LP each for the generator and collector. Each production route is treated as a single LP. With such an arrangement, the original algorithm [2] would have taken a significant number of super-steps, but the modified algorithm only consists of three super-steps: generation of lots, independent processing for all production routes, and gathering of lots at the collector. Because the execution is now embarrassingly parallel, the program performance depends on the efficiency of the runtime systems.

3. Preliminary Implementation

We did a preliminary comparison of four runtime libraries [9]: POSIX threads [4], Active threads [3], Cilk [1], and Oxford BSP [6] which is an implementation of Bulk Synchronous Parallel (BSP) model. Our choices were determined mainly by our target platforms which are machines that support shared-address spaces, whether it be Non-Uniform Memory Access (NUMA) (e.g. SGI Origin 2000) or UMA (e.g. Sun Ultra2 Enterprise 3000).

Because multithreading is a common programming model on such platforms, three of our choices are thread-based libraries. They however offer different synchronization mechanisms and have different system performance. We included POSIX in our comparison, because it is an industry standard. Active threads has a similar interface to POSIX threads, and is especially targeted for fine-grain irregular parallel computations. Cilk has an efficient thread implementation, and a provably good scheduling and load balancing mechanism. While it is thread-based, its synchronization mechanism is unlike that for POSIX and Active threads. A Cilk parent thread only synchronizes with its children by waiting for their termination. Last but not least, we included Oxford BSP in our study, because it has a synchronous message-passing model, an alternative different from the other thread-based libraries.

We obtained our timings on a 4-CPU Ultra2 using models which were simpler than the benchmark in this paper. In general, the POSIX threads' overheads are still too high for fine-grain computation. The other three research libraries all show speedups on 4 processors, but to different extents. Cilk speedup curves improve with larger thread granularity, while Active threads' speedup is consistent across different thread granularity's. After considering the ease of programming and efficiency, we decided to use Active Threads as the runtime library.

We ran our updated benchmark application (Section 2.1) on a 4-CPU Sun Enterprise 3000 UltraSparc 2. A major difference between the original benchmark used in [9] and the current benchmark is that the latter incorporates the additional rules for each lot-processing machine, and there are now more intermediate calculations which allocates and frees objects dynamically.

The timings are shown in Table 1. We found that the parallel version on 1-CPU was actually faster than the sequential version, probably because the sequential version utilizes a global event list, while the events are distributed into smaller lists at different LP's in the parallel version. The parallel version ran slower on 4 processors than a single processor. We took a profile of the memory management calls in the benchmark. The results are shown in Table 2, with the turn-around time, and the total time spent on memory allocations (by all the threads). The turnaround time on 4 processors (in Table 2) is greater than the corresponding timings in Table 1, because of the additional overheads in calling *gethrtime()* in the profiling. The efficiency of a runtime's memory management was not a prominent factor during our preliminary study, because then the emphasis was on thread creation and synchronization overheads, and our model then had simple event-handling computations.

From the profile, it was clear that we need to find a more efficient memory management library, to replace that provided by Active Threads. We found two packages that appear to be suitable: (a) ptmalloc library [5], and (b) Vmalloc library [7]. A preliminary test showed that Vmalloc performs better than ptmalloc. We therefore modified our program to use Vmalloc's memory management calls, while retaining Active Threads for its threads and synchronization facilities.

Table 1. Initial timings (in sec) of Sematech wafer fabrication datasets using Active Threads

	set1	set2	set3	set4	set5	set6
Sequential	1.46	3.02	6.23	0.20	1.56	1.51
1-CPU	1.29	2.46	5.02	0.18	1.24	1.20
4-CPU	1.75	5.00	11.40	0.26	2.23	2.48

Table 2. Profiled timings (in seconds) of benchmark

	Exec. time on 4 CPU's	Total time on mem. mgt.	No. of allocations	No. of deallocations
set1	4.01	4.61	678321	654374
set2	8.07	21.24	1484824	1394356
set3	24.02	76.26	3655131	3461240
set4	0.37	0.23	95051	88958
set5	3.74	12.24	1314554	1119870
SET6	4.40	14.80	1143974	974112

4. Improved Implementation

We first describe the features of the Vmalloc library and how it is incorporated into the application.

Table 3. Improved timings (in seconds) using Vmalloc+Active Threads

	set1	set2	set3	set4	set5	set6
Sequential	1.46	3.02	6.23	0.20	1.56	1.51
1-CPU	1.53	2.94	6.08	0.21	1.49	1.43
4-CPU	1.36	1.69	2.14	0.21	0.72	0.70

The Vmalloc library provides facilities for the programmer to allocate different regions of memory with different allocation policies. The program can then allocate blocks from the separate regions according to its usage pattern at different points of execution. The original Vmalloc library did not take into account parallel access by the separate regions to obtain their blocks from a global pool. We modified the library to protect access to the global pool, and make use of the feature of separate regions as follows.

- The modified program allocates a region for each thread. Each thread then allocates and frees memory blocks from its own region.
- It is however incorrect to allocate a memory block in region A and free it in region B. Because event objects are passed from one LP to another, we therefore cannot simply allocate event objects from a thread's region. But since event objects are allocated from independent event pool managers which in turn, get their blocks

from a global event pool manager, we assign a Vmalloc memory region to the global event pool manager.

Table 4. Breakdown of time (in seconds) spent on memory management using Vmalloc+Active Threads

	set1	set2	set3	set4	set5	set6
Exec. time on 4 CPU's	2.04	2.62	4.02	0.38	1.17	0.97
Total time on mem. mgt.	1.28	3.20	8.55	0.19	3.49	2.78

We made these changes and obtained improved timings for the same benchmark (Table 3). The parallel program now demonstrates speedups on 4 processors over the sequential version, and also as compared to the 1-processor timings. Table 4 gives a similar breakdown of the memory allocation timings and turn-around time. The times spent on memory management are now drastically reduced from those in Table 2.

From our experience, it is encouraging to find that there are public-domain research libraries which are both efficient and stable for developing parallel simulations. More importantly, because the functionality's of the libraries are well-defined, we are able to install them separately, and use them as independent but interacting components within an application. We can envision that other well-defined parallel libraries can be added as independent components, when the application requirements change. The prerequisite for a library to be used as a component independently (whether unchanged or slightly modified), with others, is that it provides a well-defined set of primitives and does it efficiently. For example, on a distributed network of multiprocessors, an Active Message library providing fast communication primitives, may complement libraries like Active Threads and Vmalloc to build parallel applications.

At the moment, our experiments are only conducted on a Sun UltraSparc2 which is a common platform for most of the research software. The "plug-and-play" nature of the software will however be limited for parallel programmers on other less research-software-friendly machines, e.g. SGI. If such component libraries are also portable, they will help greatly to make parallel programming more accessible.

5. Conclusion

In this paper, we have described the relevance of building parallel support libraries, so that they can be used in a "plug-and-play" fashion within an application. We initially chose the Active Threads library based on an evaluation of four different runtime libraries, on a much simplified simulation model. When we elaborated the model using more realistic datasets (Sematech) and more complex event-handling, the bottleneck due to Active Threads' memory allocation became more apparent.

We found two memory management libraries as possible candidates to complement Active Threads. They are ptmalloc and Vmalloc. The latter is more efficient, and achieves speedups for the application. An interesting observation is that the changes to the simulation code are minimal, and both Active Threads and Vmalloc are now independent components for a larger program. Another example of a component library that we might need in future is a parallel number generator.

Making such component libraries generally available and portable will allow parallel programmers to implement more complex applications (e.g. simulations), and make parallel programming more manageable. The important prerequisite is that a library be well-encapsulated, with well-defined interface and functionality. For example, Vmalloc library's interface is strictly for memory allocation/deallocation.

Our simulation model is still relatively simple because it only looks at wafer fabrication. We are currently integrating various aspects of a virtual factory model, including business processes, manufacturing and communications network support, and evaluating the different protocols to find out which will give better performance for our application. We also foresee the need to study load balancing and scheduling issues when the implementation work on the prototype gets further underway.

References

1. R. D. Blumofe, C. F. Joerg, B. C. Kuszmaul, C. E. Leiserson, K. H. Randall and Y. Zhou. Cilk: An Efficient Multithreaded Runtime System. *Journal of Parallel and Distributed Computing*, Vol.37, No.1, pp.55-69, 1996.
2. Wentong Cai, E. Letertre and S. J. Turner. Dag Consistent parallel Simulation: a Predictable and Robust Conservative Algorithm. In *Proceedings of 11th Workshop on Parallel and Distributed Simulation (PADS'97)*, pp. 178-181, Lockenhaus Austria, June 1997.
3. Boris Weissman. Active threads manaul. International Computer Science Institute, Berkeley, CA 94704. Technical Report TR-97-037. 1997.
4. The Institute of Electrical and Electronics Engineers. Portable Operating System Interface (POSIX) -Part 1: Amendment 2: Threads Extensions [C Language]. *POSIX P1003.4a/D7*. April 1993.
5. Wolfram Gloger. ptmalloc Library. ftp://ftp.dent.med.uni-muenchen.de/pub/wmglo / ptmalloc.tar.gz
6. Jonathan M.D. Hill. Installation and User Guide for the Oxford BSP toolset (v1.1) implementation of BSPlib. Oxford Parallel Computing Laboratory, Oxford University. June 1997.
7. Kiem-Phong Vo. Vmalloc: A General and Efficient Memory Allocator. Software – Practice and Experience. Vol. 26 (3), pp. 357 – 374, March 1996.
8. Sanjay Jain. Virtual Factory Framework: A Key Enabler for Agile Manufacturing. *Proceedings of 1995 INRIA/ IEEE Symposium on Emerging Technologies and Factory Automation*, Paris, Oct. 1995, Vol. 1, pp. 247-258, IEEE Computer Society Press, Los Alamitos, CA.
9. Chu-Cheow Lim, Yoke-Hean Low et al. An Empirical Comparison of Runtime Systems for Conservative Parallel Simulation. 2nd Workshop on Runtime Systems for Parallel Programming (RTSPP 98). Orlando, Florida - USA, March 30, 1998.
10. David M. Nicol, "The Cost of Conservative Synchronization in Parallel Discrete Event Simulation", *Journal of the ACM*, Vol.40, No.2, pp.304-333, April 1993.
11. Sematech. Modeling Data Standards, version 1.0. Technical report, Sematech, Inc., Austin, TX78741, 1997.

A Coordination Layer for Exploiting Task Parallelism with HPF

Salvatore Orlando[1] and Raffaele Perego[2]

[1] Dip. di Matematica Appl. ed Informatica, Università Ca' Foscari di Venezia, Italy
[2] Istituto CNUCE, Consiglio Nazionale delle Ricerche (CNR), Pisa, Italy

Abstract. This paper introduces $COLT_{HPF}$, a run–time support for exploiting task parallelism within HPF programs, which can be employed by a compiler of a high-level coordination language to structure a set of data-parallel HPF tasks according to popular paradigms of *task-parallelism*. We use $COLT_{HPF}$ to program a computer vision application and report the results obtained by running the application on an SGI/Cray T3E.

1 Introduction

Although HPF-1 [8] permits programmers to express data-parallel computations in a portable, high-level way, it is widely accepted that many important parallel applications cannot be efficiently implemented following a pure data-parallel paradigm. The promising possibility of exploiting a mixture of task and data parallelism, where data parallelism is restricted within HPF tasks and task parallelism is achieved by their concurrent execution, has recently received much attention [6,5]. Depending on the applications, HPF tasks can be organized according to patterns which are structured to varying degrees. For example, applications may be modeled by a fixed but unstructured task dependency graph, where edges correspond to data-flow dependencies. However, it is more common for parallel applications to process streams of input data, so that a more regular *pipeline* task structure can be exploited [11]. When the bandwidth of a given pipeline stage has to be increased, it is often better to replicate it rather than using several processors for its data-parallel implementation. Replication entails using a *processor farm* structure [7], where incoming jobs are dispatched on one of the stage replicas by adopting either a simple round-robin or a dynamic self-scheduling policy.

This paper presents $COLT_{HPF}$ (COordination Layer for Tasks expressed in HPF), a coordination/communication layer for HPF tasks. $COLT_{HPF}$ provides suitable mechanisms for starting distinct HPF data-parallel tasks on disjoint groups of processors, along with optimized primitives for inter-task communication where data to be exchanged may be distributed among the processors according to user-specified HPF directives. We discuss how $COLT_{HPF}$ can be used to structure data-parallel computations that cooperate according to popular forms of task parallelism like pipelines and processor farms [11,7]. We present

D. O'Halloran (Ed.): LCR'98, LNCS 1511, pp. 386–393, 1998.
© Springer-Verlag Berlin Heidelberg 1998

templates which implement these forms of task parallelism and we discuss the exploitation of these templates to design a structured, high-level, coordination language. We claim that the use of such a language simplifies program development and restructuring, while effective automatic optimizations (mapping, choice of the degree of parallelism for each task, program transformations) can be easily devised because the specific structure of the parallel programs is restricted and statically known. Unfortunately, this approach requires a new compiler in addition to HPF, though the templates proposed can also be exploited to design libraries of *skeletons* [4,1]. However, the compiler is very simple, though its complexity may increase depending on the level of optimization supported.

2   Task-Parallel Structures to Coordinate HPF Tasks

To describe the features of $COLT_{HPF}$ we refer to a particular class of applications which exploit a mixture of task and data parallelism. More specifically, we focus on applications which transform an input data stream into an output one of the same length. As regards the structures of task parallelism used to coordinate

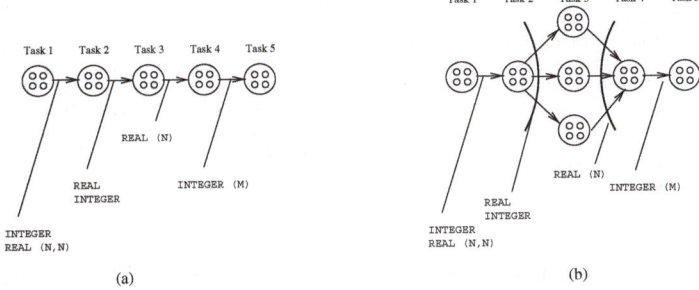

Fig. 1. Two examples of the same application implemented (a) by means of a pipeline, and (b) by hierarchically composing the same pipeline with a processor farm.

these HPF tasks, we focus on a few forms of parallelism, namely *pipelines* and *processor farms*. Figure 1.(a) shows the structure of an application obtained by composing five data-parallel tasks according to a *pipeline* structure, where the first and the last stages of the pipeline only produce and consume, respectively, the data stream. The data types of the input/output channels connecting each pair of interacting tasks are also shown. Figure 1.(b) shows the same application where Task 3 has been replicated. In this case, besides computing their own job by transforming their input data stream into the output one, Task 2 has to dispatch the various elements of the output stream to the three replicas of Task 3, while Task 4 has to collect the elements received from any of the three replicas.

Each form of parallelism can be associated with an *implementation template*. A template can be considered as the code scheme of a set of communicating HPF tasks which cooperate according to a fixed interaction pattern. In order to obtain the actual implementation of a user application, the template corresponding to the chosen parallel structure must be instantiated by inserting the user-provided code, as well as the correct calls to the $COLT_{HPF}$ primitives to initialize channels and to exchange data between tasks.

Since most of the code production needed to instantiate a template can be automated, we believe that the best usage of $COLT_{HPF}$ is through a simple high-level coordination language. Roughly speaking, the associated compiler should in this case be responsible for instantiating templates for users. To use such a coordination language a programmer should only be required to provide the HPF code of each task, its parameter lists to specify the types of the elements composing the input and the output streams, and finally the language constructs to express how these tasks must be coordinated, e.g. according to a pipeline or a processor farm form of parallelism. A simple coordination language to express this kind of structured parallel programming strategy, P^3L, has already been proposed elsewhere [1], even if the host language adopted was sequential (C) rather than parallel (HPF). For example, a P^3L-like code to express the structure represented in Figure 1.(b) would be:

```
task_3 in(INTEGER a, REAL b) out(REAL c(N,N))      pipe in() out()
   hpf_distribution(DISTRIBUTE C(BLOCK, *))            task_1 in()      out(INTEGER a, REAL b(N,N))
   hpf_code_init(<initialiaze the task status>)        task_2 in(a,b) out(INTEGER c, REAL d)
   hpf_code(<use a and b, compute, and produce c>)     foo      in(c,d) out(REAL e(N,N))
end                                                    task_4 in(e)    out(INTEGER f(M))
                                                       task_5 in(f)    out()
                                                     end pipe
farm foo in(INTEGER a, REAL b) out(REAL c(N,N))
   task_3 in(a, b) out(c)
end farm
```

Note the definition of Task 3, with the relative input and the output lists of parameters, the specification of the layout for distributed parameters, and the HPF user code. Since Task 3 must be replicated, a *farm* named foo is thus defined, whose identical workers are replicas of Task 3. Finally, the farm must be composed with the other tasks to obtain the final *pipeline* structure of Figure 1.(b)[1]. Note the hierarchical composition of the task-parallel constructs: there is a pipe, which invokes a farm, which, in turn, invokes a simple HPF data-parallel task. The specification of the structure of the application is concise, simple, and high-level. Moreover, by only modifying this high-level description we can radically change the parallel structure of the application to test alternative implementations.

The code shown does not specify the number of processors to be exploited by each task, nor the number of workers of the farm (e.g. the number of replicas of Task 3). Suitable directives could be provided, so that a programmer can tune these parameters to optimize performance (*performance debugging*), although, since we are concentrating on a set of restricted and structured forms of parallelism, the compiler could use suitable performance models, profiling information

---

[1] For the sake of brevity, the definition of the other tasks of the pipe is not reported.

and also architectural constraints (e.g. the number of available processors) to optimize resource allocation [1,11].

3 $COLT_{HPF}$ Implementation

The current implementation of $COLT_{HPF}$ [9] is bound with an HPF compiler, Adaptor [2], which has been configured to exploit MPI. We believe that our technique is very general, so that a similar binding might easily be made with other HPF compilers that use MPI too. The binding is based on a simple modification of the Adaptor run-time support, so that each HPF task exploits a different MPI communicator. For each disjoint processor group on which the various HPF tasks have to be mapped, we create a distinct communicator, namely MPI_LOCAL_COMM_WORLD, by using the MPI_Comm_split primitive. To this end, a configuration file must be provided to define the processor groups and the mapping of the various HPF tasks. Thus, while MPI_LOCAL_COMM_WORLD is now used for all Adaptor-related MPI calls within each HPF task, the default communicator MPI_COMM_WORLD is used for intertask communications implemented by $COLT_{HPF}$.

Communicating distributed data between a pair of HPF tasks may involve all the processors of the two corresponding groups. Moreover, when data and processor layouts of the sender and receiver tasks differ, it also entails the redistribution of the data exchanged. Since many of these inter-task communications may need to be repeated due to the presence of an input/output stream, $COLT_{HPF}$ provides primitives to establish *persistent typed channels* between tasks. These channels, on the basis of the knowledge about data distributions on the sender and the receiver processor groups, thus store the *Communication Schedule*, which is used by the send/receive primitives for packing/unpacking data and for carrying out the "minimal" number of point-to-point communications between the processors of the two groups. To open a channel, both the sender and receiver have to inquire the HPF run-time support to find out the corresponding array data distributions. This information is then exchanged, and, by using Ramaswamy and Banerjee's *pitfalls* redistribution algorithm [10], each processor derives its *Communication Schedule*. $COLT_{HPF}$ also supplies primitives to exchange scalar data between processor groups, where these data are replicated on all the processors of the groups.

Finally, $COLT_{HPF}$ provides primitives to signal simple events between tasks, where the reception of messages may be carried out *non-deterministically*. These signals are useful, for example, to implement processor farms that adopt a dynamic self scheduling policy to dispatch jobs. According to this policy, the farm dispatcher, e.g. Task 2 in Figure 1.(b), receives *ready* signals from any of the various farm workers, where these signals state the completion of a job dispatched beforehand and a request for further jobs.

$COLT_{HPF}$ primitives are implemented as HPF_LOCAL EXTRINSIC subroutines. When an EXTRINSIC subroutine is invoked by an HPF task, all the processors executing the task switch from the single thread of control provided by HPF to an

SPMD style of execution. According to the HPF language definition, HPF_LOCAL subroutines have to be written in a restricted HPF language where, for example, it is not possible to transparently access data stored on remote processors, but each processor can only refer its own section of any distributed array.

The techniques adopted in the implementation of $COLT_{HPF}$ are similar to those exploited by Foster et al. to design their HPF binding for MPI [5]. In [9] we survey their work and other related ones.

4   Template Examples

In this section we exemplify the concept of *implementation template* by illustrating the *task template* of a generic pipeline stage, and its instantiation starting from a $P^3L - like$ high level specification of the stage.

A pipeline stage is an HPF task which cyclically reads an element of the input stream and produces a corresponding output element, where an incremental mark is associated with each element of the stream. The transmission of each stream element is thus preceded by the transmission of the related mark. The end of the stream is identified by a particular END_OF_STREAM mark.

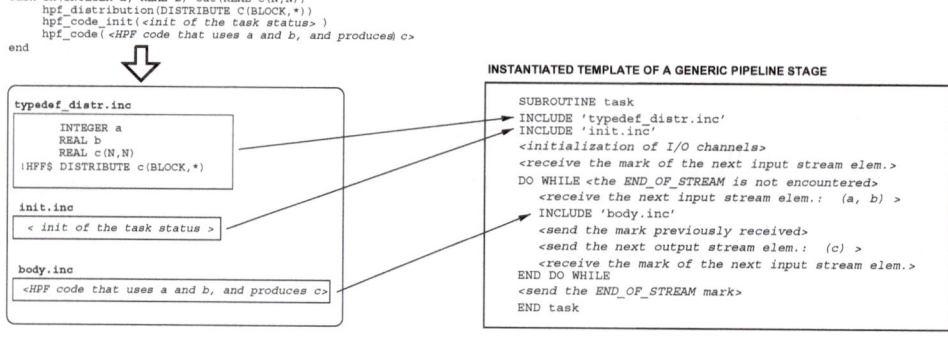

Fig. 2. A *task template* of a pipeline stage, where its instantiation is shown starting from a specific construct of a high-level coordination language.

Figure 2 shows the process template of a pipeline stage and its instantiation. As can be seen, the input/output lists of data, along with their distribution directives, are used by the compiler to generate an include file typedef_distr.inc. Moreover, the declaration of the task local variables, along with the relative code for their initialization is included in another file, init.inc. Finally, the code to be executed to consume/produce each data stream element is contained in the include file body.inc. These files are directly included in the source code of the template which is also shown in the figure. To complete the instantiation of the template, the appropriate calls to the $COLT_{HPF}$ layer which initialize the input/output channels and send/receive the elements of the input/output stream, also have to be generated and included. The correct generation of these calls relies on the knowledge of the task input/output lists, as well as the mapping of the tasks onto the disjoint groups of processors.

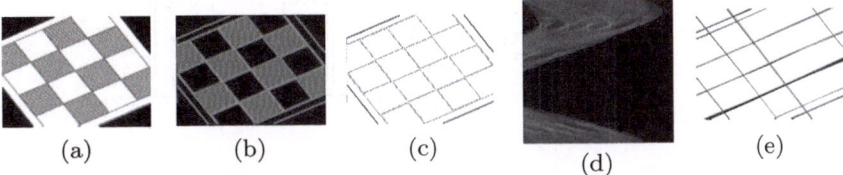

(a)   (b)   (c)   (e)

(d)

Fig. 3. Example of the input/output images produced by the various stages of the computer vision application: (a)⇒(b): Sobel filter stage for edge enhancement – (b)⇒(c): Thresholding stage to produce a bit map – (c)⇒(d): Hough transform stage to detect straight lines – (d)⇒(e): de-Hough transform stage to plot the most voted straight lines.

5   Experimental Results

To show the effectiveness of our approach we used $COLT_{\text{HPF}}$ to implement a complete high-level computer vision application which detects in each input image the straight lines that best fit the edges of the objects represented in the image itself. For each grey-scale image received in input (for example, see Figure 3.(a)), the application enhances the edges of the objects contained in the image, detects the straight lines lying on these edges, and finally builds a new image containing only the most evident lines identified at the previous step. The application can be naturally expressed according to a three stage pipeline structure. The first stage reads from the file system each image, and applies a low-level Sobel filter to enhance the image edges. Since the produced image (see Figure 3.(b)) is still a grey-scale one, it has to be transformed into a black-white bitmap (see Figure 3.(c)) to be processed by the following stage. Thus a thresholding filter is also applied by the first stage before sending the resulting bitmap to the next stage. The second stage performs a Hough transform, a high-level vision algorithm which tries to identify in the image specific patterns (in this case straight lines) from their analytical representation (in this case the equations of the straight lines). The output of the Hough transformation is a matrix of accumulators $H(\rho, \theta)$, each element of which represents the number of black pixels whose spatial coordinates (x, y) satisfy the equation $\rho = x \cos \theta + y \sin \theta$. Matrix H can be interpreted as a grey-scale image (see Figure 3.(d)), where lighter pixels correspond to the most "voted for" straight lines. Finally, the third stage chooses the most voted for lines, and produces an image where only these lines are displayed. The resulting image (see Figure 3.(e)) is then written to an output file.

Table 1. Computation and I/O times (in secs) for the HPF implementation of the three stages of the pipeline.

Procs	Sobel&Thresh			Hough	de-Hough		
	I/O	Comp.	Total	Comp.	I/O	Comp.	Total
1	9.6	11.9	21.5	148.3	1.0	21.4	22.4
2	10.0	5.8	15.8	78.0	1.2	17.3	18.5
4	10.2	2.4	12.6	43.5	1.3	13.7	15.0
8	10.4	0.9	11.3	24.7	1.3	12.3	13.6
16	10.5	0.7	11.2	15.9	1.3	11.8	13.1
32	11.6	0.7	12.3	12.3	1.4	11.6	13.0

Table 1 illustrates some results of experiments conducted on an SGI/Cray T3E. It shows the completion times of each of the three stages, where the input stream is composed of 60 256×256 images. Note that the I/O times of the first and the third stage do not scale with the number of processors used. If the total completion times reported in the table is considered, it is clear that it is no point exploiting more than 4/8 processors for these stages. On the other hand, the Hough transform stage scales better. We can thus assign enough processors to the second stage so that its bandwidth becomes equal to that of the other stages. For example, if we use 2 processors for the first stage, we should use 4 processors for the third stage, and 16 for the second one to optimize the throughput of the pipeline. Alternatively, since the costs of the Hough transform algorithm very much depends on the input data [3], we may decide to exploit a processor farm for the implementation of the second stage. For example, a farm with two replicated workers, where the bandwidth of each worker is half the bandwidth of the first and the last stages, allows the overall pipeline throughput to be optimized, provided that a dynamic self scheduling policy is implemented to balance the workers' workloads.

Table 2 shows the execution times and the speedups measured on a Cray T3E executing our computer vision application, where we adopted a self-scheduling processor farm for the second stage of the pipeline. The column labeled *Structure* in the table, indicates the mapping used for the $COLT_{\mathrm{HPF}}$ implementations. For example, (4 (8,8) 4) means that 4 processors were used for both the first and last stage of the pipeline, while each one of the two farm workers was run on 8 processors. The table also compares the results obtained by the $COLT_{\mathrm{HPF}}$ implementations with those obtained by pure HPF implementations exploiting the same number of processors. The execution times measured with the $COLT_{\mathrm{HPF}}$ implementations were always better than the HPF ones. The performance improvements obtained are quite impressive and range from 60% to 160%.

6   Conclusions

In this paper we have discussed $COLT_{\mathrm{HPF}}$, a run-time support to coordinate HPF tasks. We have shown how $COLT_{\mathrm{HPF}}$ can be exploited to design implementation templates for common forms of parallelism, and how these templates can be used

Table 2. Comparison of execution times (in seconds) obtained with the HPF and $COLT_{HPF}$ implementation of the computer vision application.

	$COLT_{HPF}$			HPF		$HPF/COLT_{HPF}$ ratio
Procs	*Structure*	Exec. Time	Speedup	Exec. Time	Speedup	
8	1 (3,3) 1	30.7	6.26	49.7	3.87	1.6
16	2 (4,4,4) 2	19.9	9.66	40.3	4.77	2.0
24	4 (8,8) 4	15.8	12.14	38.2	5.03	2.4
32	8 (8,8,8) 8	14.4	13.34	37.6	5.11	2.6

by a compiler of a structured, high-level coordination language. We have also presented some encouraging experimental results, conducted on an SGI/Cray T3E, where pipeline and farm templates have been instantiated to implement a complete computer vision application.

Acknowledgments Our greatest thanks are for Thomas Brandes, for many valuable discussions about task parallelism and Adaptor. We also wish to thank Ovidio Salvetti for his suggestions about the computer vision application and the CINECA Consortium of Bologna for the use of the SGI/Cray T3E.

References

1. B. Bacci, M. Danelutto, S. Orlando, S. Pelagatti, and M. Vanneschi. P^3L: a Structured High-level Parallel Language and its Structured Support. *Concurrency: P&E*, 7(3):225–255, 1995, Wiley.
2. T. Brandes. ADAPTOR Programmer's Guide Version 5.0. Internal Report Adaptor 3, GMD-SCAI, Sankt Augustin, Germany, April 97.
3. S. C. Orphanoudakis D. Gerogiannis. Load Balancing Requirements in Parallel Implementations of Image Feature Extraction Tasks. *IEEE TPDS*, 4(9), Sept. 1993.
4. J. Darlington et al. Parallel Programming Using Skeleton Functions. In *Proc. of PARLE '93*, pages 146–160, Munich, Germany, June 1993. LNCS 694, Spinger-Verlag.
5. Ian Foster, David R. Kohr, Jr., Rakesh Krishnaiyer, and Alok Choudhary. A Library-Based Approach to Task Parallelism in a Data-Parallel Language. *JPDC*, 45(2):148–158, Sept. 1997, Academic Press.
6. T. Gross, D. O'Hallaron, and J. Subhlok. Task parallelism in a high performance fortran framework. *IEEE Parallel and Distr. Technology*, 2(2):16–26, 1994.
7. A.J.G. Hey. Experiments in MIMD Parallelism. In *Proc. of PARLE '89*, pages 28–42, Eindhoven, The Netherlands, June 1989. LNCS 366 Spinger-Verlag.
8. C.H. Koebel, D.B. Loveman, R.S. Schreiber, G.L. Steele Jr., and M.E. Zosel. *The High Performance Fortran Handbook*. The MIT Press, 1994.
9. S. Orlando and R. Perego. $COLT_{HPF}$, a Coordination Layer for HPF Tasks. Technical Report TR-4/98, Dip. di Mat. Appl. ed Informatica, Università di Venezia, March 1998. Available at `http://raffaele.cnuce.cnr.it//papers.html`.
10. S. Ramaswamy and P. Banerjee. Automatic generation of efficient array redistribution routines for distributed memory multicomputers. In *Frontiers '95: The 5th Symp. on the Frontiers of Massively Paral. Comp.*, pages 342–349, Feb. 1995.
11. J. Subhlok and G. Vondran. Optimal Latency-Throughput Tradeoffs for Data Parallel Pipelines. In *Proc. of 8th Annual ACM SPAA*, June 1996.

InterAct: Virtual Sharing for Interactive Client-Server Applications *

Srinivasan Parthasarathy and Sandhya Dwarkadas

Department of Computer Science
University of Rochester
Rochester, NY 14627–0226

{srini,sandhya}@cs.rochester.edu

Abstract. *We describe InterAct, a framework for interactive client-server applications. InterAct provides an efficient mechanism to support object sharing while facilitating client-controlled consistency. Advantages are two-fold: the ability to cache relevant data on the client to help support interactivity, and the ability to extend the computation boundary to the client in order to reduce server load. We examine its performance on the interactive data-mining domain, and present some basic results that indicate the flexibility and performance achievable.*

1 Introduction

Many applications require interaction among disparate components, often running in different environments. Simulation of interactive virtual environments, interactive speech recognition, interactive vision (object recognition systems), and interactive data mining, are some examples. A large number of such applications are client-server in nature and involve processes that exchange data in an irregular fashion.

In such application domains, both the data sharing mechanisms and the consistency models are important. While the use of shared memory improves ease-of-use, employing a spatial memory model such as release consistency [6] is not always the most efficient alternative. Roughly speaking, release consistency guarantees a coherent view of *all* shared data at synchronization points. This can have an adverse effect on performance especially in high-latency message-based environments.

Interactive client-server applications can often use consistency mechanisms that are more flexible, with client-controlled consistency and object sharing. For instance, some clients might require updates to shared objects at regular intervals instead of whenever the object is modified, while others might require updates whenever the object is modified "by a certain amount". In other words, such applications may tolerate stale data based on a temporal or change-based

---

* This work was supported in part by NSF grants CDA–9401142, CCR–9702466, and CCR–9705594; and an external research grant from Digital Equipment Corporation.

D. O'Hallaron (Ed.): LCR'98, LNCS 1511, pp. 394–401, 1998.

criterion, thereby reducing communication overhead and improving efficiency. Since traditional shared memory environments do not provide such alternatives, developers of interactive applications are forced to use cumbersome and unsuitable programming interfaces in order to achieve efficiency.

InterAct is a runtime system that provides both efficiency and ease-of-use. It presents the user with a transparent and efficient data sharing mechanism across disparate processes. This feature enables clients to cache relevant shared data locally, enabling faster response times to interactive queries. Further, InterAct provides flexible client-controlled mechanisms to map and specify consistency requirements for shared objects. The consistency specifications are exploited by our system to enhance application performance. We evaluate our system on an interactive data mining application. Our results show upto a 3-fold improvement in client side response times to interactive queries.

The rest of this paper is organized as follows. Section 2 describes our overall goals, and the design of the runtime interface. Section 3 describes the implementation details of maintaining address independence and enforcing consistency requirements. Section 4 describes our experimental results. Section 5 describes related work. Our conclusions and on-going work are outlined in Section 6.

2 The Runtime Interface

In order to accomplish its goal of transparently supporting interactive applications, Interact must provide an interface that:

- Defines a data (structure) format for shared objects that is address space and architecture independent.
- Identifies, defines, and supports the types of consistency required.

We illustrate the design using the interactive data mining domain in particular an association mining system [12]. Data mining algorithms typically operate on large data sets and are compute intensive. The process is also largely repetitive, with the user perturbing the input parameters to a given task in order to arrive at the desired result. Due to the large datasets involved, some functions must be performed on the server since they would otherwise involve huge amounts of communication with the client. However, the interactive querying component is naturally performed on the client. This creates a natural split in work allocation. An efficient split entails sharing data summaries between client and server. This sharing can improve interaction efficiency while potentially reducing the server load.

In Figure 1, we describe a general-purpose interactive mining algorithm mapped onto InterAct. The client has mapped an array, a DAG, and a list onto the virtual shared dataspace. An element in the list points to the DAG object, represented by the dotted connection. Once mapped, a client can synchronize the local version of the data structure with the server at appropriate points. The server is responsible for creating and updating the data structures in the virtual dataspace. InterAct transparently handles all consistency and sharing-related updates as well as client-server communication.

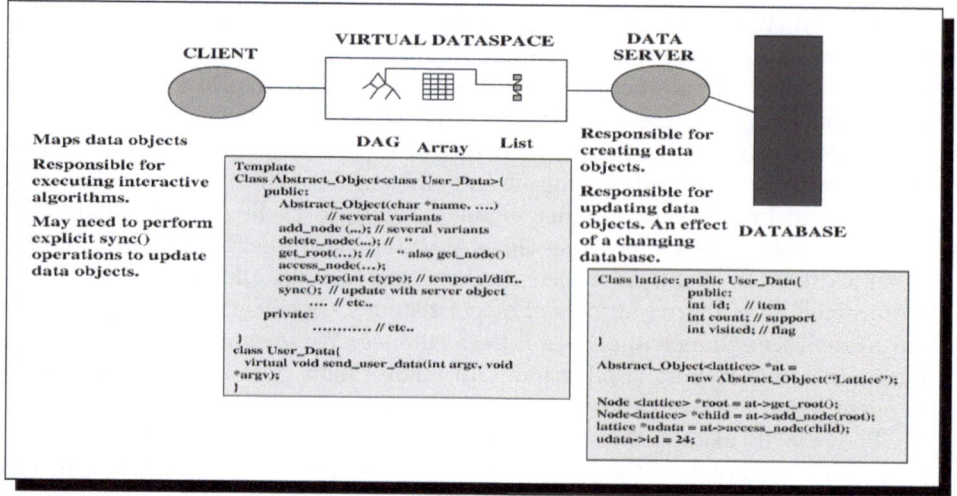

Fig. 1. Interactive Client-Server Mining

2.1 Data Declaration

In order to make the system both address-space and architecture-independent, the runtime system must define a suitable format for data representation. Our implementation relies on the use of C++ and some programmer annotation to identify the relevant information about shared data to the runtime system.

In Figure 1, we describe the current interface available to the user within the two greyed rectangular regions . The left-hand side is the InterAct object template/interface. Our interface is essentially a set of template classes with pre-defined functions for creating objects (`Abstract_Object`), defining (`User_Data`), adding (`add_node`), and accessing (`access_node`) nodes within an object, and functions for synchronizing (`sync`) and defining the required consistency type (`cons_type`). The right-hand side represents a sample declaration and usage of an InterAct object. For the association mining application each node contains 3 variables as shown in the the figure. The application creates an abstract object called "Lattice" (the DAG in Figure 1) consisting of such nodes. It then creates and accesses nodes in the lattice.

2.2 Consistency Types

As mentioned in the previous section our API includes mechanisms to express desired client consistency types, and an explicit way to make data consistent. The API also requires that changes to objects are made within explicitly identified *intervals*, which are similar to a transaction start and commit. Sharing and caching is facilitated in our system by the provision of several consistency guarantees. The following consistency types are defined:

- **One Time Updates** specifies a one-time request for data by the client. No history need be maintained. This is the default consistency type.
- **Polled Updates** specifies that the client will make requests for updates when necessary.
- **Immediate Updates** specifies that the server should notify the client whenever there are any changes to the mapped data in any interval.
- **Diff Content Updates** specifies that the client must be updated if the data changes by a specified amount.
- **Temporal Updates** specifies that the client must be updated every x units of time. In other words, the data cannot be out of sync for $> x$ time units.

The different consistency types can be exploited by our system to enhance application performance. For instance, in some data mining applications, where a visual map is evaluated over equispaced time points, changes to the visual map need not be communicated immediately .Identifying this requirement using **Temporal Update** allows the runtime to make this optimization. In the process of discretization, it has been shown that small changes to the probability density function estimate does not severely affect the result quality. Identifying this property using **Diff-Content Update**, indicating that the application can live with stale data, allows the runtime to reduce the frequency of updates. Similarly, knowing that a client requires a **Polled Update** as opposed to a **One Time Update** tells the runtime system that shipping object changes might be more beneficial than resending the object on each poll.

3   Implementation Issues

The key to the efficient support of sharing is efficient address translation while maintaining address independence, efficiently identifying modifications to an object, and minimizing when these changes are communicated. We address each of these issues here.

3.1   Address Translation

InterAct objects request memory in page chunks using a segment-based memory placement library [9]. The library, which uses the Unix malloc routines, provides mechanisms to control memory placement policies for dynamic data structures. Using the library functions, we can identify the pages that belong to a given **object**. An **object** refers to a recursive data structure such as a tree or graph. Each such **object** is composed of a set of **nodes** that may be interconnected. Determining the address of a particular node within an object is similar to array indexing, since the size of each node is fixed. Communication is also simplified, since we communicate changes to the object at the granularity of a node.

Like any distributed object system, our interface identifies any pointers and their associated types to the runtime system in order to provide address-independence. During object creation, the object's internal representation is divided into data and connection pages. Data pages contain all the data information for an object. Similarly, connection pages store the actual connection information for nodes within an object. Information in the connection pages identify the object (in the case of inter-object pointers) and the node within the object in terms of an index, making address independence feasible. Separating connection and data information, co-locates all the pointers, enabling the runtime to perform rapid address translation.

3.2   Object Modification Detection

The technique we use to detect modifications is similar to that used by multiple-writer page-based software distributed shared memory systems [4,2]. At the beginning of every interval, all relevant object pages are marked read-only using the *mprotect* VM call. When a processor incurs a write fault, it creates a write notice (*WN*) for the faulting page and appends the *WN* to a list of *WN*s associated with the current interval. It simultaneously saves a pristine copy of each page called a *twin* and enables write permissions [4]. The *twin* serves two purposes. First, if a client request comes in during an interval, data is delivered from the twin, thereby ensuring atomicity. Second, at the end of an interval the *twin* is used to identify the nodes modified within an interval.

When an interval completes, all objects that have been modified within the transaction interval (identified through the *WN* list) increment their associated object timestamp. Each object has an associated timestamp map. A timestamp map contains an entry for each node indicating the last time at which it was modified. The timestamp map for all the nodes contained in pages in the *WN* list are updated. Work is thus limited only to those pages that are actually modified. The update is done by comparing the page to its *twin* to determine the nodes that have been modified.

When asked for changes by the client, the object compares its timestamp map entries for each node against the last time the client has been appraised of object updates. The result of the timestamp comparison is a run-length encoding of the node data and node connections that have been modified, which constitute the *diff* of the object. Header information also specifies the object identifier, and number of node data and connection updates.

On the client side, we maintain information corresponding to the objects that are mapped and where they are stored in local memory. On receiving a diff message, we update the corresponding object by decoding the header to determine the object identifier. This object identifier is then used to determine the local location of the object. Data and connection information for nodes within the object are similarly address independent.

3.3   Consistency Maintenance

The runtime system optimizes data communication by using the consistency types specified by the user to determine when communication is required. The goal is to reduce messaging overhead and allow the overlap of computation and communication. Implementation of the **Immediate Update, Polled Update**, and **One-Time Update** consistency guarantees are fairly straightforward. **One-Time Update** does not require any meta-data maintenance. **Immediate Update** and **Polled Update** are implemented by having the client send the most recent timestamp of the object it has seen. Only those nodes with timestamps greater than this value are communicated. **Temporal Updates** are supported by having the runtime system on the client's side poll for updates at the intervals defined by the user. To keep track of **Diff Content Updates**, an additional element in the client timestamp array maintains a cumulative count of nodes modified since the last client update. If this cumulative count exceeds a preset (by the user) number, the client is sent an update. For this case the server has to maintain the last timestamp seen by the respective clients.

4   Experimental Evaluation

We evaluate our framework on the interactive association mining algorithm, used as a running example in this paper (Figure 1). In this application, the data server is responsible for creating a shared data structure (itemset lattice [12]) based on the local database. This lattice is subsequently mapped by the client. The client executes some non-trivial interactions on the lattice, as described in previous work [1]. The server updates the mapped data structure corresponding to changes in the database (which we simulate), and commits these changes. Updates are transmitted to the client on a client poll.

In our experimental setup, the server was running on a 143 MHz Sun UltraSparc machine, with 128 MB of memory. We evaluated the framework on 3 separate client configurations. **Client1** was a 50 MHz Sun SPARCstation-LX with 24 MB of memory, **Client2** was an 85 MHz Sun SPARCstation-4 with 32 MB of memory, and **Client3** was a 143 MHz Sun UltraSparc with 64 MB of memory. Our network was a 10 Mbps Ethernet.

Communication Performance: We evaluated the effectiveness of using diffs (with **Polled_Updates**) as opposed to resending the entire object (using **One_Time_Send**). We found sending diffs could be 10-30 times faster than resending the entire object for reasonable sized changes. The size of the diff message is much smaller, resulting in reduced communication overhead. The gains due to reduction in communication cost also reflect the reduction in overhead from client-server flow control due to finite buffer sizes.

Client Info	Client Side	Exec-Server	Speedup
Client1	4.74	6.0+0.54	1.4
Client2	1.65	3.8+0.54	2.6
Client3	0.83	1.7+0.54	2.7

Table 1. Interactive Performance (times in seconds, object sizes in bytes)

Interactive Performance: In order to estimate the benefits of permitting interactivity (through client side caching), in Table 1, we compare executing a mining query on the locally mapped data structure (Client-Side) as opposed to executing it on the server side and shipping the results to the client (Exec-Server[communication time + execution time]). For this particular query, the response time is reduced by about a factor of two when executing on the client-side. The faster the client, the bigger the speedup, since the difference in raw query execution times between client-side execution and server-side execution is reduced, resulting in higher relative communication overhead.

Runtime Overhead: We evaluated the overhead imposed by our system on the server side during normal execution without client connections. To evaluate this overhead we compared the test application written using the **InterAct** interface against a program written using standard C++. We found the runtime overhead imposed by adhering to our framework, for the above interactive experiments, to be less than 6%.

5   Related Work

Remote Procedure Call (RPC) mechanisms, and Remote Method Invocation (RMI) mechanisms have been used for building client-server applications. Distributed object systems such as Emerald [8], Rover [7], and Globe [11], also permit object sharing in the presence of replicated objects and object migration. Clearly, InterAct shares some features with such systems, such as support for address-independent objects (serialization/marshalling), and a need to identify where the pointers are and what they point to. However, in these systems, shared objects can be kept consistent only in one of two ways: modifications result in the entire data structure being communicated, or object logs keep track of method invocations and these methods are re-executed on object replicas. The former results in extra communication, while the latter may not be possible for interactive applications if the methods require data available only on the server side as in data mining applications. Our system provides a transparent mechanism to identify modifications made to these data structures, thereby reducing data communication.

Computer Supported Collaborative Work (CSCW) [5] systems share some of the features of our system (supporting interactive sessions across disparate systems, update notification etc.). However, most such applications support only a particular aspect of work, e.g., informal communication, distributed meetings, document co-authoring etc. This leads to a proliferation of isolated tools with little or no inter-operability.

Our work derives some of its characteristics from the distributed shared memory domain. In particular, the way we compute changes to our objects is a hybrid combination of the approaches described in TreadMarks [2] and Midway [13]. Orca [3] is similar in some respects to our work, particularly in that it provides an address independent object format similar to ours. Beehive [10] is a distributed shared memory system that also supports a temporal notion of consistency called delta consistency. This is similar to temporal updates in InterAct.

Our system differs from the above distributed shared memory approaches in that it supports sharing across disparate processes. Further, InterAct differs from these related approaches in its flexible supports for relaxed consistency types on a per client basis rather than on a per application basis. For instance, in InterAct, two clients can map the same data structure using a different consistency type.

6   Conclusions

We have described a general framework that supports efficient data structure sharing with client-controlled consistency for interactive client-server applications. The interface enables clients to cache relevant shared data locally, enabling faster response times to interactive queries. The interface eliminates the complexity of determining exactly what data to communicate among clients and servers, as well as when that data must be communicated. We are in the process of using the framework to develop applications in the interactive data-mining domain.

References

1. C. Aggarwal and P. Yu. Online generation of association rules. In *ICDE*, Feb 1998.
2. C. Amza, A.L. Cox, S. Dwarkadas, P. Keleher, H. Lu, R. Rajamony, and W. Zwaenepoel. TreadMarks: Shared memory computing on networks of workstations. *IEEE Computer*, 29(2):18–28, Feb 1996.
3. H.E. Bal, M.F. Kaashoek, and A.S. Tanenbaum. Orca: A language for parallel programming of distributed systems. *IEEE TSE*, Jun 1992.
4. J.B. Carter, J.K. Bennett, and W. Zwaenepoel. Implementation and performance of Munin. In *Proceedings of the 13th ACM SOSP*, Oct 1991.
5. Prasun Dewan. A Survey of Applications of CSCW Including Some in Educational Settings. *ED-MEDIA*, pages 147–152, Jun 1993.
6. K. Gharachorloo, D. Lenoski, J. Laudon, P. Gibbons, A. Gupta, and J. Hennessy. Memory consistency and event ordering in scalable shared-memory multiprocessors. In *Proceedings of the 17th ISCA*,May 1990.
7. A.D. Joseph, A.F. deLespinasse, J.A. Tauber, D.K. Gifford, and M.F. Kaashoek. Rover: A toolkit for mobile information access. In *15th SOSP*, Dec 1995.
8. E. Jul, H. Levy, N. Hutchinson, and A. Black. Fine-grained mobility in the Emerald system. *ACM TOCS*, 6(1):109–133, Feb 1988.
9. S. Parthasarathy, M. J. Zaki, and W. Li. Memory placement for parallel data mining on shared-memory systems. To appear in *KDD*, Aug 1998.
10. A. Singla, U. Ramachandran, and J. Hodgins. Temporal notions of synchronization and consistency in beehive. In *PROC of the 9TH SPAA*, Jun 1997.
11. M. vanSteen, P. Homburg, and A.S. Tanenbaum. The architectural design of globe: A wide-area distributed system. In *Technical Report (Vrije University) IR-431*, Mar 1997.
12. M. J. Zaki, S. Parthasarathy, M. Ogihara, and W. Li. New parallel algorithms for fast discovery of association rules. *Data Mining and Knowledge Discovery: An International Journal*, Dec 1997.
13. M.J. Zekauskas, W.A. Sawdon, and B.N. Bershad. Software write detection for distributed shared memory. In *PROC of first OSDI*, pages 87–100, Nov 1994.

Standard Templates Adaptive Parallel Library (STAPL)

Lawrence Rauchwerger, Francisco Arzu, and Koji Ouchi

Dept. of Computer Science
Texas A&M University
College Station, TX 77843-3112
http://www.cs.tamu.edu/faculty/rwerger
{rwerger,farzu,kouchi}@cs.tamu.edu

Abstract. STAPL (Standard Adaptive Parallel Library) is a parallel C++ library designed as a superset of the STL, sequentially consistent for functions with the same name, and executes on uni- or multiprocessors. STAPL is implemented using simple parallel extensions of C++ which provide a SPMD model of parallelism supporting recursive parallelism. The library is intended to be of generic use but emphasizes irregular, non-numeric programs to allow the exploitation of parallelism in areas such as geometric modeling or graph algorithms which use dynamic linked data structures. Each library routine has several different algorithmic options, and the choice among them will be made adaptively based on a performance model, statistical feedback, and current run-time conditions. Built–in performance monitors can measure actual performance and, using an extension of the BSP model predict the relative performance of the algorithmic choices for each library routine. STAPL is intended to possibly replace STL in a user transparent manner and run on small to medium scale shared memory multiprocessors which support OpenMP.

1 Motivation

Although multi-processors have become commercially viable, exploiting their potential to obtain scalable speedups has remained an elusive goal, and today their use is still mostly confined to research environments. This lack of popularity among users is due to the difficulty of developing parallel applications that can efficiently exploit the hardware. We believe that parallel processing can be successful only when the effort to achieve scalable performance across a variety of applications and architectures is comparable to that of developing sequential codes.

In sequential computing, standardized libraries have proven to be valuable tools for simplifying the program development process by providing routines for common operations that allow programmers to concentrate on higher level problems. Similarly, libraries of elementary, generic, parallel algorithms would provide important building blocks for parallel applications or specialized libraries [2,3,6]. Due to the added complexity of programming parallel machines, we

D. O'Hallaron (Ed.): LCR'98, LNCS 1511, pp. 402–409, 1998.

believe that the potential impact of libraries on the future of parallel computing will be more profound than for sequential computing. Properly designed libraries could insulate naive users from managing parallelism by providing routines that are easily interchangeable with their sequential counterparts, while allowing more sophisticated users to use their expertise to extract higher performance gains.

Unfortunately, however, designing parallel libraries that are both portable and efficient is a challenge that has so far not been met. This is due mainly to the difficulty of managing concurrency and the wide variety of parallel and distributed architectures. For example, due to the differing costs of an algorithm's communication patterns on different memory systems, the best algorithm on one machine is not necessarily the best on another. On a given machine, the algorithm of choice may vary depending upon the data and run-time conditions (e.g., network traffic and system load). We believe programmers should be liberated from such concerns by parallel libraries that automatically determine which algorithm to use and how to schedule it based on a performance model, statistical feedback, and run-time conditions.

An important constraint on the development of any software is its interoperability with existing codes and standards. The dissemination and eventual adoption by the public of any new library depends on how well programmers can interface the old programs with the new software packages. At the same time, extending or building on top of existing work can greatly reduce both the developing efforts as well as the users' learning experience. It is for this reason that we have chosen to develop a parallel template library (STAPL) that offers full compatibility with the recently ANSI adopted Standard Template Library (STL) [5].

In a departure from previous approaches to libraries which have almost exclusively targeted scientific, numerical applications, STAPL will emphasize irregular, non-numeric programs. It will allow users to exploit parallelism when dynamic linked data structures replace vectors as the fundamental data structure in application areas such as geometric modeling or when algorithms operate on graphs. While we understand the difficulty of this task we believe that modern applications in all fields are rapidly evolving in this direction.

For STAPL to gain widespread acceptance and use, it is essential that the library routines achieve reasonable performance across a wide spectrum of applications and architectures and free its users from problems related to portability and algorithm choice. In STAPL, each library routine will have several different algorithmic options, and the choice among them will be made adaptively based on a performance model, statistical feedback, and current run-time conditions. Built–in performance monitors will measure actual performance and, using a an extension of the BSP model [1] that incorporates system specific information, STAPL will predict the relative performance of the algorithmic choices for each library routine and thus become an adaptive library.

2   STAPL General Specifications

STAPL will be a parallel C++ library with functionality similar to STL. To ease the transition to parallel programming and to insure portability and continuity for the current use of STL, STAPL will be a superset of the STL, it will be sequentially consistent for functions with the same name, and will execute on uni- or multi-processors. These characteristics will have the added benefit of introducing programmers to parallelism in a rather smooth and painless manner.

STAPL will be implemented using simple parallel extensions of C++ which provide a SPMD model of parallelism and will support recursive (nested) parallelism (as in NESL [2]). Although nested parallelism is not widely supported in the currently targeted commercial DSM machines we believe that it is an important feature that needs to be provided from the very beginning for several reasons: (i) large parallel processors have a hierarchical topology and will support a hierarchical run-time system in the near future, (ii) current compilers do not exploit well parallelism at the multi- and microprocessor level (at the same time) – but we believe improvement will come soon, and (iii) library functions are used as basic, elementary blocks which can be themselves nested or incorporated in a larger parallel application, thus requiring appropriate support. We intend to use the machine native run-time system and, as soon as it becomes available, generate OpenMP directives, thus insuring portability across platforms.

We have defined and have initial implementations of the three key extensions: (i) `pforall`, (ii) `prange`, and (iii) `pcontainer`. The `pforall` function applies a function to every object in a container in parallel and its implementation is so far the only architecture specific component of STAPL. The `prange` class is a parallel equivalent of the iterator class in STL that allows random access to all objects in a (certain range) in a container. The `pcontainer` is the parallel equivalent of the STL container and offers (semi–) random access to its elements, a pre-condition for parallel processing.

We will embrace the STL design philosophy of separating container from generic algorithm, which will be connected by `pranges`. There will be three types of parallel algorithms in STAPL. First, parallel algorithms with semantics identical to their sequential counterparts (e.g., sort, merge, reverse). Second, parallel algorithms with enhanced semantics. For example, a sequential `find` operation might return the first element found while a parallel `find` operation might return any (or all) elements found. Third, parallel algorithms with no sequential equivalent in STL, e.g., parallel prefix, a basic operation in many parallel algorithms. These algorithms will be implemented in the extended C++ language mentioned above and the containers will be manipulated through `pranges`. STAPL will use its own specially designed `pcontainers` that will allow pseudo-random access to its elements and thus be usable in parallel computation. For compatibility STL containers and `pcontainers` can co-exist in the same program. Furthermore, STAPL functions can use STL containers which, when necessary, can be translated internally into their parallel counterparts (`pcontainers`). For example, a linked list which does not support random access will be translated internally (without changing the interface) into a parallel linked list (e.g., one sublist for each processor). Initial speedups are not expected to be very high because of the translation overhead. Thus, we will also provide the user with the means to directly use `pcontainers` which will avoid this translation cost. For example, directly invoking a parallel sorting algorithm

```
void psort(container.prange);
```

would avoid any internal translation required to run the original STL `sort` in parallel.

Adding Adaptive Capabilities to STAPL. The goal of this phase is to add features to the STAPL routines that optimize performance by selecting the best algorithm, the number of processors, scheduling, and data layout, thus guaranteeing a certain level of performance across platforms and applications. The two major components that will confer adaptive capabilities to STAPL are execution-time instrumentation for performance monitoring and a relatively simple yet accurate performance model for parallel computation.

For example, load imbalance, network congestion, and cache miss ratios are factors that should be taken into account when determining which and how many processors should be used; hardware monitors now available on modern machines (e.g., SGI Origin2000) provide low overhead performance monitoring capabilities. Also, the algorithm's impact on system resources (e.g., memory traffic and workload) should be considered.

The performance model, a modified BSP model [1] is currently being developed and experimentally validated by our collaborators. Finally, the library will provide performance feedback to the programmer, either during or after program execution which can be used to design more efficient methods.

3   STAPL Components Overview

In this section we briefly present the basic STAPL components and their overall organization.

STL consists of three major components; `containers`, `iterators` and generic algorithms. Containers are data structures such as vectors, lists, sets and maps, and generic algorithms are operations such as searching, sorting and merging. Algorithms are generic in the sense that every algorithm can work on a variety of containers. This is accomplished by defining algorithms in terms of `iterators` which are generalized C++ pointers. Iterator types are specific to the different type of container they traverse, e.g., forward, backward, random.

STAPL consists of five major components: p_containers, `iterators`, p_ranges, the function p_for_all and p_algorithms. Although p_for_all() is the main component which manages parallelism, it is usually hidden from users. Users can write STAPL parallel programs just by using p_containers, p_ranges and p_algorithms. Also, **p_ranges** can be constructed via STL (sequential) containers and iterators.

Parallelism is embedded as follows. A p_range is a collection of iterators to which parallel processing is applied. A p_range is divided into subranges of type s_range each of which is a minimum quantum processed by a single processor

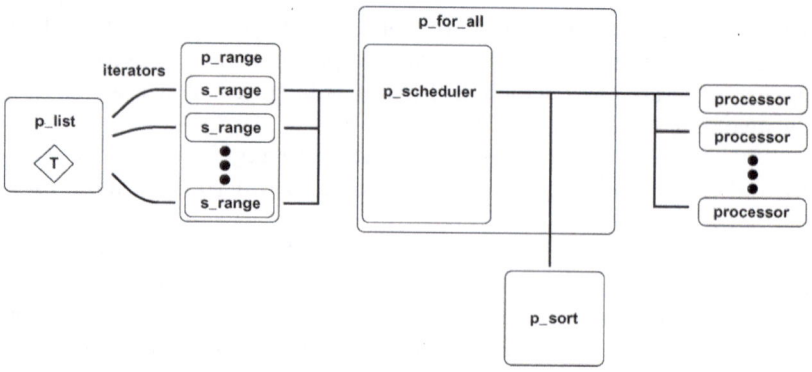

Fig. 1. STAPL Components

at a time. The function **p_for_all()** has a subcomponent **p_scheduler** which gets another s_range, associates it with a copy of p_algorithm and executes the algorithm over the s_range on some processor. Note that we provide random access to the set of s_ranges. Figure 1 shows the overal organization of STAPL's major components.

3.1   P_ranges and P_containers

The p_range class in STAPL is a generalization of the STL iterator. It allows, in essence, semi-parallel access to all objects in a container or within a certain range. The p_range type provides the same begin() and end() functions that the container provides, since a p_range can be seen as a parallel adapter to the container. p_ranges allow the programmer to work with different containers in a uniform manner.

To support nested parallelism the p_range is partioned in a set of sub-p_ranges. At the lowest level of parallelism every p_range will hold a group of serial ranges, called s_ranges, which are a range of contiguous elements in the container. The s_range is the minimum quantum that the scheduler can send to a processor for parallel processing. The union of all s_ranges constitutes the p_range of a container (or p_container). At the limit this means that if we have a list of N elements and every s_range has only one element, we obtain full random access to the list. The ratio between the number of s_ranges of a container to the number of processors (currently kept at 1:1) is a user modifiable parameter and will be adaptively tunable. The scheduler maps each s_range to a specific processor at run time. The p_range class provides methods for partitioning the container or p_container in an efficient way. Any modification of the STAPL P_container (e.g., dynamic insertion or deletion of elements) will be reflected in the information kept by its associated p_range and will be memorized for future instantiations. On the other hand, a STL container is unable to inform its associated p_range of any structural change and the responsibility of keeping its associated p_range up-to-date rests with the programmer.

Every STL container type, has a STAPL counterpart (e.g., `p_vector`, `p_list`). In addition STAPL includes new, complex data structures which are not trivially parallelized (e.g., `p_graph`, `p_hash`) but are necessary in modern, non-numeric applications.

While similar to and backwards compatible to sequential STL containers, p_containers support p_ranges via new member functions and record their distribution information. For example, the p_list (Parallel List) can reuse its per processor distribution information from previous instances, thus avoiding an expensive re-distribution operation. The beginning and ending of each sub-list or s_range (sequential range) can be randomly accessed via its s_range index, but the components inside this s_range will be traversed with the same limitations as that of the sequential iterators for that container (e.g., forward iterators for lists, random iterators for vectors) . This organization offers "semi-random" access to the p_container (and containers). All generic parallel algorithms in STAPL have to follow this rule to work with the different types of containers.

3.2   P_Forall Function Template

P_forall is, so far, the only STAPL parallel programming primitive and is the only machine dependent function template. The function p_forall() applies in parallel the function passed in as an argument to the container p_range. It can work with one or many p_ranges at the same time, depending on the needs of the parallel operation.

On every processor the argument function used in p_forall() is applied to its corresponding s_range (group of elements). The p_forall() construct does not guarantee by itself that its application is correct, i.e. that it will satisfy all the data dependence conditions associated with the concurrent application of the chosen function. This responsibility will rest with the programmer, as in most other languages that support parallel extensions.

The current version of STAPL generates calls to the native run time systems, e.g., the SGI's m_fork library, to implement its parallel processing environment. p_forall() will generate Open-MP standard directives in the near future. When the run-time system allows it, p_forall() supports nested parallelism.

An instantiation of a p_forall causes each processor to create its own copy of the argument function class via its copy constructor. Any instance variables in the function are automatically privatized to each processor's stack. It is expected that most private storage will be allocated and initialized in the prologue() method and freed up in the epilogue() method of this function.

The p_forall() also accepts an optional parameter through which the programmer can provide their own scheduler. If not specified, a default scheduler provided by STAPL will be used.

3.3   Generic P_algorithms

P_algorithms are generic parallel algorithms. P_algorithms are written in terms of p_ranges and iterators. There are three types of parallel algorithms in STAPL.

1. Parallel algorithms with semantics identical to their sequential counterparts (e.g., sort, merge, reverse)
2. Parallel algorithms with enhanced semantics. For example, a sequential find operation might return the first element found while a parallel find operation might return any (or all) elements found.
3. Useful parallel algorithms which are often used in parallel programs (e.g., p-way merge, parallel prefix.).

Figures 3 and 2 represent examples of the speedup obtained for two sorting algorithms, radix sort and merge sort respectively, that have been implemented in STAPL and executed on an SGI Power Challenge. Note that the represent the STL implementation as a baseline (number of processors = 0) followed by the speedup obtained with STAPL on 1, 2, 4 and 8 processors.

In the following section we present some criteria for adaptively choosing and tuning the parallel algorithm.

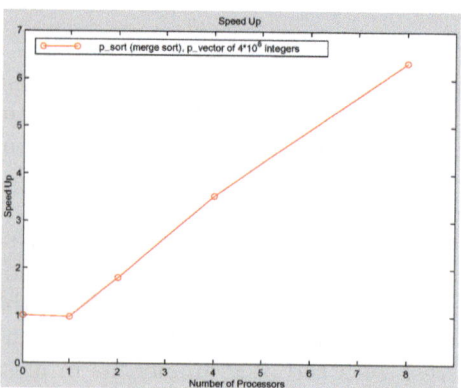

Fig. 2. STAPL Merge Sort Speedup

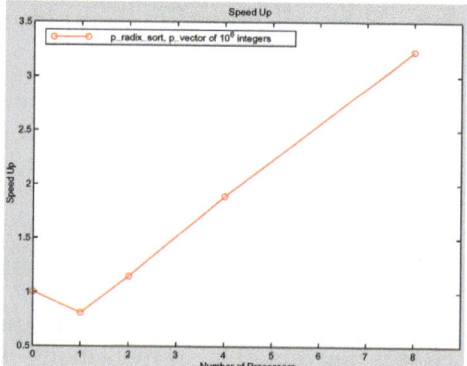

Fig. 3. STAPL Radix Sort Speedup

3.4   Adaptive Features of STAPL

STAPL will provide mechanisms for both programmer directed and automatic algorithm selection. Optional arguments will allow programmers to use *a priori* knowledge of the input to specify which method to employ. If the choice of algorithm is left to STAPL, then a newly developed performance model [1] will be used to determine the best algorithm (possibly sequential) for the given system and data size. Also, the library will be able to sample the input data and to help choose the most appropriate method. Then, the algorithm selection feature will compute the best algorithm based on the performance model and other information such as sensitivity to input data. We will provide methods that automatically analyze this information at execution-time and determine the algorithm of choice.

The Modified BSP model. The BSP is an attractive performance model due to its relative simplicity. Briefly, it measures the time complexity of an algorithm by breaking it into so called *supersteps* (computation and communication taking place between barrier synchronizations) and analyzing each superstep separately. The machine independent complexity is expressed in terms the data size n, number of processors p, and parameters g and l accounting for communication costs such as bandwidth and synchronization. Each machine has different values of g and l which are measured experimentally. The algorithm selection is made by evaluating the complexities using the machine's values for g and l, the available processors p, and the data size n. Amato *et al.*[1] have recently enhanced this model by taking into account more general architectural features and predicting upper and lower bounds on performance, thus making it a more practical model of parallel performance.

Performance Monitoring. Adaptive tuning of performance requires real time data; it is therefore imperative for such an adaptive library to incorporate from the very beginning execution-time instrumentation for performance monitoring. We have started early on with the implementation of execution-time instrumentation for performance monitoring. For example, load imbalance, network congestion, and cache miss ratios, factors that may determine which and how many processors should be used can be easily measured by using the hardware monitors now available on modern machines (e.g., SGI Origin2000). Finally, the library will provide performance feedback to the programmer either during or after program execution, to be used to design more efficient methods.

3.5   Relation to Other Work.

The goal of this research is not to substitute but to complement other current efforts to parallelize C++ with static, compile-time methods. The other parallel STL implementations known to us (e.g., [4]) target scientific applications which employ array data structures (which support random access). STAPL tries to explore linked dynamic structures (for which random access iterators do not exist) and their application in non-numeric applications.

References

1. N. M. Amato, A. Pietracaprina, G. Pucci, L. K. Dale and J. Perdue, "A Cost Model for Communication on a Symmetric Multiprocessor", TR 98004, Dept. of Computer Science, Texas A&M University, January, 1998.
2. G.E. Blelloch, "NESL: A nested data-parallel language," Technical Report CMU-CS-92-103, School of Computer Science, Carnegie Mellon University, April 1993.
3. G.E. Blelloch, *Vector Models for Data-Parallel Computing*, MIT Press, 1990.
4. E. Johnson and D. Gannon, *HPC++: Experiments with the Parallel Standard Library*, In *Proc. of the 1997 Int. Conf. on Supercomputing*, 1997, pp. 124–131.
5. D. Musser and A. Saini, *STL Tutorial and Reference Guide*, Addison-Wesley, 1996.
6. R. Sedgewick, *Algorithms in C++*, Addison-Wesley, 1992.

Author Index